The Character of Americans
A BOOK OF READINGS

The
Character
of
Americans
A BOOK OF READINGS

Edited by

Michael McGiffert

Professor of History, University of Denver

Revised Edition · 1970

THE DORSEY PRESS   HOMEWOOD, ILLINOIS

IRWIN-DORSEY LIMITED, GEORGETOWN, ONTARIO

REVISED EDITION

First Printing, June, 1970
Second Printing, April, 1971
Third Printing, September, 1972

Library of Congress Catalog Card No. 70–124170
Printed in the United States of America

To
David Morris Potter

Foreword to the First Edition

"What, then, is the American, this new man?" The study of American national character began with that question, posed by a French immigrant on the morn of American independence in 1782. The fascination of Crèvecoeur's query has not been diminished by reiteration; for nearly two centuries Americans have been trying to explain themselves to themselves, and they are still actively engaged in the undertaking. This collection of readings offers a sampling of observations, conjectures, and interpretations, drawn from several fields of scholarship and different periods of history. Essays by American authors are supplemented by the writings of visitors from overseas to whom Americans have turned an interested, if often irritable, ear. The perspectives of the past, by which continuities and changes in the American character can be appraised, are presented by several historians. Some of the selections—and all of them to some extent—are impressionistic and intuitive: they carry the mark and merit, as well as the liabilities, of highly individualized perception and reflection. Others represent the work of anthropologists, sociologists, and psychologists who have held up a mirror to America and, over the last two decades, have developed a formal theory for the analysis of national character as an enterprise of the behavioral sciences. Among these documents the reader will find materials from which to fashion or refashion an understanding of what it has meant, and what it means, to be an American.

Crèvecoeur's *Letters from an American Farmer,* from which a selection is given below, are noteworthy as the pioneer examination of American character. They command abiding interest also for what they reveal respecting the problems of dealing with so complex a subject—problems which continue to challenge Crèvecoeur's successors. When the French observer remarked, "The difficulty consists in the manner of viewing so extensive a scene," he was referring not merely to the formidable spaciousness of a country that stretched from the rocky bays of Maine to the pine barrens of Georgia and extended indefinitely westward beyond the Appalachian ridges, nor was he speaking only, if at all, of the inconveniences of travel by horse and stage over a land which was only partially redeemed from the primeval forest. The real "difficulty" was more fundamental: it was essentially a problem of procedure and perspective, and it arose less from the spread of the land than from the social and cultural heterogeneity of its inhabitants.

No special acuity was needed to perceive that America consisted of a patchwork of peoples who were not yet accustomed to thinking of themselves, either collectively or individually, as Americans. For scarcely more than one generation the term "American" had been occasionally used to distinguish the British colonists in North America from their countrymen across the sea, and less than 20 years had passed, when Crèvecoeur wrote, since Christopher Gadsden's memorable declaration at the Stamp Act Congress, "There ought to be no New England man, no New Yorker, known on the Continent, but all of us Americans." Though a political union had been contrived, and national independence proclaimed, the former subjects of George III were far from possessing a sense of common nationality. The viability of the Confederation was likewise doubtful. Many observers, both American and foreign, concurred with Alexander Hamilton in 1783 that "the centrifugal is much stronger than the centripetal force in these states—the seeds of disunion much more numerous than those of union."[1]

If it was venturesome to believe that a durable nation could be created out of the 13 disparate and disputatious states, it was still more audacious to posit, as Crèvecoeur did, the existence of a normative American character, definable in national terms. What congruities could be located among persons so diverse as the hardy Nantucket fishermen, the aristocratic planters of the Chesapeake, the plain Yankee farmers, and the rough backwoodsmen who occupied the far expanding fringes of settlement? Though the ready availability of land, the prevalence of opportunities for social and economic advancement, and the selective factors of immigration reduced the disparities of class status among white Americans, so that, as Crèvecoeur noted, "the rich and poor are not so far removed from each other as they are in Europe," yet there were diversities enough to baffle the search for a pattern in the patchwork of population.

Crèvecoeur was keenly sensitive to the heterogeneity of the people. Americans, he wrote, were "not only Americans in general, but either Pennsylvanians, Virginians, or provincials under some other name," and he predicted that the "strong differences" which they exhibited would grow increasingly evident in time. Yet back of all distinctions he perceived a common type, forged from a common experience—the type of the "American in general"—and he detected the leading characteristics of that type in the figure of the industrious, self-sufficient, prosperous farmer whose sturdy republican virtues Thomas Jefferson also celebrated. This was *Homo Americanus* in his most representative role and guise. The United States of Crèvecoeur's acquaintance was in fact a nation of

[1]Harold C. Syrett and Jacob E. Cooke, eds., *The Papers of Alexander Hamilton* (New York: Columbia University Press, 1962), III, 304.

farmers, and Crèvecoeur's *Letters* are the *locus classicus* of the stereotype of the agrarian hero in whom were concentrated those personal and civil qualities which, to Crèvecoeur's eye, were most characteristically American.

Like his successors, Crèvecoeur was interested not only in the *product,* labeled standard American, but in the *process* whereby transplanted Europeans were transformed into "a new race of men" by the action upon them of the natural and cultural environment. A thorough-going environmental determinist, he employed a horticultural metaphor to describe the making of Americans. "Every thing has tended to regenerate them; new laws, a new mode of living, a new social system; here they are become men: in Europe they were as so many useless plants, wanting vegetative mould, and refreshing showers; they withered, and were mowed down by want, hunger, and war; but now by the power of transplantation, like all other plants they have taken root and flourished!" The outcome was a radically "new man," the archetypical man of the West, shaped by the experience of emancipation from the rigid constraints of Old World society and by the opportunities which the New World proffered with an open hand. "*He* is an American, who, leaving behind him all his ancient prejudices and manners, receives new ones from the new mode of life he has embraced, the new government he obeys, and the new rank he holds. He becomes an American by being received in the broad lap of our great *Alma Mater."* Crèvecoeur thus boldly espoused a doctrine of American exceptionalism. The "new man" sprang fresh and virile from the New World soil; his ways of thinking and doing were distinctively different from those of his European forebears.

Crèvecoeur's observations and major propositions have been substantially modified by later writers. His vivid portrait of the happy husbandman has been disputed on the ground that it expressed more the bucolic romanticism of the European pastoral mystique than the actual character of the enterprising, restless, acquisitive American farmer to whom the land was something less to hold than to have, less to cherish over the passage of generations than to exploit for profit. Few scholars, moreover, have shared Crèvecoeur's belief that the dominant traits of American character are epitomized by a single representative figure, although fruitful studies have been made of the changing conventions of the hero in America—the fortunate farmer, the frontiersman, the self-made man and others, not excluding the contemporary antiheroic types of the gray-flannel "organization man" and the "other-directed" personality—in quest of clues to the structure of values which such popular images body forth. Crèvecoeur's comparatively unsophisticated theses of environmentalism and exceptionalism, later cast in the form of an influential explanation of American character by the historian Frederick Jackson Turner, have also been appreciably qualified and refined. These modifications having been noted, however, the major themes which Crèvecoeur explored continue to control the analysis of American character, and the objectives remain essentially the same: to trace whatever characterological patterns may exist (with a watchful eye to variations as well as to norms), to examine the ways in which Americans differ, whether markedly or marginally, from the people of other nations in point of values, behavior, and traits of personality, and to inquire into the factors and forces which have conditioned the experience by which the national character has been formed and may be altered.

The principal problems also persist, among them the problem of generalization. Unlike the artist who is concerned with the idiosyncratic and intensely personal experience of individuals or the historian who, eschewing the quest for general laws, modestly prefers to chronicle the sequences of unique and unrepeatable events,[2] the student of national character is a generalizer by necessity. In this respect his enterprise is related to the social or behavioral sciences, yet it also partakes of art insofar as he engages to depict a composite character by selecting and ordering the complex data which the modern nation presents to the inquiring eye. The "portrait" that results is necessarily a synthetic abstraction, derived from extensive observation disciplined by sagacity. It has the look of what the German sociologist Max Weber called an "ideal-type," that is, not an exact empirical description but a construction designed for conceptual clarity and analytical utility.[3] It also has the appearance of myth: "I speak," said the philosopher George Santayana, "of the American in the singular, as if there were not millions of them, north and south, east and west, of both sexes, of all ages, and of various races, professions, and religions. Of course the one American I speak of is mythical; but to speak in parables is inevitable in such a subject, and it is perhaps as well to do so frankly."[4] In its treatment of dominant and recessive features, the portrait is thus rather a caricature than a photographic likeness of, say, the passport type, but what it sacrifices in literal exactitude it may recoup by revelation of essentials. Blurring detail and risking distortion for the sake of expressive emphasis and manageable simplicity, the student of national character works in broad strokes on an immense canvas to delineate the distinctive qualities of a nation's people.

These observations on the identification of a normative national character lead to some remarks on the problem of exceptionalism, with particular reference to the American case. To what extent can it be justly stated that the American has been, through his historical career, a "new man" or at least a distinctively different man, as Crèvecoeur thought him to be? Popular sentiment endorses belief in the exceptionality of the inhabitants of the United States. Since the landing of the Puritans in the 1630s, Americans have regarded themselves as a "peculiar people," specially favored by God or nature, exempt from many of the ordinary tribulations of mankind, commissioned to enact a singularly significant role in human history. This presumption of a distinctive national status

---

[2]Cf. Fred A. Shannon's review of David M. Potter's *People of Plenty* in *The Mississippi Valley Historical Review,* XLI (March, 1955), p. 733: "I can envision 162,000,000 different American characters, perhaps divisible into 327 categories with wide divergencies in each, but I still cannot see an American national character."

[3]Cf., for example, David Riesman, "Some Observations on the Study of American Character," *Psychiatry,* XV (August, 1952), p. 333.

[4]Santayana, *Character and Opinion in the United States* (New York: George Braziller, 1955), pp. 94–95.

and destiny was reinforced by long years of political and military isolation from the Old World, by the achievements of democracy and economic enterprise, by the heady experience of conquering a continent, and by the commentaries of visitors from abroad who expatiated, curiously or critically, on the peculiarities of Americans. Such writers as Crèvecoeur, Tocqueville, and Turner, as the selections given in this volume show, worked within the convention of American exceptionalism, either assuming or attempting to demonstrate its validity.

Because an understanding of the ways in which Americans see and have seen themselves is essential to an understanding of American character, the conviction of peculiarity constitutes a significant subject for inquiry; it is one of the data with which the student of American character is concerned.[5] The issue of its validity, however, poses another sort of problem, one which requires circumspect treatment. No doubt the concept of exceptionality contains an important truth: the *total constellation* of American characteristics is evidently unique. At the same time, the concept stands in need of qualification by the recognition that, taken singly and out of context, most, if not all, of those characteristics are exemplified elsewhere. As David Riesman aptly remarks, "It is often said that a burger of Lyons is closer in type to a burger of Bremen or Buffalo than any of them is to a factory worker in his own country."[6] To say that Americans are different—which collectively they are, though the implications need not be invidious—is not to say that they are radically different—which is not necessarily so. The task of investigation is to check the proposition of exceptionalism by examining the nature and extent of supposed characterological differences.

Critics of the concept of national character sometimes object that excessive attention to the peculiarities of nations is pernicious because it impedes the realization of an international or supranational community of mankind. It is contended that "men are more alike" and that the differences which divide the nations ought to be de-emphasized in the interest of world order and concord.[7] Such remonstrances, however well intended, appear to be misdirected: national differences will not be wished away by refusal to examine them, let alone by denying that they exist. On the contrary, quite aside from national strategies of survival, the general interests of humanity are better served by candid assessment of differences to the end that erroneous stereotypes may be corrected and avenues of international communication may be improved. Furthermore, the investigation of national character is not restricted to the elements of contrast; correctly conceived, although the inquiry may sometimes be warped to the purposes of chauvinism and propaganda, it is concerned as much with the transna-

---

[5]See, among other writings, Ralph Henry Gabriel, *The Course of American Democratic Thought* (2nd ed.; New York: Ronald Press Co., 1956), and Edward McNall Burns, *The American Idea of Mission: Concepts of National Purpose and Destiny* (New Brunswick, N.J.: Rutgers University Press, 1957).

[6]"Psychological Types and National Character: An Informal Commentary," *American Quarterly*, V (Winter, 1953), p. 328.

[7]See, for example, Boyd Shafer, *Nationalism: Myth and Reality* (New York: Harcourt, Brace & World, 1955), ch. 12.

tional congruities of character as with culturally conditioned differences.[8] This fact furnishes an additional argument for comparative studies of national character.

The acknowledgment of these and other difficulties by contemporary scholars may be taken to mark the coming of age of national character study as a collaborative project of the social sciences. Fortunately, the value of the undertaking does not entirely depend on the solution of such problems. Useful results may be obtained from less than perfect methods, provided the investigator is cognizant of the hazards that he runs, and only the most rigorous theoretician would insist that all analysis be suspended until the apparatus be made scientifically impeccable. At the very least, recognition of obstacles to be overcome imposes a discipline of modesty which was often lacking among the impressionistic writers who dominated the field until about the time of World War II. At its best, fortified by wisdom and experience, impressionism could produce such masterwork as Alexis de Tocqueville's *Democracy in America,* from which a selection appears in this volume. At its worst, it exhibited the shoddy defects of prejudice, superficiality, stereotypical opinion, and fragmentary observation. When these deficiencies were compounded with a malignant ethnocentrism, as in the Aryan dogma of Nazi Germany, the idea of national character itself was discredited among sober scholars.

During the last 20-odd years national character has been restored to respectability as a legitimate subject for inquiry by the allied forces of the behavioral sciences. From the disciplines of social psychology, psychoanalysis, and cultural anthropology, linked in the study of "culture and personality," national character has acquired formulas which, though not altogether free of imperfection, have greatly reduced the liabilities under which the concept formerly labored. . . . When the findings of the behavioral scientists are illuminated by a knowledge of history it becomes evident that never before has there been better hope and more adequate intellectual equipment for discovering what the American is, has been, and may become.

Denver, Colorado   MICHAEL MCGIFFERT
July, 1964

---

[8]For a caustic indictment of the misuse of the idea of national character see Hamilton Fyfe, *The Illusion of National Character* (London, 1940).

Foreword to the
Revised Edition

Shifts in the foci of the study of national character—occasioned chiefly by deepening misgivings about the applicability of the formulas of culture and personality to the explanation of large, complex, modern national societies—together with the appearance of fresh interpretive writings, require revisions in a book that, like this one, seeks to be useful as an introduction to an important general field of learning. Of the first edition's 25 selections, 9 have been dropped; 14 have been added. The sections on child-rearing and on values are substantially enlarged; the readings from the characterology of the 1950's, centered in the work of David Riesman, are reduced in number and scope; a group of essays on contemporary American issues composes the collection's new concluding section. For helpful suggestions on what to take out and what to put in, I am indebted to students at the University of Denver and the University of Colorado Denver Center, as well as to the many social scientists and historians who have shared with me their knowledge of the literature and their experience in teaching this anthology. The editorial effort has been subsidized by a grant from the Graduate School of the University of Denver.

My interest in studying the character of Americans was first inspired, and has been greatly instructed, by David M. Potter, professor of history at Stanford University, to whom this volume is gratefully dedicated.

Denver, Colorado
May, 1970

MMcG

Contents

V. AMERICAN VALUES

VI. THE ONGOING INQUIRY

INTRODUCTION I

INTRODUCTION I

Each of the three following selections is concerned with the quest for an American identity; together they introduce most of the major themes of this volume. Contending that it is characteristically American to be intensely inquisitive about the American character, John A. Kouwenhoven, Professor of English at Barnard College, locates the sources of our national self-consciousness in the discontinuities of American experience and the mixture of cultural heritages to which Americans lay claim. A people of varied pasts whose national character is a matter more of achievement than of birthright, Americans derive a common identity from their experience of "estrangement" from the past. Kouwenhoven's essay, subtitled "Some Un-American Advice to Non-Americans," grew out of a talk to a group of foreign students in 1959.

The second reading comes from the book *America as a Civilization* (1957), an encyclopedic examination of contemporary life and thought in the United States, by Max Lerner, newspaper columnist, lecturer, teacher, and author of many books on American culture and public affairs. Dealing circumspectly with the problems of defining the character of Americans, Lerner argues that the American is at once "the archetypal modern man" and the exemplar of a pattern of culture which is unique. To solve the riddle posed by these apparently contradictory propositions, he advances a qualified doctrine of exceptionalism: "The idea of American exceptionalism and the idea of American integration into the broader Western pattern are not mutually exclusive," for America "has developed its own characteristic institutions, traits, and social conditions within the larger [Western] frame." With respect to American character Lerner discovers no simple formula, no single organizing principle, no all-embracing explanation, but rather a diversity of traits, values, and impulses so great that American civilization must be viewed as "a highly polarized field of meaning."

In the third selection, the historian David M. Potter, of Stanford University, surveys important definitions of American character from Thomas Jefferson to David Riesman and reflects on the problem of reconciling the contrasting images of the American as individualist and idealist (depicted by Jefferson and by

Frederick Jackson Turner in his "frontier hypothesis") and as materialist and conformist (described by Alexis de Tocqueville). These seemingly contrary appraisals, Potter suggests, may be harmonized as expressions of the fundamental value of equality, especially that "strand of equalitarianism which stresses the universal dignity of all men, and which hates rank as a violation of dignity. . . ." Herein Potter discerns a possible "key to various facts of the national character, even to contradictory aspects" of it, so that where Max Lerner emphasizes "the polar impulses" of American culture, Potter finds evidence of an essential inner consistency. As the readings in this collection show, the study of American character derives vitality from the tension, illustrated by Lerner and Potter, between the stress on diversity and the stress on unity.

The Dispraising of America

JOHN A. KOUWENHOVEN

I imagine that one of the most curious, one of the oddest, things that non-Americans notice in America is what might be called the American's self-consciousness about his American-ness. We have been like that for many years—from the very beginning, in fact.

The first published answer to the question "What is an American?" appeared in 1782—just one year after the battle of Yorktown victoriously ended six years of fighting for American independence. The question forms the title of a much-quoted chapter in *Letters from an American Farmer; Describing Certain Provincial Situations, Manners, and Customs, Not Generally Known.*

This book, which first posed the self-conscious "American" question, was written in the English language, for an English audience, by a man born and educated in France, who lived while writing it in New York, but who referred to himself as a Pennsylvanian, and who stopped off in London, to arrange for the book's publication there, while he was on his way back to his native France—whence he would soon return to America as French consul in New York where (as he told his friend Benjamin Franklin) he enjoyed "The Privileges of double citizenship."

I have deliberately emphasized the mix-up of tradition in Hector St. John de Crèvecoeur's background because I want to suggest that, in a sense, the American's self-consciousness about his American-ness is still—as it was in 1782—in great part the result of a feeling or sense of "double citizenship." We Americans are all, in one way or another, aware of a double or bifurcated heritage. The eleventh-generation descendant of immigrants from Holland and the second-generation descendant of immigrants from China are no different in this respect from the eleventh-generation descendant of Negro slaves imported from the

Reproduced by permission of the author from John A. Kouwenhoven, *The Beer Can by the Highway: Essays on What's "American" about America* (Garden City, N.Y.: Doubleday & Co., Inc., 1961).

Congo. Each of us is conscious of a heritage as an American, and each of us is conscious of another heritage—or, more commonly, of a complex mixture of heritages—from cultures whose values are, in varying degrees, unlike those we have acquired as Americans.

In some sense this is no doubt true of other peoples as well as Americans. One thinks of the Canadians and Australians, for example, or the Liberians or the Israelis. Canada, with its bilingual culture, presents a special problem. It lives with a clear-cut, external duality between English-speaking Canadians and French Canadians, a cleavage which is marked by geographical as well as linguistic boundaries. But in so far as the French Canadian has been cut off from his French heritage, he was cut off from it by the Englishmen who have become his fellow Canadians, not by an act of his own will. Neither the English-speaking nor the French Canadians, nor the Australians, have voluntarily shattered the continuity of their non-Canadian or non-Australian heritage by an appeal to revolutionary violence, with its inevitable aftermath of resentment and passionate self-assertion.

As for the Liberians and Israelis, however diverse their national origins may be, their motive in immigrating to the countries in which they now live was to re-establish their ties to a heritage even older and more deeply rooted in them than that of the nation from which they came. The immigrant to the United States, however, has always been required (or has deliberately sought) to attach himself to a heritage-in-the-making—a heritage which is not in any sense one to which he is entitled by his ancestry, but one to whose shaping he, as much as (but no more than) anyone else, has the right and duty to contribute.

What James Baldwin, the American novelist, once said of the American Negro can be said with some justice of the white American as well: he arrives at his identity "by virtue of the absoluteness of his estrangement from his past." We Americans do, of course, nourish illusions of recovering the European or African or Asian or American-Indian half of our dual heritage. Some of us even maintain an illusory sort of psychologically dual citizenship. Such illusions may, indeed, be necessary as long as men are uncertain about the legitimacy of their status, and the American—white or non-white—has never been quite sure what his status is. For we are all, as it were, the younger sons, the disinherited, the bastard offspring of the past. The American estate to which we lay claim is not, and cannot be, ours by right of primogeniture. It is ours only by squatters' right, or by virtue of conquest or piracy or love.

For all these reasons it is true, I think, that the citizens of no other major world power share the special sense of "double citizenship" which from Crèvecoeur's time to ours has made the Americans so self-consciously inquisitive about "What is an American?" A century after Crèvecoeur, Henry James, one of the greatest American novelists, devoted his major energies to the imaginative exploration of the implications of that question, and entitled one of his major novels *The American*. I do not know of (and cannot imagine) any important French author writing a novel called *The Frenchman*, or any Russian writing one called *The Russian*. Our libraries are full of disputatious writings by Americans with titles like *The American Spirit in Art* and *The American Style in Politics*. There *is*, of course, a book called *The Englishness of English Art*—but it was not written by an Englishman, I assure you. Until recently, at least, the English have confidently known what was English about England and therefore have not had to be self-conscious about it. But the Americans have never been sure what it was to be Americans—which is why, from the beginning, they have asserted so loudly and so inconclusively that they *were* sure. I have a shelfful of books purporting to define the American spirit or the American character and they offer as many different definitions as there are books—all mistaken definitions, too, except one (the one I wrote), and even that one strikes me as slightly tinted by its author's myopia.

Now, the reason for dwelling at some length on this characteristic in remarks which are addressed to non-Americans is that if you are a visitor or temporary resident in the United States, you probably have some reason to want to understand what the "American spirit" is, or what the "American character's" characteristics are. If you are curious about such things, we will be delighted; and if, when you return to your homes, you write a book about us, telling your countrymen the truth about America, be sure to get the book published in this country, too. It will almost certainly be a best seller—especially if it is very critical and says disagreeable things about the "Snow Queen" frigidity of American women; the low, materialistic interests of American men (and their humble subservience to their womenfolk); the disparity between our professions of democratic equality and our economic and educational segregation of Negroes; our addiction to comic books and bottled pop; and the rest.

If you write a book giving the lowdown on America from a foreign observer's point of view, you will be in good company. Some very intelligent foreigners have written some very interesting books about us—ranging from the Frenchman De Tocqueville's great work on *Democracy in America*, down through Lord Bryce's study of the *American Commonwealth*, to the Swedish Gunnar Myrdal's *The American Dilemma*. Each of these was and is popular with American readers. But you don't have to be as judicious and encyclopedic as De Tocqueville, Bryce, and Myrdal to be a hit with us. You can be as intemperate as Mrs. Trollope, who flatly told her English countrymen in 1832 that she had discovered the Americans to be horrid: "I do not like their principles," she wrote, "I do not like their manners, I do not like their opinions." And for her courtesy we have rewarded her by buying up unnumbered editions of her book—which is still—after a hundred and twenty years—in print.

The Derogatory Stance

This appetite of ours for comment about us, abusive or judicious, may seem an endearing quality, especially if you are looking forward to getting substantial royalty checks from an American publisher, but you should be warned that from other points of view it might prove to be a trap.

Put it this way, to start with. Our appetite for criticism and analysis of America by foreigners is an aspect of our self-conscious interest in discovering what "an American" is, and this in turn is a symptom of our not knowing. Since we don't know, and wish very much that we did (our philanthropic foundations spend hundreds of thousands of dollars a year subsidizing studies of precisely this question), we love to listen to anyone who talks as if he knew. If he bases what he says on statistical studies and the paraphernalia of sociological research, so much the better. But if he spins it all out of his head, we don't mind that either.

Being an essentially modest people—or shall I say a people who by education and admonition have been taught that the architecture of Greece, and the Roman code of law, and the painting of Flanders and France, and the ethical wisdom of the Orient, and the poetry and drama of England are unsurpassed and unsurpassable, and that even in technology and science the basic work is all European and we have merely applied the principles ingeniously—being whatever you want to call this, a modest or fundamentally unself-assured people—we find it easier to believe the derogatory things about ourselves than the approving ones. We also find it easier to say the derogatory things—in fiction, drama, and the expressive arts in general.

Of course there was a time when we could (and did) say the self-approving things. But nobody but an ass could have taken us very seriously in our moods of slapping ourselves on the back, and—as a matter of fact—few people did take it seriously. It was too obviously a kind of whistling in the dark. Not even the writers who "made the eagle scream," as the saying was in the nineteenth century, took themselves seriously; often they were being intentionally funny and fooled nobody except humorless English travelers and some uncommonly stuffy politicians. (I am, of course, oversimplifying here—but it is generally true, I think, that whenever an American says anything very flattering about American civilization, he hastens to counteract it with something unflattering, in order to avoid what he feels would be an air of "I'm better than you," in order to "take himself down a peg.")

The result is that in serious writing about the nature and quality of the American experience, both fiction and non-fiction, whether written by foreigners or by Americans, you are likely to find more that is derogatory than that is approving. And most of what is approving can easily be discounted as ignorant, or superficial, or mere high spirits.

Furthermore—and this is the root of the difficulty, if one is really intent upon learning what America means—it is very easy to mistake the significance of the literature which criticizes or rejects American culture for its bourgeois values, its materialism, its complacency, and so on. We are all quite likely to take such criticism at its face value, and thereby miss the point. We are likely either to praise it for its success in embodying values "superior" to America's standardized middle-class mediocrity, or, if we are in a chauvinistic or jingoistic mood, to damn it out of hand for its wrongheadedness.

The significance of a novel like Sinclair Lewis's *Babbitt* is, I believe, missed if you conclude from it either that Lewis was "un-American" because he disapproved of businessmen like Babbitt or that his book represents a set of values "superior" to (and therefore not characteristic of) the values of the civilization men like Babbitt had created in America. For Lewis was not writing as one who has descended from a "higher" plane to observe our civilization. He writes as one of us, who has seen—from a perspective which he assumes his fellow Americans can share—the inadequacies, the forlorn limitations of certain aspects of American life—aspects which his readers will reject just as he does. And of course he was right. His novel was a great popular success. His readers, most of whom were in business or commerce, saw in Babbitt some of the very things that they saw in themselves, and toward which they felt, like Lewis, an odd mixture of sardonic amusement and of loyalty.

What I am trying to suggest is that, if a foreign reader concluded, from the quality of photographic, tape-recorded reality which Lewis's technique imparts to his novel, that Babbitt was the typical American businessman of the 1920's— and if he further concluded that, since American civilization is a business civilization, he could draw from the novel some conclusions about the inadequacies and forlorn limitations of the civilization itself, he would have run a serious risk. Hitler and his cohorts took such a risk, gambling that a nation of Babbitts would not rise to the challenge of Nazi domination of Europe. The leaders of other nations may make a similar mistake if they get the impression from our current non-fiction that we are a nation of juvenile delinquents or if they conclude from our young poets and novelists that our young people are beatniks. For Jack Kerouac and Ginsberg, like Lewis and Mencken in the twenties, do not quite signify what they appear to be saying. Their significance, I think, is that they are witnesses to the basic and never-ceasing drive within our culture to lift itself, to be dissatisfied with its limitations, to try—at whatever cost in self-distrust or self-reproach—to discover what, indeed, is an American.

Citizens of a New World

I am afraid I am beginning to sound apocalyptic, as if, like the cheap politician whom the nineteenth-century humorists burlesqued, I were about to make the American eagle scream. I hope that is not what I am about to do.

For what interests me about American civilization is that it is not—even in name—the civilization of the United States. As that name "American" suggests, it is something whose relevance is not confined in political boundaries. I know that we use it that way some of the time. I know that our neighbors in Latin America sometimes are hurt by what they assume to be our arrogance in speaking of ourselves as Americans; for geographically, they are as much Americans as we who live in the United States. But I like to think that at least some of the time we know this as well as they do, and that when we call ourselves Americans we are not implying that they are *not* Americans, but are—on the contrary—thinking of ourselves not merely as citizens of the United States but as people living in a New World. For in a very real sense we, like all people whose lives have felt the impact of the twin energies of democracy and technology, *are* living in a New World—not merely the hemispheric New World of the geographers, but the New World which the great seventeenth-century English physician, Sir Thomas Browne, called "the America and untravelled parts of truth." Everyone who lives in *this* America, in *this* new and untraveled world, is as much concerned as are those of us who live in the United States to discover "What is an American?"

I am sure that I forget from time to time, as most of my fellow citizens forget, that this New World is not coextensive with my nation, or—more provincial still—with my precinct. I know that United States foreign policy is often not synonymous with a policy which would be genuinely American in the sense of that word I have tried to suggest. But our tendency to behave, much of the time, as citizens of the United States is as human and natural as it is for people in other lands to behave as citizens of Ghana or India or France. We cannot ignore, nor should non-Americans who wish to understand us ignore, the national heritage of the United States and the privileges and obligations of its citizens. But if I am not mistaken what we all really want to know is what Crèvecoeur wanted to know a century and three quarters ago: what is an American? And that question can be answered, I think, only when we discover that non-geographical "America" which is, in fact, the community in whose citizenship all our bifurcated heritages, our dual citizenships, are ultimately involved. We shall know "what is an American," I suspect, only when we know who is fit to be a citizen of the New World to whose dynamics and energies the United States has made large contributions, but which is being shaped by people in all lands where the influence of modern technology, and of a democratic faith in man's unexplored potentialities, have been felt. For America, in this sense, is still in the making—is still the New World to which mankind has for so many centuries been adventuring.

The Idea of American Civilization

MAX LERNER

Archetypal Man of the West

Commentators on American traits delight in quoting De Crèvecoeur's classic remark that "the American is a new man who acts on new principles." One should add that while the American was a *novus homo* when De Crèvecoeur wrote his *Letters from an American Farmer* toward the end of the eighteenth century, he is no longer so in the mid-twentieth. He is no longer an experiment: he has been proved a success, by every standard of wealth, glitter, prestige, freedom, and power. Wherever history pours fresh molten metal, in industrial achievement, living standards, and political freedom, inevitably it makes him at least in part the mold. The American has become the "New World man"—the archetypal man of the West.

For an American to write thus may seem too boastful, yet I try to write it as if I were not American but a detached observer noting a new phenomenon. Americans are not loved in the world today, although they deeply desire affection. In the countries of color there is a good deal of suspicion of them, and even some hatred. In the older civilizations of Europe there is a kind of patronizing contempt which passes for anti-Americanism. Throughout the world there is a fear of the current American stress on arms and money. Yet it remains true that the principal imperialism the American exercises is the imperialism of attraction. If he is not admired, he is envied; and even his enemies and rivals pay him the homage of imitation. People throughout the world turn almost as by a tropism to the American image. To be American is no longer to be only a

Reproduced by permission of the author from Max Lerner, *America as a Civilization: Life and Thought in the United States Today* (New York: Simon and Schuster, 1957). Footnotes omitted.

nationality. It has become, along with Communism and in rivalry with it, a key pattern of action and values.

So summary a conquest of the world's imagination, never before achieved without arms and colonization, is proof of an inner harmony between America and the modern spirit. It is because of this harmony that America has acted as a suction force, drawing from everywhere people attuned to its basic modes of life. The migration to America, from the start, of capital and of human labor and talent, was followed by the migration from America of capital, talent, economic and military strength. Both migrations, to and from America, have multiplied its influence. Having absorbed the world's strength to form its own, America has been fusing its own strength with the world's.

There has been from the start a marriage of true minds between the American and the type-man of the modern era, the New World man. To the question, wonderfully put in 1782 by De Crèvecoeur in his *American Farmer,* "What then is the American, this new man?" De Tocqueville sought an answer on his visit in the 1830s. The greatness of his book lay at least partly in its portrayal of a young civilization in which incipient European forces could reach their climactic form. In America the main trends of tendency that were dammed up in Europe itself were to find expression. As Robert Payne has put it, "America is Europe with all the walls down." Although I have insisted that America is a definable civilization in itself, it first emerged as an offshoot from the larger entity of the West which was seeking a New World form. The American is thus the concentrated embodiment of Western man, more sharply delineated, developed under more urgent conditions, but with most of the essential traits present.

Consider some of these traits. I am trying here to describe, not the American alone, but a type which has cropped up all over Europe as well since the Reformation and the rise of science.

He is mobile, restless. He has largely broken with status and moves more freely than Old World man moved up and down the ladder of wealth and class rank, as he moved over large areas, conquering space. He rifles the sciences as he opens up the continents, quenchless in his thirst for experience. He is this-worldly and not otherworldly, with a sharp sense of time and its uses: the objects of his ambition are secular rather than sacred. Accustomed to thinking in terms of the attainable, he is optimistic, with a belief in progress and a respect for technical skills and material success. He is *homo faber,* stamping his imprint on products and on machines that make products and on machines that run machines, and increasingly in the same spirit on art and ideas. He believes in whatever can be touched, grasped, measured. He is a technical man, whose absorption is not with *to what good* but with *how.* He is non-ascetic, with a taste for comfort and a belief that the means, if not the goal, of life are found in a higher living standard.

He is *l'homme moyen sensuel,* not too finicky in his sexual life about caste or class lines or about rigid standards of virtue. Hungering for a sense of personal worth, he is torn between the materialisms he can achieve and the feeling of wholeness which eludes him. He has a disquieting sense that the old gods too have eluded him and wonders when the new ones will arrive. Yet, unlike men of previous ages, it is not salvation he is after, nor virtue, nor saintliness, nor beauty, nor status. He is an amoral man of energy, mastery, and power. Above all else, he is a man for whom the walls have been broken down. He is the double figure in Marlowe, of Tamerlane and Dr. Faustus, the one sweeping like a footloose barbarian across the plains to overleap the barriers of earlier civilizations, the other breaking the taboos against knowledge and experience, even at the cost of his soul.

For this modern man the world has not yet become one world, and as the contemporary tensions attest, some time will elapse before it does. Yet what is likely to count in this direction is less the outlook of the diplomats than of the new geographers who complete the work of the cartographers of the Renaissance. Being technical men, they turn the globe around every possible way, but basically theirs is the airman's view for whom political boundaries are minor, and the heavens arch over them to be pierced and the earth stretches out to be engirded by flight. For the airman, racial boundaries do not exist either: what he sees from the air is not the color of men but how well the fields are laid out and irrigated and cultivated, what has been done in uncovering and using Nature's resources, what chimneys and spires are the witnesses of industry and culture, what clusters of community life there are in villages, cities, metropolitan areas. This was the glimpse that Wendell Willkie had—that despite divergences of economic systems, of race and color and language and social structure, the world is compassable, interdependent, organic.

Thus the great themes of the Renaissance and Reformation are fulfilled in the American as the archetypal modern man—the discovery of new areas, the charting of the skies, the lure of power, the realization of self in works, the magic of science, the consciousness of the individual, the sense of the unity of history. These are the themes that have left their mark on modern man. Perceiving this, Wyndham Lewis said of America that "the logic of the geographical position and history of the U. S. leads . . . to the ultimate formation of a society that will not be as other societies, but an epitome of all societies." He had in mind specifically the ethnic pluralism and democratic inclusiveness of America which hold the world in microcosm. It is this trans-national character of American society which, despite the surviving American tribalisms, makes it congruous with the strivings of other peoples. The same applies to the structure of the American personality, which is mobile, ethnically diverse, energy-charged, amoral, optimistic, genial, technic-minded, power-oriented. The question is not whether these traits are admirable or lovable but whether they polarized the energies of much of the world—as they do.

American Exceptionalism

The portrait of American—and New World—man I have just drawn is not meant to be an idealized one. It has shadows as well as lights. And it poses a riddle of both logic and history: logically, how we can speak of the American as the "archetypal" man of the modern world and at the same time assert that American civilization is a pattern within itself, whole and unique; historically, how America has developed out of the common conditions of the modern world, yet developed with such an acceleration of energy and power; and whether the future arc of its development is likely to recapitulate the course of experience of European and Asiatic civilizations.

I do not underestimate the difficulties of this riddle. That is why I am little inclined to see America within any of the rather grandiose schemes of historical determinism, whose real value is to suggest lines of study and not to close them. The seduction of historical parallels should not lure us away from studying America as a civilization pattern in itself—its tensions, its lines of development, its weaknesses and strengths. The learning of Vico and Hegel, of Marx, of Spengler and Toynbee, of Sorokin, would still leave unexplained the unlikely genesis of America, its rapid rise to power, the contrast of its outer image and its inner qualities, its materialism and idealism, its isolationism and leadership role. Whether such a civilization will survive or is doomed will depend less on grand historical "laws" than upon how Americans grapple with their problems and use their characteristic resources and energies.

If I do not subscribe to the cry of "America is doomed," neither am I pleading for the distorted version of "American exceptionalism" which has been the pious theme of spread-eagle theorists seeking to depict America as immune from the forces of history and the laws of life. This version of exceptionalism is easily used as an idea weapon in the anti-democratic struggle, as Schlesinger shows in citing the attack on the efforts to organize trade-unions in the Jacksonian period. Ever since then the cry that "America is different" has been an unfailing answer to any challenge that might disturb the structure of existing power, and the carriers of the challenge have been regarded as "un-American," "alien," and therefore "subversive."

But these distortions should not blind us to the valid elements in the theory of exceptionalism. The fact is that while American civilization is not immune to the surging beat of world forces, it has developed its own characteristic institutions, traits, and social conditions within the larger frame. America represents, as I have stressed above, the naked embodiment of the most dynamic elements of modern Western history. What this implies is that exceptionalism *includes* an acceptance of the European ties and does not reject them. The idea of American exceptionalism and the idea of American integration into the broader Western pattern are not usually exclusive but are polar facets of the same field of energy. When you speak of American uniqueness, you must speak also in the same framework about the European diversity. It is in this sense of what is *characteristically American* that I use the idea of exceptionalism.

A rapid listing of some of the outstanding books on America will show that almost every commentator has fixed on some unique elements in it. De Tocqueville saw the whole of American life as a new form of society which he called *democracy*. Charles Dickens had never seen anything to equal American money-mad materialism. Bryce was impressed with the uniqueness of the Federal system and the party system. Whitman, castigating American corruption, nevertheless glimpsed democratic vistas beyond them more stirring than ever before in history. Henry and Brooks Adams saw the degradation of the democratic dogma stretched further in America than anywhere else in the democratic world. Thorstein Veblen, who felt that American capitalism had been carried to a unique degree of power, concentration, and finesse, did a series of studies in absentee ownership showing how business enterprise in modern times had taken characteristic forms in the case of America—developing such home-grown products as the country town, the independent farmer, the captain of industry, the technology of physics and chemistry.

Herbert Croly found a peculiar "promise" in American life he found nowhere else. Waldo Frank, in his "rediscovery" of America, found equally a characteristically excessive power and excessive childishness in the American mind. D. H. Lawrence found in "classical" American literature a mixture of the primitive and the bourgeois, in the clash of which he located the characteristic split in the American soul. H. L. Mencken, studying the one feature of American life which might have been expected to follow the pattern of its English parent—its speech—found elements of originality in it so marked as to make it a separate American language. André Siegfried, explaining America in the 1920s and again in the 1950s, saw its peculiar problems in the clash between the "Anglo-Saxon tradition" and the later immigrant strains; but he also asserted that America was a new civilization that had left the European far behind. Robert and Helen Lynd, in their two *Middletown* studies, wryly found the distillation of American thinking in the "Middletown spirit"—a body of folk-belief that set Americans off from any other culture. Margaret Mead saw the core of the American character in the distinctive effects of the authority-and-freedom pattern on the interaction of the sexes and the growing-up process within the family. D. W. Brogan saw an interrelation between the paradoxes within the American political system and within the national character. Geoffrey Gorer, arguing that the child in America is conditioned to seek love and success above all else, deduced from it a different but still characteristic American personality pattern. Wyndham Lewis saw in the ethnic mixtures of the American stock, and their ways of living together, the seeds of "cosmic man."

David Riesman explored the American character in terms of its increasing submission to the tyranny of opinion and the failure of the individual to heal his loneliness in the crowd. David M. Potter saw the Americans as a "people of plenty" and the crucial traits of the American character as arising from situations of abundance and opportunity. Daniel Boorstin saw the genius of American politics in the American's habit of taking his own premises and values for granted as "givens," not to be thought about. Louis Hartz saw the specific character of an institution as shaped by the fact that Americans never had an old feudal order to destroy by revolutionary overturn, as the Europeans did.

I do not mean to imply that each of these writers was an adherent of the theory of American exceptionalism. I do say that these important studies of the whole or some segment of American life use, as a practical matter, the working hypothesis of an American character and culture which are set off distinctively from others in history and in the contemporary world.

National Character and the Civilization Pattern

The convenient way to deal with the problem of national character is to list a people's traits, presenting them as "American traits," the "American mind," or the "American spirit." Some of the commentators enumerate the traits mechanically, as if it were a question of a grocery list or a warehouse inventory of odds-and-ends items. One trouble with this method of delineating character by enumeration is that the lists tend to cancel each other out. Lee Coleman, culling the lists of American traits from the available commentaries on America, found he could spot the exact opposite in some other list. Thus Americans are generous and niggardly, sympathetic and unfeeling, idealistic and cynical, visionary and practical—which leaves us with the conclusion, true but not novel, that Americans are bewilderingly human. Another difficulty is that the traits change over the generations. Compare the Garden of Eden picture of American traits in De Crèvecoeur at the end of the eighteenth century with De Tocqueville's for the late 1830s and 1840s, Bryce's contemporary picture for the 1880s and 1890s, or (retrospectively) Commager's *The American Mind* for the same period.

There are, however, certain salient traits which commentators attribute to the American in every period: Coleman finds that these are the tendency to club together or "join" in associations, the belief in democracy, the belief in equality, individual freedom, "direct action" in disregard of law, stress on local government, practicality, prosperity and material well-being, Puritanism, the influence of religion, uniformity and conformity.

It is hard to define the American national character by listing traits or even "value clusters," mainly because there are difficulties inherent in the idea of national character itself. Many writers are wary of it because it has been used cynically in war and power struggles to blacken the enemy symbol or sustain the conceit of a God-given or history-given national superiority. Caught between the Fascist theorists who have used it to bolster their doctrine of racist purity and pollution, and the Marxist theorists who reject it for placing too little stress on class interest and class militancy, the idea of national character has become a thorny and controversial one.

While it is risky to attribute a national character to any people, as if its qualities and destiny could be ripped out of the living body of history, it is also true that nations are realities, that their cultures develop along different paths, and that the world inside the heads of their people is a characteristic world. Much of the chauvinist and racist treachery of the term can be avoided if it is remembered that national character is a doctrine not of blood but of culture. It consists of a body of values, social habits, attitudes, traits held in common by most members of the culture. Thus the psychological field of action, thought, and emotion into which an American is born differs not only from the Russian or Chinese but even from that of an Englishman.

Traditionally, national character has been used as a semi-literary rule-of-thumb to differentiate one nationality type from another or give impressionistic force to generalization about a whole people. One of the classics here is Emerson's *English Traits,* which is witness that literary insight may be worth more than all the paraphernalia of recent social science. Yet the new anthropological and psychiatric techniques did mark a turning point in the approach to national character. First they were applied to the study of primitive personality structure, and then to psychological warfare in World War II. The psychiatrists knew from their experience that diagnosis and therapy vary with individuals of differing character types, and that these character types apply not only to neurotics and psychotics but to presumably normal persons. At the same time the anthropologists, studying contemporary primitive groups, found that each culture has its own pattern, within which there are also several different variants of character and personality. In World War II, before the military strategists could lay their plans for an assault on the enemy mind, they had to know what the enemy mind was like—hence the American studies of the Germans and Japanese, in which the theory of national character was tested in the crucible of life-and-death action. Thus the war studies converged with the work of the psychiatrists and anthropologists to form a new strain, one whose by-product has been an effort to apply the same techniques to contemporary America.

This strain of inquiry now makes possible a new way of getting at what has usually been called the "American character" or the "American spirit." It is not a disembodied presence in the sky or some mystical force inherent in race or history. Neither is it the body of folk-belief that Americans derive from their mass media and their whole cultural environment. It is best sought at the point where cultural norms in America shape personality and character, and where in turn the human material and the energies of Americans leave their impact on the fabric of the culture.

I may cite as an example of this process the way children are brought up in America, how their personalities are shaped by the emotional atmosphere of the family and the structure of authority and freedom within it, how the whole tone of growing up is set by the inordinate concentration on the child, the pervasive influence of the new big-audience media, the seeping in of the cultural values of success, prestige, and security, and the clash between permissive and restrictive codes as it is reflected in the child's mind. One can find similar examples in what is happening to the American character and spirit today as a result of suburban living, or the conditions of work and incentive within the new corporate structures, or the wave of "do-it-yourself" amateurism which has come as a recoil from the trend toward complete mechanization, or the sense of encirclement that leads to a stress on "loyalty" and "security," or the virtual ending of immigration, or the emergence of new elites and a complex, far-reaching middle class. These are only a few instances of how the energies of the individual American are channeled by characteristic cultural conditions of training and living, shaping certain common character traits for whole groups of individuals and weaving them into the fabric of the civilization.

This does not mean that, by some necromantic determinism, every little American who is born alive comes out stamped with exactly the same traits or propensities. There are in-groups, out-groups, and marginal groups; there are regional, class, and ethnic variations; there is a bewildering variety of individual personality patterns and traits. Yet the central stream of tendency remains, and with it the shaping interrelations of American personality and culture.

What are some of the ways of uncovering this interrelation? One way is a study of mental disorders, asking, as the psychiatrists do, what are the characteristic sources of personality breakdown—what it is that makes Americans crack up when and as they do? To answer this means to get some insight into the strains under which men live in America, the expectations the culture sets up in them as against the satisfactions it places within their reach, the norms of conduct and thought it seeks to enforce, the fault lines and frustrations that develop within them. Another way is to ask what personality types can be most clearly discerned among Americans, and what modes of life and striving within the culture account for the impulse toward those personality types. A third is to ask what life goals the Americans set up for themselves and what they make a cult of and are obsessed with, making sure to distinguish between the conscious and irrational levels of their striving.

One can dig deeper, perhaps, and seek some hidden dimension of the American character which symbolizes the basic American life view. Thus F. S. C. Northrop (The Meeting of East and West) takes the deepest thing about any civilization to be its metaphysic—its assumptions and beliefs about the constitution of the unseen universe, and he suggests that it was the reception by America of the atomistic metaphysics of Locke and Hume which has influenced the individualism and fragmentation of American life. Thus also Charles W. Morris (Six Ways of Life) attempts an approach through symbolic value systems. He lists the crucial systems in history as the Dionysian (surrender to the instinctual life), the Buddhist (annihilation of self for serenity), the Christian (purifying of self for spiritual values), the Mohammedan (merging of self in a holy war against the enemies of the true way), the Apollonian (conserving of traditional values), and the Promethean (conquest and organization of the environment by science and technology). He sees American civilization as primarily Promethean, but with elements of the Christian and the Apollonian, pointing out that the Promethean strain puts the emphasis on the instrumental, that the Apollonian has hardened into a Toryism of the spirit which could mean a static civilization, and that the Christian strain has had to be subordinated when it has conflicted with the more dominant elements of the civilization. I cite this suggestive scheme to illustrate how the study of the great world myths can shed light on what Americans are like and what they live by.

Since most of this is speculative, American observers have tried to approach their own civilization by the very different and more modest road of community surveys and cross-section area studies—of "Middletown," "Jonesville," "Yankeetown," "Elmtown," "Southern Town," "Plainville." What these studies offer is a degree of verification for certain theoretical leads, or of doubt cast upon others; they can show the extent to which the members of the American culture verbalize the articles in the American creed, and how they see themselves (and others) in the class system and the success-and-rating system of their time. But the community studies can never be broader or deeper than the issues they pose, nor more imaginative than the questions they raise.

Discussions of national character sometimes remind you of one of Cagliostro's magical spells or the incantatory hokum of a side-show barker telling the virtues of some nostrum. There is no talismanic quality in any of the newer approaches to national character. The hard work of giving contour to the mass of known material on American civilization cannot be dispensed with. The insights of the psychiatrists and anthropologists are all to the good, if they do not overstress some single symbolic key to the national character. The method of Gorer, for example, as used in the Gorer-Rickman study, *The People of Great Russia*, has been sharply satirized as the "swaddling theory" because it takes the infantile experience of the Russian peasant child, who was closely swaddled in the early months of his life, as a pre-verbal emotional conditioning to the rage, guilt, and violent alternations of emotion in the Russian as an adult. In *The American People*, Gorer put stress on the cult of the mother, the rejection of the father, the child's craving for affection, and the fear of loneliness, and again saw them as clue—if not cause—to the national character. A good deal depends on how hard the thesis is pushed. If we take it not as a verified truth but as impressionistic lead for further research and analysis, it is all to the good. The course of wisdom is to recognize the limits of any study of personality traits and to see the whole of the national character as one phase of the total civilization pattern.

Single Key—or Polar Pattern?

The question then arises whether there is some single organizing principle in this civilization pattern, some key that unlocks all the doors. For generations Western thinkers have been haunted by the dream of finding the single factor that shapes all else in its image. It might be Hegel or Spencer, Marx or Sorel, Spengler, Freud or Jung, Veblen, Henry George, Brooks Adams or Henry Adams, but it was always a form of cabala. I can offer the reader no single talisman to the secret of American civilization.

The temptation is great to seek it. Following the lead of Marx or Veblen, one might stress the march of technology and the system of business power, and build all the rest on that. After Laski's *American Democracy,* which applied that method unsparingly to the analysis of contemporary America, such an approach would yield sharply decreasing returns. While Laski's theme is democracy, as with De Tocqueville and Bryce, it is the subject of the book only as a corpse is the subject of a murder mystery. The real theme is the system of capitalist power and its business civilization: between these and democracy Laski depicts a bitter feud. Democracy in Laski's study is a little like the hero of Clifford Odet's early play, *Waiting for Lefty:* the stage is set for the hero, everyone measures his life and aspirations by him, but he never shows up because he has fallen victim to the forces of greed and reaction. Obviously economic power and class structure are important themes in the American civilization pattern, and I shall dwell a good deal on them. But an analysis which makes them the sole key distorts a good deal and misses many of the most dramatic recent changes in American life.

Laski's approach, like Veblen's, marked a recoil from the school of political idealism, which seemed to make political institutions and ideas the end and beginning and everything in the middle. In one sense De Tocqueville belonged to that tradition, since he started with the idea of democracy and traced its ramifications through phase after phase of American life. But De Tocqueville set an example of breadth of view which could not be matched by the later students of America, even someone with the insight of Bryce, whose approach was more narrowly through the political institutions of *The American Commonwealth,* while De Tocqueville's traced out imaginatively the political and moral ramifications of the democratic idea. Bryce, moreover, had lost much of the sense of wonder and excitement one finds in De Tocqueville about the revolutionary implications of democracy and was more interested in how the political actuality had worked out. In both cases, however, the organizing principle is political.

Another approach lays the key stress on psychological and moral values. It gives primacy to beliefs and attitudes, and the creative force of religion and ideas, and derives the technology and economic achievement of America from them rather than the other way round. The unacknowledged assumption is that the way to understand America is to start with the human psyche in its American form and with its whole intellectual and moral world. One finds this approach, with mystical overtones, in Waldo Frank's *Rediscovery of America;* one finds it, with religious overtones in Toynbee and Niebuhr; one finds it, in its more direct psychological form, in the writing of the young American scholars today who are exploring the relation of culture and personality.

My own view is that both economic man and psychological man—the materialist emphasis and the individualist emphasis—are each stripped of meaning without the other. The problem of social analysis is only partially illumined by the search for causes. In much of our thinking, causation is giving way to relation and interaction. "America is this," says one observer of American life.

"America is that," says another. It is likely that America is both, because America is a highly polarized field of meaning, but that neither can be fully understood except in relation to the other and to the whole intricate civilization pattern. The study of American civilization becomes thus the study of the polar pattern itself, not a search for some single key that will unlock causation. It is largely a question of what you focus upon, and against what background. The problem of American interpretation is best seen in a figure-ground perspective: but what will be figure and what will be ground will vary with the purpose at hand.

Thus my concern will be neither with the material world alone nor with the moral-psychological world alone, but with the interplay between them. If there is a figure-ground relation in American civilization it must be sought in the relation between power and ideas, science and conscience, the revolutionary machine and the conservative crust of tradition, mass production and social creativeness, individualist values and collective action, capitalist economics and democratic freedom, class structure and the image of prestige and success in the American mind, elite power and the popular arts, the growth of military power and the persistence of civilian control, the fact of an American imperium and the image of an open constitutional world.

One may see in these polar impulses the proof that American life is deeply split. One may prefer to see them as contradictory parts of a bewildering puzzle. Or one may see them as signs of an effort, on a grander scale than ever in history, to resolve the conflicting impulses that are to be found in every civilization but each of which occurs here with a strength and tenacity scarcely witnessed elsewhere.

The Quest for the National Character

DAVID M. POTTER

Unlike most nationality groups in the world today, the people of the United States are not ethnically rooted in the land where they live. The French have remote Gallic antecedents; the Germans, Teutonic; the English, Anglo-Saxon; the Italians, Roman; the Irish, Celtic; but the only people in America who can claim ancient American origins are a remnant of Red Indians. In any deep dimension of time, all other Americans are immigrants. They began as Europeans (or in the case of 10 per cent of the population, as Africans), and if they became Americans it was only, somehow, after a relatively recent passage westbound across the Atlantic.

It is, perhaps, this recency of arrival which has given to Americans a somewhat compulsive preoccupation with the question of their Americanism. No people can really qualify as a nation in the true sense unless they are united by important qualities or values in common. If they share the same ethnic, or linguistic, or religious, or political heritage, the foundations of nationality can hardly be questioned. But when their ethnic, religious, linguistic, and political heritage is mixed, as in the case of the American people, nationality can hardly exist at all unless it takes the form of a common adjustment to conditions of a new land, a common commitment to shared values, a common esteem for certain qualities of character, or a common set of adaptive traits and attitudes. It is partly for this reason that Americans, although committed to the principle of freedom of thought, have nevertheless placed such heavy emphasis upon the obligation to accept certain undefined tenets of "Americanism." It is for this same reason, also, that Americans have insisted upon their distinctiveness from the Old World from which they are derived. More than two centuries ago Hec-

Reprinted by permission of Harper & Row, Publishers, from John Higham (ed.), *The Reconstruction of American History,* copyright 1962.

tor St. John de Crèvecoeur asked a famous question, "What then is the American, this new man?" He simply assumed, without arguing the point, that the American is a new man, and he only inquired wherein the American is different. A countless array of writers, including not only careful historians and social scientists but also professional patriots, hit-and-run travellers, itinerant lecturers, intuitive-minded amateurs of all sorts, have been repeating Crèvecoeur's question and seeking to answer it ever since.

A thick volume would hardly suffice even to summarize the diverse interpretations which these various writers have advanced in describing or explaining the American character. Almost every trait, good or bad, has been attributed to the American people by someone,[1] and almost every explanation, from Darwinian selection to toilet-training, has been advanced to account for the attributed qualities. But it is probably safe to say that at bottom there have been only two primary ways of explaining the American, and that almost all of the innumerable interpretations which have been formulated can be grouped around or at least oriented to these two basic explanations, which serve as polar points for all the literature.

The most disconcerting fact about these two composite images of the American is that they are strikingly dissimilar and seemingly about as inconsistent with one another as two interpretations of the same phenomenon could possibly be. One depicts the American primarily as an individualist and an idealist, while the other makes him out as a conformist and a materialist. Both images have been developed with great detail and elaborate explanation in extensive bodies of literature, and both are worth a close scrutiny.

For those who have seen the American primarily as an individualist, the story of his evolution as a distinctive type dates back possibly to the actual moment of his decision to migrate from Europe to the New World, for this was a process in which the daring and venturesome were more prone to risk life in a new country while the timid and the conventional were more disposed to remain at home. If the selective factors in the migration had the effect of screening out men of low initiative, the conditions of life in the North American wilderness, it is argued, must have further heightened the exercise of individual resourcefulness, for they constantly confronted the settler with circumstances in which he could rely upon no one but himself, and where the capacity to improvise a solution for a problem was not infrequently necessary to survival.

In many ways the colonial American exemplified attitudes that were individualistic. Although he made his first settlements by the removal of whole communities which were transplanted bodily—complete with all their ecclesiastical and legal institutions—he turned increasingly, in the later process of settlement, to a more and more individualistic mode of pioneering, in which one separate family would take up title to a separate, perhaps an isolated, tract of land, and would

---

[1] Lee Coleman, "What is American: a Study of Alleged American Traits," in *Social Forces*, XIX (1941), surveyed a large body of the literature on the American character and concluded that "almost every conceivable value or trait has at one time or another been imputed to American culture by authoritative observers."

move to this land long in advance of any general settlement, leaving churches and courts and schools far behind. His religion, whether Calvinistic Puritanism or emotional revivalism, made him individually responsible for his own salvation, without the intervention of ecclesiastical intermediaries between himself and his God. His economy, which was based very heavily upon subsistence farming, with very little division of labor, also impelled him to cope with a diversity of problems and to depend upon no one but himself.

With all of these conditions at work, the tendency to place a premium upon individual self-reliance was no doubt well developed long before the cult of the American as an individualist crystallized in a conceptual form. But it did crystallize, and it took on almost its classic formulation in the thought of Thomas Jefferson.

It may seem paradoxical to regard Jefferson as a delineator of American national character, for in direct terms he did not attempt to describe the American character at all. But he did conceive that one particular kind of society was necessary to the fulfillment of American ideals, and further that one particular kind of person, namely the independent farmer, was a necessary component in the optimum society. He believed that the principles of liberty and equality, which he cherished so deeply, could not exist in a hierarchical society, such as that of Europe, nor, indeed, in any society where economic and social circumstances enabled one set of men to dominate and exploit the rest. An urban society or a commercial society, with its concentration of financial power into a few hands and its imposition of dependence through a wage system, scarcely lent itself better than an aristocracy to his basic values. In fact, only a society of small husbandmen who tilled their own soil and found sustenance in their own produce could achieve the combination of independence and equalitarianism which he envisioned for the ideal society. Thus, although Jefferson did not write a description of the national character, he erected a model for it, and the model ultimately had more influence than a description could ever have exercised. The model American was a plain, straightforward agrarian democrat, an individualist in his desire for freedom for himself, and an idealist in his desire for equality for all men.

Jefferson's image of the American as a man of independence, both in his values and in his mode of life, has had immense appeal to Americans ever since. They found this image best exemplified in the man of the frontier, for he, as a pioneer, seemed to illustrate the qualities of independence and self-reliance in their most pronounced and most dramatic form. Thus in a tradition of something like folklore, half-legendary figures like Davy Crockett have symbolized America as well as symbolizing the frontier. In literature, ever since J. Fenimore Cooper's Leatherstocking tales, the frontier scout, at home under the open sky, free from the trammels of an organized and stratified society, has been cherished as an incarnation of American qualities.[2] In American politics the voters showed

---

[2]Henry Nash Smith, *Virgin Land: the American West as Symbol and Myth* (1950), brilliantly analyzes the power which the image of the Western pioneer has had upon the American imagination.

such a marked preference for men who had been born in log cabins that many an ambitious candidate pretended to pioneer origins which were in fact fictitious.

The pioneer is, of course, not necessarily an agrarian (he may be a hunter, a trapper, a cowboy, a prospector for gold), and the agrarian is not necessarily a pioneer (he may be a European peasant tilling his ancestral acres), but the American frontier was basically an agricultural frontier, and the pioneer was usually a farmer. Thus it was possible to make an equation between the pioneer and the agrarian, and since the pioneer evinced the agrarian traits in their most picturesque and most appealing form there was a strong psychological impulse to concentrate the diffused agrarian ideal into a sharp frontier focus. This is, in part, what Frederick Jackson Turner did in 1893 when he wrote *The Significance of the Frontier in American History.* In this famous essay Turner offered an explanation of what has been distinctive in American history, but it is not as widely realized as it might be that he also penned a major contribution to the literature of national character. Thus Turner affirmed categorically that "The American intellect owes its striking characteristics to the frontier. That coarseness and strength, combined with acuteness and acquisitiveness; that practical inventive turn of mind, quick to find expedients; that masterful grasp of material things, lacking in the artistic but powerful to effect great ends; that restless, nervous energy; that dominant individualism, working for good and for evil; and withal, that buoyancy and exuberance which comes with freedom—these are traits of the frontier, or traits called out elsewhere because of the existence of the frontier."[3]

A significant but somewhat unnoticed aspect of Turner's treatment is the fact that, in his quest to discover the traits of the American character, he relied for proof not upon descriptive evidence that given traits actually prevailed, but upon the argument that given conditions in the environment would necessarily cause the development of certain traits. Thus the cheapness of land on the frontier would make for universal land-holding which in turn would make for equalitarianism in the society. The absence of division of labor on the frontier would force each man to do most things for himself, and this would breed self-reliance. The pitting of the individual man against the elemental forces of the wilderness and of nature would further reinforce this self-reliance. Similarly, the fact that a man had moved out in advance of society's institutions and its stratified structure would mean that he could find independence, without being overshadowed by the institutions, and could enjoy an equality unknown to stratified society. All of this argument was made without any sustained effort to measure exactly how much recognizable equalitarianism and individualism and self-reliance actually were in evidence either on the American frontier or in American society. There is little reason to doubt that most of his arguments were valid or that most of the traits which he emphasized did actually prevail, but it is nevertheless ironical that Turner's interpretation, which exercised such vast influence upon historians, was not based upon the historian's kind of proof, which is from

[3]Frederick J. Turner, *The Frontier in American History* (Henry Holt and Co., 1920), p. 37.

evidence, but upon an argument from logic which so often fails to work out in historical experience.

But no matter how he arrived at it, Turner's picture reaffirmed some by-now-familiar beliefs about the American character. The American was equalitarian, stoutly maintaining the practices of both social and political democracy; he had a spirit of freedom reflected in his buoyance and exuberance; he was individualistic—hence "practical and inventive," "quick to find expedients," "restless, nervous, acquisitive." Turner was too much a scholar to let his evident fondness for the frontiersman run away with him entirely, and he took pains to point out that this development was not without its sordid aspects. There was a marked primitivism about the frontier, and with it, to some extent, a regression from civilized standards. The buoyant and exuberant frontiersman sometimes emulated his Indian neighbors in taking the scalps of his adversaries. Coarse qualities sometimes proved to have more survival value than gentle ones. But on the whole this regression was brief, and certainly a rough-and-ready society had its compensating advantages. Turner admired his frontiersman, and thus Turner's American, like Jefferson's American, was partly a realistic portrait from life and partly an idealized model from social philosophy. Also, though one of these figures was an agrarian and the other was a frontiersman, both were very much the same man—democratic, freedom-loving, self-reliant, and individualistic.

An essay like this is hardly the place to prove either the validity or the invalidity of the Jeffersonian and Turnerian conception of the American character. The attempt to do so would involve a review of the entire range of American historical experience, and in the course of such a review the proponents of this conception could point to a vast body of evidence in support of their interpretation. They could argue, with much force, that Americans have consistently been zealous to defend individualism by defending the rights and the welfare of the individual, and that our whole history is a protracted record of our government's recognizing its responsibility to an ever broader range of people—to men without property, to men held in slavery, to women, to small enterprises threatened by monopoly, to children laboring in factories, to industrial workers, to the ill, to the elderly, and to the unemployed. This record, it can further be argued, is also a record of the practical idealism of the American people, unceasingly at work.

But without attempting a verdict on the historical validity of this image of the American as individualist and idealist, it is important to bear in mind that this image has been partly a portrait, but also partly a model. In so far as it is a portrait—a likeness by an observer reporting on Americans whom he knew—it can be regarded as authentic testimony on the American character. But in so far as it is a model—an idealization of what is best in Americanism, and of what Americans should strive to be, it will only be misleading if used as evidence of what ordinary Americans are like in their everyday lives. It is also important to recognize that the Jefferson-Turner image posited several traits as distinctively American, and that they are not all necessarily of equal validity. Particularly,

Jefferson and Turner both believed that love of equality and love of liberty go together. For Jefferson the very fact, stated in the Declaration of Independence, that "all men are created equal," carried with it the corollary that they are all therefore "entitled to [and would be eager for] life, liberty, and the pursuit of happiness." From this premise it is easy to slide imperceptibly into the position of holding that equalitarianism and individualism are inseparably linked, or even that they are somehow the same thing. This is, indeed, almost an officially sanctioned ambiguity in the American creed. But it requires only a little thoughtful reflection to recognize that equalitarianism and individualism do not necessarily go together. Alexis de Tocqueville understood this fact more than a century ago, and out of his recognition he framed an analysis which is not only the most brilliant single account of the American character, but is also the only major alternative to the Jefferson-Turner image.

After travelling the length and breadth of the United States for ten months at the height of Andrew Jackson's ascendancy, Tocqueville felt no doubt of the depth of the commitment of Americans to democracy. Throughout two volumes which ranged over every aspect of American life, he consistently emphasized democracy as a pervasive factor. But the democracy which he wrote about was far removed from Thomas Jefferson's dream.

"Liberty," he observed of the Americans, "is not the chief object of their desires; equality is their idol. They make rapid and sudden efforts to obtain liberty, and if they miss their aim resign themselves to their disappointment; but nothing can satisfy them without equality, and they would rather perish than lose it."[4]

This emphasis upon equality was not, in itself, inconsistent with the most orthodox Jeffersonian ideas, and indeed Tocqueville took care to recognize that under certain circumstances equality and freedom might "meet and blend." But such circumstances would be rare, and the usual effects of equality would be to encourage conformity and discourage individualism, to regiment opinion and to inhibit dissent. Tocqueville justified this seemingly paradoxical conclusion by arguing that:

When the inhabitant of a democratic country compares himself individually with all those about him, he feels with pride that he is the equal of any one of them; but when he comes to survey the totality of his fellows, and to place himself in contrast with so huge a body, he is instantly overwhelmed by the sense of his own insignificance and weakness. The same equality that renders him independent of each of his fellow citizens, taken severally, exposes him alone and unprotected to the influence of the greater number. The public, therefore, among a democratic people, has a singular power, which aristocratic nations cannot conceive; for it does not persuade others to its beliefs, but it imposes them and makes them permeate the thinking of everyone by a sort of enormous pressure of the mind of all upon the individual intelligence.[5]

[4]Alexis de Tocqueville, *Democracy in America*, edited by Phillips Bradley (Alfred A. Knopf, 1946), I, pp. 53–4.
[5]*Ibid.*, II, p. 94; II, p. 10.

At the time when Tocqueville wrote, he expressed admiration for the American people in many ways, and when he criticized adversely his tone was abstract, bland, and free of the petulance and the personalities that characterized some critics, like Mrs. Trollope and Charles Dickens. Consequently, Tocqueville was relatively well received in the United States, and we have largely forgotten what a severe verdict his observations implied. But, in fact, he pictured the American character as the very embodiment of conformity, of conformity so extreme that not only individualism but even freedom was endangered. Because of the enormous weight with which the opinion of the majority pressed upon the individual, Tocqueville said, the person in the minority "not only mistrusts his strength, but even doubts of his right; and he is very near acknowledging that he is in the wrong when the greater number of his countrymen assert that he is so. The majority do not need to force him; they convince him." "The principle of equality," as a consequence, had the effect of "prohibiting him from thinking at all," and "freedom of opinion does not exist in America." Instead of reinforcing liberty, therefore, equality constituted a danger to liberty. It caused the majority "to despise and undervalue the rights of private persons," and led on to the pessimistic conclusion that "Despotism appears . . . peculiarly to be dreaded in democratic times."[6]

Tocqueville was perhaps the originator of the criticism of the American as conformist, but he also voiced another criticism which has had many echoes, but which did not originate with him. This was the condemnation of the American as a materialist. As early as 1805 Richard Parkinson had observed that "all men there [in America] make it [money] their pursuit," and in 1823 William Faux had asserted that "two selfish gods, pleasure and gain, enslave the Americans." In the interval between the publication of the first and second parts of Tocqueville's study, Washington Irving coined his classic phrase concerning "the almighty dollar, that great object of universal devotion throughout the land."[7] But it remained for Tocqueville, himself, to link materialism with equality, as he had already linked conformity.

Of all passions, he said, which originate in or are fostered by equality, there is one which it renders peculiarly intense, and which it also infuses into the heart of every man: I mean the love of well-being. The taste for well-being is the prominent and indelible feature of democratic times. . . . The effort to satisfy even the least wants of the body and to provide the little conveniences of life is uppermost in every mind.

He described this craving for physical comforts as a "passion," and affirmed that "I know of no country, indeed, where the love of money has taken stronger hold on the affections of men."[8]

[6]*Ibid.*, II, p. 261; II, p. 11; I, p. 265; II, p. 326; II, p. 322.
[7]Richard Parkinson, *A Tour in America in 1798–1800* (2 vols., 1805), vol. II, p. 652; William Faux, *Memorable Days in America* (1823), p. 417; Washington Irving, "The Creole Village," in *The Knickerbocker Magazine*, November 1836.
[8]Tocqueville, *Democracy in America*, II, p. 26; II, p. 128; II, p. 129; I, p. 51.

For more than a century we have lived with the contrasting images of the American character which Thomas Jefferson and Alexis de Tocqueville visualized. Both of these images presented the American as an equalitarian and therefore as a democrat, but one was an agrarian democrat while the other was a majoritarian democrat; one an independent individualist, the other a mass-dominated conformist; one an idealist, the other a materialist. Through many decades of self-scrutiny Americans have been seeing one or the other of these images whenever they looked into the mirror of self-analysis.

The discrepancy between the two images is so great that it must bring the searcher for the American character up with a jerk, and must force him to grapple with the question whether these seemingly antithetical versions of the American can be reconciled in any way. Can the old familiar formula for embracing opposite reports—that the situation presents a paradox—be stretched to encompass both Tocqueville and Jefferson? Or is there so grave a flaw somewhere that one must question the whole idea of national character and call to mind all the warnings that thoughtful men have uttered against the very concept that national groups can be distinguished from one another in terms of collective group traits.

Certainly there is a sound enough basis for doubting the validity of generalizations about national character. To begin with, many of these generalizations have been derived not from any dispassionate observation or any quest for truth, but from superheated patriotism which sought only to glorify one national group by invidious comparison with other national groups, or from a pseudoscientific racism which claimed innately superior qualities for favored ethnic groups. Further, the explanations which were offered to account for the ascribed traits were as suspect as the ascriptions themselves. No one today will accept the notions which once prevailed that such qualities as the capacity for self-government are inherited in the genes, nor will anyone credit the notion that national character is a unique quality which manifests itself mystically in all the inhabitants of a given country. Between the chauvinistic purposes for which the concept of national character was used, and the irrationality with which it was supported, it fell during the 1930's into a disrepute from which it has by no means fully recovered.

Some thinkers of a skeptical turn of mind had rejected the idea of national character even at a time when most historians accepted it without question. Thus, for instance, John Stuart Mill as early as 1849 observed that "of all vulgar modes of escaping from the consideration of the effect of social and moral influences on the human mind, the most vulgar is that of attributing diversities of character to inherent natural differences." Sir John Seely said, "no explanation is so vague, so cheap, and so difficult to verify."[9]

But it was particularly at the time of the rise of Fascism and Naziism, when the vicious aspects of extreme nationalism and of racism became glaringly con-

---

[9]Mill, *The Principles of Political Economy* (1849), I, p. 390; Seely, quoted by Boyd C. Shafer, "Men Are More Alike," in *American Historical Review*, LVII (1952), p. 606.

spicuous, that historians in general began to repudiate the idea of national character and to disavow it as an intellectual concept, even though they sometimes continued to employ it as a working device in their treatment of the peoples with whose history they were concerned. To historians whose skepticism had been aroused, the conflicting nature of the images of the American as an individualistic democrat or as a conformist democrat would have seemed simply to illustrate further the already demonstrated flimsiness and fallacious quality of all generalizations about national character.

But to deny that the inhabitants of one country may, as a group, evince a given trait in higher degree than the inhabitants of some other country amounts almost to a denial that the culture of one people can be different from the culture of another people. To escape the pitfalls of racism in this way is to fly from one error into the embrace of another, and students of culture—primarily anthropologists, rather than historians—perceived that rejection of the idea that a group could be distinctive, along with the idea that the distinction was eternal and immutable in the genes, involved the ancient logical fallacy of throwing out the baby along with the bath. Accordingly, the study of national character came under the special sponsorship of cultural anthropology, and in the 'forties a number of outstanding workers in this field tackled the problem of national character, including the American character, with a methodological precision and objectivity that had never been applied to the subject before. After their investigations, they felt no doubt that national character was a reality—an observable and demonstrable reality. One of them, Margaret Mead, declared that "In every culture, in Samoa, in Germany, in Iceland, in Bali, and in the United States of America, we will find consistencies and regularities in the way in which new born babies grow up and assume the attitudes and behavior patterns of their elders—and this we may call 'character formation.' We will find that Samoans may be said to have a Samoan character structure and Americans an American character structure."[10] Another, the late Clyde Kluckhohn, wrote: "The statistical prediction can safely be made that a hundred Americans, for example, will display certain defined characteristics more frequently than will a hundred Englishmen comparably distributed as to age, sex, social class, and vocation."[11]

If these new students were correct, it meant that there was some kind of identifiable American character. It might conform to the Jeffersonian image; it might conform to the Tocquevillian image; it might conform in part to both; or it might conform to neither. But in any event discouraged investigators were enjoined against giving up the quest with the conclusion that there is no American character. It has been said that a philosopher is a blind man in a dark room looking for a black cat that isn't there; the student of national character might also, at times, resemble a blind man in a dark room, looking for a black cat, but

---

[10]Margaret Mead, *And Keep Your Powder Dry* (William Morrow and Co., 1942), p. 21. Miss Mead also says, "The way in which people behave is all of a piece, their virtues and their sins, the way they slap the baby, handle their court cases, and bury their dead."

[11]Clyde Kluckhohn and Henry A. Murray, *Personality in Nature, Society and Culture* (Alfred A. Knopf, 1949), p. 36.

the cultural anthropologists exhorted him to persevere in spite of the problems of visibility, for the cat was indubitably there.

Still confronted with the conflicting images of the agrarian democrat and the majoritarian democrat, the investigator might avoid an outright rejection of either by taking the position that the American character has changed, and that each of these images was at one time valid and realistic, but that in the twentieth century the qualities of conformity and materialism have grown increasingly prominent, while the qualities of individualism and idealism have diminished. This interpretation of a changing American character has had a number of adherents in the last two decades, for it accords well with the observation that the conditions of the American culture have changed. As they do so, of course the qualities of a character that is derived from the culture might be expected to change correspondingly. Thus, Henry S. Commager, in his *The American Mind* (1950), portrayed in two contrasting chapters "the nineteenth-century American" and "the twentieth-century American." Similarly, David Riesman, in *The Lonely Crowd* (1950), significantly sub-titled *A Study of the Changing American Character,* pictured two types of Americans, first an "inner-directed man," whose values were deeply internalized and who adhered to these values tenaciously, regardless of the opinions of his peers (clearly an individualist), and second an "other-directed man," who subordinated his own internal values to the changing expectations directed toward him by changing peer groups (in short, a conformist).

Although he viewed his inner-directed man as having been superseded historically by his other-directed man, Riesman did not attempt to explain in historical terms the reason for the change. He made a rather limited effort to relate his stages of character formation to stages of population growth, but he has since then not used population phase as a key. Meanwhile, it is fairly clear, from Riesman's own context, as well as from history in general, that there were changes in the culture which would have accounted for the transition in character. Most nineteenth-century Americans were self-employed; most were engaged in agriculture; most produced a part of their own food and clothing. These facts meant that their well-being did not depend on the goodwill or the services of their associates, but upon their resourcefulness in wrestling with the elemental forces of Nature. Even their physical isolation from their fellows added something to the independence of their natures. But most twentieth-century Americans work for wages or salaries, many of them in very large employee groups; most are engaged in office or factory work; most are highly specialized, and are reliant upon many others to supply their needs in an economy with an advanced division of labor. Men now do depend upon the goodwill and the services of their fellows. This means that what they achieve depends less upon stamina and hardihood than upon their capacity to get along with other people and to fit smoothly into a co-operative relationship. In short the culture now places a premium upon the qualities which will enable the individual to function effectively as a member of a large organizational group. The strategic importance of this institutional factor has been well recognized by William H. Whyte, Jr., in his significantly titled book *The Organization Man* (1956)—for the conformity of Whyte's bureaucratized individual results from the fact that he lives under an imperative to succeed in a situation where promotion and even survival depend upon effective inter-action with others in an hierarchical structure.

Thus, by an argument from logic (always a treacherous substitute for direct observation in historical study), one can make a strong case that the nineteenth-century American should have been (and therefore must have been) an individualist, while the twentieth-century American should be (and therefore is) a conformist. But this formula crashes headlong into the obdurate fact that no Americans have ever been more classically conformist than Tocqueville's Jacksonian democrats—hardy specimens of the frontier breed, far back in the nineteenth century, long before the age of corporate images, peer groups, marginal differentiation, and status frustration. In short, Tocqueville's nineteenth-century American, whether frontiersman or no, was to some extent an other-directed man. Carl N. Degler has pointed out this identity in a very cogent paper not yet published, in which he demonstrates very forcibly that most of our easy assumptions about the immense contrast between the nineteenth-century American and the twentieth-century American are vulnerable indeed.[12]

This conclusion should, perhaps, have been evident from the outset, in view of the fact that it was Tocqueville who, in the nineteenth century, gave us the image which we now frequently identify as the twentieth-century American. But in any case, the fact that he did so means that we can hardly resolve the dilemma of our individualist democrat and our majoritarian democrat by assuming that both are historically valid but that one replaced the other. The problem of determining what use we can make of either of these images, in view of the fact that each casts doubt upon the other, still remains. Is it possible to uncover common factors in these apparently contradictory images, and thus to make use of them both in our quest for a definition of the national character? For no matter whether either of these versions of the American is realistic as a type or image, there is no doubt that both of them reflect fundamental aspects of the American experience.

There is no purpose, at this point in this essay, to execute a neat, pre-arranged sleight-of-hand by which the individualist democrat and the conformist democrat will cast off their disguises and will reveal themselves as identical twin Yankee Doodle Dandies, both born on the fourth of July. On the contrary, intractable, irresolvable discrepancies exist between the two figures, and it will probably never be possible to go very far in the direction of accepting the one without treating the other as a fictitious image, to be rejected as reflecting an anti-democratic bias and as at odds with the evidence from actual observation of the behavior of *Homo americanus* in his native haunts. At the same time, however, it is both necessary to probe for the common factors, and legitimate to

[12]Delivered on 30 December 1960, at the annual meeting of the American Historical Association in New York. [See citation below, p. 418.—Ed.]

observe that there is one common factor conspicuous in the extreme—namely the emphasis on equality, so dear both to Jefferson's American and to Tocqueville's. One of these figures, it will be recalled, has held no truth to be more self-evident than that all men are created equal, while the other has made equality his "idol," far more jealously guarded than his liberty.

If the commitment to equality is so dominant a feature in both of these representations of the American, it will perhaps serve as a key to various facets of the national character, even to contradictory aspects of this character. In a society as complex as that of the United States, in fact, it may be that the common factors underlying the various manifestations are all that our quest should seek. For it is evident that American life and American energy have expressed themselves in a great diversity of ways, and any effort to define the American as if nearly two hundred million persons all corresponded to a single type would certainly reduce complex data to a blunt, crude, and oversimplified form. To detect what qualities Americans share in their diversity may be far more revealing than to superimpose the stereotype of a fictitious uniformity. If this is true, it means that our quest must be to discover the varied and dissimilar ways in which the commitment to equality expresses itself—the different forms which it takes in different individuals—rather than to regard it as an undifferentiated component which shows in all individuals in the same way. Figuratively, one might say that in seeking for what is common, one should think of the metal from which Americans are forged, no matter into how many shapes this metal may be cast, rather than thinking of a die with which they all are stamped into an identical shape. If the problem is viewed in this way, it will be readily apparent that Tocqueville made a pregnant statement when he observed that the idea of equality was "the fundamental fact from which all others seem to be derived."

The term "equality" is a loose-fitting garment and it has meant very different things at very different times. It is very frequently used to imply parity or uniformity. The grenadiers in the King of Prussia's guard were equal in that they were all, uniformly, over six feet six inches tall. Particularly, it can mean, and often does mean in some social philosophies, uniformity of material welfare—of income, of medical care, etc. But people are clearly not uniform in strength or intelligence or beauty, and one must ask, therefore, what kind of uniformity Americans believed in. Did they believe in an equal sharing of goods? Tocqueville himself answered this question when he said, "I know of no country . . . where a profounder contempt is expressed for the theory of the permanent equality of property."[13]

At this point in the discussion of equality, someone, and very likely a business man, is always likely to break in with the proposition that Americans believe in equality of opportunity—in giving everyone what is called an equal start, and in removing all handicaps such as illiteracy and all privileges such as monopoly or special priority, which will tend to give one person an advantage over another. But if a person gains the advantage without having society give it to him, by

[13]Tocqueville, *Democracy in America*, I, p. 57–8.

being more clever or more enterprising or even just by being stronger than someone else, he is entitled to enjoy the benefits that accrue from these qualities, particularly in terms of possessing more property or wealth than others.

Historically, equality of opportunity was a particularly apt form of equalitarianism for a new, undeveloped frontier country. In the early stages of American history, the developed resources of the country were so few that an equality in the division of these assets would only have meant an insufficiency for everyone. The best economic benefit which the government could give was to offer a person free access in developing undeveloped resources for his own profit, and this is what America did offer. It was an ideal formula for everyone: for the individual it meant a very real chance to gain more wealth than he would have secured by receiving an equal share of the existing wealth. For the community, it meant that no one could prosper appreciably without activities which would develop undeveloped resources, at a time when society desperately needed rapid economic development. For these reasons, equality of opportunity did become the most highly sanctioned form of equalitarianism in the United States.

Because of this sanction, Americans have indeed been tolerant of great discrepancies in wealth. They have approved of wealth much more readily when they believed that it had been earned—as in the case, for instance, of Henry Ford—than when they thought it had been acquired by some special privilege or monopoly. In general, however, they have not merely condoned great wealth; they have admired it. But to say that the ideal of equality means only equality of opportunity is hardly to tell the whole story. The American faith has also held, with intense conviction, the belief that all men are equal in the sense that they share a common humanity—that all are alike in the eyes of God—and that every person has a certain dignity, no matter how low his circumstances, which no one else, no matter how high *his* circumstances, is entitled to disregard. When this concept of the nature of man was translated into a system of social arrangements, the crucial point on which it came to focus was the question of rank. For the concept of rank essentially denies that all men are equally worthy and argues that some are better than others—that some are born to serve and others born to command. The American creed not only denied this view, but even condemned it and placed a taboo upon it. Some people, according to the American creed, might be more fortunate than others, but they must never regard themselves as better than others. Pulling one's rank has therefore been the unforgivable sin against American democracy, and the American people have, accordingly, reserved their heartiest dislike for the officer class in the military, for people with upstage or condescending manners, and for anyone who tries to convert power or wealth (which are not resented) into overt rank or privilege (which are). Thus it is permissible for an American to have servants (which is a matter of function), but he must not put them in livery (which is a matter of rank); permissible to attend expensive schools, but not to speak with a cultivated accent; permissible to rise in the world, but never to repudiate the origins from which he rose. The most palpable and overt possible claim of rank is, of course, the effort of one individual to assert authority, in a personal sense, over others, and accordingly the rejection of authority is the most pronounced of all the concrete expressions of American beliefs in equality.

In almost any enterprise which involves numbers of people working in conjunction, it is necessary for some people to tell other people what to do. This function cannot be wholly abdicated without causing a breakdown, and in America it cannot be exercised overtly without violating the taboos against authority. The result is that the American people have developed an arrangement which skillfully combines truth and fiction, and maintains that the top man does not rule, but leads; and does not give orders, but calls signals; while the men in the lower echelons are not underlings, but members of the team. This view of the relationship is truthful in the sense that the man in charge does depend upon his capacity to elicit the voluntary or spontaneous co-operation of the members of his organization, and he regards the naked use of authority to secure compliance as an evidence of failure; also, in many organizations, the members lend their support willingly, and contribute much more on a voluntary basis than authority could ever exact from them. But the element of fiction sometimes enters, in terms of the fact that both sides understand that in many situations authority would have to be invoked if voluntary compliance were not forthcoming. This would be humiliating to all parties—to the top man because it would expose his failure as a leader and to the others because it would force them to recognize the carefully concealed fact that in an ultimate sense they are subject to coercion. To avoid this mutually undesirable exploration of the ultimate implications, both sides recognize that even when an order has to be given, it is better for it to be expressed in the form of a request or a proposal, and when compliance is mandatory, it should be rendered with an appearance of consent.

It is in this way that the anti-authoritarian aspect of the creed of equality leads to the extraordinarily strong emphasis upon permissiveness, either as a reality or as a mere convention in American life. So strong is the taboo against authority that the father, once a paternal authority, is now expected to be a pal to his children, and to persuade rather than to command. The husband, once a lord and master, to be obeyed under the vows of matrimony, is now a partner. And if, perchance, an adult male in command of the family income uses his control to bully his wife and children, he does not avow his desire to make them obey, but insists that he only wants them to be co-operative. The unlimited American faith in the efficacy of discussion as a means of finding solutions for controversies reflects less a faith in the powers of rational persuasion than a supreme reluctance to let anything reach a point where authority will have to be invoked. If hypocrisy is the tribute that vice pays to virtue, permissiveness is, to some extent, the tribute that authority pays to the principle of equality.

When one recognizes some of these varied strands in the fabric of equalitarianism it becomes easier to see how the concept has contributed to the making, both of the Jeffersonian American and the Tocquevillian American. For as one picks at the strands they ravel out in quite dissimilar directions. The strand of equality of opportunity, for instance, if followed out, leads to the theme of individualism. It challenged each individual to pit his skill and talents in a competition against the skill and talents of others and to earn the individual rewards which talent and effort might bring. Even more, the imperatives of the competitive race were so compelling that the belief grew up that everyone had a kind of obligation to enter his talents in this competition and to "succeed." It was but a step from the belief that ability and virtue would produce success to the belief that success was produced by—and was therefore an evidence of—ability and virtue. In short, money not only represented power, it also was a sign of the presence of admirable qualities in the man who attained it. Here, certainly, an equalitarian doctrine fostered materialism, and if aggressiveness and competitiveness are individualistic qualities, then it fostered individualism also.

Of course, neither American individualism nor American materialism can be explained entirely in these terms. Individualism must have derived great strength, for instance, from the reflection that if all men are equal, a man might as well form his own convictions as accept the convictions of someone else no better than himself. It must also have been reinforced by the frontier experience, which certainly compelled every man to rely upon himself. But this kind of individualism is not the quality of independent-mindedness, and it is not the quality which Tocqueville was denying when he said that Americans were conformists. A great deal of confusion has resulted, in the discussion of the American character, from the fact that the term individualism is sometimes used (as by Tocqueville) to mean willingness to think and act separately from the majority, and sometimes (as by Turner) to mean capacity to get along without help. It might be supposed that the two would converge, on the theory that a man who can get along by himself without help will soon recognize that he may as well also think for himself without help. But in actuality, this did not necessarily happen. Self-reliance on the frontier was more a matter of courage and of staying power than of intellectual resourcefulness, for the struggle with the wilderness challenged the body rather than the mind, and a man might be supremely effective in fending for himself, and at the same time supremely conventional in his ideas. In this sense, Turner's individualist is not really an antithesis of Tocqueville's conformist at all.

Still, it remains true that Jefferson's idealist and Tocqueville's conformist both require explanation, and that neither can be accounted for in the terms which make Jefferson's individualist and Tocqueville's materialist understandable. As an explanation of these facets of the American character, it would seem that the strand of equalitarianism which stresses the universal dignity of all men, and which hates rank as a violation of dignity, might be found quite pertinent. For it is the concept of the worth of every man which has stimulated a century and a half of reform, designed at every step to realize in practice the ideal that every human possesses potentialities which he should have a chance to fulfill. Whatever has impeded this fulfillment, whether it be lack of education, chattel slavery, the exploitation of the labor of unorganized workers, the hazards of unemployment, or the handicaps of age and infirmity, has been the object, at one time or another, of a major reforming crusade. The whole American commitment to progress would be impossible without a prior belief in the perfectibility of man and in the practicability of steps to bring perfection nearer. In this sense, the American character has been idealistic. And yet its idealism is not entirely irreconcilable with its materialism, for American idealism has often framed its most altruistic goals in materialistic terms—for instance of raising the standard of living as a means to a better life. Moreover, Americans are committed to the view that materialistic means are necessary to idealistic ends. Franklin defined what is necessary to a virtuous life by saying "an empty sack cannot stand upright," and Americans have believed that spiritual and humanitarian goals are best achieved by instrumentalities such as universities and hospitals which carry expensive price tags.

If the belief that all men are of equal worth has contributed to a feature of American life so much cherished as our tradition of humanitarian reform, how could it at the same time have contributed to a feature so much deplored as American conformity? Yet it has done both, for the same respect of the American for his fellow men, which has made many a reformer think that his fellow citizens are worth helping, has also made many another American think that he has no business to question the opinions that his neighbors have sanctioned. True, he says, if all men are equal, each ought to think for himself, but on the other hand, no man should consider himself better than his neighbors, and if the majority have adopted an opinion on a matter, how can one man question their opinion, without setting himself up as being better than they. Moreover, it is understood that the majority are pledged not to force him to adopt their opinion. But it is also understood that in return for this immunity he will voluntarily accept the will of the majority in most things. The absence of a formal compulsion to conform seemingly increases the obligation to conform voluntarily. Thus, the other-directed man is seen to be derived as much from the American tradition of equalitarianism as the rugged individualist, and the compulsive seeker of an unequally large share of wealth as much as the humanitarian reformer striving for the fulfillment of democratic ideals.

To say that they are all derived from the same tradition is by no means to say that they are, in some larger, mystic sense, all the same. They are not, even though the idealism of the reformer may seek materialistic goals, and though men who are individualists in their physical lives may be conformists in their ideas. But all of them, it may be argued, do reflect circumstances which are distinctively American, and all present manifestations of a character which is more convincingly American because of its diversity than any wholly uniform character could possibly be. If Americans have never reached the end of their quest for an image that would represent the American character, it may be not because they failed to find one image but because they failed to recognize the futility of attempting to settle upon one, and the necessity of accepting several.

II

AS OTHERS HAVE SEEN US

INTRODUCTION II

In times past the American craving for definition was constantly fed, but never sated, by a host of foreign visitors who came on errands of inquiry to these shores. Many came to scoff, and some remained to praise; either way, whether sympathetic or censorious, their writings found an avid audience in the United States. Though their perceptions were more or less deeply colored by their pre-conceptions, the travelers from abroad held up a mirror in which Americans could see themselves as others saw them. The image provoked an occasional flurry of ruffled patriotism, yet on the whole young America's self-esteem was flattered by old Europe's attentions. What was said, even when derogatory, mattered less than the gratifying fact that Europeans found so much to say.

America figured ambiguously in the European imagination. To some onlook-ers it represented a primitive stage of culture in which the charms of agrarian innocence were mingled with the repugnant features of democratic barbarity. Observers like Mrs. Trollope, mother of the British novelist, were repelled by the adolescent braggadocio and uncultivated manners of rough-cut Jonathans who asserted their equality with any English "gent" by squirting tobacco juice indis-criminately in public places. To other writers America appeared as Europe's lost paradise: it was the golden land of opportunity, the asylum of liberty, the new Garden of Eden beyond the western sea; its inhabitants, however unrefined their deportment, displayed the rudiments of natural nobility.

These dual versions of the theme of primitivism were linked together in J. Hector St. John de Crèvecoeur's *Letters from an American Farmer,* published in London in 1782. To his celebration of the simple pleasures of farming—the dominant stress of his account—Crèvecoeur coupled a disparaging report on the crudities of the forest frontier where "men appear to be no better than carnivo-rous animals of a superior rank," together with a horrified indictment of the cruelties of the slave system in the South. Two images stood side by side in striking contrast: in the idyl of innocence, a little boy rides happily upon his father's plow along the "odoriferous furrow"; in the portrait of barbarism, a Negro slave, found guilty of murdering an overseer, hangs caged and dying in

38

the woods while rapacious birds, like Harpies, tear his flesh and peck out his eyes. America was thus depicted as the nearest modern approximation to the original state of nature, itself a highly ambivalent concept.

To numerous observers America prefigured the destiny of Western society: they located its significance in time to come rather than in time gone by. In fact, the primitivist and futurist visions were closely related. As Europe's fresh start, America was the place where the bonds of hoary tradition were relaxed, where the carapace of convention had not yet hardened, where things could be done over and done better. On this virgin ground, uncluttered by the debris of history, a fairer civilization might in time arise—but whether fair or foul, the career of the United States was portentous. Believing that the prospects of Europe were foreshadowed in America, many travelers came to learn what the New World republic was doing, where it was going, and what the Old World might have to hope or fear from its development.

That was why Alexis de Tocqueville, a young French aristocrat, passed several months in the United States in the early 1830s. His report, the two-volume *Democracy in America,* was published in 1835 and 1840. Tocqueville's method was bifocal: he brought to the inquiry a preconception of democracy, fashioned from the experience of France and polarized against an ideal-typical definition of aristocracy; he checked that concept by direct observation of the democratic example of Jacksonian America. Weaving together induction and deduction, he constructed a model of the democratic society; equalitarianism was its governing dogma and equality of conditions its primary attribute. Convinced that democracy was the wave of the future, Tocqueville hoped, by easing its advance in Europe, to forestall further revolutionary upheaval and fortify the elements of liberty against the antagonistic thrust, as he saw it, of the equalitarian principle. Though he was less interested in America for its own sake than in the monitory lessons that Europe might draw from the American record—"America," he remarked, "was only my framework; democracy was the subject"—*Democracy in America* ranks as the classic analysis of American political institutions and national character. The selection groups Tocqueville's reflections on the central themes of individualism and association, conformity and autonomy, mobility and materialism. It is taken from the original translation by the Englishman, Henry Reeve.

A half-century later, James Bryce came from England to survey the maturing American republic, publishing his *The American Commonwealth* in two volumes in 1888. A friendly critic whose judicious appraisal of American politics furnished ammunition for the reform movements of the period, Bryce found much to admire in America. Democracy, though its performance fell somewhat short of its promises, was no longer experimental, and the United States, whatever its defects, had arrived at "the highest level, not only of material well-being but of intelligence and happiness which the race has yet obtained." Insisting on rigorously empirical investigation and sharply critical of writers—Tocqueville among them—who, in his judgment, "preferred abstract speculation to the humble task of ascertaining and weighing the facts," Bryce worked close to the realities of American life. More than most foreigners, he was sensitive to the ways in which a peculiar historical experience had given a singular shape to the American character. Though Bryce's account was less apprehensive as well as less prophetic than Tocqueville's, their major findings ran so nearly parallel that the sagacity of the Frenchman's spacious conjectures was confirmed in important respects by the Englishman's observations.

For the student of American national character much of the value of the writings of Crèvecoeur, Tocqueville, and Bryce resides in their cosmopolitan scope. Each adopted an explicitly comparative method which, if not altogether free from diffractions of vision, gave exceptional clarity to the distinctive contours of American character. They did not disregard the diversities of American society, yet when viewed from a distance those diversities, disproportionately prominent to American eyes, tended to blur into a common form. Perhaps they overstated the elements of uniformity; nevertheless, their trans-national perspective helped to correct the myopia to which Americans, excepting a few (one thinks of Henry Adams, Henry James, and even James Fenimore Cooper) whose experience included a sojourn overseas, were generally subject. That the people of the United States possessed a *national* character these foreign observers had no doubt, and their cosmopolitan outlook lent authority to their descriptions of it.

What Is an American?

J. HECTOR ST. JOHN DE CRÈVECOEUR

I wish I could be acquainted with the feelings and thoughts which must agitate the heart and present themselves to the mind of an enlightened Englishman, when he first lands on this continent. He must greatly rejoice that he lived at a time to see this fair country discovered and settled; he must necessarily feel a share of national pride, when he views the chain of settlements which embellishes these extended shores. When he says to himself, this is the work of my countrymen, who, when convulsed by factions, afflicted by a variety of miseries and wants, restless and impatient, took refuge here. They brought along with them their national genius, to which they principally owe what liberty they enjoy, and what substance they possess. Here he sees the industry of his native country displayed in a new manner, and traces in their works the embrios of all the arts, sciences, and ingenuity which flourish in Europe. Here he beholds fair cities, substantial villages, extensive fields, an immense country filled with decent houses, good roads, orchards, meadows, and bridges, where an hundred years ago all was wild, woody and uncultivated! What a train of pleasing ideas this fair spectacle must suggest; it is a prospect which must inspire a good citizen with the most heartfelt pleasure. The difficulty consists in the manner of viewing so extensive a scene. He is arrived on a new continent; a modern society offers itself to his contemplation, different from what he had hitherto seen. It is not composed, as in Europe, of great lords who possess every thing, and of a herd of people who have nothing. Here are no aristocratical families, no courts, no kings, no bishops, no ecclesiastical dominion, no invisible power giving to a few a very visible one; no great manufacturers employing thousands, no great refinements of luxury. The rich and the poor are not so far removed from each other as they are in Europe. Some few towns excepted, we are all tillers of the earth, from Nova Scotia to West Florida. We are a people of cultivators, scattered over an immense territory, communicating with each other by means of good roads

41

and navigable rivers, united by the silken bands of mild government, all respecting the laws, without dreading their power, because they are equitable. We are all animated with the spirit of an industry which is unfettered and unrestrained, because each person works for himself. If he travels through our rural districts he views not the hostile castle, and the haughty mansion, contrasted with the clay-built hut and miserable cabbin, where cattle and men help to keep each other warm, and dwell in meanness, smoke, and indigence. A pleasing uniformity of decent competence appears throughout our habitations. The meanest of our log-houses is a dry and comfortable habitation. Lawyer or merchant are the fairest titles our towns afford; that of a farmer is the only appellation of the rural inhabitants of our country. It must take some time ere he can reconcile himself to our dictionary, which is but short in words of dignity, and names of honour. There, on a Sunday, he sees a congregation of respectable farmers and their wives, all clad in neat homespun, well mounted, or riding in their own humble waggons. There is not among them an esquire, saving the unlettered magistrate. There he sees a parson as simple as his flock, a farmer who does not riot on the labour of others. We have no princes, for whom we toil, starve, and bleed: we are the most perfect society now existing in the world. Here man is free as he ought to be; nor is this pleasing equality so transitory as many others are. Many ages will not see the shores of our great lakes replenished with in'and nations, nor the unknown bounds of North America entirely peopled. Who can tell how far it extends? Who can tell the millions of men whom it will feed and contain? for no European foot has as yet travelled half the extent of this mighty continent!

. . . .

In this great American asylum, the poor of Europe have by some means met together, and in consequence of various causes; to what purpose should they ask one another what countrymen they are? Alas, two thirds of them had no country. Can a wretch who wanders about, who works and starves, whose life is a continual scene of sore affliction or pinching penury; can that man call England or any other kingdom his country? A country that had no bread for him, whose fields procured him no harvest, who met with nothing but the frowns of the rich, the severity of the laws, with jails and punishments; who owned not a single foot of the extensive surface of this planet? No! urged by a variety of motives, here they came. Every thing has tended to regenerate them; new laws, a new mode of living, a new social system; here they are become men: in Europe they were as so many useless plants, wanting vegetative mould, and refreshing showers; they withered, and were mowed down by want, hunger, and war; but now by the power of transplantation, like all other plants they have taken root and flourished! Formerly they were not numbered in any civil lists of their country, except in those of the poor; here they rank as citizens. By what invisible power has this surprising metamorphosis been performed? By that of the laws and that of their industry. The laws, the indulgent laws, protect them as they arrive, stamping on them the symbol of adoption; they receive ample rewards for their labours; these accumulated rewards procure them lands; those lands confer on them the title of freemen, and to that title every benefit is affixed which men can possibly require. This is the great operation daily performed by our laws. From whence proceed these laws? From our government. Whence the government? It is derived from the original genius and strong desire of the people.

. . . .

What attachment can a poor European emigrant have for a country where he had nothing? The knowledge of the language, the love of a few kindred as poor as himself, were the only cords that tied him: his country is now that which gives him land, bread, protection, and consequence: *Ubi panis ibi patria,* is the motto of all emigrants. What then is the American, this new man? He is either an European, or the descendant of an European, hence that strange mixture of blood, which you will find in no other country. I could point out to you a family whose grandfather was an Englishman, whose wife was Dutch, whose son married a French woman, and whose present four sons have now four wives of different nations. *He* is an American, who leaving behind him all his ancient prejudices and manners, receives new ones from the new mode of life he has embraced, the new government he obeys, and the new rank he holds. He becomes an American by being received in the broad lap of our great *Alma Mater.* Here individuals of all nations are melted into a new race of men, whose labours and posterity will one day cause great changes in the world. Americans are the western pilgrims, who are carrying along with them that great mass of arts, sciences, vigour, and industry which began long since in the east; they will finish the great circle. The Americans were once scattered all over Europe; here they are incorporated into one of the finest systems of population which has ever appeared, and which will hereafter become distinct by the power of the different climates they inhabit. The American ought therefore to love this country much better than that wherein either he or his forefathers were born. Here the rewards of his industry follow with equal steps the progress of his labour; his labour is founded on the basis of nature, *self-interest;* can it want a stronger allurement? Wives and children, who before in vain demanded of him a morsel of bread, now, fat and frolicsome, gladly help their father to clear those fields whence exuberant crops are to arise to feed and to clothe them all; without any part being claimed, either by a despotic prince, a rich abbot, or a mighty lord. Here religion demands but little of him; a small voluntary salary to the minister, and gratitude to God; can he refuse these? The American is a new man, who acts upon new principles; he must therefore entertain new ideas, and form new opinions. From involuntary idleness, servile dependence, penury, and useless labour, he has passed to toils of a very different nature, rewarded by ample subsistence.—This is an American.

. . . .

Men are like plants; the goodness and flavour of the fruit proceeds from the peculiar soil and exposition in which they grow. We are nothing but what we derive from the air we breathe, the climate we inhabit, the government we obey, the system of religion we profess, and the nature of our employment. . . .

Those who live near the sea, feed more on fish than on flesh, and often encounter that boisterous element. This renders them more bold and enterprising; this leads them to neglect the confined occupations of the land. They see and converse with a variety of people; their intercourse with mankind becomes extensive. The sea inspires them with a love of traffic, a desire of transporting produce from one place to another; and leads them to a variety of resources which supply the place of labour. Those who inhabit the middle settlements, by far the most numerous, must be very different; the simple cultivation of the earth purifies them, but the indulgences of the government, the soft remonstrances of religion, the rank of independent freeholders, must necessarily inspire them with sentiments, very little known in Europe among people of the same class. What do I say? Europe has no such class of men; the early knowledge they acquire, the early bargains they make, give them a great degree of sagacity. As freemen they will be litigious; pride and obstinacy are often the cause of law suits; the nature of our laws and governments may be another. As citizens it is easy to imagine, that they will carefully read the newspapers, enter into every political disquisition, freely blame or censure governors and others. As farmers they will be careful and anxious to get as much as they can, because what they get is their own. As northern men they will love the chearful cup. As Christians, religion curbs them not in their opinions; the general indulgence leaves every one to think for themselves in spiritual matters; the laws inspect our actions, our thoughts are left to God. Industry, good living, selfishness, litigiousness, country politics, the pride of freemen, religious indifference, are their characteristics. If you recede still farther from the sea, you will come into more modern settlements; they exhibit the same strong lineaments, in a ruder appearance. Religion seems to have still less influence, and their manners are less improved.

Now we arrive near the great woods, near the last inhabited districts; there men seem to be placed still farther beyond the reach of government, which in some measure leaves them to themselves. How can it pervade every corner; as they were driven there by misfortunes, necessity of beginnings, desire of acquiring large tracks of land, idleness, frequent want of economy, ancient debts; the re-union of such people does not afford a very pleasing spectacle. When discord, want of unity and friendship; when either drunkenness or idleness prevail in such remote districts; contention, inactivity, and wretchedness must ensue. There are not the same remedies to these evils as in a long established community. The few magistrates they have, are in general little better than the rest; they are often in a perfect state of war; that of man against man, sometimes decided by blows, sometimes by means of the law; that of man against every wild inhabitant of these venerable woods, of which they are come to dispossess them. There men appear to be no better than carnivorous animals of a superior rank, living on the flesh of wild animals when they can catch them, and when they are not able, they subsist on grain. He who would wish to see America in its proper light, and have a true idea of its feeble beginnings and barbarous rudiments, must visit our extended line of frontiers where the last settlers dwell, and where he may see the first labours of settlement, the mode of clearing the earth, in all their different appearances; where men are wholly left dependent on their native tempers, and on the spur of uncertain industry, which often fails when not sanctified by the efficacy of a few moral rules. There, remote from the power of example, and check of shame, many families exhibit the most hideous parts of our society. They are a kind of forlorn hope, preceding by ten or twelve years the most respectable army of veterans which come after them. In that space, prosperity will polish some, vice and the law will drive off the rest, who uniting again with others like themselves will recede still farther; making room for more industrious people, who will finish their improvements, convert the loghouse into a convenient habitation, and rejoicing that the first heavy labours are finished, will change in a few years that hitherto barbarous country into a fine fertile, well regulated district. Such is our progress, such is the march of the Europeans toward the interior parts of this continent. In all societies there are off-casts; this impure part serves as our precursors or pioneers; my father himself was one of that class, but he came upon honest principles, and was therefore one of the few who held fast; by good conduct and temperance, he transmitted to me his fair inheritance, when not above one in fourteen of his contemporaries had the same good fortune.

Forty years ago this smiling country was thus inhabited; it is now purged, a general decency of manners prevails throughout, and such has been the fate of our best countries.

Exclusive of those general characteristics, each province has its own, founded on the government, climate, mode of husbandry, customs and peculiarity of circumstances. Europeans submit insensibly to these great powers, and become, in the course of a few generations, not only Americans in general, but either Pennsylvanians, Virginians, or provincials under some other name. Whoever traverses the continent must easily observe those strong differences, which will grow more evident in time. The inhabitants of Canada, Massachuset, the middle provinces, the southern ones will be as different as their climates; their only points of unity will be those of religion and language.

. . . .

There is no wonder that this country has so many charms, and presents to Europeans so many temptations to remain in it. A traveller in Europe becomes a stranger as soon as he quits his own kingdom; but it is otherwise here. We know, properly speaking, no stranger; this is every person's country; the variety of our soils, situations, climates, governments, and produce, hath something which must please every body. No sooner does an European arrive, no matter of what condition, than his eyes are opened upon the fair prospect; he hears his language spoken, he retraces many of his own country manners, he perpetually hears the names of families and towns with which he is acquainted; he sees happiness and prosperity in all places disseminated; he meets with hospitality, kindness, and plenty every where; he beholds hardly any poor, he seldom hears of punishments and executions; and he wonders at the elegance of our towns, those miracles of industry and freedom. He cannot admire enough our rural districts, our convenient roads, good taverns, and our many accommodations; he involuntarily loves a country where every thing is so lovely. When in England, he was a mere Englishman; here he stands on a larger portion of the globe, not less than its fourth part, and may see the productions of the north, in iron and naval stores; the provisions of Ireland, the grain of Egypt, the indigo, the rice of China. He does not find, as in Europe, a crouded society, where every place is over-stocked; he does not feel that perpetual collision of parties, that difficulty of beginning, that contention which oversets so many. There is room for every body in America; has he any particular talent, or industry? he exerts it in order to procure a livelihood, and it succeeds. Is he a merchant? the avenues of trade are infinite; is he eminent in any respect? he will be employed and respected. Does he love a country life? pleasant farms present themselves; he may purchase what he wants, and thereby become an American farmer. Is he a labourer, sober and industrious? he need not go many miles, nor receive many informations before he will be hired, well fed at the table of his employer, and paid four or five times more than he can get in Europe. Does he want uncultivated lands? thousands of acres present themselves, which he may purchase cheap. Whatever be his talents or inclinations, if they are moderate, he may satisfy them. I do not mean that every one who comes will grow rich in a little time; no, but he may procure an easy, decent maintenance, by his industry. Instead of starving he will be fed, instead of being idle he will have employment; and these are riches enough for such men as come over here. The rich stay in Europe, it is only the middling and the poor that emigrate. Would you wish to travel in independent idleness, from north to south, you will find easy access, and the most chearful reception at every house; society without ostentation, good cheer without pride, and every decent diversion which the country affords, with little expence. It is no wonder that the European who has lived here a few years, is desirous to remain; Europe with all its pomp, is not to be compared to this continent, for men of middle stations, or labourers.

An European, when he first arrives, seems limited in his intentions, as well as in his views; but he very suddenly alters his scale; two hundred miles formerly appeared a very great distance, it is now but a trifle; he no sooner breathes our air than he forms schemes, and embarks in designs he never would have thought of in his own country. There the plenitude of society confines many useful ideas, and often extinguishes the most laudable schemes which here ripen into maturity. Thus Europeans become Americans.

Democracy in America

ALEXIS DE TOCQUEVILLE

Introduction

Among the novel objects that attracted my attention during my stay in the United States, nothing struck me more forcibly than the general equality of conditions. I readily discovered the prodigious influence which this primary fact exercises on the whole course of society, by giving a certain direction to public opinion, and a certain tenor to the laws; by imparting new maxims to the governing powers, and peculiar habits to the governed. I speedily perceived that the influence of this fact extends far beyond the political character and the laws of the country, and that it has no less empire over civil society than over the Government; it creates opinions, engenders sentiments, suggests the ordinary practices of life, and modifies whatever it does not produce. The more I advanced in the study of American society, the more I perceived that the equality of conditions is the fundamental fact from which all others seem to be derived, and the central point at which all my observations constantly terminated.

. . . .

It is evident to all alike that a great democratic revolution is going on among us; but there are two opinions as to its nature and consequences. To some it appears to be a novel accident, which as such may still be checked; to others it seems irresistible, because it is the most uniform, the most ancient, and the most permanent tendency which is to be found in history. . . .

. . . .

. . . Gradually the . . . ranks mingle; the divisions which once severed mankind are lowered; property is divided, power is held in common, the light of intelligence spreads, and the capacities of all classes are equally cultivated; the State becomes democratic, and the empire of democracy is slowly and peaceably introduced into the institutions and the manners of the nation. I can conceive a society in which all men would profess an equal attachment and respect for the

47

laws of which they are the common authors; in which the authority of the State would be respected as necessary, though not as divine; and the loyalty of the subject to the chief magistrate would not be a passion, but a quiet and rational persuasion. Every individual being in the possession of rights which he is sure to retain, a kind of manly reliance and reciprocal courtesy would arise between all classes, alike removed from pride and meanness. The people, well acquainted with its true interests, would allow that in order to profit by the advantages of society it is necessary to satisfy its demands. In this state of things the voluntary association of the citizens might supply the individual exertions of the nobles, and the community would be alike protected from anarchy and from oppression.

I admit that, in a democratic State thus constituted, society will not be stationary; but the impulses of the social body may be regulated and directed forward; if there be less splendour than in the halls of an aristocracy, the contrast of misery will be less frequent also; the pleasures of enjoyment may be less excessive, but those of comfort will be more general; the sciences may be less perfectly cultivated, but ignorance will be less common; the impetuosity of the feelings will be repressed, and the habits of the nation softened; there will be more vices and fewer crimes. In the absence of enthusiasm and of an ardent faith, great sacrifices may be obtained from the members of a commonwealth by an appeal to their understandings and their experience; each individual will feel the same necessity for uniting with his fellow-citizens to protect his own weakness; and as he knows that if they are to assist he must co-operate, he will readily perceive that his personal interest is identified with the interest of the community. The nation, taken as a whole, will be less brilliant, less glorious, and perhaps less strong; but the majority of the citizens will enjoy a greater degree of prosperity, and the people will remain quiet, not because it despairs of amelioration, but because it is conscious of the advantages of its condition. If all the consequences of this state of things were not good or useful, society would at least have appropriated all such as were useful and good; and having once and forever renounced the social advantages of aristocracy, mankind would enter into possession of all the benefits which democracy can afford.

. . . .

. . . I confess that in America I saw more than America; I sought the image of democracy itself, with its inclinations, its character, its prejudices, and its passions, in order to learn what we have to fear or to hope from its progress.

Individualism and Association

I have shown how it is that in ages of equality every man seeks for his opinions within himself; I am now about to show how it is that, in the same ages, all his feelings are turned toward himself alone. Individualism is a novel expression, to which a novel idea has given birth. Our fathers were only acquainted with egotism. Egotism is a passionate and exaggerated love of self, which leads a man to connect everything with his own person, and to prefer himself to everything in the world. Individualism is a mature and calm feeling, which disposes each member of the community to sever himself from the mass of his fellow-creatures; and to draw apart with his family and his friends; so that, after he has thus formed a little circle of his own, he willingly leaves society at large to itself. Egotism originates in blind instinct: individualism proceeds from erroneous judgment more than from depraved feelings; it originates as much in the deficiencies of the mind as in the perversity of the heart. Egotism blights the germ of all virtue; individualism, at first, only saps the virtues of public life; but, in the long run, it attacks and destroys all others, and is at length absorbed in downright egotism. Egotism is a vice as old as the world, which does not belong to one form of society more than to another; individualism is of democratic origin, and it threatens to spread in the same ratio as the equality of conditions.

Among aristocratic nations, as families remain for centuries in the same condition, often on the same spot, all generations become, as it were, contemporaneous. A man almost always knows his forefathers, and respects them: he thinks he already sees his remote descendants, and he loves them. He willingly imposes duties on himself toward the former and the latter; and he will frequently sacrifice his personal gratifications to those who went before and to those who will come after him. Aristocratic institutions have, moreover, the effect of closely binding every man to several of his fellow-citizens. As the classes of an aristocratic people are strongly marked and permanent, each of them is regarded by its own members as a sort of lesser country, more tangible and more cherished than the country at large. As in aristocratic communities all the citizens occupy fixed positions, one above the other, the result is that each of them always sees a man above himself whose patronage is necessary to him, and below himself another man whose co-operation he may claim. Men living in aristocratic ages are therefore almost always closely attached to something placed out of their own sphere, and they are often disposed to forget themselves. It is true that in those ages the notion of human fellowship is faint, and that men seldom think of sacrificing themselves for mankind; but they often sacrifice themselves for other men. In democratic ages, on the contrary, when the duties of each individual to the race are much more clear, devoted service to any one man becomes more rare; the bond of human affection is extended, but it is relaxed.

Among democratic nations new families are constantly springing up, others are constantly falling away, and all that remain change their condition; the woof of time is every instant broken, and the track of generations effaced. Those who went before are soon forgotten; of those who will come after no one has any idea: the interest of man is confined to those in close propinquity to himself. As each class approximates to other classes, and intermingles with them, its members become indifferent and as strangers to one another. Aristocracy had made a chain of all the members of the community, from the peasant to the king: democracy breaks that chain, and severs every link of it. As social conditions become more equal, the number of persons increases who, although they are neither rich enough nor powerful enough to exercise any great influence over their fellow-creatures, have nevertheless acquired or retained sufficient education and fortune to satisfy their own wants. They owe nothing to any man, they expect nothing from any man; they acquire the habit of always considering themselves as standing alone, and they are apt to imagine that their whole destiny is in their own hands. Thus not only does democracy make every man forget his ancestors, but it hides his descendants, and separates his contemporaries from him; it throws him back forever upon himself alone, and threatens in the end to confine him entirely within the solitude of his own heart.

. . . .

The Americans have combated by free institutions the tendency of equality to keep men asunder, and they have subdued it. The legislators of America did not suppose that a general representation of the whole nation would suffice to ward off a disorder at once so natural to the frame of democratic society, and so fatal: they also thought that it would be well to infuse political life into each portion of the territory, in order to multiply to an infinite extent opportunities of acting in concert for all the members of the community, and to make them constantly feel their mutual dependence on each other. The plan was a wise one. The general affairs of a country only engage the attention of leading politicians, who assemble from time to time in the same places; and as they often lose sight of each other afterward, no lasting ties are established between them. But if the object be to have the local affairs of a district conducted by the men who reside there, the same persons are always in contact, and they are, in a manner, forced to be acquainted, and to adapt themselves to one another.

It is difficult to draw a man out of his own circle to interest him in the destiny of the state, because he does not clearly understand what influence the destiny of the state can have upon his own lot. But if it be proposed to make a road across the end of his estate, he will see at a glance that there is a connection between this small public affair and his greatest private affairs; and he will discover, without its being shown to him, the close tie which unites private to general interest. Thus, far more may be done by intrusting to the citizens the administration of minor affairs than by surrendering to them the control of important ones, toward interesting them in the public welfare, and convincing them that they constantly stand in need one of the other in order to provide for it. A brilliant achievement may win for you the favour of a people at one stroke; but to earn the love and respect of the population which surrounds you, a long succession of little services rendered and of obscure good deeds—a constant habit of kindness, and an established reputation for disinterestedness—will be required. Local freedom, then, which leads a great number of citizens to value the affection of their neighbours and of their kindred, perpetually brings men together, and forces them to help one another, in spite of the propensities which sever them.

In the United States the more opulent citizens take great care not to stand aloof from the people; on the contrary, they constantly keep on easy terms with the lower classes: they listen to them, they speak to them every day. They know that the rich in democracies always stand in need of the poor; and that in democratic ages you attach a poor man to you more by your manner than by benefits conferred. The magnitude of such benefits, which sets off the difference of conditions, causes a secret irritation to those who reap advantage from them; but the charm of simplicity of manners is almost irresistible: their affability carries men away, and even their want of polish is not always displeasing. This truth does not take root at once in the minds of the rich. They generally resist it as long as the democratic revolution lasts, and they do not acknowledge it immediately after that revolution is accomplished. They are very ready to do good to the people, but they still choose to keep them at arm's length; they think that is sufficient, but they are mistaken. They might spend fortunes thus without warming the hearts of the population around them—that population does not ask them for the sacrifice of their money, but of their pride.

It would seem as if every imagination in the United States were upon the stretch to invent means of increasing the wealth and satisfying the wants of the public. The best-informed inhabitants of each district constantly use their information to discover new truths which may augment the general prosperity; and if they have made any such discoveries, they eagerly surrender them to the mass of the people.

. . . .

It would be unjust to suppose that the patriotism and the zeal that every American displays for the welfare of his fellow-citizens are wholly insincere. Although private interest directs the greater part of human actions in the United States as well as elsewhere, it does not regulate them all. I must say that I have often seen Americans make great and real sacrifices to the public welfare; and I have remarked a hundred instances in which they hardly ever failed to lend faithful support to each other. The free institutions which the inhabitants of the United States possess, and the political rights of which they make so much use, remind every citizen, and in a thousand ways, that he lives in society. They every instant impress upon his mind the notion that it is the duty, as well as the interest of men, to make themselves useful to their fellow-creatures; and as he sees no particular ground of animosity to them, since he is never either their master or their slave, his heart readily leans to the side of kindness. Men attend to the interests of the public, first by necessity, afterward by choice: what was intentional becomes an instinct; and by dint of working for the good of one's fellow-citizens, the habit and the taste for serving them is at length acquired.

. . . .

. . . Americans of all ages, all conditions, and all dispositions, constantly form associations. They have not only commercial and manufacturing companies, in which all take part, but associations of a thousand other kinds—religious, moral, serious, futile, extensive or restricted, enormous or diminutive. The Americans make associations to give entertainments, to found establishments for education, to build inns, to construct churches, to diffuse books, to send missionaries to the antipodes; and in this manner they founded hospitals, prisons, and schools. If it be proposed to advance some truth, or to foster some feeling by the encouragement of a great example, they form a society. Wherever, at the head of some new undertaking, you see the Government in France, or a man of rank in England, in the United States you will be sure to find as association. . . .

. . . Aristocratic communities always contain, among a multitude of persons who by themselves are powerless, a small number of powerful and wealthy citizens, each of whom can achieve great undertakings single-handed. In aristocratic societies men do not need to combine in order to act, because they are strongly held together. Every wealthy and powerful citizen constitutes the head of a permanent and compulsory association, composed of all those who are dependent upon him, or whom he makes subservient to the execution of his designs. Among democratic nations, on the contrary, all the citizens are independent and feeble; they can do hardly anything by themselves, and none of them can oblige his fellow-men to lend him their assistance. They all, therefore, fall into a state of incapacity, if they do not learn voluntarily to help each other. If men living in democratic countries had no right and no inclination to associate for political purposes, their independence would be in great jeopardy; but they might long preserve their wealth and their cultivation: whereas if they never acquired the habit of forming associations in ordinary life, civilization itself would be endangered. A people among whom individuals should lose the power of achieving great things single-handed, without acquiring the means of producing them by united exertions, would soon relapse into barbarism.

. . . .

Feelings and opinions are recruited, the heart is enlarged, and the human mind is developed by no other means than by the reciprocal influence of men upon each other. I have shown that these influences are almost null in democratic countries; they must therefore be artificially created, and this can only be accomplished by associations.

When the members of an aristocratic community adopt a new opinion, or conceive a new sentiment, they give it a station, as it were, beside themselves, upon the lofty platform where they stand; and opinions or sentiments so conspicuous to the eyes of the multitude are easily introduced into the minds or hearts of all around. In democratic countries the governing power alone is naturally in a condition to act in this manner; but it is easy to see that its action is always inadequate, and often dangerous. A government can no more be competent to keep alive and to renew the circulation of opinions and feelings among a great people than to manage all the speculations of productive industry. No sooner does a government attempt to go beyond its political sphere and to enter upon this new track, than it exercises, even unintentionally, an insupportable tyranny; for a government can only dictate strict rules, the opinions which it favours are rigidly enforced, and it is never easy to discriminate between its advice and its commands. Worse still will be the case if the government really believes itself interested in preventing all circulation of ideas; it will then stand motionless, and oppressed by the heaviness of voluntary torpor. Governments, therefore, should not be the only active powers: associations ought, in democratic nations, to stand in lieu of those powerful private individuals whom the equality of conditions has swept away.

As soon as several of the inhabitants of the United States have taken up an opinion or a feeling that they wish to promote in the world, they look out for mutual assistance; and as soon as they have found each other out, they combine. From that moment they are no longer isolated men, but a power seen from afar, whose actions serve for an example, and whose language is listened to. The first time I heard in the United States that a hundred thousand men had bound themselves publicly to abstain from spirituous liquors, it appeared to me more like a joke than a serious engagement; and I did not at once perceive why these temperate citizens could not content themselves with drinking water by their own firesides. I at last understood that these hundred thousand Americans, alarmed by the progress of drunkenness around them, had made up their minds to patronize temperance. They acted just in the same way as a man of high rank who should dress very plainly, in order to inspire the humbler orders with a contempt of luxury. It is probable that if these hundred thousand men had lived in France, each of them would singly have memorialized the government to watch the public-houses all over the kingdom.

Nothing, in my opinion, is more deserving of our attention than the intellectual and moral associations of America. The political and industrial associations of that country strike us forcibly; but the others elude our observation, or if we discover them, we understand them imperfectly, because we have hardly ever seen anything of the kind. It must, however, be acknowledged that they are as necessary to the American people as the former, and perhaps more so. In democratic countries the science of association is the mother of science; the progress of all the rest depends upon the progress it has made. Among the laws that rule human societies there is one that seems to be more precise and clear than all others. If men are to remain civilized, or to become so, the art of associating together must grow and improve in the same ratio in which the equality of conditions is increased.

. . . .

Democracy does not attach men strongly to each other; but it places their habitual intercourse upon an easier footing. If two Englishmen chance to meet at the Antipodes, where they are surrounded by strangers whose language and manners are almost unknown to them, they will first stare at each other with much curiosity and a kind of secret uneasiness; they will then turn away, or, if one accosts the other, they will take care only to converse with a constrained and absent air upon very unimportant subjects. Yet there is no enmity between these men; they have never seen each other before, and each believes the other to be a respectable person. Why, then, should they stand so cautiously apart? We must go back to England to learn the reason.

When it is birth alone, independent of wealth, which classes men in society, every one knows exactly what his own position is upon the social scale; he does not seek to rise, he does not fear to sink. In a community thus organized, men of different castes communicate very little with each other; but if accident brings them together, they are ready to converse without hoping or fearing to lose their own position. Their intercourse is not upon a footing of equality, but it is not constrained. When moneyed aristocracy succeeds to aristocracy of birth, the case is altered. The privileges of some are still extremely great, but the possibility of acquiring those privileges is open to all: whence it follows that those who possess them are constantly haunted by the apprehension of losing them, or of other men's sharing them; those who do not yet enjoy them long to possess them at any cost, or, if they fail, to appear at least to possess them—which is not impossible. As the social importance of men is no longer ostensibly and permanently fixed by blood, and is infinitely varied by wealth, ranks still exist, but it is not easy clearly to distinguish at a glance those who respectively belong to them. Secret hostilities then arise in the community; one set of men endeavour by innumerable artifices to penetrate, or to appear to penetrate, among those who are above them; another set are constantly in arms against these usurpers of their rights; or rather the same individual does both at once, and while he seeks to raise himself into a higher circle, he is always on the defensive against the intrusion of those below him.

Such is the condition of England at the present time; and I am of opinion that the peculiarity before adverted to is principally to be attributed to this cause. An aristocratic pride is still extremely great among the English, and as the limits of aristocracy are ill defined, everybody lives in constant dread lest advantage should be taken of his familiarity. Unable to judge at once of the social position of those he meets, an Englishman prudently avoids all contact with them. Men are afraid lest some slight service rendered should draw them into an unsuitable acquaintance; they dread civilities, and they avoid the obtrusive gratitude of a stranger quite as much as his hatred. Many people attribute these singular anti-social propensities, and the reserved and taciturn bearing of the English, to purely physical causes. I may admit that there is something of it in their race, but much more of it is attributable to their social condition, as is proved by the contrast of the Americans.

In America, where the privileges of birth never existed, and where riches confer no peculiar rights on their possessors, men unacquainted with each other are very ready to frequent the same places, and find neither peril nor advantage in the free interchange of their thoughts. If they meet by accident, they neither seek nor avoid intercourse; their manner is therefore natural, frank, and open: it is easy to see that they hardly expect or apprehend anything from each other, and that they do not care to display, any more than to conceal, their position in the world. If their demeanour is often cold and serious, it is never haughty or constrained; and if they do not converse, it is because they are not in a humour to talk, not because they think it their interest to be silent. In a foreign country two Americans are at once friends, simply because they are Americans. They are repulsed by no prejudice; they are attracted by their common country. For two Englishmen the same blood is not enough; they must be brought together by the same rank. The Americans remark this unsociable mood of the English as much as the French do, and they are not less astonished by it. . . .

. . . .

It has been universally remarked that in our time the several members of a family stand upon an entirely new footing toward each other; that the distance which formerly separated a father from his sons has been lessened; and that paternal authority, if not destroyed, is at least impaired. Something analogous to this, but even more striking, may be observed in the United States. In America the family, in the Roman and aristocratic signification of the word, does not exist. All that remains of it are a few vestiges in the first years of childhood, when the father exercises, without opposition, that absolute domestic authority which the feebleness of his children renders necessary, and which their interest, as well as his own incontestable superiority, warrants. But as soon as the young American approaches manhood, the ties of filial obedience are relaxed day by day; master of his thoughts, he is soon master of his conduct. In America there is, strictly speaking, no adolescence: at the close of boyhood the man appears, and begins to trace out his own path. It would be an error to suppose that this is preceded by a domestic struggle, in which the son has obtained by a sort of moral violence the liberty that his father refused him. The same habits, the same principles which impel the one to assert his independence, predispose the other to consider the use of that independence as an incontestable right. The former does not exhibit any of those rancorous or irregular passions which disturb men long after they have shaken off an established authority; the latter feels none of that bitter and angry regret which is apt to survive a by-gone power. The father foresees the limits of his authority long beforehand, and when the time arrives he surrenders it without a struggle: the son looks forward to the exact period at which he will be his own master; and he enters upon his freedom without precipitation and without effort, as a possession which is his own and which no one seeks to wrest from him.

It may perhaps not be without utility to show how these changes which take place in family relations are closely connected with the social and political revolution which is approaching its consummation under our own observation. There are certain great social principles which a people either introduces everywhere or tolerates nowhere. In countries which are aristocratically constituted with all the gradations of rank, the Government never makes a direct appeal to the mass of the governed: as men are united together, it is enough to lead the foremost; the rest will follow. This is equally applicable to the family, as to all aristocracies which have a head. Among aristocratic nations, social institutions recognize, in truth, no one in the family but the father; children are received by society at his hands; society governs him, he governs them. Thus the parent has not only a natural right, but he acquires a political right, to command them; he is the author and the support of his family; but he is also its constituted ruler. In democracies, where the government picks out every individual singly from the mass, to make him subservient to the general laws of the community, no such intermediate person is required: a father is there, in the eye of the law, only a member of the community, older and richer than his sons.

When most of the conditions of life are extremely unequal, and the inequality of these conditions is permanent, the notion of a superior grows upon the imaginations of men: if the law invested him with no privileges, custom and public opinion would concede them. When, on the contrary, men differ but little from each other, and do not always remain in dissimilar conditions of life, the general notion of a superior becomes weaker and less distinct: it is vain for legislation to strive to place him who obeys very much beneath him who commands; the manners of the time bring the two men nearer to one another, and draw them daily toward the same level. . . .

When men live more for the remembrance of what has been than for the care of what is, and when they are more given to attend to what their ancestors thought than to think themselves, the father is the natural and necessary tie between the past and the present—the link by which the ends of these two chains are connected. In aristocracies, then, the father is not only the civil head of the family, but the oracle of its traditions, the expounder of its customs, the arbiter of its manners. He is listened to with deference, he is addressed with respect, and the love which is felt for him is always tempered with fear. When the condition of society becomes democratic, and men adopt as their general principle that it is good and lawful to judge of all things for one's self, using former points of belief not as a rule of faith but simply as a means of information, the power which the opinions of a father exercise over those of his sons diminishes as well as his legal power.

. . . .

Thus, at the same time that the power of aristocracy is declining, the austere, the conventional, and the legal part of parental authority vanishes, and a species of equality prevails around the domestic hearth. I know not, upon the whole, whether society loses by the change, but I am inclined to believe that man individually is a gainer by it. I think that, in proportion as manners and laws become more democratic, the relation of father and son becomes more intimate and more affectionate; rules and authority are less talked of; confidence and tenderness are oftentimes increased, and it would seem that the natural bond is drawn closer in proportion as the social bond is loosened. In a democratic family the father exercises no other power than that with which men love to invest the affection and the experience of age; his orders would perhaps be disobeyed, but his advice is for the most part authoritative. Though he be not hedged in with ceremonial respect, his sons at least accost him with confidence; no settled form of speech is appropriated to the mode of addressing him, but they speak to him constantly, and are ready to consult him day by day; the master and the constituted ruler have vanished—the father remains. Nothing more is needed, in order to judge of the difference between the two states of society in this respect, than to peruse the family correspondence of aristocratic ages. The style is always correct, ceremonious, stiff, and so cold that the natural warmth of the heart can hardly be felt in the language. The language, on the contrary, addressed by a son to his father in democratic countries is always marked by mingled freedom, familiarity, and affection, which at once show that new relations have sprung up in the bosom of the family.

A similar revolution takes place in the mutual relations of children. In aristocratic families, as well as in aristocratic society, every place is marked out beforehand. Not only does the father occupy a separate rank, in which he enjoys extensive privileges, but even the children are not equal among themselves. The age and sex of each irrevocably determine his rank, and secure to him certain privileges: most of these distinctions are abolished or diminished by democracy. . . .

. . . Under democratic laws all the children are perfectly equal, and consequently independent: nothing brings them forcibly together, but nothing keeps them apart; and as they have the same origin, as they are trained under the same roof, as they are treated with the same care, and as no peculiar privilege distinguishes or divides them, the affectionate and youthful intimacy of early years easily springs up between them. Scarcely any opportunities occur to break the tie thus formed at the outset of life; for their brotherhood brings them daily together, without embarrassing them. It is not, then, by interest, but by common associations and by the free sympathy of opinion and of taste, that democracy unites brothers to each other. It divides their inheritance, but it allows their hearts and minds to mingle together. . . .

Conformity and Autonomy

I know no country in which there is so little true independence of mind and freedom of discussion as in America. In any constitutional state in Europe every sort of religious and political theory may be advocated and propagated abroad; for there is no country in Europe so subdued by any single authority as not to contain citizens who are ready to protect the man who raises his voice in the cause of truth from the consequences of his hardihood. If he is unfortunate enough to live under an absolute government, the people is upon his side; if he inhabits a free country, he may find a shelter behind the authority of the throne, if he require one. The aristocratic part of society supports him in some countries, and the democracy in others. But in a nation where democratic institutions exist, organized like those of the United States, there is but one sole authority, one single element of strength and of success, with nothing beyond it.

In America, the majority raises very formidable barriers to the liberty of opinion: within these barriers an author may write whatever he pleases, but he will repent it if he ever step beyond them. Not that he is exposed to the terrors of an auto-da-fé, but he is tormented by the slights and persecutions of daily obloquy. His political career is closed forever, since he has offended the only authority which is able to promote his success. Every sort of compensation, even that of celebrity, is refused to him. Before he published his opinions he imagined that he held them in common with many others; but no sooner has he declared them openly than he is loudly censured by his over-bearing opponents, while those who think like him, without having the courage to speak, abandon him in silence. He yields at length, oppressed by the daily efforts he has been making, and he subsides into silence, as if he was tormented by remorse for having spoken the truth.

Fetters and headsmen were the coarse instruments which tyranny formerly employed; but the civilization of our age has refined the arts of despotism, which seemed, however, to have been sufficiently perfected before. The excesses of monarchical power had devised a variety of physical means of oppression: the democratic republics of the present day have rendered it as entirely an affair of the mind as that will which it is intended to coerce. Under the absolute sway of an individual despot the body was attacked in order to subdue the soul, and the soul escaped the blows which were directed against it and rose superior to the attempt; but such is not the course adopted by tyranny in democratic republics; there the body is left free, and the soul is enslaved. The sovereign can no longer say, "You shall think as I do on pain of death"; but he says: "You are free to think differently from me, and to retain your life, your property, and all that you possess; but if such be your determination, you are henceforth an alien among your people. . . ."

. . . .

If great writers have not at present existed in America, the reason is very simply given in these facts; there can be no literary genius without freedom of opinion, and freedom of opinion does not exist in America. The Inquisition never has been able to prevent a vast number of anti-religious books from circulating in Spain. The empire of the majority succeeds much better in the United States, since it actually removes the wish of publishing them. Unbelievers are to be met with in America, but, to say the truth, there is no public organ of infidelity. Attempts have been made by some governments to protect the morality of nations by prohibiting licentious books. In the United States no one is punished for this sort of works, but no one is induced to write them; not because all the citizens are immaculate in their manners, but because the majority of the community is decent and orderly.

In these cases the advantages derived from the exercise of this power are unquestionable, and I am simply discussing the nature of the power itself. This irresistible authority is a constant fact, and its judicious exercise is an accidental occurrence.

The tendencies to which I have just alluded are as yet very slightly perceptible in political society, but they already begin to exercise an unfavourable influence upon the national character of the Americans. I am inclined to attribute the singular paucity of distinguished political characters to the ever-increasing activity of the despotism of the majority in the United States. . . .

. . . .

In that immense crowd which throngs the avenues to power in the United States I found very few men who displayed any of that manly candour and that masculine independence of opinion which frequently distinguished the Americans in former times, and which constitutes the leading feature in distinguished characters, wheresoever they may be found. It seems, at first sight, as if all the minds of the Americans were formed upon one model, so accurately do they correspond in their manner of judging. . . .

. . . .

. . . In the ages of aristocracy which preceded our own, there were private persons of great power, and a social authority of extreme weakness. The outline of society itself was not easily discernible, and constantly confounded with the different powers by which the community was ruled. The principal efforts of the men of those times were required to strengthen, aggrandize, and secure the supreme power; and, on the other hand, to circumscribe individual independence within narrower limits, and to subject private interests to the interests of the public. Other perils and other cares await the men of our age. Among the greater part of modern nations, the government, whatever may be its origin, its constitution, or its name, has become almost omnipotent, and private persons are falling, more and more, into the lowest stage of weakness and dependence. In olden society everything was different; unity and uniformity were nowhere to be met with. In modern society everything threatens to become so much alike, that the peculiar characteristics of each individual will soon be entirely lost in the general aspect of the world. Our forefathers were prone to make an improper use of the notion that private rights ought to be respected; and we are naturally prone, on the other hand, to exaggerate the idea that the interest of a private individual ought always to bend to the interest of the many. . . .

. . . .

I think that in no country in the civilized world is less attention paid to philosophy than in the United States. The Americans have no philosophical school of their own; and they care but little for all the schools into which Europe is divided, the very names of which are scarcely known to them. Nevertheless it is easy to perceive that almost all the inhabitants of the United States conduct their understanding in the same manner, and govern it by the same rules—that is to say, that without ever having taken the trouble to define the rules of a philosophical method, they are in possession of one, common to the whole people. To evade the bondage of system and habit, of family-maxims, class-opinions, and, in some degree, of national prejudices; to accept tradition only as a means of information, and existing facts only as a lesson used in doing otherwise and doing better; to seek the reason of things for one's self, and in one's self alone; to tend to results without being bound to means, and to aim at the substance through the form—such are the principal characteristics of what I shall call the philosophical method of the Americans. But if I go further, and if I seek among these characteristics that which predominates over and includes almost all the rest, I discover that in most of the operations of the mind each American appeals to the individual exercise of his own understanding alone. America is therefore one of the countries in the world where philosophy is least studied, and where the precepts of Descartes are best applied. Nor is this surprising. The Americans do not read the works of Descartes, because their social condition deters them from speculative studies; but they follow his maxims because this very social condition naturally disposes their understanding to adopt them. In the midst of the continual movement which agitates a democratic community the tie which unites one generation to another is relaxed or broken; every man readily loses the trace of the ideas of his forefathers or takes no care about them. Nor can men living in this state of society derive their belief from the opinions of the class to which they belong; for, so to speak, there are no longer any classes, or those which still exist are composed of such mobile elements that their body can never exercise a real control over its members. As to the influence which the intelligence of one man has on that of another, it must necessarily be very limited in a country where the citizens, placed on the footing of a general similitude, are all closely seen by each other; and where, as no signs of incontestable greatness or superiority are perceived in any one of them, they are constantly brought back to their own reason as the most obvious and proximate source of truth. It is not only confidence in this or that man which is then destroyed, but the taste for trusting the ipse dixit of any man whatsoever. Every one shuts himself up in his own breast, and affects from that point to judge the world.

The practice which obtains among the Americans of fixing the standard of their judgment in themselves alone, leads them to other habits of mind. As they perceive that they succeed in resolving without assistance all the little difficulties which their practical life presents, they readily conclude that everything in the world may be explained, and that nothing in it transcends the limits of the understanding. Thus they fall to denying what they can not comprehend; which leaves them but little faith for whatever is extraordinary, and an almost insurmountable distaste for whatever is supernatural. As it is on their own testimony that they are accustomed to rely, they like to discern the object which engages their attention with extreme clearness; they therefore strip off as much as possible all that covers it, they rid themselves of whatever separates them from it, they remove whatever conceals it from sight, in order to view it more closely and in the broad light of day. This disposition of the mind soon leads them to contemn forms, which they regard as useless and inconvenient veils placed between them and the truth.

The Americans, then, have not required to extract their philosophical method from books; they have found it in themselves. . . .

. . . .

A principle of authority must . . . always occur, under all circumstances, in some part or other of the moral and intellectual world. Its place is variable, but a place it necessarily has. The independence of individual minds may be greater, or it may be less: unbounded it can not be. Thus the question is, not to know whether any intellectual authority exists in the ages of democracy, but simply where it resides and by what standard it is to be measured.

I have shown ... how equality of condition leads men to entertain a sort of instinctive incredulity of the supernatural, and a very lofty and often exaggerated opinion of the human understanding. The men who live at a period of social equality are not, therefore, easily led to place that intellectual authority to which they bow either beyond or above humanity. They commonly seek for the sources of truth in themselves, or in those who are like themselves. This would be enough to prove that at such periods no new religion could be established, and that all schemes for such a purpose would be not only impious but absurd and irrational. It may be foreseen that a democratic people will not easily give credence to divine missions; that they will turn modern prophets to a ready jest; and that they will seek to discover the chief arbiter of their belief within, and not beyond, the limits of their kind.

When the ranks of society are unequal, and men unlike each other in condition, there are some individuals invested with all the power of superior intelligence, learning, and enlightenment, while the multitude is sunk in ignorance and prejudice. Men living at these aristocratic periods are therefore naturally induced to shape their opinions by the superior standard of a person or a class of persons, while they are averse to recognize the infallibility of the mass of the people.

The contrary takes place in ages of equality. The nearer the citizens are drawn to the common level of an equal and similar condition, the less prone does each man become to place implicit faith in a certain man or a certain class of men. But his readiness to believe the multitude increases, and opinion is more than ever mistress of the world. Not only is common opinion the only guide which private judgment retains among a democratic people, but among such a people it possesses a power infinitely beyond what it has elsewhere. At periods of equality men have no faith in one another, by reason of their common resemblance; but this very resemblance gives them almost unbounded confidence in the judgment of the public; for it would not seem probable, as they are all endowed with equal means of judging, but that the greater truth should go with the greater number.

When the inhabitant of a democratic country compares himself individually with all those about him, he feels with pride that he is the equal of any one of them; but when he comes to survey the totality of his fellows, and to place himself in contrast to so huge a body, he is instantly overwhelmed by the sense of his own insignificance and weakness. The same equality which renders him independent of each of his fellow-citizens taken severally exposes him alone and unprotected to the influence of the greater number. The public has therefore among a democratic people a singular power, of which aristocratic nations could never so much as conceive an idea; for it does not persuade to certain opinions, but it enforces them, and infuses them into the faculties by a sort of enormous pressure of the minds of all upon the reason of each.

In the United States the majority undertakes to supply a multitude of ready-made opinions for the use of individuals, who are thus relieved from the necessity of forming opinions of their own. Everybody there adopts great numbers of theories, on philosophy, morals, and politics, without inquiry, upon public trust; and if we look to it very narrowly, it will be perceived that religion herself holds her sway there, much less as a doctrine of revelation than as a commonly received opinion. . . .

. . . In the principle of equality I very clearly discern two tendencies; the one leading the mind of every man to untried thoughts, the other inclined to prohibit him from thinking at all. And I perceive how, under the dominion of certain laws, democracy would extinguish that liberty of the mind to which a democratic social condition is favourable; so that, after having broken all the bondage once imposed on it by ranks or by men, the human mind would be closely fettered to the general will of the greatest number.

. . . .

Whenever social conditions are equal, public opinion presses with enormous weight upon the mind of each individual; it surrounds, directs, and oppresses him; and this arises from the very constitution of society, much more than from its political laws. As men grow more alike, each man feels himself weaker in regard to all the rest; as he discerns nothing by which he is considerably raised above them, or distinguished from them, he mistrusts himself as soon as they assail him. Not only does he mistrust his strength, but he even doubts of his right; and he is very near acknowledging that he is in the wrong, when the greater number of his countrymen assert that he is so. The majority do not need to constrain him—they convince him. In whatever way, then, the powers of a democratic community may be organized and balanced, it will always be extremely difficult to believe what the bulk of the people reject, or to profess what they condemn.

This circumstance is extraordinarily favourable to the stability of opinions. When an opinion has taken root among a democratic people, and established itself in the minds of the bulk of the community, it afterward subsists by itself and is maintained without effort, because no one attacks it. Those who at first rejected it as false, ultimately receive it as the general impression; and those who still dispute it in their hearts, conceal their dissent; they are careful not to engage in a dangerous and useless conflict. . . .

. . . .

The principle of equality, which makes men independent of each other, gives them a habit and a taste for following, in their private actions, no other guide but their own will. This complete independence, which they constantly enjoy toward their equals and in the intercourse of private life, tends to make them look upon all authority with a jealous eye, and speedily suggests to them the notion and the love of political freedom. Men living at such times have a natural bias to free institutions. Take any one of them at a venture, and search if you can his most deep-seated instincts; you will find that of all governments he will soonest conceive and most highly value that government whose head he has himself elected, and whose administration he may control. Of all the political effects produced by the equality of conditions, this love of independence is the first to strike the observing, and to alarm the timid; nor can it be said that their alarm is wholly misplaced, for anarchy has a more formidable aspect in democratic countries than elsewhere. As the citizens have no direct influence on each other, as soon as the supreme power of the nation fails, which kept them all in their several stations, it would seem that disorder must instantly reach its utmost pitch, and that, every man drawing aside in a different direction, the fabric of society must at once crumble away.

I am, however, persuaded that anarchy is not the principal evil that democratic ages have to fear, but the least. For the principle of equality begets two tendencies: the one leads men straight to independence, and may suddenly drive them into anarchy; the other conducts them by a longer, more secret, but more certain road, to servitude. Nations readily discern the former tendency, and are prepared to resist it; they are led away by the latter, without perceiving its drift; hence it is peculiarly important to point it out. For myself, I am so far from urging as a reproach to the principle of equality that it renders men untractable, that this very circumstance principally calls forth my approbation. I admire to see how it deposits in the mind and heart of man the dim conception and instinctive love of political independence, thus preparing the remedy for the evil which it engenders; it is on this very account that I am attached to it.
. . . .

. . . As in ages of equality no man is compelled to lend his assistance to his fellow-men, and none has any right to expect much support from them, every one is at once independent and powerless. These two conditions, which must never be either separately considered or confounded together, inspire the citizen of a democratic country with very contrary propensities. His independence fills him with self-reliance and pride among his equals; his debility makes him feel from time to time the want of some outward assistance, which he can not expect from any of them, because they are all impotent and unsympathizing. In this predicament he naturally turns his eyes to that imposing power which alone rises above the level of universal depression. Of that power his wants and especially his desires continually remind him, until he ultimately views it as the sole and necessary support of his own weakness. This may more completely explain what frequently takes place in democratic countries, where the very men who are so impatient of superiors patiently submit to a master, exhibiting at once their pride and their servility.

The hatred which men bear to privilege increases in proportion as privileges become more scarce and less considerable, so that democratic passions would seem to burn most fiercely at the very time when they have least fuel. I have already given the reason of this phenomenon. When all conditions are unequal, no inequality is so great as to offend the eye; whereas the slightest dissimilarity is odious in the midst of general uniformity: the more complete is this uniformity, the more insupportable does the sight of such a difference become. Hence it is natural that the love of equality should constantly increase together with equality itself, and that it should grow by what it feeds upon. This never-dying, ever-kindling hatred, which sets a democratic people against the smallest privileges, is peculiarly favourable to the gradual concentration of all political rights in the hands of the representative of the State alone. The sovereign, being necessarily and incontestably above all the citizens, excites not their envy, and each of them thinks that he strips his equals of the prerogative which he concedes to the crown. The man of a democratic age is extremely reluctant to obey his neighbour who is his equal; he refuses to acknowledge in such a person ability superior to his own; he mistrusts his justice, and is jealous of his power; he fears and he contemns him; and he loves continually to remind him of the common dependence in which both of them stand to the same master. Every central power which follows its natural tendencies courts and encourages the principle of equality; for equality singularly facilitates, extends, and secures the influence of a central power.

In like manner it may be said that every central government worships uniformity: uniformity relieves it from inquiry into an infinite number of small details which must be attended to if rules were to be adapted to men, instead of indiscriminately subjecting men to rules: thus the government likes what the citizens like, and naturally hates what they hate. These common sentiments, which, in democratic nations, constantly unite the sovereign and every member of the community in one and the same conviction, establish a secret and lasting sympathy between them. The faults of the government are pardoned for the sake of its tastes; public confidence is only reluctantly withdrawn in the midst even of its excesses and its errors, and it is restored at the first call. Democratic nations often hate those in whose hands the central power is vested; but they always love that power itself.

Thus by two separate paths I have reached the same conclusion. I have shown that the principle of equality suggests to men the notion of a sole, uniform, and strong government: I have now shown that the principle of equality imparts to them a taste for it. To governments of this kind the nations of our age are therefore tending. They are drawn thither by the natural inclination of mind and heart; and in order to reach that result, it is enough that they do not check themselves in their course. I am of opinion that, in the democratic ages which are opening upon us, individual independence and local liberties will ever be the produce of artificial contrivance; that centralization will be the natural form of government.

. . . .

I seek to trace the novel features under which despotism may appear in the world. The first thing that strikes the observation is an innumerable multitude of men all equal and alike, incessantly endeavouring to procure the petty and paltry pleasures with which they glut their lives. Each of them, living apart, is as a stranger to the fate of all the rest—his children and his private friends constitute to him the whole of mankind; as for the rest of his fellow-citizens, he is close to them, but he sees them not—he touches them, but he feels them not; he exists but in himself and for himself alone; and if his kindred still remain to him, he may be said at any rate to have lost his country. Above this race of men stands an immense and tutelary power, which takes upon itself alone to secure their gratifications, and to watch over their fate. That power is absolute, minute, regular, provident, and mild. It would be like the authority of a parent, if, like that authority, its object was to prepare men for manhood; but it seeks, on the contrary, to keep them in perpetual childhood: it is well content that the people should rejoice, provided they think of nothing but rejoicing. For their happiness such a government willingly labours, but it chooses to be the sole agent and the only arbiter of that happiness: it provides for their security, foresees and supplies their necessities, facilitates their pleasures, manages their principal concerns, directs their industry, regulates the descent of property, and subdivides their inheritances—what remains, but to spare them all the care of thinking and all the trouble of living? Thus it every day renders the exercise of the free agency of man less useful and less frequent; it circumscribes the will within a narrower range, and gradually robs a man of all the uses of himself. The principle of equality has prepared men for these things: it has predisposed men to endure them, and oftentimes to look on them as benefits.

After having thus successively taken each member of the community in its powerful grasp, and fashioned them at will, the supreme power then extends its arm over the whole community. It covers the surface of society with a network of small complicated rules, minute and uniform, through which the most original minds and the most energetic characters can not penetrate, to rise above the crowd. The will of man is not shattered, but softened, bent, and guided: men are seldom forced by it to act, but they are constantly restrained from acting: such a power does not destroy, but it prevents existence; it does not tyrannize, but it compresses, enervates, extinguishes, and stupefies a people, till each nation is reduced to be nothing better than a flock of timid and industrious animals, of which the government is the shepherd.

I have always thought that servitude of the regular, quiet, and gentle kind which I have just described might be combined more easily than is commonly believed with some of the outward forms of freedom; and that it might even establish itself under the wing of the sovereignty of the people. Our contemporaries are constantly excited by two conflicting passions; they want to be led, and they wish to remain free: as they can not destroy either one or the other of these contrary propensities, they strive to satisfy them both at once. They devise a sole, tutelary, and all-powerful form of government, but elected by the people. They combine the principle of centralization and that of popular sovereignty; this gives them a respite; they console themselves for being in tutelage by the reflection that they have chosen their own guardians. Every man allows himself to be put in leading-strings, because he sees that it is not a person or a class of persons, but the people at large, that holds the end of his chain. . . .

Mobility and Materialism

In America the passion for physical well-being is not always exclusive, but it is general; and if all do not feel it in the same manner, yet it is felt by all. Carefully to satisfy all, even the least wants of the body, and to provide the little conveniences of life, is uppermost in every mind. . . . All the revolutions which have ever shaken or destroyed aristocracies, have 'shown how easily men accustomed to superfluous luxuries can do without the necessaries of life; whereas men who have toiled to acquire a competency can hardly live after they have lost it.

. . . When . . . the distinctions of ranks are confounded together and privileges are destroyed—when hereditary property is subdivided, and education and freedom widely diffused, the desire of acquiring the comforts of the world haunts the imagination of the poor, and the dread of losing them that of the rich. Many scanty fortunes spring up; those who possess them have a sufficient share of physical gratifications to conceive a taste for these pleasures—not enough to satisfy it. They never procure them without exertion, and they never indulge in them without apprehension. They are, therefore, always straining to pursue or to retain gratifications so delightful, so imperfect, so fugitive.

If I were to inquire what passion is most natural to men who are stimulated and circumscribed by the obscurity of their birth or the mediocrity of their fortune, I could discover none more peculiarly appropriate to their condition than this love of physical prosperity. The passion for physical comforts is essentially a passion of the middle classes: with those classes it grows and spreads, with them it preponderates. From them it mounts into the higher orders of society, and descends into the mass of the people. I never met in America with any citizen so poor as not to cast a glance of hope and envy on the enjoyments of the rich, or whose imagination did not possess itself by anticipation of those good things which fate still obstinately withheld from him. On the other hand, I never perceived among the wealthier inhabitants of the United States that proud contempt of physical gratifications which is sometimes to be met with even in the most opulent and dissolute aristocracies. Most of these wealthy persons were once poor: they have felt the sting of want; they were long a prey to adverse fortunes; and now that the victory is won, the passions which accompanied the contest have survived it: their minds are, as it were, intoxicated by the small enjoyments which they have pursued for forty years. Not but that in the United States, as elsewhere, there are a certain number of wealthy persons who, having come into their property by inheritance, possess, without exertion, an opulence they have not earned. But even these men are not less devotedly attached to the pleasures of material life. The love of well-being is now become the predominant taste of the nation; the great current of man's passions runs in that channel, and sweeps everything along in its course.

. . . .

The especial taste that the men of democratic ages entertain for physical enjoyments is not naturally opposed to the principles of public order; nay, it often stands in need of order that it may be gratified. Nor is it adverse to regularity of morals, for good morals contribute to public tranquility and are favourable to industry. It may even be frequently combined with a species of religious morality: men wish to be as well off as they can in this world, without foregoing their chance of another. Some physical gratifications can not be indulged in without crime; from such they strictly abstain. The enjoyment of others is sanctioned by religion and morality; to these the heart, the imagination, and life itself are unreservedly given up; till, in snatching at these lesser gifts, men lose sight of those more precious possessions which constitute the glory and the greatness of mankind. The reproach I address to the principle of equality is not that it leads men away in the pursuit of forbidden enjoyments, but that it absorbs them wholly in quest of those which are allowed. By these means, a kind of virtuous materialism may ultimately be established in the world, which would not corrupt, but enervate the soul, and noiselessly unbend its springs of action.

. . . .

... In America I saw the freest and most enlightened men placed in the happiest circumstances that the world affords: it seemed to me as if a cloud habitually hung upon their brow, and I thought them serious and almost sad even in their pleasures. ... It is strange to see with what feverish ardour the Americans pursue their own welfare; and to watch the vague dread that constantly torments them lest they should not have chosen the shortest path which may lead to it. A native of the United States clings to this world's goods as if he were certain never to die; and he is so hasty in grasping at all within his reach that one would suppose he was constantly afraid of not living long enough to enjoy them. He clutches everything, he holds nothing fast, but soon loosens his grasp to pursue fresh gratifications.

In the United States a man builds a house to spend his latter years in it, and he sells it before the roof is on: he plants a garden, and lets it just as the trees are coming into bearing: he brings a field into tillage, and leaves other men to gather the crops: he embraces a profession, and gives it up: he settles in a place, which he soon afterward leaves, to carry his changeable longings elsewhere. If his private affairs leave him any leisure, he instantly plunges into the vortex of politics; and if at the end of a year of unremitting labour he finds he has a few days' vacation, his eager curiosity whirls him over the vast extent of the United States, and he will travel fifteen hundred miles in a few days to shake off his happiness. Death at length overtakes him, but it is before he is weary of his bootless chase of that complete felicity which is forever on the wing.

At first sight there is something surprising in this strange unrest of so many happy men, restless in the midst of abundance. The spectacle itself is, however, as old as the world; the novelty is to see a whole people furnish an exemplification of it. Their taste for physical gratifications must be regarded as the original source of that secret inquietude that the actions of the Americans betray, and of that inconstancy of which they afford fresh examples every day. He who has set his heart exclusively upon the pursuit of worldly welfare is always in a hurry, for he has but a limited time at his disposal to reach it, to grasp it, and to enjoy it. The recollection of the brevity of life is a constant spur to him. Besides the good things which he possesses, he every instant fancies a thousand others which death will prevent him from trying if he does not try them soon. This thought fills him with anxiety, fear, and regret, and keeps his mind in ceaseless trepidation, which leads him perpetually to change his plans and his abode. If in addition to the taste for physical well-being a social condition be superadded, in which the laws and customs make no condition permanent, here is a great additional stimulant to this restlessness of temper. Men will then be seen continually to change their track, for fear of missing the shortest cut to happiness. It may readily be conceived that if men, passionately bent upon physical gratifications, desire eagerly, they are also easily discouraged: as their ultimate object is to enjoy, the means to reach that object must be prompt and easy, or the trouble of acquiring the gratification would be greater than the gratification itself. Their prevailing frame of mind, then, is at once ardent and relaxed, violent and enervated. Death is often less dreaded than perseverance in continuous efforts to one end.

The equality of conditions leads by a still straighter road to several of the effects which I have here described. When all the privileges of birth and fortune are abolished, when all professions are accessible to all, and a man's own energies may place him at the top of any one of them, an easy and unbounded career seems open to his ambition, and he will readily persuade himself that he is born to no vulgar destinies. But this is an erroneous notion, which is corrected by daily experience. The same equality which allows every citizen to conceive these lofty hopes renders all the citizens less able to realize them: it circumscribes their powers on every side, while it gives freer scope to their desires. Not only are they themselves powerless, but they are met at every step by immense obstacles, which they did not at first perceive. They have swept away the privileges of some of their fellow-creatures which stood in their way, but they have opened the door to universal competition: the barrier has changed its shape rather than its position. When men are nearly alike, and all follow the same track, it is very difficult for any one individual to walk quick and cleave a way through the dense throng which surrounds and presses him. This constant strife between the propensities springing from the equality of conditions and the means it supplies to satisfy them harasses and wearies the mind.

It is possible to conceive men arrived at a degree of freedom which should completely content them; they would then enjoy their independence without anxiety and without impatience. But men will never establish any equality with which they can be contented. Whatever efforts a people may make, they will never succeed in reducing all the conditions of society to a perfect level; and even if they unhappily attained that absolute and complete depression, the inequality of minds would still remain, which, coming directly from the hand of

God, will forever escape the laws of man. However democratic, then, the social state and the political constitution of a people may be, it is certain that every member of the community will always find out several points about him that command his own position; and we may foresee that his looks will be doggedly fixed in that direction. When inequality of conditions is the common law of society, the most marked inequalities do not strike the eye: when everything is nearly on the same level, the slightest are marked enough to hurt it. Hence the desire of equality always becomes more insatiable in proportion as equality is more complete.

Among democratic nations men easily attain a certain equality of conditions: they can never attain the equality they desire. It perpetually retires from before them, yet without hiding itself from their sight, and in retiring draws them on. At every moment they think they are about to grasp it; it escapes at every moment from their hold. They are near enough to see its charms, but too far off to enjoy them; and before they have fully tasted its delights they die. To these causes must be attributed that strange melancholy that oftentimes will haunt the inhabitants of democratic countries in the midst of their abundance, and that disgust at life that sometimes seizes upon them in the midst of calm and easy circumstances. . . .

In democratic ages enjoyments are more intense than in the ages of aristocracy, and especially the number of those who partake in them is larger: but, on the other hand, it must be admitted that man's hopes and his desires are oftener blasted, the soul is more stricken and perturbed, and care itself more keen.

. . . .

. . . Among aristocratic nations every man is pretty nearly stationary in his own sphere; but men are astonishingly unlike each other—their passions, their notions, their habits, and their tastes are essentially different: nothing changes, but everything differs. In democracies, on the contrary, all men are alike and do things pretty nearly alike. It is true that they are subject to great and frequent vicissitudes; but as the same events of good or adverse fortune are continually recurring, the name of the actors only is changed, the piece is always the same. The aspect of American society is animated, because men and things are always changing, but it is monotonous, because all these changes are alike.

Men living in democratic ages have many passions, but most of their passions either end in the love of riches or proceed from it. The cause of this is, not that their souls are narrower, but that the importance of money is really greater at such times. When all the members of a community are independent of or indifferent to each other, the co-operation of each of them can only be obtained by paying for it: this infinitely multiplies the purposes to which wealth may be applied, and increases its value. When the reverence that belonged to what is old has vanished, birth, condition, and profession no longer distinguish men, or scarcely distinguish them at all: hardly anything but money remains to create strongly marked differences between them, and to raise some of them above the common level. The distinction originating in wealth is increased by the disappearance and diminution of all other distinctions. Among aristocratic nations money only reaches to a few points on the vast circle of man's desires—in democracies it seems to lead to all. The love of wealth is therefore to be traced, either as a principal or an accessory motive, at the bottom of all that the Americans do: this gives to all their passions a sort of family likeness, and soon renders the survey of them exceedingly wearisome. This perpetual recurrence of the same passion is monotonous; the peculiar methods by which this passion seeks its own gratification are no less so.

In an orderly and constituted democracy like the United States, where men can not enrich themselves by war, by public office, or by political confiscation, the love of wealth mainly drives them into business and manufactures. Although these pursuits often bring about great commotions and disasters, they can not prosper without strictly regular habits and a long routine of petty uniform acts. The stronger the passion is, the more regular are these habits, and the more uniform are these acts. It may be said that it is the vehemence of their desires which makes the Americans so methodical; it perturbs their minds, but it disciplines their lives.

The remark I here apply to America may indeed be addressed to almost all our contemporaries. Variety is disappearing from the human race; the same ways of acting, thinking, and feeling are to be met with all over the world. This is not only because nations work more upon each other, and are more faithful in their mutual imitation; but as the men of each country relinquish more and more the peculiar opinions and feelings of a caste, a profession, or a family, they simultaneously arrive at something nearer to the constitution of man, which is everywhere the same. Thus they become more alike, even without having imitated each other. Like travellers scattered about some large wood, which is intersected by paths converging to one point, if all of them keep their eyes fixed upon that point and advance toward it, they insensibly draw nearer together—though they seek not, though they see not, though they know not each other; and they will be surprised at length to find themselves all collected on the same spot. . . .

The American Character in the 1880s

JAMES BRYCE

National Character and Public Opinion

As the public opinion of a people is even more directly than its political institutions the reflection and expression of its character, we may begin the analysis of opinion in America by noting some of those general features of national character which give tone and colour to the people's thoughts and feelings on politics. There are, of course, varieties proper to different classes, and to different parts of the vast territory of the Union; but it is well to consider first such characteristics as belong to the nation as a whole, and afterwards to examine the various classes and districts of the country. And when I speak of the nation, I mean the native Americans. What follows is not applicable to the recent immigrants from Europe, and, of course, even less applicable to the Southern negroes.

The Americans are a good-natured people, kindly, helpful to one another, disposed to take a charitable view even of wrong-doers. Their anger sometimes flames up, but the fire is soon extinct. Nowhere is cruelty more abhorred. Even a mob lynching a horse thief in the West has consideration for the criminal, and will give him a good drink of whiskey before he is strung up. Cruelty to slaves was unusual while slavery lasted, the best proof of which is the quietness of the slaves during the war when all the men and many of the boys of the South were serving in the Confederate armies. As everybody knows, juries are more lenient to offences of all kinds but one, offences against women, than they are anywhere in Europe. The Southern "rebels" were soon forgiven; and though civil wars are proverbially bitter, there have been few struggles in which the combatants did so

Reprinted with permission of The Macmillan Company from *The American Commonwealth* by James Bryce. Copyright, 1910, by The Macmillan Company.

many little friendly acts for one another, few in which even the vanquished have so quickly buried their resentments. It is true that newspapers and public speakers say hard things of their opponents; but this is a part of the game, and is besides a way of relieving their feelings: the bark is sometimes the louder in order that a bite may not follow. Vindictiveness shown by a public man excites general disapproval, and the maxim of letting bygones be bygones is pushed so far that an offender's misdeeds are often forgotton when they ought to be remembered against him.

All the world knows that they are a humorous people. They are as conspicuously the purveyors of humour to the nineteenth century as the French were the purveyors of wit to the eighteenth. Nor is this sense of the ludicrous side of things confined to a few brilliant writers. It is diffused among the whole people; it colours their ordinary life, and gives to their talk that distinctively new flavour which a European palate enjoys. Their capacity for enjoying a joke against themselves was oddly illustrated at the outset of the Civil War, a time of stern excitement, by the merriment which arose over the hasty retreat of the Federal troops at the battle of Bull Run. When William M. Tweed was ruling and robbing New York, and had set on the bench men who were openly prostituting justice, the citizens found the situation so amusing that they almost forgot to be angry. Much of President Lincoln's popularity, and much also of the gift he showed for restoring confidence to the North at the darkest moments of the war, was due to the humorous way he used to turn things, conveying the impression of not being himself uneasy, even when he was most so.

That indulgent view of mankind which I have already mentioned, a view odd in a people whose ancestors were penetrated with the belief in original sin, is strengthened by this wish to get amusement out of everything. The want of seriousness which it produces may be more apparent than real. Yet it has its significance; for people become affected by the language they use, as we see men grow into cynics when they have acquired the habit of talking cynicism for the sake of effect.

They are a hopeful people. Whether or no they are right in calling themselves a new people, they certainly seem to feel in their veins the bounding pulse of youth. They see a long vista of years stretching out before them, in which they will have time enough to cure all their faults, to overcome all the obstacles that block their path. They look at their enormous territory with its still only half-explored sources of wealth, they reckon up the growth of their population and their products, they contrast the comfort and intelligence of their labouring classes with the condition of the masses in the Old World. They remember the dangers that so long threatened the Union from the slave power, and the rebellion it raised, and see peace and harmony now restored, the South more prosperous and contented than at any previous epoch, perfect good feeling between all sections of the country. It is natural for them to believe in their star. And this sanguine temper makes them tolerant of evils which they regard as transitory, removable as soon as time can be found to root them up.

They have unbounded faith in what they call the People and in a democratic system of government. The great States of the European continent are distracted by the contests of Republicans and Monarchists, and of rich and poor,—contests which go down to the foundations of government, and in France are further embittered by religious passions. Even in England the ancient Constitution is always under repair, and while some think it is being ruined by changes, others hold that further changes are needed to make it tolerable. No such questions trouble native American minds, for nearly everybody believes, and everybody declares, that the frame of government is in its main lines so excellent that such reforms as seem called for need not touch those lines, but are required only to protect the Constitution from being perverted by the parties. Hence a further confidence that the people are sure to decide right in the long run, a confidence inevitable and essential in a government which refers every question to the arbitrament of numbers. There have, of course, been instances where the once insignificant minority proved to have been wiser than the majority of the moment. Such was eminently the case in the great slavery struggle. But here the minority prevailed by growing into a majority as events developed the real issues, so that this also has been deemed a ground for holding that all minorities which have right on their side will bring round their antagonists, and in the long run win by voting power. If you ask an intelligent citizen why he so holds, he will answer that truth and justice are sure to make their way into the minds and consciences of the majority. This is deemed an axiom, and the more readily so deemed because truth is identified with common sense, the quality which the average citizen is most confidently proud of possessing.

This feeling shades off into another, externally like it, but at bottom distinct—the feeling not only that the majority, be it right or wrong, will and must prevail, but that its being the majority proves it to be right. This idea, which appears in the guise sometimes of piety and sometimes of fatalism, seems to be no contemptible factor in the present character of the people. . . .

The native Americans are an educated people, compared with the whole mass of the population in any European country except Switzerland, parts of Germany, Norway, Iceland, and Scotland; that is to say, the average of knowledge is higher, the habit of reading and thinking more generally diffused, than in any other country. They know the Constitution of their own country, they follow public affairs, they join in local government and learn from it how government must be carried on, and in particular how discussion must be conducted in meetings, and its results tested at elections. The Town Meeting was for New England the most perfect school of self-government in any modern country. In villages, men used to exercise their minds on theological questions, debating points of Christian doctrine with no small acuteness. Women in particular, pick up at the public schools and from the popular magazines far more miscellaneous information than the women of any European country possess, and this naturally tells on the intelligence of the men. Almost everywhere one finds women's clubs in which literary, artistic, and social questions are discussed, and to which men of mark are brought to deliver lectures.

That the education of the masses is nevertheless a superficial education goes without saying. It is sufficient to enable them to think they know something about the great problems of politics: insufficient to show them how little they know. The public elementary school gives everybody the key to knowledge in making reading and writing familiar, but it has not time to teach him how to use the key, whose use is in fact, by the pressure of daily work, almost confined to the newspaper and the magazine. So we may say that if the political education of the average American voter be compared with that of the average voter in Europe, it stands high; but if it be compared with the functions which the theory of the American government lays on him, which its spirit implies, which the methods of its party organization assume, its inadequacy is manifest. This observation, however, is not so much a reproach to the schools, which generally do what English schools omit—instruct the child in the principles of the Constitution—as a tribute to the height of the ideal which the American conception of popular rule sets up.

For the functions of the citizen are not, as has hitherto been the case in Europe, confined to the choosing of legislators, who are then left to settle issues of policy and select executive rulers. The American citizen is one of the governors of the Republic. Issues are decided and rulers selected by the direct popular vote. Elections are so frequent that to do his duty at them a citizen ought to be constantly watching public affairs with a full comprehension of the principles involved in them, and a judgment of the candidates derived from a criticism of their arguments as well as a recollection of their past careers. The instruction received in the common schools and from the newspapers, and supposed to be developed by the practice of primaries and conventions, while it makes the voter deem himself capable of governing, does not fit him to weigh the real merits of statesmen, to discern the true grounds on which questions ought to be decided, to note the drift of events and discover the direction in which parties are being carried. He is like a sailor who knows the spars and ropes of the ship and is expert in working her, but is ignorant of geography and navigation; who can perceive that some of the officers are smart and others dull, but cannot judge which of them is qualified to use the sextant or will best keep his head during a hurricane.

They are a moral and well-conducted people. Setting aside the *colluvies gentium* which one finds in Western mining camps, now largely filled by recent immigrants, and which popular literature has presented to Europeans as far larger than it really is, setting aside also the rabble of a few great cities and the negroes of the South, the average of temperance, chastity, truthfulness, and general probity is somewhat higher than in any of the great nations of Europe. The instincts of the native farmer or artisan are almost invariably kindly and charitable. He respects the law; he is deferential to women and indulgent to children; he attaches an almost excessive value to the possession of a genial manner and the observance of domestic duties.

They are also—and here again I mean the people of native American stock, especially in the Eastern and Middle States—on the whole, a religious people. It is not merely that they respect religion and its ministers, for that one might say of Russians or Sicilians, not merely that they are assiduous church-goers and Sunday-school teachers, but that they have an intelligent interest in the form of faith they profess, are pious without superstition, and zealous without bigotry. The importance which some still, though all much less than formerly, attach to dogmatic propositions, does not prevent them from feeling the moral side of their theology. Christianity influences conduct, not indeed half as much as in theory it ought, but probably more than it does in any other modern country, and far more than it did in the so-called ages of faith.

Nor do their moral and religious impulses remain in the soft haze of self-complacent sentiment. The desire to expunge or cure the visible evils of the world is strong. Nowhere are so many philanthropic and reformatory agencies at work. Zeal outruns discretion, outruns the possibilities of the case, in not a few of the efforts made, as well by legislation as by voluntary action, to suppress vice, to prevent intemperance, to purify popular literature.

Religion apart, they are an unreverential people. I do not mean irreverent,— far from it; nor do I mean that they have not a great capacity for hero-worship, as they have many a time shown. I mean that they are little disposed, especially in public questions—political, economical, or social—to defer to the opinions of those who are wiser or better instructed than themselves. Everything tends to make the individual independent and self-reliant. He goes early into the world; he is left to make his way alone; he tries one occupation after another, if the first or second venture does not prosper; he gets to think that each man is his own best helper and adviser. Thus he is led, I will not say to form his own opinions, for few are those who do that, but to fancy that he has formed them, and to feel little need of aid from others towards correcting them. There is, therefore, less disposition than in Europe to expect light and leading on public affairs from speakers or writers. Oratory is not directed towards instruction, but towards stimulation. Special knowledge, which commands deference in applied science or in finance, does not command it in politics, because that is not deemed a special subject, but one within the comprehension of every practical man. Politics is, to be sure, a profession, and so far might seem to need professional aptitudes. But the professional politician is not the man who has studied statesmanship, but the man who has practised the art of running conventions and winning elections.

Even that strong point of America, the completeness and highly popular character of local government, contributes to lower the standard of attainment expected in a public man, because the citizens judge of all politics by the politics they see first and know best,—those of their township or city,—and fancy that he who is fit to be selectman, or county commissioner, or alderman, is fit to sit in the great council of the nation. Like the shepherd in Virgil, they think the only difference between their town and Rome is in its size, and believe that what does for Lafayetteville will do well enough for Washington. Hence when a man of statesmanlike gifts appears, he has little encouragement to take a high and statesmanlike tone, for his words do not necessarily receive weight from his position. He fears to be instructive or hortatory, lest such an attitude should expose him to ridicule; and in America ridicule is a terrible power. Nothing escapes it. Few have the courage to face it. In the indulgence of it even this humane race can be unfeeling.

They are a busy people. I have already observed that the leisured class is relatively small, is in fact confined to a few Eastern cities. The citizen has little time to think about political problems. Engrossing all the working hours, his avocation leaves him only stray moments from this fundamental duty. It is true that he admits his responsibilities, considers himself a member of a party, takes some interest in current events. But although he would reject the idea that his thinking should be done for him, he has not leisure to do it for himself, and must practically lean upon and follow his party. It astonished me in 1870 and 1881 to find how small a part politics played in conversation among the best educated classes and generally in the cities. Since 1896 there has been a livelier and more constant interest in public affairs; yet even now business matters so occupy the mind of the financial and commercial classes, and athletic competitions the minds of the uneducated classes and of the younger sort in all classes, that political questions are apt, except at critical moments, to fall into the background.[1] In a presidential year, and especially during the months of a presidential campaign, there is, of course, abundance of private talk, as well as of public speaking, but even then the issues raised are largely personal rather than political in the European sense. But at other times the visitor is apt to feel—more, I think, than he feels anywhere in Britain—that his host has been heavily pressed by his own business concerns during the day, and that when the hour of relaxation arrives he gladly turns to lighter and more agreeable topics than the state of the nation. This remark is less applicable to the dwellers in villages. There is plenty of political chat round the store at the cross roads, and though it is rather in the nature of gossip than of debate, it seems, along with the practice of local government, to sustain the interest of ordinary folk in public affairs.[2]

The want of serious and sustained thinking is not confined to politics. One feels it even more as regards economical and social questions. To it must be ascribed the vitality of certain prejudices and fallacies which could scarcely

[1] The increased space given to athletics and games of all sorts in the newspapers marks a change in public taste no less striking here than it is in Britain. As it is equally striking in the British colonies, one may take it as a feature common to the modern English-speaking world, and to that world only, for it is scarcely discernible in Continental Europe.

[2] The European country where the common people best understand politics is Switzerland. That where they talk most about politics is, I think, Greece. I remember, for instance, in crossing the channel which divides Cephalonia from Ithaca, to have heard the boatmen discuss a recent ministerial crisis at Athens, during the whole voyage, with the liveliest interest and apparently some knowledge.

survive the continuous application of such rigorous minds as one finds among the Americans. Their quick perceptions serve them so well in business and in the ordinary affairs of private life that they do not feel the need for minute investigation and patient reflection on the underlying principles of things. They are apt to ignore difficulties, and when they can no longer ignore them, they will evade them rather than lay siege to them according to the rules of art. The sense that there is no time to spare haunts an American even when he might find the time, and would do best for himself by finding it.

Some one will say that an aversion to steady thinking belongs to the average man everywhere. True. But less is expected from the average man in other countries than from a people who have carried the doctrine of popular sovereignty further than it has ever been carried before. They are tried by the standard which the theory of their government assumes. In other countries statesmen or philosophers do, and are expected to do, the solid thinking for the bulk of the people. Here the people are supposed to do it for themselves. To say that they do it imperfectly is not to deny them the credit of doing it better than a European philosopher might have predicted.

They are a commercial people, whose point of view is primarily that of persons accustomed to reckon profit and loss. Their impulse is to apply a direct practical test to men and measures, to assume that the men who have got on fastest are the smartest men, and that a scheme which seems to pay well deserves to be supported. Abstract reasonings they dislike, subtle reasonings they suspect; they accept nothing as practical which is not plain, downright, apprehensible by an ordinary understanding. Although open-minded, so far as willingness to listen goes, they are hard to convince, because they have really made up their minds on most subjects, having adopted the prevailing notions of their locality or party as truths due to their own reflection.

It may seem a contradiction to remark that with this shrewdness and the sort of hardness it produces, they are nevertheless an impressionable people. Yet this is true. It is not their intellect, however, that is impressionable, but their imagination and emotions, which respond in unexpected ways to appeals made on behalf of a cause which seems to have about it something noble or pathetic. They are capable of an ideality surpassing that of Englishmen or Frenchmen.

They are an unsettled people. In no State of the Union is the bulk of the population so fixed in its residence as everywhere in Europe; in some it is almost nomadic. Except in the more stagnant parts of the South, nobody feels rooted to the soil. Here to-day and gone to-morrow, he cannot readily contract habits of trustful dependence on his neighbours. Community of interest, or of belief in such a cause as temperance, or protection for native industry, unites him for a time with others similarly minded, but congenial spirits seldom live long enough together to form a school or type of local opinion which develops strength and becomes a proselytizing force. Perhaps this tends to prevent the growth of variety in opinion. When a man arises with some power of original thought in politics, he is feeble if isolated, and is depressed by his insignificance, whereas if he grows up in favourable soil with sympathetic minds around him, whom he can in prolonged intercourse permeate with his ideas, he learns to speak with confidence and soars on the wings of his disciples. One who considers the variety of conditions under which men live in America may certainly find ground for surprise that there should be so few independent schools of opinion.

But even while an unsettled, they are nevertheless an associative, because a sympathetic people. Although the atoms are in constant motion, they have a strong attraction for one another. Each man catches his neighbour's sentiment more quickly and easily than happens with the English. That sort of reserve and isolation, that tendency rather to repel than to invite confidence, which foreigners attribute to the Englishman, though it belongs rather to the upper and middle class than to the nation generally, is, though not absent, yet less marked in America.[3] It seems to be one of the notes of difference between the two branches of the race. In the United States, since each man likes to feel that his ideas raise in other minds the same emotions as in his own, a sentiment or impulse is rapidly propagated and quickly conscious of its strength. Add to this the aptitude for organization which their history and institutions have educed, and one sees how the tendency to form and the talent to work combinations for a political or any other object has become one of the great features of the country. Hence, too, the immense strength of party. It rests not only on interest and habit and the sense of its value as a means of working the government, but also on the sympathetic element and instinct of combination ingrained in the national character.

They are a changeful people. Not fickle, for they are if anything too tenacious of ideas once adopted, too fast bound by party ties, too willing to pardon the errors of a cherished leader. But they have what chemists call low specific heat; they grow warm suddenly and cool as suddenly; they are liable to swift and vehement outbursts of feeling which rush like wildfire across the country, gaining glow, like the wheel of a railway car, by the accelerated motion. The very similarity of ideas and equality of conditions which makes them hard to convince at first makes a conviction once implanted run its course the more triumphantly. They seem all to take flame at once, because what has told upon one, has told in the same way upon all the rest, and the obstructing and separating barriers which exist in Europe scarcely exist here. Nowhere is the saying so applicable that nothing succeeds like success. The native American or so-called Know-nothing party had in two years from its foundation become a tremendous force, running, and seeming for a time likely to carry, its own presidential candidate. In three years more it was dead without hope of revival. Now and then as for instance in the elections of 1874–75, and again in those of 1890, there comes

---

[3] I do not mean that Americans are more apt to unbosom themselves to strangers, but that they have rather more adaptiveness than the English, and are less disposed to stand alone and care nothing for the opinion of others. It is worth noticing that Americans travelling abroad seem to get more easily into touch with the inhabitants of the country than the English do; nor have they the English habit of calling those inhabitants—Frenchmen, for instance, or Germans—"the natives."

a rush of feeling so sudden and tremendous, that the name of Tidal Wave has been invented to describe it.

After this it may seem a paradox to add that the Americans are a conservative people. Yet any one who observes the power of habit among them, the tenacity with which old institutions and usages, legal and theological formulas, have been clung to, will admit the fact. Moreover, prosperity helps to make them conservative. They are satisfied with the world they live in, for they have found it a good world, in which they have grown rich and can sit under their own vine and fig tree, none making them afraid. They are proud of their history and of their Constitution, which has come out of the furnace of civil war with scarcely the smell of fire upon it. It is little to say that they do not seek change for the sake of change, because the nations that do this exist only in the fancy of alarmist philosophers. There are nations, however, whose impatience of existing evils, or whose proneness to be allured by visions of a brighter future, makes them under-estimate the risk of change, nations that will pull up the plant to see whether it has begun to strike root. This is not the way of the Americans. They are no doubt ready to listen to suggestions from any quarter. They do not consider that an institution is justified by its existence, but admit everything to be matter for criticism. Their keenly competitive spirit and pride in their own ingenuity have made them quicker than any other people to adopt and adapt inventions: telephones were in use in every little town over the West, while in the city of London men were just beginning to wonder whether they could be made to pay. The Americans have doubtless of late years become, especially in the West, an experimental people, so far as politics and social legislation are concerned. Yet there is also a sense in which they are at bottom a conservative people, in virtue both of the deep instincts of their race and of that practical shrewdness which recognizes the value of permanence and solidity in institutions. They are conservative in their fundamental beliefs, in the structure of their governments, in their social and domestic usages. They are like a tree whose pendulous shoots quiver and rustle with the lightest breeze, while its roots enfold the rock with a grasp which storms cannot loosen.

. . . .

The Uniformity of American Life

To the pleasantness of American life there is one, and perhaps only one, serious drawback—its uniformity. Those who have been struck by the size of America, and by what they have heard of its restless excitement, may be surprised at the word. They would have guessed that an unquiet changefulness and turmoil were the disagreeables to be feared. But uniformity, which the European visitor begins to note when he has travelled for a month or two, is the feature of the country which Englishmen who have lived long there, and Americans who are familiar with Europe, most frequently revert to when asked to say what is the "crook in their lot."

· ·

It is most clearly not with Europe, but with each of the leading European peoples that we must compare the people of America. So comparing them with the peoples of Britain, France, Germany, Italy, Spain, one discovers more varieties between individuals in these European peoples than one finds in America. Scotchmen and Irishmen are more unlike Englishmen, the native of Normandy more unlike the native of Provence, the Pomeranian more unlike the Wurtemberger, the Piedmontese more unlike the Neapolitan, the Basque more unlike the Andalusian, than the American from any part of the country is to the American from any other. Differences of course there are between the human type as developed in different regions of the country,—differences moral and intellectual as well as physical. You can generally tell a Southerner by his look as well as by his speech, and the South, as a whole, has a character of its own, propagated from the older Atlantic to the newer Western States. A native of Maine will probably differ from a native of Kentucky, a Georgian from an Oregonian. But these differences strike even an American observer much as the difference between a Yorkshireman and a Warwickshire man strikes the English, and is slighter than the contrast between a middle-class southern Englishman and a middle-class Scotchman, slighter than the differences between a peasant from Northumberland and a peasant from Dorsetshire. Or, to take another way of putting it: If at some great gathering of a political party from all parts of the United Kingdom you were to go round and talk to, say, one hundred, taken at random, of the persons present, you would be struck by more diversity between the notions and tastes and mental habits of the individuals comprising that one hundred than if you tried the same experiment with a hundred Americans of similar education and position, similarly gathered in a convention from every State in the Union.

I do not in the least mean that people are more commonplace in America than in England, or that the Americans are less ideal than the English. Neither of these statements would be true. On the contrary, the average American is more alive to new ideas, more easily touched through his imagination or his emotions, than the average Englishman or Frenchman. He has a keen sense of humour, and an unquenchable faith in the future. I mean only that the native-born Americans appear to vary less, in fundamentals, from what may be called the dominant American type than Englishmen, Germans, Frenchmen, Spaniards, or Italians do from any type which could be taken as the dominant type in any of those nations. Or, to put the same thing differently, it is rather more difficult to take any assemblage of attributes in any of these European countries and call it the national type than it is to do the like in the United States.

These are not given as the impressions of a traveller. Such impressions, being necessarily hasty, and founded on a comparatively narrow observation, would deserve little confidence. They sum up the conclusions of Europeans long resident in America, and familiar with different parts of the country. They are, I think, admitted by the most acute Americans themselves. I have often heard the

latter dilate on what seems to them the one crowning merit of life in Europe—
the variety it affords, the opportunities it gives of easy and complete changes of
scene and environment. The pleasure which an American finds in crossing the
Atlantic, a pleasure more intense than any which the European enjoys, is that of
passing from a land of happy monotony into regions where everything is redo-
lent with memories of the past, and derives from the past no less than from the
present a wealth and a subtle complexity of interest which no new country can
possess.

Life in America is in most ways pleasanter, simpler, less cumbered by conventions than in Europe; it floats in a sense of happiness like that of a radiant
summer morning. But life in any of the great European centres is capable of an
intensity, a richness blended of many elements, which has not yet been reached
in America. There are more problems in Europe calling for solution; there is
more passion in the struggles that rage round them; the past more frequently
kindles the present with a glow of imaginative light. In whichever country of
Europe one dwells, one feels that the other countries are near, that the fortunes
of their peoples are bound up with the fortunes of one's own, that ideas are
shooting to and fro between them. The web of history woven day by day all over
Europe is vast and of many colours: it is fateful to every European. But in
America it is only the philosopher who can feel that it will ultimately be fateful
to Americans also; to the ordinary man the Old World seems far off, severed by
a dissociating ocean, its mighty burden with little meaning for him.

Those who have observed the uniformity I have been attempting to describe
have commonly set it down, as Europeans do most American phenomena, to
what they call Democracy. Democratic government has in reality not much to
do with it, except in so far as such a government helps to induce that deference
of individuals to the mass which strengthens a dominant type, whether of ideas,
of institutions, or of manners. More must be ascribed to the equality of material
conditions, still more general than in Europe, to the fact that nearly every one is
engaged either in agriculture, or in commerce, or in some handicraft, to the
extraordinary mobility of the population, which, in migrating from one part of
the country to another, brings the characteristics of each part into the others, to
the diffusion of education, to the cheapness of literature and universal habit of
reading, which enable every one to know what every one else is thinking, but
above all, to the newness of the country, and the fact that four-fifths of it have
been made all at a stroke, and therefore all of a piece, as compared with the slow
growth by which European countries have developed. Newness is the cause of
uniformity, not merely in the external aspect of cities, villages, farmhouses, but
in other things also, for the institutions and social habits which belonged a
century ago to a group of small communities on the Atlantic coast, have been
rapidly extended over an immense area, each band of settlers naturally seeking
to retain its customs, and to plant in the new soil shoots from which trees like
those of the old home might spring up. The variety of European countries is due,
not only to the fact that their race-elements have not yet become thoroughly

commingled, but also that many old institutions have survived among the new ones; as in a city that grows but slowly, old buildings are not cleared away to make room for others more suited to modern commerce, but are allowed to stand, sometimes empty and unused, sometimes half adapted to new purposes. This scarcely happens in America. Doubtless many American institutions are old, and were old before they were carried across the Atlantic. But they have generally received a new dress, which, in adapting them to the needs of to-day, conceals their ancient character; and the form in which they have been diffused or reproduced in the different States of the Union is in all those States practically identical.

III

PERSPECTIVES, PAST
AND PRESENT

INTRODUCTION III

In this section four historians and an anthropologist plot the developing design of the national character over the years from 1815 to the present day. The readings are noteworthy not only for what they have to say about the character of Americans but also for what they exhibit with respect to the shifting foci and advancing analytical sophistication of the study of national character.

Henry Adams concluded the ninth and final volume of his *History of the United States of America during the Administrations of Jefferson and Madison* in 1891 with a chapter, reproduced here in part, on the character of the American people at the close of the War of 1812, an event which has been aptly called the second war for American independence. Adams was the first professional historian to take cognizance of the national character as a legitimate subject for investigation. Disparaging the conventional themes of political, constitutional, diplomatic, and military history, he contended that, to write significantly, the historian should concern himself with the totality of an evolving culture. That was what Adams meant when he declared that "of all historical problems, the nature of a national character is the most difficult and the most important," and when he asserted that the study of national character was "more important than that of politics or economics." For a generation of historians who were trained in the German "scientific" school of Leopold von Ranke and who concurred with the English historian Edward A. Freeman that history was "past politics," Adams was breaking new ground, anticipating the extension of interest into the uncharted fields of social, intellectual, and cultural history.

Adams himself stopped short on the threshold of those unexplored regions. Boldly opening the first volume of the *History* with six chapters on the character of the nation in 1800, he presented a portrait of a people prosperous, industrious, ambitious, mobile, optimistic, intensely practical, and deeply conservative. The description might have been drawn from Tocqueville's *Democracy in America;* some two decades earlier, Adams had adopted Tocqueville's work as "the Gospel of my private religion." Adams faltered, however, at the close of his study. In contrast to the careful craftsmanship and penetrating erudition which marked

his best work and set him in the front rank of American historians, the concluding essay on the American character was marred by hasty and superficial execution. To the traits of "intelligence, rapidity, and mildness" which, in his judgment, were "fixed in the national character as early as 1817," Adams gave
inadequate definition and merely cursory examination. As a result, his observations were more suggestive than conclusive.

The reason was partly that Adams was first in the field: His inquiry was
hampered by paucity of appropriate data. It was also partly, perhaps fundamentally, personal: The tragic suicide of his wife in 1885, during the writing of the
History, cut his life in two. Six years later he told an intimate friend that the last
two volumes had been composed "in a very different frame of mind from that in
which the work was begun. . . . If you compare the tone of my first volume . . .
with that of the ninth volume when it appears, you will feel that the light has
gone out." And there was one other reason. In his autobiography, *The Education of Henry Adams,* the historian traced his futile search for "some great
generalization which would finish one's clamor to be educated." As in his life, so
in his *History:* He could neither discover nor contrive a formula to explain the
shaping of American character. Adams' descriptions of that character were perceptive, but he was not content with mere description; he sought an organizing
principle—and found it not. His discussion of causal factors was negative for the
most part; it was mainly devoted to repudiation of those foreign observers who
made "rapacity the accepted explanation of American peculiarities." But if the
thesis of "rapacity" was not adequate or even accurate, what could be put in its
place? Adams' inability to frame a satisfactory answer to that question was
reflected in the insufficiency of his final assessment of the national character.

What Adams missed, Frederick Jackson Turner found. In a paper presented
to the American Historical Association in 1893, just two years after the publication of the last volume of Adams' *History,* the younger historian from the Mid-
west discussed "The Significance of the Frontier in American History." The
selection below, excerpted from that epoch-making essay and from Turner's
article of 1910 entitled "Contributions of the West to American Democracy,"
offers a concise statement of the main elements of Turner's "frontier hypothesis"
which dominated the interpretation of American history and character through
the first four or five decades of the present century.

Turner regarded the frontier experience as the pre-eminent factor in the forming of an American character; he named the pioneer as the archetypical American. His interpretation, like Crèvecoeur's, was governed by the conjoined principles of environmentalism and exceptionalism, succinctly expressed in the magis-
terial dictum that "American democracy . . . was not carried in the *Susan Constant* to Virginia, nor in the *Mayflower* to Plymouth. It came out of the American forest, and it gained new strength each time it touched a new frontier." The
distinctive features of the national character—indeed, its distinctively *national*
features—were sculptured by the people's triumphant encounter with the western wilderness over the course of nearly three centuries. America possessed, and

took possession of, what Europe lacked: an abundance of free or cheap land; it was the occupation of that land and the exploitation of its bounty that made Americans American.

In another way, also, Turner's exposition resembled Crèvecoeur's: The front of settlement advanced across the continent in cycles of regeneration wherein society was temporarily reduced, on the raw moving margins of civilization, to its bare essentials, subsequently to be reconstructed in novel, ever more characteristically American, patterns. The receding frontier was the place where institutions were dismantled and re-formed; where European and Eastern complexity yielded to elemental simplicity; where individuals were freed, however briefly, from social controls; where, in the outcome, the promise of America was fulfilled and an authentically American style came into being. Thus the primitivist thesis which Crèvecoeur had adumbrated was elaborated by Turner into a general formula of cultural transformation.

Thematic congruities aside, Turner broke company with Crèvecoeur at several major points, betokening the Americanization of the interpretation of American character. Where the Frenchman's European sensibilities led him to emphasize the continuity of land ownership over familial generations—his American husbandman aspired to no greater blessing than to cultivate his ancestral acres and bequeath them to his children after him—Turner stressed the restive mobility of the typical American farmer and his exploitative attitude toward the soil. Crèvecoeur's agrarian mystique bespoke the yearning of the European peasant rather than the acquisitive and wasteful enterprise of the westering Yankee who was not content to pin his life within the narrow domestic bounds of the parental fields. Crèvecoeur wrote harshly of the backwoodsmen whose manners compared unfavorably, to his eye, with those of the Indians; Turner presented a more sanguine appraisal. In short, Turner's pioneer was Crèvecoeur's "new man" responding to the attraction of a rich and accessible continent, shucking off his European garments as he entered the forest, and rejoicing to find his fortunes magnified, his stature enhanced, and his spirits rejuvenated by his movement through American space. The Pennsylvania farm which marked the *terminus ad quem* for Crèvecoeur's liberated peasant became the *terminus a quo* of Turner's newer and more American frontiersman.

By about 1930 the frontier hypothesis, embellished and extended by Turner's followers, had established a near monopoly of American historiography and acquired the sanctity of orthodox doctrine. Thereafter it came under mounting criticism from historians who sharply questioned its presuppositions, its scholarship, and its adequacy as a theory of American history and character.[1] Facts were turned up which did not fit the formula—nor could the formula be stretched to accommodate the facts. Especially strenuous objections were elicited by the inapplicability of the interpretation, as Turner himself admitted, to the

---

[1]Selections from the literature of controversy can be found in George Rogers Taylor (ed.), *The Turner Thesis* (Boston: D. C. Heath and Company, 1949). See also "Interpretations of the American West: A Descriptive Bibliography," annotated by Walter Rundell, Jr., in *Arizona and the West,* III (Spring, 1961; Summer, 1961), pp. 69–88, 148–68.

emergent industrial-urban complex of American life, by its exclusivist or isolationist connotations, and by its insufficient regard for the continuities of culture and the tough conservative character of institutions.

Alternative emphases and approaches were suggested by such scholars as the late Arthur M. Schlesinger, professor of history at Harvard University, whose essay on American character, originally published in 1943, is reprinted here in full. While concurring with Turner in stressing the prime importance of "New World conditions"—"The undeveloped continent prescribed the conditions of living the new life, the mold within which the American character took shape"—Schlesinger insisted that due attention be given to "Old World influences" on American culture as well as to the formative significance of other frontiers than that of the land. His essay can be read as an expansion of Turner's thesis, as a qualification of it, and as a post-Turnerian inquiry into the modifications of character that occurred when "the primacy of rural life gave way to the rise of urbanism."[2]

Among Turner's most acute critics were historians who, acknowledging their debt to the master and attempting to salvage whatever was valid in his work, reinterpreted the frontier experience as a special case of some more general phenomenon of American life. Turner had defined the frontier as, among other things, the abundance of open land; by the 1950s historians were exploring the implications of abundance in general for the development of the national character.[3] Turner had stressed the movement of Americans across the face of the continent; later writers, drawing on the resources of sociology and psychology, developed a general theory of social mobility, both horizontal and vertical, in which the settlement of the West occupied an important but restricted place.[4] In the fourth selection, George W. Pierson, professor of history at Yale University, rings changes on that latter theme with some provocative comments on the relation of American character to the "M-Factor" of migration, mobility, and movement. Pierson's article was originally presented as a lecture at the University of Munich in 1961; it invites comparison with Tocqueville's observations on the same large topic of the American as man in motion.

In the frontier hypothesis the factor of vertical mobility was subordinated to the factor of horizontal mobility; movement on the ladder of social class was treated as a function or by-product of movement over land-space, and vertical mobility as an independent variable in the formation of American character received less than adequate attention from the Turnerians. By way of corrective, the concluding essay in this section examines the characterological significance of the American "race towards success" in which each generation strives to climb higher than its fathers. The author, Margaret Mead, is one of America's

[2]For an extended statement of Schlesinger's "urban interpretation" see his essay, "The City in American Civilization," in *Paths to the Present* (New York: The Macmillan Company, 1949), chap. XI.

[3]See especially David M. Potter, *People of Plenty: Economic Abundance and the American Character* (Chicago: University of Chicago Press, 1954), chap. VII.

[4]See, e.g., Everett S. Lee, "The Turner Thesis Re-examined," *American Quarterly*, XIII (Spring, 1961), pp. 77–83.

leading anthropologists. The book from which the reading is excerpted, *And Keep Your Powder Dry* (1943), commands a prominent position in the literature of national character as a pioneer application of culture-and-personality analysis to the character and culture of a complex modern nation.

The Shaping of National Character

HENRY ADAMS

Until 1815 nothing in the future of the American Union was regarded as settled. As late as January, 1815, division into several nationalities was still thought to be possible. Such a destiny, repeating the usual experience of history, was not necessarily more unfortunate than the career of a single nationality wholly American; for if the effects of divided nationality were certain to be unhappy, those of a single society with equal certainty defied experience or sound speculation. One uniform and harmonious system appealed to the imagination as a triumph of human progress, offering prospects of peace and ease, contentment and philanthropy, such as the world had not seen; but it invited dangers, formidable because unusual or altogether unknown. The corruption of such a system might prove to be proportionate with its dimensions, and uniformity might lead to evils as serious as were commonly ascribed to diversity.

The laws of human progress were matter not for dogmatic faith, but for study; and although society instinctively regarded small States, with their clashing interests and incessant wars, as the chief obstacle to improvement, such progress as the world knew had been coupled with those drawbacks. The few examples offered by history of great political societies, relieved from external competition or rivalry, were not commonly thought encouraging. War had been the severest test of political and social character, laying bare whatever was feeble, and calling out whatever was strong; and the effect of removing such a test was an untried problem.

In 1815 for the first time Americans ceased to doubt the path they were to follow. Not only was the unity of their nation established, but its probable divergence from older societies was also well defined. Already in 1817 the differ-

From *History of the United States* by Henry Adams (Charles Scribner's Sons, 1890).

ence between Europe and America was decided. In politics the distinction was more evident than in social, religious, literary, or scientific directions; and the result was singular. For a time the aggressions of England and France forced the United States into a path that seemed to lead toward European methods of government; but the popular resistance, or inertia, was so great that the most popular party leaders failed to overcome it, and no sooner did foreign dangers disappear than the system began to revert to American practices; the national government tried to lay aside its assumed powers. When Madison vetoed the bill for internal improvements he could have had no other motive than that of restoring to the government, as far as possible, its original American character.

The result was not easy to understand in theory or to make efficient in practice; but while the drift of public opinion, and still more of practical necessity, drew the government slowly toward the European standard of true political sovereignty, nothing showed that the compromise, which must probably serve the public purpose, was to be European in form or feeling. As far as politics supplied a test, the national character had already diverged from any foreign type. Opinions might differ whether the political movement was progressive or retrograde, but in any case the American, in his political character, was a new variety of man.

The social movement was also decided. The war gave a severe shock to the Anglican sympathies of society, and peace seemed to widen the breach between European and American tastes. Interest in Europe languished after Napoleon's overthrow. France ceased to affect American opinion. England became an object of less alarm. Peace produced in the United States a social and economic revolution which greatly curtailed the influence of New England, and with it the social authority of Great Britain. The invention of the steamboat counterbalanced ocean commerce. The South and West gave to society a character more aggressively American than had been known before. That Europe, within certain limits, might tend toward American ideas was possible, but that America should under any circumstances follow the experiences of European development might thenceforward be reckoned as improbable. American character was formed, if not fixed.

The scientific interest of American history centered in national character, and in the workings of a society destined to become vast, in which individuals were important chiefly as types. Although this kind of interest was different from that of European history, it was at least as important to the world. Should history ever become a true science, it must expect to establish its laws, not from the complicated story of rival European nationalities, but from the economical evolution of a great democracy. North America was the most favorable field on the globe for the spread of a society so large, uniform, and isolated as to answer the purposes of science. There a single homogeneous society could easily attain proportions of three or four hundred million persons, under conditions of undisturbed growth.

In Europe or Asia, except perhaps in China, undisturbed social evolution had been unknown. Without disturbance, evolution seemed to cease. Wherever disturbance occurred, permanence was impossible. Every people in turn adapted itself to the law of necessity. Such a system as that of the United States could hardly have existed for half a century in Europe except under the protection of another power. In the fierce struggle characteristic of European society, systems were permanent in nothing except in the general law, that, whatever other character they might possess they must always be chiefly military.

The want of permanence was not the only or the most confusing obstacle to the treatment of European history as a science. The intensity of the struggle gave prominence to the individual, until the hero seemed all, society nothing; and what was worse for science, the men were far more interesting than the societies. In the dramatic view of history, the hero deserved more to be studied than the community to which he belonged; in truth, he was the society, which existed only to produce him and to perish with him. Against such a view historians were among the last to protest, and protested but faintly when they did so at all. They felt as strongly as their audiences that the highest achievements were alone worth remembering either in history or in art, and that a reiteration of commonplaces was commonplace. With all the advantages of European movement and color, few historians succeeded in enlivening or dignifying the lack of motive, intelligence, and morality, the helplessness characteristic of many long periods in the face of crushing problems, and the futility of human efforts to escape from difficulties religious, political, and social. In a period extending over four or five thousand years, more or less capable of historical treatment, historians were content to illustrate here and there the most dramatic moments of the most striking communities. The hero was their favorite. War was the chief field of heroic action, and even the history of England was chiefly the story of war.

The history of the United States promised to be free from such disturbances. War counted for little, the hero for less; on the people alone the eye could permanently rest. The steady growth of a vast population without the social distinctions that confused other histories,—without kings, nobles, or armies; without church, traditions, and prejudices,—seemed a subject for the man of science rather than for dramatists or poets. To scientific treatment only one great obstacle existed. Americans, like Europeans, were not disposed to make of their history a mechanical evolution. They felt that they even more than other nations needed the heroic element, because they breathed an atmosphere of peace and industry where heroism could seldom be displayed; and in unconscious protest against their own social conditions they adorned with imaginary qualities scores of supposed leaders, whose only merit was their faculty of reflecting a popular trait. Instinctively they clung to ancient history as though conscious that of all misfortunes that could befall the national character, the greatest would be the loss of the established ideals which alone ennobled human weakness. Without heroes, the national character of the United States had few charms of imagination even to Americans.

Historians and readers maintained Old World standards. No historian cared to hasten the coming of an epoch when man should study his own history in the same spirit and by the same methods with which he studied the formation of a crystal. Yet history had its scientific as well as its human side, and in American history the scientific interest was greater than the human. Elsewhere the student could study under better conditions the evolution of the individual, but nowhere could he study so well the evolution of a race. The interest of such a subject exceeded that of any other branch of science, for it brought mankind within sight of its own end.

Travellers in Switzerland who stepped across the Rhine where it flowed from its glacier could follow its course among mediaeval towns and feudal ruins, until it became a highway for modern industry, and at last arrived at a permanent equilibrium in the ocean. American history followed the same course. With prehistoric glaciers and mediaeval feudalism the story had little to do; but from the moment it came within sight of the ocean it acquired interest almost painful. A child could find his way in a river-valley, and a boy could float on the waters of Holland; but science alone could sound the depths of the ocean, measure its currents, foretell its storms, or fix its relations to the system of Nature. In a democratic ocean science could see something ultimate. Man could go no further. The atom might move, but the general equilibrium could not change.

Whether the scientific or the heroic view were taken, in either case the starting-point was the same, and the chief object of interest was to define national character. Whether the figures of history were treated as heroes or as types, they must be taken to represent the people. American types were especially worth study if they were to represent the greatest democratic evolution the world could know. Readers might judge for themselves what share the individual possessed in creating or shaping the nation; but whether it was small or great, the nation could be understood only by studying the individual. For that reason, in the story of Jefferson and Madison individuals retained their old interest as types of character, if not as sources of power.

. . . .

That the individual should rise to a higher order either of intelligence or morality than had existed in former ages was not to be expected, for the United States offered less field for the development of individuality than had been offered by older and smaller societies. The chief function of the American Union was to raise the average standard of popular intelligence and well-being, and at the close of the War of 1812 the superior average intelligence of Americans was so far admitted that Yankee acuteness, or smartness, became a national reproach; but much doubt remained whether the intelligence belonged to a high order, or proved a high morality. From the earliest ages, shrewdness was associated with unscrupulousness; and Americans were freely charged with wanting honesty. The charge could neither be proved nor disproved. American morality was such as suited a people so endowed, and was high when compared with the morality of many older societies; but, like American intelligence, it discouraged excess. Probably the political morality shown by the government and by public men during the first sixteen years of the century offered a fair gauge of social morality. Like the character of the popular inventions, the character of the morals corresponded to the wants of a growing democratic society; but time alone could decide whether it would result in a high or low national ideal.

Finer analysis showed other signs of divergence from ordinary standards. If Englishmen took pride in one trait more than in another, it was in the steady uniformity of their progress. The innovating and revolutionary quality of the French mind irritated them. America showed an un-English rapidity in movement. In politics, the American people between 1787 and 1817 accepted greater changes than had been known in England since 1688. In religion, the Unitarian movement of Boston and Harvard College would never have been possible in England, where the defection of Oxford or Cambridge, and the best educated society in the United Kingdom, would have shaken Church and State to their foundations. In literature the American school was chiefly remarkable for the rapidity with which it matured. The first book of Irving was a successful burlesque of his own ancestral history; the first poem of Bryant sang of the earth only as a universal tomb; the first preaching of Channing assumed to overthrow the Trinity; and the first paintings of Allston aspired to recover the ideal perfection of Raphael and Titian. In all these directions the American mind showed tendencies that surprised Englishmen more than they struck Americans. Allston defended himself from the criticism of friends who made complaint of his return to America. He found there, as he maintained, not only a growing taste for art, but "a quicker appreciation" of artistic effort than in any European land. If the highest intelligence of American society were to move with such rapidity, the time could not be far distant when it would pass into regions which England never liked to contemplate.

Another intellectual trait . . . was the disposition to relax severity. Between the theology of Jonathan Edwards and that of William Ellery Channing was an enormous gap, not only in doctrines but also in methods. Whatever might be thought of the conclusions reached by Edwards and [Samuel] Hopkins, the force of their reasoning commanded respect. Not often had a more strenuous effort than theirs been made to ascertain God's will, and to follow it without regard to weaknesses of the flesh. The idea that the nature of God's attributes was to be preached only as subordinate to the improvement of man, agreed little with the spirit of their religion. The Unitarian and Universalist movements marked the beginning of an epoch when ethical and humanitarian ideas took the place of metaphysics, and even New England turned from contemplating the omnipotence of the Deity in order to praise the perfections of his creatures.

The spread of great popular sects like the Universalists and Campbellites, founded on assumptions such as no Orthodox theology could tolerate, showed a growing tendency to relaxation of thought in that direction. The struggle for existence was already mitigated, and the first effect of the change was seen in the increasing cheerfulness of religion. Only when men found their actual world almost a heaven, could they lose overpowering anxiety about the world to come. Life had taken a softer aspect, and as a consequence God was no longer terrible. Even the wicked became less mischievous in an atmosphere where virtue was easier than vice. Punishments seemed mild in a society where every offender could cast off his past, and create a new career. For the first time in history, great bodies of men turned away from their old religion, giving no better reason than that it required them to believe in a cruel Deity, and rejected necessary conclusions of theology because they were inconsistent with human self-esteem.

The same optimism marked the political movement. Society was weary of strife, and settled gladly into a political system which left every disputed point undetermined. The public seemed obstinate only in believing that all was for the best, as far as the United States were concerned, in the affairs of mankind. The contrast was great between this temper of mind and that in which the Constitution had been framed; but it was no greater than the contrast in the religious opinions of the two periods, while the same reaction against severity marked the new literature. The rapid accumulation of wealth and increase in physical comfort told the same story from the standpoint of economy. On every side society showed that ease was for a time to take the place of severity, and enjoyment was to have its full share in the future national existence.

The traits of intelligence, rapidity, and mildness seemed fixed in the national character as early as 1817, and were likely to become more marked as time should pass. A vast amount of conservatism still lingered among the people; but the future spirit of society could hardly fail to be intelligent, rapid in movement, and mild in method. Only in the distant future could serious change occur, and even then no return to European characteristics seemed likely. The American continent was happier in its conditions and easier in its resources than the regions of Europe and Asia, where Nature revelled in diversity and conflict. If at any time American character should change, it might as probably become sluggish as revert to the violence and extravagances of Old-World development. The inertia of several hundred million people, all formed in a similar social mould, was as likely to stifle energy as to stimulate evolution.

With the establishment of these conclusions, a new episode in American history began in 1815. New subjects demanded new treatment, no longer dramatic but steadily tending to become scientific. The traits of American character were fixed; the rate of physical and economical growth was established; and history, certain that at a given distance of time the Union would contain so many millions of people, with wealth valued at so many millions of dollars, became thenceforward chiefly concerned to know what kind of people these millions were to be. They were intelligent, but what paths would their intelligence select? They were quick, but what solution of insoluble problems would quickness hurry? They were scientific, but what control would their science exercise over their destiny? They were mild, but what corruptions would their relaxations bring? They were peaceful, but by what machinery were their corruptions to be purged? What interests were to vivify a society so vast and uniform? What ideals were to ennoble it? What object, besides physical content, must a democratic continent aspire to attain? For the treatment of such questions, history required another century of experience.

The Frontier Experience

FREDERICK JACKSON TURNER

. . . In the settlement of America we have to observe how European life entered the continent, and how America modified and developed that life and reacted on Europe. . . . The frontier is the line of most rapid and effective Americanization. The wilderness masters the colonist. It finds him a European in dress, industries, tools, modes of travel, and thought. It takes him from the railroad car and puts him in the birch canoe. It strips off the garments of civilization and arrays him in the hunting shirt and the moccasin. It puts him in the log cabin of the Cherokee and Iroquois and runs an Indian palisade around him. Before long he has gone to planting Indian corn and plowing with a sharp stick; he shouts the war cry and takes the scalp in orthodox Indian fashion. In short, at the frontier the environment is at first too strong for the man. He must accept the conditions which it furnishes, or perish, and so he fits himself into the Indian clearings and follows the Indian trails. Little by little he transforms the wilderness, but the outcome is not the old Europe. . . . The fact is, that here is a new product that is American. At first, the frontier was the Atlantic coast. It was the frontier of Europe in a very real sense. Moving westward, the frontier became more and more American. As successive terminal moraines result from successive glaciations, so each frontier leaves its traces behind it, and when it becomes a settled area the region still partakes of the frontier characteristics. Thus the advance of the frontier has meant a steady movement away from the influence of Europe, a steady growth of independence on American lines. And to study this advance, the men who grew up under these conditions, and the political, economic, and social results of it, is to study the really American part of our history.

. . . .

... The frontier promoted the formation of a composite nationality for the American people. The coast was preponderantly English, but the later tides of continental immigration flowed across to the free lands. This was the case from the early colonial days. The Scotch-Irish and the Palatine Germans, or "Pennsylvania Dutch," furnished the dominant element in the stock of the colonial frontier. With these peoples were also the freed indented servants, or redemptioners, who at the expiration of their time of service passed to the frontier. Governor Spotswood of Virginia writes in 1717, "The inhabitants of our frontiers are composed generally of such as have been transported hither as servants, and, being out of their time, settle themselves where land is to be taken up and that will produce the necessarys of life with little labour." Very generally these redemptioners were of non-English stock. In the crucible of the frontier the immigrants were Americanized, liberated, and fused into a mixed race, English in neither nationality nor characteristics. The process has gone on from the early days to our own.

. . . .

From the conditions of frontier life came intellectual traits of profound importance. The works of travelers along each frontier from colonial days onward describe certain common traits, and these traits have, while softening down, still persisted as survivals in the place of their origin, even when a higher social organization succeeded. The result is that to the frontier the American intellect owes its striking characteristics. That coarseness and strength combined with acuteness and inquisitiveness; that practical, inventive turn of mind, quick to find expedients; that masterful grasp of material things, lacking in the artistic but powerful to effect great ends; that restless, nervous energy; that dominant individualism, working for good and for evil, and withal that buoyancy and exuberance which comes with freedom—these are traits of the frontier, or traits called out elsewhere because of the existence of the frontier.

. . . .

It was because Andrew Jackson personified these essential Western traits that in his presidency he became the idol and the mouthpiece of the popular will. In his assault upon the Bank as an engine of aristocracy, and in his denunciation of nullification, he went directly to his object with the ruthless energy of a frontiersman. For formal law and the subtleties of State sovereignty he had the contempt of a backwoodsman. Nor is it without significance that this typical man of the new democracy will always be associated with the triumph of the spoils system in national politics. To the new democracy of the West, office was an opportunity to exercise natural rights as an equal citizen of the community. Rotation in office served not simply to allow the successful man to punish his enemies and reward his friends, but it also furnished the training in the actual conduct of political affairs which every American claimed as his birthright. Only in a primitive democracy of the type of the United States in 1830 could such a system have existed without the ruin of the State. National government in that period was no complex and nicely adjusted machine, and the evils of the system were long in making themselves fully apparent.

The triumph of Andrew Jackson marked the end of the old era of trained statesmen for the Presidency. With him began the era of the popular hero. Even Martin Van Buren, whom we think of in connection with the East, was born in a log house under conditions that were not unlike parts of the older West. Harrison was the hero of the Northwest, as Jackson had been of the Southwest. Polk was a typical Tennesseean, eager to expand the nation, and Zachary Taylor was what Webster called a "frontier colonel." During the period that followed Jackson, power passed from the region of Kentucky and Tennessee to the border of the Mississippi. The natural democratic tendencies that had earlier shown themselves in the Gulf States were destroyed, however, by the spread of cotton culture, and the development of great plantations in that region. What had been typical of the democracy of the Revolutionary frontier and of the frontier of Andrew Jackson was now to be seen in the States between the Ohio and the Mississippi. As Andrew Jackson is the typical democrat of the former region, so Abraham Lincoln is the very embodiment of the pioneer period of the Old Northwest. Indeed, he is the embodiment of the democracy of the West. . . .

The pioneer life from which Lincoln came differed in important respects from the frontier democracy typified by Andrew Jackson. Jackson's democracy was contentious, individualistic, and it sought the ideal of local self-government and expansion. Lincoln represents rather the pioneer folk who entered the forest of the great Northwest to chop out a home, to build up their fortunes in the midst of a continually ascending industrial movement. In the democracy of the Southwest, industrial development and city life were only minor factors, but to the democracy of the Northwest they were its very life. To widen the area of the clearing, to contend with one another for the mastery of the industrial resources of the rich provinces, to struggle for a place in the ascending movement of society, to transmit to one's offspring the chance for education, for industrial betterment, for the rise in life which the hardships of the pioneer existence denied to the pioneer himself, these were some of the ideals of the region to which Lincoln came. The men were commonwealth builders, industry builders. Whereas the type of hero in the Southwest was militant, in the Northwest he was industrial. It was in the midst of these "plain people," as he loved to call them, that Lincoln grew to manhood. As Emerson says, "He is the true history of the American people in his time." The years of his early life were the years when the democracy of the Northwest came into struggle with the institution of slavery which threatened to forbid the expansion of the democratic pioneer life in the West. In President Eliot's essay on "Five American Contributions to Civilization," he instances as one of the supreme tests of American democracy its attitude upon the question of slavery. But if democracy chose wisely and worked effectively toward the solution of this problem, it must be remembered that Western democracy took the lead. The rail-splitter himself became the nation's President in that fierce time of struggle, and armies of the woodsmen and pioneer farmers recruited in the Old Northwest made free the Father of Waters, marched through Georgia, and helped to force the struggle to a conclusion at Appomattox. The free pioneer democracy struck down the slave-holding aristocracy on its march to the West.

The last chapter in the development of Western democracy is the one that deals with its conquest over the vast spaces of the new West. At each new stage of Western development, the people have had to grapple with larger areas, with bigger combinations. The little colony of Massachusetts' veterans that settled at Marietta received a land grant as large as the State of Rhode Island. The band of Connecticut pioneers that followed Moses Cleaveland to the Connecticut Reserve occupied a region as large as the parent State. The area which settlers of New England stock occupied on the prairies of northern Illinois surpassed the combined area of Massachusetts, Connecticut, and Rhode Island. Men who had become accustomed to the narrow valleys and the little towns of the East found themselves out on the boundless spaces of the West dealing with units of such magnitude as dwarfed their former experience. The Great Lakes, the Prairies, the Great Plains, the Rocky Mountains, the Mississippi and the Missouri, furnished new standards of measurement for the achievement of this industrial democracy. Individualism began to give way to cooperation and to governmental activity. Even in the earlier days of the democratic conquest of the wilderness, demands had been made upon the government for support in internal improvements, but this new West showed a growing tendency to call to its assistance the powerful arm of national authority. In the period since the Civil War, the vast public domain has been donated to the individual farmer, to States for education, to railroads for the construction of transportation lines.

Moreover, with the advent of democracy in the last fifteen years upon the Great Plains, new physical conditions have presented themselves which have accelerated the social tendency of Western democracy. The pioneer farmer of the days of Lincoln could place his family on a flatboat, strike into the wilderness, cut out his clearing, and with little or no capital go on to the achievement of industrial independence. Even the homesteader on the Western prairies found it possible to work a similar independent destiny, although the factor of transportation made a serious and increasing impediment to the free working-out of his individual career. But when the arid lands and the mineral resources of the Far West were reached, no conquest was possible by the old individual pioneer methods. Here expensive irrigation works must be constructed, cooperative activity was demanded in utilization of the water supply, capital beyond the reach of the small farmer was required. In a word, the physiographic province itself decreed that the destiny of this new frontier should be social rather than individual.

Magnitude of social achievement is the watchword of the democracy since the Civil War. From petty towns built in the marshes, cities arose whose greatness and industrial power are the wonder of our time. The conditions were ideal for the production of captains of industry. The old democratic admiration for the self-made man, its old deference to the rights of competitive individual development, together with the stupendous natural resources that opened to the conquest of the keenest and the strongest, gave such conditions of mobility as enabled the development of the large corporate industries which in our own decade have marked the West.

. . . If now in the way of recapitulation, we try to pick out from the influences that have gone to the making of Western democracy the factors which constitute the net result of this movement, we shall have to mention at least the following:—

Most important of all has been the fact that an area of free land has continually lain on the western border of the settled area of the United States. Whenever social conditions tended to crystallize in the East, whenever capital tended to press upon labor or political restraints to impede the freedom of the mass, there was this gate of escape to the free conditions of the frontier. These free lands promoted individualism, economic equality, freedom to rise, democracy. Men would not accept inferior wages and a permanent position of social subordination when this promised land of freedom and equality was theirs for the taking. Who would rest content under oppressive legislative conditions when with a slight effort he might reach a land wherein to become a co-worker in the building of free cities and free States on the lines of his own ideal? In a word, then, free lands meant free opportunities. Their existence has differentiated the American democracy from the democracies which have preceded it, because ever, as democracy in the East took the form of highly specialized and complicated industrial society, in the West it kept in touch with primitive conditions, and by action and reaction these two forces have shaped our history.

In the next place, these free lands and this treasury of industrial resources have existed over such vast spaces that they have demanded of democracy increasing spaciousness of design and power of execution. Western democracy is contrasted with the democracy of all other times in the largeness of the tasks to which it has set its hand, and in the vast achievements which it has wrought out in the control of nature and of politics. It would be difficult to overemphasize the importance of this training upon democracy. Never before in the history of the world has a democracy existed on so vast an area and handled things in the gross with such success, with such largeness of design, and such grasp upon the means of execution. In short, democracy has learned in the West of the United States how to deal with the problem of magnitude. The old historic democracies were but little states with primitive economic conditions.

But the very task of dealing with vast resources, over vast areas, under the conditions of free competition furnished by the West, has produced the rise of those captains of industry whose success in consolidating economic power now raises the question as to whether democracy under such conditions can survive. For the old military type of Western leaders like George Rogers Clark, Andrew Jackson, and William Henry Harrison have been substituted such industrial leaders as James J. Hill, John D. Rockefeller, and Andrew Carnegie.

The question is imperative, then, What ideals persist from this democratic experience of the West; and have they acquired sufficient momentum to sustain themselves under conditions so radically unlike those in the days of their origin? ... Under the forms of the American democracy is there in reality evolving such a concentration of economic and social power in the hands of a comparatively few men as may make political democracy an appearance rather than a reality? The free lands are gone. The material forces that gave vitality to Western democracy are passing away. It is to the realm of the spirit, to the domain of ideals and legislation, that we must look for Western influence upon democracy in our own days.

. . . .

This, at least, is clear: American democracy is fundamentally the outcome of the experiences of the American people in dealing with the West. Western democracy through the whole of its earlier period tended to the production of a society of which the most distinctive fact was the freedom of the individual to rise under conditions of social mobility, and whose ambition was the liberty and well-being of the masses. This conception has vitalized all American democracy, and has brought it into sharp contrasts with the democracies of history, and with those modern efforts of Europe to create an artificial democratic order by legislation. The problem of the United States is not to create democracy, but to conserve democratic institutions and ideals. . . .

What Then Is the American, This New Man?

ARTHUR M. SCHLESINGER

The question which forms the title of this essay has never ceased to arouse interest since Crèvecoeur posed it in the last years of the Revolution. If we can learn why the American has come to be what he is, how he reacts instinctively to life, wherein he differs from other peoples, we shall have gained a deep insight into the springs of national behavior. Crèvecoeur's own answer, the considered opinion of a Frenchman long resident in the New World, may still be read with profit. The American, he said, "is either an European, or the descendant of an European, hence that strange mixture of blood which you will find in no other country. . . . *He* is an American, who leaving behind him all his ancient prejudices and manners, receives new ones from the new mode of life he has embraced, the new government he obeys, and the new rank he holds. . . . From involuntary idleness, servile dependence, penury, and useless labor, he has passed to toils of a very different nature.—This is an American."

I

Crèvecoeur, of course, was one of a long procession of Europeans who have tried to describe and appraise the American. Their writings, though of varying merit, possess the common advantage of presenting an outsider's point of view, free from the predilections and prepossessions which blur the American's vision of himself. Viewing the scene from a different background, they are also sensitive to national divergences of which the native-born are usually unaware. Though bias may influence the individual observer's judgment, the total number of visitors has been so great as to render far more significant their points of agreement.

The composite portrait that emerges deserves thoughtful consideration. The attributes most frequently noted are a belief in the universal obligation to work; the urge to move from place to place; a high standard of average comfort; faith in progress; the eternal pursuit of material gain; an absence of permanent class barriers; the neglect of abstract thinking and of the aesthetic side of life; boastfulness; a deference for women; the prevalence of spoiled children; the general restlessness and hurry of life, always illustrated by the practice of fast eating; and certain miscellaneous traits such as overheated houses, the vice of spitting and the passion for rocking chairs and ice water.

This inventory, so far as it goes, reveals qualities and attitudes recognizably American. Moreover, the travelers express no doubt as to the existence of a distinctive national character. The native-born looking at their fellow countrymen readily identify them as New Englanders and Middle Westerners or Southerners, as products of old American stock or newcomers of immigrant origin; and they remember that at one period of their history the differences between Northerner and Southerner sharpened into a tragic war. But the detached observer from Europe has always been less impressed by these regional deviations than by the evidences of fundamental kinship, even in slavery times.

James Bryce, most perspicacious of the commentators, goes so far as to say, "Scotchmen and Irishmen are more unlike Englishmen, the native of Normandy more unlike the native of Provence, the Pomeranian more unlike the Wurtemberger, the Piedmontese more unlike the Neapolitan, the Basque more unlike the Andalusian, than the American from any part of the country is to the American from any other part." His conclusion is that "it is rather more difficult to take any assemblage of attributes in any of these European countries and call it the national type than it is to do the like in the United States." The preoccupation of American historians with local and sectional diversities has tended to obscure this underlying reality.

But the particular "assemblage of attributes" recorded by the travelers leaves much to be desired. Not only is the list incomplete, but it carelessly lumps the significant with the trivial. Since the typical European tried to cover as much ground as possible in a short time, his attention was caught by externals, with the result that annoying traits and ways assumed undue importance, much as dust in the eye of a wayfarer distorts the appearance of the landscape. The gospel of work, for example, hardly deserves to be equated with the addiction to spitting. Though the more thoughtful sought to correlate what they noticed with the avowed ideals of the people, they usually lacked sufficient knowledge of the deeper historical trends to grasp either the true import of the ideals or how they manifested themselves in action. Finally, the traveler gave little attention to the crucial problem of why the special combination of qualities and attitudes had become endemic within the borders of the United States.

Hence the judgment of these onlookers, though often clear-sighted and frequently valuable as a corrective, leaves ample room for the student of United States history to venture an answer to Crèvecoeur's question. If the native-born historian be suspect as a party in interest, he may at least strive to observe that counsel of objectivity which his professional conscience reveres.

II

What then is the American from a historian's point of view? The answer, briefly expressed, is so simple as to be a platitude. This "new man" is the product of the interplay of Old World influences and New World conditions. But just what heritage did the colonists bring with them from Europe, and why and how was it changed? Predominantly it involved that part of Europe's social experience in which they themselves had shared. The great bulk of the settlers, like the immigrants of later times, belonged to the poorer classes. They and their ancestors, whether in England or on the Continent, had been artisans, small tradesmen, farmers, day laborers—the broad foundation which supported the fine superstructure of European civilization. Shut out from a life of wealth, leisure and aesthetic enjoyment, they had tended to regard the ways of their social superiors with misgiving, if not resentment, and by the same token they magnified their own qualities of sobriety, diligence and thrift. Even when many of them, as notably in England, improved their economic position in the sixteenth and seventeenth centuries as a result of the great growth of commerce and industry, they continued to exalt the ancient proprieties.

This attitude found its classic spiritual expression in Calvinism. As Professor Tawney has said, Calvinism was "perhaps the first systematic body of religious teaching which can be said to recognize and applaud the economic virtues." It neatly fitted the glove of divine sanction to the hand of prudential conduct, thereby giving a sense of personal rectitude to the business of getting ahead in the world. But whether in Britain or elsewhere, whether in the religious groups directly concerned or those more remotely affected, Calvinism merely intensified a pre-existing bent. It is similarly true that the stringent code of morals often attributed to Calvinism, and more particularly to the Puritans, represented a lower-middle-class mentality long antedating the Geneva teachings.

This, then, was the type of humanity upon which the untamed New World wielded its influence. It has often been observed that plants and animals undergo modification when removed to America. These mutations arise from differences in climate and geography. But other factors as well affected transplanted people. One was the temperament of the settler, the fact that he was more adventurous, more ambitious or more rebellious against conditions at home than his fellows. It is not necessary to believe with William Stoughton in 1670 that "God sifted a whole Nation that he might send Choice Grain over into this Wilderness," but undoubtedly the act of quitting a familiar existence for a strange and perilous one demanded uncommon attributes of hardihood, self-reliance and imagination. Once the ocean was crossed, sheer distance from the old country and the challenge of new experiences further weakened the bonds of custom, evoked latent capacities and awakened the settler to possibilities of improvement hitherto unsuspected.

The undeveloped continent prescribed the conditions of living the new life, the mold within which the American character took shape. Farming was the primary occupation. At first resorted to to keep from starvation, it quickly became the mainstay of existence. The Revolution was fought by a people of whom nineteen out of twenty tilled the soil. With good land obtainable for more than a century after Independence, agriculture continued, though with gradually diminishing effect, to provide the pervasive atmosphere of American life and thought. "The vast majority of the people of this country live by the land, and carry its quality in their manners and opinions," wrote Ralph Waldo Emerson in 1844. Even when the hosts from Continental Europe began to swell the population after the middle of the nineteenth century, the rural temper of the nation remained pretty much unaltered, for many of the immigrants also turned to farming. This long apprenticeship to the soil made an indelible impress on the developing American character, with results which the modern age of the city has not wholly effaced.

Agriculture in the New World, however, differed from agriculture in the Old. This was the initial lesson which the colonists were compelled to learn. Those who had been farmers in their homelands found many of the traditional methods unsuitable. Those who had worked at urban occupations suffered an even greater handicap. Densely forested land must be cleared; the wildness taken out of the soil; a knowledge gained of indigenous plants and of the best means of growing them. The settlers of Jamestown were barely able to struggle through the early years. "There were never Englishmen left in a forreigne Country in such miserie as wee," wrote one of them. "Unsufferable hunger" caused them to eat horses, dogs, rats and snakes, and instances even of cannibalism are recorded. As is well known, the Plymouth colonists experienced similar trials. Yet in both cases the woods abounded with native fruits, berries, roots and nuts, game was plentiful, and near-by waters teemed with fish.

Had these courageous men been more readily adaptable, they could have enjoyed a gastronomic abundance beyond the dreams of the wealthiest classes at home. But they had never faced such an experience before, and reversion to a stage of civilization which the white man had long since outgrown was not easy. At the very first, all the early settlements actually imported food supplies; the Swedish colony on the Delaware did so for twenty years. A knowledge of self-sufficient farming came slowly and painfully, with untold numbers of men, women and children perishing in the process. In the long run, however, the settlers learned how to master their environment. Utilizing native crops and Indian methods of tillage, they abandoned the intensive cultivation required by the limited land resources of the Old World. It was simpler to move on to new fields when the fertility of the old was exhausted. The typical farm was a small one, worked by the owner and his family. Even when the system of staple production developed in the South, the small independent farmers considerably outnumbered the great slaveholding planters.

Though the colonial agriculturalist owed much to the savage, he had no wish to live like one. Accustomed in the old country to simple comforts and mechanical devices in the home and about the farm, he duplicated them in the wilderness. Every husbandman became a manufacturer and every farmhouse a small factory, producing flour, soap and candles, tanning skins, preparing the winter's meat supply, making nails, harness, hats, shoes and rugs, contriving tools, churns, casks, beds, chairs and tables. Such activities he supplemented with trapping, hunting and fishing. As cold weather closed in, he used his spare time getting out rough timber products, such as shingles and planks, or spent the long evenings before the open fireplace carving gunstocks or making brooms while his womenfolk knitted, spun or wove.

Under pressure of circumstances the farmer thus became a Jack-of-all-trades. As Chancellor Livingston wrote, "being habituated from early life to rely upon himself he acquires a skill in every branch of his profession, which is unknown in countries where labour is more divided." Take the case of a typical New Englander, John Marshall of Braintree, early in the eighteenth century. Besides tending his farm, he bought and sold hogs, was a painter, brickmaker and carpenter, turning out as many as three hundred laths in a day, and served as a precinct constable. The primitive state of society fostered a similar omnicompetence in other walks of life, as the career of Benjamin Franklin so well exemplifies. Lord Cornbury, the governor of New York, characterized Francis Makemie as "a Preacher, a Doctor of Physick, a Merchant, an Attorney, or Counsellor at Law, and," he ruefully added, "which is worse of all, a Disturber of Governments."

The pioneer farmer of later times was the colonial farmer reborn. Up and down the Mississippi Valley he faced the same difficulties and opportunities as his forefathers, and he dealt with them in much the same way. As time went on, to be sure, he managed to buy more and more of his tools and household conveniences. He also took advantage of new inventions like the iron plow and the reaper, while increasingly he raised crops for sale in a general market. Meanwhile along the Atlantic Seaboard similar changes occurred. But whether in the older or newer communities these innovations affected the surface rather than the substance of the traditional mode of life. Nor did the advent of cities at first do much to alter the situation. Mere islands in a sea of forests and farms, they long retained marked rural characteristics and depended for a large part of their growth on continued accessions from the countryside.

III

What elements of the national character are attributable to this long-time agrarian environment? First and foremost is the habit of work. For the colonial farmer ceaseless striving constituted the price of survival; every member of the community must be up and doing. When anyone failed to do his part, the authorities, whether Puritan, Anglican or otherwise, laid a heavy hand upon the culprit. The Virginia Assembly in 1619 ordered the slothful to be bound over to compulsory labor. A few years later the Massachusetts Bay Company instructed Governor John Endecott that "noe idle drone bee permitted to live amongst us," and the General Court followed this up in 1633 with a decree that "noe prson, howse houlder or othr, shall spend his time idlely or unproffitably, under paine of such punishmt as the Court shall thinke meete to inflicte." Such regulations had long existed in England, where it was hoped, vainly, they might combat the unemployment and vagrancy of a surplus laboring class; in America the object was to overcome a labor shortage—that exigent problem of every new country. Of course, most of the settlers, having been inured to toil in the homeland, needed no official prodding. They were the hardest-working people on earth, their only respite being afforded by strict observance of the Sabbath as demanded by both church and state.

The tradition of toil so begun found new sustenance as settlers opened up the boundless stretches of the interior. "In the free States," wrote Harriet Martineau in 1837, "labour is more really and heartily honoured than, perhaps, in any other part of the civilised world." Alonzo Potter voiced the general opinion of the American people when he asserted a few years later, "Without a definite pursuit, a man is an excrescence on society. ... In isolating himself from the cares and employments of other men, he forfeits much of their sympathy, and can neither give nor receive great benefit." Even when the usual motives for work did not exist, the social compulsion remained. As William Ellery Channing put it, "The rich man has no more right to repose than the poor," for nobody should so live as to "throw all toil on another class of society."

One source of Northern antagonism to the system of human bondage was the fear that it was jeopardizing this basic tenet of the American creed. "Wherever labor is mainly performed by slaves," Daniel Webster told the United States Senate, "it is regarded as degrading to freemen"; and the Kentucky abolitionist David Rice pointed out that in the South "To labour, is to *slave;* to work, is *to work like a Negroe.*" After the Civil War, General W. T. Sherman found public occasion to thank God that now at long last Southern whites would have "to earn an honest living."

Probably no legacy from our farmer forebears has entered more deeply into the national psychology. If an American has no purposeful work on hand, the fever in his blood impels him nevertheless to some visible form of activity. When seated he keeps moving in a rocking chair. A European visitor in the 1890's saw more fact than fancy in a magazine caricature which pictured a foreigner as saying to his American hostess, "It's a defect in your country, that you have no leisured classes." "But we have them," she replied, "only we call them tramps." The traveler's own comment was: "America is the only country in the world, where one is ashamed of having nothing to do."

This worship of work has made it difficult for Americans to learn how to play. As Poor Richard saw it, "Leisure is the Time for doing something useful"; and James Russell Lowell confessed,

> Pleasure doos make us Yankees kind o' winch,
> Ez though 't wuz sunthin' paid for by the inch;
> But yit we du contrive to worry thru,
> Ef Dooty tells us thet the thing's to du.

The first mitigations of the daily grind took the form of hunting, fishing, barn-raisings and logrollings—activities that had no social stigma because they contributed to the basic needs of living. As the years went on, the great Southern planters, imitating the landed gentry in England, developed rural diversions of an elaborate sort; but their example, like that of the fashionable circles in the Northern cities, merely made the common man all the more self-conscious when he turned to recreation. Nor did the mid-nineteenth-century German and Irish immigrants, who indulged in spontaneous enjoyments when the day was over, have any other effect upon the native stock than to reinforce suspicions of the newcomers formed on other grounds. "The American," wrote the New Yorker, Henry T. Tuckerman, in 1857, "enters into festivity as if it were a serious business." And a serious business it has in considerable degree continued to be ever since.

Into it goes all the fierce energy that once felled the forests and broke the prairies. Americans play games not for fun but to win. They attend social gatherings grimly determined to have a "good time." Maxim Gorky said of Coney Island, "What an unhappy people it must be that turns for happiness here." The "rich gift of extemporizing pleasures," of taking leisure leisurely, seems alien to the national temper. It is significant that the English *Who's Who* includes the recreations of the notables listed, while the American does not.

The importance attached to useful work had the further effect of helping to make "this new man" indifferent to aesthetic considerations. To the farmer a tree was not a thing of beauty and a joy forever, but an obstacle to be replaced as quickly as possible with a patch of corn. In the words of an eighteenth-century American, "The Plow-man that raiseth Grain is more serviceable to Mankind, than the Painter who draws only to please the Eye. The Carpenter who builds a good House to defend us from the Wind and Weather, is more serviceable than the curious Carver, who employs his Art to please the Fancy." The cult of beauty, in other words, had nothing to contribute to the stern business of living; it wasn't "practical." The bias thus given to the national mentality lasted well into America's urban age. One result has been the architectural monotony and ugliness which have invariably offended travelers used to the picturesque charm of Old World cities.

IV

On the other hand, the complicated nature of the farmer's job, especially during the first two and a half centuries, afforded an unexcelled training in mechanical ingenuity. These ex-Europeans and their descendants became a race of whittlers and tinkers, daily engaged in devising, improving and repairing tools and other utensils until, as Emerson said, they had "the power and habit of invention in their brain." "Would any one but an American," asked one of Emerson's contemporaries, "have ever invented a milking machine? or a machine to beat eggs? or machines to black boots, scour knives, pare apples, and do a hundred things that all other peoples have done with their ten fingers from time immemorial?"

As population increased and manufacturing developed on a commercial scale, men merely turned to new purposes the skills and aptitudes that had become second nature to them. Thus Eli Whitney, who as a Massachusetts farm youth had made nails and hatpins for sale to his neighbors, later contrived the cotton gin and successfully applied the principle of interchangeable parts to the production of muskets; and Theodore T. Woodruff, a New York farm boy, won subsequent fame as the inventor of a sleeping car, a coffee-hulling machine and a steam ploy. In this manner another trait became imbedded in the American character.

The farmer's success in coping with his multitudinous tasks aroused a pride of accomplishment that made him scorn the specialist or expert. As a Jack-of-all-trades he was content to be master of none, choosing to do many things well enough rather than anything supremely well. Accordingly, versatility became another outstanding American attribute. In public affairs the common man agreed with President Jackson that any intelligent citizen could discharge the duties of any governmental office. He had an abiding suspicion of the theorist or the "scholar in politics," preferring to trust his own quick perceptions and to deal from day to day with matters as they arose. In his breadwinning pursuits the American flitted from job to job in marked contrast to the European custom of following occupations which often descended from father to son.

The most casual scrutiny of the *Dictionary of American Biography* discloses countless instances reminiscent of John Marshall and Francis Makemie in colonial times. Thomas Buchanan Read, born on a Pennsylvania farm, was in turn a tailor's apprentice, grocer's assistant, cigar maker, tombstone carver, sign painter and actor before he became a portrait painter, novelist and poet. Another personage is listed as "ornithologist and wholesale druggist"; another as "preacher, railway president, author"; and still another as "physician, merchant, political leader, magazine editor, poet, and critic." The wonder is that, despite such a squandering of energies, they could yet gain sufficient distinction in any phase of their activities to be recalled by posterity.

Even in his principal occupation of growing food, the farmer encountered harsh criticism from foreign observers because of the way he wore out the land, neglected livestock and destroyed forest resources. But Old World agriculture rested on a ratio of man to land which in the New World was the reverse. It was as logical for the American farmer to "mine" the soil and move on to a virgin tract as it was for the European peasant to husband his few acres in the interest of generations unborn. Not till the opening years of the twentieth century, when the pressure of population dramatized the evils of past misuse, did the conservation of natural resources become a set national policy.

Meanwhile the tradition of wasteful living, bred by an environment of plenty, had fastened itself upon the American character, disposing men to condone extravagance in public as well as in private life. Even governmental corruption could be winked at on the ground that a wealthy country like the United States could afford it. In their daily living, Americans were improvident of riches that another people would have carefully preserved. One newcomer from England in the early nineteenth century wrote that the apples and peaches rotting in Ohio orchards were more "than would sink the British fleet." Another said of her neighbors that she wished "the poor people of England had the leavings of their tables, that goes to their dogs and hogs." A great national emergency like that of the Axis war reveals the extent to which the practice still prevails. People learned that, by responding to the government's appeal to salvage kitchen fats, old iron and other materials usually discarded, they could make a substantial contribution to the war effort.

Toward women the American male early acquired an attitude which sharply distinguished him from his brother in the Old World. As in every new country, women had a high scarcity value, both in the colonies and later in the pioneer West. They were in demand not only as sweethearts and wives, but also because of their economic importance, for they performed the endless work about the house and helped with the heavy farm labor. "The cry is everywhere for girls; girls, and more girls!" wrote a traveler in 1866. He noted that men outnumbered women in thirty-eight of the forty-five states and territories. In California the proportion was three to one; in Colorado, twenty to one. "Guess my husband's got to look after me, and make himself agreeable to me, if he can," a pretty Western girl remarked—"if he don't, there's plenty will." In the circumstances men paid women a deference and accorded them a status unknown in older societies. European observers attributed the high standard of sex morals largely to this fact, and it is significant that the most rapid strides toward equal suffrage took place in those commonwealths whose rural characteristics were strongest.

V

Since the agriculturalist regarded his farm as only a temporary abode—an investment rather than a home—he soon contracted the habit of being "permanently transitory." Distance that would have daunted the stoutest-hearted European deterred "this new man" not at all. Many an Atlantic Coast family migrated from place to place across the continent until the second or third generation reached the rim of the Pacific, then the next one began the journey back. "In no State of the Union," wrote James Bryce in 1888, "is the bulk of the population so fixed in its residence as everywhere in Europe; in many it is almost nomadic."

But for this constant mingling of people and ideas the spirit of sectionalism would have opened far deeper fissures in American society than it did, for the breadth of the land, the regional diversification of economic interests and the concentration of European immigrants in certain areas were all factors conducive to disaffection and disunity. Apart from the crisis of 1861, however, it has always been possible to adjust sectional differences peaceably. The war between North and South might itself have been avoided if the system of slave labor had not increasingly stopped the inflow of persons from other parts of the country as well as from Europe. Denied such infusions of new blood, the Southerners lived more and more to themselves, came to exalt their peculiarities over the traits they had in common with their fellow countrymen and, in the end, determined to establish an independent state.

As the nation grew older and its institutions took on a more settled aspect, the locomotive tendencies of the Americans showed no signs of abatement. According to a study in 1936, "over the last few decades mobility has been increasing rather than decreasing." The Department of Agriculture noted that the average farm family remained in the same place only five or six years and that nearly half the children ultimately abandoned the farm. Urban dwellers are no more likely to stay put, shifting about from city to city. On the principle of the man biting the dog, the *New York Times,* June 14, 1942, reported that a resident of Sebastapol, California, had lived in the same house for fifty years, though it admitted that his ten brothers and sisters had left the town.

With the advent of the low-priced automobile and the passion for long-distance touring, the rippling movement of humanity came to resemble the waves of the ocean. In 1940 the American people owned more motorcars than bathtubs. It seemed as though the pursuit of happiness had become the happiness of pursuit. Foreigners had earlier expressed amazement at the spectacle of dwellings being hauled along the streets from one site to another, but even before the late war, more than half a million Americans had discovered in the automobile trailer a means of living constantly on wheels.

Geographic or horizontal mobility, however, was a less fundamental aspect of American life than social or vertical mobility, though the two were not unrelated. The European conception of a graded society, with each class everlastingly performing its allotted function, vanished quickly amidst primitive surroundings that invited the humblest to move upward as well as outward. Instead of everybody being nobody, they found that anybody might become somebody. In the language of James Russell Lowell, "Here, on the edge of the forest, where civilized man was brought face to face again with nature and taught mainly to rely on himself, mere manhood became a fact of prime importance." This emancipation from hoary custom was "no bantling of theory, no fruit of forethought," but "a gift of the sky and of the forest."

Accordingly, there arose the ingrained belief in equality of opportunity, the right of all men to a free and fair start—a view which in one of its most significant ramifications led to the establishment of free tax-supported schools. This was far from being a dogma of enforced equality. To benefit from equality of opportunity a man must be equal to his opportunities, with the government serving principally as an umpire to supervise the game with a minimum of rules. The upshot was a conception of democracy rigorously qualified by individualism.

This individualistic bias sometimes assumed forms that defied government. The colonists in their relations with the mother country evaded unwelcome regulations and, prompted by their theologians and lawyers, insisted that acts of Parliament contrary to their "unalienable rights" were void. Within the colonies those who dwelt remote from centers of law and order adopted a like attitude toward the provincial authorities. The Scotch-Irish who illegally occupied Pennsylvania soil in the early eighteenth century contended "it was against the laws of God and nature, that so much land should be idle while so many Christians wanted it to labor on and to raise their bread." As a substitute for constituted authority the settlers sometimes created their own unofficial tribunals, which adjudicated property titles and punished offenders against the public peace. In other instances they resorted to the swifter retribution of individual gunplay, or of mob action and lynch law, for from taking the law into one's hands when it could not function it was but a step to taking the law into one's hands when it did not function as one wanted it to.

The tendency to violence so generated has continued to condition the national mentality to the present time. Thoreau, the great philosopher of individualism, knew of no reason why a citizen should "ever for a moment, or in the least degree, resign his conscience to the legislator," declaring that "we should be men first, and subjects afterward." A similar conviction undoubtedly inspired William H. Seward's flaming declaration to the proslavery Senators in 1850 that "there is a higher law than the Constitution," just as it actuated the thousands of churchgoing Northerners who secretly banded together to violate the Fugitive Slave Act. But generally it has been self-interest or convenience, rather than conscience, that has provided the incentive to lawbreaking, as in the case of the businessman chafing against legislative restrictions or of the motorist disobeying traffic regulations. Sometimes the attitude has paraded under such high-sounding names as states' rights and nullification. This lawless streak in the American character has often been directed to wrong purposes, but it has also served as a check on the abuse of governmental powers and as a safeguard of minority rights.

In still another aspect, the individualism of the pioneer farmer does much to explain the intense cultivation of the acquisitive spirit. In the absence of hereditary distinctions of birth and rank the piling up of wealth constituted the most obvious badge of social superiority, and once the process was begun, the inbred urge to keep on working made it difficult to stop. "The poor struggle to be rich, the rich to be richer," remarked an onlooker in the mid-nineteenth century. Thanks to equality of opportunity with plenty for all, the class struggle in America has consisted in the struggle to climb out of one class into a higher one. The zest of competition frequently led to sharp trading, fraud and chicanery, but in the popular mind guilt attached less to the practices than to being caught at them. Financial success was accepted as the highest success, and not till the twentieth century did a religious leader venture to advance the un-American doctrine that ill-gotten wealth was "tainted money," even when devoted to benevolent uses.

VI

It would be a mistake, however, to think of the American simply as a mechanism set in motion by dropping a coin in the slot. When President Coolidge made his famous remark, "The business of America is business," he quite properly added, "The chief ideal of the American people is idealism. I cannot repeat too often that America is a nation of idealists." This ambivalence puzzled foreign commentators, who found it difficult, for example, to reconcile worship of the Almighty Dollar with the equally universal tendency to spend freely and give money away. In contrast to Europe, America has had practically no misers, and one consequence of the winning of Independence was the abolition of primogeniture and entail. Harriet Martineau was among those who concluded that "the eager pursuit of wealth does not necessarily indicate a love of wealth for its own sake."

The fact is that, for a people who recalled how hungry and oppressed their ancestors had been through long centuries in the Old World, the chance to make money was like the sunlight at the end of a tunnel. It was the means of living a life of human dignity. It was a symbol of idealism rather than materialism. Hence "this new man" had an instinctive sympathy for the underdog, and even persons of moderate substance freely shared it with the less fortunate, helping to endow charities, schools, hospitals and art galleries and to nourish humanitarian undertakings which might otherwise have died a-borning.

The energy that entered into many of these causes was heightened by another national attitude: optimism. It was this quality that sustained the European men and women who with heavy hearts left ancestral homes to try their fortunes in a wild and far-off continent. The same trait animated the pioneer farmers confronted by the hardships, loneliness and terrors of the primeval forest, and served also to spur their successors who, though facing less dire conditions, were constantly pitted against both the uncertainties of the weather and the unpredictable demands of the market. When Thomas Jefferson remarked, "I steer my bark with Hope in the head, leaving Fear astern," he spoke for his compatriots. To doubt the future was to confess oneself a failure since the life history of almost any American documented the opposite view. A belief in progress blossomed spontaneously in such a soil.

If this belief made some men tolerant of present abuses in the confident expectation that time would provide the cure, it fired others with an apostolic zeal to hasten the happy day. As a keen observer in the middle of the last century said of his countrymen, "Americans are sanguine enough to believe that no evil is without a remedy, if they could only find it, and they see no good reason why they should not try to find remedies for all the evils of life." Not even fatalism in religion could long withstand the bracing atmosphere of the New World. This quality of optimism sometimes soared to dizzy heights, impelling men to strive for earthly perfection in communistic societies or to prepare to greet the imminent return of Christ.

It attained its most blatant expression, however, in the national addiction to bragging. At bottom, this habit sprang from pride in a country of vast distances and huge elevations plus an illimitable faith in its possibilities of being great as well as big. The American glorified the future in much the same spirit as the European glorified the past, both tending to exalt what they had the most of. And by a simple transition the American went on to speak of expected events as though they had already happened, being prompted perhaps by an urge to compensate for an inner sense of inferiority. This frame of mind led statesmen to cultivate spreadeagle oratory—a style which the *North American Review* in 1858 defined as "a compound of exaggeration, effrontery, bombast, and extravagance, mixed metaphors, platitudes, defiant threats thrown at the world, and irreverent appeals flung at the Supreme Being."

For the same reason the ordinary citizen resorted to hyperbole. In the thinly settled sections this manner of speech went by the name of tall talk, causing the backwoods to be known as a "paradise of puffers." A Frenchman, however, referred to a national, not a regional, trait when he said Americans seemed loath to admit that Christopher Columbus himself had not been an American, and it was an Easterner writing in an Eastern magazine who soberly averred, "It is easier, say the midwives, to come into this world of America . . . than in any other world extant." In business life this indulgent attitude toward truth lent itself to deliberate attempts to defraud, and made the land speculator with his "lithographed mendacity" the natural forerunner of the dishonest stock promoter of later times. Boastfulness is an attribute of youth which greater national maturity has helped to temper. Still the War Department in its manual of behavior for Yankee soldiers in England during the Axis war thought it prudent to admonish them: "Don't show off or brag or bluster."

This facility for overstatement has lent a distinctive quality to American humor. In the United States humor has never been part of a general gaiety of spirit. It has had to break through a crust of life thick with serious purpose. Hence it has had to be boisterous and bold, delighting in exaggeration, incongruities and farcical effects and reaching a grand climax in the practical joke. Out of a comic mood so induced arose such folk heroes as Mike Fink, Paul Bunyan, Pecos Bill and the myth-embroidered Davy Crockett, whose fabulous exploits flourished in oral tradition long before they were reduced to print. In deference to the national sobriety of temperament the most successful professional humorists have been those who told their yarns while preserving a decorous gravity of expression.

VII

If this analysis of national characteristics is well-founded, then certain modifications of the pattern were inevitable when the primacy of rural life gave way to the rise of urbanism. That change began to take place in the latter years of the nineteenth century. In 1860 only a sixth of the people lived in towns of eight thousand or more, but by 1900 a third dwelt in such communities and today well over half do. Along with urban concentration went a remarkable development of means of communication and transport—the telephone, rural free delivery, interurban electric transit, good roads, the automobile, the movie, the radio—that carried city ideas and ways to "the very finger-tips of the whole land." Though most of the historic traits continued to thrive in this new milieu, some were moderated and a few disappeared. The time is too short to gauge the full consequences, but several of the reversals of attitude are noteworthy.

One is the importance which Americans have come to attach to cultural achievement. The ancient prejudice against "useless" activities could not long withstand the compelling opportunities of the city. In the city were to be found the best schools and colleges, the best newspapers and magazines, and practically all the bookstores, libraries, publishing houses, concert halls, conservatories of music, art museums and theaters. There, too, America made closest contact with the vital thought of Europe. Stimulated by such an atmosphere, the writer or artist could also command an appreciative audience and financial support. Who can ever know how dreadful a toll the two and a half centuries of agricultural life exacted in terms of creative advances of the mind and spirit, how many a mute inglorious Milton succumbed to the unremitting struggle with Nature? For persons like these the city meant a glad release, giving them a chance to mature their powers, consort with kindred spirits and enter the lists for fame and fortune. Even in earlier times cultural stirrings had centered in the towns and cities. Now as the urban influence became uppermost, Americans commenced to make contributions to scholarship, science, literature and the fine arts that challenged comparison with the best Europe could offer.

As a necessary consequence, much of the former aversion to specialization of talent vanished. In a civilization rapidly growing more complex, men began to place a higher value on thoroughly mastering a skill or conquering a particular intellectual domain. The business of making a living tended to fall into compartments, with the men best equipped by training or experience reaping the greatest rewards. This trend characterized not only industry and trade but also the arts and sciences. Even in public life expert knowledge steadily played a larger part, notably in the administrative services of city, state and nation. The derisive references to the New Deal's "Brain Trust" came from political opponents who, however, did not intend to forgo the same advantage when they returned to power.

A further result of the altered aspect of American society has been the great impetus given to voluntary associative activity. In a country environment the gregarious instinct was constantly balked by the dearth of neighbors. The hunger for companionship could discover only occasional outlet, as at the county fair or in the agitated throng gathered from far and near for a camp meeting. Now, to the rural birthright of liberty and equality the city added the boon of fraternity. In a crowded community, like could find like. The reformer, the businessman, the wage earner, the intellectual worker, the sports lover, the ancestor worshiper—all these and many others gravitated into special groups to further interests held in common—and these local societies seldom failed to expand into nation-wide federations. Soon the population became divided between the organized and those who organized them, until, if the late Will Rogers is to be believed, "Americans will join anything in town but their own family. Why, two Americans can't meet on the street without one banging a gavel and calling the other to order." Thus the passion for associative activity came to be a sovereign principle of life.

Quite as noteworthy has been another effect of city growth: the discrediting of individualism as the automatic cure of social and economic ills. As the nineteenth century advanced, the increasing domination of the national economy by urban magnates of business and finance caused the farmers to demand that the government intercede to protect their right to a decent livelihood. In the cities the cramped living quarters, the growing wretchedness of the poor and the rise of difficult social problems also created doubts as to the sufficiency of the laissez-faire brand of democracy. Only the rich and powerful seemed now to profit from a reign of unbridled individualism. Though the solid core of ancient habit yielded stubbornly, the average man came gradually to believe that under the changed conditions it was the duty of the government of all to safeguard the opportunities of all. After the American fashion it was a doctrineless conviction, the product of an adjustment to new times for the sake of preserving the traditional spirit of self-reliance and free competition.

Though the gospel of work continued as unquestioned as ever, willing workers could no longer be certain of regular employment, particularly in the towns and cities. Every sudden jar to the nation's business structure rendered large numbers idle. Through no fault of his own, the laborer was being denied an essential part of his heritage. As early as 1893 the American Federation of Labor resolved that "the right to work is the right to life," and declared that "when the private employer cannot or will not give work the municipality, state or nation must." But it was not till the Great Depression destroyed the livelihood of people in all walks of life that this novel view became an article of American faith. The New Deal assumed the obligation not merely of succoring the hungry, but of creating jobs for the idle and of guarding against such hazards in the future by means of unemployment insurance, retirement pay for aged wage earners and special provisions for farmers. Thus what had started originally because of the community's need that all should work became transformed, first into a doctrine of the right to work, and then into the duty of society to provide the means of work.

VIII

The national character, as we at present know it, is thus a mixture of long-persisting traits tempered by some newly acquired ones. Based upon the solid qualities of those Europeans who planted the colonies, it assumed distinctive form under pressure of adaptation to the radically different situation. "Our ancestors sought a new continent," said James Russell Lowell. "What they found was a new condition of mind." The protracted tutelage to the soil acted as the chief formative influence, dispelling ancient inhibitions, freeing dormant energies, revamping mental attitudes. The rise of the city confirmed or strengthened many of the earlier characteristics while reshaping others. Probably no one of the traits is peculiar to the American people; some occasion apology rather than pride; but the aggregate represents a way of life unlike that of any other nation.

Just as the American character has undergone modification in the past, so it will doubtless undergo modification in the future. Nevertheless, certain of its elements seem so deeply rooted as to withstand the erosion of time and circumstance. Of this order are the qualities that made possible the development of the continent, the building of a democratic society and the continuing concern for the welfare of the underprivileged. These are attributes better suited to peace than to war, yet every great crisis has found the people ready to die for their conception of life so that their children might live it. The American character, whatever its shortcomings, abounds in courage, creative energy and resourcefulness, and is bottomed upon the profound conviction that nothing in the world is beyond its power to accomplish.

The M-Factor in American History

GEORGE W. PIERSON

Is there any such thing as "national character"? In particular, is there, or has there ever been, an American Character? Many critics question, or even deny the idea. Students of American civilization generally seem to start out by thinking there must be an American Character. But then they encounter great difficulties in defining this character—that is, they find too many different or contradictory types, none of the types unique, all of them appearing also in other cultures, a few of them perhaps unstable across the years. The result? Conscientious scholars are driven to despair, and decide that American society is neither consistent nor original nor completely different; therefore we have no distinctive character.

Now this, I submit, may be just a little foolish. For theoretically it isn't scientific, and practically it doesn't make sense. Theoretically, is it not a poor kind of science which says that, because you and I cannot wholly know a thing or exactly define it, it doesn't exist? Just because we cannot scientifically define Americanism would seem a quite insufficient reason for ignoring its existence. What has not existed, rather, may be that intuition of causes, that exact grasp of detail, that art of proportion, that science of social structure, which will enable us to say: this is, in a sum total way, different, *sui generis,* peculiar. After all, a combination does not have to be unique in all its elements, or even in a single one of these elements, to be different in sum total. I will assert that theoretically there may be an American Character, even though that character may have been composed of familiar elements, even though it is only the proportions which have been different, even though the resulting society may be mixed, contradic-

Reprinted with permission from George W. Pierson, "The M-Factor in American History," *American Quarterly,* XIV, No. 2, Pt. 2 (1962), pp. 275–89. Copyright, 1962, Trustees of the University of Pennsylvania.

tory, pluralistic, unjelled. The very indeterminism of a society may be a distinguishing mark. Theoretically, I see no barrier to believing that an American Character may exist.

On the contrary, on the grounds of common sense, I see many reasons to believe that there is and has been an American Character, for one thing because the most intelligent thinkers and observers have thought so, and have kept on thinking so, across the years. These observers may have differed in the labels they attached to us, they may have argued about the causes of our American peculiarities, but every one of them has thought that the Americans are a little odd in their psychology, and a little different in their social institutions. Crèvecoeur went so far as to call the American a "New Man." And he defined this new man as the Progressive: "He is an American who leaves behind his ancient prejudices and manners." But whatever the definition, from Crèvecoeur to Tocqueville to André Siegfried, from Dickens to Bryce to Denis Brogan, from Lieber to Keyserling or Robert Jungk, the most thoughtful commentators have asserted that there is and has been (and, alas, will continue to be) an American Character.

What caused this Americanism to emerge? Many things, no doubt; far too many even to list in this paper. So I shall confine my attention to a single prevailing characteristic of our people: the migration factor in our history, our excessive mobility. Yet before I take up the Moving American, allow me to recall some classic interpretations which have exercised a strong influence on the writing of American history, and on thinking about America generally.

How are Americans different? In the beginning was the Word, and the Word had it that we were a Chosen People, a seed sifted out of the populations of Europe, a community of saints destined to create a better society on this earth. Like the Israelites of old, we were a people under divine command. As we sang in the old hymn: "O God, beneath thy guiding hand our exiled fathers crossed the sea!"

After about one hundred and fifty years, there succeeded to this Biblical interpretation the thought that, if we were not always more holy, we were at least more free. As an independent nation, our destiny was to bring liberty, self-government, republicanism, the art of federal decentralization to the succor of oppressed mankind. So to the religious mission there succeeded a political mission—which was what Alexis de Tocqueville came to study.

From the beginning, also, there had always been an economic mission. America was El Dorado: the golden opportunity, the country of get-rich-quick, the land of the second chance, the asylum for the poverty-stricken. So, as foreign and native observers alike commented, America was (1) the land of goodness, (2) the land of liberty, and (3) the land of plenty.

For a long while these three national myths satisfied. Toward the end of the nineteenth century, however, there emerged a series of more sophisticated, or "scientific," explanations, and, in particular, one which has exercised enormous influence. What was it changed Europeans into Americans?

For historians of the past generation, the Frontier Hypothesis of Frederick Jackson Turner supplied the classic answer. It was the *frontier* experience which made us different. That is, it was our struggle with the wilderness—it was exploiting the vast free lands of the interior—it was freeing ourselves from the past, "breaking the cake of custom," leaving behind the fetters of settled society and the refinements of civilization to start over again in the woods—it was the lonely pioneers chopping out clearings on the road westward—it was getting together with other pioneers to rebuild a simpler, freer society—it was pulling up stakes and repeating the process—it was moving and moving again until in 1890 the free land and the West were all used up. On the frontier, said Turner, society became atomic, individualism flourished, democracy was generated, national legislation was encouraged. The opportunities of the West also opened a gate of escape for the oppressed of the East, and so contributed to the democratization and Americanization of the seaboard. The frontier also transformed personal character. As Turner phrased it:

That coarseness and strength combined with acuteness and inquisitiveness; that practical, inventive turn of mind, quick to find expedients; that masterful grasp of material things, lacking in the artistic but powerful to effect great ends; that restless, nervous energy; that dominant individualism, working for good and evil, and withal that buoyancy and exuberance which comes with freedom—these are traits of the frontier, or traits called out elsewhere because of the existence of the frontier.

In effect, said Turner, it was primarily the molding influence of the Frontier which had transformed so many European materials into a new American amalgam. In his oft-quoted phrase, the frontier was "the line of most rapid and effective Americanization."

For a long while this satisfied. But about thirty years ago, when Turner died, and his imaginative idea was making its way into popular speech, and Franklin Delano Roosevelt was using the disappearance of the frontier to justify a welfare state, a number of people discovered political reasons for questioning the doctrine. Historians themselves grew uneasy. For one thing, the hypothesis seemed too nationalistic, too provincial. For another, the Frontier concept embraced too many overlapping or discordant influences. Again, the frontier cause seemed to be credited with inconsistent results: it made Americans both sectional and nationalistic, cooperative and individualistic, repetitive yet original. Once again, one wondered how many Americans could have been affected. And how were we to stay American after 1890, when the frontier disappeared? In the upshot, the frontier theory seemed to explain far too much by far too little.

Yet, for all this, it was a difficult theory to discard. For if the frontier did not produce the effects ascribed to it, what did?

I believe we now have at least a small part of the answer. It has been hinted by many perceptive observers, not least by Tocqueville or by Francis Lieber or by Sarmiento. I call it the M-Factor in American history.

What made and kept us different was not just the wildness of the North American continent, nor its vast empty spaces, nor even its wealth of resources, powerful as must have been those influences. No. It was, first of all, the M-Factor: the factor of movement, migration, mobility. Colonization was one part of it; immigration, another; the westward movement itself was a fraction, but only a fraction, of the whole. This whole began with many old-world uprootings. It gathered force with the transatlantic passage. It flooded on to the farmlands of the mid-continent. But increasingly it meant movement also *away* from the frontier, from farm to town, from region to region, from city to city. Individuals, families, churches, villages, on occasion whole countrysides have participated—and continue to participate. Francis Lieber said that in America he felt as if tied to the arms of a windmill. To him, movement had become our "historical task." And Sarmiento was so staggered by our propensity for traveling around that he predicted that, if the trump of doom were suddenly to sound, it would surprise two-thirds of the Americans, out on the roads like ants.

In all this, I repeat, the frontier played an important but limited part. For if people moved to the frontier, they moved also before there was a frontier, moved behind and away from the frontier, and kept on moving even more enthusiastically when the frontier closed.

Let us put it this way: Frederick Jackson Turner was a great poet-historian, who more than half sensed the power that was in migration, but then imprisoned this giant in the rough homespun of the vanishing pioneers. So we of a later generation must once again return to the great question: What has made and still makes Europeans into restless Americans? I venture herewith some tentative speculations, in the hope that we will find in them ideas worth working out.

My basic proposition is obvious: Movement means change. To transfer is in some part to transform. *"Wanderung meint wandlung,"* as the Germans put it. And all forms of movement, from mass exodus to simple milling around, have shared in this subtle process of alteration.

Why should motion cause change? First, because *institutions* do not move easily. A few will be destroyed; many more are damaged; nearly all are shaken, and have to be pruned, simplified, or otherwise adjusted to survive the transplanting. To a degree *displacement* means *replacement* of institutions.

Why again should migration cause modification? Because the migrants are not average people. As a group they do not represent a fair cross-section of the society they are leaving; as individuals they tend toward exaggerations of one sort or another; as settlers they won't wish to reproduce the society they have left, or succeed in reproducing it even should they so desire.

This brings us to the third great reason for change, the new circumstances: that is, the hardships and accidents of the crossing, the strangers encountered on the road, the unaccustomed climate and geography of their new environment. Movement means exposure, and successive exposures compel unexpected changes.

It may be urged that more credit should go to the strangers and the new countries. Or it may be observed that migrations are often the result or the symptom of changes that have already taken place in the parent society. And with both these ideas I agree. On the one hand, many immigrants were Americanized only long after they got over. On the other, not a few American types, like the puritan and the businessman, had already appeared in sixteenth-century Europe. So migration served both as prologue and as epilogue; it has been the means of change and the effect of change (as well as the cause). Yet no movement of people or institutions, however started or motivated, can take place without further alterations. For migration selects special types for moving; it subjects them to exceptional strains on the journey; and it then compels them to rebuild, with liberty to choose or refuse from the mail-order catalogue of Western experience. On top of all that, repeated movements, such as we in our country have known, seem to have a cumulative, or progressive, effect.

What parts of a civilization, what elements in a society, does the M-Factor attack? Apparently, all parts. Before his death Ellsworth Huntington, who was one of the earliest American scientists to become curious about this phenomenon, came to see in migration a selective force so strong that it affected the stock and temperament of a people as well as its culture. After some hesitations, I believe we will concur. For I believe it can be demonstrated that movement changes the physical population, the institutions and group structures, the social habits and traditions, the personal character and attitudes of the migrants.

Allow me to offer some random, familiar illustrations at this point.

The American population? It was formed and re-formed by migration. To begin with we were all immigrants. Moreover, because the Atlantic was open, people from many lands and nations came to these shores, until we were the leading conglomerate of the West, a Rainbow Division of Europe. Political scientists call us a pluralistic society. Sociologists find culture conflicts endemic.

Again because the migrants did not all come at once, but in intermittent surges, and because in free movements the later comers, as strangers, are handicapped and must enter the lower levels of their class and occupation, the natives or earlier-comers have repeatedly found themselves pushed upstairs, to the more skilled jobs, to the managerial posts, to the position of employers and capitalists. At the same time, moving upstairs was difficult, so difficult that the older stock felt it had to cut down on the number of its own children, if it was to graduate them into the higher levels of living—so difficult that the next-to-last comers tended to resent the labor competition of the newcomers and tried to exclude them. Thus the Yankees industrialized with the aid of other people's children. Meanwhile these laboring generations, as they matured, tried to keep the jobs for themselves and, whether as skilled artisans or later trade union bosses, as Know-Nothings in the 1850s or McCarthyites a century later, became the strongest champions of immigration restriction, the most suspicious of new foreigners, the uncompromising 100 percenters. So from 1820 to 1920 what ought to have been for the Anglo-American population a series of European additions became instead a progressive physical substitution. And after 1920 the freedom to immigrate was shut off by the votes of the very groups which had benefited from it earlier. But why did not and has not this stepladder movement of infiltration produced a stratified, hierarchical, skyscraper society? The answer is again the M-Factor, but this time internal migration. Inside, the freedom to move remained, and a man could get out of his cellar in town by building a one-story cabin up-country, or he could come off his eroded acres into Chicago, where the rising buildings and professions had elevators in them.

If we now turn from questions of nationality and occupation to the age and sex characteristics of our population, we find that here, too, the M-Factor has left deep marks. For three hundred years, or at least until the great depression, we were a young country. We boasted of it. Foreigners rarely failed to mention the childlike innocence, the boyish enthusiasm, the youthful drive and bustle and activity-for-activity's sake of these strange Americans. The youth of America, quipped Oscar Wilde, is its oldest tradition. And perhaps we were guilty of a certain "shortage of adults." At least the demographers have proved that our Constitution was made for adolescents—as late as 1820 the median age of the population was only 16 years, and it was not until well into the twentieth century that that median soared above 25. That is, it was only after preventive medicine had started to prolong the lives of the infirm, and immigration restriction had cut down on the annual influx of bachelors and young marrieds, that we first really began to feel middle-aged. How does the M-Factor figure in this? Well, students of migration have rediscovered the fact that it is overwhelmingly the young, between the ages of 15 and 25, who move—and in the first waves or pioneer phases, it is primarily the young men. The frontiers, whether of farm or factory, start emphatically male (Oh Susannah, don't you cry for me!).

Yet the men were not to have it all their own way, for the M-Factor can give things a sardonic twist. Migration has perennially represented rebellion against past tyrannies or authorities, against the father no less than against the lord or priest, against the husband no less than against the father. Thus, after the first settlements had been established, the open spaces and open opportunities of this country just invited the younger generation to leave home and strike out on their own, and the able young men accepted the invitation. Even today it is the rare son of ability who does not insist on leaving the town where he was born to try to make his way in a larger world. Meanwhile the pioneer women, being scarce as well as weak, found that they had inadvertently acquired a scarcity value. For them, as well as for the children, migration meant progressive emancipation—an emancipation eventually crowned by woman suffrage, Mother's Day and much symbolic statuary. Thus, as our lonely forefathers pushed relentlessly westward, and the idea of equality came galloping up behind, the Pioneer Mother replaced the Pilgrim Father on the sculptor's pedestal in the town square. (Whether the statuesque Miss America has now replaced her bronzed mother in the popular imagination I leave to braver men to say—we may note only the querulous complaints of our English and Continental friends that we are today a woman-run and child-dominated subcivilization.)

If we next pursue the M-Factor from our population to our economy, what will we find? An economy in which transportation has loomed extraordinarily large—witness the railroads, the automobile age and the airplane industry of today—witness also in our myths how prairie schooners and pony express, paddle wheelers and the long whistle of the trains, Ford cars and the Spirit of St. Louis have entered into the folklore of our people.

> *The wheels are singing on the railroad track*
> *If you go, you can't come back.*
> *Hear the whistle blow*

For Americans, it has been said, the automobile restates a national principle, since, after all, the settler was the first auto-mobile. In the U.S. a mile is something to put behind you. Where else would you find a place named Stillwater Junction?

More soberly, if our interest runs rather to our religious peculiarities, it might be observed that the need for settlers, and the ease of exit and entrance from one colony to the other, made toleration and disestablishment of churches almost inevitable from the start. The same ease of escape then long made it difficult for the states to impose adequate taxation, or any other really burdensome regulation, on their footloose citizens. A Virginian did not have to stay in Virginia. A Yorker could go to Michigan. If a business failed, or a marriage, the simplest thing was to decamp. Other states would welcome you. So, by and by, Reno became a monument to our vagrant fancies in matters matrimonial.

Again, politically our moving habits not only made possible but reinforced a decentralizing, federal tendency. Legally, the absence of customary law in the new settlements must have fostered the excessive American dependence on statute law. Migration also splintered our first establishments of higher education, in the sense that it led to the founding of many colleges instead of concentration on a few national universities. Thus my own institution, through the efforts of its migrating graduates, became a mother of colleges a full century before it could accumulate enough substance in New Haven to rival the great foundations of Europe. Finally, our peculiar instability of family homesite, and the lack of a national capital or home, shifted emotional loyalties to things that could be carried with us, such as declarations of principle and constitutional theories. And eventually, to bind ourselves together, we were forced to insist with an unusual, almost tyrannical, emphasis on such assimilative codes and social practices as are commonly summed up in that telltale phrase: "The American *Way* of Life."

But enough of such random illustrations.

Let us now proceed to ask, on a more systematic basis, how, just how, have migration and movement acted to convert Europeans into something rich and strange?

Considering the matter first on a broad social scale, I would propose that the M-Factor has been (turn by turn or even all at once): (1) the great Eliminator; (2) the persistent Distorter; (3) an arch-Conservator; (4) an almost irresistible Disintegrator or Atomizer; (5) a heart Stimulant or Energizer; and (6) the prime source of Optimism in the American atmosphere, a never-failing ozone of hope. Also, (7) the Secularizer and Externalizer of our beliefs, and (8) the Equalizer and Democratizer of social classes. Indeed a little reflection will suggest still other ways in which migration has shaken its European ingredients into new patterns. But on this occasion let us consider merely some of these eight, with just a hint or two of historic events by way of illumination.

Migration was the great Eliminator? Nothing could be plainer. In theory you can't take everything with you when you move. Some goods are too bulky or delicate to be put on ship; some household possessions will fall out of the covered wagon. Again, in a free migration, not all elements in a society will wish to move; the dregs will be too spiritless and impoverished to emigrate unaided; the ruling classes entirely too successful and satisfied. Check this theory against history and what do we find? In the early colonization there came out of England the rising middle classes, with some admixture of the lowest elements, but with only a few aristocratic leaders. Ours started, therefore, as a decapitated society, virtually without nobles or bishops, judges or learned lawyers, artists, playwrights or great poets. Taking a hopeful view, a student of mine once maintained that settlement transferred the accent from *nobility* to *ability*. Considering the transfer culturally, however, one must recognize a tragic impoverishment. Despite all our gains of goodness or plenty or freedom, the men of the highest attainments and greatest skills had stayed home—and with them their arts and refinements, their leisure-class culture. The same process of abandonment, of flight from the elite and their standards, would be discernible later in the settlement of the West. Axiomatically, the fine arts, the theoretical sciences, the most advanced tools and machinery, are not found or produced on moving frontiers. Like war or fire or inflation, migration has been a great destroyer of inherited treasure.

At first glance such destruction may seem only temporary, to be replaced "when we have time." Yet meanwhile some elements are missing, the balance is changed, the old society has been distorted—and before long one may get reconciled to doing without. On top of this, the M-Factor has promoted distortion in an even more drastic way. For moving forces the reclassification of values. Why? Because the land of destination attracts more strongly for one or two presumed goods than for the others (as for economic opportunity perhaps, or political freedom, or the right to worship in one's own way). So if a family is to go, they have to believe, or persuade themselves, that the particular goods to be realized are more important to them than all the other social goods, which may be diminished, or even be left behind altogether. If similar movements are made by later generations for like reasons, then these cherished values may rise almost to the status of holy commandments or natural rights, and in the nineteenth century become the polar magnets in a new value system. By elimination and wilful distortion a moving people becomes a narrower society: thinner and shallower, yet in some things much more intense.

This calls attention to a third and almost paradoxical characteristic of migration: its conservatism. People moved to save as well as to improve. But when they found they couldn't take everything with them, then a curious thing often happened. They came to value even more highly what they had succeeded in preserving. Having suffered such privations, having sacrificed so many other possessions, they clung to what was saved with a fiercer passion. Witness the Puritans with their Wilderness Zion, the Mormons under Brigham Young, or even Turner's leapfrogging pioneers. For these last, as for so many others, it had become easier to move than to change their vocation, their habits, their antiquated methods. To put this bluntly, for them the cheap lands of the West made it easier to keep on with their soil-mining and strip-farming, and possible to avoid such painful changes as learning a proper care of the land, or the new crop rotation of the advanced parts of Europe and the East. So for the American farmer—or agriculturally speaking—the westward movement became the great postponement of American history. They profited personally, but it was a postponement nonetheless—just as in the flight of the New England textile industry to the South in our times. In France, before De Gaulle, the peasant and small shopkeeper clung stubbornly to his land or shop, but politically moved constantly to the left. That is, economically, he might be a selfish reactionary, and even vote for Poujade, but by changing the name of his party leftward he was sure he was making "progress." Did not some of our American pioneers give themselves the same feeling of progress by moving westward? Migration, I would suggest, could be a way of promoting change—and of avoiding it, too. Flight can be an escape from the future as well as from the past.

The M-Factor, we must next realize, was an almost irresistible Disintegrator or Atomizer. Few authoritarian institutions from Europe could stand the strain of Atlantic distances or the explosion of American space. So either they decentralized or died. Witness the early church. In Virginia the episcopal organization proved so little suited to the far-flung tobacco plantations that the Church of England almost withered away, whereas in New England the Puritan branch of the same church developed a localized or Congregational organization, and flourished. Then, later, when the Irish immigration poured life and vigor into American Catholicism, the hierarchy, intuitively recognizing that moving out on the lands might cripple the Church as well as weaken the individual's faith, did their best to hold the new arrivals in the seaport towns, at least until some interior communities could be effectively churched. Ultimately, I believe it will be found that our Catholics have moved less often, less widely and less soon than their Protestant neighbors, hence have missed certain corrosive acids and opportunities in the M-Factor.

One of these opportunities, of course, was to stand on your own feet, to make your own way, and if need be to move again. In our expanding settlements the arm of the State (like the authority of the bishops) shriveled, and a kind of physical individualism sprouted. On the trail, society tended to break down into chance parties of moving families or individuals. And at the destination everything was to be reconstructed. It took energy and courage to move, and more energy to make the move succeed. Hence migration was a great stimulant to action—and when such action repeatedly succeeded (or, as we may say, "worked"), then perhaps the beginnings of a habit of action had been established, both for oneself and for one's neighbor. The American reputation for activism, as for self-help and neighborly helpfulness, surely needs no underlining.

Migration was not only the Destroyer, Distorter, Conservator, Atomizer and Energizer of western society, but its most effective "Optimizer." First of all, out of the welter of old-world classes and temperaments it selected the up-and-coming and the hopeful. Pessimists didn't bother; you had to be an optimist to move. Next it required sacrifice and waiting, and so captured many believers, the men of faith. Finally, it rewarded the successful—and those who weren't lucky were given a second try. America the Golden was the land of the second chance. And from failure it offered a full timetable of escapes.

I realize that it is customary at this point to do a ritualistic dance around the statue of the golden calf—and credit our optimism or success primarily to the sheer wealth of the continent. But if we did become a "people of plenty," and if that plenty left its mark even on the size of our automobiles, let us not forget that the beginnings were almost invariably hard, and what the land long offered most of was tough places and violent weather. What kind of plenty was it converted the gravel patch of New England into smiling farms? Lots of hard work, I should say, and plenty of faith. Again, who but a lunkheaded optimist would grow wheat in western Kansas? Or who in his right mind would go settle in Dakota? No. The Black Hills gold and the U.S. farm bounties, these bonanzas were later and almost accidental discoveries. In my book, optimism made more states than vice versa. Many a town existed first, or only, in the imagination. "Boost, don't knock" has been the slogan of new communities just abuilding, and the booster is Mr. Johnny-come-lately. We began as migrants, that is, wishful thinkers, and each wave of immigration, each boatload from abroad, brought us fresh injections of this heart stimulant. For Europe's poor, the freedom to come changed "tomorrow" from a threat into a promise. For its men of faith, the act of moving and moving again substituted "the future" for "the heavenly hereafter." And with time the mission of American idealists came to be in and for this world. From infant damnation to the social gospel is but a long tramp.

I hope I may be forgiven if I now pass over the secularizing and externalizing influences of mobility (which Sorokin has explored) in favor of its equalitarian and leveling effects. For these democratic tendencies seem to me particularly important, and I have stumbled on some odd illustrations.

Here the theoretical argument would be that the M-Factors are often democratic in their consequences, first because for the lower classes emigration means *"getting out from under,"* the first step on the road up; secondly because the hardships of the journey are no respecters of birth (witness the miserable failure of the early "Gentlemen" of the Jamestown Colony in Virginia). In the third place, and most significantly, the process of resettlement is a process of making new mixtures, out of a gathering of strangers, each without authority, credentials, reputation or other priority than that of arrival. In a new community (frontier or town) family and past performance hardly count. Everyone has to make his own mark, and stands equal with his fellow-strangers. The social competition, as it were, starts over, with all the camaraderie and "gamesmanship" of a new catch-as-catch-can. Migration has been a great Mixmaster. And mixtures of anonymous elements are necessarily more democratic, at least at first. So much for doctrine. Now for my illustrations.

My first illustration, if you will allow the personal reference, comes out of an effort to understand my own university. How explain Yale College of the 1890s, a college that prided itself on its democracy? It is true there were a few Whitneys, Vanderbilts or Harknesses, with social pretensions and inordinate allowances. Yet evidently the game was wide open, and any self-help student from no matter how humble a background or obscure a school had a chance to show what he could do and rise to the top and be the honor man in the Senior Society elections, if he had what it took. Now how was it possible that a college like Yale, with almost two hundred years of tradition and family attachments, could still offer so fair and square an opportunity to all comers? Because Yale was, in a sense, an annually renewed community, and because its constituents came, not just from around New Haven or New England but from all over the country, without prior knowledge of each other or claims to authority. It was a skeptical Harvard professor, European born, who first taught me this truth. Listen to George Santayana:

The relations of one Yale student to another are completely simple and direct. They are like passengers in a ship. . . . They live in a sort of primitive brotherhood with a ready enthusiasm for every good or bad project, and a contagious good humor.
. . . Nothing could be more American. . . . Here is sound, healthy principle, but no scrupulousness, love of life, trust in success, a ready jocoseness, a democratic amiability, and a radiant conviction that there is nothing better than oneself. It is a boyish type of character, earnest and quick in things practical, hasty and frivolous in things intellectual, but the boyishness is a healthy one, and in a young man, as in a young nation, it is perfection to have only the faults of youth.

What Yale College and the Frontier, and indeed much of the rest of America, had in common, Santayana suggests, was young Americans in a new mixture.

If this first illustration comes with a strange sound, let me hasten to propose my second. It concerns dogs. In France, on sabbatical a few years ago, I seemed to run into only two kinds of dogs. One was the pampered, pedigreed poodle, sitting with his mistress in the restaurants, even eating from her plate: the fine flower of canine aristocracy, and most grandly indifferent to strangers. The second type was nondescript and fierce, the savage watchdog at peasant doorway or château gate, guarding the family domain and inherited possessions, *"les situations acquises."* This character disliked strangers on sight, and promptly tried to chew them up. After one or two close calls with such receptionists, I came back to the States—and found dogs of all sorts of ancestry, chiefly mixed. But what they showed mostly was curiosity, and a sort of friendly expectancy. Their tails said: "Howdy, stranger." For they were not guarding any particular place. They belonged to traveling men, and had been around.

My third illumination, if we can call it that, concerns money. Foreigners still accuse us of being excessively money-minded, of measuring everything by the almighty dollar. Our defenders answer: it's not the money, it's the power and the achievement. You make a million to prove you're a man; then, like as not, you give it away. After all, you can't take it with you.

Yet can't you? As I was once thinking about the M-Factor, it suddenly came to me that on a journey, or in a new community, money was one of the few things that you could take along. Cash took the place of your pedigree or family letter of credit. It spoke with a certain authority, East or West. Money was power? Yes. But especially it was currency: the power that you could take with you. So on the moving frontier, in the new towns, it was differentiation by dollars that first disturbed the democracy of new mixtures.

Having got diverted by some of the social consequences of the M-Factor, I cannot do justice to some of the most interesting effects of all: the influence of migration on personal character and attitudes. In the moment remaining let me merely suggest possibilities.

Was it not the psychological imperatives of migration, even more than frontier land, that helped make and keep us a nation of optimists? Was it not the physical demands of colonization and resettlement, as well as Calvinism and middle-class origins, that made us into such a nation of workers, activists, materialists, instrumentalists? The difference between what André Siegfried calls "homo faber" or the American, and homo sapiens or the European, is it not perhaps that one of these characters has been sitting still? Whereas we, poor pilgrims, have itching feet. Restless to start with, we have become more so with repeated displacement. *Here today and gone tomorrow.* The wandering mania has got into our blood, our houses, our attention, our very ways of speech. *Come on! Get going! Don't be a stick-in-the-mud! You don't want to get left, do you? It's a good year to make the move. So long! I don't know where I'm going, but I'm on my way. Anywhere I hang my hat is home, sweet home, to me.*

In the revealing American vernacular it is impressive to observe how many things are defined in terms of movement. A man *on the road* to success is a *comer, a go-getter. That's going some,* we say—and by and by we listen for the magic words that we also have *arrived.* So also with failure *He missed the bus.* Or, *he missed the boat. He is not getting anywhere. She got left in the lurch. He got bogged down with administration.* A man who is growing old is *slowing up,* and then by and by he reaches *the end of the trail.* Death itself used to be spoken of as *crossing the divide.*

Reinforcing the testimony of our vernacular are our social habits. Unable to stay put, thrown among fellow transients, having newcomers flood in about us, we have perforce become hospitable, and genial with strangers. Not knowing their ancestry, and caring less, first names have been all we needed. There is a fellowship in our country, known to some of you perhaps, where last names are absolutely prohibited. And, incidentally, this illustrates another American trait: our propensity for "joining." Lonely from disassociation, we will make ten lodges grow where but one *bierstube* stood before. Frightened and not quite able to bear our independence, we oscillate between assertiveness and timidity, between an almost violent aggression and an almost cowardly conformity. Imaginative and suggestible, we are notorious for our fads and our instability. Insecure in our values, we have become adept at inventing dogmas to comfort ourselves. Not quite sure that our abandonment of the old world and of the past was justified, we have long been haunted by ambivalent feelings: a mixture of scorn and guilt complex about the older civilizations of Europe.

"It is a complex fate, being an American," said Henry James, "and one of the responsibilities it entails is fighting against a superstitious valuation of Europe." Ralph Waldo Emerson felt the same way: "Can we never extract the tapeworm of Europe from the brain of our countrymen?"

Finally, because migration appealed for diverse reasons especially to extremists—to saints and real sinners, to fundamentalists and free thinkers, to dreamers and "tough bastards," to groupists and individualists side by side—our society has never received its fair share of balanced, equable, middle-of-the-road temperaments, but has been shot through with violent contradictions. Hence so many of our seeming inconsistencies, to this very day.

To me the migrant seems not a single or a simple character, but is he not recognizably different—and American?

Paradoxically, if we turn up the other side of the coin, there are the Europeans, fearful of becoming Americanized. Is this entirely out of weakness, or envy, or admiration? Hardly. Let us rather take note of a curious and unappreciated development. In the last generation mobility has swept the continent. With their *vacances payés,* their *campings,* their folkwagons, our cousins have found a new freedom. So, if today there is Americanization in Europe, and if our ways of life seem to be coming closer together, may it not be in part because the Old World societies are as never before in movement, and because Siegfried's "homo sapiens," too, is taking to the roads?

We Are All Third Generation

MARGARET MEAD

What then is this American character, this expression of American institutions and of American attitudes which is embodied in every American, in everyone born in this country and sometimes even in those who have come later to these shores? What is it that makes it possible to say of a group of people glimpsed from a hotel step in Soerabaja or strolling down the streets of Marseilles, "There go some Americans," whether they have come from Arkansas or Maine or Pennsylvania, whether they bear German or Swedish or Italian surnames? Not clothes alone, but the way they wear them, the way they walk along the street without awareness that anyone of higher status may be walking there also, the way their eyes rove as if by right over the facade of palaces and the rose windows of cathedrals, interested and unimpressed, referring what they see back to the Empire State building, the Chrysler tower, or a good-sized mountain in Montana. Not the towns they come from—Sioux City, Poughkeepsie, San Diego, Scotsdale—but the tone of voice in which they say, "Why, I came from right near there. My home town was Evansville. Know anybody in Evansville?" And the apparently meaningless way in which the inhabitant of Uniontown warms to the inhabitant of Evansville as they name over a few names of people whom neither of them know well, about whom neither of them have thought for years, and about whom neither of them care in the least. And yet, the onlooker, taking note of the increased warmth in their voices, of the narrowing of the distance which had separated them when they first spoke, knows that something has happened, that a tie has been established between two people who were lonely before, a tie which every American hopes he may be able to establish as he hopefully asks every stranger: "What's your home town?"

Americans establish these ties by finding common points on the road that all are expected to have traveled, after their forebears came from Europe one or two

131

or three generations ago, or from one place to another in America, resting for long enough to establish for each generation a "home town" in which they grew up and which they leave to move on to a new town which will become the home town of their children. Whether they meet on the deck of an Atlantic steamer, in a hotel in Singapore, in New York or in San Francisco, the same expectation underlies their first contact—that both of them have moved on and are moving on and that potential intimacy lies in paths that have crossed. Europeans, even Old Americans whose pride lies not in the circumstance that their ancestors have moved often but rather in the fact that they have not moved for some time, find themselves eternally puzzled by this "home town business." Many Europeans fail to find out that in nine cases out of ten the "home town" is not where one lives but where one did live; they mistake the sentimental tone in which an American invokes Evansville and Centerville and Unionville for a desire to live there again; they miss entirely the symbolic significance of the question and answer which say diagrammatically, "Are you the same kind of person I am? Good, how about a coke?"

Back of that query lies the remembrance and the purposeful forgetting of European ancestry. For a generation, they cluster together in the Little Italies, in the Czech section or around the Polish Church, new immigrants clinging together so as to be able to chatter in their own tongue and buy their own kind of red peppers, but later there is a scattering to the suburbs and the small towns, to an "American" way of life, and this is dramatized by an over-acceptance of what looks, to any European, as the most meaningless sort of residence—on a numbered street in Chicago or the Bronx. No garden, no fruit trees, no ties to the earth, often no ties to the neighbors, just a number on a street, just a number of a house for which the rent is $10 more than the rent in the old foreign district from which they moved—how can it mean anything? But it does.

For life has ceased to be expressed in static, spatial terms as it was in Europe, where generation after generation tied their security to the same plot of ground, or if they moved to a city, acted as if the house there, with its window plants, was still a plot of ground anchored by fruit trees. On a plot of ground a man looks around him, looks at the filled spaces in the corner of the garden. There used to be plum trees there, but father cut them down when he was a child; now he has planted young peaches—the plot is filled up again. And he can lean over the wall and talk to the neighbor who has planted plums again—they are the same kind of people, with the same origins and the same future. Having the same origins and the same future, they can dwell in the present which is assumed to be part of one continuous way of life.

But for two Americans, chance met on a train or at adjacent desks in a big office building, working in a road gang or a munition plant or on the same ground crew at an airport, there are no such common origins or common expectations. It is assumed, and not mentioned, that grandparents likely were of different nationality, different religion, different political faith, may have fought on opposite sides of the same battles—that great-great-grandparents may have burned each other at the stake. . . .

. . . Each and every American has followed a long and winding road; if the roads started in the same spot in Europe, best forget that—that tie leads backwards to the past which is best left behind. But if the roads touched here, in this vast country where everyone is always moving, that is a miracle which brings men close together.

In our behavior, however many generations we may actually boast of in this country, however real our lack of ties in the old world may be, we are all third generation, our European ancestry tucked away and half forgotten, the recent steps in our wanderings over America immortalized and over-emphasized. When a rising man is given an administrative job and a chance to choose men for other jobs, he does not, if he is an American, fill those jobs with members of his family—such conduct is left to those who have never left their foreign neighborhoods, or to the first generation. He does not fill them exclusively with members of his own class; his own class is an accidental cross-section which wouldn't contain enough skills. He can't depend upon his golfing mates or this year's neighbors to provide him with the men he needs. Instead, he fills the jobs with men from somewhere along the road he has traveled, his home town, his home state, his college, his former company. They give him the same kind of assurance that a first-generation Hollywood producer felt when he put his cousins in charge of the accounts—their past and his past are one—at one spot anyway—just as in a kin-oriented society common blood assures men of each other's allegiance. The secretary, trying to shield her boss from the importunities of the office seeker, knows it's no use trying to turn away a man from that little North Dakota college that the boss went to. The door is always open to them, any one of them, any day. And a newspaper headline screams: "Rock of Chickamauga blood still flows in soldiers' veins."

European social scientists look at this picture of American intimacy and fail to understand it. In the first place, they cannot get inside it. An Englishman, who has never been in America before, arriving in Indianapolis and trying to establish relationships with an American who has never been in England, finds himself up against what seems to be a blank wall. He meets hearty greetings, eager hospitality, an excessive attempt to tie the visitor to the local scene by taking him rapidly over its civic wonders, an equally excessive attempt to tie in Uncle Josiah's trip to India with the fact that the guest was reared in the Punjab—and then blankness. But if the Englishman then takes a tour in the Northwest, spends a week in the town where his Indiana host lived as a boy and then returns to Indianapolis, he will find a very different greeting awaiting him, which he may mistakenly put down to the fact that this is a second meeting. Only if he is a very astute observer will he notice how the path he has taken across the United States has the power to thaw out any number of hosts at any number of dinner parties.

The wife of the European scientist, now living as a faculty wife in a small university town in Colorado, will find herself similarly puzzled. She doesn't seem to get anywhere with the other faculty wives. Their husbands and her husband have the same status, the same salary, perhaps the same degree of world-wide reputation. She has learned their standards of conspicuous consumption; she can make exactly the same kind of appetizers, set a bridge table out with prizes just as they do—and yet, there is no intimacy. Only when both have children can she and some faculty wife really get together. She thinks it is the common interest in the children which forms the tie; actually it is the common experience of the children, who have something in common which the two women will never have in the same way—the same home town, which provides the necessary link, so fragile, and from a European point of view so meaningless and contentless, and yet, for an American, so essential. Later, even if they have lived childlessly beside each other, should they meet again in Alaska or Mississippi, they would be friends—with no real accession of common interests that the European wife could see. For she does not realize that to Americans only the past can give intimacy, nor can she conceive how such an incredibly empty contact in the past can be enough.

. . . .

But it is impossible for all Americans who must work or play together to have a bit of identical past, to have lived, even in such rapidly shifting lives, within a few miles of the spot where the others have lived, at some different period for some different reason. Thin and empty as is the "home town" tie, substitutes for it must be found; other still more tenuous symbols must be invoked. And here we find the enthusiastic preferences for the same movie actor, the same brand of peaches, the same way of mixing a drink. Superficially it makes no sense at all that preference for one brand of cigarette over another may call forth the same kind of enthusiasm that one might expect if two people discovered that they had both found poetry through Keats or both nearly committed suicide on account of the same girl. Only by placing these light preferences against a background of idiosyncratic experience—by realizing that every American's life is different from every other American's; that nowhere, except in parts of the Deep South and similar pockets, can one find people whose lives and background are both identical or even similar—only then do these feverish grabs at a common theme make sense. English or Dutch residents in the colonies will spend hours sighing over the names of the shops or drinks of their respective Bond Streets, creating in their nostalgia a past atmosphere which they miss in the harsh tropical landscape about them. Americans, in a sense colonials in every part of America, but colonials who have come to have no other home, also create a common atmosphere within which to bask in the present as they criticize or approve the same radio program or moving picture actor.

There is also that other American method of forming ties, the association—the lodge, fraternity, club which is such a prominent feature of American life. Lloyd Warner has described our societies of veterans of past wars as comparable to a cult of the dead which binds a community together, with the veterans of the most distant war lowest in the social scale. Seen from the point of view which I have been discussing, each war creates a magnificent common past for large numbers of men. It is not surprising that those who have the fewest ties among themselves—those whose poverty-stricken way of life admits of few associations—cling longest to this common experience.

. . . .

Social scientists, taking their cues from Eastern colleges or from Sinclair Lewis, have been inclined to sneer at the American habit of "joining," at the endless meetings, the clasp of fellowship, the songs, the allegedly pseudoenthusiasm with which "brothers" greet each other. Safe on the eminence of available intellectual ties and able to gossip together about the famous names and the scandals of their professions, they have failed to appreciate that these associational ties give not the pseudo-security which some European philosopher feels he would get out of them if he had to share in them, but very real security. Not until he has been marooned—his train missed, no taxi available—and driven sixty miles across bad roads in the middle of the night by someone who belongs to another chapter of the same national organization does he begin to realize that the tie of common membership, flat and without content as it is, bolstered up by sentimental songs which no one really likes to sing but which everyone would miss if they weren't sung, has an intensity of its own; an intensity measured against the loneliness which each member would feel if there were no such society.

If this then, this third-generation American, always moving on, always, in his hopes, moving up, leaving behind him all that was his past and greeting with enthusiasm any echo of that past when he meets it in the life of another, represents one typical theme of the American character structure, how is this theme reflected in the form of the family, in the upbringing of the American child? For to the family we must turn for an understanding of the American character structure. We may describe the adult American, and for descriptive purposes we may refer his behavior to the American scene, to the European past, to the state of American industry, to any other set of events which we wish; but to understand the regularity of this behavior we must investigate the family within which the child is reared. Only so can we learn how the newborn child, at birth potentially a Chinaman or an American, a Pole or an Irishman, becomes an American. By referring his character to the family we do not say that the family is the cause of his character and that the pace of American industry or the distribution of population in America are secondary effects, but merely that all the great configuration of American culture is mediated to the child by his parents, his siblings, his near relatives, and his nurses. He meets American law first in the warning note of his mother's voice: "Stop digging, here comes a cop." He meets American economics when he finds his mother unimpressed by his offer to buy another copy of the wedding gift he has just smashed: "At the 5 and 10 cent store, can't we?" His first encounter with puritan standards may come through his mother's "If you don't eat your vegetables you can't have any dessert." He learns the paramount importance of distinguishing between vice and virtue; that it is only a matter of which comes first, the pleasure or the pain. All his great lessons come through his mother's voice, through his father's laughter, or the tilt of his father's cigar when a business deal goes right. Just as one way of understanding a machine is to understand how it is made, so one way of understanding the typical character structure of a culture is to follow step by step the way in which it is built into the growing child. Our assumption when we look at the American family will be that each experience of early childhood is contributing to make the growing individual "all of a piece," is guiding him towards consistent and specifically American inconsistency in his habits and view of the world.

What kind of parents are these "third-generation" Americans? These people who are always moving, always readjusting, always hoping to buy a better car and a better radio, and even in the years of Depression orienting their behavior to their "failure" to buy a better car or a better radio. Present or absent, the better car, the better house, the better radio are key points in family life. In the first place, the American parent expects his child to leave him, leave him physically, go to another town, another state; leave him in terms of occupation, embrace a different calling, learn a different skill; leave him socially, travel if possible with a different crowd. Even where a family has reached the top and actually stayed there for two or three generations, there are, for all but the very, very few, still larger cities or foreign courts to be stormed. Those American families which settle back to maintain a position of having reached the top in most cases moulder there for lack of occupation, ladder-climbers gone stale from sitting too long on the top step, giving a poor imitation of the aristocracy of other lands. At the bottom, too, there are some without hope, but very few. Studies of modern youth dwell with anxiety upon the disproportion between the daydreams of the under-privileged young people and the actuality which confronts them in terms of job opportunities. In that very daydream the break is expressed. The daughter who says to her hard-working mother: "You don't know. I may be going to be a great writer," is playing upon a note in her mother's mind which accepts the possibility that even if her daughter does not become famous, she will at least go places that she, the mother, has never gone.

In old societies such as those from which their grandparents and great-grandparents came (and it is important to remember that Americans are oriented towards the Europe from which their ancestors emigrated, not to the Europe which exists today) parents had performed an act of singular finality when they married, before ever a child was born. They had defined its probable place in the sun. If they maintained the same status throughout the child's growing life, kept the necessary bit of ground or inheritance to start him off as befitted him, reared him to act and feel and believe in a way appropriate to "that state of life to which it has pleased God to call him," the parents had done their share. Their service to their child was majorly the maintenance of their own place in the world. His care, his food, his shelter, his education—all of these were by-products of the parents' position. But in America, such an attitude, such a concentration on one's own position makes one, in most cases, a bad parent. One is not just restaking the same old claim for one's child, nor can one stake out the child's new claim for him. All one can do is to make him strong and well equipped to go prospecting for himself. For proper behavior *in* that state of life to which it has pleased God to call one, is substituted proper behavior *towards* that state of life to which God, if given enough assistance, may call one's son and daughter. Europeans laugh at the way in which parents pick for their newborn babies colleges which they have never seen. It does, of course, make sense to plan one's affairs so that one's son goes to the same school one went to oneself; but this fantastic new choice—for a squirming bit of humanity which may after all not have the brains to get through the third grade—is inexplicable. Parenthood in America has become a very special thing, and parents see themselves not as giving their children final status and place, rooting them firmly for life in a dependable social structure, but merely as training them for a race which they will run alone.

With this orientation towards a different future for the child comes also the expectation that the child will pass beyond his parents and leave their standards behind him. . . .

By and large, the American father has an attitude towards his children which may be loosely classified as autumnal. They are his for a brief and passing season, and in a very short while they will be operating gadgets which he does not understand and cockily talking a language to which he has no clue. He does his best to keep ahead of his son, takes a superior tone as long as he can, and knows that in nine cases out of ten he will lose. If the boy goes into his father's profession, of course, it will take him a time to catch up. He finds out that the old man knows a trick or two; that experience counts as over against this new-fangled nonsense. But the American boy solves that one very neatly: he typically does not go into his father's profession, nor take up land next to his father where his father can come over and criticize his plowing. He goes somewhere else, either in space or in occupation. And his father, who did the same thing and expects that his son will, is at heart terrifically disappointed if the son accedes to his ritual request that he docilely follow in his father's footsteps and secretly suspects the imitative son of being a milksop. He knows he is a milksop—or so he thinks—because he himself would have been a milksop if he had wanted to do just what his father did.

This is an attitude which reaches its most complete expression in the third-generation American. His grandfather left home, rebelled against a parent who did not expect final rebellion, left a land where everyone expected him to stay. Come to this country, his rebellious adventuring cooled off by success, he begins to relent a little, to think perhaps the strength of his ardor to leave home was overdone. When his sons grow up, he is torn between his desire to have them succeed in this new country—which means that they must be more American than he, must lose entirely their foreign names and every trace of allegiance to a foreign way of life—and his own guilt towards the parents and the fatherland which he has denied. So he puts on the heat, alternately punishing the child whose low marks in school suggest that he is not going to be a successful American and berating him for his American ways and his disrespect for his father and his father's friends from the old country. When that son leaves home, he throws himself with an intensity which his children will not know into the American way of life; he eats American, talks American, dresses American, he will be American or nothing. In making his way of life consistent, he inevitably makes it thin; the overtones of the family meal on which strange, delicious, rejected European dishes were set, and about which low words in a foreign tongue wove the atmosphere of home, must all be dropped out. His speech has a certain emptiness; he rejects the roots of words—roots lead back, and he is going forward—and comes to handle language in terms of surfaces and clichés. He rejects half of his life in order to make the other half self-consistent and complete. And by and large he succeeds. Almost miraculously, the sons of the Polish day laborer and the Italian fruit grower, the Finnish miner and the Russian garment worker become Americans.

Second generation—American-born of foreign-born parents—they set part of the tone of the American eagerness for their children to go onward. They have left their parents; left them in a way which requires more moral compensation than was necessary even for the parent generation who left Europe. The immigrant left his land, his parents, his fruit trees, and the little village street behind him. He cut the ties of military service; he flouted the king or the emperor; he built himself a new life in a new country. The father whom he left behind was strong, a part of something terribly strong, something to be feared and respected and fled from. Something so strong that the bravest man might boast of a successful flight. He left his parents, entrenched representatives of an order which he rejected. But not so his son. He leaves his father not a part of a strong other-way of life, but bewildered on the shores of the new world, having climbed only halfway up the beach. His father's ties to the old world, his mannerisms, his broken accent, his little foreign gestures are not part and parcel of something strong and different; they are signs of his failure to embrace this new way of life. Does his mother wear a kerchief over her head? He cannot see the generations of women who have worn such kerchiefs. He sees only the American women who wear hats, and he pities and rejects his mother who has failed to become—an American. And so there enters into the attitude of the second-generation American—an attitude which again is woven through our folkways, our attitude towards other languages, towards anything foreign, towards anything European—a combination of contempt and avoidance, a fear of yielding, and a sense that to yield would be weakness. His father left a father who was the representative of a way of life which had endured for a thousand years. When he leaves his father, he leaves a partial failure; a hybrid, one who represents a step towards freedom, not freedom itself. His first-generation father chose between freedom and what he saw as slavery; but when the second-generation American looks at his European father, and through him, at Europe, he sees a choice between success and failure, between potency and ignominy. He passionately rejects the halting English, the half-measures of the immigrant. He rejects with what seem to him equally good reasons "European ties and entanglements." This second-generation attitude which has found enormous expression in our culture especially during the last fifty years, has sometimes come to dominate it—in those parts of the country which we speak of as "isolationist." Intolerant of foreign language, foreign ways, vigorously determined on being themselves, they are, in attitude if not in fact, second-generation Americans.

When the third-generation boy grows up, he comes up against a father who found the task of leaving his father a comparatively simple one. The second-generation parent lacks the intensity of the first, and his son in turn fails to reflect the struggles, the first against feared strength and the second against guiltily rejected failure, which have provided the plot for his father and grandfather's maturation. He is expected to succeed; he is expected to go further than his father went; and all this is taken for granted. He is furthermore expected to feel very little respect for the past. Somewhere in his grandfather's day there was an epic struggle for liberty and freedom. His picture of that epic grandfather is a little obscured, however, by the patent fact that his father does not really respect him; he may have been a noble character, but he had a foreign accent. The grandchild is told in school, in the press, over the radio, about the founding fathers, but they were not after all *his* founding fathers; they are, in ninety-nine cases out of a hundred, somebody else's ancestors. Any time one's own father, who in his own youth had pushed his father aside and made his own way, tries to get in one's way, one can invoke the founding fathers—those ancestors of the real Americans; the Americans who got here earlier—those Americans which father worked so very hard, so slavishly, in fact, to imitate. This is a point which the European observer misses. He hears an endless invocation of Washington and Lincoln, of Jefferson and Franklin. Obviously, Americans go in for ancestor worship, says the European. Obviously, Americans are longing for a strong father, say the psycho-analysts. These observers miss the point that Washington is not the ancestor of the man who is doing the talking; Washington does not represent the past to which one belongs by birth, but the past to which one tries to belong by effort. Washington represents the thing for which grandfather left Europe at the risk of his life, and for which father rejected grandfather at the risk of his integrity. Washington is not that to which Americans passionately cling but that to which they want to belong, and fear, in the bottom of their hearts, that they cannot and do not.

This odd blending of the future and the past, in which another man's great-grandfather becomes the symbol of one's grandson's future, is an essential part of American culture. "Americans are so conservative," say Europeans. They lack the revolutionary spirit. Why don't they rebel? Why did President Roosevelt's suggestion of altering the structure of the Supreme Court and the Third-Term argument raise such a storm of protest? Because, in education, in attitudes, most Americans are third generation, they have just really arrived. Their attitude towards this country is that of one who has just established membership, just been elected to an exclusive club, just been initiated into the rites of an exacting religion. Almost any one of them who inspects his own ancestry, even though it goes back many more generations than three, will find a gaping hole somewhere in the family tree. Campfire girls give an honor to the girl who can name all eight great-grandparents, including the maiden names of the four great-grandmothers. Most Americans cannot get this honor. And who was that missing great-grandmother? Probably, oh, most probably, not a grand-niece of Martha Washington.

We have, of course, our compensatory mythology. People who live in a land torn by earthquakes have myths of a time when the land was steady, and those whose harvests are uncertain dream of a golden age when there was no drought. Likewise, people whose lives are humdrum and placid dream of an age of famine and rapine. We have our rituals of belonging, our DAR's and our Descendants of King Philip's Wars, our little blue book of the blue-blooded Hawaiian aristocracy descended from the first missionaries, and our *Mayflower,* which is only equaled in mythological importance by the twelve named canoes which brought the Maoris to New Zealand. The mythology keeps alive the doubt. The impressive president of a patriotic society knows that she is a member by virtue of only one of the some eight routes through which membership is possible. Only one. The other seven? Well, three are lost altogether. Two ancestors were Tories. In some parts of the country she can boast of that; after all, Tories were people of substance, real "old families." But it doesn't quite fit. Of two of those possible lines, she has resolutely decided not to think. Tinkers and tailors and candlestick makers blend indistinctly with heaven knows what immigrants! She goes to a meeting and is very insistent about the way in which the Revolutionary War which only one-eighth of her ancestors helped to fight should be represented to the children of those whose eight ancestors were undoubtedly all somewhere else in 1776.

On top of this Old American mythology, another layer has been added, a kind of placatory offering, a gesture towards the Old World which Americans had left behind. As the fifth- and sixth- and seventh-generation Americans lost this zest which came with climbing got to the top of the pecking order[1] in their own town or city and sat, still uncertain, still knowing their credentials were shaky, on the top of the pile, the habit of wanting to belong—to really belong, to be accepted absolutely as something which one's ancestors had NOT been—became inverted. They turned towards Europe, especially towards England, towards presentation at Court, towards European feudal attitudes. And so we have had in America two reinforcements of the European class attitudes—those

---

[1]Pecking order is a very convenient piece of jargon which social psychologists use to describe a group in which it is very clear to everybody in it, just which bird can peck which, or which cow butt which other cow away from the water trough. Among many living creatures these "pecking orders" are fixed and when a newcomer enters the group he has to fight and scramble about until everybody is clear just where he belongs—below No. 8 chick, for instance, and above old No. 9.

hold-overs of feudal caste attitudes, in the newly-come immigrant who carries class consciousness in every turn and bend of his neck, and the new feudalism, the "old family" who has finally toppled over backwards into the lap of all that their remote ancestors left behind them.

When I say that we are most of us—whatever our origins—third-generation in character structure, I mean that we have been reared in an atmosphere which is most like that which I have described for the third generation. Father is to be outdistanced and outmoded, but not because he is a strong representative of another culture, well entrenched, not because he is a weak and ineffectual attempt to imitate the new culture; he did very well in his way, but he is out of date. He, like us, was moving forwards, moving away from something symbolized by his own ancestors, moving towards something symbolized by other people's ancestors. Father stands for the way things were done, for a direction which on the whole was a pretty good one, in its day. He was all right because he was on the right road. Therefore, we, his children, lack the mainsprings of rebellion. He was out of date; he drove an old model car which couldn't make it on the hills. Therefore it is not necessary to fight him, to knock him out of the race. It is much easier and quicker to pass him. And to pass him it is only necessary to keep on going and to see that one buys a new model every year. Only if one slackens, loses one's interest in the race towards success, does one slip back. Otherwise, it is onward and upward, *towards* the world of Washington and Lincoln; a world in which we don't fully belong, but which we feel, if we work at it, we some time may achieve.

AS THE TWIG IS BENT

IV

INTRODUCTION IV

Twenty years ago the American psychoanalyst Erik H. Erikson called attention to the need for studies of the upbringing of children in relation to the development of national character. "One may scan work after work on history, society, and morality and find little reference to the fact that all people start as children and that all peoples begin in their nurseries."[1] With Erikson, students of the interactions of personality and culture contend that national character cannot be defined or explained solely in reference to the experiences of adults, whether on the frontier or in the city, whether winning bread or striving for higher social status. The modes of adult response to experience—the sense that is made of it, the ways by which problems are met or evaded, the modifications or confirmations of character that occur in consequence—are so profoundly conditioned by upbringing that it can be affirmed, without exaggeration, that the basic elements of mature character are formed in the crib, in the bathroom, and on the playground—at every point, in short, where the malleable personalities of the young are shaped by the impress of culture, mediated by parents and peers.

When Erikson wrote in 1950, behavioral scientists had already recognized the relevance of child-training to national character. Freudian and other psychoanalytic theories had been deployed, with mixed effect, in the interpretation of national character, and anthropologists such as Margaret Mead, whose trailblazing account of the *Coming of Age in Samoa* was published in 1928, had reported on the processes of personality formation among primitive peoples. Since Erikson wrote, the techniques of inquiry have been further refined, the conceptual apparatus of culture-and-personality analysis has been more fully developed, and promising efforts have been made to engage the resources of history with those of the behavioral sciences in interdisciplinary liaison.

Examples of progress in this field are furnished by the following selections from the work of two historians and an anthropologist. No historian has done more than David M. Potter of Stanford University to foster cooperation among academic disciplines in the investigation of American character. His book, *Peo-*

[1] *Childhood and Society* (New York: W. W. Norton & Company, 1950), p. 12.

144

ple of Plenty: Economic Abundance and the American Character (1954), from which the first selection is taken, shows how abundance has been a ruling factor in the shaping of personality in the United States. The second reading comes from *Americans and Chinese: Two Ways of Life* (1953), a transnational study of national character by Francis L. K. Hsu, Professor of Anthropology at Northwestern University. Born and brought up in China before World War II, Hsu calls himself a "marginal man" in whom two contrasting cultures meet: "He paces the border where they confront each other within himself, and he can reach out to touch them both." Hsu's reflections on differences in child training in these two cultures illustrate the utility of comparative analysis of national character.

Foreign observers have consistently pointed, with mingled approval and alarm, to the child-centeredness of the American family. In the third selection Richard L. Rapson, who teaches history at the University of Hawaii, traces the roots of this cultural pattern as far back as the early nineteenth century. In contemporary America, child-centeredness has been exemplified by the well known "baby book" of Dr. Benjamin Spock, from which the concluding selection is drawn. First published in 1946, Dr. Spock's manual, *Baby and Child Care*, is declared by its publisher to be the best selling American book of the twentieth century. Its author has been widely regarded as the leading proponent of permissiveness; it is therefore worth noting that in the latest edition (1968) he remarks that "the principal change that has occurred in my own outlook on child rearing has been the realization that what is making the parent's job most difficult is today's child-centered viewpoint." Another generation or two at least will be needed to show what effect, if any, this change in Dr. Spock's thinking may have on the character of Americans.

Economic Abundance and the Formation of American Character

DAVID M. POTTER

... The questions recur: What, if anything, does the factor of abundance have to do with the process of personality formation (in so far as this process is understood) in the United States? How does the process differ from that in countries where the measure of abundance is not so great?

To these questions, I believe, some highly explicit answers are possible. Let us therefore be entirely concrete. Let us consider the situation of a six-month-old American infant, who is not yet aware that he is a citizen, a taxpayer, and a consumer.

This individual is, to all appearances, just a very young specimen of *Homo sapiens,* with certain needs for protection, care, shelter, and nourishment which may be regarded as the universal biological needs of human infancy rather than specific cultural needs. It would be difficult to prove that the culture has as yet differentiated him from other infants, and, though he is an American, few would argue that he has acquired an American character. Yet abundance and the circumstances arising from abundance have already dictated a whole range of basic conditions which, from his birth, are constantly at work upon this child and which will contribute in the most intimate and basic way to the formation of his character.

To begin with, abundance has already revolutionized the typical mode of his nourishment by providing for him to be fed upon cow's milk rather than upon

Reprinted from *People of Plenty: Economic Abundance and the American Character* by David M. Potter, by permission of The University of Chicago Press. Copyright 1954 by The University of Chicago.

his mother's milk, taken from the bottle rather than from the breast. Abundance contributes vitally to this transformation, because bottle feeding requires fairly elaborate facilities of refrigeration, heating, sterilization, and temperature control, which only an advanced technology can offer and only an economy of abundance can make widely available. I will not attempt here to resolve the debated question as to the psychological effects, for both mother and child, of bottle feeding as contrasted with breast feeding in infant nurture. But it is clear that the changeover to bottle feeding has encroached somewhat upon the intimacy of the bond between mother and child. The nature of this bond is, of course, one of the most crucial factors in the formation of character. Bottle feeding also must tend to emphasize the separateness of the infant as an individual, and thus it makes, for the first time, a point which the entire culture reiterates constantly throughout the life of the average American. In addition to the psychic influences which may be involved in the manner of taking the food, it is also a matter of capital importance that the bottle-fed baby is, on the whole, better nourished than the breast-fed infant and therefore likely to grow more rapidly, to be more vigorous, and to suffer fewer ailments, with whatever effects these physical conditions may have upon his personality.

It may be argued also that abundance has provided a characteristic mode of housing for the infant and that this mode further emphasizes his separateness as an individual. In societies of scarcity, dwelling units are few and hard to come by, with the result that high proportions of newly married young people make their homes in the parental ménage, thus forming part of an "extended" family, as it is called. Moreover, scarcity provides a low ratio of rooms to individuals, with the consequence that whole families may expect as a matter of course to have but one room for sleeping, where children will go to bed in intimate propinquity to their parents. But abundance prescribes a different regime. By making it economically possible for newly married couples to maintain separate households of their own, it has almost destroyed the extended family as an institution in America and has ordained that the child shall be reared in a "nuclear" family, so-called, where his only intimate associates are his parents and his siblings, with even the latter far fewer now than in families of the past. The housing arrangements of this new-style family are suggested by census data for 1950. In that year there were 45,983,000 dwelling units to accommodate the 38,310,000 families in the United States, and, though the median number of persons in the dwelling unit was 3.1, the median number of rooms in the dwelling unit was 4.6. Eighty-four per cent of all dwelling units reported less than one person per room.[1] By providing the ordinary family with more than one room for sleeping, the economy thus produces a situation in which the child will sleep either in a

[1]Data from United States Department of Commerce, *Census of Housing: 1950*, Vol. 1, Part I (Washington: Government Printing Office, 1953), p. xxx. For purposes of enumeration kitchens were counted as rooms, but bathrooms, hallways, and pantries were not. Many dwelling units were, of course, occupied by single persons or others not falling under the definition of a family, but the number of households—43,468,000—was also less than the number of dwelling units.

room alone or in a room shared with his brothers or sisters. Even without allowing for the cases in which children may have separate rooms, these conditions mean that a very substantial percentage of children now sleep in a room alone, for, with the declining birth rate, we have reached a point at which an increasing proportion of families have one child or two children rather than the larger number which was at one time typical. For instance, in the most recent group of mothers who had completed their childbearing phase, according to the census, 19.5 per cent had had one child and 23.4 had had two. Thus almost half of all families with offspring did not have more than two children throughout their duration. In the case of the first group, all the children were "only" children throughout their childhood, and in the second group half of the children were "only" children until the second child was born. To state this in another, and perhaps a more forcible, way, it has been shown that among American women who arrived at age thirty-four during the year 1949 and who had borne children up to that time, 26.7 per cent had borne only one child, and 34.5 per cent had borne only two.[2] If these tendencies persist, it would mean that, among families where there are children, hardly one in three will have more than two children.

The census has, of course, not got around to finding out how the new-style family, in its new-style dwelling unit, adjusts the life-practice to the space situation. But it is significant that America's most widely circulated book on the care of infants advises that "it is preferable that he [the infant] not sleep in his parents' room after he is about 12 months old," offers the opinion that "it's fine for each [child] to have a room of his own, if that's possible," and makes the sweeping assertion that "it's a sensible rule not to take a child into the parents' bed for any reason."[3] It seems clear beyond dispute that the household space provided by the economy of abundance has been used to emphasize the separateness, the apartness, if not the isolation, of the American child.

Not only the nourishment and housing, but also the clothing of the American infant are controlled by American abundance. For one of the most sweeping consequences of our abundance is that, in contrast to other peoples who keep their bodies warm primarily by wearing clothes, Americans keep their bodies warm primarily by a far more expensive and even wasteful method: namely, by heating the buildings in which they are sheltered. Every American who has been abroad knows how much lighter is the clothing—especially the underclothing—of Americans than of people in countries like England and France, where the

[2]Clyde V. Kiser, "Fertility Trends in the United States," *Journal of the American Statistical Association,* XLVII (1952), 31–33. Figures given by Kiser, based on research by P. K. Whelpton, also include childless women; but my concern here is with the sibling relationships of children and not with the fertility of women, and I have therefore based my statements upon the record of women who have borne children rather than upon women of childbearing age. My statement has no way of allowing for half-brothers and sisters born of different mothers or for differentiating the number of children who survive from the number born.

[3]Benjamin Spock, *The Pocket Book of Baby and Child Care* (New York: Pocket Books, Inc., 1946), pp. 96–97.

winters are far less severe than ours, and every American who can remember the conditions of a few decades ago knows how much lighter our clothing is than that of our grandparents. These changes have occurred because clothing is no longer the principal device for securing warmth. The oil furnace has not only displaced the open fireplace; it has also displaced the woolen undergarment and the vest.

This is a matter of considerable significance for adults but of far greater importance to infants, for adults discipline themselves to wear warm garments, submitting, for instance, to woolen underwear more or less voluntarily. But the infant knows no such discipline, and his garments or bedclothes must be kept upon him by forcible means. Hence primitive people, living in outdoor conditions, swaddle the child most rigorously, virtually binding him into his clothes, and breaking him to them almost as a horse is broken to the harness. Civilized peoples mitigate the rigor but still use huge pins or clips to frustrate the baby's efforts to kick off the blankets and free his limbs. In a state of nature, cold means confinement and warmth means freedom, so far as young humans are concerned. But abundance has given the American infant physical freedom by giving him physical warmth in cold weather.

In this connection it may be surmised that abundance has also given him a permissive system of toilet training. If our forebears imposed such training upon the child and we now wait for him to take the initiative in these matters himself, it is not wholly because the former held a grim Calvinistic doctrine of child-rearing that is philosophically contrary to ours. The fact was that the circumstances gave them little choice. A mother who was taking care of several babies, keeping them clean, making their clothes, washing their diapers in her own washtub, and doing this, as often as not, while another baby was on the way, had little choice but to hasten their fitness to toilet themselves. Today, on the contrary, the disposable diaper, the diaper service, and most of all the washing machine, not to mention the fact that one baby seldom presses upon the heels of another, make it far easier for the mother to indulge the child in a regime under which he will impose his own toilet controls in his own good time.

Thus the economy of plenty has influenced the feeding of the infant, his regime, and the physical setting within which he lives. These material conditions alone might be regarded as having some bearing upon the formation of his character, but the impact of abundance by no means ends at this point. In so far as it has an influence in determining what specific individuals shall initiate the infant into the ways of man and shall provide him with his formative impressions of the meaning of being a person, it must be regarded as even more vital. When it influences the nature of the relationships between these individuals and the infant, it must be recognized as reaching to the very essence of the process of character formation.

The central figures in the dramatis personae of the American infant's universe are still his parents, and in this respect, of course, there is nothing peculiar either to the American child or to the child of abundance. But abundance has at least provided him with parents who are in certain respects unlike the parents of children born in other countries or born fifty years ago. To begin with, it has given him young parents, for the median age of fathers at the birth of the first child in American marriages (as of 1940) was 25.3 years, and the median age of mothers was 22.6 years. This median age was substantially lower than it had been in the United States in 1890 for both fathers and mothers. Moreover, as the size of families has been reduced and the wife no longer continues to bear a succession of children throughout the period of her fertility, the median age of mothers at the birth of the last child has declined from 32 years (1890) to 27 years (1940). The age of the parents at the birth of both the first child and the last child is far lower than in the case of couples in most European countries. There can be little doubt that abundance has caused this differential, in the case of the first-born by making it economically possible for a high proportion of the population to meet the expenses of homemaking at a fairly early age. In the case of the last-born, it would also appear that one major reason for the earlier cessation of childbearing is a determination by parents to enjoy a high standard of living themselves and to limit their offspring to a number for whom they can maintain a similar standard.

By the very fact of their youth, these parents are more likely to remain alive until the child reaches maturity, thus giving him a better prospect of being reared by his own mother and father. This prospect is further reinforced by increases in the life-span, so that probably no child in history has ever enjoyed so strong a likelihood that his parents will survive to rear him. Abundance has produced this situation by providing optimum conditions for prolonging life. But, on the other hand, abundance has also contributed much to produce an economy in which the mother is no longer markedly dependent upon the father, and this change in the economic relation between the sexes has probably done much to remove obstacles to divorce. The results are all too familiar. During the decade 1940–49 there were 25.8 divorces for every 100 marriages in the United States, which ratio, if projected over a longer period, would mean that one marriage out of four would end in divorce. But our concern here is with a six-month-old child, and the problem is to know whether this factor of divorce involves childless couples predominantly or whether it is likely to touch him. The answer is indicated by the fact that, of all divorces granted in 1948, no less than 42 per cent were to couples with children under eighteen, and a very large proportion of these children were of much younger ages. Hence one might say that the economy of abundance has provided the child with younger parents who chose their role of parenthood deliberately and who are more likely than parents in the past to live until he is grown, but who are substantially less likely to preserve the unbroken family as the environment within which he shall be reared.

In addition to altering the characteristics of the child's parents, it has also altered the quantitative relationship between him and his parents. It has done this, first of all, by offering the father such lucrative opportunities through work outside the home that the old agricultural economy in which children worked alongside their fathers is now obsolete. Yet, on the other hand, the father's new employment gives so much more leisure than his former work that the child may, in fact, receive considerably more of his father's attention. But the most vital transformation is in the case of the mother. In the economy of scarcity which controlled the modes of life that were traditional for many centuries, an upper-class child was reared by a nurse, and all others were normally reared by their mothers. The scarcity economy could not support many nonproductive members, and these mothers, though not "employed," were most decidedly hard workers, busily engaged in cooking, washing, sewing, weaving, preserving, caring for the henhouse, the garden, and perhaps the cow, and in general carrying on the domestic economy of a large family. Somehow they also attended to the needs of a numerous brood of children, but the mother was in a sense a full-time attendant upon any one child. Today, however, the economy of abundance very nearly exempts a very large number of mothers from the requirement of economic productivity in order that they may give an unprecedented share of their time to the care of the one or two young children who are now the usual number in an American family. Within the home, the wide range of labor-saving devices and the assignment of many functions, such as laundering, to service industries have produced this result. Outside the home, employment of women in the labor force has steadily increased, but the incidence of employment falls upon unmarried women, wives without children, and wives with grown children. In fact, married women without children are two and one-half times as likely to be employed as those with children. Thus what amounts to a new dispensation has been established for the child. If he belongs to the upper class, his mother has replaced his nurse as a full-time attendant. The differences in character formation that might result from this change alone could easily be immense. To mention but one possibility, the presence of the nurse must inevitably have made the child somewhat aware of his class status, whereas the presence of the mother would be less likely to have this effect. If the child does not belong to the upper class, mother and child now impinge upon each other in a relationship whose intensity is of an entirely different magnitude from that which prevailed in the past. The mother has fewer physical distractions in the care of the child, but she is more likely to be restive in her maternal role because it takes her away from attractive employment with which it cannot be reconciled.

If abundance has thus altered the relationship of the child with his parent, it has even more drastically altered the rest of his social milieu, for it has changed the identity of the rest of the personnel who induct him into human society. In the extended family of the past, a great array of kinspeople filled his cosmos and guided him to maturity. By nature, he particularly needed association with children of his own age (his "peers," as they are called), and he particularly responded to the values asserted by these peers. Such peers were very often his brothers and sisters, and, since they were all members of his own family, all came under parental control. This is to say that, in a sense, the parents controlled the peer group, and the peer group controlled the child. The point is worth making because we frequently encounter the assertion that parental control of the child has been replaced by peer-group control; but it is arguable that what is really the case is that children were always deeply influenced by the peer group and that parents have now lost their former measure of control over this group, since it is no longer a familial group. Today the nursery school replaces the large family as a peer group, and the social associations, even of young children, undergo the same shift from focused contact with family to diffused contact with a miscellany of people, which John Galsworthy depicted for grown people in the three novels of the *Forsyte Saga*. Again, the effects upon character may very well be extensive.

Abundance, then, has played a critical part in revolutionizing both the physical circumstances and the human associations which surround the American infant and child. These changes alone would warrant the hypothesis that abundance has profoundly affected the formation of character for such a child. But to extend this inquiry one step further, it may be worth while to consider how these altered conditions actually impinge upon the individual. Here, of course, is an almost unlimited field for investigation, and I shall only attempt to indicate certain crucial points at which abundance projects conditions that are basic in the life of the child.

One of these points concerns the cohesive force which holds the family together. The family is the one institution which touches all members of society most intimately, and it is perhaps the only social institution which touches young children directly. The sources from which the family draws its strength are, therefore, of basic importance. In the past, these sources were, it would seem, primarily economic. For agrarian society, marriage distinctively involved a division of labor. Where economic opportunity was narrowly restricted, the necessity for considering economic ways and means in connection with marriage led to the arrangement of matches by parents and to the institution of the dowry. The emotional bonds of affection, while always important, were not deemed paramount, and the ideal of romantic love played little or no part in the lives of ordinary people. Where it existed at all, it was as an upper-class luxury. (The very term "courtship" implies this upper-class orientation.) This must inevitably have meant that the partners in the majority of marriages demanded less from one another emotionally than do the partners of romantic love and that the emotional factor was less important to the stability of the marriage. Abundance, however, has played its part in changing this picture. On the American frontier, where capital for dowries was as rare as opportunity for prosperous marriage was plentiful, the dowry became obsolete. Later still, when abundance began to diminish the economic duties imposed upon the housewife, the function of marriage as a division of labor ceased to seem paramount, and the romantic or emotional factor assumed increasing importance. Abundance brought the luxury of romantic love within the reach of all, and, as it did so, emotional harmony became the principal criterion of success in a marriage, while lack of such harmony became a major threat to the existence of the marriage. The statistics of divorce give us a measure of the loss of durability in marriage, but they give us no measure of the factors of instability in the marriages which endure and no measure of the increased focus upon emotional satisfactions in such marriages. The children of enduring marriages, as well as the children of divorce, must inevitably feel the impact of this increased emphasis upon emotional factors, must inevitably sense the difference in the foundations of the institution which holds their universe in place.

In the rearing of a child, it would be difficult to imagine any factors more vital than the distinction between a permissive and an authoritarian regime or more vital than the age at which economic responsibility is imposed. In both these matters the modern American child lives under a very different dispensation from children in the past. We commonly think of these changes as results of our more enlightened or progressive or humanitarian ideas. We may even think of them as results of developments in the specific field of child psychology, as if the changes were simply a matter of our understanding these matters better than our grandparents. But the fact is that the authoritarian discipline of the child, within the authoritarian family, was but an aspect of the authoritarian social system that was linked with the economy of scarcity. Such a regime could never have been significantly relaxed within the family so long as it remained diagnostic in the society. Nor could it have remained unmodified within the family, once society began to abandon it in other spheres.

Inevitably, the qualities which the parents inculcate in a child will depend upon the roles which they occupy themselves. For the ordinary man the economy of scarcity has offered one role, as Simon N. Patten observed many years ago, and the economy of abundance has offered another. Abundance offers "work calling urgently for workmen"; scarcity found the "worker seeking humbly any kind of toil."[4] As a suppliant to his superiors, the worker under scarcity accepted the principle of authority; he accepted his own subordination and the obligation to cultivate the qualities appropriate to his subordination, such as submissiveness, obedience, and deference. Such a man naturally transferred the principle of authority into his own family and, through this principle, instilled into his children the qualities appropriate to people of their kind—submissiveness, obedience, and deference. Many copybook maxims still exist to remind us of the firmness of childhood discipline, while the difference between European and American children—one of the most clearly recognizable of all national differences—serves to emphasize the extent to which Americans have now departed from this firmness.

This new and far more permissive attitude toward children has arisen, significantly, in an economy of abundance, where work has called urgently for the workman. In this situation, no longer a suppliant, the workman found submis-

---

[4]Simon Nelson Patten, *The New Basis of Civilization* (New York: Macmillan Co., 1907), pp. 187–88. I am indebted to Arthur Schlesinger, Jr., for calling my attention to Patten's important observations on this subject.

siveness no longer a necessity and therefore no longer a virtue. The principle of authority lost some of its majesty, and he was less likely to regard it as the only true criterion of domestic order. In short, he ceased to impose it upon his children. Finding that the most valuable trait in himself was a capacity for independent decision and self-reliant conduct in dealing with the diverse opportunities which abundance offered him, he tended to encourage this quality in his children. The irresponsibility of childhood still called for a measure of authority on one side and obedience on the other, but this became a means to an end and not an end in itself. On the whole, permissive training, to develop independent ability, even though it involves a certain sacrifice of obedience and discipline, is the characteristic mode of child-rearing in the one country which most distinctively enjoys an economy of abundance. Here, in a concrete way, one finds something approaching proof for Gerth and Mills's suggestion that the relation of father and child may have its importance not as a primary factor but rather as a "replica of the power relations of society."

If scarcity required men to "seek humbly any kind of toil," it seldom permitted women to seek employment outside the home at all. Consequently, the woman was economically dependent upon, and, accordingly, subordinate to, her husband or her father. Her subordination reinforced the principle of authority within the home. But the same transition which altered the role of the male worker has altered her status as well, for abundance "calling urgently for workmen" makes no distinctions of gender, and, by extending economic independence to women, has enabled them to assume the role of partners rather than of subordinates within the family. Once the relation of voluntarism and equality is introduced between husband and wife, it is, of course, far more readily extended to the relation between parent and child.

If abundance has fostered a more permissive regime for the child, amid circumstances of democratic equality within the family, it has no less certainly altered the entire process of imposing economic responsibility upon the child, hence the process of preparing the child for such responsibility. In the economy of scarcity, as I have remarked above, society could not afford to support any substantial quota of nonproductive members. Consequently, the child went to work when he was as yet young. He attended primary school for a much shorter school year than the child of today; only a minority attended high school; and only the favored few attended college. Even during the brief years of schooling, the child worked, in the home, on the farm, or even in the factory. But today the economy of abundance can afford to maintain a substantial proportion of the population in nonproductive status, and it assigns this role, sometimes against their will, to its younger and its elder members. It protracts the years of schooling, and it defers responsibilities for an unusually long span. It even enforces laws setting minimal ages for leaving school, for going to work, for consenting to sexual intercourse, or for marrying. It extends the jurisdiction of juvenile courts to the eighteenth or the twentieth year of age.

Such exemption from economic responsibility might seem to imply a long and blissful youth free from strain for the child. But the delays in reaching economic maturity are not matched by comparable delays in other phases of growing up. On the contrary, there are many respects in which the child matures earlier. Physically, the child at the lower social level will actually arrive at adolescence a year or so younger than his counterpart a generation ago, because of improvement in standards of health and nutrition.[5] Culturally, the child is made aware of the allurements of sex at an earlier age, partly by his familiarity with the movies, television, and popular magazines, and partly by the practice of "dating" in the early teens. By the standards of his peer group, he is encouraged to demand expensive and mature recreations, similar to those of adults, at a fairly early age. By reason of the desire of his parents that he should excel in the mobility race and give proof during his youth of the qualities which will make him a winner in later life, he is exposed to the stimuli of competition before he leaves the nursery. Thus there is a kind of imbalance between the postponement of responsibility and the quickening of social maturity which may have contributed to make American adolescence a more difficult age than human biology alone would cause it to be. Here, again, there are broad implications for the formation of character, and here, again, abundance is at work on both sides of the equation, for it contributes as much to the hastening of social maturity as it does to the prolongation of economic immaturity.

Some of these aspects of the rearing of children in the United States are as distinctively American, when compared with other countries, as any Yankee traits that have ever been attributed to the American people. In the multiplicity which always complicates social analysis, such aspects of child-rearing might be linked with a number of factors in American life. But one of the more evident and more significant links, it would seem certain, is with the factor of abundance. Such a tie is especially pertinent in this discussion, where the intention of the whole book has been to relate the study of character, as the historian would approach it, to the same subject as it is viewed by the behavioral scientist. In this chapter, especially, the attempt has been made to throw a bridge between the general historical force of economic abundance and the specific behavioral pattern of people's lives. Historical forces are too often considered only in their public and over-all effects, while private lives are interpreted without sufficient reference to the historical determinants which shape them. But no major force at work in society can possibly make itself felt at one of these levels without also having its impact at the other level. In view of this fact, the study of national character should not stand apart, as it has in the past, from the study of the process of character formation in the individual. In view of this fact, also, the effect of economic abundance is especially pertinent. For economic abundance is a factor whose presence and whose force may be clearly and precisely recognized in the most personal and intimate phases of the development of personality in

[5]Alfred C. Kinsey et al., *Sexual Behavior in the Human Male* (Philadelphia: W. B. Saunders Co., 1948), p. 397.

the child. Yet, at the same time, the presence and the force of this factor are recognizable with equal certainty in the whole broad, general range of American experience, American ideals, and American institutions. At both levels, it has exercised a pervasive influence in the shaping of the American character.

Americans and Chinese: The Beginnings of Contrast

FRANCIS L. K. HSU

How have Chinese and Americans acquired their contrasting ways of life? I am convinced that the most plausible and probable answer to this question must be broadly Freudian. That is, these contrasts are to be found first and foremost in the family, the first external mold of the vast majority of mankind.

All students of man today accept the general theorem that, except for extreme cases such as geniuses and idiots, personality is chiefly the result of conditioning by culture. Personality is the sum total of the individual's characteristic reactions to his environment, while culture consists of the accepted patterns of behavior in every society. The contrasts between Chinese and American ways of life may be viewed, therefore, as contrasts between the sum totals in their respective personality and culture.

The personality of the individual and the culture of his society are by no means identical. No individual is an automaton, just as no society is without variation. However, each society offers rewards to those of its members who act according to its accepted pattern of behavior and it punishes those who do not.

Since cultural conditioning begins in the family, it is logical for us to inquire first into the broad contrasts in the family systems in which the two ways of life are taught and propagated.

In doing so, however, we must exercise great restraint. There is ample temptation to stretch Freudian theory to absurd lengths. Gregory Bateson, a British anthropologist, suggested, for example, that British and American attitudes toward their respective colonies are copies of the respective parent-child rela-

Reprinted with permission from Francis L. K. Hsu, *Americans and Chinese: Two Ways of Life* (New York: Abelard-Schuman, 1953). A new enlarged edition (new subtitle: *Purpose and Fulfillment in Great Civilizations)* is scheduled for publication by The Natural History Press, New York City.

tionships in the two countries. The American parents encourage in their children "certain sorts of boastful and exhibitionistic behavior, while still in a position somewhat subordinate to and dependent upon the parents," but in England the parent-child relationship is characterized by "dominance and succoring." The American parent-child relationship "contains within itself factors for psychologically weaning the child, while in England, among the upper classes, the analogous breaking of the succoring dependent link has to be performed by . . . the boarding school." Since "colonies cannot be sent to a boarding school . . . England has very great difficulty in weaning her non-Anglo Saxon colonies, while these colonies have had corresponding difficulty in attaining maturity—in sharp contrast with the history of the Philippines."[1]

Geoffrey Gorer, another British anthropologist, is equally daring. He considers America's two houses of Congress as a sort of extension of a certain sibling relationship in the American family. The House, being the younger brother of the family, is erratic and less responsible in its actions, knowing full well that the Senate, its older brother, will come to its rescue.[2]

Neither of these are examples of true science or even of sound logic. To avoid such pitfalls, we shall, instead of concentrating on details (which tend to vary because of geography, class, occupation, and many other factors), look at the broader phases of the family pattern in which the two peoples differ greatly, but consistently.

The Home

Let us begin with Chinese and American homes. An American house usually has a yard, large or small. It may have a hedge, but rarely is there a wall so high that a passer-by cannot see the windows. The majority of American houses have neither hedge nor wall whatsoever. Usually the interior is shielded from exterior view only by window curtains or blinds, and then during but part of the day.

The majority of Chinese houses are, in the first place, surrounded by such high walls that only the roofs are visible from the outside, and solid gates separate the interior grounds from the outside world. In addition there is usually a shadow wall placed directly in front of the gates on the other side of the street[3] as well as a four-leafed wooden screen standing about five feet behind the gates. The outside shadow wall keeps the home from direct exposure to the unseen spirits. The inside wooden screen shields the interior courtyard from pedestrians' glances when the gates are ajar.

Inside the home, the contrast between China and America is reversed. The

---

[1] Gregory Bateson, "Some Systematic Approaches to the Study of Culture and Personality," in *Character and Personality*, 11:76–82, 1942, reprinted in D. Haring, *Personal Character and Social Milieu*, 1949, pp. 110–16.

[2] Geoffrey Gorer, *The American People*, N.Y., 1949.

[3] Many streets are lined with houses on one side only. Where both sides of the street are occupied, it is still possible to erect shadow walls since home entrances do not as a rule directly face each other.

American emphasis within the home is on privacy. There are not only doors to the bathrooms but also to the bedrooms, to the living room, and even to the kitchen. Space and possessions are individualized. Thus parents have little liberty in the rooms of the children, and children cannot do what they want in those parts of the house regarded as pre-eminently the domain of the parents. Among some sections of the American population this rule of privacy extends to the husband and wife, so that each has a separate bedroom.

Within the Chinese home, on the other hand, privacy hardly exists at all, except between opposite sexes who are not spouses. Chinese children, even in the homes which have ample room, tend to share the same chambers with their parents until they reach adolescence. Not only do parents have freedom of action with reference to the children's belongings, but the youngsters can also use the possessions of the parents if they can lay their hands on them. If children damage their parents' possessions they are scolded not because they touched things that were not theirs but because they are too young to handle them with proper care.

The lack of privacy within the home finds its extreme expression in many well-to-do families of North China. Here the rooms are arranged in rows like the cars of a train. But instead of each room having a separate entrance, all the rooms are arranged in sequence, one leading into another. Thus, if there are five rooms, the front door of the house opens into the center room, which serves as the kitchen and dining room. There are two doors on opposite walls of the kitchen, each leading into a room which has in turn another door opening into the end rooms. Beginning at one end of the house, call it room A, one can walk in a straight line from there to room B, into the kitchen-dining room C, into room D, and finally into room E. The parents will occupy room B, nearest the kitchen, leaving room A free for a married daughter when she and her children come for a prolonged visit. If the family has two married sons, the older brother and his wife and children will occupy room D, while the younger brother and his wife will occupy room E. The occupants of rooms A and E will have to cross, respectively, rooms B and D in order to go in and out of the house. Actual arrangements vary somewhat from family to family, but this simplified picture is generally true.

Such an arrangement in living quarters would be very offensive to Americans. For even within the family Americans hew to the line as to what is yours and what is mine. But many Chinese adhere to a variation of the common linear arrangement even when they have more rooms in which to spread out. For they consider all within the four walls as being one body. The American child's physical environment establishes strong lines of individual distinction within the home but there is very little stress on separation of the home from the community. The Chinese child's environment is exactly the reverse. He finds a home with few demarcation lines within it but separated by high walls and multiple gates from the outside world.

Parents and Children

The difference between Chinese and American homes reflects their contrasting patterns of behavior in the family. In no country on earth is there so much attention paid to infancy[4] and so much privilege accorded childhood as in the United States. From every point of view this country is a paradise on earth for children. In contrast, it may be said without exaggeration that China is a country in which children come last.

The contrast can be seen in a myriad of ways. Americans are very verbal about their children's rights. There is not only state and federal legislation to protect the young ones, but there are also various juvenile protective associations to look after their welfare. Not only is infanticide treated like murder, but parents can get into legal trouble if they discipline their children with some enthusiasm.

In China parents have a completely free hand with their children. Popular misconception notwithstanding, infanticide has always been rare in China, and certainly no parents would brag about it. Yet even in modern times parents who have committed infanticide have almost always been free from legal action. It is literally true that from the viewpoint of American children, parents have practically no rights; but from the viewpoint of Chinese parents, children have little reason to expect protection from their elders. If an American were to point with justifiable pride to his country's many child protective associations, a Chinese would simply counter with an equally proud boast about his nation's numerous "societies for saving papers with written characters on" or "societies for giving away coffins."

American parents are so concerned with the welfare of their children, and they are so determined to do the right thing, that they handsomely support a huge number of child specialists, scientific or quack, to supply them with advice on what children like best. Chinese parents have taken their children so much for granted that pediatrics as a separate branch of medicine was unknown until modern times. As far as I know there is no piece of traditional literature aimed at making the Chinese better parents, and even during the days of the Republic there was hardly any scientific inquiry into what the children might think and desire. Articles on how to treat children appeared only sporadically in a few Chinese newspapers and magazines.

But Americans do not only study their children's behavior—they glorify it.

[4]The attention-attracting value of children's photographs, recognized both by advertisers and the proverbial baby-kissing politician, is confirmed as well by newspaper readership surveys. In September 1947, the Journalism Quarterly published figures on reader reaction to 2,200 general news photographs published in newspapers from coast to coast. Among males, pictures in the "children and baby" category caught the attention of 59 percent, which was a slightly higher response than that produced by the photo categories of "beauty queens and glamor girls," "international and general news," "accidents and disasters" (each 58 percent), and even "sports" (57 percent). Among women, the children's photos attracted the attention of 77 percent, slightly lower than the "weddings and engagements" classification (79 percent) but somewhat above the "society and club news" category (76 percent).

Chinese do not only take their children for granted—they minimize them. The important thing to Americans is what parents should do for their children; to Chinese, what children should do for their parents.

The American emphasis on children has gone so far that even strangers can interfere with parents without regard to the circumstances. An Eastern European immigrant friend of mine once related to me the following experience. He was riding in an elevated train with his six-year-old son. The youngster continued to ignore his cautions against standing close to the entrance. He cuffed the boy a few times. Thereupon another passenger arose, advanced menacingly and said angrily: "If you dare to strike that child again I'll have you arrested."

The extent to which some American parents go to suit the convenience of their children is exemplified by a mid-Western couple I know. To make their little ones happy, they installed a fancy slide in their living room. Guests entered the apartment by bending under it, and then they attempted to enjoy a conversation within reach of the boisterous sideshow provided by the young ones going up and down.

That this is unusual even for the United States is indicated by the fact that this couple felt compelled to justify their action every time they had a visitor and by the fact that their friends remarked about it. On the other hand, no Chinese parents could have kept the respect of the community if they permitted anything remotely resembling this.

For many centuries Chinese were both entertained and instructed by some tales known as "The Twenty-Four Examples of Filial Piety." These stories were illustrated in paintings, dramatized on the stage, recited by story-tellers in tea houses and in market places all over the country. Here is one of these "examples":

A poor man by the name of Kuo and his wife were confronted with a serious problem. His aged mother was sick in bed. She needed both medicine and nourishment which Kuo could ill afford. After consultation between themselves, Kuo and his wife decided that the only way out was to get rid of their three-year-old only son. For Kuo and his wife said to each other. 'We have only one mother, but we can always get another child.' Thereupon the two went out to the field to dig a pit for the purpose of burying their child alive. But shortly after the man had started to dig he suddenly struck gold. It transpired that the gods were moved by the spirit of their filial piety, and this was their reward. Both the child and the mother were amply provided for and the family thrived happily ever after.

To the Chinese this story dramatized their most important cultural ideal, that support of the parents tops all other obligations and that this obligation must be fulfilled even at the expense of the children.

Economic support is not, however, the only way in which Chinese children are obligated to their parents. Their social duty toward their parents is even more striking. The son not only has to follow the Confucian dictum that "parents are always right," but at all times and in all circumstances he must try to satisfy their wishes and look after their safety. If the parents are indisposed, the son should spare no trouble in obtaining a cure for them. If a parent is sentenced to prison, the son must arrange to take that parent's place. If the parents are displeased with their daughter-in-law, the good son does not hesitate to think about divorce. In the service of the elders, no effort is too extraordinary or too great.

Here again folktales are useful indications of the actual values. One classical story tells how a man gave up his hard-won official post in order to walk many miles in search of his long-lost mother. Another tells how a youngster of four-teen jumped on and strangled a tiger when the beast was about to devour his father. In a third story, a man cut a piece of flesh from his arm and boiled it in the pot with his father's medicine, believing that the soup would help the elder to recover from his long illness. Yet another tells us:

When the mother of the dutiful Wang Low was still alive in the days of the Wei dynasty, she was greatly afraid of thunder. After her death she was buried in a mountain forest. Whenever Low heard a thunderstorm he immediately ran to the graveyard, kneeled, and tearfully said: 'Low is here, Mother, do not be afraid.'

Moreover, many Chinese stories did not remain mere literature but were sometimes copied to the letter by over-filial sons. In the thousands of volumes of district histories and genealogical records to be found in every part of the country are many individual biographies of local greats. After a cursory reading of about fifty of them, I found at least five instances in which men and women were said to have sliced flesh from their arms to be boiled in the medicine pot of one or another of their parents. One man did this twice during one of his father's illnesses. Because the elder's condition remained serious, the filial son decided to take a more drastic course of action. He cut out a piece of what he thought was his "liver" instead. Both he and his father died shortly afterwards. Hundreds of other biographies contain less dramatic episodes, but all are variations on the same theme.

It is not suggested that all Chinese youngsters are indoctrinated in filial piety on the day of their birth, or that more than a handful of American parents have ever had occasion to be rebuked by strangers for the way they handled their own children. It is important to realize, however, that incidents and lore like the ones given are symptomatic of the different social climates in which parents and children in the two countries react to one another.

Given the American type of atmosphere, parents do not only wish to help their children according to the parents' experiences. They must try to find out by elaborate research what the youngsters really want, so that the elders can better satisfy the youngsters' individual predilections. Although it is true that children all over the world are inclined to play, American parents do not stop at giving their children every conceivable kind of toy. They feel compelled to reduce even the rudiments of a child's education to a matter of fun. Recently I came across two books advertised as *Playbooks That Teach Your Child to Dress,* one for boys and one for girls.

The toy industry of America rose from an annual business of a mere $150,000,000 in 1939 to $750,000,000 in 1951. We may expect that this figure will increase in the next decade because of the increasing number of commercially profitable events such as local "baby weeks," the acceleration of learning by playing, and the coming and going of fashions in playthings as in other products. The annual business catering to all infant needs has reached, in 1951, an astronomical $5,000,000,000. Television today, as has radio for years, has scores of programs designed for children. Their announcers advise the kiddies to tell parents that they will eat nothing but "Snapcrackles" for breakfast. The children do so, and most parents obey by purchasing the desired product.

The relations of Chinese parents and children exhibit none of these tendencies. Chinese parents are amused by infantile behavior and youthful exuberance, but the measure of their children's worth is determined primarily by the degree to which they act like adults. The sooner they do so the better. Chinese parents are rather proud of a child who acts "older than his age" where American parents are likely to take a similar child to a specialist. Or Chinese parents are apt to be upset by certain aspects of a child's behavior which would bring joy to American parents.

Take toys again for an example. Chinese children occasionally receive a toy. When I was six years of age my mother bought me a cart made of tinfoil. Soldered above the entrance to the cart was an ornamental rectangle. Having seen movable curtains on real carts, I attempted to lower the curtain at the entrance of my toy cart and yanked the stationary ornament out of place. An American mother would have gloated over the creative impulse of her "budding genius"; but my mother was very much displeased because she thought me destructive and temperamental. Had I acted the model child that the Chinese mother hoped for, by nursing one old toy for a couple of years, an American mother might have worried about the retarded or warped state of my mind.

The specific mechanisms through which Chinese and American children begin their contrasting ways of life are many. To begin with, the average size of the Chinese family is, contrary to popular belief, about five persons. The average number in an American family is three. More important than size is the fact that when an American speaks of a family he refers to a group composed of parents and unmarried children, whereas the Chinese term for family includes grandparents and in-laws. Even if Chinese grandparents and in-laws do not live under the same roof, they usually reside in the same village, a neighboring village, or at the farthest a neighboring district. On the other hand, Americans related by blood or legal bonds usually live so far from one another that this broader group does not come together except on such occasions as Easter, Thanksgiving, Christmas, or other holidays.

These differences mark the point of departure in the early experiences of Chinese and American children. The Chinese child grows up amidst continuing or frequent contacts with a number of related individuals besides his own parents and siblings, but his American counterpart grows up in much greater physical isolation. Very early in life the former is conditioned to appreciate the importance of getting along with a wide circle of relatives while the latter is not.

Far more crucial, however, is the manner of interaction between the growing child and individuals other than those making up his immediate family. American parents are the sole agents of control over their children until the latter are of age. The grandparents and in-laws do not ordinarily occupy a disciplinary role, whether they live in the same house or not. Even when grandparents take over during an emergency such as sickness or childbirth, the older people are supposed to do no more than administer things according to the laws laid down by the younger couple, more likely by the younger woman. The usual response of an American elder to any request made by his or her little grandchild is, "Does your mother want you to?" When control is exercised over an American child, it is the parental arm that does so, no other.

Chinese parents have much less exclusive control over their children. In cases where grandparents do not share the same roof with them, during a brief visit the older couple can do almost anything that they see fit in regard to the children, even if it means going over the parents' heads. The liberty taken by most Chinese aunts, uncles, and in-laws might break up most American families. Furthermore, while an American mother exhibits her displeasure with an over-indulgent grandmother and is considered right by others, a Chinese mother doing the same thing is an object of censure rather than sympathy. The strength of the Chinese parental authority, far from being overpowering, usually varies with circumstances.

The inevitable result of the omnipresent and exclusive control of American parents over their children is greater and deeper emotional involvement. Since parents are all-powerful, their images in the mind of the growing child naturally are elevated above all else. To the extent that they are the only objects of worship, they also are liable to become the only oppressors. Accordingly, when an American child likes his parents, they are his idols. When he dislikes them, they are his enemies. A conscious or unconscious attachment to one parent at the expense of the other, a situation which gave Freud ground for postulating his famed Oedipus complex, is the extreme expression of this situation.

Not knowing the American kind of close and exclusive relationship, the mutual affection of Chinese parents and children is toned down. Since parental authority varies with circumstances, the parental image in the mind of the growing child must necessarily share the spotlight with men and women held in much higher esteem, such as grandparents, and with those regarded as the equals of the parents, such as uncles and aunts. The feeling toward parents being divided and diluted, the child does not develop a paralyzing attachment to, or strong repulsion against, the elders. There is still less reason for the emergence of the Oedipal triangle, in which the child is allied to one parent against the other. Consequently, when the Chinese child likes his parents he fails to raise them to high heaven; when he dislikes them he still vents his displeasure with great reserve.

Contrary to popular belief, it is a fact that Chinese parents, though much more respected, revered, or even feared by their children than are American parents by theirs, actually leave much less of an impression on the character of their progeny, since the parent-child relationship is neither so close nor so emotionally charged.

The beginnings of the contrasts between the two ways of life now become apparent. In the American scene the child soon learns to follow his own predilections. For his environment is sensitive to *him*. In the Chinese scene the child soon learns to appreciate the importance of changing circumstances. For he is obliged to be sensitive to his *environment.*

Similarly, the American child tends to develop strong feelings of love or hate. For the exclusive parent-child bond inevitably concentrates emotions at a few points. The Chinese child tends to moderate his feelings in general. For his diffused relationship with parents and relatives likewise tempers his emotional involvements.

As Chinese and American children grow older the contrast between their experiences is intensified. American parents encourage their children to do things for themselves. At the age of three or four, American children are exhorted to be big boys and girls, to dress themselves, feed themselves, and defend themselves against bullies.

Chinese parents are pleased if their children can do any of these or similar things. They do not, however, make a point of encouraging them or bragging about them. As to defending themselves, the characteristic advice to Chinese children is "don't get into trouble outside, and run home if there is danger."

Yet, though consciously encouraging their children to grow up in some ways, American parents firmly refuse to let the youngsters enter the real world of the adults. For one thing, they leave their children with sitters when they go to parties. If they entertain at home they put the youngsters to bed before the guests arrive. Children have no part in parents' social activities.

Chinese parents take their children with them not only to wedding feasts, funeral breakfasts, and religious celebrations, but also to purely social or business gatherings. A father in business thinks nothing of bringing his boy of six or seven to an executives' conference.

This pattern is still adhered to by the majority of second, third and fourth generation Chinese-Americans in Hawaii. Like their Caucasian neighbors, Chinese organizers in Hawaii also resort to "family picnics" and "family evenings" and even athletics for the purpose of maintaining or increasing club or church enrollment. But, unlike their Caucasian neighbors, Chinese parents in Hawaii take their very young children with them on many more occasions, for example on social and business visits which regularly last until late at night.

The result is that while Chinese youngsters unobtrusively enter into the world of the adults, American youngsters tend to develop a world of their own. This is further accentuated by the Chinese parents' insistence on complete community of interests with children, as much as by the American parents' insistence on privacy for all individuals.

The business of American parents, social and commercial, is their private reserve, and no trespassing by children is allowed except on those rare and eventful occasions when an explicit invitation is extended. Newspaper "psychologists" frequently advise that a well-adjusted personality will result if parents do not burden their children with adult difficulties. By the same token, parents are also supposed to refrain from entering into the doings of their youngsters. These same advisors admonish worried mothers to disappear when their teen-age daughters entertain at home.

Not so among the Chinese. Chinese children consider it a matter of course to witness or even participate in adult negotiations, exactly as Chinese adults think nothing about joining in their children's activities. This reciprocity goes so far that neither has any qualms about opening letters addressed to the other.

Nothing is more strikingly symbolic of these profound differences than the fact that American children celebrate their birthdays among themselves, their parents being assistants or servants, while Chinese children's birthdays are occasions for adult celebration, in which children may be present, as in wedding or funeral feasts, but they are certainly not the center of attraction.

The line of demarcation between the adult and the child worlds is drawn in many other ways. For instance, many American parents may be totally divorced from the church, or entertain grave doubts about the existence of God, but they send their children to Sunday schools and help them to pray. American parents struggle in a world of tough competition where sheer cunning and falsehood are often rewarded and respected, but they feed their children with nursery tales in which the morally good is pitted against the bad, and in the end the good is invariably rewarded and the bad inevitably punished. When American parents are in serious domestic trouble, they maintain a front of sweetness and light before their children. Even if American parents suffer a major business catastrophe, they feel obliged to turn their tearful eyes to their children and fake a smile, saying, "Honey, everything is all right." This American desire to maintain the children's world separate from that of the adults is exemplified also by the practice of delaying transmission of the news to children when their parents have been killed in an accident, or concealing the facts from them when one of the parents goes to jail. Thus, in summary, American parents face a world of reality while their children live in the near ideal realm of the fairy tales where the rules of the parental world do not apply, are watered down, or are even reversed.

Chinese children, however, share the same world with their parents. While there is not complete accord between what Chinese parents teach and what they do, for all human beings are prone to leave some gap between the lesson and the deed, parents make little effort to hide their problems and real selves from their children. In triumph the children celebrate with the adults; in disaster the little ones suffer with them. Very early in life Chinese children learn that reward and punishment are not necessarily consistent with the established rules of conduct, and that justice and love do not always prevail. Yet at the same time they are more likely than American children to become conscious of the power exercised by the environment. For theirs is an environment that is very exposed, and young eyes without blinkers see their parents' faults as well as their virtues. From the beginning they see their parents not as giants astride the earth, moving mountains and slaying dragons, which is the American child's Bunyanesque interpretation of the scene, but as ordinary mortals succeeding at times but failing at others, following inevitably the paths marked by custom and tradition.

Thus the American child is not only increasingly convinced of the importance of his individual predilections, he is equally sure that no eventuality can deter him, the invincible individual, from realizing them in thought or action. In his restricted and comforting world he has experienced few irreparable setbacks and known few situations in which he is entirely frustrated by reality. Just as joy and good proceed from the parents, who focus upon themselves all attention and draw to themselves all power, it is they alone who can impose restrictions that the child may see as barriers to his own advancement.

The Chinese child is not only fully aware that he should obey his parents and other seniors, but even when he succeeds in circumventing them he still faces the hurdles presented by custom and tradition. Through his active observation of and participation in adult activities, he is already well versed, by hard knocks on the head, in his own shortcomings and the real nature of his society. The foci of attention and power being many, the restrictions imposed upon the individual come not from the parents, but the society at large. Even if he resents these barriers he can still see no point at which to center his attack, for they are too numerous and too diffuse.

. . . .

Chinese school children . . . are not shocked by injustice, slights, or untruths because they have experienced or learned to expect these trials. At 12 or 14 most of them are not merely acquainted with their future places and problems in society—they are already full-fledged members of society and have known its tribulations and disappointments.

This realistic orientation is assisted further by the Chinese ideal of mutual dependence, which is the exact opposite of the American spirit of self-reliance. In a previous connection we noted that the Chinese son has to support his father. We must now point out that the Chinese father is no less bound to the support of his son. This reciprocal obligation is a social contract that lasts for life. The idea of a legal "will" is alien to Chinese thought. A Chinese father's assets, no less than his liabilities, automatically and equally go to his several sons before or after his death.[5]

[5]This pattern survives today in spite of laws to the contrary. Even as late as 1944 villagers could not dispose of their property without consent of their adult male children.

The Chinese child learns about this in diverse ways. For one thing, he never has to manage an allowance.[6] He is free to spend whatever he can get out of his parents. The idea of earning money from one's parents is considered laughable by Chinese. Consequently, while necessity causes poor Chinese children to learn the value of money, youngsters from wealthier families have little financial worry in sight.

The social tie between Chinese parents and sons is equally automatic, irretrievable, and lasting for the lifetime of all parties. A proverb truly expresses the essence of the pattern: "First thirty years, one looks at the father and respects the son; second thirty years, one looks at the son and respects the father." That is to say, while the son is young the father's social status determines that of the son; but later the son's social status determines that of the father.

For this reason the sons of the powerful, however young, are as powerful as their fathers, while the fathers can, even after retirement, always wield the authority derived from the position of their sons. Thus the son of a Chinese warlord always commanded, and was respected, as a little warlord, just as the father of a Chinese emperor was unquestionably a sort of super-emperor.

Furthermore, while the American father who basks in his son's glory or the son who profits from his father's fame will always object to any suggestion that this is the real situation, a similarly situated Chinese father or son has no such desire to conceal his source of strength. In case the identity of such an individual is temporarily obscured, he is likely to glorify it in just so many words. Karl Eskelund, a Danish news reporter, in his book, *My Chinese Wife* (N.Y., 1945), tells of a fight he had one night in Chungking during World War II. Instead of returning blow for blow, his young Chinese opponent shouted: "Do you know who I am? I am Chiang Ching-Kuo—the Generalissimo's son!"

The performance of Chiang's offspring may seem cowardly to most Americans. But most Chinese would understand that it befitted the exalted station of his father. In fact, he did not even have to be the Generalissimo's son. The Generalissimo's nephews, or remoter relatives, if there were any, could also act similarly.

Thus the Chinese pattern of mutual dependence, instead of encouraging self-reliance, induces satisfaction in reliance. For the parent-child ties are permanent rather than transitory. It is taken for granted that they are immutable, and so not subject to individual acceptance or rejection. Secure in the shadow of their ancestors, Chinese youngsters at school age have no great psychological urge to seek any alliance outside the kin group.

For Chinese youngsters, therefore, the call of the gang possesses none of the dictatorial compulsion that it has for their American brethren. It is not that Chinese boys and girls will purposely differ from their schoolmates or friends.

---

[6]In some parts of China, married sons each have a yearly allowance from the head of the family called something like "clothes money." This sum meets the clothing and other pocket expenses of the man and his wife. But if there is only one son in the family, he may spend as much as the family can afford.

But they seem to get along with their play groups without having to part with the things their parents represent. My own experience illustrates the point. When my parents moved their home from a South Manchurian village to an East Manchurian town I was for the first time in my life confronted with a dialect difference. My first grade schoolmates spoke a dialect considerably different from mine. Within six weeks I had changed over to the speech prevailing in school, but at home I spoke in my original tongue, although my parents never suggested that I do so. This transition occurred again when I went to Peking and once more when I went to Shanghai. Each time I acquired a new dialect. But each new dialect was merely added to the list of those at my command. This pattern was true of all Chinese youngsters whom I knew, even with reference to entirely foreign languages, for Russian and Japanese were widely known in Manchuria, French in Yunnan, and English in the rest of China. Furthermore, this pride in individual achievement in foreign languages prevailed even at the height of anti-British or anti-Japanese feeling.

Chinese parents, on their part, have little reason for anxiety as their children grow older. First, never having been complete masters of their children, they do not feel rejected when the youngsters become more independent. Second, the Chinese parent-child relationship is permanent. A father is always a father, whether or not he is loving or kind. A son is always a son; rarely is he disowned because he is not dutiful. Lastly, Chinese social organization is such that age, far from being a defect, is a blessing. Chinese parents have no reason to regret their children's coming of age, for it assures not a lesser role but a more respected place for themselves.

The Chinese pattern of mutual dependence thus forms the basis of a psychological security for both the old and the young. When children have little urge to depart, parents have little need to hold. The result is a way of life in which individual predilections are minimized not because there is strong restraint that demands conformity, but because the emotions of the individual are neutralized when he is satisfied with things as they are.

The American Child as Seen by British Travelers, 1845-1935

RICHARD L. RAPSON

While British travelers to American shores disagreed with one another on many topics between the years 1845 and 1935, they spoke with practically one voice upon two subjects: American schools and American children.[1] On the whole they thought the public school system admirable; with near unanimity they found the children detestable.

This adds up to a paradox, for if the innovation of free public education was, as most of these visitors contended, the best thing about America, surely some decent effect upon the schools' young charges should have been faintly discernible. Yet the British were not at all charmed by the youngsters, and the foreign observers had very few kind things to say in behalf of American children.

The paradox as stated must leave one unsatisfied. In any nation one should expect the child to stamp his impress upon the climate of the entire society; the detestable child should become the detestable adult. But especially in a nation which the British characterized by the term "youthful"—the epithet more often used in a complimentary rather than a deprecatory fashion—one would with reason expect to find some association between the word and the actual young people of the country.

There was no question as to what quality in the children did most to nettle the Englishmen. As David Macrae said in 1867: "American children are un-

Reprinted with permission from Richard L. Rapson, "The American Child as Seen by British Travelers, 1845-1935," *American Quarterly*, XVII, No. 3 (1965), pp. 520-34. Copyright, 1965, Trustees of the University of Pennsylvania.
[1]The evidence for this article derives from a reading of over 260 published books composed by Britons who wrote of the United States on the basis of visits made here between 1845 and 1935. The essay itself is drawn from my dissertation at Columbia, *The British Traveler in America, 1860-1935.*

doubtedly precocious."[2] In the same year, Greville Chester explained a little this theme, which appeared with more monotonous regularity than did any other in these books. "Many of the children in this country," he said, "appear to be painfully precocious—small stuck-up caricatures of men and women, with but little of the fresh ingenuousness and playfulness of childhood."[3]

Again in that same uneventful year of 1867, the Robertsons embellished this developing portrait thus:

Their infant lips utter smart sayings, and baby oaths are too often encouraged . . . even by their own parents, whose counsel and restraint they quickly learn wholly to despise. It is not uncommon to see children of ten calling for liquor at the bar, or puffing a cigar in the streets. In the cars we met a youth of respectable and gentlemanly exterior who thought no shame to say that he learned to smoke at eight, got first 'tight' at twelve, and by fourteen had run the whole course of debauchery.[4]

Every year American youth was similarly berated for its precocity. "Precocity" politely expressed the British feeling that American children were pert, impertinent, disrespectful, arrogant brats. But "precocious" meant more than that; it implied that American children weren't children at all. Three British mothers made this point. Therese Yelverton exclaimed that "in the course of my travels I never discovered that there were any American *children*. Diminutive men and women in process of growing into big ones, I have met with; but the child in the full sense attached to that word in England—a child with rosy cheeks and bright joyous laugh, its docile obedience and simplicity, its healthful play and its disciplined work, is a being almost unknown in America."[5]

Daniel Boorstin in the introduction to a new edition of *A Lady's Life in the Rocky Mountains* wrote of how Isabella Bird "saw a society where, in a sense, everyone was young, yet where the most painful sight was 'the extinction of childhood. I have never seen any children, only debased imitations of men and women.' "[6] And Lady Emmeline Stuart-Wortley, before the Civil War, commented: "Little America is unhappily, generally, only grown-up America, seen through a telescope turned the wrong way. The one point, perhaps, in which I must concur with other writers on the United States, is there being no real child-like children here."[7]

Eyre Crowe tells how he and his traveling companion, William Makepeace Thackeray, came across a youngster reading a newspaper, "already devouring the toughest leaders, and mastering the news of the world whilst whiffing his

[2]Macrae, *The Americans at Home* (New York, 1952), p. 45. (First edition, Edinburgh, 1870).
[3]Chester, *Transatlantic Sketches* (London, 1869), pp. 230–31.
[4]William and W. F. Robertson, *Our American Tour* (Edinburgh, 1871), pp. 9–10.
[5]Therese Yelverton, *Teresina in America* (London, 1875), I, 263. She also found them to be "insolent, unruly, and rude." *Ibid.*, p. 269. Oscar Wilde thought that little girls were more charming in their precocity than little boys. *Writings* (New York, 1907), III, 251.
[6]Isabella Lucy Bird, *A Lady's Life in the Rocky Mountains.* The edition by Daniel Boorstin (Norman, Okla., 1960) was used, p. xxii. (First edition, London, 1875).
[7]Stuart-Wortley, *Travels in the United States* (Paris, 1851), p. 67.

cigar, and not without making shies at a huge expectorator close at hand."[8] The picture of the cigar-smoking cherub flashed recurrently in these accounts.

The visitors did not have to search far for an explanation—at least a superficial explanation—for this disconcerting childhood behavior. Although a few of them remarked at the leniency of the common schools and regretted the lack of corporal punishment handed out there,[9] many more felt that the only doses of discipline ever received by the child were administered, even if in small quantities, in the schoolrooms. No, it was unquestionably in the home that the child was indulged, and indulgence gave him his swagger.

His parents either could not or else chose not to discipline their offspring. To be sure, the school system was not blameless. Many, like Fraser, regarded the school "as an extension of the family," which, by its very effectiveness made matters more difficult for mother and father.[10]

... it must be allowed that schools are robbing parents of the power to control their families. The school has drawn to itself so much of the love and veneration of the young that in the homes missing its spell they grow unruly. Parents are not experts in the management of children, nor have they the moral weight of an institution to back them up, hence they fail to keep up the smooth ascendancy of the school.[11]

P. A. Vaile blamed the American mother: "She is refusing to perform her part of the contract. First she 'went back' on raising her children, now she does not want to have any children at all."[12] Mrs. Humphreys raged at "the conspicuous absence of maternal instinct as a feature of American marriages."[13]

Many others accused fathers, but usually with greater sympathy. After all, the father simply worked too hard all day to have much time, interest or energy to devote to his little ones. "The husband has his occupations, friends, and amusements."[14]

No matter which parent had to bear the burden of guilt, many an Englishman simply felt that home life in the United States just wasn't homelike; it lacked atmosphere, comfort, love, play and warmth. It never became the cozy, friendly hearth which imparted to a family a sense of kinship, identity or oneness. Long after young couples had forsaken the custom of dwelling in boarding houses or hotels and exposing their tiny ones to the dregs of society—a custom deplored by every Englishman—long after this, W. L. George, along with most others, refused to admit that Americans still had any idea as to what constituted a "real" home.

[8]Eyre Crowe, *With Thackeray in America* (London, 1893). p. 21.
[9]John Strathesk [John Tod]. *Bits About America* (Edinburgh, 1887), p. 149; Richard DeBary, *The Land of Promise* (London, 1908), p. 131.
[10]James Nelson Fraser, *America, Old and New* (London, 1910), p. 280.
[11]*Ibid.,* p. 282.
[12]P. A. Vaile, *Y., America's Peril* (London, 1909). p. 111.
[13]Mrs. Desmond Humphreys, *America Through English Eyes* (London, n.d. [1913?]), p. 165.
[14]*Ibid.,* p. 161. Horace Vachell said that in the West at least "you will find fathers and mothers the slaves of their children." *Life and Sport on the Pacific Slope* (New York, 1901), p. 74.

The hard child [he said] suggests the hard home, which is characteristic of America. I visited many houses in the United States, and, except among the definitely rich, I found them rather uncomfortable. They felt bare, untenanted; they were too neat, too new . . . one missed the comfortable accumulation of broken screens, old fire irons, and seven-year-old volumes of the *Illustrated London News,* which make up the dusty, frowsy feeling of home. The American house is not a place where one lives, but a place where one merely sleeps, eats, sits, works.[15]

George may have been a bit unfair to expect to find "seven-year-old volumes of the *Illustrated London News*" lying about, but he had a right to notice the lack of age; it takes years for a family to implant its brand on a structure of brick and mortar.[16] Perhaps, as many visitors rightly pointed out, Americans were too much on the go, too mobile for them ever to fulfill George's requirements for home-ness.[17] This nonetheless did not excuse the parents from their failure to bring up their children appropriately. Joseph Hatton, in 1881, begged the mothers and fathers to take their responsibilities as parents more seriously than they were and to realize, as any sensible person must, that their overindulgence of the child was "excessive and injurious."[18]

Little Fritz, a pretty little American boy who sat as the subject for one of Philip Burne-Jones' paintings, told his grandmother, in the artist's presence, "I'll kick your head!" After being chided and asked to apologize there was "dead silence on the part of Fritz." Finally, after some more pleading, Fritz relented and uttered "a few perfunctory and scarcely audible sounds, which were generously construed by the family as expressive of contrition and penitence; and Fritz started again with a clear record, for a brief period. His mother had absolutely no influence on him whatever, and she admitted as much."[19]

Other American parents admitted as much also; they were fully aware of their inability to control their little ones, but they just didn't know what to do about it. L. P. Jacks, in 1933, let an American mother speak her heart about her utter helplessness and frustration in a way that was rather revealing and even poignant:

We mothers are rapidly losing all influence over our children, and I don't know how we can recover it. We have little or no control over them, whether boys or girls. The schools and the colleges take them out of our hands. They give them everything for nothing, and that is what the children expect when they come home. Their standards and their ideals are formed in the school atmosphere, and more by their companions than their teachers. They become more and more intractable to home influence and there is nothing for it but to let them go their own way.[20]

[15]Walter L. George, *Hail Columbia!* (New York, 1921), p. 199.

[16]At least "if ever so humble, the abodes in America are invariably neat and cleanly," claimed Alfred Pairpont in 1890 in *Rambles in America* (Boston, 1891), p. 166.

[17]Said George Steevens, *The Land of the Dollar* (Edinburgh, 1897): "You cannot call a people who will never be happy ten years in the same place . . . home-loving in the English sense." p. 313.

[18]Joseph Hatton, *Today in America* (New York, 1881), p. 7.

[19]Sir Philip Burne-Jones, *Dollars and Democracy* (New York, 1904), p. 36.

[20]L. P. Jacks, *My American Friends* (New York, 1933), p. 149. Notice the young mother's stress on the influence which the peer-group culture held over her children.

But the majority of the Britons did not accept either the influence of the schools or the social fact of mobility as sufficient explanations for the precocious child; they would have had little justification for disliking the child with the fervor they did and deploring the parents' follies so strongly if these impersonal forces accounted adequately for the situation.

They felt, rather, that causes ran deeper, in more insidious channels. Not only did the parents spoil their children, but they *wanted* to spoil them. Not only did the mothers and fathers put up with more than they should have, but they were actually proud of their babies. The Britons were especially distressed when they decided that parents felt, as a rule, not the least bit guilty over their own efforts or over the way their boys and girls were turning out. The travelers came not to the conclusion that American parents were unable to discipline their sons and daughters, but that they deliberately chose to "let them go their own way." This either infuriated the by now bewildered visitor, or else made him desperate to figure out just how this insanity could possibly reign.

William Howard Russell could not accept the excuse that the schools pre-empted parental power since "there is nothing in the American [school] system to prevent the teaching of religious and moral duties by parents at home; but it would seem as if very little of that kind of instruction was given by the busy fathers and anxious mothers of the Republic. . . ." [21]

Horace Vachell, as did many others, told a child story that turned into a mother story. It seems that one day the author was in the parlor of a ship filled with ailing people, including the author's own mother who was suffering with a bad headache. Into this sickly assemblage trooped our hero—a small American boy who decided to soothe the aches of all by playing on the bagpipes! "The wildest pibroch ever played in Highland glen was sweet melody compared to the strains produced by this urchin." [22] He naturally continued to play, louder than ever, despite the daggered glances hurled at him from all around the parlor; he stopped only when he tired. Then, instead of permitting sweet peace, "he flung down the pipes, walked to the piano, opened it, sat down, and began to hammer the keys with his feet." [23]

At this turn of events, our long-suffering author had had enough. " 'You play very nicely with your feet,' I ventured to say, as I lifted him from the stool, "but some of these ladies are suffering with headache, and your music distresses them. Run away, like a good boy, and don't come back again.' " [24]

But Vachell's story did not end here because, in the final analysis, this is more of a mother tale than a child story. "The mother was furious. Had I been Herod the Great, red-handed after the slaughter of the Innocents, she could not have looked more indignant or reproachful. I was interfering with the sacred rights of

[21] William Howard Russell, *Hesperothen: Notes from the West* (London, 1882), II, 156.
[22] Vachell, p. 80.
[23] *Ibid.*, p. 80.
[24] *Ibid.*, p. 80.

the American child to do what he pleased, where he pleased, and when he pleased."[25]

Vachell's first conclusion inevitably was that American children were unspeakable monsters, utterly lacking in "sense of duty, reverence, humility, obedience."[26] His second conclusion was, however, more interesting and more important, namely that parents actually "encourage the egoism latent in all children, till each becomes an autocrat."[27]

Once this appalling discovery had been verified, it occurred to the more curious of the Britons to raise the appropriate question: how could the American parents be proud of these diminutive devils?

Sir Edwin Arnold presented a question of this sort, in more general form, to one whom he regarded as an expert on this strange *genus Americanus:* Walt Whitman. " 'But have you reverence enough among your people?' I asked. 'Do the American children respect and obey their parents sufficiently, and are the common people grateful enough to the best men, their statesmen, leaders, teachers, poets, and "betters" generally?' "[28]

To this most fundamental of all inquiries Whitman responded: " 'Allons, comrade!, your old world has been soaked and saturated in reverentiality. We are laying here in America the basements and foundation rooms of a new era. And we are doing it, on the whole, pretty well and substantially. By-and-by, when that job is through, *we will look after the steeples and pinnacles.*' "[29]

Whitman and Arnold included childhood precocity within the larger framework of a new people refusing to pay homage to their betters, refusing to revere their "superiors." Such reverence constitutes one of the necessary ingredients of an aristocratically-oriented society. Lack of that reverence suggests an egalitarian society, and these two distinguished men of letters were implying that the precocious child was symptomatic not merely of weak, stupid, willful parents, but rather of the pervasiveness in American society of the principle of equality. In fact no generalization about America was made more forcefully or repeatedly by the commentators en masse than that the thrust of the American belief in equality (understood as opportunity to rise more than as classlessness) was ubiquitous; it extended into every corner of the daily institutional fabric of American life—into the schools wherein all children had the right to a free education, into politics where all had the right to vote, into the enhanced place of women in American society, into the fluid class structure, into the churches wherein voluntary religion was the rule, and, perhaps most astonishing of all, apparently even into the homes where little boys and little girls were granted unheard-of liberties.

[25] *Ibid.,* p. 80.
[26] *Ibid.,* p. 79.
[27] *Ibid.,* p. 79. One should bear in mind at all times the difficulties the travelers had of meeting representative American families since, as W. L. George candidly admitted, "truly representative families generally keep themselves rather to themselves." George, p. viii.
[28] Sir Edwin Arnold, *Seas and Lands* (New York, 1891), pp. 78–79.
[29] *Ibid.,* p. 79.

Captain Marryat, as early as 1839, related a well-known example illustrating this last point:

Imagine a child of three years old in England behaving thus:—

"Johnny, my dear, come here," says his mamma.

"I won't," cries Johnny.

"You must, my love, you are all wet, and you'll catch cold."

"I won't," replies Johnny.

"Come, my sweet, and I've something for you."

"I won't."

"Oh! Mr. —, do, pray make Johnny come in."

"Come in, Johnny," says the father.

"I won't."

"I tell you, come in directly, sir—do you hear?"

"I won't," replies the urchin, taking to his heels.

"A sturdy republican, sir," says his father to me, smiling at the boy's resolute disobedience.[30]

In 1845 Francis Wyse generalized upon incidents like these, placing them in a broad social context. "There is seldom any very great restraint," he noted, "imposed upon the youth of America whose precocious intellect, brought forth and exercised at an early, and somewhat premature age, and otherwise encouraged under the republican institutions of the country, has generally made them impatient of parental authority."[31]

Parental authority did not sensibly differ from any other exercise of power: royal, military, governmental or private. Americans had established their independence in rebellion against authority; they had rejected all artificially imposed forms of superiority; and they had proclaimed the equality of man. Surely these principles should extend to the family. Indeed, Jacks talked aptly of the way in which children had applied (with considerable parental approval) the Declaration of Independence to themselves.[32] And James Fullarton Muirhead, who composed one of the most informative chapters on this topic, formulated the grand generalization thus: "The theory of the equality of man is rampant in the nursery."[33] He referred to the infants as "young republicans," "democratic sucklings," "budding citizens of a free republic."[34]

Here then was another application of the theory of equality—one which even the friendly Muirhead could not get himself to smile upon. It "hardly tends," he patiently tried to explain, "to make the American child an attractive object to the stranger from without. On the contrary, it is very apt to make said stranger

[30]Quoted in Lawrence A. Cremin, *The American Common School* (New York, 1951), p. 217.

[31]*America: Its Realities and Resources* (London, 1846), p. 295.

[32]*My American Friends*, pp. 150–51.

[33]Muirhead, *America, The Land of Contrasts* (London, 1902), p. 64. (First edition, London, 1898).

[34]*Ibid.*, pp. 63, 65.

long strenuously to spank these budding citizens of a free republic, and to send them to bed *instanter*."[35]

One must, of course, sympathize with the British traveler as he suffered through each encounter with these young specimens of the New World. But their hate affair is as much beside the point as their love affair with the schools. Both child-rearing at home and the nation-wide system of compulsory public education were faithful to the omnipresent force of equality, and the paradox which began this chapter turns out to be no paradox at all. The commentators liked what they saw in the classrooms because authority was being exercised. It was being exercised by teachers who wielded it in the interests of learning and morality. When the visitors confronted the child outside the schools and in the context of home and family they were appalled by what they believed to be the universal and inexcusable betrayal of authority by the parents.

This reversal in the roles of authority vis-à-vis children disoriented the observers to such an extent that many of them never realized that, just a few chapters before their excoriation of the American child, they had been blessing his development in the schoolrooms. Although the traveler frequently sensed that the "success" of the teachers and the indulgent "failures" of the parents were related to each other, and that both stemmed from the same peculiar general assumptions in which American society was rooted, not one of them ever managed to pose squarely the problem of how and whether dual authority *could* be exerted on the child, of just how parent and teacher *should* combine their efforts in child-rearing, given the public school system and the widespread assumption that the child was an equal partner in the family "team."

The origins of this dilemma may be traced back to colonial days when, under the pressure of new conditions, the familiar family pattern brought over from the Old World suffered major transformations affecting both child-rearing practices and the role of education.

The traditional family was the wide kinship group with the source of power vested in the father and extending outward to include not only wife and children, but cousins, other relatives and servants as well. The father was the chief educator, transferring the traditions of his culture and vocational training itself to his sons. But authority and traditionalism were, as revealed in an excellent study by Bernard Bailyn, inadequate for conditions in the New World where problems were new, land abundant, labor scarce and old solutions to old problems irrelevant.[36] In these circumstances "the young—less bound by prescriptive memories, more adaptable, more vigorous—stood often at advantage. Learning faster, they came to see the world more familiarly, to concede more readily to unexpected necessities, to sense more accurately the phasing of a new life. They and not their parents became the effective guides to a new world, and they

---

[35] *Ibid.*, p. 65.
[36] Bernard Bailyn, *Education in the Forming of American Society* (Chapel Hill, N.C., 1960).

thereby gained a strange, anomalous authority difficult to accommodate within the ancient structure of family life."[37]

While the details need not concern us here, the traditional family and educative pattern could not survive these challenges.

By the middle of the eighteenth century the classic lineaments of the American family as modern sociologists describe them—the "isolation of the conjugal unit," the "maximum of dispersion of the lines of descent," partible inheritances, and multilineal growth—had appeared. The consequences can hardly be exaggerated. Fundamental aspects of social life were affected. In the reduced, nuclear family, thrown back upon itself, traditional gradations in status tended to fall to the level of necessity. Relationships tended more toward achievement than ascription. The status of women rose; marriage, even in the eyes of the law, tended to become a contract between equals. Above all, the development of the child was affected.[38]

One of the effects on the child cited by Bailyn concerned the passage of the child into society as "the once elaborate interpenetration of family and community dissolved." A result was that "the individual acquired an insulation of consciousness," a "heightened . . . sense of separateness" from society, and particularly from the state which no longer could "command his automatic involvement."[39] Perhaps this is what the British meant by precocity.

A second result came as the Puritans transferred the primary educative responsibilities from "the maimed . . . family to formal instructional institutions, and in so doing not only endowed schools with a new importance but expanded their purpose beyond pragmatic vocationalism toward vaguer but more basic cultural goals."[40] Perhaps this explains why the British abused American parents.

The commentators who believed that parents must exercise authority over children were not pleased by what they saw in American families. In order to muster any kind words it was necessary to revise traditional conceptions of the family and accept a measure of equality in the home, accept the notion that the various family members could be close friends.

Dicey was one who was able to take this step. He concluded one of his volumes in 1863 in praise of "the great charm which surrounds all family relations in the North. Compared with Europe, domestic scandals are unknown; and between parents and their grown-up children, there exists a degree of familiarity and intimacy which one seldom witnesses in this country."[41]

There were other companions besides the parents and grown-up children. Growing boys and their fathers were companions, wrote Zincke in 1868. "In America the father never loses sight of his child, who thus grows up as his companion, and is soon treated as a companion, and is in some sort an equal."[42]

[37] *Ibid.*, pp. 22–23.
[38] *Ibid.*, pp. 25–26.
[39] *Ibid.*, pp. 24–25.
[40] *Ibid.*, p. 27.
[41] Edward Dicey, *Six Months in the Federal States* (London, 1863), I, 310.
[42] Foster Barham Zincke, *Last Winter in the United States* (London, 1868), pp. 70–71.

Zincke went on to relate a pleasant incident he observed on a train between a fourteen-year-old boy and his father.

They had long been talking on a footing of equality. . . . At last, to while away the time, they began to sing together. First they accompanied each other. Then they took alternate lines; at last alternate words. In this of course they tripped frequently, each laughing at the other for his mistakes. There was no attempt at keeping up the dignity of a parent, as might have been considered necessary and proper with us. There was no reserve. They were in a certain sense already on an equal footing of persons of the same age.[43]

Mothers and daughters were companions, Low maintained. "Daughters are much with their mothers, and they become their companions younger than they do in Europe. At an age when the French girl, for instance, is still demurely attending her convent, or the English girl is in the hands of her governess, her more emancipated sister across the Atlantic is calling with her mother on her friends, or assisting her in the drawing-room on her reception days."[44]

Sons and daughters received equal treatment, claimed Saunders. Whereas "in an English family, as a rule, the greatest consideration is shown to the boys," in America, if anything, "the wishes of the girls would be first listened to, and their education provided for." The boy, after all, "is as eager to start life on his own account as is a greyhound to rush after the hare." "In the matter of early independence both sexes are equal."[45]

Even husbands and wives were companions. While the wife "will not consent to being submerged by her children, she gives much of her time to them, and is still able to find time to be with her husband. The average American husband makes a confidante and a companion of his wife. . . . "[46]

The patriarchies and matriarchies of the past had been replaced by a family team composed of equals. The British perceived this family revolution as being directly parallel to the fundamental cultural difference between the New World which blurred distinctions and the Old which honored and preserved them. As Muirhead put it: "The reason—or at any rate one reason—of the normal attitude of the American parent towards his child is not far to seek. It is almost undoubtedly one of the direct consequences of the circumambient spirit of democracy. The American is so accustomed to recognize the essential equality of others that he sometimes carries a good thing to excess. . . . The present child may be described as one of the experiments of democracy."[47]

Americans enthroned their children not merely out of blind obedience to some social ethos which compelled them to do in the home something consonant

[43] *Ibid.*, p. 71.
[44] A. M. Low, *America at Home* (London, 1905), p. 74.
[45] William Saunders, *Through the Light Continent* (London, 1879), pp. 399–400. Also enlightening on these leveling tendencies in the home are J. Nelson Fraser, p. 246 and Harold Spender, *A Briton in America* (London, 1921), pp. 253–54.
[46] Low, p. 82.
[47] Muirhead, pp. 70–71.

with what the nation proclaimed to the world as its faith. Americans, as Zincke's story of the singing father and son so nicely shows, were often quite fond of their children, and rather than being harried or intimidated, they were not infrequently joyful parents. In fact, the Americans, according to the British, believed in their young ones in much the same way that they believed in their future. Let the youths' natural spirit triumph and they would not only participate in a grand future, but they would be the chief forgers of that future; the child was the future. Children could be heard as well as seen because they represented hope in "the land of youth." "Nowhere," said Muirhead, "is the child so constantly in evidence; nowhere are his wishes so carefully consulted; nowhere is he allowed to make his mark so strongly on society in general."[48] Richard DeBary chimed in that "America is wholly convinced . . . that the young child can take it all in. The child is given kingship and becomes the king."[49]

Those few Englishmen who thought well of American children praised precisely the same qualities which the detractors abominated. Arnold Bennett, for example, came across one "captivating creature whose society I enjoyed at frequent intervals throughout my stay in America. . . . [She] was a mirror in which I saw the whole American race of children—their independence, their self-confidence, their adorable charm, and their neat sauciness."[50] The reformer George Holyoake liked "the American habit of training their children to independence" more than he did England's "unwise domestic paternalism, which encourages a costly dependence."[51]

John Strathesk did not employ the term "precocious" in a deprecating manner when he decided that "the girls and boys of America are very frank, even precocious."[52] And Sir Philip Gibbs expanded upon this theme. "The children of America," he said, "have the qualities of their nation, simplicity, common sense, and self-reliance. They are not so bashful as English boys and girls, and they are free from the little constraints of nursery etiquette which make so many English children afraid to open their mouths. They are also free entirely from that juvenile snobbishness which is still cultivated in English society, where boys and girls of well-to-do parents are taught to look down with contempt upon children of the poorer classes."[53]

It may be noticed that the adjectives used to depict the child are similar, whether used in delight or disgust: saucy, self-reliant, wild, spontaneous, immodest, independent, demanding, irreverent. It may furthermore be observed

[48] *Ibid.*, p. 63.
[49] DeBary, p. 128. "Young America does not sit at the master's feet and worship: it has definite opinions, which it deems as much deserving of hearing as other people's, and it gives them forth with the bold confidence born of youthful inexperience and immaturity." Emily Faithfull, *Three Visits to America* (Edinburgh, 1884), p. 89.
[50] Arnold Bennett, *Your United States* (New York, 1912), pp. 147–48.
[51] George Jacob Holyoake, *Among the Americans* (Chicago, 1881), p. 183.
[52] Strathesk, p. 149.
[53] Philip Gibbs, *Land of Destiny* (New York, 1920), p. 88.

that they bear resemblance to adjectives which some Englishmen thought applicable to the young nation as a whole.[54] Some visitors also found the terms suitable for characterizing American adults as well.

The blurring of lines between young and old in the New World furnished an invitation to some British writers to caricature both American parents and children. But to Margaret Mead this leveling tendency forms an explicable part of a peculiarly national approach to child-rearing which she has called "third-generation American."[55] The American child, contends this anthropologist, is expected to traverse a course very different from his father's, and "with this orientation towards a different future for the child comes also the expectation that the child will pass beyond his parents and leave their standards behind him."[56] Thus "it comes about that American parents lack the sure hand on the rudder which parents in other societies display."[57] Or, approaching the matter from a different perspective than either the historian Bailyn or Miss Mead, Erik Erikson supports their findings when he writes that "the psychoanalysis of the children of immigrants clearly reveals to what extent they, as the first real Americans in their family, become their parents' cultural parents."[58]

As Erikson and many other psychologists have stressed, the high prestige accorded youth, understandable though it may be considering the abundant resources, the scarcity of labor, the virgin conditions, and the rapid pace of change in the egalitarian New World, is not without cost to Americans. The child himself has to pay a price for his exalted place; the compulsion to achieve, to succeed, can be taxing and perhaps ultimately futile. Unlike his Old World counterpart who begins life with a position of ascribed status which he knows is his own, the American child can never let up.

The society, too, has to pay a price for its cult of youth. It is paid not only in the primitive music, the puerile television and the domestic tyranny to which the adult world is exposed at the command of teenagers, and to which the adults meekly succumb. It is paid also in the sacrifice of wisdom, of standards, of permanence, of serenity under the frantic injunction to constantly "think young." The quiet contemplation of the past and the present is sacrificed when all must worship at the alter of the future.

The most repeated consensus at which the travelers arrived concerning the "American character" was that that character resembled, at heart, the character of a child. If there were no childlike children, if there were only miniature adults in "the land of youth," then the reverse was equally true—there were few adultlike adults; there were only adults trying to be young. "There are no old in America at all," said George Steevens in 1900.[59] By this he meant two things.

[54]Even Vachell, who told the story of the boy with the bagpipes, had to confess to the "originality, independence, pluck, and perspicuity" of the children (p. 83).
[55]Margaret Mead, *And Keep Your Powder Dry: An Anthropologist Looks at America* (New York, 1942), p. 45.
[56]*Ibid.*, p. 41.
[57]*Ibid.*, p. 43.
[58]Erik Erikson, *Childhood and Society* (2nd ed.; New York, 1963), p. 294.
[59]George Steevens, p. 314.

First, that adult virtues are uncultivated in the New World; the American "retains all his life a want of discipline, an incapacity for ordered and corporate effort."[60]

Steevens' second meaning centered on the fate of those who were actually aged. "They are shouldered unmercifully out of existence," he claimed. "I found in New York a correspondence on the open question whether the old have any right to respect. Many of the public thought, quite seriously, they had no right even to existence."[61]

The dearest price of all is paid neither by the children nor by the society but by the adults who have to be "boys" at the office, who as parents must "live for their children," who as mature women must forever look and act like eighteen-year-olds, who as elderly must join the other aged in some zippy retirement community quarantined from the rest of mankind.

The cult of youth has perhaps permitted a more spontaneous family life to develop, and it has, no doubt, lent to our national life a special vigor and freshness. But in exalting childhood and early youth to the consummatory positions in life, it follows that maturity and old age should become anti-climactic. Indeed, in America, as one ages, one declines, and the reward of lower movie admission fees for "senior citizens" furnishes rather ineffectual solace. One can only guess at the extent to which the American fixation on the earlier stages of the life cycle is related to our tendency to deny the reality of old age and to put from our minds all thoughts of death. And it is not possible to do more here than to raise the question which then becomes inescapable: what kinds of spiritual reserves might this habit of mind take from the individual as he passes through life?[62]

Thirty years after his 1869 visit to America, the Rev. Mr. Macrae returned and noted that the "independence and precocious intellect of the American children" had not diminished; but he was "less struck with these features this time."[63] The reason he was less struck was precisely the same that made Harold Spender think better of the American children in 1920, twenty years after *his* first visit. "Our English child in the interval," said Spender, substituting his native land for Macrae's Scotland, "has become a little more American."[64] By the early years of the twentieth century, America's startling departure in raising children and in inflating the status of the youngsters in the family hierarchy was, like various other American innovations, becoming more general in the Old World also.

[60] *Ibid.*, p. 314.

[61] *Ibid.*, p. 314.

[62] The seeds of the thoughts in the above paragraph, and in many others in this paper, were planted by Richard Hofstadter, both in conversation and in an early draft of an as-yet unpublished article called "Foreign Observers and American Children"—an article from which Professor Hofstadter was kind enough to let me read.

[63] David Macrae, *America Revisited and Men I Have Met* (Glasgow, 1908), p. 24.

[64] Harold Spender, p. 271.

Baby and Child Care

BENJAMIN SPOCK

ENJOY YOUR BABY

Don't be afraid of him. You'd think from what some people say about babies demanding attention that they come into the world determined to get their parents under their thumb by hook or by crook. This isn't true. Your baby is born to be a reasonable, friendly human being.

Don't be afraid to feed him when you think he's really hungry. If you are mistaken, he'll merely refuse to take much.

Don't be afraid to love him and enjoy him. Every baby needs to be smiled at, talked to, played with, fondled—gently and lovingly—just as much as he needs vitamins and calories. That's what will make him a person who loves people and enjoys life. The baby who doesn't get any loving will grow up cold and unresponsive.

Don't be afraid to respond to other desires of his as long as they seem sensible to you and as long as you don't become a slave to him. When he cries in the early weeks, it's because he's uncomfortable for some reason or other—maybe it's hunger or indigestion, or fatigue, or tension. The uneasy feeling you have when you hear him cry, the feeling that you want to comfort him, is meant to be part of your nature, too. Being held, rocked or walked may be what he needs.

Spoiling doesn't come from being good to a baby in a sensible way, and it doesn't come all of a sudden. Spoiling comes on gradually when a mother is too afraid to use her common sense or when she really wants to be a slave and encourages her baby to become a slave driver. . . .

Enjoy him as he is—that's how he'll grow up best. . . . Love and enjoy your child for what he is, for what he looks like, for what he does, and forget about the qualities that he doesn't have. I don't give you this advice just for sentimental reasons. There's a very important practical point here. The child who is appreciated for what he is, even if he is homely, or clumsy, or slow, will grow up with confidence in himself, happy. He will have a spirit that will make the best of all the capacities that he has, and of all the opportunities that come his way. He will make light of any handicaps. But the child who has never been quite accepted by his parents, who has always felt that he was not quite right, will grow up lacking confidence. He'll never be able to make full use of what brains, what skills, what physical attractiveness he has. If he starts life with a handicap, physical or mental, it will be multiplied tenfold by the time he is grown up. . . .

STRICTNESS OR PERMISSIVENESS?

This looms as a big question for many new parents. A great majority of them find the right answer in a little while. For a few parents it remains a worrisome question, no matter how much experience they've had.

I may as well let the cat out of the bag right away as far as my opinion goes and say that strictness or permissiveness is not the real issue. Good-hearted parents who aren't afraid to be firm when it is necessary can get good results with either moderate strictness or moderate permissiveness. On the other hand, a strictness that comes from harsh feelings or a permissiveness that is timid or vacillating can each lead to poor results. The real issue is what spirit the parent puts into managing the child and what attitude is engendered in the child as a result.

We've been through a big transition. It's hard to get any perspective on this topic without taking a historical view. Styles in strictness vary from one period to another. The Victorian Age was quite strict, for instance, about manners and modesty. In the twentieth century, especially after World War I, a reaction set in. Several factors pushed it along. The great American pioneers in educational research, like John Dewey and William Kilpatrick, showed that a child learns better and faster with a method of teaching that makes allowance for his particular readiness to progress and that recognizes his eagerness to learn if the subject matter is suitable. Freud and his followers showed that harsh toilet training or frightening a child about sex can distort his personality and lead to neurosis. Studies of delinquents and criminals revealed that most of them had suffered more from lack of love in childhood than from lack of punishment. These discoveries, among others, encouraged a general relaxation in child discipline and a greater effort to give children what they seemed to need as individuals. Several wise leaders in American pediatrics, Aldrich and Powers and Gesell, began to introduce a similar philosophy into the medical care of babies and children. But physicians remained strict about infant feeding right into the 1940's, because they still feared that irregular schedules and irregular amounts of formula might bring on the severe diarrheal diseases that used to cause so many infant deaths. Then the experiments of Dr. Preston McLendon and Mrs. Frances P. Simsarian with the "self-demand" schedule, published in 1942, helped to convince doctors that most babies can do very well choosing their own feeding times and will remain healthy. Since then, there has been a rapid and widespread shift in medical practice. Today a majority of American babies are being put on more or less flexible schedules at first.

Doctors who used to conscientiously warn young parents against spoiling are now encouraging them to meet their baby's needs, not only for food, but for comforting and loving.

These discoveries and these changes of attitudes and methods have benefited most children and parents. There are fewer tense ones, more happy ones.

But it's not possible for a civilization like ours to go through such a change of philosophy—it really amounts to a revolution—without raising doubts in many parents' minds and without getting some parents thoroughly mixed up. It's basic human nature to tend to bring up your children about as you were brought up. It's easy enough to pick up new ideas about vitamins and inoculations. But if your upbringing was fairly strict in regard to obedience, manners, sex, truthfulness, it's natural, it's almost inevitable, that you will feel strongly underneath about such matters when raising your own children. You may have changed your theories because of something you've studied or read or heard, but when your child does something that would have been considered bad in your own childhood, you'll probably find yourself becoming more tense, or anxious, or angry than you imagined possible. This is nothing to be ashamed of. This is the way Nature expects human beings to learn child care—from their own childhood. This is how different civilizations have managed to remain stable and carry on their ideals from generation to generation.

The reason that most parents have been able to do a good job with their children during the past fifty years of changing theory is that they themselves had been brought up reasonably happily, were comfortable about raising their children the same way, and didn't follow any new theory to extremes. When doctors were emphasizing regularity, confident parents followed a regular schedule in general (and *most* babies adjusted to it *most* of the time), but they weren't afraid to make an occasional exception when the baby became painfully hungry ahead of time, because they felt in their bones that this was right.

When doctors more recently have been emphasizing flexibility, confident parents haven't carried this to extremes, either. They don't let a sleepy but obstinate baby refuse to be put to bed, because they know very well (mostly from their own childhood) that bedtime is bedtime and that theories of flexibility have very little to do with this situation.

Parents who become confused with new theories are often of two kinds. There are, first of all, those who have been brought up with too little confidence in their own judgment. If you don't dare trust yourself, you *have* to follow what someone else says, willy-nilly. A second group are those parents who feel that they were brought up too severely. They remember the resentment they felt toward their parents at times, and they don't want their children to feel that way about them. But this is a very difficult approach. If you want to raise your children the way you were raised, you have a definite pattern to follow. You know just how obedient, how helpful, how polite, you want them to be. You don't have to stop and think. But if you want to treat them quite differently than the way you were treated—more indulgently, for instance, or more as equals—you don't have any pattern of how far to carry it. If things begin to get out of hand—if, for example, your child begins to take advantage of your permissiveness—it's harder to find your way back onto the right track. The child makes you mad, all right, but the madder you get the guiltier you feel for fear you'll step into the very pattern you were determined to avoid.

Of course, I'm making all this sound too black or white. We all start out as young parents partly agreeing, partly disagreeing, with the methods our parents used. It's a matter of degree. And most of us find a compromise that works reasonably well. I have been exaggerating in order to make clear the difficulty that some parents have had.

Stick to your convictions. I think that good parents who naturally lean toward strictness should stick to their guns and raise their children that way. Moderate strictness—in the sense of requiring good manners, prompt obedience, orderliness—is not harmful to children so long as the parents are basically kind and so long as the children are growing up happy and friendly. But strictness *is* harmful when the parents are overbearing, harsh, chronically disapproving, and make no allowances for a child's age and individuality. This kind of severity produces children who are either meek and colorless or mean to others.

Parents who incline to an easygoing kind of management, who are satisfied with casual manners as long as the child's attitude is friendly, or who happen not to be particularly strict—for instance, about promptness or neatness—can also raise children who are considerate and cooperative, as long as the parents are not afraid to be firm about those matters that do seem important to them.

When parents get unhappy results from too much permissiveness, it is not so much because they demand too little, though this is part of it. It is more because they are timid or guilty about what they ask or because they are unconsciously encouraging the child to rule the roost.

WHAT ARE YOUR AIMS IN RAISING A CHILD?

The rearing of children is more and more puzzling for parents in the twentieth century because we've lost a lot of our old-fashioned convictions about what kind of morals and ambitions and characters we want them to have. We've even lost our convictions about the purpose of human existence. Instead we have come to depend on psychological concepts. They've been helpful in solving many of the smaller problems but they are of little use in answering the major questions.

You may not be conscious of these changes—because you are so much a part of these times or because you grew up in an unusually stable family.

Other countries and times. In the past it was assumed in many countries that man's main function in the world—over and above making a living—was to serve God, by carrying out his purposes as revealed by religion. That's why in the Middle Ages the churches were by far the most imposing buildings. Much the same was true in America in the Colonial period. Children never had any idea that life was for their fulfillment. They were constantly exhorted to overcome their base natures in order to grow up to be pleasing in God's eyes.

In other places, especially in the past hundred years or so, it has been taught that man's purpose is to serve his country. This was true to a degree of France in Napoleon's time, the British empire, the German empire. It has been even more true of some modern states, not only of a Communist state like the Soviet Union but of a democratic one like Israel. Parents and teachers are in agreement with leaders about what virtues are to be encouraged in children: cooperativeness, studiousness, dedication to the specific principles of the nation. Parents don't have to keep wondering and worrying—about whether they are doing the right thing.

In even more parts of the world, it has always been assumed that children are born and raised to serve the aims of the family—what sociologists call the extended family or the clan. In childhood and youth they are to prepare themselves for work at the jobs which are considered the valuable ones by their particular family. They must as children and later as grown-ups revere and defer to their elders. Even in marrying, in many countries, they can't be allowed to be carried away by their foolish hearts but must accept marriages that are arranged by their parents for the purpose of advancing the family's welfare.

Child-centered America. In America very few children are raised to believe that their principal destiny is to serve their family, their country or God. Generally we've given them the feeling that they are free to set their own aims and occupations in life according to their inclinations. In a majority of cases these aims are visualized mainly in material terms.

The tendency is for American parents to consider the child at least as important as themselves—perhaps potentially more important. An Enlgish anthropologist said that whereas in other countries children are taught to look up to their parents as rather distinguished superior people, whatever their actual place in the society, the remarkable thing about America is that a father will say to his son, "Son, if you don't do better than I've done, I won't think much of you." This is an upsidedown respect. This is why America has often been called child-centered.

In other lands young parents gain confidence about aims and methods for rearing their children from family traditions and from having the grandparents nearby to advise and help them. These comforts have often been lacking in America. Our ancestors left their homelands because they were impatient with old ways and had the courage to try the unknown. Their descendants ever since have been restlessly moving from place to place in search of opportunity, often raising their children hundreds of miles away from any relatives. So they've had to turn to professional advisers and books and new theories for the help they needed.

I want to give a couple of small examples of how the child-centered, psychological approach can leave parents in the lurch unless it is backed up by a moral sense. Jealous quarreling between brothers and sisters has recently been tolerated *much more* than it was in previous generations. The psychological reasoning has been that jealousy is normal; if it is inhibited too severely, by making a child feel excessively guilty, it can cause various distortions of the personality. Parents shouldn't be badgering their children over *every little* thing anyway. There is considerable truth in these concepts. But when parents have followed them too exclusively, without consideration for the rights of the family or the ethics of society, the jealous child has been allowed to be much too mean to the younger one, has kept the family in an uproar and ended up with a guilty conscience anyway, because of the cruelty he has gotten away with.

A student of 19 is becoming increasingly rude and even verbally abusive toward his mother, who is a highly conscientious person. She has come to the guilty conclusion—incorrectly—that she must have failed him somehow, so she responds submissively to his reproaches. He senses that it is not right for him to pick on his mother just because he is out of sorts in some other department of his life yet, instinctively, he behaves worse and worse in order to get her to crack down.

You can see that psychological concepts don't help unless they are backed up by a sense of what's right and proper; they can seriously interfere with the operation of the parents' good sense; they can create further problems.

I doubt that Americans will ever want their children's ambitions to be subordinated to the wishes of the family or the needs of the country. However, I think that more of our children would grow up happier and more stable if they were acquiring a conviction, all through childhood, that the most important and the most fulfilling thing that human beings can do is to serve humanity in some fashion and to live by their ideals. (This does not preclude their earning a living or seeking advancement.) This is why human beings behave better, feel more purposeful, have better mental health during wartime, when they have a common purpose. And statistics show that there is less crime and less suicide during financial depressions, when people face a greater challenge. It's also *much easier* for the parents themselves, in meeting the hundred issues that come up every day with children—for instance, about politeness, chores, quarreling, schoolwork, dating—if they have their own principles. Then the answers to the detailed questions come more readily.

We are disillusioned. Fortunate are the parents with a strong religious faith. They are supported by a sense of conviction and serenity in all their activities. Usually they can pass on their faith to at least a majority of their children.

Many of the people who have no religious faith are doubly deprived today, because they don't have much belief in man either. We live in a disenchanted, disillusioned age—not about things, but about human beings.

This has been evident in the increasing tendency in literature, plays and movies in the past fifty years to play down the kindly and spiritual aspects of man and to focus on his crude, animal side. Manners in social life have been coarsened, especially among women. Even greeting cards, instead of wishing invalids and relatives well, jeer at them. Art rarely shows attractive people; it omits them altogether or makes them hideous. Many youths cultivate dishevelment as if they are ashamed to be human and a few of them withdraw from society altogether.

The disenchantment has been caused in part by the rapid strides in the sciences of biology, psychology and sociology, which have seemed to stress man's closeness to other animals, the crudeness of his basic instincts, the mechanicalness of his behavior patterns. Perhaps even more basic has been the weakening of the authority of religion in the minds of many people, caused by the increased authority of the sciences. This has greatly diminished man's former feeling that he was a very special and noble creature created in God's image.

The realization that the Biblical description of Creation cannot be taken literally has made many people question whether religious teachers have a solid basis for prescribing man's conduct and aims.

I believe that man's disillusionment is based on a misunderstanding of his nature. It's true he is related by evolution to other animals. But he is also vastly different. He is idealistic in his aspirations. His relationships are predominantly spiritual. His capacity for abstract reasoning has enabled him to discover much of the meaning of the universe. He has invented fantastic machines. He has created beauty in all the arts. All this has been made possible by the aspirations kindled in him in early childhood by his adoration of his parents. Whether or not man has religious faith, he can believe in the power of love and in man's potentialities for good, if he understands the spiritual development of a child.

AMERICAN VALUES

V

INTRODUCTION V

Since 1944, when the Swedish social analyst Gunnar Myrdal, exploring the problem of race relations in the United States, essayed a tentative summary of "the American Creed,"[1] behavioral scientists and historians have devoted systematic attention to the task of identifying, validating, classifying, and interpreting those values or configurations of values which may be said to be characteristically American. Formerly regarded as supplemental to the study of personality traits, behavioral patterns, and institutional structures, the examination of values has now been widely accepted as a coordinate approach in national character analysis; many scholars have found in it a key to aspects of the American character which are less accessible by other avenues of investigation. The readings in this section sample the results of the inquiry into values and constitute a report on its progress. They also point to certain difficulties that have been encountered in the attempt to define the values of a nation as complex and various as the United States.

Prominent among those difficulties is the problem of tracing a coherent pattern of demonstrably *national* values, a problem that divides the ranks of social science into camps which may be loosely characterized as pluralist and monist. The difference between the two positions is essentially a matter of emphasis: While it is generally agreed that the system of values is not altogether uniform or harmonious, opinions differ in regard to the *degree* of integration in the system. The pluralists stress the evidences of diversity; the monists accent the elements of consensus. Numerous observers have been deeply impressed by the inner tensions, inconsistencies, and unresolved contradictions which they detect in the structure of American values, while others, discerning a "strain toward consistency" and impatient of paradoxes and polarities which they judge to be more apparent than real, have identified certain "core" or "focal" values by which the value system—or substantial portions of it—is ordered and unified.

A second major problem relates to the tracing of changes and continuities in

---

[1] *An American Dilemma: The Negro Problem and Modern Democracy* (New York: Harper & Bros., 1944), ch. 1.

values over time. Historians have chronicled the transformation of the United States from a loosely knit country composed predominantly of yeoman farmers into an urban-industrial Gargantua characterized by metropolitan clusters of population, an advanced technology managed by corporate and governmental bureaucracies, an instant communications system, an elevated standard of living, and a high degree of social and economic interdependence. How have American values been affected by such vast changes in the scale, quality, and complexity of life? In what ways, to what ends, and with what effects have these changes been responsive to or influenced by the value system itself? Pursuing these questions we enter the shadowy region where the character of a people is formed out of the interpenetrations of values and experience.

These themes are treated in the first three readings in this section. The essay by Ethel M. Albert, professor of anthropology and speech at Northwestern University, discusses conflicts and changes in American values in relation to the uncertainty about values that is reported to be characteristic of many Americans today. In the second selection, Robin M. Williams, Jr., professor of sociology at Cornell University, presents evidence to support the thesis that recent changes in American values, while important, are not fundamental: "For the most part they grow directly out of elements already present at the beginning of our period of review [about 1900] and show strong continuity with the past." Williams' scheme of value categories is derived from his book, *American Society: A Sociological Interpretation,* which set forth a pluralist interpretation of the nation's values. "American society," he wrote, "does not have a completely consistent and integrated value-structure. We do not seem to find a neatly unified 'ethos' or an irresistible 'strain toward consistency.' "[2] A contrasting position is taken in the third reading in this section by Professor Francis L. K. Hsu, whose work appears for the second time in this collection. Hsu's critical review of the literature on American values develops the proposition that "what we need to see is that the contradictory American 'values' noted by sociologists, psychologists, and historians are but manifestations of one core value," namely self-reliance. This dictum, though it may state the monist contention too emphatically, bespeaks the principle of *e pluribus unum* to which the general logic of the social sciences is keyed and expresses the "strain toward consistency" which governs the monistic analysis of values.

The recent study of American values has been greatly influenced by the views of David Riesman, professor of social relations at Harvard University, whose brilliant study, *The Lonely Crowd,*[3] published in 1950, reflected the concern of post-World War II intellectuals with problems of individuality, conformity, and autonomy in a mass society. His central thesis, broadly stated, was that a momentous change had occurred and was still occurring in the character and val-

[2] *American Society: A Sociological Interpretation* (2nd ed., rev.; New York: Alfred A. Knopf, 1960), pp. 413–14.

[3] *The Lonely Crowd: A Study of the Changing American Character* (New Haven: Yale Univ. Press, 1950)—written in collaboration with Reuel Denney and Nathan Glazer.

ues of urban upper-middle-class Americans. Using a conceptual apparatus of "ideal types," he described a shift from "inner direction" to "other direction"—from a personality type in which norms are implanted by parental precept, example, and pressure, to one in which peer group influence predominates. These categories and their implications are more fully defined in the fourth selection below. The fifth selection, also by Riesman, sets out the ethical imperative in his characterology. Social reform, he contends, can be accomplished by "the saving remnant," viz., that minority of self-directed persons who are not implacably driven to conform to the expectations and directions of others. Such people are psychologically "capable of freedom"; they are to some degree "autonomous," and because the essence of autonomy is "heightened self-consciousness," the other-directed society—whose members are trained to be sensitive to themselves as well as responsive to others—may be a singularly congenial milieu for the development of autonomous personalities.

Riesman's ideas on the degree and direction of value change are criticized in the next two readings by Seymour Martin Lipset, professor of sociology at Harvard University, and Fred I. Greenstein, professor of government at Wesleyan University. Drawing on the reports of foreign visitors, Lipset contends that persistent values of equality and individual achievement have played and continue to play vital roles in the determination of social character through their influence on technological and economic change. While traits of other-direction may be more plainly exhibited by middle-class urban Americans today than by their counterparts a century ago, the difference is held to be one of degree rather than one of kind. Lipset's essay is not only an illuminating critique of Riesman's work, but a valuable contribution in its own right to the literature of American character.

Professor Greenstein concludes from studies of children's exemplars for the period 1896–1958 that, Riesman and others to the contrary notwithstanding, Americans have not come to value personal achievement less in the past two or three generations. Greenstein's findings, like Lipset's, challenge the historical sociology which sets the alleged "passivity of contemporary Americans" against an idealized picture of "a much more vigorous, optimistic, upwardly striving folk" at the beginning of the present century.

In the final selection, Thomas L. Hartshorne, who teaches American history at Cleveland State University, places Riesman's views in the context of the social criticism of the 1950's. *The Lonely Crowd,* Hartshorne writes, was a tract for the times: at the same time that it tried to define and explain the character of an important segment of Americans, it revealed, in its concepts and concerns, some of the salient traits and tensions of that character. Hartshorne also remarks that Riesman's ideas were often misunderstood for the same reasons that they enjoyed so great a vogue: "Americans brought up on the conflict between conformity and individualism . . . were deluded by the apparent similarity of Riesman's concepts to the older ideas and simply assumed that they *were* the older ideas slightly refurbished." Though Hartshorne locates Riesman's work in relation to the intellectual interests of two decades ago, he leaves open the question of whether and how Riesman's characterology may validly apply to the character of Americans in the 1970's. Have we grown more other-directed? Are there signs of progress toward personal autonomy? These are questions to which each reader may wish to seek his own answers.

Conflict and Change in American Values

ETHEL M. ALBERT

In the learned and popular literature on contemporary American values, uncertainty about values is regularly reported. Value problems, in America and in the Western cultural tradition generally, are in no sense novel, as witness the long history of value philosophy and social criticism. Focused social-scientific studies of values are by contrast relatively new. The relationship between descriptive studies of values and philosophical value theory remains unclear. For those who adopt the view that they are mutually relevant, the outcome of the "is-ought" issue depends less on a priori considerations than on the actual results and contents of empirical studies. Definition and resolution of value problems are not a matter of theoretical speculation. They depend on whatever research reveals about the factual nature of values. The programmatic position, that the factual aspect of values is relevant to value theory, becomes a hypothesis or guiding principle. It is, in the present state of social-scientific studies of values, confronted by the plain fact that the data are far from descriptively adequate, the methods and theories neither well defined nor well established.

There is no single social science value theory. There are a multiplicity of approaches, historical, psychological, sociological, or anthropological, and, within each special social science, numerous conflicting schools of thought. Tentativeness about the specific meaning of the general proposition that the descriptive is relevant to the philosophic treatment of values is dictated by the tentativeness of any hypotheses that can at present be formulated about the descriptive character of values. Here, to account for the reported uncertainty about values

Reprinted with permission from Ethel M. Albert, "Conflict and Change in American Values: A Culture-Historical Approach," *ETHICS an International Journal of Social, Political, and Legal Philosophy,* LXXIV (Oct., 1963), pp. 19–33. Copyright 1963 by the University of Chicago. Footnotes omitted.

in America, preliminary hypotheses will be formulated that utilize historical and contemporary data, and anthropological documentation and theories of contrasting cultural patterns.

Conflict and Change

Contemporary value uncertainty may be viewed in part, perhaps in very large part, as a response to value conflicts associated with significant historical changes that reached a critical point in the mid-twentieth century and to the persistence of competing, alternative value systems of the different cultures that make up American society. The uncertainty may also be in part a reaction to consistent failure to foresee the outcomes, favorable and unfavorable, of the considerable changes in values and in the conditions of life and ways of thought initiated by modern science, which have in our time reached proportions probably inconceivable to those who initiated these changes.

The relations of change and conflict are not simple. Change may bring conflicts, but it may also resolve them—as, in the course of time, it has settled the conflict between inherited privilege and the common good, between legalized slavery and liberty as a universal right. Persistence may as easily as change lead to conflicts. If conditions change, but values do not, the resulting lag will probably cause disturbing currents. The degree of integration of values with life-conditions, whether there is change or persistence, is critical, when we seek the sources of value-conflicts. Specifically, it is necessary to know which changes and which failures to change have generated conflicts. Not all value-conflicts lead to uncertainty about values. If A and B disagree, and each is absolutely sure he is right, conflict inevitably results. These are external conflicts that may very well strengthen conviction and opposition. When an individual seriously entertains alternative means or ends, value-conflicts can and often do give rise to internal conflicts. These are virtually certain to shake confidence, or to generate uncertainty.

Value uncertainty is often represented as leading inevitably to the disorganization of persons and of societies. Yet, conflict and uncertainty have been utilized for constructive reintegration of values to suit the realities of changed conditions of existence. Change and conflict are universal processes in human affairs, not unlike motion in physics. They are part of the dynamics of life that produce resolutions as well as conflicts, conviction as well as uncertainty. If then, attention is here concentrated on value conflicts related to uncertainty, it is only for the sake of understanding one phase of values that needs further clarification.

Values as Systems

Values are most easily understood as elements of value systems. Anthropological research suggests that value systems are distinctively culturally patterned. Individual value systems may be treated as variations of the cultural value system. Each element of a cultural value system is in various ways related to other values, to relevant social institutions, and to individual actions. Each may change and in changing may bring about alterations elsewhere in the value system or in the way of life. When realization of values repeatedly brings unforeseen consequences, it indicates ignorance of the systematic interconnections of values with each other and with environing conditions. It is more fruitful to use failure to predict as a guide to further social scientific inquiry than to conclude from it that values are non-logical in character and operation.

Values are by definition criteria, that is, ideals, goals, norms, and standards. Accessible principally through analyses of verbal behavior, values are not the same as the actualities of conduct. Actualization may reveal that values in the fact are not so elegant as they seemed when they were theoretic, shining ideals; that performance does not measure up to intentions; that practice does not vindicate theory. Realization may bring in its train highly undesirable, unforeseen side effects and may bring to light value conflicts that were invisible while the values remained verbal statements only.

Each value system may be assumed to rest on value premises that tend to be implicit: the more a value is taken for granted, the less likely it is to be stated explicitly or examined. When events occur that cause doubt, values may become objects of conscious and critical awareness. Moreover, in the course of time, unnoticed changes in meanings and in the internal relationships among values are likely to occur. Hence, actualization may bring surprises when such values are enacted. Further, particularly in Indo-European cultures, high-level ideals are not intended for universal, literal realization. Secondary values are in fact found in every cultural value system. They are the practical rather than the ideal guides to behavior. When the contrast between ideal and realistic values becomes visible, uneasiness and uncertainty may result. Precisely because it is believed that the realization of values should bring happiness, betterment, satisfaction—this is virtually a defining characteristic of cultural systems of values— it is necessary for adequate study to examine the actual as well as the hoped-for results of the realization of values.

Traditional American Values

Observers of the American scene often disagree in their interpretation of values, but there is a commonly accepted pool of data—historical, sociological, and anthropological—and some stable analytical results. These include the set of explicit, central values of the United States, as these have developed since about 1776, and as they are reported by observers from Tocqueville to such contemporary writers as Myrdal, Lerner, and Kluckhohn.

In the Declaration of Independence, in the Constitution, and in other formal as well as informal statements of basic American values, the central values comprise: equality; liberty; justice; democracy, understood as the sovereignty of the people; the right of private property; and individual responsibility, freedom and initiative, circumscribed only by avoiding harm to others and by concern for the general welfare. These values were conceived in direct opposition to eighteenth-century tyranny and aristocracy. The significance of these values has by now changed from opposition to a clearly defined enemy to uncertain status in a long-established democratic republic. When the Declaration of Independence was written, there was slavery. Slaves were not, of course, counted as citizens. Property qualifications were assumed a natural prerequisite of suffrage. Women were legal minors. Now, at least in law, liberty and equality are the rights of all, irrespective of race, color, creed, sex, or previous condition of servitude.

The "American character"—that victim of so much abuse, foreign and domestic—was, and to some extent for some Americans still is, conceived as governed by optimism; confidence in the future; a belief in progress to be achieved by effort; a high evaluation of success understood as prosperity, to be achieved by individual initiative; high moral character, more or less in keeping with the Puritan ethic, namely, an orientation to duty, industriousness, seriousness, or sobriety; morality interpreted largely as respectability; religious faith, with or without church attendance; also, practicality; respect for education and skill; self-reliance; physical and spiritual courage; neighborly tolerance of diversity within the limits of law and order and moral decency; patriotism, qualified by the right to criticize and change the law; an activistic approach to life, with accomplishment, good deeds, improvement and success central; and, in general, the maintenance of high hopes and high ideals, even when realities require departures from accepted rules. The conviction was and is still general that the order of the universe at large and the organization of life in the country are such that men get pretty much what they deserve, although some luck is needed.

The American creed, with its assurance of rights to life, liberty, and the pursuit of happiness, was at first conceived as self-evident. Questions, not rhetorical, now are asked: What has become of the ideals envisaged for individual well-being and social progress? In the abstract, the ideals seem unexceptionable and promising of a good life and a happy future. And so in large part they have been, as conditions have favored their realization. To the changes in their meaning and application briefly indicated above may be added a type of general alteration in American society upon which there is virtual unanimity among observers, the secularization of American values, as seen in a decrease in the role of religion and of the sacred in American life and a corresponding increase in concern with material, fleshly and other mundane, secular values.

Secularization

Secularization in economic affairs must seem the most "natural" locus of such change. The relationship between religious values and economic enterprise is vastly altered, since the early days of the American republic. For the founding fathers, money-making was a virtue, poverty a proof of laziness and moral unworthiness. But business became increasingly secularized, as money-making became easier. Civil War profiteering opened the way for the notions that "money does not care to whom it belongs," and "anybody can make a million dollars, but nobody can get rich honestly." The money-making methods of the nineteenth-century "captains of industry" made great fortunes but drove a deep wedge between religious ethics and business ethics. Yet, recent studies of the values of American businessmen indicate that those "at the top" preserve the ethical outlook of their Puritan predecessors, only very little changed. For the general public, however, economic well-being is less a virtue than a human right which the government ought to guarantee. Although money-making is still highly regarded, the change in the American economy from small, individual enterprise to huge industry has taken the moral glory out of it. Readjustment has not yet been made to the modifications in the contents and relations of the values of economic success, progress, self-reliance, and high moral character.

General American morality has, of course, also been affected by secularization. To some extent a response to secularization in economics, changes in morality have also been critically influenced by the increasing implementation of humanistic values. The same scientific humanism that furthered the values of universal well-being has destroyed their traditional foundation. Although there is close correspondence between traditional Christian values and modern scientific values, the authoritative religious basis of Western morality has been lost. The moral principles remain, but they are left dangling, in effect waiting for a new foundation to be built beneath them. Social science has tried to provide new foundations. It is nevertheless truly a queer spectacle: the traditional Christian virtue of charity and the traditional American value of tolerance are now being supported or justified by psychoanalytical and anthropological theory.

Although dogmatic and bigoted viewpoints persist, they are not the generally accepted model of American values. Sympathy and friendliness, easy-going, uncritical attitudes are widespread and are fostered by the mass media. At the same time, there is much concern about education, juvenile delinquency, the impressions made by Ugly Americans abroad, the quality of television shows, the new downward trend in church attendance, the supposed trend to conformism in teen-agers and in organization men, and general moral values. The high volume and persistence of such concerns in America are made more interesting by the fact that violence and conformity, long part of the American scene, have again been rediscovered and that some of these problems trouble other countries of the world, where they appear not to be taken quite so seriously.

Preoccupation with material and technological goals and a devotion to quantification and to "bigness" tend perhaps to obscure the persistence of moral sensitivity as a traditional American characteristic. Secularization seems to have destroyed moralism and reformism, but this appearance is perhaps due to the contrast between the relatively permissive ideal of current morality and the harsh, intolerant model of Puritanism in its prime. Serious Americans in the past examined their consciences, chiefly in the churches; today, serious Americans often examine their unconscious on the psychoanalyst's couch or in the public press. There has been a change in content and method, but Americans are still much more given to anxious examination of the inner self than the peoples of other Western nations.

The Sorcerer's Apprentice

Secularization may be viewed as an unforeseen result of simultaneously realizing the ideals of economic prosperity, humanism, and progress in theoretical and applied science. Each of these values is by itself beyond reproach. The results of their joint progressive realization are good but far from flawless, and through their mutual interaction, they have been radically transformed. Nobody set out to undermine high ethical standards in business or the value of self-reliance. These and other side effects resulted from extending science and education and from increasing the scope and power of the economy. Moreover, as mental illness figures suggest, wealth, health, education, political rights, and the myriad other goods provided by the modern way of life have not produced the "good life" for all their beneficiaries. Looking back to the time these defining characters of happiness were formulated, we see that, for the poor, the promise of wealth seemed happiness; for the sick, health was the greatest good; for the illiterate, education was the panacea; for the unfree, freedom was the dream. Desirable though the removal of ills undeniably is, negatively determined values do not appear adequate for constructing an effective, satisfying value system.

Examination of other facets of the traditional American value system can only reinforce the sobering view of what happens to even the best of ideals when they become realities. What has happened to "efficiency"—in this age of gadgets, chromium, fins, and overmechanization? What of "rationality" as a value? What should constitute the educational curriculum, now that Latin is out of date and a B.A. is a minimal requirement for socioeconomic respectability? What can religion be, in an age of science? What of the family, when experts in child-rearing, child-feeding, and progressive education contradict so firmly the maxim that "mother knows best"? Progress—another word that increasingly evokes anxieties—has a price.

It is not surprising that the surprises produced by the realization of American values should have led to uncertainty. History has contradicted the assumptions made about the basic values. Even when, as now, these values have been or are close to being realized beyond the fondest dreams of those who first proposed them, the changes they bring about unsettle the patterns of life to which we are accustomed. Flexibility was no part of the original charter. Readjustment takes time, but because there are many rapid changes in the modern world and because so much of what happens is unexpected, there is a prolongation of a mood of questioning and uncertainty.

The Premise of Homogeneity

Another unexpected development in the growth of the United States and of Western civilization generally is related to a conflict of values that has remained hidden until recently. It is usual to refer to American values as though there were one kind of American, one American value system, due allowance being made for individual personality differences. However, the United States has long been decidedly a multicultural community. The internal diversity of the American population—in language, religion, values, and customs—is very great and is a source of fundamental value conflicts. The fact of value diversity within the United States touches a very tender spot in the value system of the dominant official pattern of values sketched above. The publicly sanctioned attitude toward diversity is tolerance. But in the beginning and still today for not a few Americans, "diversity" refers only to variations on one cultural base, the English-speaking, Protestant, Caucasian. It has already been noted that the intended beneficiaries of early American values did not include slaves, poor men, or women, nor were Orientals, "foreigners," or American Indians included.

After the pacification of the American Indians, the problem of dealing with these culturally very different peoples was dissolved in the belief that they were "vanishing Americans." Far from having vanished, the American Indians are now at least ten times more numerous than they were at the close of the Civil War. The millions of immigrants from Europe, it was earnestly believed, would in a generation's time become like other Americans through the process of assimilation. The idea of the melting-pot functioned as a safeguard against the problems of basic cultural diversity. "Hyphenated" Americans, however, are still numerous, even in the third and fourth generations.

Within the culturally and numerically dominant American population, clearly visible differences of wealth, customs, and tastes were assumed to be in some sense temporary. Economic development would end the more offensive economic contrasts, and mass public education would alter manners, customs, and tastes toward uniform American standard models. It is only very recently that sociologists have explicitly addressed themselves to the study of what is now recognized as a centuries-old phenomenon of "social class" in America.

The belief in rapid elimination of class and cultural differences reflected a general European belief. It was supposed that Westernization would raise "primitives" to the level of "civilization" and bring the world's many "pagans" and "heathens" into Christendom. A social adaptation of evolutionary theory was a strong support: upward progress was inevitable, and it needed only the patient help of colonial governments, foreign investments, and missionaries to bring about a brotherhood of all men. The theory of progress through Westernization was based on the belief in ultimate homogeneity, conjoined with the assumption that Western culture was the highest expression of the evolution of society and civilization.

That there has been some degree of cultural homogenization in the United

States is more than likely, although it is very difficult to estimate correctly. There may not be a net reduction in the actual number of life-ways. The same is essentially true around the world. Even the most Westernized Africans are still African, and Oxford-educated Hindus are still Asians. Indeed, when cultures meet, new syntheses are made that exist side by side with the parent traditions. The persistence and possible increase of cultural diversity signifies the persistence of different systems of values. The relation between the premise of homogeneity and the persistence of fundamental cultural differences is a general problem of western European culture.

Varieties of Americans

Within the United States, the simplest and most obvious set of subcultural differences follow regional lines. Although the divisions are not clear-cut or absolute, it is not difficult to distinguish the North or North East from the South, or the East from the Mid West, or those from the Southwest and Pacific Far West. Regional differences reflect with surprising fidelity the widely different national and cultural origins of their original settlers, each with a distinctive value system. Regional-cultural contrasts are often intensified by the contrasts between rural and urban patterns and by social differences related to variations in social status, occupation, economic level, and education. Observers have noted that America is still predominantly rural in its outlook; for example, until very recently, Americans did not elect "city-slickers" to the presidency. The rural way of life is still associated with the good life, the city with the "unstable" and "anonymous," with sin and temptation—wherein lie its chief attractions.

That there are common core American values related to the traditional model described above is doubtless true. Judgment of what they mean concretely and of different rates and types of change can be reliable only when account has been taken of the differences that have characterized the American social-cultural system since the beginning of American history. There are, to repeat, similarities that crosscut the differences. Automobiles, television, and other mass media have contributed to an increase of uniformity over wide geographical and social areas. Nevertheless, few if any of us would have any difficulty distinguishing a southern accent from other ways of speaking American English, or a Madison Avenue man-in-the-gray-flannel-suit from a Texas ranch hand, or a Boston lady from a Hollywood star.

Another set of differences comes into view when we consider the range of religions in the United States. Some 80 per cent of Americans are called Protestant. An illusion of uniformity is created by the label but is quickly dispelled by a simple statistic: there are some three hundred varieties of Protestantism in the United States. The Amish, the Hutterites, and the Mormons not only disagree among themselves about doctrines and ways of life but also disagree very strongly with Lutherans, Baptists, Methodists, Unitarians, and others, all of whom disagree among themselves. There are in addition many millions of Roman

Catholics; a large number of Greek Orthodox Christians; many Jews, themselves divided among orthodox, reform, and other interpretations; representatives of such non-European world religions as Buddhism and Islam; affiliates of Bahai and of numerous other special sects associated with creeds originating in other parts of the world. The Constitution guarantees freedom of belief also to those who are firm in their disbelief in any religion. There are no indications that diversity in respect of religious affiliation is diminishing. On the contrary, the proliferation of new sects and conversions away from Christianity to other religions continue apace.

Language difference is a significant clue to cultural variation. Within the United States, there are, to the delight of dialect geographers and linguists, a great variety of local versions of English, some virtually or totally incomprehensible to other Americans. Time has not diminished the local flavor of Elizabethan "hillbilly" speech, or of the English spoken by Pennsylvania Dutch. In New Glarus, Wisconsin, where much of American Swiss cheese is made, third- and fourth-generation American children speak English with a thick accent, for at home, they speak only Swiss German. For generations, there have been Syrians and Norwegians settled on the south shore of Brooklyn, New York; Armenians in Boston and elsewhere; Italians, Italian Swiss, and other vineyard operators in New York, California, and elsewhere; Portuguese fishermen in California. For many of them, the first language learned is not English. In Louisiana, French is a second official language. Several million native-born as well as naturalized American citizens are native speakers of Spanish. The addition of the states of Hawaii and Alaska has greatly increased the linguistic inventory. The list is swelled by the languages of American Indians—and there are scores of them, mutually incomprehensible as English and Russian—and of several Semitic and Oriental languages. "Ghettos" make it possible for American citizens to go through life with no more than a smattering of English.

Differences of language are important in themselves, because they are a direct though potentially surmountable barrier to communication. More than that, they are a highly reliable though not absolute index of deep cultural differences, including differences in values, in outlook on life, in customs. Americans of different cultural affiliations have widely different attitudes and values, including evaluations of the fact of diversity as such. Internal cultural differences enable us to view dominant American, or Western, values in the perspective of crosscultural comparison.

Diversity and Conflict

The assumption that diversity leads to conflict while uniformity assures harmony is one of the principal currents of traditional Western thought. It is neither logically inevitable nor universally believed. Diversity implies conceptual conflict when it is accompanied by the assumption that there is only one right way of life, only one truth, only one set of values that is right. Conjoined with the directive that action should be taken to assure that the right way shall prevail, diversity leads to physical, personal, or political conflict. Diversity does not lead to conflict if it is interpreted in a "live-and-let-live" framework. Tolerance for diversity is a minor though persistent and ambiguous theme in the Western world, but it is the dominant view of many American Indian and non-Western peoples.

The ideal of progress and its concomitant optimism and effort are attached to reformist zeal. Possession of "the right way," from the beginning of Western culture, has carried a directive to pass it on to others—sometimes whether they like it or not. Difference is interpreted, consciously or not, as implying "higher" and "lower" on the value scale. On the domestic scene, determined wives persist in their efforts to cure errant husbands of their bad habits; political clean-up campaigns are not infrequent; religious missions and technological missions earnestly carry modern, Western ideas and methods to non-Western peoples and to those Western peoples whose past has stayed too long with them. In the face of failures or of persistent diversity—that is, in the face of data that call into question the reliability of the premise of ultimate homogeneity and universal Westernization—optimism and reformist zeal can and do rely upon time: the future is an indispensable dimension of Western values.

Similarity of life-ways, values, or beliefs does not necessarily exclude conflict, though the premise of homogeneity presupposes that it does. Some of the most bitter doctrinal disputes, past and present, are found within systems of belief and values. Civil war, it has been observed, is more envenomed than quarrels between strangers. The numerous Christian sects, the various Moslem sects, the diverse versions of Buddhism reflect internal disagreements about details, not about major value premises. In no small measure, the present conflict of western European political and economic theory with eastern European and now Asian doctrines is a matter of means, not of ends. Both sides are agreed that the well-being of all mankind is the goal and that democracy and independence are necessary conditions of political well-being. Both sides are committed to material welfare as a fundamental value, and each is determinedly convinced of the correctness of one way, its own, and of the wrong-headedness and immorality of the opposing view. The ideologies are different, seen from within, but their common roots in Platonism and other ancient Mediterranean ways of thought are easily visible when history is consulted. Differences between capitalism and communism are negligible by contrast with, for example, Hindu or Buddhist antimaterialistic mysticism or with the past-oriented traditionalism of various cultures. Not only Nehru of India but others as well find the analogy of Tweedledee and Tweedledum irresistible.

The history of ideas in the West is largely a history of conflicting "absolutes." Each of the combatants is sure that he has "the" truth. Even relativism in the Western world is absolutely opposed to absolutisms. The absolutism-relativism conflict, one of the perennials of Western philosophy, is literally meaningless in many of the world's cultures. The pre-Communist Chinese doctrine, "let one hundred flowers bloom," is a valid model for the interpretation of diversity of most American Indians and of many of the cultures of Africa, Asia, and Oceania. It would not be astonishing if it continues for a very long time as private opinion in China. Where this model is appropriate, diversity in outlook is considered perfectly natural. Social order in much of the world is preserved without attention to creeds or dogmas: the demand for uniformity and the use of social sanctions are directed to actions, not to thoughts, beliefs, or values.

Studies of the effects of Western on non-Western cultures reveal that the rational-scientific-technological world view is not an obviously correct and immediately attractive one. But one of the distinguishing characteristics of any world view is its invisibility. Thoroughly taken for granted, it is like a transparent lens of which the viewer is unaware. Comparison and contrast make implicit assumptions evident. A full inventory of the premises of the Western world view and an understanding of its structure and significance depend in large measure on point-by-point comparison with alternative systems.

The Western attitude toward nature is generally one of exploitation of inanimate nature for human welfare, an easy consequence of the assumptions that man and nature are different in kind and that man is superior to the merely material. However, many peoples hold the land in deep reverence and are horrified at the sight of metal tools cutting into its tender side. Their attitude toward technological changes in agriculture is understandably negative. Or many peoples—for example, the Navaho and Zuni Indians—believe that man is a part of nature, relative of the animals, the clouds, the trees. They see no conflict or essential difference of kind between man and the natural environment, and even their gods are part of one unified, harmonious universe. Or, in Hinduism, where all living things are essentially one with the deity and salvation is conceived as reabsorption in the Ultimate One Being, preoccupation with salvation tends to minimize attention to such relatively unimportant details as an adequate food supply, protection against the elements, or medicine to cure the sick.

Another facet of the Western world view is revealed by contrasting conceptions of the relationships proper among men. The modern industrialized world appreciates the utility of impersonal organizations, of impersonal relationships among men, especially in economic and political situations. For an American Indian who leaves the reservation to live and work in the surrounding society, or for an African who leaves the bush to work in a mine or in a European-type African city, there is no experience with the notion of impersonal personal relationships. Individuals regarded as employees by Europeans and Americans regard themselves as their employer's charge or dependent relative.

Almost anywhere in the world outside the industrialized areas, most types of change are considered undesirable. Generations of trial and error have painfully produced a traditional way of life and thought that is deeply venerated. Still another critical difference between modern technology and traditionalist views of nature has to do with the measure of man's power over nature. Fatalism in various forms is very widespread. The ups and downs of human life are interpreted as the result of the workings of fate or other great forces beyond human control or comprehension. Misfortune is then considered inevitable; it evokes no resolve to study its causes and no attempt to avert recurrence. Good fortune is equally unpredictable, coming to whom it chooses. Fatalism thus teaches a negative view of knowledge, of effort, of human power to determine events, of planning or foresight. It is the very opposite of the premise of the modern Western world view in which man is nature's master. In fatalistic cultures, "progress" has no meaning or has a negative meaning, because it means change.

The general assumption of the West when it is confronted by failures or by stubborn cultural differences in non-Western peoples is characteristically optimistic. In due course, the obstacles will be overcome; the American way or Western ways will prevail. Not infrequently, alterations more or less forced upon non-Western peoples in the name of progress have only confirmed the fear of change of conservative peasants or simple fisherfolk or herders. Established methods and theories in agriculture and medicine, applied in geographic areas not studied in sufficient detail for mastery of local peculiarities, have all unwittingly killed off fish in lakes or increased erosion or aggravated health problems. Changes intended as purely economic have unsettled family life and caused great social confusion. Some unforeseen consequences of programs designed to increase well-being have been embarrassingly at variance with original intentions. The outlawing of polygamy in certain parts of the world on grounds of its immorality was promptly followed by the appearance of the previously unknown practices of adultery and prostitution, and "illegitimate" children were born to communities that lacked even a word for infants born out of wedlock.

Many programs designed to improve life have turned out well. Nevertheless, the common human tendency to pay more attention to pains suffered than to good things enjoyed has tended to reinforce unfavorable impressions of the effects of Western ways. The enthusiastic espousal of Western values by the leaders of the new nations does not resolve the problems of applying Western ideas to traditionalist patterns. Voluntary or involuntary, grafts of new ways and new values on the old tend to be unsettling at least temporarily, a great hardship for the many who do not live in the future. Regard for the systematic, patterned nature of values and for their relation to the rest of culture is necessary to effect orderly transition to new ways.

As a view of diversity, the Western premise of ultimate homogeneity is in direct opposition to the Western value of respect for individual differences, belief in the right of both individual and national self-determination, and the value of tolerance. This is by no means a novel conflict in Western thought but is rather the continuation of a conflict that is thousands of years old. Tolerance of diversity in its weakest form is not much more than indifference to diversity, maintained as long as other ways and other values keep their distance. A stronger form of opposition to absolutes is the kind of relativism that demands preserving diversity as itself valuable, respecting each value system and each life-way as equally good with every other. Such extreme tolerance tends to be impracticable.

Genocide, sadism, murder, and other such phenomena raise the issue of drawing the line somewhere. The question has then to arise, where shall it be drawn? Neither an absolutist view nor a flaccid, undiscriminating relativism of accepting everything is satisfactory for theory or for solving practical problems. There is not yet a workable answer to the question of the right way to deal with diversity within the general Western world view or in its specifically American manifestations. The frame of reference is deficient and needs to be replaced.

Utopias and Realities

Viewed in historical and comparative cultural perspective, the dominant, formal American value system may be seen as a distinctive cultural pattern, reacting to a distinctive historical development. Western society is, by its own decision, progressive and changing. It is also "utopian." As we have seen, the realization of the dominant ideal values of the United States, as of the wider Western world of which it is an integral part, brought in its wake a series of surprises, only some of which were pleasant. In no small part, the surprises are a consequence of the fact that Western values tend to be utopian. The tendency to propose utopias intended for realization on this earth is very strong in the Western world and takes many forms, just as perfection in the hereafter is characteristic for Indo-European cultures more generally.

In social science and everyday life, as in the unrolling of its history, the West is harassed by the problem of unpredictability in human affairs. This may be because its own outlook on life, its own values, make Westerners so unpredictable, by comparison with the traditionalistic, empirically minded, practical peoples of other cultural traditions. For high ideals determine expectations much of the time but conduct only some of the time, and not even the acting individual can be sure which values will govern his conduct at a given moment.

When they are newly proposed, utopian values are in the nature of the case untested. Lack of experience with their actual consequences accounts for the low level of predictive power, compared with the empirically tested values of traditionalistic societies. Traditionalistic societies know the strengths and weaknesses of their values and know what to expect of them when they are realized. The cost of such security is patent: little or no improvement or embellishment of life conditions is effected. The cost of utopian values is also patent. When the contrast between the high level of stated ideas and the relatively low level and unforeseen negative effects of actual performance appears, when it is realized that many men live by very different values from those they proclaim, individuals in Western cultures easily move from uncritical moral idealism to uncritical cynicism. The term "hypocrisy" has much currency in Western moral and social criticism. Reformist zeal and cynicism are opposite but probably equally natural responses to the conflict between the utopian character of Western values and the stubbornness of "realities."

Attached to "utopianism" is what might be called a "millennial" attitude:

when the utopia in question is realized, all will be so perfect that no further changes will ever be necessary. This sort of notion—that a time will come when there will be no change—conflicts with the idea of progress. The combination of utopian and millennial thinking is very familiar to us, like so much else a "footnote to Plato." *The Republic* promised that once philosophers were kings, government would be so perfect that no further change would be needed. The Hebraic tradition promised the kingdom of God on earth, an arrangement of human life so perfect that further change would be nonsensical. The passage of several millenniums of history has not altered the pattern. The *Utopia* of More and the ideal societies of the eighteenth- and nineteenth-century writers were also intended to establish the perfect social order—universal peace, health, prosperity, cultivated tastes, and more. Marx's classless society belongs here: with the removal of class differences, conflict would be removed from social life, further changes would not be needed—and the dialectical pendulum would stop swinging. The scientific-technological utopia of the twentieth century inherited all the major characteristics of its forebears. All these utopias, it must be noted, presuppose universal acceptance as a condition of success. They share the premise of ultimate homogeneity and thus fail to deal realistically with diversity, even those proclaiming respect for individuality.

It is too soon to conclude that none of the utopias now trying to prove their worth, to say nothing of utopias as yet in the making, will succeed in bringing about a condition of life so perfect that everyone will be persuaded of its excellence and that no further changes will be necessary. For the present, however, none has succeeded in defeating the competition or in reducing diversity. On the contrary, contemporary utopian plans are confronted with essentially the same realities: (*a*) the actualization of utopian values not previously tested, however great the benefits, has produced unexpected and often undesirable side effects; (*b*) changes in values and life-ways occur piecemeal and rarely, if ever, in entire value systems or entire cultures; as a result, differences persist and may even be intensified, at the same time that there are some changes toward uniformity; (*c*) more specifically for the value cluster associated with economic-technological-educational progress, (*i*) realization of the relevant values has produced the problem of survival represented by potential military uses of atomic energy; (*ii*) the contrast in well-being between those who already enjoy the realization of these values and those who are waiting for the benefits is greater now than in earlier and less affluent days; (*iii*) the reception accorded the values themselves, the means necessary to their realization and the other facets of the world view and value system tendered with them to non-Western peoples has been very variable, ranging from flat refusal by some to impatient enthusiasm for overnight modernization by others.

The alternative responses to the situation, characteristic of Western culture, include (*a*) the persistence of confidence in one's own beliefs and values as the only correct ones for all mankind and the concomitant persistence of head-on collisions with those who have other ideas of "the" right way; (*b*) occasionally, recommendations for a return to the prescientific, traditionalistic ways of thought and action; (c) explicit relativistic recognition of conflicting claims as each having something of value, followed often by a sense of uncertainty generated by the implicit premise that there can be only one correct system, and leading not infrequently to a demand for new values, preferably a new utopia. The data on which uncertainty feeds include the facts, at any given time, of out-and-out failures of some values, especially the highest ideals, to be realized; of disappointing or disorganizing results of realizing key values; and of the unsettled claims of competing values or value systems.

Conclusion

Risk and uncertainty are probably permanent features of human existence. They are interpreted and responded to in diverse ways. Among fatalists, for example, courageous resignation to whatever chance or fortune turns up seems the logical reaction. Within the Western tradition, however, uncertainty tends to be acutely uncomfortable, psychologically and intellectually. In economics the theory of games, in characteristically Western fashion, provides a mathematical method to minimize risk. Uncertainty in the field of values has in some instances led to vacillation or paralysis of judgment and action. This is neither practically nor theoretically welcome. However, uncertainty produced by sober observation and interpreted as a temporary suspension of judgment is, in the philosophical-scientific tradition, considered both an intellectual and a moral virtue. It may be regarded as willingness to admit ignorance and refusal to accept easy and probably false or misleading solutions to the persistent and probably permanent human problems of values. This is generally the view adopted by John Dewey and others who have attempted to utilize scientific methods in value theory. It would seem inconsistent with the denial of the possibility of final certainty to seek a new utopia in which scientific or any other methods are put forward with the idea of terminating problems of values for all time.

The common assumption that science can gain universal agreement, albeit only in the realm of facts, may be viewed as another manifestation of the ancient Western preoccupation with achieving homogeneity. Whatever merit the assumption has in theory, it has so far failed signally in practice. It offers no workable solution to the problems generated by the actual persistence of diversity, as much in the realm of facts or beliefs as in the realm of values. Whatever applications may be attempted of scientific methods to the description of values or to the construction of a philosophical value theory, these cannot be of much practical utility if they, too, proceed on the assumption that everyone everywhere can be converted to one point of view about facts and values and that such unanimity would assure harmony and co-operation.

The need to examine and probably to revise the assumption of homogeneity is one of the theoretical implications for value theory that emerges from examination of the culture-historical development of values in the United States and in

Western culture generally. There is a concomitant need to examine and probably to revise the utopian-millennial aspirations of value theories in the direction of taking seriously the descriptive realities. Attention to specific problems and their specific circumstances rather than to universal, eternal, ideal proposals appears to be in order. A generalized theory of values can better follow from than precede an examination of specific actual problems and solutions.

If anthropological theories about cultures as distinctively patterned are correct, there is little likelihood that value uncertainty in the United States can be dealt with by direct borrowing of a philosophy developed in some other cultural tradition where pluralism has never been problematic. Resolution in this as in so many other realistic difficulties must come from within, more specifically, from a well-documented statement of the nature of the problem to be solved. If the interpretation of value uncertainty suggested above—granting its obvious tentativeness and incompleteness—is at least in the right direction, it justifies the hope that uncertainty associated with serious consideration of the historical and anthropological facts about values will issue in appreciation of the constructive value of uncertainty as an invitation to further inquiry. The understanding of the way values work out in relation to the conditions of their actual realization may reduce the disagreeable surprises that have played so large a part in generating uncertainty that is psychologically and intellectually paralyzing. Research may point a way toward resolving or avoiding conflicts implicit in seemingly compatible values prior to their actualization. Reliable information about the contents and consequences of values in different cultures and different historical eras may contribute to refinement of criteria for a meaningful "evaluation of values." Since the internal conflicts of American society and the results of its historical development are so much like those of the contemporary international scene, one may even indulge the hope—utopian, to be sure—that a resolution of practical and theoretical problems of American values will contribute to resolving the urgent problems of world-wide survival, peace, and well-being.

Changing Value Orientations and Beliefs on the American Scene

ROBIN M. WILLIAMS, JR.

The term "values" has been used to refer to interests, pleasures, likes, preferences, duties, moral obligations, desires, wants, needs, aversions and attractions, and many other kinds of selective orientation. However, one of the widely accepted definitions in the social science literature restricts values to *conceptions of the desirable,* influencing selective behavior, and sharply distinguishes between what is desired and what is desirable, equating the latter with what we ought to desire. In this restrictive definition, values regulate ". . . impulse satisfaction in accord with the whole array of hierarchical enduring goals of the personality, the requirements of both personality and sociocultural system for order, the need for respecting the interests of others and of the group as a whole in social living."[1] Clearly, this is a highly socialized view of value, which rules out, e.g., purely hedonic interests and gratifications.

In a broader view, anything good or bad is a value, or a value is anything of interest to a human subject. Men are not indifferent to the world; they do not stop with a sheerly factual view of their experience. Explicitly or implicitly they are continually regarding things as good or bad, pleasant or unpleasant, beautiful or ugly, appropriate or inappropriate, true or false, as virtues or vices. A

Reprinted with permission from Robin M. Williams, Jr., "Changing Value Orientations and Beliefs on the American Scene," *Illinois in Transition: Proceedings of the Illinois State of Society Conference for Church Leaders* (Cooperative Extension Service, University of Illinois, no date—mimeographed).

[1]Clyde Kluckhohn: "Values and Value-Orientations in the Theory of Action: An Exploration in Definition and Classification." Talcott Parsons and Edward A. Shils (editors): *Toward a General Theory of Action,* Harvard University Press, Cambridge, 1951, p. 399.

comprehensive initial view of the total field of valuing seems most useful; more specific conceptions can then be developed for particular purposes.[2]

Accordingly, we look first to the common features of all value-phenomena. It seems that all values contain some cognitive elements (although some definitions do not include this), that they have a selective or directional quality, and that they involve some affective component. Values serve as criteria for selection in action. When most explicit and fully conceptualized, values become criteria for judgment, preference, and choice. When implicit and unreflective, values nevertheless perform as if they constituted grounds for decisions in behavior. Men do prefer some things to others; they do select one course of action rather than another out of a range of possibilities; they do judge the conduct of other men.[3]

On the basis of an earlier extended analysis, we may begin our present discussion with a listing of 15 major value-belief themes that are salient in American culture:[4]

1. Activity and work.

2. Achievement and success.

3. Moral orientation.

4. Humanitarianism.

5. Efficiency and practicality.

6. Science and secular rationality.

7. Material comfort.

8. Progress.

9. Equality.

10. Freedom.

11. Democracy.

12. External conformity.

13. Nationalism and patriotism.

14. Individual personality.

15. Racism and related group-superiority themes.

Taken as a total set, these complex orientations imbue the culture as a whole with a tendency to emphasize active mastery rather than passive acceptance of events; an external rather than an inward view of the world; an outlook that perceives society and history as open-ended, not static; a faith in rationalism as opposed to traditionalism; an interest in orderliness; a universalistic rather than a particularistic social ethic; horizontal or equalitarian rather than hierarchical social relationships; and a high evaluation of individual personality rather than collective identity and responsibility.[5]

---

[2]Cf. Stephen C. Pepper: *The Sources of Value,* University of California Press, Berkeley and Los Angeles, 1958; Ralph Barton Perry: *Realms of Value: A Critique of Human Civilization,* Harvard University Press, Cambridge, 1954.

[3]Adapted from an article to be published in the *New International Encyclopedia of the Social Sciences.*

[4]Robin M. Williams, Jr.: *American Society* (2nd edition), Alfred A. Knopf, New York, 1960, Chapter XI.

[5]*Op. cit.,* Robin M. Williams, Jr., p. 469–470.

As we examine *values* (standards), we shall have to find our evidence in various admixtures with *knowledges* and *beliefs*, for in any evaluative act there are cognitive elements. Our judgments of what should be are always related to our judgments of what is. Thus our present view of mental illness as illness (rather than as possession by demons, or as the result of morally culpable behavior) points to humane medical treatment, rather than punishment, as a "good." The change from older orientations is partly a change in biological, psychological, and sociological knowledge, but the changed beliefs in the long run profoundly affect evaluative standards, even as changes in values in turn will affect our perception and conceptions of reality.

But perhaps we are leaping to unwarranted conclusions by the very way we have stated our topic, for we seem to be assuming that changes in values actually have occurred. It is conceivable that we are bedazzled by the obvious and dramatic changes in technology and economic life in the United States together with changes in superficial customs and in surface ideologies. It would be conceivable that a great many conspicuous changes in these easily observable matters could leave essentially untouched an "underlying" substrate of basic values. In other words, specific norms, beliefs, and patterns of overt behavior might change while the fundamental *standards* for judging desirability were preserved intact, changing only in the surface forms of expression.

Perhaps the strongest statement of the thesis that the major values in American life have not been radically changed even over a long period has come from Seymour Martin Lipset,[6] who argues that ". . . the value system is perhaps the most enduring part of what we think of as society, or a social system,"[7] and that massive technological and social changes have left relatively intact the main values and such enduring tensions as "democratic equalitarianism" versus "achievement orientation." He reminds us that the observations by foreign visitors of American life during the past century and a half cast doubt on the idea that value-patterns have changed greatly. In particular, he notes the persistence from very early times of emphasis on the themes of *equality* and *achievement* and of "other-direction" and *conformity*. He views with approval the conclusion of W. W. Rostow that a distinctive pattern of American values and institutions goes back at least to the end of the 18th century.

Clearly, whether we see change or no change depends partly upon how value is defined, especially upon the level of generality. At one extreme are highly abstract principles, such as universal brotherhood; at the other, quite specific norms prescribing details of behavior. The more abstract and generalized the values we define, the less likely they are to show change over time. Thus Talcott Parsons, working with such generalized cultural values as "instrumental activ-

[6] *The First New Nation: The United States in Historical and Comparative Perspective,* Basic Books, Inc., New York, 1963, Chapter 3.
[7] *Ibid,* p. 123.

ism" favors the thesis of *relative* constancy rather than *fundamental* change in American values over a relatively long period.[8]

At the most generalized level, it seems correct to say that during the last half century or so no completely new major value-orientations have appeared, nor have any main values completely disappeared. The most important changes have been, on the one hand, changes in beliefs and, on the other, changes in emphasis, accent, and arrangement of values. Yet these changes are filled with consequences for human experience and the direction of societal development. On this ground we are reassured that we may legitimately deal with real and important changes in both beliefs and values.

In a much-cited article Clyde Kluckhohn has suggested that our society has experienced a set of changes in values resulting in heightened emphasis on group rather than individual goals, on security rather than future success, on adjustment rather than competitive achievement, on expressive rather than instrumental values. More specifically he suggests:

1.   Strictly personal values have given way in favor of more publicly standardized "group values," whether those of a community, an organization, a social class, a profession, or an interest group.

2.   More emphasis is being placed on psychological *desiderata* relating to mental health, the education and training of children, and self-cultivation (as an adaptation to "normality" in group living).

3.   "Respectable and stable security" has risen in the scale of values at the expense of high aspirations and effort directed at long-time future success.

4.   Aesthetic values have received increasing favor.

5.   Participation in organized religion has risen in approval, but the emphasis seems to be heavily on group affiliation and stability rather than on intensified personal religious commitment.

6.   Heterogeneity in certain respects is becoming a principle of organizing the value system; variety is valued.

7.   Ideals for women have changed, as have sexual codes.

8.   There is increased concern for abstract standards; greater value is placed on explicit values.[9]

This insightful but avowedly impressionistic inventory provides a point of departure, and forces us to confront the question of where to look for the more important rather than the less important changes.

Let us emphasize again that generalizations concerning values in American society are limited by the fact that the available data are scanty, unsystematic, and often difficult to interpret. Generalizations concerning *changes* in values are

---

[8]"The Point of View of the Author," Max Black (ed.): *The Social Theories of Talcott Parsons,* Prentice-Hall, Inc., Englewood Cliffs, N. J. 1961, p. 346–347.

[9]Clyde Kluckhohn: "Have There Been Discernible Shifts in American Values During the Past Generation?" Elting E. Morison (ed.): *The American Style,* Harper & Brothers, New York, 1958, p. 204.

even more difficult to make than are descriptions of the current value patterns, for comparable information usually is not available for both the past and the present periods. Even when certain values can be identified and located, it is rare that we also have reliable information concerning their salience, intensity, and exact relation to specified kinds of overt behavior. Also, we must be aware continually that great diversity of values is certain to be found when analysis has to deal with something as complicated as a highly differentiated society of more than 195 million people. Any value we can identify will be found in association with other values that oppose, contradict, and modify its influence upon behavior.

It is this kind of complex interpenetration and tension and opposition that characterizes large-scale and complex societies, so that it is quite impossible to give any neat over-all summary or label to an entire nation without misleading simplification. For instance, I would hold that in the southern states there is a value system sufficiently distinctive to be more than a mere variant of a unitary national system. It seems essential to stress this diversity or "pluralism" in the sense of marked differences in values within different segments, sections, strata, and other divisions within America's social structure. Nevertheless, when all the necessary qualifications have been taken into account, we believe that some fairly important general conclusions can be drawn.

Modes of Change in Values and Beliefs

Among the ways in which values and beliefs can change, the following are noteworthy:

1. CREATION.   A new standard or belief is developed out of experience and becomes effective, at some level, in regulating behavior.

2. ABRUPT DESTRUCTION.   Although extremely rare, there are some instances in which a massive event results in the relatively sudden disappearance of previously accepted orientations.

3. ATTENUATION.   Withdrawal of affect and commitment is relatively slow; intensity diminishes; fewer and fewer persons will promote, support, teach, or defend the belief or value orientation.

4. EXTENSION.   The orientation is applied to objects and events in addition to those included in the original sphere of relevance.

5. ELABORATION.   The value or belief is progressively rationalized, symbolized, dramatized, documented, and otherwise made more complex or more embedded in its socio-cultural context.

6. SPECIFICATION.   A generalized orientation increasingly is defined in terms of the particular contexts in which it is considered applicable. Thus: "In the American case, the implications of certain initially given values have been explored in a great variety of specific social contexts, resulting in numerous modifications and restrictions in applications. Thus 'freedom' is now felt to be compatible with compulsory vaccination, compulsory school attendance, and

peacetime military conscription. It is now also clear that the eminently democratic 'equality of opportunity' can intensify the competition for invidious distinction."[10]

7. LIMITATION.   Through confronting *other* values, any given value position necessarily comes to be altered—even if only in the direction of rigid absolutism. A frequent outcome, however, is that a particular value, by being tested in relation to other values, comes to be bounded or limited by the recognized claims of other values. So it is that American democratic philosophies and practices always have been obliged to accommodate a persisting strain between *freedom* and *equality:* each is necessary for the other, but neither can be pushed to extremes without negating its companion.

8. EXPLICATION.   In the form of folk virtues, values are typically implicit—indeed, often altogether incapable of explicit formulation by the people who orient their behavior to these covert but powerful standards. At the opposite extreme, highly detailed explicit values are stated in creedal or philosophical systems. Again to quote an earlier statement:

American society has long been characterized by a vast oral and written accumulation of explicit value-statements. Although it would be difficult to demonstrate a clear trend . . . it seems likely that the past half century has brought increasingly explicit articulation of major values. Explicit statement of values is encouraged both by rapid changes in specific social norms and by direct challenges, including the rise and spread of totalitarian political movements.[11]

9. CONSISTENCY.   It comes as no surprise that two sharply opposed diagnoses are with us: (1) American values are becoming more consistent; (2) American values are becoming less consistent. Our suggestion is that no immediate global generalization is warranted. Greater systematic explicitness at the level of national political assertions and mass-media creeds almost certainly implies "contradiction," "inconsistency," and "hypocrisy" when viewed against the daily realities of behavior in particular localities, urban or rural. What often is overlooked by both popular commentaries and social science analysis is that the structural separation of collectivities and groups permits the peaceful co-existence of radically incompatible values within the same integrated political and economic orders.

10. INTENSITY (ABSOLUTISM).   A value formerly accepted as one among many *desiderata* may become so intensely held and promoted as to become the center of life. A value formerly the focus of all other criteria may lose its central intellectual and emotional *raison d'etre,* become relativized, and recede into the ranks of the ordinary criteria of daily life.

The sudden disappearance of a widely accepted value-orientation is a very rare event. What may appear to be an abrupt rejection of a hitherto prevailing

---

[10]James H. Copp (ed.): *Our Changing Rural Society: Perspectives and Trends,* Iowa State University Press, Ames, 1964, p. 27.

[11]*Op. cit.,* James H. Copp, p. 28.

value or set of values usually turns out upon closer inspection to have been preceded by long-term diminution in strength of commitment and by a gradual withdrawal of attention and effort. To be maintained, values require investment—of time, attention, effort, affect. Unless exercised, values atrophy. As Rodman has said:

At the heart of our analysis lies the issue of when old values die and new values develop. It is precisely because old values never die, and because new values only gradually appear, that it may, at times, be difficult to state categorically that a particular value is effectively held by a particular individual or shared by a particular group.[12]

Analysis of value-change is greatly indebted to Florence Kluckhohn's insistence that all major types of value-orientations are found in all societies at all times—with varying degrees of emphasis and dominance and in varying combinations.[13] If this view is accepted, it follows that,

Given an array of value orientations and a reasonable estimate of the proportion of people who hold to them, it is possible to see empirically that there is always some segment of the population that is congenial to the adoption of almost any change. Such a segment does not necessarily have to subscribe to the dominant or major variant value orientations of the society in order to make itself felt.[14]

From the considerations just reviewed, it is clear that changes in values and beliefs may occur in many different ways. A few of these modes of transformation will be illustrated by the particular changes in American values, to which we now turn.

Activity and Work

For most of its history, the United States has been noted for its activity and bustle, its high evaluation of being busy, its aversion to idleness, and its glorification of the man of action. Work itself, as a highly purposive and organized form of being active, has been regarded with especially strong approval. What Goetz Briefs called "the metaphysical drive to work" often had direct connections with religious convictions. The goodness of work became for a time for some segments of the population an unquestioned virtue and was inculcated as such in several generations of American children. In a society of farmers and individually owned and managed business firms, the connection between work and visible accomplishment was immediate and close.

It was in this way that the value-commitment to work as a virtue came to be

[12]Hyman Rodman: "The Lower Class Value Stretch," in Louis A. Ferman, Joyce L. Kornbluh, and Alan Haber (eds.): *Poverty in America,* The University of Michigan Press, Ann Arbor, 1965, p. 282.

[13]Florence R. Kluckhohn and Fred L. Strodtbeck: *Variations in Value Orientations,* Evanston, 1961.

[14]William Caudill and Harry A. Scarr: "Japanese Value Orientations and Culture Change," *Ethnology,* Vol. I, No. 1, January 1962, p. 90.

tied historically to the belief that this virtue would be rewarded. There is now more than a hint that " . . . the emphasis has shifted from the importance of work and striving to the urgency of appearing to be successful . . . , as measured by the power and property which one openly consumes."[15] The President of the American Academy of Political and Social Science calls for " . . . the courage to pronounce that work for work's sake is philosophically bad and can only result in mortification of the spirit and the flesh."[16] At the same time that the cults of success and lavish consumption cast doubt on the intrinsic merit of work as such, unemployment and under-employment for many workers, together with automation and computerized industry (the "Cybernetic Revolution") and with certain kinds of chronic social disorganization, may be creating the conditions for a permanent *Lumpenproletariat* of poor persons who are defeated, alienated, and outside the labor force. Few new jobs are being created for the less skilled workers in the private sectors of the economy (except in poorly paid service occupations). As Secretary of Labor Wirtz put it, many of the new sophisticated machines have the equivalent of a high school diploma. Short of more massive and imaginative public action than now exists, many of the uneducated and unskilled simply will not be able to find work. At the upper income levels, the connection between work and income often is slight, e.g., when persons live on income from investments. The new phenomenon of poverty in the midst of affluence suggests that income is also divorced from work for the very poor. Indeed, one already hears from the Ad Hoc Committee on the Triple Revolution the following:

As the first step to a new consensus it is essential to realize that the traditional link between jobs and income is being broken. . . . We urge, therefore, that society, through its appropriate legal and governmental institutions, undertake an unqualified commitment to provide every individual and every family with an adequate income as a matter of right.[17]

The idea of guaranteed annual income is bound to appear the less startling the more workers come to see their jobs as primarily "busy work" that will soon be done by automated devices in any case.

Our impression therefore is that activity and work are coming to be less highly regarded and less often used as criteria of the good man or the good life. It must be emphasized, however, that this is a *relative* statement and that instrumental activism continues to be very strongly valued indeed.

Achievement and Success

Another central theme in the American value heritage is the emphasis upon

---

[15]Melvin M. Tumin: "Some Unapplauded Consequences of Social Mobility in a Mass Society," *Social Forces,* Vol. 36, No. 1, October 1957, p. 32–37.

[16]James C. Charlesworth: "A Comprehensive Plan for the Wise Use of Leisure," in *Leisure in America: Blessing or Curse?,* Monograph No. 4, American Academy of Political and Social Science, Philadelphia, April 1964, p. 35.

[17]Statement reprinted in Ferman *et al.* (eds.): *op. cit.,* p. 451.

competitive achievement in which individual performance is judged against a standard of excellence. The strength and pervasiveness of this value-complex have been conspicuous throughout most of national history. However, many observers and commentators in the 1950s and 1960s have called attention to an alleged decline in achievement values, as well as in the ethic of hard work and ascetic self-discipline.[18] The older "principled" orientation is said to be changing in favor of security, social approval, conformity (to *other people* rather than to a *tradition* or an ethical code or principle), and smooth interpersonal relations. Although these assertions have been challenged and although some contrary evidence has been brought forward, it is true that scattered studies of cultural products consistently suggest a long-term decline in expressed *achievement* values. Analysis of a random sample of editorials in the *National 4-H Club News* from 1924 to 1958 showed a significant decline in emphasis on the value of achievement (and no significant change in *affiliation* or *cooperation* values).[19] Similar results were found in an analysis of advertising in the *Ladies' Home Journal* from 1890 to 1956.[20] Magazine fiction and mass heroes (e.g., entertainers) also show indications of lessened stress on excellence of achievement and more on the "rewards" of being successful.

Our own impression from all the bits and pieces of information that are available is that achievement has receded in salience and intensity in relation to success, but that the change is a shift in emphasis rather than a reversal of values and that achievement remains an outstanding value-orientation.

Moral Orientation and Humanitarianism

An obviously central part of American value-orientations is bound together in a distinctive moral orientation, including the idea of obligatory moral principles that transcend immediate expediency and that apply universally to everyone. Because moral principles of this kind run counter to very strong interests, impulses, and other values, the record shows much deviant behavior and violation. Whether commitment and conformity have decreased, remained the same, or increased during this century is difficult to say. By picking and choosing examples, one can easily make a plausible case for any view. In our judgment, admittedly impressionistic, there has been some decrease in the binding power of such absolute values as honesty, but a probable increase in the effective implementation of humanitarian values. The prevailing ethic in personal relations is perhaps less stern and rigid and possibly more kindly than previously.

The tendency to shift away from punitive-moralistic to medical-humanitarian

[18]For example, David Riesman: *The Lonely Crowd*, Yale University Press, New Haven, 1950; William H. Whyte: *The Organization Man*, Doubleday Anchor Books, New York, 1956.

[19]Murray A. Straus and Lawrence J. Houghton: "Achievement, Affiliation, and Cooperation Values as Clues to Trends in American Rural Society, 1924–1958," *Rural Sociology*, Vol. 25, No. 4, December 1960, p. 394–403.

[20]S. M. Dornbusch and L.C. Hickman: "Other-Directedness in Consumer-Goods Advertising: A Test of Riesman's Historical Theory," *Social Forces*, Vol. 38. No 2, December 1959, p. 99–102.

approaches is prominent, for instance, in the evaluation of mental illness and its treatment.[21] For example, Woodward in a local study has noted a loss of faith in repressive and punitive approaches and documents widespread acceptance of the view of mental illness as " . . . a sickness that should evoke sympathetic understanding and that requires some form of professional treatment."[22] A general movement to apply universalistic criteria and to accept humanitarian values seems evident in public policies toward ethnic and racial minorities, poor people, the physically disabled, children, women workers, and others subject to special stresses, disabilities, and discrimination. Such sensitivity does not seem marked, on the other hand, with regard to enemies in war, to communists, and to those who dissent radically from prevailing beliefs.

Changes in moral codes—whether called religious or secular—are likely to be affected by and to have effects upon organized religion.[23] Since World War II, we have heard much of an alleged revival of religious interest and activity. The statistics show rising membership, and surveys show much testimony to acceptance of generalized religious beliefs. On the other hand, the number of clergy have not increased proportionally to expanded memberships, financial contributions apparently have not outdistanced the rise in dollar incomes, and studies show an impressive degree of popular ignorance of religious history and doctrine. Even the conspicuous intellectual ferment in the seminaries and among prominent theologians seems to have had little impact on a rather placid kind of popular piety. At the same time, evangelical forms of fundamentalistic Protestantism attract much involvement in certain parts of the total society.[24] Internal secularization may be glimpsed in the many activities and interests in church programs that do not seem fully permeated with religious symbols and values. Religious tolerance and ecumenical interests have grown.

Many bits of evidence point to a process of secularization of certain aspects of religious beliefs, values, and practices. For instance, Barnett has traced the way in which Easter came to be treated in the popular press as a commercial opportunity rather than as a sacred occasion.[25] A study (B. J. Crawford) of the changing content of hymns over the century beginning in 1835 showed a marked decrease in transcendental and supernatural topics and references and a marked increase in social and ethical content. Many topics formerly defined and discussed in a religious context have come under the sway of scientists and other professionalized secular agents.

With many reservations and qualifications, we can say that religiously connected beliefs and values have, over the last half century, moved from personal

[21]Julian L. Woodward: "Changing Ideas on Mental Illness and Its Treatment," *American Sociological Review*, Vol. 16, No. 4, August 1951, p. 443–454.

[22]*Ibid*, p. 444.

[23]See: "Religion in American Society," *The Annals of the American Academy of Political and Social Science*, Vol. 332, November 1960.

[24]Cf. Louis Gasper: *The Fundamentalist Movement*, Mouton & Co., Paris and The Hague, 1961.

[25]James H. Barnett: "The Easter Festival: A Study of Cultural Change," *American Sociological Review*, Vol. 14, No. 1, February 1949, p. 62–70.

salvation to social ethics, from concerns with the supernatural order and the after-life to greater interest in the pressing concerns and sufferings of men in the here-and-now,[26] from sacramental and ritualistic activities to social service and to involvement in the great domestic and international issues of the times. Personal fulfillment in devotion and service is more often emphasized, and asceticism, sacrifice, and impersonal duty are less often stressed.

Science and Secular Rationality

The theme of science and secular rationality is a complex and changing mix of beliefs, knowledge, and values. Certain values are indispensable for the very existence of science—it cannot be practiced save on the basis of objectivity, honesty, tentativeness, rationality, and openness to criticism.[27] There is no doubt that the tremendous growth in scientific activity over the last hundred years has entailed the spread of scientific values more and more widely through the social system. The emphasis upon applied science and technology has strengthened and extended the theme of instrumental activism in nearly every area of human interests, eventually including society and social man himself. In the systematic pursuit of empirical validity, science has produced highly desired by-products in mastery of the physical environment, greater material comfort, conquest of diseases, and increases in social power. At the same time, it is in the very nature of science that it will arouse fear and resistance and moral revulsion if it relentlessly pursues the goal of increasing knowledge. As it saves lives through modern medical practice, it is capable of providing megadeaths through nuclear, chemical, and biological warfare. Even as it increases national wealth, it creates economic dislocations of great magnitude. And its (necessary) organized scepticism is often felt to be threatening to cherished ideologies and established belief-systems.

Nevertheless, over the sweep of the last century, science (together with technology) has permeated more and more of our culture and society. The extension of scientific methods and concepts and styles of thought into the study of human biology, psychology, and the social sciences means that no areas of experience are now closed to scientific approaches.

Efficiency and Practicality

In passing we may note that verbal deference to both efficiency and practicality apparently remains great. Our society has always put great store in quick

---

[26]As one small illustration, Crawford found that hymns dealing with sin, salvation, evangelism, death, and judgment were 44 percent of the Methodist hymnal in 1836 but had declined to 12 percent by 1935.

[27]Merton speaks of four institutional imperatives of science: universalism, communalism of findings, disinterestedness, and systematic skepticism. (Robert K. Merton: *Social Theory and Social Structure*, Revised Edition, The Free Press, Glencoe, Illinois, 1957, p. 522.)

pragmatic solutions to technical and instrumental problems. Whether this orientation has become increasingly dangerous in the world of today is a question we feel obliged to raise, but to which we have no adequate answer.

Material Comfort and Hedonic Enjoyment

Values, we have said, are standards of desirability that are invested with affect and that function as points of reference for selectivity in actual behavior, not merely in fantasy. According to this conception, it seems correct to identify a normative preference for material comfort as a major theme in the American constellation of values. It is difficult, however, to trace the theme through time in order to say whether it has remained unchanged or has risen or declined in the hierarchy of values; systematic and comparable data bearing directly on the matter simply are not available, and inferences must be based on historical materials whose precise meanings are not always certain. Certainly the "Gilded Age" of the 1890s was marked by conspicuous consumption on the part of the newly wealthy, by a great preoccupation with money and material opulence, and by much single-minded and ruthless economic acquisitiveness. Religiously tinged praise of asceticism has been found in all periods of national history, but undoubtedly has declined markedly during the 20th century.

Under the long-term influence of affluence and of the commercialized pressures to consume, the ideal of self-denial has come to be less and less acceptable[28] Appreciation of material abundance at times grows into a preoccupation with creature comfort. Having a good time often comes to be semi-obligatory.[29] On the whole, however, there is now a more relaxed acceptance of comforts and pleasures, without a sense of sin or guilt and simply as part of a good life here and now.

Progress

Generations of foreign observers have been struck by the seemingly boundless optimism and faith in progress they found in the United States. Although this tendency to believe that the future will be better, in some sense, than the past remains widespread and strong, the 20th century experience clearly has reduced the conviction that progress is inevitable.

[28]A content-analysis of best-seller novels for 1900–1904 and 1946–1950 showed that " . . . the writers of popular fiction presented alcohol in positive rather than negative terms, and the tendency to see drinking as supportive and good increased during the half-century span." (Harold W. Pfantz: "The Image of Alcohol in Popular Fiction: 1900–1904 and 1946–1950," *Quarterly Journal of Studies on Alcohol,* Vol. 23, No. 1, March 1962, p. 146.)

[29]Martha Wolfenstein: "The Emergence of Fun Morality," *Journal of Social Issues,* Vol. 7, 1951, p. 15–25.

Aesthetic Values

American society often has been criticized for an alleged lack of commitment to and support of aesthetic values, and more particularly of the creative arts. In the perspective of historical comparison with Western Europe, it seems clear that our business civilization indeed has not strongly encouraged an emphasis upon aesthetic values and artistic activity. In the most recent decades, however, many evidences point to increased appreciation and support of these aspects of our culture, e.g., the rapidly growing numbers of local symphony orchestras, theater groups, and opera groups; the vogue of amateur painting and sculpture; the rising attendance at art galleries and museums and at concerts and theatre; and the national political interest in the arts.

One can only speculate on this, but it may well be that increased attention to and participation in art activities and in a self-conscious search for beauty has had to wait upon a slackening of instrumental activism in the world of work. We may be seeing the beginning of a shift from instrumental to expressive interests. At the same time, it is quite likely that aesthetic standards are themselves being changed by immersion in American culture.[30]

Equality

On the whole, although the evidences are fragmentary and sometimes contradictory, it seems that the value of *equality* has received increased attention and implementation during the last generation. There has not been a steady or continuous movement, but rather two great periods of change, i.e., the early New Deal and the developments associated with the Civil Rights Movement of the 1950s and 1960s. At the level of national law and administrative policy, there has been substantial movement toward establishing equality of political and civil rights for segments of the population formerly subject to discrimination and disadvantage—women, the propertyless, Negroes, aliens, unpopular religious sects, and so on. To this extent, a universalistic ethic has become more firmly institutionalized.

Obviously there still is great economic inequality; nor is there any potent political movement to reduce the differentials between rich and poor. Minimal aid for the most severely deprived is as far as the current consensus will go in this direction. The general economic development of the nation, however, has resulted in substantial leveling up, so that a very large middle-income stratum has developed. At the same time, the increased differentiation of the society has produced a number of strategic elites rather than a single ruling class. Less than

---

[30]"The trend toward broadening the scope of aesthetics, making it more descriptive and empirical in aim and method, is part of a larger trend in American thought away from metaphysical idealism and dualism and toward a more naturalistic orientation. . . . The trend . . . (the so-called 'Twilight of the Absolute,' which seems new and revolutionary to some French writers) has long prevailed in the United States." (Thomas Munro: "Recent Developments in Aesthetics in America," *ACLS Newsletter*, Vol. XV, No. 2, Feb. 1964, p. 2–3, American Council of Learned Societies.)

formerly is there a unitary focus of power and authority in a clearly discernible and socially integrated ruling class. Instead we have several functional elites, performing different major sets of societal tasks. A highly differentiated society combines functional inequality with relatively rapid and massive movement toward " . . . a good measure of economic equality . . . [in addition] . . . to the civil and political equality won during the past three centuries."[31]

Freedom

By the value of *freedom* we mean that criterion of conduct which holds it desirable that men be subject to minimal external constraint in seeking the ends they desire by the means they deem most appropriate. Of course, there is no such thing as unconditional and unlimited freedom in human society; at some point one man's freedom becomes an infringement of the equally valid and precious freedom of another man. To insist upon freedom as a value is only to insist that it is always a relevant criterion for behavior; to the advocate of freedom the burden of proof is upon him who would curtail freedom to show valid reason in terms of some other higher or more urgent value. Freedom, in the present sense, means maximum possibility for men to attain their separate goals, and it probably is maximized in a society with a stable political consensus and with plural and "balancing" centers of power.[32]

Freedom is curtailed by coercion, but it may be curtailed also by lack of positive opportunity. Freedom to work is an empty thing if no jobs are available. The formal right of access to restaurants and hotels is useless to persons who have no money. It follows that the institutional rules that forbid interference with basic freedoms are not enough, essential as they are, to guarantee an optimal situation of freedom. When Negro Americans received the protection of the Civil Rights Act of 1964, it was clear that the formal rights thus safeguarded would not touch the constraints caused by unemployment and low income.

Looking broadly across the whole complex national scene, it is reasonable to conclude that the combination of increased prosperity and widened equality of opportunity has greatly extended many areas of freedom since the turn of the century. On the other hand, suppression and intolerance of political dissent have continued to appear from time to time. Concurrently the exigencies of large-scale centralized economic and political organization and of urban life have produced numerous detailed constraints unknown to our grandparents. The freedom of the frontiersman is not the freedom of the Detroit automobile factory worker or the junior executive in a large corporation. The total picture of changes both in actual specific freedoms and in their evaluation is so qualitatively diverse that any overall estimate would be nearly meaningless. Perhaps the

[31]Suzanne Keller: *Beyond the Ruling Class: Strategic Elites in Modern Society,* Random House, New York, 1963, p. 271.

[32]DeGré: "Freedom and Social Structure," *American Sociological Review,* Vol. 11, No. 5, October 1946, p. 524–536.

most useful thing to say is that the *value* of freedom can be expressed under many different organizational forms, but that it is never easy to preserve and requires continuous defense: it is still true that the price of personal liberty is eternal vigilance.

Democracy

The term *democracy* does not point to a single clearly specified standard; rather, it refers to a quite complex set of values and beliefs, centered on but not confined to the political order. It includes the ideas that the society's key decision-makers should be elected, that they should be subject to laws not of their own making, that the people should have a set of basic civil and political rights that cannot be voted away, and that all citizens should have a voice in major decisions affecting them. As we have already noted, the counterpoised themes of equality and freedom are central to the democratic creed.

Obviously the concept of democracy can be invoked in any area of life—family, church, school, business firm, labor union, hospital, governmental agency, voluntary association, local community, and so on.

One measure of change in American political democracy is access to the franchise. A century ago only 17 percent of the population were eligible to vote in presidential elections; today over 60 percent are eligible, and the proportion of those eligible who actually vote has increased since its low point in 1920. The total "quality" of participation in political life has not been measured, but at least in the exercise of the franchise the democratic tradition clearly is viable. On the other side, as is often noted in these times, the direct participation of the large numbers of persons affected by political and economic decisions in the actual making of those same decisions is severely limited. Indeed, the growth of the size and scope of political and economic organizations has led to increased centralization of decision-making. "Town-meeting democracy" most definitely is not the mode of operation of the giant corporation or the state and federal bureaucracies. As more and more of the crucial decisions affecting the individual have moved out of the local community, a certain amount of alienation and a sense of helplessness have been observed. To what extent this has affected commitment to the *value* of democracy, however, remains uncertain.

Conformity

The debate touched off by David Riesman's thesis of a shift *from* conformity to fixed values and rules as a matter of conscience *to* conformity to the opinions of other people—from "gyroscope" to "radar"—is still going on some fifteen years later. Sometimes the thesis has been misunderstood, and bootless arguments have been conducted over the unanswerable question whether there is more conformity or less conformity now than in the past. But even the more sophisticated hypothesis does not lend itself to a definitive answer.

For one thing, it is especially difficult in this case to disentangle changes in social situations from changes in values. In the tightly interdependent social world of the large city and the giant organization, many kinds of coordination are essential that were not of concern to the independent farmer and business entrepreneur. Alertness to the opinions of others surely is in part not a loss of "conscience," but rather a realistic response to indispensable group functioning. And a well-educated and prosperous population in a political democracy has many realistic capacities for independence of belief and action not open in an earlier era to sharecroppers, sweat-shop employees, miners in company towns, steel workers on a 12-hour day and 7-day week, terrorized and disenfranchised Negroes in the South, and so on.

In opposition, there clearly are numerous and important influences working in the direction posited by Riesman: e.g., pressures for political orthodoxy, the seductive inducements of upward social mobility, the overwhelming peer-groups of adolescents, or the relentless blandishments of the mass media. Furthermore, extraordinary pressures toward conformity are created by efforts to secure coordination and reliability of behavior in large-scale organizations.

Of course it is true that the small-town and rural America of earlier days was not particularly receptive to drastic dissent, and a premium was often placed on sheer adherence to the local norms of belief and conduct almost regardless of content. (After all, de Tocqueville was commenting on a censorious "tyranny of the majority" in the America of the 1830s.) Nevertheless, an appraisal of the total force of modern developments in social structures and processes inclines us to the view that the evaluation of conformity as a good thing has increased rather than decreased since the beginning of the 20th century.

Nationalism

Obviously *nationalism* does not represent a single unitary value-orientation; rather, it is a very elaborate and changing set of concepts and evaluations. The nationalism of Manifest Destiny was very different in specific content from the nationalism of today. The high-pitched patriotism of World War I would have seemed strange to the American soldiers of the Korean War. Through all these changes, however, one can identify two persisting kinds of nationalistic sentiments. One is totalistic and self-contained; it sometimes demands unquestioning acceptance of any and all acts of the national state in international affairs ("my country, right or wrong"). The other kind of nationalism is more critical and differentiated, and its high positive evaluation of the worth of the American nation-state is predicated upon that state's representing other values, such as freedom or equality.

Over the period since World War I, nationalism in America has become less isolationistic, probably less provincial and less chauvinistic, and certainly more complex and differentiated. Nevertheless, totalistic sentiments of nationalism remain strong and are always increased by a sense of political and military threat, foreign or domestic.

Individual Personality

Central to the high tradition of our culture is the concept of the unique worth and dignity of the human individual. The concept of the autonomous and infinitely valuable individual, with its deep religious origins and overtones, has long served as a touchstone and rallying point for values of freedom, equality, democracy, and humanitarianism. Commitment to a high evaluation of individual personality, conversely, is the base for resistance to excessive demands for conformity, to racism and categorical treatment, to chauvinism, and to excessive preoccupation with success, material comfort, efficiency, and other instrumental values.

In the age of Hiroshima, of Nazi genocide, and of war-games calculated in terms of megadeaths, it may seem all too clear that the high evaluation of the individual personality has been destroyed in the mass societies of this bloodiest of all centuries. Yet when we shift attention from the mass violence of war and revolution to the quieter changes internal to American society, we find many evidences of positive reinforcement of the value of the individual. Never before has so much been done to protect, nurture, and develop the potentialities of poor people, the physically and mentally disabled and handicapped, racial and ethnic minorities, children, the unemployed, and people in other countries.

Respect for the integrity of personality means that persons are not to be manipulated as tools or exploited as objects. Correspondingly, commitment to a high evaluation of individual personality tends to be weakened by involvement in the instrumental use of persons without their consent. Since such manipulation is frequent in war and in much political and economic activity, the present generation is subjected to massive strain in this area of evaluation. The net effects have not been studied systematically and remain in doubt.

Racism and Group Superiority

Racism and related doctrines of inherent ethnic, religious, or class superiority have a long history and deep roots in American life.[33] Nevertheless there can be no question that during the past half century both racist beliefs and group-superiority beliefs and values have greatly diminished in prevalence and intensity, and a substantial reduction in gross discrimination has been achieved.[34] Studies of public attitudes show a marked increase since World War II in the acceptance by white people of racial integration in schools, public accommodations, and

[33]William Stanton: *The Leopard's Spots: Scientific Attitudes Toward Race in America, 1815–59,* The University of Chicago Press, Chicago, 1960; Mark H. Haller: *Eugenics: Hereditarian Attitudes in American Thought,* Rutgers University Press, New Brunswick, N.J., 1963.

[34]John P. Roche: *The Quest for the Dream,* The Macmillan Company, New York, 1963.

residential areas.[35] The general weakening of racist beliefs continues in spite of some strong local countermovements—and seems likely in the long run to undercut to some extent ideas of group superiority based on ethnic or religious differences as well. Racist ideology is not likely to disappear in the foreseeable future, but it is conceivable that it could cease to be a major theme within some such period as the next twenty-five years.

Conclusions

To summarize this rather lengthy and necessarily complex discussion is to run the risk of distortion and oversimplification. In the interests of brevity, however, we suggest the following very rough and tentative summary of estimated average changes in major value-belief themes.

Value-Belief Complexes	Period (approximate)	
	1900–1945	1945–1965
Activity...........................	Indeterminate	—
Work.............................	—	—
Achievement......................	—	+ (Post-Sputnik I)
Success...........................	+	+
Material comfort..................	+	+
Humanitarianism (domestic)........	+	+
Humanitarianism (war).............	+	—
"Absolute" moral orientation.......	—	No change
Practicality.......................	+	—
Efficiency........................	+	—
Science and secular rationality......	+	+
Progress..........................	+	—
Freedom..........................	Indeterminate	—
Equality..........................	+	+
Democracy........................	+	Indeterminate
Conformity (to social pressure)......	+	+
Individual personality..............	+	Indeterminate
Nationalism.......................	+	− to +
Racism—group superiority..........	—	—
Total Factors showing:		
Increase..........................	14	8
No change or indeterminate.........	2	6
Decrease..........................	4	8

Note: (−) is decrease; (+) is increase.

As we examine this summary, it is striking that in the period from around 1900 up to the end of World War II the major thrust was in the direction of further positive development of the themes analyzed. Since 1945, however, our

[35]Herbert H. Hynam and Paul B. Sheatsley: "Attitudes Toward Desegregation," *Scientific American,* Vol. 211, No. 1, July 1964, p. 16–23.

estimates suggest a shift in the pattern in the direction of lessened emphasis on instrumental activism, some disillusionment ("progress"), and possibly some loss in humanitarianism under the exigencies of war. These changes should not be overemphasized; on net balance, during the last half-century the verdict has to be "the same main values—only more so." The changes that have occurred are clearly important, but for the most part they grow directly out of elements already present at the beginning of our period of review and show strong continuity with the past.

American society today contains, along with its working consensus of values and beliefs, great variety in the standards of behavior by which men attempt to live and in terms of which they judge themselves and others. The ranges of objectively possible value-positions according to which a person may regulate his life are highly restricted in technologically undeveloped social systems in which people live close to the margin of subsistence and in which the cultural inventory contains few contrasts and variations. In the American society of today (and perhaps even more in the future), the arc of possibilities widens greatly. Affluence, sophistication, and diversity combine to encourage a positive evaluation of variety—in certain respects—and in any case open up a great range of possible values for individual selection.

Values are created in human experience, social and non-social. Although values, once formed, may persist strongly for long periods even after the conditions out of which they originally emerged have radically changed, it is reasonable to suppose that drastic changes in the objective circumstances will eventually lead to changes in values. (Of course, the relation to reciprocal:changed values may lead to alterations in the physical and social environment.) For example, it is a plausible hypothesis that *achievement values* will be stressed in a society that has both a strong consensus on moral standards and relatively good objective opportunity for goal-attainment. On the other hand, *affective* values, stressing "enjoyment," tend to come to the forefront in two different types of situations: (a) in prosperous and secure societies, or (b) in societies in which rewards for sustained achievement are low and risks high. *Collective-integrative* values, yet again, will be stressed in societies severely and persistently threatened by other societies. War and the threat of war are major stimuli to collectivism, both as a condition and as a value-orientation.

To the extent that these generalizations are valid, the values of the America of the future will be crucially affected by immediately impending decisions concerning the nation's international relations. In this interdependent world, a clear understanding of the value-implications of public policies takes on new qualities of long-range significance.

American Core Value and National Character

FRANCIS L. K. HSU

In approaching the subject of American national character, students have experienced some unusual difficulties. What they have done so far is either to present pictures of contradictions with little or no attempt to reconcile the opposing elements, or to construct models of what, in their view, ought to be, with little or no attempt to deal with what actually occurs. In this chapter I shall try to show that the difficulties are not insurmountable, that the contradictions, though numerous, are more apparent than real, and that, even the models of what ought to be, though different from reality, can be meaningful once we achieve a proper perspective.

A Picture of Contradictions

After comprehensive sampling of the literature from early times down to 1940, Lee Coleman lists the following as "American traits": "associational activity, democracy and belief and faith in it, belief in the equality of all as a fact and as a right, freedom of the individual in ideal and in fact, disregard of law—direct action, local government, practicality, prosperity and general material well-being, puritanism, emphasis on religion and its great influence in national life, uniformity and conformity (Coleman 1941:498).

It is clear at once that this list of traits not only fails to give cognizance to such obvious facts as racial and religious prejudice, but the different traits mutually contradict each other at several points. For example, values attached to "local government" and "democracy" are in direct contradiction to that of

Reprinted with permission from F. Hsu's "American Core Value and National Character" in *Psychological Anthropology*, Francis Hsu, ed. (Homewood, Ill.: The Dorsey Press, 1961).

"disregard of law" leading to "direct action." The beliefs in "equality" and in "freedom" are in direct contradiction to the emphasis on "uniformity and conformity."

Cuber and Harper, writing nearly ten years later in a book entitled *Problems of American Society: Values in Conflict,* have reduced the total number of American values enumerated but not done much else. Their list is as follows: "monogamous marriage, freedom, acquisitiveness, democracy, education, monotheistic religion, freedom and science" (Cuber and Harper 1948:369). Cuber and Harper recognize that some of these values are inconsistent with each other and with social reality. But they attempt to explain such inconsistencies as follows:

On the surface it might seem relatively easy for a society, and especially for some one person, to discover such inconsistencies as these, evaluate the two positions, choose one, and discard the other. . . . But in practice it seems not to be so easy an undertaking. In the first place, logical inconsistency may constitute social consistency—that is, a person whose values seem, inconsistent when analysed by a third party may regard himself to be quite consistent. Both values seem to him to be quite tenable because he can point out the other persons in the society as authority for the rightness of each position (Cuber and Harper 1948:372).

As we shall see later, their explanation contains the germ of truth as to why the individual is not free to act as he sees fit, to make his value orientation more self-consistent, but it has not gone far enough. If every individual adheres to his inconsistent values because he can resort to "other persons in the society as authority for the rightness of each position," then we cannot possibly explain how values in America would ever undergo change, and how some individuals are more affected by the inconsistencies than others, enough for them to espouse certain "causes" and throw their weight behind crusades for emancipation of the slaves or to bust up saloons.

Over the years the analysis of American values has remained stagnant at this level. Thus, in *American Society* Robin Williams again gives us no more than a catalogue of American values as follows: "achievement" and "success," "activity" and "work," "moral orientation," "humanitarian mores," efficiency and practicability, "progress," material comfort, equality, freedom, external conformity, science and secular rationality, nationalism-patriotism, democracy, individual personality, racism and related group-superiority themes. (The quotation marks applied to seven of these values are Williams') (Williams 1951:388–440; 1960:415–470).

Williams does realize, perhaps more than the other authors, that the values are not of equal importance and that they have to be somehow related and reconciled with each other. Accordingly, in his conclusion on value orientation, he makes a summary classification to emphasize some and to de-emphasize others:

a)   Quasi values or *gratifications:* such as material comforts.

b)   Instrumental interests or means values: such as wealth, power, work, and efficiency.

c)   Formal universalistic values of western tradition: rationalism, impersonal justice; universalistic ethics, achievement, democracy, equality, freedom, certain religious values, and values of individual personality.

d)   Particularistic, segmental or localistic values: best exemplified in racist-ethnic superiority doctrines and in certain aspects of nationalism (Williams 1951:441; 1960:468–469).

This classification accomplishes little. It is not simply a question of differences between professed values and the actual reality. Such differences are likely to be found in any society. More specifically the question is one of unresolved and unaccounted for differences between certain professed values and other professed values. We may reconcile "efficiency" as a value with the continuous blocking of modern improvements in the building trades as a matter of difference between theory and practice. But how do we reconcile the "value of individual personality" with the oppressive and increasing demand for "conformity"? The most glaring contradiction exists between "equality," "freedom," and so forth on the one hand and "racist-ethnic superiority doctrines and certain aspects of nationalism" on the other. Williams tries to expunge the "ethnic superiority doctrines and so forth" by inaccurately classifying the latter as "particularistic, segmented or localistic values."

It is easy to see how Williams errs here. If the belief in racist-ethnic superiority were truly segmental or localistic (by which I think Williams means that it is particular to the South), how can we explain the racism that is also prevalent in the North? In fact, it has been aptly observed, and I think with some justification, that the only difference between the South and the North in the matter of racial attitudes is that the South is more open and honest about it, while the North is more covert and hypocritical about it. Of course, this view fails to consider the fact that the law by and large still supports racism in some Southern states, while the law is against it in the North. Besides, practically all the broad legislative and judiciary improvements affecting race relations have originated from the North. These legal changes do not, however, erase the widespread social, economic, and other forms of discrimination which are practiced in the North as well as in the South. Furthermore, even if we say that the racist attitude is only characteristic of the South, we must inevitably be confronted with the question: How does the South reconcile its racist attitudes with its professed belief in democracy? Are the North and the South two fundamentally separate cultures?

Some students frankly take the line of least resistance by characterizing the American culture as "Schizoid" (Read Bain 1935: 266–76), or inherently "dualistic," that is to say, full of opposites (Harold J. Laski 1948:738). This is the same sort of conclusion reached by Gunnar Myrdal who, after a mammoth investigation of the Negro-White relations, left the entire matter as *An American*

Dilemma (1944). Apart from presenting many factual details on racial discrimination in this society, Myrdal said nothing more than that there is the problem of a psychological conflict between the democratic ideal of equality, on the one hand, and the existing inequalities in race relations, education, income distribution, health benefits, and so forth, on the other. The few anthropologists who have bothered to study American values have hardly improved on this state of affairs. Thus, Kluckhohn expressed himself in 1941 on this subject:

While the relative unanimity over some kind of aid to Britain demonstrates that at least in a crisis a nexus of common purposes is still effective, the diagnostic symptom of the sickness of our society is the lack of a unifying system of canons of choice, emotionally believed in as well as intellectually adhered to (Kluckhohn 1941:175).

When Kluckhohn gave us his more intensive analysis of the American culture six years later, we can readily understand why his early conclusion of American values was as it was: Because his analysis consists of another list of "orientations" and "suborientations" that are very much in the manner of Robin Williams' treatment detailed above on pages 230 and 231 (Kluckhohn and Kluckhohn 1947).

Thus, our understanding of American values is today no better than it was several decades ago. Periodically we note the conflicts and inconsistencies among the different elements, but we leave them exactly where we started.

An American Blind Spot

I have taken so much time to come to this futile point because I do not wish to be accused of setting up a nonexistent straw man and then, with the flourish of discovery, knock him down.

The reason for this lack of progress in the scientific analysis of value conflicts inherent in American culture is, I believe, to be found in the fact that many Western and especially American scholars have been so emotionally immersed in the absolute goodness of their own form of society, ethic, thought, and religion that it is hard for them to question them, even in scientific analyses. Consequently, they cannot see anything but the eventual triumph of their cultural ideals such as freedom and equality over realities such as racism and religious intolerance. Some frankly see the former as the basic American values and the latter as outright deviations which need not even be considered. This attitude is most decidedly characteristic even of eminent scholars of American history such as Henry Steele Commager. In his book *The American Mind* he practically dismisses the Negro and, in fact, all nonwhites with one sentence:

Nothing in all history had ever succeeded like America, and every American knew it. Nowhere else on the globe had nature been at once so rich and so generous, and her riches were available to all who had the enterprise to take them and the good fortune to be white (1950:5).

I would have regarded the last sentence quoted here to be Commager's satire on the prevailing attitude of the American public, if not for the fact that, in the rest of his 443 pages, he makes no more than a few passing references to the treatment of Negroes (in one of which the word "Oriental" is inserted). Furthermore, in these references, the Negroes might well have been as important as the wayside flowers trampled on by the horses drawing westward wagons driven by white Americans. When Commager comes to twentieth century America, he seems to be most exasperated by the adverse manifestations of the American mind in the form of crime, racial and religious bigotry, lawlessness, irreligion, looseness of sex mores, conformity, class formation, and so forth. He seems so intent upon denying them, yet cannot, that he speaks in the following confusing vein:

All this presented to the student of the American character a most perplexing problem. It was the business of the advertisers to know that character, and their resources enabled them to enlist in its study the aid of the most perspicacious sociologists and psychologists. Yet if their analysis was correct, the American people were decadent and depraved. *No other evidence supported this conclusion.* Advertisers appealed to fear, snobbery, and self-indulgence, yet no one familiar with the American character would maintain that these were indeed its predominant motivations, and statesmen who knew the American people appealed to higher motives, and not in vain. The problem remained a fascinating one, *for if it was clear that advertisers libeled the American character, it was equally clear that Americans tolerated and even rewarded those who libeled them* (Commager 1944:419; italics mine).

Besides its obvious one-sidedness (for example, his statement that "the statesmen who knew the American people appealed to higher motives, and not in vain" is about as true as another which reads, "the statesmen who knew the American people appealed to *baser* motives, and not in vain,"), Commager contradicts himself badly. Unable to deny the reality of facts uncovered by scientists, facts which are used profitably by advertisers, yet unable to bring himself to see them in their true perspective, he solved his academic dilemma by branding the facts as "libel."

Gordon Allport commits the same error in his book *The Nature of Prejudice.* In its entire 519 pages Allport theorizes about mankind and religion, but his mankind is Western mankind (where he occasionally refers to Negroes and Orientals, he is merely speaking about to what different extents the different Western groups reject them), and by religion he means Protestantism, Catholicism, and Judaism, with nothing even about Eastern Orthodoxy and one sentence on Islam. Limited by such a culture-bound framework Allport is not unnaturally inconsistent (1954). In discussing racial prejudice, Allport relies heavily on experimental psychology. There is a great deal of evidence that the more prejudiced personality tends to be one which is more in need of definiteness and more moralistic. For example, "he is uncomfortable with differentiated categories; he prefers them to be monopolistic" (Allport 1954:175, 398–408). Here

Allport apparently accepts the conclusion to which his evidence leads him. However, in connection with religious bigotry Allport seems to adopt a different procedure altogether. Here he first admits that religions which claim to possess final truths are bound to lead to conflicts, and that individuals who have no religious affiliations tend to show less prejudice than do church members. But these are, in his words, too "distressing" to him and so demand "closer inspection" (Allport 1954:451).

To the student, what Allport means by "closer inspection" turns out to be a surprise, for Allport departs from the acceptable principle of science by purposely attempting to negate stronger evidences in favor of much flimsier facts. He admits that, quantitatively, the correlation between greater church affiliation and greater prejudice is correct, but he also insists that it is not correct because there are "many cases" where the influence of the church "is in the reverse direction" (Allport 1954:451). In other words, Allport finds the evidences too distressing because they show the Christian churches and the Christian values in an unfavorable light. He simply cannot tolerate the fact that the absolutist Christian faith and the exclusive Christian church membership do lead to greater prejudice. Under the circumstances, Allport has no alternative but to throw overboard the quantitative evidence in favor of some qualitative statements.

Yet even so sophisticated a social scientist as Lloyd Warner is no exception. In his book *American Life, Dream and Reality* he finds the Jonesville *grade school* children's evaluation of one another to be so strongly reflective of social-class values as to blind them to the actual reality (for example, children from the top classes were rated 22 times cleaner than those from the bottom, but in fact the latter as a whole came to school cleaner and neater than the former). However, he also finds that the Jonesville *high school* children, though following a similar pattern, do not make such categorical and rigid judgments by class values. Warner's explanations of this difference are most revealing:

Since the older children are presumably more the products of their culture than the younger ones, there appears to be a contradiction here. . . . Actually, the reasons for the differences in judgment help verify our hypothesis. The children in the high school, being products of American society, have learned to be less open and more careful about what they say and how they feel on the tabooed subject of status. *Furthermore, they have learned to use American values of individualism and are able to make clearer discriminations about the worth of an individual than are the younger children* (Warner 1953:182–3; italics mine).

The interesting thing is that Warner's second explanation here not only contradicts the one preceding it but contradicts his entire thesis, which is that social class values strongly influence American behavior and ideas. It is as though this second explanation came out by accident, perhaps a Freudian slip of his research pen, for in sentiments like "the worth of the individual" many Americans find real emotional security.

What we have to see is that in the minds of a majority of our scholars the idea of democracy and Christianity, with their respective attributes of freedom and equality in one case and of love and mercy in the other, are the over-all American values par excellence. They are so consciously upheld that all explanations of American behavior must somehow begin and end with them. Any evidence contrary to this mold is therefore treated as deviation or as "regional phenomena," as "libel," as creating a "schizoid" situation, a "dilemma." This in my view is the blind spot to many of our Western social scientists today. Given this blind spot, our scientists have consistently confused what ought to be with what is. It leads many scholars to explain the kind of American behavior they deem desirable by one theory, and another kind of American behavior, which they abhor and which contradicts the first kind, by another and contradictory theory. Some even misuse the eclectic approach by pleading the multiplicity of correlates or causation in complex human affairs.

The fundamental axiom of science is to explain more and more facts by fewer and fewer theories. Anyone can explain all characteristics of a given situation with as many different theories, but his explanation will not be of value as a piece of work of science. It might be close to a factual description. Or it might be close to fantasy or rationalization. The axiom of explaining more and more facts by fewer and fewer theories is especially crucial if the facts are obviously related, as when they occur in the same organized society and often among and in the same individuals.

Once this is admitted it becomes obvious that, when confronted with contradictions in the object of his inquiry, the scientist's first duty is, instead of trying to treat them as discrete entities and explaining them with contradictory hypotheses, to explore the possibility of a link between the contradictory phenomena. In doing so the scientist is not presuming that values in any given society must be totally consistent with each other and that all contradictions must be resolved. It is perfectly possible that many societies, being large and complex, have inconsistent or contradictory values. But what our scientists so far would seem to fail or even refuse to do is to concede even the possibility of any positive connection between these contradictory values.

Self-Reliance, Fear of Dependency, and Insecurity

What we need to see is that the contradictory American "values" noted by the sociologists, psychologists, and historians are but manifestations of one core value. Furthermore, many scholars must have been aware of this core value in one way or another but, because of their blind spot, have failed to recognize its importance. The American core value in question is *self-reliance*, the most persistent psychological expression of which is the fear of dependence. It can be shown that all of the "values" enumerated thus far, the mutually contradictory ones and the mutually supportive ones, the evil ones as well as the angelic ones, spring from or are connected with self-reliance.

American self-reliance is basically the same as English individualism except that the latter is the parent of the former while the former has gone farther than the latter. However, self-reliance possesses no basic characteristics which were not inherent in individualism. Individualism developed in Europe as a demand for political equality. It insists that every individual has inalienable and God-given political rights which other men cannot take away and that every man has equal right to govern himself or choose his own governors. Self-reliance, on the other hand, has been inseparable in America from the individual's militant insistence on economic, social, and political equality. The result is while a qualified individualism, with a qualified equality, has prevailed in England and the rest of Europe, what has been considered the inalienable right of every American is an unlimited self-reliance and an unlimited equality.

It is not suggested here that all Americans do in fact possess the unlimited economic and social equality in which they firmly believe. But it is easy to observe how strongly and widely the belief in them manifests itself. For example, the English have been able to initiate a sort of socialism in reality, as well as in name, but Americans, regardless of social security, farm subsidies, and other forms of government planning, intervention, and assistance, are as firmly as ever committed to the idea of free enterprise and deeply intolerant toward other social systems. Similarly, the English still tend to respect class-based distinctions in wealth, status manners, and language, while Americans tend to ridicule aristocratic manners or Oxford speech, and resent status so much that Lloyd Warner, for example, describes it as being a "tabooed" subject in discussing Jonesville high school students. Finally, the English still consider the crown a symbol of all that is best and hereditary, Americans criticize the personal taste of their highest officials and at least have the common verbal expression that everybody can be president.

This self-reliance is also very different from self-sufficiency. Any Chinese or European village can achieve self-sufficiency as a matter of fact. The average self-sufficient Chinese farmer will have no feeling whatever about other people who are not self-sufficient. But American self-reliance is a militant ideal which parents inculcate in their children and by which they judge the worth of any and all mankind. This is the self-reliance about which Ralph Waldo Emerson has written so eloquently and convincingly in some immortal pieces. This is also the self-reliance taught in today's American schools. The following is a direct quotation from a statement of "basic beliefs" given to the students by the social science department of one of the nation's best high schools in 1959:

Self-reliance is, as it has always been, the key to individual freedom, and the only real security comes from the ability and the determination to work hard, to plan, and to save for the present and the future.[1]

American self-reliance is then not new. As a concept it is in fact well known and well understood. Yet such is the power of the blind spot that its over-all and

---

[1] A mimeographed sheet issued to its pupils by a school in the Greater Chicago area, 1959.

basic importance has so far escaped our scientific attention. How the individual-ism of Western Europe has been transformed into American self-reliance is a question outside the scope of this paper. It has been dealt with elsewhere (Hsu 1953:111–114). Suffice it to say here that under this ideal every individual is his own master, in control of his own destiny, and will advance and regress in society only according to his own efforts. He may have good or bad breaks but,

> Smile and the world smiles with you,
> Cry and you cry alone.

It is, of course, obvious that not all Americans are self-reliant. No ideal of any society is uniformly manifested in all its members. But a brief comparison will make the point clearer. A man in traditional China with no self-reliance as an ideal may not have been successful in his life. But suppose in his old age his sons are able to provide for him generously. Such a person not only will be happy and content about it, but is likely also to beat the drums before all and sundry to let the world know that he has good children who are supporting him in a style to which he has never been accustomed. On the other hand, an American parent who has not been successful in life may derive some benefit from the prosperity of his children, but he certainly will not want anybody to know about it. In fact, he will resent any reference to it. At the first opportunity when it is possible for him to become independent of his children he will do so.

Therefore, even though we may find many individuals in traditional China and elsewhere who are in fact self-sufficient, and even though we may find individuals in America who are in fact dependent upon others, the important thing is to realize that where self-reliance is not an ideal, it is neither promoted nor a matter of pride, but where it is an ideal, it is both. In American society the fear of dependence is so great that an individual who is not self-reliant is an object of hostility and called a misfit. "Dependent character" is a highly deroga-tory term, and a person so described is thought to be in need of psychiatric help.

However, it is obvious that no individual can be completely self-reliant. In fact, the very foundation of the human way of life is man's dependence upon his fellow men without which we would have no law, no custom, no art, no science, and not even language. It is not meant that an individual human being cannot be trained, from the beginning of his life, to form no relationship with any fellow human being. But if an individual wishes to lead a human existence, in this society or any other, he is bound to be dependent upon his fellow human beings intellectually and technologically as well as socially and emotionally. Individuals may have differing degrees of needs for their fellow human beings, but no one can truly say that he needs no one. It seems that the basic American value orientation of self-reliance, by its denial of the importance of other human be-ings in one's life, creates contradictions and therefore serious problems, the most ubiquitous of which is insecurity.

This insecurity presents itself to the individual American in a variety of ways. Its most important ingredient is the lack of permanency both in one's ascribed relationships (such as those of the family into which one is born) and in one's achieved relationships (such as marital relationship for a woman and business partnership for a man). Its most vital demand on the individual is to motivate him in a perpetual attempt to compete with his fellow human beings, to belong to status-giving groups, and, as a means of achieving these ends, to submit to the tyranny of organization and to conform to the customs and fads of the peer group which are vital to his climbing and/or status position at any given time and place. In other words, in order to live up to their core value orientation of self-reliance, Americans as a whole have to do much of its opposite. Expressed in the jargon of science, there is, for example, a direct relationship between self-reliance and individual freedom on the one hand and submission to organization and conformity on the other (Hsu 1960:151). Exactly the same force can be seen to link:

a)   Christian love with religious bigotry.

b)   Emphasis on science, progress, and humanitarianism with parochialism, group-superiority themes and racism.

c)   Puritan ethics with increasing laxity in sex mores.

d)   Democratic ideals of equality and freedom with totalitarian tendencies and witch hunting.

These four pairs of contradictions are not exclusive of each other. For example, Christian love is in sharp contrast with racism as with religious bigotry. Similarly emphasis on science, and so forth, is as opposed to totalitarian tendencies and witch hunting as to parochialism and group superiority themes. In fact, we can contrast the first half of any of the above pairs with the second half of any other.

Christian Love versus Christian Hate

For the purpose of this paper we shall consider some of these contradictions in a composite whole: the American emphasis on Christian love, and freedom, equality, and democracy on the one hand, and racism and religious bigotry on the other. This is a contradiction which has tested the energy of some of the best euphemistic orators and the ingenuity of some of the most brilliant scholars. Especially in the religious area they try to write off the religious wars. They try to forget about the Holy Inquisitions. They try to ignore the hundreds of thousands of witches convicted and burned on the stake. They try to deny any connection between any of these and the Nazi Germany slaughter of the Jews, especially the anti-Semitism, anti-intellectualism, and racial persecution found, here covertly and there openly, in the United States. But when some scholars do realize that the past patterns are very much alive at present, though the specific techniques have changed, they tend to make harmless observations of which the following is a typical example:

Worship in common—the sharing of the symbols of religion—has united human groups in the closest ties known to man, yet religious differences have helped to account for some of the fiercest group antagonisms (Elizabeth K. Nottingham 1954:2).

Williams, who quotes the above passage, goes a little further by suggesting two clues to the riddle as to why some worship in common has united people and some has divided them: (a) "Not all conflicts in the name of organized religion are actually "religious" and (b) there may be different degrees of involved commitment actually at work in "nominal religious affiliations" (Robin M. Williams 1956:14–15). But there is no observable basis for distinction between "true" religious conflict and religious conflicts which are only nominally religious. Are theological controversies purely religious or nominally religious? The truth is that, even if the conflict is over nothing but liturgy, or over the question of virgin birth, they are still fought between human beings each with personal, emotional involvements in specific issues.

Williams' second clue is a more sound one. Put it differently, this is that the more "involved commitment" actually at work in nominal religious affiliations the more religious dissension and bigotry there will be. Since the stronger one's commitment to an object or issue the more inflexible this commitment becomes, it is natural that more "involved commitment" will lead to more dissension and bigotry. Certain data quoted by Allport, referred to before, directly support this proposition.[2] It is interesting to note that Williams, after stating this proposition, dismisses it as "extreme." Instead he collects a conglomeration of twenty divergencies in value—orientations which, he believes but does not demonstrate, are partially the basis of religious conflicts in the United States (Williams 1956:14–17).

It is unnecessary to probe into the reasons why Williams attaches so little significance to his second clue. It is also beyond the scope of this paper to detail the irrelevancy of some of his "divergencies" to this problem on hand. We can, however, indicate how the link between the degree of involved commitment in

[2]"Over four hundred students were asked the question, 'To what degree has religion been an influence in your upbringing?' Lumping together those who report that religion was a marked or moderate factor, we find the degree of prejudice far higher than among those who report that religion was a slight or non-existent factor in their training. Other studies reveal that individuals having no religious affiliation show on the average less prejudice than do church members" (Allport 1954:451).

And again, "First, it is well to be clear concerning the existence of certain natural, and perhaps unresolvable, conflicts inherent in various aspects of religion.

"Take first the claim of certain great religions—that each has absolute and final possession of Truth. People who adhere to different absolutes are not likely to find themselves in agreement. The conflict is most acute when missionaries are actively engaged in proselytizing divergent sets of absolutes. Moslem and Christian missionaries in Africa, for example, have long been at odds. Each insists that if its creed were completely realized in practice, it would eliminate all ethnic barriers between men. So it would. But in actuality, the absolutes of any one religion have never yet been accepted by more than a fraction of mankind.

"Catholicism by its very nature must believe that Judaism and Protestantism are in error. And varieties of Judaism and Protestantism feel keenly that other varieties of their own faith are perverse in many points of belief" (Allport 1954:444–445).

nominal religious affiliations and the extent of dissension and bigotry is the source of the contradiction: Christian love versus Christian hate. It is not hard for the trained social scientist to note that religious affiliation in the United States today has become so largely a matter of associational affiliation that "the values that inhere in group affiliation and participation" far and above overshadow "the specific values espoused" by the religious body (Williams 1956:17). The overwhelming proof of this is to be found in well-known works such as the Lynds' on "Middle Town" and Lloyd Warner and associates on "Yankee City" and "Jonesville,"[3] but particularly in the results of a poll of 100,000 Protestant ministers in all parts of the United States by the *Christian Century* magazine in 1951, to determine the "outstanding" and most "successful" churches. This poll showed twelve to be the chosen ones. One of the twelve was the First Presbyterian Church of Hollywood.

The applauded "qualities" of this church have been analyzed elsewhere (Hsu 1953:273–277). Suffice it to say here that the "successful qualities" of this church seem to be that the "happiness" of the parishioners revolves about the social and material endeavors which redound to their benefit alone but that the spiritual faith and the quality of the ministers' teachings receive practically no attention.

All this is understandable once we appreciate the persistent demands that the core American value of self-reliance makes on the individual. The churches must compete and, in order to exist and to be "successful," must satisfy the status quest of its members. To achieve that "success," the churches not only have to conform to the trend toward organization, but they must try to find new ways of increasing their memberships so as to reach greater "successes."

In this psychology we can now find the common ground between religious bigotry and racial prejudice. Western religious dissensions have been associated with many things but their principal and perennial feature has been the search for original purity in ritual and belief. The Reformation was based on it. The entire evolution of Protestantism from the Lutheran church to Quakerism has had it as the central ingredient. The Holy Inquisition was instituted to ferret out impurity in Christian thought and practice. This fervent search for and jealous guard over purity expresses itself in the racial scene as the fear of genetic mixing of races which feeds the segregationist power in the North as well as in the South, no matter what rhetoric and other logic are employed. When religious affiliations have become largely social affiliations, this fear of impurity makes religious and racial prejudices undistinguishable. Religion is not the question. The point of the greatest importance is affiliation. The neighborhoods and clubs are as exclusive as the churches and church activities tend to be, in spite of all

[3]Commenting on religion George C. Homans says: "We are apt to think that the choice of a church among people brought up in the Protestant tradition is a matter of individual conscience. No doubt it is. But it is certainly also true that the membership of churches, in Hilltown as in Boston, tended to correlate roughly with that of certain social groups" (1950:346).

protestation of equality, democracy, worth of the individual, Christian love, and humility.

The individual who is enjoined to be self-reliant, unlike one who is taught to respect authority and external barriers, has no permanent place in his society. Everything is subject to change without notice. He is always anxious to look above for possible openings to climb, but he is at the same time and constantly threatened from below by possible upward encroachment. In his continuous effort at status achieving and maintaining, the self-reliant man fears nothing more than contamination by fellow human beings who are deemed inferior to him. This contamination can come about in diverse forms: sharing the same desks at the same schools, being dwellers of the same apartments, worshipping in the same churches, sitting in the same clubs, or being in any situation of free and equal contact.

In this context, as in others, individuals will vary in the extent to which they are pressed by the fear of inferiority. Some will join hate organizations, lynching mobs, and throw stones at Negro residences or paint swastikas on Jewish synagogues. These are violent acts of prejudice. Others will do everything they legally or by devious means can do to keep individuals of certain religious, racial, or ethnic groups out of residential areas, certain occupations, and social fraternities. These are active nonviolent acts of prejudice. Still others will quietly refuse to associate with members of religious, racial, or ethnic minorities and teach their children to observe this taboo because one just does not do such things. These are passive nonviolent acts of prejudice.

Under such circumstances many, perhaps most, individuals find it impossible to act in the same way as they have professed and been taught. It is not that they love contradiction or that they are, according to their critics, hypocritical. It is simply that they are oppressed by fears for losing status—fears deeply rooted in a relatively free society with a core value of self-reliance. This is also why integration of minorities, be they racial or religious, cannot reach a satisfactory destination either along the line of total assimilation into the majority way of life or along that of pluralism. There is some factual indication that Jewish youngsters who are raised as non-Jews have a much harder time adjusting to their peers in college than those who have been raised consciously and militantly to cultivate their identity in Judaic tradition and church life. In other words, their complete identity and assimilation as Americans are always subject to rejection (Samuel Teitelbaum 1953).[4] On the other hand, the rationalization in support of

---

[4]This is based on two groups of answers to a questionnaire. The first group of answers was from 230 Northwestern University students in 1951 of whom 210 were undergraduates. A condensed version of the same questionnaire was sent to a random sampling of 730 undergraduates at nine midwestern universities and colleges in 1952–53, from which 325 undergraduates responded. The results, though quantitatively inconclusive, are qualitatively suggestive. First, students of Jewish background experience relatively little anti-Semitism at high school level when mixed dates are frequent, but at the university level their social contacts become much less diversified. Second, there is more open identification with Jewish culture and institutions as the generation of Americanization advances. That is to say, the second and third generation American Jews tend to be more openly

anti-Oriental legislation was that the Oriental standard of living was too low and that they were incapable of assimilation to the American way of life.

A reverse proof of the hypothesis advanced in this paper is not hard to find. We have only to look at societies where obedience to authority and dependence relationships are encouraged and where the individual is not subject to such pressures coming with self-reliance and, therefore, more sure of his place in society. Individuals in such societies tend to have much less need for competition, status seeking, conformity, and, hence, racial and religious prejudices. For example, religious dissensions, persecutions, and conflicts have always been prominent in the West as they have always been rare in the Orient. In Japan and China, the few occasions on which religious persecutions took place were invariably of short duration, always tied to the insecurity of political rule and never involved masses of the people except as temporary mobs (Hsu 1953:246–248). The case of Hindu-Moslem violence and casteism in India is considered elsewhere (Hsu 1961). Again, religious dissensions, persecutions, and racial conflicts are today more intense and widespread in Protestant-dominated societies of the West (see Chapter 14) than in their Catholic counterparts. In this dichotomy we are contrasting the United States, Canada, Australia, Union of South Africa, and so forth, as one camp and the Latin American republics, as well as Portuguese, Belgian, and French African possessions as the other. What has happened in Protestant-dominated societies is that, by and large, persecution in the form of bloody racial and religious outbreaks has been consistently driven underground while the manifestations of prejudice have become diffused, one almost may say democratized if not for the fact that the expression smells of sarcasm. But even in the most advanced Protestant societies racial and religious violence is always around the corner, ready to erupt now and then, here and there, as indicated by the recent anti-Negro outbreaks in England and the recurrent anti-Semitic flare-ups in Europe and the United States.[5]

Three Uses of Value

It will have been clear to some readers that this analysis of the psychosocial origin of racial and religious prejudices bears some resemblance to that of Kurt Lewin on the problems of the Jews as a minority group in many a western society. But it has significant differences. According to Lewin the most basic

---

Jewish than the fresh immigrants or first generation Americans. Coupled with this, Jewish students from families of higher social statuses (such as proprietary and professional) show more open identification than those from families of lower social statuses (such as sales). Third, in spite of these facts, students of Jewish background do not seem to prefer exclusive Jewish friendship and association in college. Fourth, with the term "normal adjustment" meaning acceptance by Gentile students, "the conscious (but not self-conscious) and self-identifying Jews among the students are those most integrated with their own people and the most normally adjusted on the college or university campus" (209). These results correspond amazingly to my personal observations but any final conclusion on the subject must, of course, await further research.

[5]The place of Mohammedanism with reference to this analysis will be considered in another publication.

problem of the Jew is that of group identity. Often repudiated in the country of his birth and upbringing, yet having no homeland which he can claim as his own, he suffers from "additional uncertainty," thus "giving" him "some quality of abnormality in the opinion of the surrounding groups." He concludes that the establishment of a Jewish homeland in Palestine (which was not yet a reality at the time of his writing) might "affect the situation of Jews everywhere in the direction of greater normality" (Kurt Lewin 1935:175–187).

The Jewish minority certainly shares the central problem, with other minorities, of uncertainty of group identity. But our analysis also shows that the degree of this uncertainty depends, in the first place, on the basic value orientation of the host majority and, in the second place, on that of the minority groups themselves. There is, for example, every reason to expect the Jewish minority to have far less of a problem of identity in Latin American countries than in North American countries. As far as North America is concerned, the Jews, like other minority groups, will always have the problem of identity whether or not they have a homeland. The Latin American peoples have less of the value orientation of self-reliance and, therefore, the individual has less psychosocial need to reject minority groups to maintain his status in society. On the other hand, within the United States, there is good reason to expect the Jewish minority to have a little more of a problem of identity than the Chinese and Japanese minorities even after the establishment of Israel. This is despite the fact that the Orientals possess much greater physical distinctiveness than the Jews as a whole from the Caucasoid majority. For the Chinese and Japanese have stronger ties with their families and wider kin groups than do the Jews, and are, therefore, less self-reliant and less free but more protected from the uncertainty of identity.

In this chapter I have not differentiated the different uses to which the term value may be put. Charles Morris, in a book entitled *Varieties of Human Value*, postulated three such uses: "Operative" values refer to the "actual direction of preferential behavior toward one kind of object rather than another." "Conceived" values refers to the "preferential behavior directed by 'an anticipation or foresight of the outcome' of such behavior," and "involves preference for a symbolically indicated object." He illustrates this meaning of value by the example of the drug addict who firmly believes that it is better not to be a drug addict because "he anticipates the outcome of not using drugs." "Object" values refer not to the behavior preferred in fact (operative value) or as symbolically desired (conceived value) but to what is preferable if the holder of the value is to achieve certain ends or objectives (1956:10–12).

While it is obvious that the three usages of the term "value" are not mutually exclusive and must influence each other, it is equally obvious that they are not hard to distinguish. Applying this scheme to the American scene we shall realize that self-reliance is an operative value as well as a conceived value. It expresses itself in two directions. In the positive direction it expresses itself as the emphasis on freedom, equality in economic and political opportunities for all, Puritan virtues, Christian love, and humanitarianism. These values are far more conceived than operative. On the negative side self-reliance expresses itself as the tendency toward racial prejudice, religious bigotry, laxity in sex mores, and totalitarianism. These values are far more operative than conceived. Values which are more conceived than operative are of great symbolic importance, and will be militantly defended by the people cherishing them. The less they live up to such conceived values the more they are likely to defend them, because their failures are associated with feelings of guilt. Values which are more operative than conceived are of great practical importance, and will be strenuously pursued by the people needing them. The more they have to act according to such operative values, the less they will admit their reality, since their actions also lead to feelings of guilt. At one extreme we shall find men who will openly fight to guard these operative values most flagrantly. At the other extreme we shall find men who will practice them by devious means. Those who hold on to these operative values openly and those who do so by subterfuge will share one common characteristic: both will deny their actions are motivated by prejudice and Christian hate. They will both insist that their actions are based totally on other reasons. In the South one ubiquitous reason is states' rights. In the North a widespread reason is property value or fear of intermarriage. When the real operative values are divulged accidentally, as it were, by one of those who share them, the reaction of the rest will be resentment against the simpleton who spoke out of turn and angry denial of everything he disclosed. These mechanisms are repeated so often on so many occasions, including the most recent (1959–60) Deerfield and Park Forest, Illinois, outbursts, that they need no further illustration or elaboration.

However, the ideas of equality, freedom, and Christian love inevitably affect all Americans because they are values that are conceived more than operative. They might even be described as the conscience of the American society. That is why failure to live according to them or outright opposition to them will both lead to guilt, denial, and subterfuge. There are men and women who champion the cause of the more conceived values just as those who desperately cling to and fight for the more operative values. The attitude of both sides toward their respective values tends to turn the values they champion into object values. That is to say, the champions of equality, freedom, and Christian love can consciously use their values as tools for their ends, just as the champions of prejudice, bigotry, and Christian hate can also consciously use their values as tools for their ends.

In the hands of some politicians and all demagogues the relationship between these values and the objects they desire often becomes transparently clear and undisguisedly selfish. It has been suggested that Hitler's hate campaign against the Jews was a major secret of his power. It is not surprising, therefore, that in the recent (1959–60) Chicago area integration outbursts, as with similar scenes elsewhere before, the opponents to integration charged their adversaries for promoting integration as a means of wooing Negro votes. But the link between the more conceived American values and the more operative values is the core

American value of self-reliance. The supporters of both desire social arrangements in which their own particular nests will be feathered in their own particular ways.

As the emphasis on democratic equality and freedom and Christian love
increases with self-reliance, totalitarian racial prejudice and bigotry and Christian hate will also increase with it. When the individual is shorn of all permanent
and reliable moorings among his fellowmen, his only security must come from
personal success, personal superiority, and personal triumph. Those who are
fortunate enough to achieve success, superiority, and triumph will, of course,
bask in the sunshine. To them democratic equality and freedom and Christian
love are extremely laudable. But success, superiority, and triumph on the part of
some must of necessity be based on the failure, inferiority, and defeat on the part
of others. For the latter, and even for some of those who are in the process of
struggling for success, superiority, and triumph, the resentment against and fear
of failure, inferiority, and defeat must be widespread and often unbearable. To
them totalitarian prejudice and bigotry and Christian hate can be means to a
flitting security. By pushing others down they at least achieve the illusion of
personal success, personal superiority, and personal triumph.[6]

The Problem of Pessimism

If the conclusions of this analysis seem to lend themselves to pessimistic
inferences, I wish to assure the readers that this is neither intentional nor desired. But the rule of science is that we must contemplate whatever conclusions
our evidences lead us to, whether they are pleasant or unpleasant.

In extenuation of certain pessimistic notes in the conclusions reached we
need, however, to realize that the contribution of Western self-reliance to human
development has been great and that even the chains of conformity and organization have their salutary aspects. What gave the Western man his superiority
over the rest of the world during the last 300 years was not his religion or his
romanticism but his self-reliance and his competitive organization. It was his
self-reliance which led him to discard the shackles of paternal authority, monarchical power, and medieval magic, in favor of wider organizations such as
church and state, mercantile fleets, and industrial ventures. When the West met
the East, it was the Western man's well-organized armed might which crushed
the East. As late as 1949 one high-ranking United States official attributed civil
war-torn China's plight, in a *Harper's* magazine article, to the fact that the
Chinese were "organizationally corrupt." It is instructive to note that today, the
two giants of the West, the U.S.A. and U.S.S.R., are still most attractive to the
rest of the world by their skill in organization. In various parts of the world their

---

[6]Additional substantiation for this analysis is found in Carl J. Friedrick (ed.), *Totalitarianism,*
which contains the results of a conference of scholars in 1953 under the auspices of the American
Academy of Arts and Sciences. Its conclusion is that totalitarianism is a new disease peculiar to
modern culture. *Modern* culture here refers, of course, to Western culture.

experts are helping peoples of other nations to organize their educational systems, or their marketing arrangements, or their agricultural practices, or their industrial efforts, or their military capabilities, or their national finances.

The purpose of this paper is neither optimistic nor pessimistic. It is to place the much-lauded American values in their proper genetic perspective. When this is done, we find that the best of America is directly linked with her worst, like Siamese twins. The way out of the worst is not to deny it but to recognize it for what it is.

BIBLIOGRAPHY

ALLPORT, GORDON
  1954   The nature of prejudice. Cambridge, Addison-Wesley Publishing Company, Inc.

BAIN, READ
  1935   Our schizoid culture. Sociology and Social Research 19:266–276.

COLEMAN, LEE
  1941   What is American: a study of alleged American traits. Social Forces, Vol. XIX, No. 4.

COMMAGER, HENRY STEELE
  1950   The American mind. New Haven, Yale University Press.

CUBER, JOHN F. and ROBERT A. HARPER
  1948   Problems of American society: values in conflict. New York, Henry Holt & Co.

FRIEDRICK, CARL J. (ed.)
  1954   Totalitarianism. Cambridge, Mass., Harvard University Press.

HOMANS, GEORGE C.
  1950   The human group. New York, Harcourt Brace & Co.

HSU, FRANCIS L. K.
  1953   Americans and Chinese: two ways of life. New York, Abelard-Schuman, Inc.
  1960   Rugged individualism reconsidered. The Colorado Quarterly 9:143–162.
  1961   Clan, caste and club: a comparative study of Chinese, Hindu, and American ways of life. Princeton, N.J., Van Nostrand Co.

KLUCKHOHN, CLYDE
  1941   The way of life. Kenyon Review, Spring, pp. 160–180.

KLUCKHOHN, CLYDE and FLORENCE R. KLUCKHOHN
  1947   American culture: generalized orientation and class pattern, Chapter IX of Conflicts of power in modern culture, 1947 Symposium of Conference in Science, Philosophy and Religion, New York, Harper and Bros.

KLUCKHOHN, FLORENCE and FRED STRODBECK
  1961   Variations in value-orientations. Evanston, Ill., Row Peterson and Co.

LASKI, HAROLD J.
  1948   The American democracy. New York, The Viking Press.

LEWIN, KURT
  1948 Psycho-sociological problems of a minority group, *In* Character and Personali-
        ty, Vol. III, 1935, 175–187. (Reprinted in Kurt Lewin: Resolving Social Con-
        flicts, New York, Harper & Bros.)
MERING, OTTO VON
  1961 A grammar of human values. Pittsburgh, University of Pittsburgh Press.
MORRIS, CHARLES
  1956 Varieties of human value. Chicago, University of Chicago Press.
MYRDAL, GUNNAR
  1944 An American dilemma. New York, Harper & Bros.
NOTTINGHAM, ELIZABETH K.
  1954 Religion and society. New York, Doubleday & Co.
TEITELBAUM, SAMUEL
  1953 Patterns of adjustment among Jewish students. Northwestern University,
        Ph.D., dissertation.
WARNER, LLOYD
  1953 American life: dream and reality. Chicago, University of Chicago Press.
WILLIAMS, ROBIN M.
  1951 American society, a sociological interpretation. New York, Alfred Knopf.
        (1960, 2d ed.).
  1956 Religion, value-orientations, and intergroup conflict. The Journal of Social Is-
        sues 12:14–15.

From Morality to Morale

DAVID RIESMAN

It is a difficult problem to attempt as in this series of lectures to link the psychological understanding of people to specific political and other social phenomena. In his paper Professor Parsons tried to show how individuals play roles in a society and how these roles within a social system may harness various types of personalities. To put it more specifically, you can get the same kind of political behavior, for instance, out of quite different human types. Although the behavior has different meanings for these people, the understanding of their differences and those different meanings may be quite irrelevant to their political and public role.

Nevertheless, and this is the topic of my discourse, it seems to me that personality does influence political behavior if we look at it in a sufficiently long-run historical view. Its influence is felt not in terms of specific behavior—in terms of explaining why somebody votes for Truman or Dewey or Wallace—but only in terms of what I like to call political style, the kind of attitude a person has towards the political cosmos: how he reacts to it, how he feels it reacting to him. If one is to speak as more than a spot-news analyst of political crisis, then he must be concerned with these long-run developments both in politics and personality.[1]

In fact, I think there is a danger for the social scientist if he allows such a phrase as political crisis to make him try to be particularly relevant in talking about spot news, the atom bomb, or what not. Because curiously enough if the social scientist is any good he can't help being relevant. He lives in our society as a participant-observer and it is no problem for him to be relevant—he can't help it. If he isn't any good, and hence irrelevant, he is sometimes likely to compen-

Reprinted with permission of the publisher from *Personality and Political Crisis* edited by Alfred H. Stanton and Stewart E. Perry. Copyright 1951 by The Free Press, A Corporation.

[1]This topic is treated more fully in *The Lonely Crowd*, by David Riesman (with the collaboration of Reuel Denney and Nathan Glazer); New Haven, Yale University Press, 1950; chapters 8–12.

sate by grandiose ambitions; and when he tries to communicate about politics—to solve present crises—he is likely to say more about his own personality than he says about politics, ironically just because he is trying too hard to talk about politics.

That is at least my prologue for taking an excursion in this paper which will go back 100 years in American history. In this way we can take a look at the changes in American character and American political style as developing from the nineteenth century to the present. I know what I have to say is difficult, and I hope that in the discussion period the unanswered ambiguities in what I say can be brought up and threshed out.

Let me first present my dramatis personae. There are two types of character in the cast: one I call the inner-directed type and the other I call the other-directed type. And they orient themselves to the world in two political styles. I call the first, the style of the moralizers, and the second, the style of the inside-dopesters. And the scene on which these moralizers and inside-dopesters play their parts is in the changing power configurations of this country in the last decades. Naturally, the broad outlines of such a drama as this must be tentative, must be experimental.

Let me begin by describing what kind of people the inner-directeds are. In framing my character types, in trying to work with character types which have psychoanalytic depth and also historical relevance, I have focused on the problem of how conformity is assured; what these people conform to; what their society or their group in society expects of them. This, it seems to me, changes over historical time. In the nineteenth century—and still to a great extent in this century—it seems to me that conformity was assured by a mechanism which I call inner-direction, in which a person was socialized in an authoritative family group by impressive and often oppressive parents and in which he internalized his image of these parents. Freud's picture of the superego is a magnificent picture of this type. This was the typical American of the middle class of the last century, the parents and grandparents of most of us today. Some of us could still be called inner-directed.

Now, the inner-directed person is oriented early in childhood towards very clear goals in life. It may be money, fame, power, goodness, or any blend of these. And he is headed for these by the kind of intimate family socialization characteristic of his age. I like to use a metaphor to describe this mechanism. I speak of these people as gyroscopically-steered. The parents install a gyroscope in them and it stabilizes them all their life. They are less independent than they seem because the gyroscope keeps them on the course for which their parents headed them.

What is the kind of society in which such types will live and work? Theirs is a world in which the opening frontiers are the frontiers of production, discovery, science. We might call it the job-minded society—a society in which people are very much aware and interested in the malleability of the physical environment, the organizational environment, and in their social mobility, their ambitions.

Their preoccupation is to harness themselves to fulfilling the tasks of the expanding society which needs a large physical plant, extensive social organization, extensive military preparation. In this kind of a job-minded society people are protected from too close resonance with each other by their concentration on these necessary and rewarding tasks.

It does not follow from this that the inner-directed man, concentrated on these tasks, is not concerned with people. People may be means to the ends of his gyroscopically-installed goal—people as voters, workers, soldiers. And he may be a pretty good manipulator of them for these ends. The point that is decisive in distinguishing him from the other-directed man is that he does not need anything from these people as ends in themselves. He does not look to them for approval. He does not look to them for warmth. He looks to them for usefulness and in other more specific and more tangible ways.

Obviously I am speaking in terms of contrast, and in order to do so I create what those who have sociological training would recognize as an ideal type—ideal not in the sense of noble, but ideal in the sense of abstract. There is no pure inner-directed man. Most of us are blends. We can make a judgment of the emphasis of these tendencies within given individuals or given social epochs.

In this job-minded society in which people oriented themselves early towards clearly defined goals, young people had clear models to follow. They might be very ambitious and hitch themselves to some star in the ancestral firmament. If they were going to be scientists, they might want to imitate Pasteur; or if painters, they might want to imitate Renoir. They thought in terms of great men. Maybe they thought their parents were great men; and they headed for that. They modeled themselves on these people. This was possible because the personal star developed in this way did not become obsolete but was good for a lifetime. In the case of the personality market, the market on which people sell themselves, there was a fair amount of stability so that a person who decided, when he was very young, that he wanted to be like, let us say, Henry Ford or Abraham Lincoln was not likely to find people calling him quaint by the time he was fifty—because others had gyroscopes too, spinning at about the same pace, moving in the same direction. People who had this type of character found themselves on the whole rewarded, found their lives unproblematical in the sense of concern with whether they fitted or not. To put the matter more generally, there was a certain fit between social structure and character structure.

Having said this, I think I have to stop at once and suggest that one should not get nostalgic about "life with father." As a play it may be amusing; but if he is your father, if he has hurt you, that may be a different matter. I think this nostalgia is actually an important social and political force in our time, and I want to come back to it later on.

Let me now introduce the next person in the dramatis personae, the other-directed. A new source of conformity is required, it seems to me, for the urban upper middle class in our big cities, a conformity for which gyroscopic adaption is not sufficiently flexible, not sufficiently resonant with other people. And for this new source of conformity I like to use the metaphor of the radar set. The other-directed child has a radar set installed, by which he can understand the interpersonal environment and see its signals around him. He is oriented very early in life, not to his ancestors, not to his parents or to his image of their exalted selves, but to his peers; that is, the other kids on the block, the other kids at school, the people who will do a great deal of the job of socializing him. In fact, those who are familiar with the work of Harry Stack Sullivan can see that he has become in a sense the analyst of this age because he was the person above all others who called attention to the importance of the peer group in the process of socialization.

One can see that the parents play a hand in this by their concern with whether the child is popular, how he is getting along with the other kids. One can see that the school also is concerned today more with morale than with morality— concerned with the social atmosphere. I speak now obviously of the progressive schools in the suburban and urban areas where the other-directed as a character type is emerging. The school puts a youngster in with the five-year-olds to see if he fits with the five-year-olds, not in terms of how much he knows, but in terms of how he gets along. And the parents are anxious and judge their success with their children by how the children get along, how popular they are; the parents act as chauffeurs and managers for the continuous stage performance of their children in the peer group.

It is important to see what the radar brings to the other-directed child. It brings direction; it brings a sense of what is worth having in life, what is worth experiencing, what is worth talking about, thinking about. And the goals obviously change with what the radar senses rather than being set for a lifetime as in the earlier epoch. Obviously I don't mean to imply that parents set about consciously to create little paragons who will fit into the society of 1950 or 1960 or 1970. They aren't that calculating, even if they would like to be. It is a long and complicated story and one, I am sure, many social investigators have worked on and thought about: how it happens that the parents, without actually being consciously aware of their role in this process, produce the children whom the next society makes use of. It is a story I cannot go into here. But I want to remark on just one of the changes from inner-direction to other-direction which might be called the change from bringing up children to bringing up father, for children may bring up parents in the other-directed society.

I think one might recognize, if he is interested in historical questions, that this does not sound so new. Perhaps the other-directed American is in a way the American as he appeared to the eyes of 150 years of European observation. The European always thought that the American was a person who cared more for what his fellows thought than anything else, that the American was more concerned with indiscriminate approval and with warmth, more dependent on his neighbors than the European was—or at least more than the European who came to America to look around. And certainly there is very much in the way of social change and so on which helps to explain why it is we have a comic strip called "Bringing Up Father" in which the daughter as well as the mother cooperates.

Now, what is the kind of society in which the other-directed person moves? For him the frontiers are not the frontiers of production but the frontiers of consumption, the frontiers of much more abundant leisure and consumer goods. He moves in a society where—at least in his picture of it—the main productive job is done. The steel mills are built, the railroads are built, the mines are dug, the government organizations are set up. And his concern is to live as a consumer. Those who may be economists can recognize the touch of Keynesian economics in that. But I want to make clear that I am not talking about conspicuous consumption—I am not talking about keeping up with the Joneses. That is an older, perhaps a traditional pattern. As long as one is concerned only with what goods he is getting out of society, out of its physical productiveness, he is still inner-directed. A person is other-directed only when his interest is not in the goods—he takes those for granted. After all, the middle-class family can have a car, a mink coat, good food, and so on. Consumption itself is no issue for most of these people. The problem for the other-directed person is not the goods themselves, but the right attitudes about the goods. Is he having the right experiences vis-à-vis the wine he drinks, the car he drives, the girl he sleeps with, and so on? That is the problem. And he looks to others for guidance as to whether he is experiencing the right experiences on the frontiers of consumption. He takes more or less for granted that he has the wherewithal, the ability to pay unremittingly to provide himself with the goods themselves.

This is another way of saying that in America we have moved from a job-minded society to a people-minded society in which one's concern is no longer with the malleability of the material but with the malleability of the personnel. It is a society in which people are no longer protected from each other by the objectivity of their workaday tasks and in which response from others becomes an end in life as well as a means.

In fact, I think it is quite interesting to look at specific individuals and see to what extent they may rationalize their need for warmth, their need for approval from others, in terms of, let us say, some sensible and easily rationalized goal such as money or security.

Think of Willy Loman, in the play, *Death of a Salesman,* as a man who looked to selling, not primarily for money—that too—but as a source of affection, a means of justifying himself, a *Weltanschauung*—all these things wrapped up in the job of the salesman. Incidentally, the play seemed quite incomprehensible to Londoners. They couldn't understand why anybody was that interested in selling and why people responded in terms other than cash. The English response showed that they didn't understand Americans. Obviously in such a society the old clear goals of ambition, the old stars of the heavenly firmament by which the inner-directed man guided himself no longer guide people.

The Saving Remnant

DAVID RIESMAN

In 1794 the Marquis de Condorcet, in hiding from the French Revolutionary Terror, ill and near death, wrote his *Sketch of an Historical View of the Progress of the Human Spirit,* a great monument to faith in human power to shape human destiny. Condorcet refused to be dismayed either by his own experience of human meanness and savagery or by his wide historical reading in the annals of cruelty and error. For he rested his hopes, not only on "observation on what man has heretofore been, and what he is at present," but also on his understanding of the *potentialities* of human nature.

It has proven more difficult than he had perhaps supposed to develop those potentialities. Today we are aware that the raw material of human nature is shaped by what we call culture into the organized force of a particular character structure; that this character structure tends to perpetuate itself from parent to child; that, largely determined by early experience, it determines in turn the adult modes of life and interpretations of new experience. The combination of character structure and social structure in a given culture is therefore relatively intractable to change. Though in America we are near Condorcet's dream of the conquest of poverty, his dream of the conquest of happiness seems ever more remote. It has become fashionable to sneer at him and other philosophers of the Enlightenment for lacking a sense of the human limitations on improvement. The sneer, however, is unimaginative. Condorcet's scientific, empirical method urges us to see precisely how recent changes in character structure, as well as in the conditions that gave rise to them, have helped to deny utopia. His philosophy then invites us to apply human reason and effort to the improvement of the human condition as thus understood.

. . . .

From *Years of the Modern,* edited by John W. Chase. Used by courtesy of David McKay Company.

While our helplessness in the world is historically the condition of every advance in our mastery of it, the feeling of helplessness may today be so overpowering that regression, and not advance, ensues. But only when we have understood those forces that make for helplessness can we assay the probable outcome, and see what might be required for the new leap to security and freedom envisaged by Condorcet. One requirement is a type of character structure that can tolerate freedom, even thrive on it; I call persons of such type "autonomous," since they are capable of conscious self-direction. The very conditions that produce other-direction on the part of the majority today, who are heteronomous—that is, who are guided by voices other than their own—may also produce a "saving remnant" who are increasingly autonomous, and who find strength in the face of their minority position in the modern world of power.

. . . .

Individual helplessness and collective power play leapfrog with each other throughout history. Today, the helplessness foreseen by a few thinkers, and sensed even in the earlier age of frontiers by many who failed, has become the common attribute of the mass of men. . . .

Today, in the advanced industrial countries, there is only one frontier left—that of consumption—and this calls for very different types of talent and character.

The inner-directed type fitted the conditions of essentially open capitalism, which rewarded ability to envisage new possibilities for production, and zeal to realize those possibilities. To a degree, this is still the case. Nevertheless, we think that, on the whole, contemporary society, especially in America, no longer requires and rewards the old enterprise and the old zeal. This does not mean that the economic system itself is slowing down; total production may continue to rise; but it can be achieved by institutionalizing technological and organizational advance, in research departments, management counsel, and corporate planning staffs. The invention and adoption of new improvements can be routinized, built into the system, so to speak, rather than into the men who run the system. Therefore, the energies of management turn to industrial and public relations, to oiling the frictions not of machines but of men.

Likewise, with the growth of monopolistic competition, the way to get ahead is not so much to make a better mousetrap but rather to "package" an old mousetrap in a new way, and then to sell it by "selling" oneself first. People feel they must be able to adapt themselves to other people, both to manipulate them and to be manipulated by them. This requires the ability to manipulate oneself, to become "a good package," to use a phrase current among personnel men. These pressures are, of course, not confined to business, but operate also in the professions, in government, and in academic life.

As work becomes less meaningful and intense, however, leisure grows and men who are discarded as workers are cultivated in the one role that still matters, that of consumer. This is not an easy role, and people become almost as preoccupied with getting the "best buys" as they once were with finding their proper "calling" in the production economy. They turn, then, to the mass media of communication for advice in how to consume; at the same time, these media help make them anxious lest they fail in the role of consumer. We speak here not merely of "keeping up with the Joneses"—this is part of an older pattern—but rather of the much more unsettling fear of missing those leisure-time experiences, including sex, love, art, friendship, food, travel, which people have been induced to feel they should have.

These changes in the nature of work and leisure have made themselves felt most strongly among the middle classes of the American big cities in the last twenty-five years or so. It is here that we find developing the character type that I call other-directed, a type whose source of direction is externalized. The clear goals and generalized judgments of the inner-directed types are not implanted in the other-directed person in childhood. Rather, he is taught, vaguely, to do the "best possible" in any given situation. As soon as he can play with other children, he is made sensitive to the judgments of this play group, looking to it for approval and direction as to what is best. Parents and other adults come to value the child in terms of his ability to live up to the group's expectations and to wrest popularity from it.

The adult never loses this dependence, but continues to live psychologically oriented to his contemporaries—to what might be called his "peer group." Of course, it matters very much who these others are: whether they are his immediate circle of the moment, or a higher circle he aspires to, or the anonymous circles of whose doings he learns from the mass media of communication.[1] But the great psychological difference from inner-direction is that this modern type needs open approval and guidance from contemporaries. This new need for approval goes well beyond the human and opportunistic reasons that lead people in any age to care very much what others think of them. People in general want and need to be liked, but it is only the other-directed character type that makes others its chief source of direction and its chief area of sensitivity and concern.

These differences in the source looked to for direction lead to different modes of conformity in the two types. The inner-directed person will ordinarily have had an early choice made for him among the several available destinies of the middle-class child. What holds him on course is that he has internalized from his elders certain general aims and drives—the drive to work hard, or to save money, or to strive for rectitude or for fame. His conformity results from the fact that similar drives have been instilled into others of his social class. As against this, the other-directed person grows up in a much more amorphous social system, where alternative destinations cannot be clearly chosen at an early age. The "best possible" in a particular situation must always be learned from the others in that situation. His conformity to the others is thus not one of generalized drives, but of details—the minutiae of taste or speech or emotion

---

[1] These are some of the "anonymous authorities" of whom Erich Fromm has written in *Escape from Freedom* and *Man for Himself*.

which are momentarily "best." Hence he internalizes neither detailed habits nor generalized drives, but instead an awareness of and preoccupation with the *process* of securing direction from others.

We can find exemplars of the other-directed character in leisured urban circles of the past, where the preoccupations were those of consumption, not production, and where status depended on the opinion of influential others. What is new is the spread of such an outlook over large sectors of a middle class that was once inner-directed. Elements of this outlook, moreover, have now filtered down in America to many members of the lower-middle class.

It is my tentative conclusion that the feeling of helplessness of modern man results from both the vastly enhanced power of the social group and the incorporation of its authority into his very character. And the point at issue is not that the other-directed character is more opportunistic than the inner-directed—if anything, the contrary is true. Rather, the point is that the individual is psychologically dependent on others for clues to the meaning of life. He thus fails to resist authority or fears to exercise freedom of choice even where he might safely do so.

An illustration may clarify my meaning. I have sometimes asked university students why they come to class so regularly day after day, why they do not—as they are technically free to do—take two or three weeks off to do anything they like on their own. The students have answered that they must come to class or otherwise they will flunk, though the fact is that many students get ahead when they finally do break through the routines. It has become apparent that the students cling to such "rational" explanations because, in their feeling of helplessness, freedom is too much of a threat. They fail to see those loopholes of which they could take advantage for their own personal development; they feel safer if they are obeying an authoritative ritual in sympathetic company. Their attendance at class has much the same meaning as the Pueblo Indian's rain-making dance, only the student has less confidence that his "prayer" will be heard. For he has left "home" for good, and all of modern thought teaches him too much for comfort and too little for help.

. . . .

Let us examine several . . . factors that have robbed the middle-class individual of his defenses against the pressure of the group. We shall deal . . . with changes in the nature of private property, of work, and of leisure, all of which at one time functioned as defenses.

In the feudal era, the individual was attached to property, largely land, by feudal and family ties. The breakdown of feudalism meant helplessness for many peasants, who were thrown off the land; but for the middle class the result was a gradual gain in consciousness of strength. A new type of relationship between persons and property developed: the person was no longer attached to property, but attached property to himself by his own energetic actions. Property, including land, became freely alienable; at the same time, it was felt to be an individual, not a family, possession. And property was satisfying, substantial—an extended part of the self. Inside the shell of his possessions, the inner-directed person could resist psychological invasion.

Today, however, property is not much of a defense. Taxes and other state activities, inflation and the panicky desire for liquid assets, have made it factually friable. Moreover, the fears of property-holders outrun the actual dangers. Thus, even powerful groups in America feel more frightened of Communism than its actual power warrants. Property no longer represents the old security for those who hold it, and the fear that it may vanish any day makes it as much a source of anxiety as of strength. The rich no longer dare flaunt wealth, but tread softly, guided by considerations of "public relations." Wealthy students often act as if ashamed of their wealth; I have sometimes been tempted to point out that the rich are a minority and have rights, too.

The change in the meaning of work is even plainer. For the inner-directed person, work seemed self-justifying: the only problem was to find the work to which one felt called. As we have seen, the age of expanding frontiers provided the individual with an inexhaustible list of tasks. Work, like property, moreover, was considered a mode of relating oneself to physical objects, and only indirectly to people. Indeed, the work-hungry inner-directed types of this period sometimes found that they were cut off from family and friends, and often from humanity in general, by their assiduity and diligence. And work, like property, was a defense against psychological invasion, a "do not disturb" sign guarding the industrious man of the middle class.

Today the meaning of work is a very different one, psychologically, though in many professions and industries the older modes still persist. To an increasing degree, the self is no longer defined by its productive accomplishments but by its role in a "Friendship" system. As the "isolate" or "rate-buster" is punished and excluded from the work force in the shop, so the lone wolf is weeded out of management; up-to-date personnel men use deep-probing psychological tests to eliminate applicants, whatever their other gifts, who lack the other-directed personality needed for the job.

To be sure, out of anxiety, a lingering asceticism, and a need for an impressive agenda, the professional and business men and women of the big cities continue to work hard, or more accurately, to spend long hours in the company of their fellow "antagonistic cooperators": "work" is seen as a network of personal relationships that must be constantly watched and oiled. Increasingly, both work and leisure call on the same sort of skills—sociability, sensitivity to others' feelings and wants, and the exercise of taste-preferences freed from direct considerations of economic advantage. Work in this case has a certain unreality for people, since it has almost floated free from any connection with technical crafts. The latter have been built into machines, or can be easily taught; but people must still go to the office and find ways of keeping, or at least looking, busy. Thus in many circles work and leisure are no longer clearly distinguished—as we can see by observing a luncheon or a game of golf among competitors.

The feeling of powerlessness of the other-directed character is, then, the result in part of the lack of genuine commitment to work. His life is not engaged in a direct struggle for mastery over himself and nature; he has no long-term goals since the goals must constantly be changed. At the same time, he is in competition with others for the very values they tell him are worth pursuing; in a circular process, one of these values is the approval of the competing group itself. Hence, he is apt to repress overt competitiveness both out of anxiety to be liked and out of fear of retaliation. In this situation, he is likely to lose interest in the work itself. With loss of interest, he may even find himself little more than a dilettante, not quite sure that he is really able to accomplish anything.

From this it follows that this type of other-directed person is not able to judge the work of others—for one thing, he is no longer sufficiently interested in work as such. He must constantly depend on specialists and experts whom he cannot evaluate with any assurance. That dependence is an inevitable and indeed a valuable fruit of the division of labor in modern society; but the inability even to dare to pass personal judgment is a defect rooted in the character of the other-directed person.

When we turn from the sphere of work to the sphere of leisure, we see again that roles in which the individual could once find refuge from and defense against the group have become stylized roles, played according to the mandates and under the very eyes of the group. The individual in the age of inner-direction had little leisure; often he was so work-driven he could not even use the leisure given him. On occasion, however, he could escape from the pressures and strains of the workaday world into a private hobby or into the resources of culture, either "high-brow" or popular. In either case, the stream of entertainment and communication was intermittent; to come into contact with it required effort. Leisure, therefore, by its very scarcity, provided a change of pace and role. Moreover, beyond these actual leisure roles stood a group of fantasy roles—roles of social ascent, of rebellion against work and inhibition, dreams of world-shaking achievement; the individual was protected against invasion at least of his right to these dreams.

Today, leisure is seldom enjoyed in solitude, nor is it often used for unequivocal escape. Hobbies of the older craft type seem to have declined, and a baseball game is perhaps the only performance where the mass audience can still judge competence. The torrent of words and images from radio, the movies, and the comics begins to pour on the child even before he can toddle; he starts very early to learn his lifelong role of consumer. The quantity of messages impinging on the child becomes increasingly "realistic"; instead of "Just-So Stories" and fairy tales, children are given "here and now" stories of real life, and escape into imaginative fantasy is therefore held at a minimum.

Likewise, movies, fiction, and radio for adults increasingly deal with "here and now" problems: how to handle one's relations with children, with the opposite sex, with office colleagues away from the office. Story writers for the better woman's magazines are instructed to deal with the intimate problems faced by the readers, and soap opera is one long game of Going to Jerusalem: when one problem sits down, another is left standing. Indeed, we might claim, there is no "escape" from leisure. Wherever we turn, in work or in popular culture, we are faced by our peers and the problems they present, including the pressure they put on us to "have fun." A kind of ascetic selflessness rules much of the greatly expanded leisure of the other-directed person: selflessness disguised by the craving for comfort, fun, and effortlessness, but ascetic nonetheless in its tense use of leisure for preparing oneself to meet the expectations of others.

Thus, the newly reached horizons of leisure and consumption made possible by our economic abundance have not been as exhilarating for the individual as the realized horizons of work and production proved to be for many in the age of expanding frontiers. On the frontiers of consumption, limitless in quality and almost equally so in quantity, men stand anxiously, haunted by the fear of missing some consumption-experience which they are supposed to have enjoyed. Young men and women today, for instance, in some urban middle-class circles, often feel they must walk a tightrope in their sex lives: they must have "experiences," yet they must not become involved emotionally on any deep level of human tenderness and intimacy. And the while they are worried lest they are incapable of loving anyone. The word of the "wise" to the young—"don't get involved"—has changed its meaning in a generation. Once it meant: don't get, or get someone, pregnant; don't run afoul of the law; don't get in the newspapers. Today the injunction is more deeply psychological; it seeks to control, not the overt experience, but its emotional interpretation in terms of smooth, unruffled manipulation of the self. This transformation is characteristic of the change from inner-direction, with its clear and generalized mandates, to other-direction, with its emphasis on the process of receiving from others very detailed stage directions in the work-play of life.

To sum up, the inner-directed person had a sense of power as he faced the group because of his relationship to property, to work, and to leisure; and because both he and the group accepted certain specific rights that encouraged any individual to be himself. Such persons often became men of substance and men of the world—they made the world *theirs*. If we look at the portraits of the more eminent men in a centuries-long gallery stretching from Holbein to John Singer Sargent, we can see that they were indeed solid citizens. Today the solid citizen has given way to the "solid sender," the "good Joe," not solid enough to risk offending anyone and afraid of disobeying the subtle and impermeable injunctions of the contemporary "peer group" to whom he looks for approval. He is a sender and receiver of messages in a network of personal ties which, unlike the personal ties of a folk society, neither warm nor protect him.

On the surface, it might appear that the individual today feels powerless because he finds no protection from the hazards of war and depression. He feels weak because he has no control over these vast matters that are decisive for him; to avert war or internal catastrophe he cannot even turn to a ritual. Yet, granting these objective reasons for anxiety and weakness, we must nevertheless ask, why is war so likely, when few people want it? I suggest that one reason—certainly not the only one!—is simply that great numbers of people do not in fact enjoy life enough. They are not passionately attached to their lives, but rather cling to them. The very need for direction that is implied in our phrases of inner-direction and other-direction signifies that one has turned over one's life to others in exchange for an agenda, a program for getting through the day.

To be sure, the abdication is not complete. But the fact remains that the person who is not autonomous loses much of the joy that comes through strength—through the effort to live one's life, not necessarily heroically, but, come what may, in full commitment to it. Modern life, for many people, is full of tense and anxious relationships to people, to production and consumption; therefore, these people are prepared to resign themselves to war which does, after all, promise certain compensations in group companionship and shared meanings.

Thus, we have come full circle from Hobbes' view of man. For him, people risked war because they were selfish individualists, and he reasoned with them that they were better off in the *Leviathan*. Modern man does not want to risk war, but allows it to come with astonishingly little protest because, fundamentally, he is not an individualist. It is tractable men who operate the intractable institutions that now precipitate war, and when it comes, it is they who conduct it.

I do not mean to imply that our society "produces" other-directed people because such people are in demand in an increasingly monopolistic, managerial economy. The relations between character and society are not that simple. Moreover, neither character nor society changes all at once. But it would take us too far afield to trace the many formative agencies in the still far-from-complete shift from inner-direction to other-direction in the middle classes.

Furthermore, I must guard against the implication that I think inner-direction is a way of life preferable to other-direction. Each type has its virtues and its vices: the inner-directed person tends to be rigid and intolerant of others; the other-directed person, in turn, is likely to be flexible and sensitive to others. Neither type is altogether comfortable in the world. But in different ways each finds the discomforts it needs psychologically in order, paradoxically, to feel comfortable. The inner-directed person finds the struggle to master himself and the environment quite appropriate; he feels comfortable climbing uphill. The other-directed person finds equally appropriate the malaise that he shares with many others. Engrossed in the activities that the culture provides, he can remain relatively unconscious of his anxiety and tonelessness. Moreover, the character type must always be judged in context. Many persons who are inner-directed and who, in an earlier age, would have gone through life in relative peace, today find themselves indignant at a big-city world in which they have not felt at home. Other-directed persons also may not feel at home, but home never had the same meaning for them. It would appear to the envious inner-directed observer, that the other-directed manage their lives better in a mass society. Conversely, the other-directed may envy the seeming firmness of the inner-directed, and look longingly back on the security of nineteenth-century society, while failing to see that firmness was often merely stubbornness and security merely ignorance.

What I have said about the loss of the individual's defenses is recognized by many thinkers who, however, feel that through voluntary associations people can attain securities analogous to those which family and clan provided in the era of primary ties, and for which work and property made additional provision in the days of expanding frontiers. They see labor unions as giving a feeling of solidarity to the working class, and even to increasing numbers of white-collar employees; they see racial minorities protected by their defense organizations, and farmers by their cooperatives; they see "group belongingness," in some sort of informal association, available to all but the most depressed. The advocacy of this as the chief remedy for the loneliness of the individual is an admission of his weakness. But it is more than that. It bolsters another set of power-combinations, only slightly democratized by individual participation. And it adds to the pressure on the individual to *join,* to submerge himself in the group—any group—and to lower still further not only his feeling that he can, but that he has a right, to stand on his own.

Conceivably, these associations in the future will succeed in strengthening the individual's feeling of his own powers by providing him with defenses, political, economic, and psychological, and by encouraging him to gain, outside his work, a variety of skills, encounters, and experiences. In the meantime, however, with the balance between helplessness and power tipped in favor of the former, the "voluntary" associations are not voluntary enough to do this job.

I turn now to examine another voluntary association, that between the sexes, whose nature, in our age as in any age, provides a profound clue to the state of subjective feelings of power and helplessness. In this context, the rapid change I discern in the denigration by American women of their own sex seems ominous. Eighty years ago, John Stuart Mill (turning to a theme touched on by Condorcet's *On the Admission of Women to the Rights of Citizenship*) wrote *The Subjection of Women* in order to show how attitudes toward this "minority" poisoned all social life; how both men and women suffered from the power-relations that prevailed between them; and how women's potentialities, even more than those of men, were crushed by social pressure. He observed that "the greater part of what women write about women is mere sycophancy to men." But he was gentle with women for he added, "no enslaved class ever asked for complete liberty at once. . . . "

In the intervening period, women did not attain "complete liberty," but they came a long way toward equality with men. In the years after 1890 and until recently, American young women of the middle class insisted on sharing with men the tasks and excitements of civilization. Today there is some evidence that many women of this class have retreated; they have again become enemies of emancipation of their sex; as the weaker power, they judge each other through the eyes of men.

Women today feel under almost as great a pressure to get married as did their pre-emancipation ancestors. In a certain way, they are under greater pressure, since all sorts of psychological aspersions are cast at them if they stay single too long.[2]

Perhaps all this means simply that women have won the battle of emancipation and can relax. I am inclined, however, to think that there is an increasing submissiveness of women to what men want of them, and to the world as men have largely made it. I interpret this, in part, as testimony to the fact that men today are far too anxious, too lacking in psychological defenses against each other, to tolerate critically-minded women. The women they want must be intelligent enough to flatter their vanity but not to challenge their prerogatives as men. Men once complained to their mistresses that their wives did not understand them; now they would complain if they did. For in their own competitive orientation to the world, men would interpret understanding from the side of women as still another, and underhanded, form of competition. This is partly because, since Mill's day, the economic and social power of women has grown; they can no longer be so obviously kept in their places. Hence their gifts, their critical powers, can no longer be patronized by powerful men, but must be subtly destroyed by anxious ones and their willing allies among the women themselves. Men and women, in their weakness, act like those minorities who throughout history have kept each other in subjection in the face of an oppressive power.[3]

In sum, men and women eye each other not as allies, but, at best, as antagonistic cooperators. In their roles as parents, they are uncertain of their children and whether they will be liked by them; in turn, this anxiety is absorbed by the children. In earlier epochs of history, events outside the home were interpreted, often somewhat narrowly, through the perspective of family needs and family morality. Today, the situation is reversed, and the home must be adjusted to the values of the outside. As with the state, "domestic policy" and "foreign policy" are interdependent, and the conflicts and strains of each sphere add to weakness in the other.

We come, then, to a conclusion that would seem paradoxical: certain groups

[2]Indeed, men, too, feel under pressure to get married early—among other reasons, lest they be thought homosexual.

[3]Something of the same transformation has occurred in the relation between parents and children. Even as men are worried lest they might not pass the test with women, so parents are afraid that their children will not approve of them—a problem that would hardly have troubled the person of inner-directed character. While parents appear to be terribly concerned to give their children approval—as they are told by all the textbooks to do—this disguises the parents' own dependence on being approved of by the children, who stand, as Margaret Mead has noted, for the New, for Youth, for the American Way—or, as I might say, for better other-direction. Moreover, parents assume the role of advisors and managers of their children's competitive struggles. This new family constellation is in fact one of the changes that may partly account for the formation of the other-directed character.

in society have grown weaker, but others have not gained in strength at their expense; rather, weakness has engendered weakness. And the state, the beneficiary of individual weakness, is ruled by men who are themselves no less weak than the rest. Even the dictators and their henchmen only seem strong under the imagery of modern propaganda. While the savage believes he will gain in potency by drinking the blood or shrinking the head of his enemy, in the modern world no individual gains in strength of character from the weakness of his fellows.

Nevertheless, even under modern conditions, and out of the very matrix of other-directed modes of conformity, some people strive toward an autonomous character. An autonomous person has no compulsive need to follow the other-direction of his culture and milieu—and no compulsive need to flout it, either. We know almost nothing about the factors that make for such positive results; it is easier to understand the sick than to understand why some stay well. It hardly helps to repeat our point that man's helplessness is the condition for his every advance, because this generalization tells us too little about individual cases. However, it seems that the helplessness of modern man in a world of power has been one element in the genesis of some of the extraordinary human achievements of our age. Some of these achievements are the physical and literary productions of men's hands and minds, but other achievements lie in the internal "productions" of men—their characters; it is of these that I speak here.

There were autonomous people of course, in the era of inner-direction, but they were made of sterner stuff; the barriers they encountered were the classic ones: family, religion, poverty. On the other hand, the person who seeks autonomy today in the upper socio-economic levels of the Western democracies is not faced with the barriers that normally restricted him in the past. The coercions against his independence are frequently invisible. An autonomous person of the middle class must work constantly to detach himself from shadowy entanglements with his culture—so difficult to break with because its demands appear so "reasonable," so trivial.

For our study of autonomy, we have drawn freely on Erich Fromm's concept of the "productive orientation" in *Man for Himself.* Fromm shows the orientation of a type of character that can relate itself to people through love, and to objects and the world generally through the creative gift. The struggle for a productive orientation becomes exigent at the very moment in history when solution of the problem of production itself, in the technical sense, is in sight.

All human beings, even the most productive, the most autonomous, are fated, in a sense, to die the death of Ivan Ilyitch, in Tolstoy's "The Death of Ivan Ilyitch," who becomes aware only on his deathbed of his underlived life and his unused potentialities for autonomy. All of us realize only a fraction of our potentialities. Always a matter of degree, always blended with residues of inner-direction or other-direction, autonomy is a process, not an achievement. Indeed, we may distinguish the autonomous by the fact that his character is never a finished product, but always a lifelong growth.

I speak of autonomy as an aspect of character structure, and not in terms of independence of overt behavior. The autonomous person may or may not conform in his behavior to the power-requirements of society; he can choose whether to conform or not. (The Bohemians and rebels are not usually autonomous; on the contrary, they are zealously tuned in to the signals of a defiant group that finds the meaning of life in a compulsive non-conformity to the majority group.) Yet the separation of "freedom in behavior" from "autonomy in character" cannot be complete. Autonomy requires self-awareness about the fact of choice, about possible ways of living. The autonomous person of today exists precisely because we have reached an awareness of the problem of choice that was not required among the Pueblos, or, for the most part, in the Middle Ages, or even in the period after the Reformation, when the concepts of God's will and of duty confined choice for many within fairly narrow bounds.

The very fluidity of modern democratic social systems, that, for the mass of people, results in anxiety and "escape from freedom," forces those who would become autonomous to find their own way. They must "choose themselves," in Sartre's phrase, out of their very alienation from traditional ties and inner-directed defenses which inhibited true choice in the past. However, I think Sartre mistaken in his Kantian notion that men can choose themselves under totalitarian conditions. Likewise, if the choices that matter are made for us by the social system, even if it is in appearance a democratic system, then our sense of freedom also will atrophy: most people need the opportunity for some freedom of behavior if they are to develop and confirm their autonomy of character. Nevertheless, the rare autonomous character we have been describing, the man of high, almost precarious, quality, must arise from that aloneness, that helplessness of modern man, that would overwhelm a lesser person. It is in this quality, and in the mode of life he is groping to achieve, that he has made a contribution to the problem of living in a power-world. Often, in vanity, we judge our own era as the most advanced or the most retrograde, yet the type of perspective on the world and the self that thousands of people have today were probably matched in the past by only a few.

The people I speak of live under urbanized conditions in every land, but they are world citizens in thought and feeling. Sensitive to wide perspectives of time and space, they have largely transcended prejudices of race or time or class. Their guides are diverse, and they feel empathy and solidarity with their colleagues across all national boundaries. There have been cosmopolitans before, but their horizons were limited by want of knowledge, and their view of man was necessarily abstract. There have been internationalists before, but they have been restricted by class and region. The contemporary autonomous person has all the sensitivity to others of the other-directed type: he needs some interpersonal warmth, and close friends mean much to him; but he does not have an irrational craving for indiscriminate approval.

In one relationship, that between the sexes, the men and women who are striving for autonomy are seeking an equality that takes account of differences, an equality of which Mill would have approved. Here women are not the subtle slaves of men, nor do they flatter them as the feminists did by seeking to adopt men's particular privileges and problems. Though we have as yet to attain a new model of marriage, grounded neither in contract nor in sex alone but in mutual growth towards autonomy, we see new sets of roles developed by people who have achieved relationships to which both partners contribute from their productive gifts. It is unlikely, however, that beyond such families, and small groups of friends or colleagues, there exist any sizeable institutions or organizations predominantly composed of autonomous folk. It is hard to imagine an autonomous society coming into being now, even on a small scale, or perhaps especially on a small scale.[4]

The fact is, moreover, that the autonomous group is hardly aware of its own existence. Those who are to some degree autonomous may not always reveal themselves as such, preferring to conform overtly out of conscious choice. As a result, the potentially autonomous often do not discover each other, though they would in that very process strengthen and defend their own autonomy.

Indeed, the potentially autonomous person tends to bewail as a tragedy his isolation from the masses and from power. He passes by the opportunity of his lot—an opportunity to develop his individuality and its fruits in art and character. Hence he wishes he could undergo a metamorphosis and rid himself of the problem of choice, indeed of his very autonomous strivings; he wishes he were like the others—whose adjustment he often overemphasizes—thus revealing his own other-directed components. By these very tendencies to betray himself and his partially achieved autonomy, he becomes weaker and less autonomous.

The autonomous few can do little enough to reduce the strength of atom bombs and of the hands that now hold them, but some can at least defend their own and others' individuality, and pioneer in various ways of living autonomously. They will enjoy this pioneering to a degree, though it will be held against them by the envious and frightened ones who have abandoned the effort toward autonomy.

If these conjectures are accurate, then it follows that, by a process of unconscious polarization which is going on in society, a few people are becoming more self-consciously autonomous than before, while many others are losing their social and characterological defenses against the group. The latter, though politically strong, are psychically weak, and the autonomous minority, by its very existence, threatens the whole shaky mode of adaptation of the majority.

Nevertheless, joy in life has its own dynamic. We have said that people today are not sufficiently attached to life. We have traced this to their other-directed

---

[4]Mary McCarthy describes with humor and insight the fate of an imaginary enclave of intellectuals seeking autonomy in her story "The Oasis." (*Horizon,* 19, [1949], 75; see, also, for some of the institutional problems, my article, "Some Observations on Community Plans and Utopia," *Yale Law Journal,* 57, [1947], 173.)

character structure, and this in turn to large-scale social changes. Yet character structure is not completely fixed for the individual, so long as life lasts, or for the group. Men have some control over the fate by which their characters are made. By showing how life can be lived with vitality and happiness even in time of trouble, the autonomous people can become a social force, indeed a "saving remnant." By converting present helplessness into a condition of advance, they lay the groundwork for a new society, though, like Condorcet, they may not live to see it.

A Changing American Character?

SEYMOUR MARTIN LIPSET

Two themes, equality and achievement, emerged from the interplay between the Puritan tradition and the Revolutionary ethos in the early formation of America's institutions. In this section the thesis is advanced that the dynamic interaction of these two predominant values has been a constant element in determining American institutions and behavior. As we have seen, equalitarianism was an explicit part of the revolt against the traditions of the Old World, while an emphasis upon success and hard work had long been a part of the Protestant ethic. In addition, the need to maximize talent in the new nation's search to "overtake" the Old World placed an added premium on an individual's achievement, regardless of his social station. The relatively few changes that Andrew Jackson made in the civil service, despite his aggressive equalitarian ethos, and the fact that his appointments were well-trained, highly educated men, show that ability was valued along with equality in the young republic.

The relationship between these themes of equality and success has been complex. On the one hand, the ideal of equal opportunity institutionalized the notion that success should be the goal of *all*, without reference to accidents of birth or class or color. On the other hand, in actual operation these two dominant values resulted in considerable conflict. While everyone was supposed to succeed, obviously certain persons were able to achieve greater success than others. The wealth of the nation was never distributed as equally as the political franchise. The tendency for the ideal of achievement to undermine the fact of equality, and to bring about a society with a distinct class character, has been checked by the

Reprinted with permission from Chapter 3, "A Changing American Character?" of *The First New Nation* by Seymour Martin Lipset, © 1963 by Seymour Martin Lipset, Basic Books, Inc., Publishers, New York. Footnotes omitted except where reference is made to a direct quotation in the text.

recurrent victories of the forces of equality in the political order. Much of our political history, as Tocqueville noted, can be interpreted in terms of a struggle between proponents of democratic equality and would-be aristocracies of birth or wealth.

In recent years, many social analysts have sought to show how the increasing industrialization, urbanization, and bureaucratization of American society have modified the values of equality and achievement. In both the 1930's and the 1950's American social scientists were certain that the country was undergoing major structural changes. In the 1930's they were sure that these changes were making status lines more rigid, that there was a movement away from achieved status back to ascribed status, and that the equalitarian ethic was threatened as a consequence. Such typical writers of the 1950's as David Riesman and William H. Whyte contend that it is the achievement motive and the Protestant ethic of hard work that are dying: they think that the new society prefers security, emotional stability, and "getting along with others." Riesman posits a transformation of the American character structure from "inner direction" (i.e., responding to a fixed internal code of morality) to "other direction" (i.e., responding to demands of others in complex situations).[1] Whyte believes that values themselves have changed. He argues that the old value system of the Protestant ethic, which he defines as the "pursuit of individual salvation through hard work, thrift, and competitive struggle," is being replaced by the "social ethic," whose basic tenets are a "belief in the group as the source of creativity; a belief in 'belongingness' as the ultimate need of the individual; and a belief in the application of science to achieve the belongingness."[2]

If the changes suggested by the critics of the 1930's or the 1950's were occurring in the drastic form indicated in their books, then America no longer could be said to possess the traits formed as a consequence of its origin as a new nation with a Protestant culture. As I read the historical record, however, it suggests that there is more continuity than change with respect to the main elements in the national value system. This does not mean that our society is basically static. Clearly, there have been great secular changes—industrialization, bureaucratization, and urbanization are real enough—and they have profoundly affected other aspects of the social structure. Many American sociologists have documented changes in work habits, leisure, personality, family patterns, and so forth. But this very concentration on the obvious social changes in a society that has spanned a continent in a century, that has moved from a predominantly rural culture as recently as 1870 to a metropolitan culture in the 1950's, has introduced a fundamental bias against looking at what has been relatively constant and unchanging.

Basic alterations of social character or values are rarely produced by change in the means of production, distribution, and exchange alone. Rather, as a socie-

---

[1]David Riesman, *The Lonely Crowd* (New Haven, Conn.: Yale University Press, 1950).
[2]William H. Whyte, *The Organization Man* (New York: Simon & Schuster, 1956).

ty becomes more complex, its institutional arrangements make adjustments to new conditions within the framework of a dominant value system. In turn, the new institutional patterns may affect the socialization process which, from infancy upward, instills fundamental character traits. Through such a process, changes in the dominant value system develop slowly—or not at all. There are constant efforts to fit the "new" technological world into the social patterns of the old, familiar world.

In this section I examine the thesis that a fundamental change has occurred in American society by treating [a] ... topic ... which has been widely discussed as reflecting important modifications in the basic value system. This [section] deals with the arguments and evidence of changes in the basic predominant character traits of Americans as suggested by men like David Riesman and William Whyte. . . . I attempt in this section to present some of the evidence for my thesis that it is the basic value system, as solidified in the early days of the new nation, which can account for the kinds of changes that have taken place in the American character and in American institutions as these faced the need to adjust to the requirements of an urban, industrial, and bureaucratic society.

Marcus Cunliffe has remarked on the American tendency to assert that a wondrous opportunity has been ruined, "that a golden age has been tarnished, that the old ways have disappeared, or that they offer no useful guide to a newer generation."[3] He points out that, American belief to the contrary, there has been surprising continuity in American history as compared with the histories of European nations. This American propensity to feel that the country is going through a major change at any "present time" is related to an almost "inherent American tendency to believe that one has been cut off decisively from the past as if by a physical barrier." Cunliffe attributes this tendency to three main elements:

First it is a consequence of the undeniable fact of continuous and rapid social change since the origins of settlement. This process has, understandably, revealed itself in regrets and neuroses as well as in pride and exuberance. Second, the tendency is rooted in the constant American determination to repudiate Europe—Europe equated with the Past, in contrast with America as the Future—and so to lose the Past altogether. Third, the tendency is a consequence of the American sense of a society which is uniquely free to choose its own destiny. The sense of mission, of dedication and of infinite possibility, in part a fact and in part an article of faith, has led to acute if temporary despairs, to suspicions of betrayal and the like, as well as to more positive and flamboyant results.[4]

In a sense, Cunliffe's analysis shows how some of the values we have seen arising from America's revolutionary origins continue to be a part of its image of itself. And perhaps more important, his observation that there has been more continuity in American history than in European history suggests that the values around which American institutions are built have not changed abruptly.

[3]Marcus Cunliffe, "American Watersheds," *American Quarterly*, 13 (1961), pp. 479-494.
[4]*Ibid.*, pp. 489–490.

Others have pointed out that America is an example of a country where social change does not have to destroy the fabric of society, precisely because it is based upon an ideological commitment to change.

The thesis that the same basic values which arose in the American Revolution have shaped the society under changing geographical and economic conditions, has also been advanced by many historians. Thus Henry Nash Smith has sought to show how the rural frontier settlements established in the West on the Great Plains reflected not only the physical environment but also "the assumptions and aspirations of a whole society."[5] He has argued that revisions in the Homestead Act, which would have permitted large farms and a more economical use of arid land, were opposed by the new settlers because they believed in the ideal of the family farm. Walt Rostow suggests there is a "classic American style [which] . . . emerged distinctively toward the end of the seventeenth century as the imperatives and opportunities of a wild but ample land began to assert themselves over various transplanted autocratic attitudes and institutions which proved inappropriate to the colonial scene . . . [and] came fully to life . . . after the War of 1812." And he further contends that this style has not changed basically, since "the cast of American values and institutions and the tendency to adapt them by cumulative experiment rather than to change them radically has been progressively strengthened by the image of the gathering success of the American adventure."[6] Commager, writing of America in general, has said: "Circumstances change profoundly, but the character of the American people has not changed greatly or the nature of the principles of conduct, public and private, to which they subscribe."[7] Three books dealing with American values, by Daniel Boorstin, Louis Hartz, and Ralph Gabriel, have each, in a different way, argued the effective continuity of the fundamental ideals of the society.

The conclusions of these historians are affirmed also in a "lexicographic analysis of alleged American characteristics, ideals, and principles" reported in a myriad of books and articles dealing with "the American way." American history was divided for the purposes of the study into four periods, "Pre-Civil War (to 1865), Civil War to World War (1866–1917), World War to Depression (1918–1929), and Depression to present (1930–1940)." For each period a list of traits alleged by observers was recorded, and "when the lists for each of the four time periods were compared, no important difference between the traits mentioned by modern observers and those writing in the earlier periods of American history was discovered." Among the traits mentioned in all four periods were "Belief in equality of all as a fact and as a right" and "uniformity and conformity."[8]

[5]Henry Nash Smith, *Virgin Land: The American West as Symbol and Myth* (Cambridge, Mass.: Harvard University Press, 1950), p. 12.

[6]W. W. Rostow, "The National Style," in Elting E. Morison, ed., *The American Style: Essays in Value and Performance* (New York: Harper & Bros., 1958), pp. 247, 259.

[7]Henry Steele Commager, *Living Ideas in America* (New York: Harper & Bros., 1951), p. xviii.

[8]Lee Coleman, "What Is American? A Study of Alleged American Traits," *Social Forces,* 19 (1941), pp. 492–499.

The Unchanging American Character

Foreign travelers' accounts of American life, manners, and character traits constitute a body of evidence with which to test the thesis that the American character has been transformed during the past century and a half. Their observations provide us with a kind of comparative mirror in which we can look at ourselves over time. It is important to note, therefore, that the type of behavior which Riesman and Whyte regard as distinctly modern, as reflecting the decline of the Protestant Ethic, was repeatedly reported by many of the nineteenth-century travelers as a peculiarly American trait in their day. Thus the English writer Harriet Martineau at times might be paraphrasing *The Lonely Crowd* in her description of the American of the 1830's:

[Americans] may travel over the world, and find no society but their own which will submit to the restraint of perpetual caution, and reference to the opinions of others. They may travel over the whole world, and find no country but their own where the very children beware of getting into scrapes, and talk of the effect of actions upon people's minds: where the youth of society determine in silence what opinions they shall bring forward, and what avow only in the family circle; where women write miserable letters, almost universally, because it is a settled matter that it is unsafe to commit oneself on paper; and where elderly people seem to lack almost universally that faith in principles which inspires a free expression of them at any time, and under all circumstances. . . .

There is fear of vulgarity, fear of responsibility; and above all, fear of singularity. . . . There is something little short of disgusting to the stranger who has been unused to witness such want of social confidence, in the caution which presents probably the strongest aspect of selfishness that he has ever seen. The Americans of the northern states are, from education and habit, as accustomed to the caution of which I speak, as to be unaware of its extent and singularity. . . .

Few persons [Americans] really doubt this when the plain case is set down before them. They agree to it in church on Sundays, and in conversation by the fireside: and the reason why they are so backward as they are to act upon it in the world, is that habit and education are too strong for them. They have worn their chains so long that they feel them less than might be supposed.[9]

Harriet Martineau is only one observer of early American life, and not necessarily more reliable than others. But it is significant that her comments on American "other-directedness" and conformism do not flow, as do those of other nineteenth-century visitors who made comparable observations, from fear or dislike of democracy. Many upper-class visitors, such as Tocqueville or Ostrogorski, saw here a threat to genuine individuality and creativity in political and intellectual life, in that democracy and equalitarianism give the masses access to elites, so that the latter must be slaves to public opinion in order to survive. Harriet Martineau, as a left-wing English liberal, did not come to America with such fears or beliefs. She remained an ardent admirer of American

[9]Harriet Martineau, *Society in America* (New York: Saunders and Otlay, 1837), Vol. III, pp. 14–15, 17.

democracy, even though she ultimately decided that "the worship of Opinion is, at this day, the established religion of the United States."[10]

The most celebrated post-Civil War nineteenth-century English visitor to America, James Bryce, saw inherent in American society "self-distrust, a despondency, a disposition to fall into line, to acquiesce in the dominant opinion. . . . " This "tendency to acquiescence and submission" is not to be "confounded with the tyranny of the majority. . . . [It] does not imply any compulsion exerted by the majority," in the sense discussed by Tocqueville. Rather Bryce, like Harriet Martineau fifty years earlier, described what he felt to be a basic psychological trait of Americans, their "fatalism," which involved a "loss of resisting power, a diminished sense of personal responsibility, and of the duty to battle for one's own opinions. . . . "[11]

Although Harriet Martineau and James Bryce stand out among nineteenth-century visitors in specifying that these other-directed traits were deeply rooted in the *personalities* of many Americans, the general *behaviors* that they and Tocqueville reported were mentioned by many other foreign travelers. For example, a summary of the writings of English travelers from 1785 to 1835 states that one important characteristic mentioned in a number of books "was the acute sensitiveness to opinion that the average American revealed."[12] A German aristocrat, who became a devotee of American democracy and a citizen of the country, stated in the 1830's that "nothing can excite the contempt of an educated European more than the continual fears and apprehensions in which even the 'most enlightened citizens' of the United States seem to live with regard to their next neighbors, lest their actions, principles, opinions and beliefs should be condemned by their fellow creatures."[13] An interpreter of nineteenth-century foreign opinion, John Graham Brooks, mentions various other writers who noted the unwillingness of Americans to be critical of each other. He quotes James Muirhead, the English editor of the *Baedeker* guide to the United States, as saying: "Americans invented the slang word 'kicker,' but so far as I could see their vocabulary is here miles ahead of their practice; they dream noble deeds, but do not do them; Englishmen 'kick' much better without having a name for it." Brooks suggested that it was the American "hesitation to face unpleasant facts rather than be disagreeable and pugnacious about them, after the genius of our English cousins, that calls out the criticism."[14]

The observation that the early Americans were cautious and sensitive has been made not only by foreign visitors but also, at different times, by Americans—as in fact many of the foreign authors report. In 1898, the American writer John Jay Chapman echoed Tocqueville's dictum of seventy years before,

[10] *Ibid.*, p. 7.

[11] James Bryce, *The American Commonwealth* (New York: Macmillan, 1912), Vol. II, pp. 351–352.

[12] Jane L. Mesick, *The English Traveller in America 1785–1835* (New York: Columbia University Press, 1922), p. 301.

[13] Francis J. Grund, *Aristocracy in America* (New York: Harper Torchbooks, 1959), p. 162.

[14] J. G. Brooks, *As Others See Us* (New York: Macmillan, 1908), p. 95.

that he knew "of no country in which there is so little independence of mind and real freedom of discussion as in America." Chapman saw the general caution and desire to please as the source of many of the ills of his day:

"Live and let live," says our genial prudence. Well enough, but mark the event. No one ever lost his social standing merely because of his offenses, but because of the talk about them. As free speech goes out the rascals come in.

Speech is a great part of social life, but not the whole of it. Dress, bearing, expression, betray a man, customs show character, all these various utterances mingle and merge into the general tone which is the voice of a national temperament; private motive is lost in it.

This tone penetrates and envelops everything in America. It is impossible to condemn it altogether. This desire to please, which has so much of the shopman's smile in it, graduates at one end of the scale into a general kindliness, into public benefactions, hospitals, and college foundations; at the other end it is seen melting into a desire to efface one's self rather than give offense, to hide rather than be noticed.

In Europe, the men in the pit at the theatre stand up between the acts, face the house, and examine the audience at leisure. The American dares not do this. He cannot stand the isolation, nor the publicity. The American in a horse car can give his seat to a lady, but dares not raise his voice while the conductor tramps over his toes.[15]

Although these accounts by travelers and American essayists cannot be taken as conclusive proof of an unchanging American character, they do suggest that the hypothesis which sees the American character changing with respect to the traits "inner-" and "other-directedness" may be incorrect.

The Unchanging American Values and Their Connection with American Character

The foreign travelers were also impressed by the American insistence on equality in social relations, and on achievement in one's career. Indeed, many perceived an intimate connection between the other-directed behavior they witnessed and the prevalence of these values, such that the behavior could not be understood without reference to them. An analysis of the writings of hundreds of British travelers in America before the Civil War reports: "Most prominent of the many impressions that Britons took back with them [between 1836 and 1860] was the aggressive egalitarianism of the people."[16] If one studies the writings of such celebrated European visitors as Harriet Martineau, the Trollopes (both mother and son), Tocqueville, or James Bryce, it is easy to find many observations documenting this point.

Baedeker's advice to any European planning to visit the United States in the late nineteenth or early twentieth century was that he "should, from the outset, reconcile himself to the absence of deference, or servility, on the part of those he

---

[15] *The Selected Writings of John Jay Chapman,* Jacques Barzun, ed. (New York: Doubleday Anchor, 1959), p. 278.

[16] Max Berger, *The British Traveller in America, 1836–1860* (New York: Columbia University Press, 1943), pp. 54-55.

considers his social inferiors."[17] A detailed examination of the comments of
European visitors from 1890 to 1910 reports general agreement concerning the
depth and character of American equalitarianism:

Whether they liked what they saw or not, most foreign observers did not doubt that
America was a democratic society. . . . Different occupations of course, brought differences in prestige, but neither the occupation nor the prestige implied any fundamental
difference in the value of individuals. . . . The similarity of conclusions based on diverse
observations was simply another indication of the absence of sharp class differences. Even
hostile visitors confirmed this judgment. . . . Some foreign observers found the arrogance
of American workers intolerable.[18]

Even today this contrast between Europe and America with respect to patterns of equality in interpersonal relations among men of different social positions is striking. A comparison of writings of European visitors at the turn of
this century with those made by British groups visiting here to study American
industrial methods since World War II states that "the foreign descriptions of
. . . America in 1890 and 1950 are remarkably similar. . . . The British teams [in
the 1950's reported] . . . the same values . . . which impressed visitors a half
century ago. Like them they found the American worker is more nearly the
equal of other members of society than the European, with respect not only to
his material prosperity, but also to . . . the attitudes of others toward him."[19]
And this attitude is apparent at other levels of American society as well. As one
commentator put it when describing the high-status Europeans who have come
to America in recent years as political refugees from Nazism and Communism:

With his deep sense of class and status, integration in American society is not easy for the
émigré. The skilled engineer or physician who . . . finally establishes himself in his profession, discovers that he does not enjoy the same exalted status that he would have had in
the old country. I met several young Croatian doctors in the Los Angeles area who were
earning $25,000 to $35,000 a year, but still felt declassed.[20]

American emphasis on equalitarianism as a dominant value is significant in
determining what to many of the Europeans were three closely related processes:
competition, status uncertainty, and conformity. Tocqueville, for example, argued that equalitarianism maximizes competition among the members of a society. But if equalitarianism fosters competition for status, the combination of the
two values of equality and achievement results, according to many of the travelers, in an amorphous social structure in which individuals are uncertain about
their social position. In fact, those travelers who were so impressed with the
pervasive equalitarianism of American society also suggested that, *precisely as a
result of the emphasis on equality and opportunity,* Americans were *more* status-

---

[17]Quoted by Philip Burne-Jones, *Dollars and Democracy* (London: Sidney Appleton, 1904), p. 69.
    [18]Robert W. Smuts, *European Impressions of the American Worker* (New York: King's Crown
Press, 1953), pp. 3–7.
    [19]*Ibid.,* p. 54.
    [20]Bogden Raditsa, "Clash of Two Immigrant Generations," *Commentary,* 25 (1958), p. 12.

conscious than those who lived in the more aristocratic societies of Europe. They believed, for example, that it was easier for the *nouveaux riches* to be accepted in European high society than in American. British travelers before the Civil War noted that Americans seemed to love titles more than Englishmen. European observers, from Harriet Martineau and Frances Trollope in the 1830's to James Bryce in the 1880's and Denis Brogan in recent years, have pointed out that the actual strength of equality as a dominant American value—with the consequent lack of any well-defined deference structure linked to a legitimate aristocratic tradition where the propriety of social rankings is unquestioned— forces Americans to *emphasize* status background and symbolism. As Brogan has remarked, the American value system has formed "a society which, despite all efforts of school, advertising, clubs and the rest, makes the creation of effective social barriers difficult and their maintenance a perpetually repeated task. American social fences have to be continually repaired; in England they are like wild hedges, they grow if left alone."[21]

Status-striving and the resultant conformism have not been limited solely, or even primarily, to the more well-to-do classes in American society. Many of the early nineteenth-century travelers commented on the extent to which workers attempted to imitate middle-class styles of life. Smuts notes that visitors at the turn of this century were struck by "what they regarded as the spend-thrift pattern of the American worker's life"; Paul Bourget, a French observer, interpreted this behavior as reflecting "the profound feeling of equality [in America which] urges them to make a show." As Werner Sombart, the German sociologist and economist, put it, "since all are seeking success . . . everyone is forced into a struggle to beat every other individual; and a steeple-chase begins . . . that differs from all other races in that the goal is not fixed but constantly moves even further away from the runners." And in an equalitarian democracy "the universal striving for success [becomes a major cause of] . . . the worker's extravagance, for, as Münsterberg [a German psychologist] pointed out, the ability to spend was the only public sign of success at earning."[22] And lest it be thought that such concerns with conspicuous consumption emerged only in the Gilded Age of the 1890's as analyzed by Veblen, sixty years earlier a medical study of the "Influence of Trades, Professions, and Occupations, in the United States, in the Production of Disease," described and analyzed behavior in much the same terms:

The population of the United States is beyond that of other countries an anxious one. All classes are either striving after wealth, or endeavoring to keep up its appearance. From the principle of imitation which is implanted in all of us, sharpened perhaps by the existing equality of conditions, the poor follow as closely as they are able the habits and manner of living of the rich . . . From these causes, and perhaps from the nature of our

[21]Denis W. Brogan, *The English People* (London: Hamish Hamilton, 1943), p. 99.
[22]Smuts, *European Impressions of the American Worker*, p. 13.

political institutions, and the effects arising from them, we are an anxious, care-worn people.[23]

While some Europeans explained American behavior that they found strange—the sensitivity, kindliness, concern for others' feelings, and moral meekness—by reference to the nature of political democracy or the overbearing desire to make money, others saw these traits as consequences of the extreme emphasis on equality of opportunity, the basic American value which they properly regarded as unique. Many argued that this very emphasis on equality, and the constant challenging of any pretensions to permanent high status, has made Americans in all social positions extremely sensitive to the opinions of others, and causes status aspirants greater anxiety about the behavior and characteristics indicative of rank than is the case with their counterparts in more aristocratic societies. Discussing the writings of various travelers, John Graham Brooks states:

One deeper reason why the English are blunt and abrupt about their rights . . . is because class lines are more sharply drawn there. Within these limits, one is likely to develop the habit of demanding his dues. He insists on his prerogatives all the more because they are narrowly defined. When an English writer (Jowett) says, "We are not nearly so much afraid of one another as you are in the States," he expressed this truth. In a democracy every one at least hopes to get on and up. This ascent depends not upon the favor of a class, but upon the good-will of the whole. This social whole has to be conciliated. It must be conciliated in both directions—at the top and at the bottom. To make one's self conspicuous and disagreeable, is to arouse enmities that block one's way.[24]

One may find an elaboration of this causal analysis among many writers at different periods. Thus Max Weber, after a visit to America in the early 1900's, noted the high degree of "submission to fashion in America, to a degree unknown in Germany" and explained it in terms of the lack of inherited class status.[25] Seven decades earlier another German, Francis Grund, who saw in American equality and democracy the hope of the world, nevertheless also believed that the ambiguous class structure made status-striving tantamount to conformity. He presents both sides of the picture in the following items:

Society in America . . . is characterized by a spirit of exclusiveness and persecution unknown in any other country. Its gradations not being regulated according to rank and title, selfishness and conceit are its principal elements. . . . What man is there in this city [New York] that dares to be independent, at the risk of being considered bad company? And who can venture to infringe upon a single rule of society?

This habit of conforming to each other's opinions, and the penalty set upon every transgression of that kind, are sufficient to prevent a man from wearing a coat cut in a

[23]Benjamin McCready, "On the Influence of Trades, Professions, and Occupations in the United States, in the Production of Disease," *Transactions of the Medical Society of the State of New York* (1836–1837), III, pp. 146–147.
   [24]Brooks, *As Others See Us*, p. 97.
   [25]H. H. Gerth and C. Wright Mills, eds., *From Max Weber: Essays in Sociology* (New York: Oxford University Press, 1946), p. 188.

different fashion, or a shirt collar no longer *à la mode,* or, in fact, to do, say, or appear anything which could render him unpopular among a certain set. In no other place, I believe, is there such a stress laid upon "saving appearances."[26]

James Bryce, a half-century later, also linked conformity to the ambiguity of the status system, particularly as it affected the wealthy classes. He pointed out that it was precisely the emphasis on equality, and the absence of well-defined rules of deference, which made Americans so concerned with the behavior of others and seemingly more, rather than less, snobbish toward each other than were comparably placed Englishmen.

It may seem a paradox to observe that a millionaire has a better and easier social career open to him in England, than in America. . . . In America, if his private character be bad, if he be mean or openly immoral, or personally vulgar, or dishonest, the best society may keep its doors closed against him. In England great wealth, skillfully employed, will more readily force these doors to open. . . . The existence of a system of artificial rank enables a stamp to be given to base metal in Europe which cannot be given in a thoroughly republican country.[27]

In comparing the reactions of Englishmen and Americans to criticism, James Muirhead (the editor of the American *Baedeker)* stated that "the Briton's indifference to criticism is linked to the fact of caste, that it frankly and even brutally asserts the essential inequality of man. . . . Social adaptability is not his [the Briton's] foible. He accepts the conventionality of his class and wears it as an impenetrable armor."[28]

A number of the foreign travelers, particularly those who visited America after the 1880's, were startled to find overt signs of anti-Semitism, such as placards barring Jews from upper-class resorts and social clubs which denied them membership. But this, too, could be perceived as a consequence of the fact that "the very absence of titular distinction often causes the lines to be more clearly drawn; as Mr. Charles Dudley Warner says: 'Popular commingling in pleasure resorts is safe enough in aristocratic countries, but it will not answer in a republic.' "[29] The most recent effort by a sociologist, Howard Brotz, to account for the greater concern about close contact with Jews in America than in England, also suggests that "in a democracy snobbishness can be far more vicious than in an aristocracy."

Lacking that natural confirmation of superiority which political authority alone can give, the rich and particularly the new rich, feel threatened by mere contact with their inferiors. . . . Nothing could be more fantastic than this to an English lord living in the country in the midst, not of other peers, but of his tenants. His position is such that he is at ease in the presence of members of the lower classes and in associating with them in recreation.

[26]Grund, *Aristocracy in America,* pp. 52, 157.
[27]James Bryce, *The American Commonwealth,* Vol. II, p. 815.
[28]James Fullerton Muirhead, *America, the Land of Contrasts: A Briton's View of His American Kin* (London: Lemson, Wolffe, 1898), p. 91.
[29]*Ibid.,* p. 27.

... It is this "democratic" attitude which, in the first instance, makes for an openness to social relations with Jews. One cannot be declassed, so to speak, by play activities.[30]

The intimate connection between other-directedness and equalitarian values perceived by these observers recalls the same connection noted by Plato in his theoretical analysis of democracy. In *The Republic* we find these words:

[In a democracy, the father] accustoms himself to become like his child and to fear his sons. ... Metic [resident alien] is like citizen and citizen like metic, and stranger like both. ... The schoolmaster fears and flatters his pupils. ... The young act like their seniors, and compete with them in speech and action, while the old men condescend to the young and become triumphs of versatility and wit, imitating their juniors in order to avoid the appearance of being sour or despotic. ... And the wonderful equality of law and ... liberty prevails in the mutual relations of men and women ... the main result of all these things, taken together, is that it makes the souls of the citizens so sensitive that they take offense and will not put up with the faintest suspicion of slavery [strong authority] that anyone may introduce.[31]

Plato's analysis points up the main question to which this chapter is addressed: Are the conformity and the sensitivity to others—"other directedness"—observed in the contemporary American character solely a function of the technology and social structure of a bureaucratic, industrialized, urban society, as Riesman and Whyte imply, or are they also to some considerable degree an expected consequence of a social system founded upon the values of equality and achievement? It seems that sociological theory, especially as expounded by Max Weber and Talcott Parsons, and much historical and comparative evidence, lend credence to the belief that the basic value system is at least a major, if not the pre-eminent, source of these traits.

As Plato noted, and as the foreign travelers testify, democratic man is deeply imbued with the desire to accommodate to others, which results in kindness and generosity in personal relations, and in a reluctance to offend. All books that are published are "exalted to the skies," teachers "admire their pupils," and flattery is general.[32] The travelers also bear out Plato's remarks about the socialization of children in a democracy. It appears that equalitarian principles were applied to child-rearing early in the history of the republic. Early British opinions of American children have a modern flavor:

The independence and maturity of American children furnished another surprise for the British visitor. Children ripened early. ... But such precosity, some visitors feared, was too often achieved at the loss of parental control. Combe claimed that discipline was lacking in the home, and children did what they pleased. Marryat corroborated this. ... Children were not whipped here [as in England], but treated like rational beings.[33]

---

[30]Howard Brotz, "The Position of the Jews in English Society." *Jewish Journal of Sociology,* 1 (1959), p. 97.
[31]Plato, *The Republic,* Ernest Rhys, ed. (London: J. M. Dent, 1935), pp. 200–226.
[32]Martineau, *Society in America,* Vol. III, pp. 63–64.
[33]Berger, *The British Traveller in America,* pp. 83–84.

Harriet Martineau's description of child-rearing in the America of Andrew Jackson sounds like a commentary on the progressive other-directed parent of the mid-twentieth century:

My [parent] friend observed that the only thing to be done [in child-rearing] is to avoid to the utmost the exercise of authority, and to make children friends from the very beginning. . . . They [the parents] do not lay aside their democratic principles in this relation, more than in others. . . . They watch and guard: they remove stumbling blocks: they manifest approbation and disapprobation: they express wishes, but, at the same time, study the wishes of their little people: they leave as much as possible to natural retribution: they impose no opinions, and quarrel with none: in short, they exercise the tenderest friendship without presuming upon it. . . . the children of Americans have the advantage of the best possible early discipline; that of activity and self-dependence.[34]

What struck the democratic Miss Martineau as progressive was interpreted quite differently by Anthony Trollope, who visited this country in 1860: "I must protest that American babies are an unhappy race. They eat and drink as they please; they are never punished; they are never banished, snubbed, and kept in the background as children are kept with us."[35] And forty years later, another English visitor, typical of the many who described American child-parent relations during a century and a half, tells us that nowhere else, as in America, "is the child so constantly in evidence; nowhere are his wishes so carefully consulted; nowhere is he allowed to make his mark so strongly on society. . . . The theory of the equality of man is rampant in the nursery. . . . You will actually hear an American mother say of a child of two or three years of age: 'I can't *induce* him to do this. . . . ' "[36]

If these reports from the middle and late nineteenth century are reminiscent of contemporary views, it is still more amazing to find, in a systematic summary of English travelers' opinion *in the last part of the eighteenth and early years of the nineteenth centuries,* that the emphasis on equality and democracy had *already* created the distinctive American child-oriented family which astonished the later visitors:

A close connection was made by the stranger between the republican form of government and the unlimited liberty which was allowed the younger generation. . . . They were rarely punished at home, and strict discipline was not tolerated in the schools. . . . It was feared that respect for elders or for any other form of authority would soon be eliminated from American life. . . . As he could not be punished in the school, he learned to regard his teacher as an inferior and to disregard all law and order.[37]

Equality was thus perceived by many of the foreign travelers as affecting the socialization of the child not only within the family but in the school as well. The German psychologist Hugo Münsterberg joins the late-eighteenth-century

[34]Martineau, *Society in America,* pp. 168, 177.
[35]Anthony Trollope, *North America* (New York: Alfred A. Knopf, 1951), p. 142.
[36]Muirhead, *America, The Land of Contrasts,* pp. 67–68. (Emphasis in original.)
[37]Mesick, *The English Traveller in America,* pp. 83–84.

visitors in complaining, over a century later in 1900, that "the feeling of equality will crop up where nature designed none, as for instance between youth and mature years. . . . Parents even make it a principle to implore and persuade their children, holding it to be a mistake to compel or punish them; and they believe that the schools should be conducted in the same spirit."[38] Various visitors were struck by the extent to which the schools did carry out this objective. The following description by an Englishman of schools in the New York area in 1833 sounds particularly modern:

The pupils are entirely independent of their teacher. No correction, no coercion, no manner of restraint is permitted to be used. . . . Parents also have as little control over their offspring at home, as the master has at school. . . . Corporal punishment has almost disappeared from American day-schools; and a teacher, who should now give recourse at such means of enforcing instruction, would meet with reprehension from the parents and perhaps retaliation from his scholars.[39]

Tocqueville also found examples of the American's mistrust of authority "even in the schools," where he marveled that "the children in their games are wont to submit to rules which they have themselves established."[40]

The educational policies which have become linked with the name of John Dewey and labeled "progressive education" actually began in a number of school systems around the country long before Dewey wrote on the subject: "To name but one example, the lower schools of St. Louis had adopted a system intended to develop spontaneously the inventive and intellectual faculties of the children by the use of games and with no formal teaching of ideas, no matter how practical."[41]

The Inadequacy of a Materialistic Interpretation of Change

Many of the foreign observers referred to above explained the other-directedness and status-seeking of Americans by the prevalence of the twin values of equality and achievement. Character and behavior were thus explained by values. They pointed out that the ethic of equality not only pervaded status relations but that it influenced the principal spheres of socialization, the family, and the school, as well.

Both Whyte's and Riesman's arguments, in contrast, explain character and values by reference to the supposed demands of a certain type of economy and its unique organization. The economy, in order to be productive, requires certain types of individuals, and requires that they hold certain values. In the final

[38]Hugo Münsterberg, The Americans (New York: McClure, Phillips, 1904), p. 28.
[39]Isaac Fidler, Observations in Professions, Literature, Manners and Emigration, in the United States and Canada, Made During a Residence There in 1832 (New York: J. and J. Harper, 1833), pp. 40–41.
[40]Tocqueville, Democracy in America, Vol. I, p. 198.
[41]Torrielli, Italian Opinion on America as Revealed by Italian Travelers, 1850–1900 (Cambridge, Mass.: Harvard University Press, 1941), p. 115.

analysis, theirs is a purely materialistic interpretation of social phenomena and is open to the criticisms to which such interpretations are susceptible.

The inadequacy of such an explanation of change in values and social character is best demonstrated by comparative analysis. British and Swedish societies, for example, have for many decades possessed occupational structures similar to that of America. Britain, in fact, reached the stage of an advanced industrial society, thoroughly urbanized, where the majority of the population worked for big business or government, long before any other nation. The occupational profiles of Sweden, Germany, and the United States have been similar for decades. If the causal connection between technology and social character were direct, then the patterns described as typical of "other-direction" or "the organization man" should have occurred in Great Britain prior to their occurrence in the United States, and should now be found to predominate in other European nations. Yet "other-direction" and the "social ethic" appear to be pre-eminently American traits. In Europe, one sees the continued, even though declining, strength of deferential norms, enjoining conformity to class standards of behavior.

Thus, comparative analysis strikingly suggests that the derivation of social character almost exclusively from the traits associated with occupational or population profiles is invalid. So important an element in a social system as social character must be deeply affected by the dominant value system. For the value system is perhaps the most enduring part of what we think of as society, or a social system. Comparative history shows that nations may still present striking differences, even when their technological, demographic, or political patterns are similar. Thus it is necessary to work out the implications of the value system within a given material setting—while always observing, of course, the gradual, cumulative effect that technological change has upon values.

In attempting to determine how American values have been intertwined with the profound changes that have taken place in American society, it is not sufficient to point out that American values are peculiarly congenial to change. Although equality and achievement have reinforced each other over the course of American history, they have never been entirely compatible either. Many of the changes that have taken place in family structure, education, religion, and "culture," as America has become a "modern" society, have manifested themselves in a constant conflict between the democratic equalitarianism, proclaimed as a national ideal in the basic documents of the American Revolution, and the strong emphasis on competition, success, and the acquisition of status—the achievement orientation—which is also deeply embedded in our national value system.

Richard Hofstadter has urged the recurring pattern of value *conflict* and *continuity* in commenting on papers presented at a conference on changes in American society:

Culturally and anthropologically, human societies are cast in a great variety of molds, but once a society has been cast in its mold—Mr. Rostow is right that our mold as a nation was established by the early nineteenth century—the number of ways in which, short of dire calamity, it will alter its pattern are rather limited. I find it helpful also to point to another principle upon which Mr. Rostow has remarked—the frequency with which commentators find societies having certain paradox polarities in them. . . . We may find in this something functional; that is, *Societies have a need to find ways of checking their own tendencies. In these polarities there may be something of a clue to social systems.* . . .

Mr. Kluckhohn's report contains some evidence that we have already passed the peak of this shift about which I have been speaking. I find some additional evidence myself in the growing revolt of middle-class parents against those practices in our education that seem to sacrifice individualism and creativity for adjustment and group values. Granted the initial polarities of the success ethic, which is one of the molds in which our society is cast, this ethic must in some way give rise, sooner or later, to a reaction. . . . I do not think that we must be persuaded that our system of values has ceased to operate.[42]

The analyses of American history and culture in the nineteenth and twentieth centuries, by both foreign and native interpreters, often differ according to whether they stress democracy and equality, or capitalism and achievement. Generally, conservatives have found fault with the decline of individuality and the pampering of children, and have seen both as manifestations of democracy and equality; while liberals have noted, with dismay, tendencies toward inequality and aristocracy, and have blamed them upon the growth of big business. These contrary political philosophies have also characterized the interpretation of American culture that predominates at any given period. Arthur Schlesinger, Sr., has even tried to measure the systematic characteristic duration of the "epochs of radicalism and conservatism [that] have followed each other in alternating order" in American history.[43]

A cursory examination of the numerous differences between the conclusions of American social scientists in the 1930's and in the 1950's shows the way in which interpretations of American culture vary with social conditions. Writers of the 1930's amassed evidence of the decline of equalitarianism and the effect of this on a variety of institutions. Karen Horney in *The Neurotic Personality of Our Time,* for example, named anxiety over chances of economic success as the curse of what she, with many of her contemporaries, regarded as a completely pecuniary, achievement-oriented culture dominated by the giant corporations. Such analysts as Robert S. Lynd, and W. L. Warner all agreed that the egalitarian emphasis in American democracy was declining sharply under the growth of the large-scale corporation, monopoly capitalism, and economic competition. They asserted categorically that mobility had decreased, and Warner predicted the development of rigid status lines based on family background.

Twenty years later, these interpretations are almost unanimously rejected.

[42]Richard Hofstadter, "Commentary: Have There Been Discernible Shifts in Values During the Past Generation?" in Elting E. Morison, ed., *The American Style: Essays in Value and Performance* (New York: Harper & Bros., 1958), p. 357. (Emphasis mine.)

[43]Arthur M. Schlesinger, Sr., *New Viewpoints in American History* (New York: Macmillan, 1922), p. 123.

Warner himself in one of his most recent works shows that chances of rising into the top echelons of the largest corporations are *greater* than they were in the 1920's. As indicated earlier in this chapter, typical writers of the 1950's are concerned that the emphasis on achievement in American society may be dying out.

In large measure, the difference between writers of the two decades reflects the contrast between the economic circumstances of the times. The depression of the 1930's inclined intellectuals toward an equalitarian radicalism, which condemned capitalism and achievement orientation as the source of evils. Even a conservative like Warner was led to emphasize the growth of inequality and the restriction of opportunity. The prosperity of the 1950's, however, renewed the legitimacy of many conservative institutions and values, and discredited some of the innovations of the previous decades. The social analyses of the 1950's, even those written by men who still considered themselves liberals or socialists, involved at least a critique of the radical excesses of the former period, if not a critique of equalitarian values themselves. Perhaps the similarity in attitudes between the analysts of the 1950's and many of the foreign travelers of the last century is due to the fact that most of the European visitors have been conservatives, or members of the elite of much more aristocratic societies, and the modern Americans reflect the post-war revival of conservative values.

While Riesman and Whyte would deny that their works contain conservative value preferences, and insist that they are simply analyzing changes, it seems fairly evident that like the more elitist travelers of the nineteenth century, they deplore many of the dominant trends. They point to the spread of progressive education, with its disbelief in rewards for hard work, as illustrating the decay of the Protestant ethic, and they assume, as a result of this, a decline in the opportunity for developing creativity. Whyte points to the shift in scientific research from individual to group projects, which in his opinion are less creative. Neither Riesman nor Whyte explicitly asserts that there is more conformity now than in the past, for the reason that men have always conformed to the values of the day; but both argue that contemporary values and personality traits emphasize accommodation to others, while the declining Protestant ethic and the inner-directed character structure stressed conformity to a fixed rule of conduct rather than to the fluctuating actions and moods of others.

This reaction against the apparent decline of the Protestant ethic of achievement and hard work, which has become a dominant theme among the intellectual middle class of the 1950's and early 1960's, should be viewed as the counterpart of the concern with the seeming breakdown of equality which moved comparable groups in the 1930's. The differences in the concerns of the two periods illustrate the important point that although the equalitarian ethos of the American Revolution and the achievement orientation of the Protestant ethic are mutually supporting, they also involve normative conflict. Complete commitment to equality involves rejecting some of the implications of valuing achievement; and the opposite is also true. Thus, when the equalitarianism of left or liberal politics is dominant, there is a reaction against achievement, and when the values of achievement prevail in a conservative political and economic atmosphere, men tend to depreciate some of the consequences of equality, such as the influence of popular taste on culture.

The supremacy of equalitarian values and liberal politics in the 1930's was reflected in the school system in the triumph of progressive education, a cause always associated with left-of-center leaders and ideologies; in industry, by the introduction of the human relations approach as an attempt to "keep the worker happy"; and in the society at large by efforts toward a general redistribution of goods and services. Social scientists and others interested in family structure criticized the supposedly typical middle-class family as too authoritarian and rigid in its treatment of children, suggesting that, in contrast to the more democratic and affectionate working-class family, it bred "authoritarian" and "neurotic" personalities. Popular psychology saw the "competitive personality" of our time as the source of many personal and social evils. Historians pictured the creators of American industry as "robber barons" and as irresponsible exploiters of American resources.

This equalitarian liberalism was perhaps strongest in the school system, where educators carried the ideal of equal treatment to a point where even intellectual differences were ignored. Special encouragement of the gifted child was regarded as an unfair privilege that inflicted psychic punishment on the less gifted: personality adjustment for *all* became the objective. In New York City, Fiorello La Guardia, the militant progressive mayor, abolished Townsend Harris High School—a special school for gifted boys in which four years of work was completed in three—on the grounds that the very existence of such a school was undemocratic, because it conferred special privileges on a minority.

In the prosperous 1950's and 1960's, these tendencies have been almost completely reversed. Big business and business careers once more have become legitimate. The Republicans held office in the 1950's, and centrists rather than liberals dominate the revived Democratic Party of the 1960's. Although Keynesian economics has remained official government policy, and is still supported by most economists, some leading members of that profession have emerged who oppose almost all government intervention. Studies of the social structure of the family have reversed the findings of the 1930's, suggesting that it is the working-class family that is more likely to be a source of "authoritarian" personality traits. Vulgarizations of the theses of Riesman and Whyte have been published in many magazines and are cited at P.T.A. meetings all over the country, where outraged middle-class parents demand a return to "old-fashioned" methods of teaching, in which hard work is rewarded and the gifted receive special attention. Many middle-class parents have placed their children in private schools. While the rapid growth of private schools in large part stems from the increasing prosperity of the country, it also reflects the desire of middle-class parents that their children receive an elite education.

The political battle between the reactions stemming from the pre-war depres-

sion and those reflecting the post-war prosperity, between equality and achievement, has been most conspicuously joined today in the debate over schools. As
the "progressive educationalists" begin to counterattack, they appeal specifically
to the values of equality and democracy. A speech by Professor A. Harry Pas-
sow of Columbia University Teachers' College attacked a proposal to create
twenty-five elite high schools for gifted children in the following terms: "It is a
perversion of democracy to set aside certain youngsters and give them privileges
which automatically set them apart as an elite group of society. It goes against
the basic idea of American education, which is to give all children an equal
opportunity for the best possible education."[44]

A leading expert, who has testified before Congressional committees for the
past twenty years or more concerning the need for educational research, once
reported that when a committee was discussing research on underprivileged or
mentally deficient children, the Democrats on the committee would exhibit great
interest; but when the committee turned to the question of the gifted child, the
Republicans perked up and the Democrats sat back. The two parties did not, of
course, oppose each other formally on these questions, since both favored research on all questions; but Republicans were simply more interested in *achievement*, or the problem of the gifted child, while Democrats were more interested
in *equality*, or the problem of the underprivileged.

To stress the coincidence of these differing interpretations of American social
trends with the political and economic cycle is not to suggest that they are
simply ideological reflections of material conditions or of the climate of opinion.
Most of them have pointed out genuine aspects of the culture, and in so doing
have improved our understanding of the functions of different institutions and
values. Both strands, the equalitarian and the achievement-oriented, remain
strong, but changing conditions sometimes fortify one at the expense of the
other, or alter the internal content of each. Thus opportunity, as measured by
the chances of success in building up a major enterprise of one's own, has given
way to opportunity measured by advancement in the bureaucratic elites. The
politics of liberalism and equality have fostered institutional changes, such as the
constant spread of public education and of training facilities within corporations, which have increased opportunities for advancement.

Conclusion

This chapter essentially has urged that a materialistic interpretation of American society sharply underestimates the extent to which basic national values,
once institutionalized, give shape to the consequences of technological and economic change. Clearly, many nations may be described as urbanized, industrialized, and capitalist, but they vary considerably in their status systems, their
political institutions, parent-child relations, and so forth. The absence of a feudal

[44]See "Plan of Schools for 'Elite' Scored," *The New York Times,* March 25, 1958, p. 25.

past, with a concomitant emphasis on equality of manners and of opportunity, has played a major role in differentiating American behavior from that of other nations.

On the other hand, it may be argued that the entire Western world has been moving in the American direction in their patterns of class relationships, family structure, and "other-directedness," and that America, which was democratic and equalitarian before industrialization, has merely led the way in these patterns. Thus, at any given time, the differences between America and much of Europe may have remained constant, but this difference might have represented little more than a time lag.

If one compares the America of the 1960's with the America of the 1880's or the 1830's one would undoubtedly note changes in the direction suggested by Riesman. The vast majority of early- and mid-nineteenth-century Americans were self-employed and lived on farms or in small towns, while today most people are employees and live in cities. This change alone has many consequences along the lines suggested by *The Lonely Crowd:*

We can contrast the small grocer who must please his individual patrons, perhaps by a "counter-side manner," with the chain-store employee who must please both the patrons and his co-workers. ... The colleague, like the peer-grouper, is the very person with whom one engages in competition for the *scarce commodity of approval* and the very person to whom one looks for guidance as to what is desirable.[45]

The entrepreneur becomes an "other-directed person [who] gives up the one-face policy of the inner-directed man for a multiface policy that he sets in secrecy and varies with each set of encounters."[46] An employee has less freedom and motivation to be individualistic than does the self-employed. Farm and small-town dwellers know each other as total human beings rather than as actors in specific relations, and are presumably less motivated to exhibit status-seeking or to seek the good opinion of those whom they have known all their lives and who are "significant others" in a variety of limited contexts. Residents of small communities are judged by their total background and personal history and by any specific set of acts. As many sociological studies of such communities have revealed, they tend to have a relatively static status system, permitting much less social mobility than that occurring in large cities. Consequently, the resident of the small town tends to be somewhat like the citizens of more rigidly stratified European states. The awareness of the relative permanence of status position reduces the anxiety to win the good opinion of others that exists where status is less stable.

There can be little question that Riesman and Whyte are right also in showing how bureaucratization and urbanization *reinforce* those social mechanisms which breed other-directedness. Success in a bureaucracy, and in the proliferat-

---

[45]P. 140. (Emphasis mine.)
[46]*Ibid.*, p. 147.

ing service occupations of modern society, depends primarily on the ability to get along well with others.

But it cannot be stressed too often that these mechanisms operate within the context of an historic American value-system and status structure that had also generated such traits in a non-bureaucratic and non-urban society. Other-direction, or, to put it less dramatically, sensitivity to the judgments of others, is an epiphenomenon of the American equalitarian ethos, of the opportunities for rapid status mobility, *and* of the general growth of an urban, bureaucratic society. The increasing complexity introduced by industrialization and urbanization makes adherence to a rigid normative code obsolete, because such a code cannot be used as a guide to the great variety of situations confronting modern, bureaucratic man. This Riesman and Whyte have well noted. However, the greater flexibility and need to adapt to others that are demanded by urban and bureaucratic life add to an already existing disposition to be concerned with the opinions of others, a disposition caused by equalitarianism and by the emphasis placed on social mobility.

Even despite the changes brought about by urbanization and bureaucratization, Americans still appear to be quite achievement oriented when compared to persons from more status-bound nations. Foreign travelers are still struck by the individual American's striving to get ahead. Indeed, there is some evidence that the higher valuation placed on social skills in present American socialization practices is precisely oriented toward upward social mobility in contemporary society. A study comparing British and American beliefs about socialization points out that while it places "getting along with others" as the most important aim of socialization, the American pattern differs from the British in that it aims "at a smoothly functioning individual, equipped for getting ahead with a varied armament of social skills."[47]

Some evidence that achievement still ranks high in the United States as compared to other nations may be seen in the data from a comparative study of the attitudes of school youth in five countries—the United States, Norway, West Germany, England, and France. Surprisingly, at least so far as concerns the expectations of the researchers, American children were less "other-directed" than those in the European countries, except Norway, as judged by their responses to the question: "Would you rather be the most popular person in your class or the one who gets the highest grades?" Among both ten-year-olds and fourteen-year-olds, Americans were more likely to prefer high grades to popularity than were German, English, and French youth.

Another indicator of the relatively high level of concern for academic achievement may be seen in the response to a question concerning anxiety over school examinations. American and French youth led in the proportion who reported worrying about exams (63 per cent); Norwegians were slightly less

[47]Maurice L. Farber, "English and American Values in the Socialization Process," *Journal of Psychology*, 36 (1953), pp. 243–250.

anxious as a group (60 per cent), while English and German students showed considerably less concern (48 and 28 per cent).

PREFERENCE FOR HIGHEST GRADES RATHER THAN
POPULARITY AMONG STUDENTS IN FIVE NATIONS

Nation	Percent Preferring Highest Grades		
	10 Year Olds	14 Year Olds	Combined Ages
Norway...............................	86%	83%	85%
United States........................	82	63	73
West Germany........................	62	50	56
England..............................	63	45	54
France...............................	53	30	42

Source: George Gallup and Evan Hill, "Is European Education Better than Ours?" *The Saturday Evening Post*, 233 (Dec. 24, 1960), p. 70.

Comparative evidence that achievement orientation and other-directedness may, in fact, be mutually reinforcing has been presented by David McClelland as a conclusion of his extensive comparative studies of the psychological processes which are related to economic development. He suggests that " 'other-directedness' is an essential feature of rapid economic development even in its early stages, rather than a special feature of advanced urban culture in the United States as Riesman suggests."[48] As he puts it:

[W]hat a modern society needs for successful development is flexibility in a man's role relationships. His entire network of relations to others should not be traditionally determined by his caste or even his occupational status. . . . The transition to the new order is certainly likely to be helped if people can learn to listen to what "other people" say is the right thing to do.[49]

An increase in other-directedness helps facilitate economic development by making individuals more receptive to "the opinion of the 'generalized other.' " It creates greater willingness to accept new norms or techniques, and it helps reduce particularistic ties, thus facilitating the operation of pure market criteria.

To test the hypothesis of the interrelationship of other-directedness and achievement orientation, McClelland analyzed children's readers from over thirty countries in 1925 and 1950 by coding the themes of the stories in terms of measures of other-directedness and achievement motivation. Countries were then classified as above or below the median score for other-directedness and achievement motivation in each period. Nations could be categorized as high on both dimensions, low on both, or high on one and low on the other. Looking then at the various countries and the extent to which they grew economically during the succeeding years (as indicated by growth in electric power), McClelland found that nations which were high on both factors greatly outperformed

[48]David C. McClelland, *The Achieving Society* (Princeton, N.J.: Van Nostrand, 1961), p. 192.
[49]*Ibid.*, p. 194.

countries which were low on both, "whereas those that were high on one and low on the other showed an average gain somewhere in between."[50]

It may come as something of a shock to realize that more could have been learned about the rate of future economic growth of a number of these countries in 1925 or 1950 by reading elementary school books than by studying such presumably more relevant matters as power politics, wars and depressions, economic statistics, or government policies governing international trade, taxation, or public finance. The reason apparently lies in the fact that the readers reflect sufficiently accurately the motives and values of key groups of men in a country which *in the long run* determine the general drift of economic and political decisions and their effect on productivity. Economic and political policies are of course the means by which economic change is brought about, but whether policies will be implemented, or even decided on in the first place, appears to depend ultimately on the motives and values of men as we have succeeded in detecting them in the stories which they think it is right for their children to read.[51]

The two orientations of other-directedness and achievement motivation, therefore, may be viewed as mutually supportive, rather than, as Riesman and Whyte suggest, mutually contradictory.

The concern with specifying how various structural changes have weakened the Protestant ethic or inner-directed traits in American life has led Riesman and others sometimes to ignore the beneficial consequences of these changes. Thus, I have pointed out elsewhere that while bureaucratization results in a heightened need to make personality adjustments to win the esteem of colleagues and supervisors, it also sets bounds to arbitrary power. By establishing rules of fair treatment, and by reducing the area of personal discretion in personnel policy, bureaucracy can reduce the fear of the employer or of the supervisor. Trade unions, found most commonly under conditions of large industry, accurately reflect their members' desires when their policies involve more, rather than less, bureaucratization of factory life. (As an example of this, unions have sought seniority rules in hiring, firing, and promoting, which increase bureaucratization and reduce arbitrary power.)

Similarly, it may be urged that some of the consequences of bureaucratization reinforce, rather than weaken, strong work and achievement orientations, particularly—but not exclusively—in the upper echelons of white-collar and executive life. The shift from the family-owned company to the management-run corporation, as Whyte pointed out, has made group activities and adjustment to group norms seem more important than before. But whatever else group dynamics in industry may be concerned with, it certainly provides an excellent way of getting men to work hard for the company. Traditionally, it has been a postulate of business management, and an empirical finding of industrial sociology, that men do not work as hard as they are able when the rewards of their work seem to be going to others. Holding other factors constant, no one works so hard as the

[50]*Ibid.*, pp. 201–202.
[51]*Ibid.*, p. 202.

head of an organization, or the self-employed or the creative professional who is directly rewarded for his labors. By extending the control of work to committees at different levels in the corporation, contemporary American business has found a means of inculcating into a large number of people a sense of responsibility for the whole organization. "Non-owners" now feel individually responsible, and the number of hard-working executives who never watch the clock, and who take work home with them, has been enormously enlarged. Thus, while other-direction may have increased, the motivation for competition and hard work remains, because the best are chosen to move up the bureaucratic hierarchy.

It is a peculiar paradox that the same structural processes may account for diverse and even sharply conflicting tendencies. Many analyses of American society have stressed the fact that individualism *and* conformism, creative innovation *and* dominance by low-level mass taste, are outgrowths of identical forces. For example, the pronounced spread of higher education and a high standard of living have caused an unprecedented increase in both the proportion of the population involved in genuinely creative, intellectual activities, and the influence by the populace on the major expressions of art, literature, and drama. Alexis de Tocqueville was fully aware of these dual tendencies when he pointed out that "the same equality that renders him [The American] independent of each of his fellow citizens, taken severally, exposes him alone and unprotected to the influence of the greater number. . . . I very clearly discern two tendencies; one leading the mind of every man to untried thoughts, the other prohibiting him from thinking at all."[52]

Today, too, there are many trends making for an increase in autonomous behavior, in free choice. Various social scientists have recently begun to document these countervailing tendencies, a phenomenon that may reflect the ever-present cyclical pattern of social analysis. Rowland Berthoff points to the seeming "gradual decline since 1920 of those make-shift communities, the fraternal lodges," which were part of the associational pattern that impressed Tocqueville, and suggests that "the psychic energy that Americans formerly expended on maintaining the jerry-built framework of such 'institutions' as these has in our more assured institutional structure of recent years been freed, at least potentially, for the creation of more valuable kinds of 'culture.' " He also infers that "the recent popular success of books deploring the unworthiness of status striving indicates that Americans are throwing off this obsession and making it, as in other societies, including pre-industrial America, merely one concern among many."[53] Robert Wood suggests, in the same vein, that "the pattern of inconspicuous consumption, the web of friendship, and the outgoing life that Whyte describes also have something of the flavor of a renaissance. Although 'keeping down with the Joneses' may indicate group tyranny, it is still better than keeping

[52]Tocqueville, *Democracy in America,* Vol. I, p. 12.

[53]Berthoff, "The American Social Order: A Conservative Hypothesis," *American Historical Review,* 65 (1960), p. 512.

up with them. At least it displays disapproval of overt snobbishness. . . . While Whyte finds pressures for benevolent conformity, he also discovers brotherhood."[54] Daniel Bell has argued that the growth in education, among other factors, has reduced conformity. He comments that "one would be hard put to find today the 'conformity' *Main Street* exacted of Carol Kennicott thirty years ago. With rising educational levels, more individuals are able to indulge a wider variety of interests," such as serious music, good books, high-level FM radio, and the like.[55]

It may be fitting to conclude this chapter with the paradox formulated by Clyde Kluckhohn, who has suggested:

Today's kind of "conformity" may actually be a step toward more genuine individuality in the United States. "Conformity" is less of a personal and psychological problem—less tinged with anxiety and guilt. . . . If someone accepts outwardly the conventions of one's group, one may have greater psychic energy to develop and fulfill one's private potentialities as a unique person. I have encountered no substantial evidence that this "conformity" is thoroughgoingly "inward."[56]

As status-seeking is the by-product of strong equalitarianism, so conformity and other-directedness may permit, or even demand, inner autonomy. . . .

[54]Robert Wood, *Suburbia: Its People and Their Politics* (Boston: Houghton Mifflin, 1959), p. 15.
[55]Bell, "The Theory of Mass Society," *Commentary,* 22 (1956), p. 82.
[56]Clyde Kluckhohn, "Have There Been Discernible Shifts in American Values during the Past Generation?" in Elting E. Morison, ed., *The American Style: Essays in Value and Performance,* p. 187.

New Light on Changing American Values

FRED I. GREENSTEIN

The values held by Americans are commonly believed to have undergone a radical change since the turn of the century. Americans, it is said, have come increasingly to prize leisure over work, accommodation to their fellows over individual achievement, in general, passivity over activity. The best known statement of the many variations on this theme is probably that of David Riesman and his associates. Riesman's thesis was presented in terms of changes in social structure and "social character"; changes from an "age of production" to an "age of consumption," which he believed had been accompanied by a shift from "inner-" to "other-direction" in the sources of Americans' "modes of conformity."[1] William Whyte's well-publicized comments on "The Declining Protestant Ethic" parallel Riesman's assertions at many points.[2]

The views of Riesman and Whyte are widely accepted. Clyde Kluckhohn reaches similar though not identical conclusions on the basis of a "massive" review of several hundred "empirical and impressionistic writings on American culture and especially American values by social scientists and others."[3] Much

Reprinted with permission from Fred I. Greenstein, "New Light on Changing American Values: A Forgotten Body of Survey Data," *Social Forces,* XLII (May, 1964), pp. 441–50. Copyright 1964, University of North Carolina Press.

[1]David Riesman with Nathan Glazer and Reuel Denney, *The Lonely Crowd: A Study of the Changing American Character* (New Haven, Conn.: Yale University Press, 1950), hereafter attributed for the sake of brevity to the senior author. A number of commentators on Riesman's work have pointed out that his discussion is less of changing character than of changing values and practices. See, for example, the articles by Sheldon L. Messinger and Burton R. Clark and by Robert Gutman and Dennis Wrong in Seymour M. Lipset and Leo Lowenthal, eds., *Culture and Social Character: The Work of David Riesman* (New York: The Free Press of Glencoe, 1961).

[2]*The Organization Man* (New York: Simon and Schuster, 1956).

[3]"Have There Been Discernible Shifts in American Values During the Past Generation?" in Elting E. Morison, ed., *The American Style* (New York: Harper and Brothers, 1958), pp. 145–217.

of the literature Kluckhohn was able to find had been "produced by writers . . . who based their reflections on their own experience rather than upon specifically pointed and systematic research."[4] Granting that these observations did not meet satisfactory standards of evidence, Kluckhohn nevertheless was impressed by the amount of broad agreement with Riesman and Whyte, although he felt it necessary to point to "the possibility that the consonance derives from Zeitgiest or from parrotings—with variations—of a few popular formulations."[5]

In addition to impressionistic accounts of changing American values, Kluckhohn was able to draw upon several studies which presented "hard" data—analyses of various indirect indices of value change, such as the variations over the years in the content of the lyrics of popular songs, best selling novels, and religious literature. The findings of a number of these studies seem to support the assertions of Riesman and Whyte. For example, after observing differences in the types of individuals who served as topics of popular magazine biographies between 1901 and 1941,[6] Leo Lowenthal concluded that contemporary audiences were being exposed to "idols of consumption" (e.g., film stars) rather than the "idols of production" (e.g., business magnates) of earlier years. Lowenthal's findings were drawn upon by Riesman to support the thesis of *The Lonely Crowd*. A more recent example of the analysis of value changes in cultural products is the study by de Charms and Moeller of a century-and-a-half of grade school textbooks.[7] Noting that "achievement imagery" in children's readers had declined consistently after the 1880's, de Charms and Moeller concluded that their findings "correspond very well" with those of Riesman and other commentators.

Lately, however, objections have been raised to the argument that one of the major twentieth century developments has been the supplanting of the Protestant Ethic with what Whyte calls "the Social Ethic." Lipset, for example, after a detailed examination of comments on the United States by nineteenth century foreign visitors, asserts that the "traits of the other-directed man have to a considerable extent always existed in the American character and that the values of achievement and individualism persist in American Society."[8] Parsons and White argue that the American "value-system has . . . remained stable . . . " and that "a major part of the phenomena that form the center of the analyses of Riesman, Kluckhohn, and others" consists merely of "new *specifications* of the [unchanged] general value system in relation to new structural and situational conditions."[9]

---

[4] *Ibid.*, p. 148.

[5] *Ibid.*, p. 182.

[6] Leo Lowenthal, "Biographies in Popular Magazines," in Paul F. Lazarsfeld and Frank N. Stanton, eds., *Radio Research 1942–43* (New York: Duell, Sloan and Pearce, 1944), pp. 507–548.

[7] Richard de Charms and Gerald H. Moeller, "Values Expressed in American Children's Readers: 1800–1950," *Journal of Abnormal and Social Psychology*, 64 (1962), pp. 136–142.

[8] Seymour M. Lipset, "A Changing American Character?" in Lipset and Lowenthal, *op. cit.*, p. 140.

[9] Talcott Parsons and Winston White, "The Link between Character and Society," in Lipset and

Ideally one would hope to resolve such disagreements by direct observation of trends over the years in people's values (a research tactic which is becoming increasingly practical as historical survey data accumulate), rather than by impressionistic reports or indirect indices of value change. As Riesman and Glazer comment, referring to questionnaires which have been devised to test Riesman's hypotheses, "we wish there were ways of finding out how nineteenth-century young people might have responded to such questionnaires . . . but history buries its dead. . . . "[10]

A Forgotten Body of Survey Data

The present article analyzes a forgotten body of survey data going back to the 1890's. Between 1896 and 1910, students of education conducted numerous investigations of the "ideals" of children and adolescents—i.e., of their statements about "what person you would most like to resemble." In later years a number of additional studies of children's exemplars were carried out, one in the 1920's and several since 1944.[11] Thus evidence is available over a 50-year period on trends in juvenile heroes and hero-worship. These data, which are probably the longest time series of reasonably reliable and comparable questionnaire findings, have the merit of providing us with a direct index of values in the

Lowenthal, *op. cit.*, p. 103. Also see Winston White, *Beyond Conformity* (New York: The Free Press of Glencoe, 1961).

[10]David Riesman with the collaboration of Nathan Glazer, *"The Lonely Crowd:* A Reconsideration in 1960,"* in Lipset and Lowenthal, *op. cit.*, p. 429.

[11]This paper draws mainly on the studies indicated with asterisks below. Following each in parentheses is the estimated or actual date of field work. In the text of the paper, these studies are indicated by date of field work rather than date of publication.

*Estelle M. Darrah, "A Study of Children's Ideals," *Popular Science Monthly*, 53 (May 1898), pp. 88–98 (Field work 1896); Earl Barnes, "Type Study on Ideals," *Studies in Education*, 2 (1902), pp. 36–42, 78–82, 115–122, 157–162, 198–202, 237–242; *Will G. Chambers, "The Evolution of Ideals," *The Pedagogical Seminary*, 10 (March 1903), pp. 101–143 (Field work ca. May 1902); *David S. Hill, "Comparative Study of Children's Ideals," *Pedagogical Seminary*, 18 (June 1911), pp. 219–231 (Field work ca. 1910); *David S. Hill, "Personification of Ideals by Urban Children," *Journal of Social Psychology*, 1 (August 1930), pp. 379-393 (Field work ca. 1928); *M. Louise Stoughton and Alice M. Ray, "A Study of Children's Heroes and Ideals," *The Journal of Experimental Education*, 15 (December 1946), pp. 156–160 (Field work ca. 1944); Robert J. Havighurst, et al., "The Development of the Ideal Self in Childhood and Adolescence," *Journal of Educational Research*, 40 (December 1946), pp. 241–257; J. B. Winkler, "Age Trends and Sex Differences in the Wishes, Identifications, Activities, and Fears of Children," *Child Development*, 20 (1949), pp. 191–200; *Fred I. Greenstein, *Children's Political Perspectives: A Study of the Development of Political Awareness and Preferences Among Pre-Adolescents*, unpublished doctoral dissertation, Yale University Library, 1959, pp. 77–102 (Field work January through March, 1958).

Chambers, *op. cit.*, presents a bibliography of a number of additional early studies. Not considered in the present discussion are several early studies of the "ideals" of foreign children, most of which are cited in Chambers' bibliography, and a study of parochial school children by Sister Mary Inez Phelan, *An Empirical Study of the Ideals of Adolescent Boys and Girls* (Washington, D. C.: Catholic University of America, 1936). A discussion of the findings in several of the early studies with respect to sex differences appears in Herbert Hyman, *Political Socialization* (Glencoe, Ill.: The Free Press, 1959), pp. 30–31. I am indebted to Hyman's book for bringing these studies to my attention.

general population. In view of the emphasis by Riesman, among others, on changing socialization practices as one determinant of value changes, it is especially interesting that the data are on the values of young people.

Several factors make possible the use of these data from a period before acceptable standards for survey research had been developed. First, although not based on random sampling, the studies draw on exceedingly large and diversified populations of children. For both the pre-World War I and the post-1944 periods (which are most important for our purposes) several studies are available from widely dispersed geographical areas, and for both periods there is enough impressionistic information about respondents' social characteristics to make it clear that the populations studied were broadly heterogeneous. Secondly, raw data are available from five of the studies—two from the early period, one from the 1920's, and two from the later period—making possible secondary analysis in terms of categories which are more revealing than those used in the original studies. In these five studies complete or nearly complete inventories of all the individuals referred to by the respondents were reported. Therefore re-analysis was possible once the identities of some of the more obscure names (ranging from turn-of-the-century Congressmen to silent screen performers) were established and a number of minor estimates were made to fill in slight gaps. Finally, the pattern of findings emerging from all the studies, a pattern which, as we shall see, supports the thesis that values have *not* changed markedly in the directions suggested by Riesman, is sufficiently clear-cut and internally consistent to eliminate doubts about the representativeness of the data.

Since the studies are of hero-worship it is useful to juxtapose them with Lowenthal's findings on changing heroes of popular biography and to discuss them in the context of both Lowenthal's and Riesman's interpretations of the former's findings.

Lowenthal and Riesman on Changing Values

Lowenthal's conclusion that "idols of consumption" had taken the place of "idols of production" was based on rather striking differences in the occupations of magazine biography subjects before and after World War I. Three major changes were found in "the professional distribution of . . . 'heroes' "; changes which Riesman saw as fitting snugly into the conclusions of *The Lonely Crowd:*

1. Perhaps the most clear-cut change followed close upon the growth in the second decade of the century of spectator sports and the mass entertainment industry. During the period before the Great War, 77 percent of the biographies of entertainers were of representatives of "serious arts" (i.e., literature, fine arts, music, dance, theatre). For each successive time period sampled there was a consistent shift in the direction of representatives of athletics and of what Lowenthal refers to as "the sphere of cheap or mass entertainment," until by 1940–41 "serious artists" made up only 9 percent of the entertainers about whom biographies were written. In all, entertainers ("serious" and "non-serious") ac-

counted for only a fourth of the pre-World War I biographies as opposed to one-half of the post-war biographies. Lowenthal concluded that "the [contemporary] idols of the masses are not, as they were in the past, the leading names in the battle of production, but the headliners of the movies, the ballparks, and the night clubs."[12]

2. The over-all decline in biographies of leaders "in the battle of production" was not as sharp as the overall increase in biographies of entertainers. Leaders of production made up 28 percent of the pre-1914 biographies and an average of about 17 percent of the biographies in the three later time-periods sampled by Lowenthal. But here also the differences were greater if one took account of the degree to which the biographical subjects represented the "serious side" of life. Early biographies were of bankers and railroad executives; the later ones concentrated on such figures as the owner of a vacation resort, a man who had organized a roadside restaurant chain, and a professional model.

3. Finally, consistent with the assertion in *The Lonely Crowd* that with the advent of other-direction politics increasingly has become a passive spectator activity rather than an arena in which to vent intense feelings,[13] biographies of political leaders were less common after World War I. Forty-six percent of the early biographies were of people in political life; less than 30 percent of the later biographies were of politicians.

Both Lowenthal and Riesman interpret the shifts in biographical heroes since the turn of the century in terms of a decline in popular aspiration levels. Biographies during the early period were "to be looked upon as examples of success which can be imitated," Lowenthal suggests. Taking note of the rhetoric in the biographies as well as the individuals who were their subjects, he concludes that during the early period such magazine articles served as "educational models." They reflected a period of "rugged individualism . . . characterized by eagerness and confidence that the social ladder may be scaled on a mass basis." The later biographies, on the other hand, "seem to lead to a dream world of the masses who no longer are capable or willing to conceive of biographies primarily as a means of orientation and education."[14]

Riesman agrees that biographies during the early period served as models which were within the aspirations of their readers, whereas today the individual "cannot imagine himself in the work role of the president of the United States or the head of a big company." However, he suggests that the contemporary biographies also are models; but these are new, other-directed models of taste, life-style, and leisure-time pursuit—"the frontiers on which the reader can himself compete. . . ."[15]

---

[12]Lowenthal, *op. cit.,* p. 517. In a brief aside, Lowenthal raises the possibility that the subjects of magazine biographies were representative merely of the "ideology" of the time, *ibid.,* p. 513. Riesman, however, seems to assume that they represent attitudes in the general population. ("Surveys of content in the mass media show a shift in the kinds of information about business and political leaders that audiences ask for.") *The Lonely Crowd, op. cit.,* p. 237.

[13] *The Lonely Crowd, op. cit.,* chap. 8.

[14]Lowenthal, *op. cit.,* p. 517.

[15] *The Lonely Crowd, op. cit.,* p. 273.

Besides using the data on trends in children's exemplars to determine whether Lowenthal's content analysis findings are valid indicators of changes in "the idols of the masses," they also may be used to establish whether one other shift in the type of exemplar chosen by children which might be anticipated from speculations in *The Lonely Crowd* has taken place.

TABLE 1

Percent of Children and Adolescents Choosing Various Classes of Public Figures as Exemplars: 1902–1958*

	Place, Approximate Date of Field Work, and Investigator				
	1902 New Castle, Penna.	1910 Nashville, Tenn.	1928 Birmingham, Montgomery, Mobile, Ala.	1944 Springfield, Mass. Stoughton,	1958 New Haven, Conn.
Exemplars	Chambers	Hill	Hill	Ray	Greenstein
Entertainment:					
"Serious"....................	4.1	4.1	5.1	—	1.8
"Non-Serious"..............	.6	.3	10.4	8.1	36.1
Business......................	1.6	1.0	1.0	—	.6
Contemporary Political:					
Incumbent President..........	3.3	.9	.2	2.7	3.3
Other......................	9.2	1.4	2.2	.4	3.0
National Hero:					
Washington..................	29.2	22.0	19.9	4.9	3.2
Lincoln.....................	3.4	.6	2.4	1.5	3.6
Other......................	3.0	9.6	5.1	4.6	3.6
Miscellaneous Figures from Wider					
Environment...............	17.2	20.6	15.6	33.4	14.8
Immediate Environment Figures..	22.4	39.5	33.8	44.4	2.0
No Response or Invalid Response.	6.0	—	4.3	—	28.0
Total....................	100.0	100.0	100.0	100.0	100.0
Ages Included in Present Tabulation	7–16	7–15	6–20	9&11	9–15
Number of Cases..............	2333	1431	8813	259	659

*A number of the percentages in Table 1 are estimates of the percentages which would have resulted if certain minor gaps in the data did not exist. All estimates are between a fraction of a percent and about three percent of what would have been found if full data were available, with the exception of the 1902 statistic for "other national heroes," which is—to some unknown degree—larger than the 3 percent indicated in the table. In each case where an estimate has been made the estimate is conservative with respect to the interpretation of the table in the text, so that any other estimate would have further strengthened the conclusions. (For example, the highest possible estimate is used for "other contemporary political figures" in 1902, and the lowest possible estimate in 1944.) Further information about the five studies summarized here, along with a discussion of the techniques of retabulation and estimation, is contained in a mimeographed technical appendix available from the author. The "miscellaneous figures from wider environment" category is residual. It includes, among others, scientists, inventors, military leaders, religious figures, and characters from fiction, as well as a small number of responses which could not be classified because the names of the exemplars were not listed or were unidentifiable.

Invalid responses (e.g., references to an occupation rather than an individual; illegible questionnaires; etc.) were eliminated from the 1910 study prior to analysis. These made up about three percent of the original 1910 sample. There is no discussion of invalid responses or of failures to respond in the 1944 study, and none are reported. The 1944 study was of second grade (age 7), fourth grade (age 9), and sixth grade (age 11) children; I have retabulated the percentages, eliminating the second grade subsample in order to bring the mean age closer to that of the other studies. Even after retabulation the mean age of this sample is still somewhat lower than that of the other samples. This evidently accounts for the greater tendency of 1944 respondents to refer to immediate environment examplars. The size of the residual "miscellaneous" category in this study is a function partly of war-time references to military heroes and partly of a somewhat larger number of unidentified exemplars.

4. Riesman suggests that identification with national heroes served an important function in the socialization of children during the period when society was "dependent on inner direction."

[In] the George Washington myth . . . [n]ot only are the little boys told in the period of inner direction that they may grow up to be president but they are given scales by which to measure and discipline themselves for the job during boyhood. If they do not tell lies, if they work hard, and so on—if, that is, they act in their boyhoods as the legendary Washington acted in his—then they may succeed to his adult role.[16]

Although Riesman does not explicitly state that the use of national heroes as childhood models has declined over the years, this conclusion is consistent with this discussion.

Trends in Children's Heroes since the Turn of the Century

In addition to drawing on the five studies (summarized in Table 1) which were suitable for retabulation, the following analysis makes impressionistic use of other internal evidence from the studies, including lengthy but not exhaustive inventories of children's statements about why they chose to be like their hero, and additional studies which did not supply sufficiently comparable or detailed data for retabulation. We shall be concerned with (1) whether the direct questionnaire data confirm the trends in "hero-worship" suggested by Lowenthal's indirect data, and (2), more fundamentally, with whether the pattern of findings in the various direct studies of children is consistent with the belief that popular aspiration levels have declined.

The first four studies summarized in Table 1 (as well as the other early studies referred to in the text and notes) employed the following item, or some slight variation thereof: "Of all persons whom you have heard, or read about, or seen, whom would you most care to be like or resemble? Why?"[17]

The fifth study used a somewhat different question: "Name a famous person you want to be like."[18]

The earlier item produced references to figures from the immediate environment by between about one-fifth and two-fifths of the respondents; the item used in 1958 produced very few such references. Therefore the latter wording may inflate the proportion of children referring to public figures, although in 1958

---

[16] *Ibid.,* p. 96.

[17] This is the wording used by Hill, "Personification of Ideals by Urban Children," *op. cit.* The item was worded as follows in the other studies: "What person of whom you have heard or read would you most like to be? Why?" Chambers, *op. cit.;* "Which person (among those you have seen, or thought of, or heard of, or read about) would you most like to resemble? Why?" Hill, "Comparative Study of Children's Ideals," *op. cit.;* "Of all the persons whom you have known, or heard about, or read about, whom would you most wish to be like? And why do you like this person?" Stoughton and Ray, *op. cit.*

[18] Greenstein, *op. cit.,* p. 76.

failure to respond is much more common than in the earlier studies. As will be seen, the variation in item and response pattern is not a serious drawback for the analysis.[19]

1. ENTERTAINERS. Following Lowenthal, I have defined "entertainer" in "the broadest sense of the word" to encompass not only popular performers such as film stars and professional athletes but also all representatives of literature and the arts. Included are figures from the past (e.g., Longfellow and even Mozart) as well as those who were living at the times of the various studies.

The long-run trends in children's responses are generally consistent with Lowenthal's findings. In particular, the change he observed in the ratio of "serious" and "non-serious" artists is clearly evident. Before World War I both the percentages in Table 1 and the authors' discussions of their findings indicate that children rarely referred to popular performers. By 1928, the proportion of popular figures referred to (e.g., Clara Bow, Rudolph Valentino, Ty Cobb, Paul Whiteman) is double that of "serious" artists; in the post-1944 samples, references to the latter category virtually disappear.[20] Because the decline of "serious artists" is accompanied by an increase in "non-serious" artists and because of the possibility that the phrasing of the 1958 item "increased" the frequency of reference to entertainers, it is not possible to determine with certainty whether over-all references to entertainers have increased.

2. BUSINESSMEN, INDUSTRIALISTS, FINANCIERS. Lowenthal's procedure was to combine business and professional occupations into a single category, the latter including such disparate types as a college president and an inventor of gadgets. Then he further analyzed the occupations in terms of whether they were "serious" or "non-serious" and whether they represented production or consumption spheres of life.

In Table 1, I have reported only the proportion of references to "captains of industry" (industrialists, financiers, and businessmen in general). This avoids a great many troublesome coding decisions about whether a profession is "seri-

---

[19]When no response and immediate environment categories in Table 1 are dropped and percentages are computed for all studies on the basis only of responses to wider environment exemplars, there is no change in the findings discussed below.

[20]Evidently none of the 1944 children referred to "serious" artists. The findings of Havighurst, et al. although presented in categories which are not strictly comparable to the present ones, provide supporting evidence that children have tended to choose popular entertainers as their exemplars in recent decades. Their study, which was of nine different populations of children and adolescents—most of them Midwesterners—seems to have been conducted in 1944 or 1945. The total number of respondents is 1,147. Havighurst, et al. present a category of exemplars labeled "glamorous adults," including "people with a romantic or ephemeral fame, due to the more superficial qualities of appearance and behavior; e.g., movie stars, military figures, athletes," as well as "characters in comic strips or radio dramas." Their discussion suggests that most of the references coded in this category were to popular entertainers. In three of the populations they studied, references to "glamorous adults" exceeded 30 percent and in four they exceeded 20 percent. In the remaining two the percentages were 14 and 2. The item used in this study permitted references both to individuals personally known by the respondents and to imaginary "composite characters," as well as to public figures. The inclusion of the "composite" category (numerous responses were classified under this heading) presumably reduces references to figures in the wider environment and therefore makes Havighurst's estimate of the frequency of "glamorous" exemplars conservative.

ous" and at the same time provides a clear-cut test of whether veneration of "idols of production" has declined.

The findings summarized in Table 1 cast serious doubt on the assumption that the frequent pre-World War I magazine biographies of captains of industry were an accurate indication of mass aspirations at the time. If such goals were prevalent in the population, it is difficult to believe that they would not have been reflected in children's statements about who they would "care to be like or resemble." But only a minute proportion (less than 2 percent) of the children in the early studies referred to men like Carnegie, Rockefeller, and Morgan as their "ideals." It is true that still fewer contemporary children make such choices (none seem to have in the 1944 study). But the decline is within an exceedingly small range.

3. CONTEMPORARY POLITICAL FIGURES.   The incumbent president and other living politicians have been placed in this category, plus individuals who were active during the adult lifetimes of parents of the children studied. Thus for the 1958 respondents, Franklin D. Roosevelt is treated as "contemporary"; Woodrow Wilson and Theodore Roosevelt have the same status for the 1928 children.

The data on contemporary political figures also cast doubt on the adequacy of Lowenthal's index. During all periods very few children chose the incumbent president. The proportion of 1902 references to Theodore Roosevelt, for example, is virtually identical with the proportion of 1944 references to Franklin Roosevelt, and in general there is no significant variation over the half-century in references to the chief executive. Studies of children's occupational goals, which were conducted around the turn of the century, further support the finding that children of that period rarely developed presidential aspirations.[21]

At first glance there seems to be partial support for Lowenthal's thesis in the

---

[21]If log cabin-to-White House mythology ever had much of an impact on children's aspirations, this must have been in the period before the 1890's, judging from the early occupational preference studies. For example, in a study of the reponses of 1,065 five through 16-year-old Brooklyn, New York, Long Branch, New Jersey, and Melrose, Mass. children to the question, "What would you like to be when you grow up?" only 11 references to the presidency emerged. Adelaide E. Wyckoff, "Children's Ideals," *The Pedagogical Seminary*, 8 (December 1901), pp. 482–492. In another early study, in which the field work took place in 1893, 1,234 Santa Rosa and San Jose, California public school children were read an anecdote describing a group of children expressing their occupational preferences. Included in the occupations listed was president. Some children made this choice, but apparently too few to be included in a table which lists occupations referred to as infrequently as six times. Hatti M. Willard, "Children's Ambitions," *Studies in Education*, 1 (January 1897), pp. 243–253. The discussions of two other early studies, neither of which present tabulations, also suggest that when children in the 1890's were asked "What would you like to be?" few of them mentioned the presidency. Will S. Monroe, "Vocational Interests of Children," *Education*, 18 (January 1898), pp. 259–264, a study of 1,755 eight to 16-year-old school children from a number of Connecticut River Valley communities in Massachusetts; and J. P. Taylor, "A Preliminary Study of Children's Hopes," *Forty-Second Annual Report of the State Superintendent for the School Year Ending July 31, 1895*, Vol. II, State of New York Department of Public Instruction, pp. 987–1015, a study of 2,000 school children from various New York State communities. These occupational preference studies present extensive quotations of children's responses and therefore are of considerable impressionistic interest. Unfortunately, they are not suitable for systematic secondary analysis.

finding that "other contemporary political figures" were chosen by about nine percent of the 1902 respondents, in contrast to less than three percent of the respondents in later studies. But two-thirds of the "other" 1902 references were to the recently assassinated President McKinley and there is evidence that during the period immediately after his death, McKinley's "martyrdom" led to a widespread idolization of him on the part of children, as well as adults.[22]

4. NATIONAL HEROES.   Riesman's discussion of the erstwhile role of national heroes in children's socialization leads us to expect that references to the *dramatis personae* of American patriotic lore will have declined. And this indeed is the case. Over 35 percent of the 1902 responses and only about 10 percent of the post-1944 responses fell in this category. In the first of the reports on children's exemplars, Darrah's 1896 study of 1440 St. Paul, Minnesota and San Mateo County, California children, references to Washington and Lincoln alone (by far the most frequently mentioned patriotic figures in all of the studies) were made by 40 percent of the ten to sixteen year-old respondents.[23] The breakdown of national heroes reported in Table 1 leads to a further observation: one individual—George Washington—seems to account for the entire declining trend in references to national heroes.

To recapitulate, the direct data on children's exemplars are consistent with only one of the three trends reported by Lowenthal. The ratio of popular over "serious" entertainers has increased over the years in roughly the same way that the content of magazine biographies has shifted. But changes in magazine biographies of "heroes of production" and of political leaders are not reflected in the direct observations of public exemplars. The direct data also support Riesman's hypothesis that contemporary children are less likely than their predecessors to identify with national heroes. We may now consider the implications of these findings.

Discussion

In general, the body of "forgotten" data discussed here provides little if any support for the notion that Americans have placed a declining value on achievement. It is true that when one compares "official" emanations (for example, addresses to high school and college graduating classes) of the past with those of today "the decline of the Protestant ethic" seems plentifully evident. But this

---

[22] A few weeks after McKinley's assassination, Earl Barnes asked 1,800 seven through 17-year-old Long Branch, New Jersey and Winfield, New York children to write essays on the topic, "Would you wish to be like Mr. McKinley? Why?" Ninety-two percent of the responses were positive and the remaining eight percent apparently consisted not of personal rejections of McKinley, but rather of statements such as "I would not like to have the care he had on his mind all the time." Earl Barnes, "Political Ideas of American Children," *Studies in Education*, 2 (1902), pp. 25–30. Barnes' discussion of his findings makes it clear that the positive responses were in the nature of vague, eulogistic statements about McKinley's character; they were not assertions of the child's desire some day to become president.

[23] Darrah, *op. cit.*, p. 94.

comparison may merely confound *fin de siècle* rationalizations with reality.[24] De Charms and Moeller find that between 1880 and 1910 "achievement imagery" in children's text books was about twice as common as it is in the contemporary period. This, they imply, indicates that achievement values were more prevalent then than now, a factor which they feel helps to explain industrial growth during those years.[25] Yet, in view of the consistently low rate of choice of businessmen as exemplars, it is difficult to believe that turn-of-the-century young people exceeded contemporary youths in the desire to excel in economic enterprise. The absence of business exemplars is especially striking in the face of what, on Lowenthal's showing, seems to have been a concerted attempt in the media to display businessmen as models for popular emulation.[26]

Similarly, rhetoric suggesting that "every boy is a potential President of the United States" abounded 60 years ago. Consider, for example, the statement by the author of one of the early studies that this "feeling . . . is one of our prized possessions. Our school literature is full of it; no address before children is complete which fails to remind them that each is on his way to the presidential chair."[27] As we have seen, the rhetoric seems to have had little impact on children's felt aspirations—choice of the incumbent president as an exemplar was exceedingly rare.

The two classes of exemplar which *did* shift over the half-century—entertainers and national heroes—are quite ambiguous indicators of aspiration levels. There is no *a priori* reason for assuming that the individual who wants to be like Enrico Caruso or Lily Pons is more driven to succeed than someone who sets up Frank Sinatra or Debbie Reynolds as an "ideal." The reverse could as easily be true. The decline in reference to national heroes (or, more precisely, references to Washington) is equally difficult to interpret. One hypothesis, which at first seems credible, is that identification with a hero such as Washington serves to channel a child's aspirations in the direction of political achievement. This seems to have been Riesman's assumption in the passage quoted above about the function of the George Washington myth in the period "dependent upon inner direction." His remarks continue: "The [presidential] role, moreover, by its very nature, is a continuing one; somebody is always president. . . . In fantasy the little boy not only identifies with the young Washington in the French and Indian wars but also with the adult role of president. . . . "[28] If this were the case

---

[24] For one likely intellectual source of such rationalizations, see Richard Hofstadter, *Social Darwinism in American Thought: 1860–1915* (Philadelphia: University of Pennsylvania Press, 1944). Cf. also, R. Richard Wohl, "The 'Rags to Riches Story': An Episode of Secular Idealism," in Reinhard Bendix and Seymour M. Lipset, eds., *Class Status and Power* (Glencoe, Ill.: The Free Press, 1953), pp. 388–395.

[25] De Charms and Moeller, *op. cit.,* pp. 193 and 141. For additional uses of children's text books as indices of achievement motivation see David C. McClelland, *The Achieving Society* (Princeton, N. J.: Van Nostrand, 1961).

[26] Further research would be desirable to determine whether the two magazines sampled by Lowenthal, *Saturday Evening Post* and *Collier's,* were representative of other periodicals of the time.

[27] Barnes, "Political Ideas of American Children," *op. cit.,* p. 27.

[28] *The Lonely Crowd, op. cit.,* p. 96.

we would expect—contrary to the present findings—that populations which were high in identification with figures such as Washington also would be high in reference to incumbent presidents.[29]

Unfortunately, in the early studies respondents' explanations of why they chose to be like their exemplars were not presented exhaustively. Therefore they cannot be retabulated. However, the extensive quotations which are given also fail to support the Riesmanian conception of an era in which the socialization process instilled in children lofty aspirations—*ad astra per aspera*.[30]

The responses reported in the early studies are not couched in the language of personal striving, nor do they carry the implication that the child expected personally to assume the role of the individual to whom he referred. The largest proportion of statements seem simply to ascribe to the child's hero what one of the early writers called "rather vague moral qualities."[31] ("I want to be like George Washington because he was good.") Other responses stress the fame of the child's exemplar, his wealth (but without the implication that by emulating his hero the child expects personally to obtain riches), his physical appearance.

Even the earliest of the studies (1896) contains quotations which, with slight alterations in prose style, might have served as epigraphs for chapters in *The Lonely Crowd* on the other-directed way of life. For example, a fifteen-year-old boy explained shortly before the election of 1896 that he wanted to be like William Jennings Bryan because Bryan "is well proportioned and well built, a good looking gentleman, and one of the smartest men in the United States . . . and is, without an exception, the greatest orator on the face of the globe."[32] In the same study, a fourteen-year-old boy selected as his idol a man he wanted to resemble "because he has not very hard work, and he has a good time and plenty of money. . . . "[33]

The assumption that achievement values have changed may, as Lipset's remarks suggest, simply be the result of inaccurate conceptions of nineteenth century America. Writers who emphasize the passivity of contemporary Americans

[29]We might also expect that age breakdowns would show identifications with Washington to be common among young children and to decline among older children, accompanied by a compensatory increase in reference to the incumbent president. Fragmentary evidence from the two earliest studies summarized in Table 1 suggests that references to Washington did indeed decrease with age, but that there was no age variation in the infrequent identifications with the incumbent president.

The discussion of trends in references to entertainers and national heroes carries no implication that the changes reported in Table 1 are irrelevant to understanding shifts in American values; it *is* being suggested that the trends do not support the thesis that there has been a shift in the direction of greater mass passivity. In explaining the changes in children's exemplars, at the very least one would have to take account of the enormously great visibility of popular entertainers to contemporary Americans as a consequence of technological change in mass communication, and of curricular changes in public education, including the advent of "social studies" as a substitute for history. On the latter see Wilhelmina Hill, *Social Studies in the Elementary School Program* (Washington, D. C.: Department of Health, Education, and Welfare, 1960), p. 24.

[30]*The Lonely Crowd, op. cit.*, pp. 118–120.

[31]Barnes, "Political Ideas of American Children," *op. cit.*, p. 28.

[32]Darrah, *op. cit.*, pp. 90–91.

[33]*Ibid.*, p. 92. Similar statements may be found in the numerous quotations of children's reasons for preferring occupations reported in the studies cited in footnote 21.

usually at least tacitly picture a much more vigorous, optimistic, upwardly striving folk who populated what Lowenthal calls the "open-minded liberal society" at the beginning of the century. But commentators on the present often find it tempting to idealize the past.[34]

Certain mistaken notions about structural changes in American society in the present century probably have contributed to the widely held belief that American aspiration levels have declined. For example, until recently it was widely assumed that upward occupational mobility has diminished in the United States. This assumption has been severely challenged by recent research.[35] Similarly, questionable assertions about the debilitating effects of contemporary "mass society" may have predisposed observers to accept over-simplified, if not erroneous hypotheses about value change.[36]

Summary

A secondary analysis of trends in children's exemplars over a period of approximately 60 years fails to support the hypothesis that American values have changed in the directions suggested by such commentators as David Riesman. Identifications with business leaders and political leaders are rare today, but were equally rare at the turn of the century. Children are less likely today to choose national heroes; more likely to choose popular entertainment figures. However, there is no reason to interpret these changes as evidence of declining aspiration levels. In general, examination of this body of studies suggests that commentators who point to the increasing passivity of contemporary Americans are able to do so only by idealizing the American past.

[34]It is interesting to compare Lowenthal's characterization of turn-of-the-century American society with the following observation by one of the early students of children's occupational preferences: "The small number of extravagant impossible hopings [among the respondents] seems quite remarkable. The apparent contentment with the lot nature has given them, the genuine delight with which the poorer children look forward to the severe monotonous labors that the future holds in store, the glad willingness to share the heavy burdens of supporting their father's family, all are witnesses to the triumph of childhood's hope and idealism over the toil and pain of the world." Taylor, *op. cit.*, p. 999. Children during this period doubtless were not devoid of mobility aspirations. Cf. the comparisons of Massachusetts children's occupational preferences with parental occupations by Monroe, *op. cit.*, which suggest, for example, that children of unskilled laborers tended to aspire toward skilled trades.

[35]Natalie Rogoff, *Recent Trends in Occupational Mobility* (Glencoe, Ill.: The Free Press, 1953); Seymour M. Lipset and Reinhard Bendix, *Social Mobility in Industrial Society* (Berkeley and Los Angeles: University of California Press, 1959).

[36]Cf., for example, Daniel Bell, "America as a Mass Society: A Critique," *Commentary*, 32 (July 1956), 75–83; Scott Greer and Peter Orleans, "Mass Society and Parapolitical Structure," *American Sociological Review*, 27 (1962), pp. 634–646.

The American Character in the 1950's

THOMAS L. HARTSHORNE

I

In the 1950's much of the discussion of the American character came to revolve around the concepts elaborated in a single book: *The Lonely Crowd* by David Riesman, Nathan Glazer, and Reuel Denney.[1] It was one of those rare books which, though intended primarily for a scholarly audience, enjoyed an enormous popular success.[2] It was probably even more popular and influential outside the academic community than within it. For non-academic intellectuals it became the basic document of social analysis in the 1950's, and discussions of contemporary society and culture frequently, if not usually, took place within the frame of reference established by *The Lonely Crowd* and used the vocabulary coined by the authors.

With hindsight, it is not difficult to explain the book's rather surprising popularity. It is obvious that it struck a responsive chord. Why? The easy answer would be that it verbalized the more or less inarticulate feelings of large numbers of people, that it systematized ideas that were in the air, that it said things that

Reprinted by permission from Thomas L. Hartshorne, *The Distorted Image: Changing Conceptions of the American Character since Turner.* Copyright 1968, The Press of Case Western Reserve University.

[1] *The Lonely Crowd: A Study of the Changing American Character* (2nd ed.; Garden City, N. Y., 1954). I have used the abridged paperback edition of the book for this study since it is more accessible to most readers than the original edition and because, at least for present purposes, it is virtually identical with the original edition. I have also taken the liberty of using the name "Riesman" as a convenient shorthand expression denoting not only Riesman himself, but also his coworkers, Glazer and Denney, whenever they collaborated with him.

[2] See Eric Larrabee, "David Riesman and His Readers," in *Culture and Social Character: The Work of David Riesman Reviewed*, eds. Seymour Martin Lipset and Leo Lowenthal (Glencoe, Ill., 1961), pp. 404–416.

people were already thinking. Many analysts of the culture of the United States were not at all convinced that the American scene was as prosperous and cheerful as it appeared to be. Beneath the glittering surface they detected evidences of profound insecurity and uncertainty, due partly to the frustrations of the Korean War and also to the necessity of living in a world all too familiar with the destructive potentialities of modern weapons. Prosperity itself was sometimes regarded with suspicion, since it was based to a considerable extent on defense spending and was thus dependent on the continued existence of a substantial threat to the nation's very existence. Many commentators believed that Americans had paid dearly for their affluence; their society was in a considerable mess. Materialism, Coca-colonization, and the heinous crimes perpetrated by the mass media in the guise of entertainment all found a prominent place in their works. Paul and Percival Goodman summed up the general feeling:

The critics have shown with pretty plain evidence that we spend our money for follies, that our leisure does not revive us, that our conditions of work are unmanly and our beautiful American classlessness is degenerating into a static bureaucracy; our mass arts are beneath contempt; our prosperity breeds insecurity; our system of distribution has become huckstering and our system of production discourages enterprise and sabotages invention.[3]

To use Henry Miller's telling phrase, America was usually pictured as an "air-conditioned nightmare."

Perhaps the most unpalatable feature of this depressing spectacle was conformity. In their frantic, even hysterical, search for security in a threatening and insecure world, Americans seemed to have made a massive retreat into conformity. American intellectuals launched what amounted to a concerted attack upon the problem. It was not, of course, a new problem—it had been one of the keynotes of analyses of the American character at least since De Tocqueville—but in the 1950's it was discussed with an intensity and on a scale rarely if ever approached before except possibly during the 1920's, the heyday of the critics of Babbittry. And it was discussed not only by disaffected litterateurs but also by social scientists. It came to be regarded as *the* American characteristic, the besetting American sin; commentators on the nation's life found in all areas of that life new evidences of the mindless conformist tendencies of the American people. Mark Twain's remark about the weather could very justly have been applied to conformity.

That there were several parallels between the social criticism of the post-war period and that of the 1920's is undeniable, but there was also one important difference: in the 1950's the villains were not so easy to identify. In the 1920's the targets had been satisfyingly concrete. All those who were unhappy with American civilization had been able to join in the game of Puritan-baiting or pioneer-baiting. In the 1950's, however, the culprit seemed to be the diffuse

---

[3] *Communitas: Means of Livelihood and Ways of Life* (2nd ed.; New York, 1960), p. 5.

entity called "mass society" or "mass culture." Assaults on the public taste were legion, but they were launched by institutions whose impersonality gave their critics some difficult moments. "We are only giving the public what it wants" turned out, dishearteningly, to be true enough to rob the critics' barbs of much of their sting. Their efforts were frustrated and frustrating. The situation seemed to call for the wholesale reform of the "public" mind, a task which would have been virtually impossible to accomplish even if someone had succeeded in determining precisely who, or what, the public was.

The Lonely Crowd found a ready response because it appeared to offer a tidy solution to this dilemma. It would be easy at this point to become involved in a discussion of one of the possible variations of the debate over the Great Man theory of history—did the book define the thinking of the time, or was it a product of the *Zeitgeist?* —but for the present let it merely be noted that it filled an important niche in the current intellectual framework. It seemed to offer a reasonably precise conceptual scheme for the analysis of contemporary American society with historical and sociological evidence to support it.

Riesman's main point was that a fundamental change was taking place in American life, a characterological shift from what he called "inner-direction" to what he called "other-direction." These terms were used to denote the different ways in which the mechanisms of social authority were brought to bear upon the individual to secure from him the conformity necessary to maintain social order and stability. In the case of inner-direction, these mechanisms were implanted in the individual early in his life by his parents or other elders, so that throughout the rest of his life he was directed by internalized rules of conduct that appeared to come from "inside" him. In the case of other-direction, the necessary social authority over the individual was exercised by his peer group, and the individual was thus directed by forces which were exerted by "others."[4]

Riesman maintained that the United States was distinctive among the nations of the world because the other-directed character type was more prevalent and more highly developed in the United States than in any other nation. But he did not feel that it was the only character type which existed in the United States. In fact, he insisted that inner-direction was still the dominant component in the characterological composition of the nation.[5] The transition from inner-direction to other-direction was still in process; it had not been completed.

II

As stimulating and provocative as Riesman's analysis of the American character was, perhaps even more interesting was the response it evoked. His book was almost universally misinterpreted. Indeed, it had the impact it did precisely

[4]*Lonely Crowd*, pp. 29–32, 34–40.
[5]Riesman and Glazer, *Faces in the Crowd: Individual Studies in Character and Politics* (New Haven, 1952), p. 5.

because it was misinterpreted, and the way in which it was misinterpreted reveals much about studies, past and present, of the American character.

Most of Riesman's readers, already concerned with conformity, saw in his analysis a sociological confirmation of their beliefs. In fact, "other-direction" fulfilled the same function for critics of American society in the 1950's that "Puritanism" had fulfilled in the 1920's. It was both the name and the cause of everything they found distasteful. But they suffered from two misapprehensions. First, they tended to assume that other-direction was the dominant mode of social conformity in the United States, while Riesman had said quite pointedly that it was not. They also tended to feel that other-direction was an exclusively American phenomenon. Riesman had implied very strongly that while there were more other-directed people in America than in any other nation, other-direction existed everywhere and would spread as socio-economic conditions in the rest of the world came to resemble those in the United States.

Second, and more interesting, is the fact that Riesman's readers tended to assume that inner-direction and other-direction were synonyms for individualism and conformity respectively. They were not. Both inner-direction and other-direction were modes of conformity, and the sole difference between them was in what the individual was conforming to. The inner-directed person *seemed* more individualistic than the other-directed person, but only because the pressures to which he conformed were less obvious. He had no more rational freedom of choice than the other-directed person. He himself was likely to be deluded into thinking that he was following his own self-determined course, but Riesman insisted that this *was* a delusion.[6]

It is therefore incorrect to assume that Riesman put a higher value on inner-direction than on other-direction. In many specific instances, in fact, he appeared to value it far less. What he did value was a state of mind and being that he called "autonomy," a state in which the individual transcended both inner-direction and other-direction and achieved a position in which he was able to make free choices about what he would conform to and, indeed, whether he would conform at all. He was not inevitably a rebel; he could choose to conform, to submit to social pressures, but if he did, it was because he had made a free, rational decision. His acceptance of authority, if he chose to accept it, was only provisional and did not indicate that he had abandoned the right or the ability to reject authority in other circumstances.[7] If any of Riesman's character types deserve the name "individualist," therefore, it is the autonomous individual and not either the inner-directed or the other-directed one.

Despite Riesman's discussion of autonomy, most of his critics and commentators have persisted in assuming an exact correspondence between inner-direction and individualism on the one hand and between other-direction and conformity

---

[6]Riesman, *Individualism Reconsidered and Other Essays* (Glencoe, Ill., 1954), pp. 101–102.

[7]*Lonely Crowd,* pp. 282–286. See also Riesman's essay "The Saving Remnant," in *Individualism Reconsidered,* pp. 99–120, where he makes the same point at greater length and in a slightly different terminology.

on the other. To be sure, the concept of autonomy is somewhat vague; there is no precise way to determine in any individual case whether a person's submission to external pressures is the result of rationality or rationalization. Still, the ambiguity is not so great as to cause the concept to be ignored completely. Inner-direction and other-direction are also rather vague, after all, and they were certainly not ignored. The mystery is deepened when it is pointed out that if Riesman was in fact talking about individualism as opposed to conformity, he went to excessive lengths in attempting to define inner-direction and other-direction. The fact that he was at some pains to devise a new vocabulary should have indicated that he did not intend to talk about individualism and conformity but about something quite different. However, it is possible that people had become so hardened to the unnecessary proliferation of jargon in the social sciences that it did not seem strange that a social scientist would coin new words when there were perfectly suitable old ones; after all, it had happened fairly frequently in the past. And because Riesman's labels were so popular, because they were seized upon so eagerly and talked about so widely, many people probably felt entitled to use them without ever having read *The Lonely Crowd.*

Many who read the book with some care, however, were still led astray. Seymour Lipset, in most ways a remarkably astute analyst of the American scene, criticized Riesman's contention that there had been a change in the American character, pointing out that many nineteenth-century commentators had stressed conformity as a distinctive American trait.[8] In other words, he also assumed that Riesman's other-direction was identical to the simple conformity stressed in so many previous treatments of the American character, and this was not the case. Conformity implies the maintenance of certain standards of external behavior, whereas other-direction describes a psychological condition and a value system. It is not mere behavioral conformity, for the autonomous individual may also conform in that sense.

Lipset's analysis raises another point. The concept of national character is by its very nature comparative. To establish his basic assumption that the nation he is dealing with is distinctive in certain respects, the analyst of national character must compare it to other nations, at least by implication. Now, much of the evidence upon which Lipset based his contention that other-direction was a distinguishing American trait in the nineteenth century was drawn from the observations of foreign travelers, and the traits they regarded as distinctively American were those which stood out as the result of comparisons, stated or implied, between the United States and Europe. Thus, they were saying in effect that nineteenth-century America was more other-directed than nineteenth-century Europe. Even granting that what they noted in the nineteenth century *was* other-direction and not simple conformity, this does not contradict Riesman's

[8]"A Changing American Character?," in *Culture and Social Character,* eds. Lipset and Lowenthal, pp. 141–156.

contention that the American character was more other-directed in the twentieth century than it had been in the nineteenth.

Riesman himself must bear part of the blame for this inability of his critics to
deal with his work. For one thing, his choice of labels for his character types was
unfortunate and probably led to considerable misunderstanding. "Inner-direction" and "other-direction" do not have the exotic flavor of many of the more
unusual terms employed by social scientists. They sound fairly familiar and seem
to be the kind of words one might use with reasonable comfort in ordinary
speech. Perhaps Riesman chose them for this very reason, hoping to avoid the
appearance of unnecessary jargonizing. But the apparent familiarity of these
terms was an unintended trap for his readers, for it seemed to make it unnecessary to determine their precise meanings. Many people were probably misled
into thinking that terms which sounded so familiar meant exactly what they
appeared to mean. Unfortunately they appeared to mean something far different
from what Riesman had intended them to mean. To people brought up to value
individualism, at least on the level of verbal affirmation, inner-direction must
have seemed much more palatable than other-direction and to have an aura of
moral superiority about it. One can easily see an individual who is unaware of
the precise meanings of the terms gladly admitting that he is inner-directed or
indignantly denying that he is other-directed. Inner-direction just sounds better.

Nor is this all. Riesman admits that he consciously modifies his ideas to suit
the specific context in which he happens to be presenting them, that he consciously adopts different positions before different audiences. He is also prone to
cast arguments in the form, "While it is true that . . . , nevertheless. . . . " And he
may reverse the order of the clauses from one work to the next. Consequently, it
is often quite difficult to discover precisely what he thinks on any given question.
It might almost be said that he forestalls all criticism by taking the critic's
position himself before anyone else has a chance to. His changeableness might
almost be taken for a mild form of intellectual dishonesty were it not for four
facts: one, he usually adopts a position likely to win him more critics than
disciples; two, playing the role of devil's advocate is a very good way of getting
people to think; three, the practice of adapting one's remarks to suit one's audience is nearly universal, and Riesman differs only in that he does it consciously
and admits it openly; four, he does not use his own modifications of his remarks
as a protective hedge, but stands behind what he has written, at the same time
showing a greater readiness than most to admit that he has been wrong and has
changed his mind. The fact remains, however, that this flexibility, admirable
though it may be in many respects, does make it difficult to deal with his work as
a whole and to comprehend it as a finished product.[9]

Lipset may thus have been led astray by Riesman himself, for Riesman did
talk at times as if he felt that other-direction and conformity were synonymous.

---

[9]See Riesman's essays "Values in Context" and "Individualism Reconsidered," in *Individualism
Reconsidered*, pp. 17–25, 26–38.

While there may be some justification for identifying other-direction with conformity, there is none at all for identifying inner-direction with individualism or for assuming that Riesman valued inner-direction more than other-direction. Yet Carl Degler did just that in his commentary on *The Lonely Crowd*. "Translated into more familiar words," he said, "the inner-directed personality is individualistic and self-reliant." Criticizing Riesman for what seemed to him to be an inaccurately laudatory treatment of the nineteenth century, Degler commented, "Undoubtedly to anyone with a spark of inner-direction in his personality the nineteenth century as depicted in *The Lonely Crowd* is almost too good to be true."[10] But the quotations which Degler cited to prove that Riesman preferred the nineteenth century to the twentieth really do nothing of the kind. If, as Degler said, "In *The Lonely Crowd* the decisive, ruthless, brusque, self-confident robber baron is taken as typical of the nineteenth century,"[11] it is difficult to see how it is possible to argue that Riesman believed nineteenth-century society to be admirable. Degler also quoted Riesman's use of words like "gloomy," "grim," and "stern" in reference to the people and culture of the past. Of course, Degler is quite correct in saying that Riesman found much to approve of in the nineteenth century, and it is obvious that he found much to disapprove of in the twentieth. However, the other-directed character, for all its deficiencies, did have certain redeeming features in Riesman's view: tolerance, sympathy, and insistence on fair play. Thus, it is possible to find in Riesman evidence that he liked certain features of the inner-directed style of the nineteenth century but disliked others, and that he disliked certain features of the other-directed style of the twentieth century but liked others. On the whole, therefore, it does not seem that Degler's argument has enough force to contradict Riesman's explicit declarations that he did not value the inner-directed past any more than he valued the other-directed present.

How can we explain this misreading of Riesman's work, a misreading more glaringly revealed in various "popular" treatments than in the work of academicians like Lipset and Degler? David Potter has pointed out—and the evidence of this study also reveals—that interpretations of the American character tend to fall into one or the other of two broad groups: they portray the American either as a materialistic conformist or as an idealistic individualist.[12] When Riesman announced the distinction between inner-direction and other-direction, therefore, Americans brought up on the conflict between conformity and individualism, and accustomed to thinking in these terms, were deluded by the apparent similarity of Riesman's concepts to the older ideas and simply assumed that they *were* the older ideas slightly refurbished.

An analysis of the types of society with which Riesman linked each of his

[10]"The Sociologist as Historian: Riesman's *The Lonely Crowd,*" *American Quarterly,* 15 (1963), 483–497. The quotations are on pp. 485 and 487 respectively.

[11]*Ibid.,* p. 485.

[12]"Quest for the National Character," in *Reconstruction of American History,* ed. Higham, pp. 197–220.

character types provides another perspective on the problem. The inner-directed personality was created in and suited to a society characterized by a state of "transitional population growth," while the other-directed personality was the product of a society in a state of "incipient population decline." This use of demographic labels should not be taken too seriously, for Riesman admitted that he used them only as a brief way of denoting a number of specific institutional characteristics.[13] Thus an inner-directed society was characterized above all by expansiveness in population, production, and space. Other-directed societies were characterized by capitalism, industrialism, urbanism, and material abundance.[14] The state of "incipient population decline" seems identical, for all practical purposes, to the state of society usually referred to by the phrase "mature industrial society." It is here that the difficulty lies.

When Riesman spoke of the inner-directed personality of the nineteenth century, his readers, regardless of Riesman's actual description, insisted on seeing Turner's individualistic frontiersman and contrasting him with the conformist security-seeker of the twentieth century. In other words, they saw in Riesman not what he actually said but what they wanted and expected him to say. They assumed that he condemned other-direction and praised inner-direction because, with their allegiance to Jeffersonian and Turnerian models of thought, *they would have done so themselves.*[15] But in fact Riesman showed a small but unmistakable preference for the industrial society of the present, feeling that such a society provided the greatest opportunities for the development of autonomous personalities, the type he really valued.[16]

---

[13] *Lonely Crowd,* pp. 23–24.

[14] *Ibid.,* pp. 28–40.

[15] This was not true of Lipset and Degler. They went astray not because they were trapped by the agrarian myth but because they assumed that Riesman was. It was an understandable mistake. Most native commentators on the American character were trapped.

[16] *Lonely Crowd,* pp. 285–286.

THE ONGOING INQUIRY ——— VI

INTRODUCTION VI

This section brings together a group of writings on subjects pertinent to the exploration of American national character in the second half of the twentieth century. Each essay treats a significant element of society—women, Southerners, blacks, the young, the "common man"—or a problematic aspect of public life. Some of the selections make explicit use of a concept of the national character. All of them contribute to a deeper understanding of it. The authors are the historian David M. Potter, two of whose essays appear elsewhere in this volume; C. Vann Woodward, professor of history at Yale University and a foremost authority on the history and culture of the South; William H. Grier and Price M. Cobbs, two black psychiatrists, whose insights challenge reassessment of the relation of definitions of American national character to the culture and experience of black Americans; Joseph Adelson, professor of psychology at the University of Michigan and author of *The Adolescent Experience;* and Peter Schrag, editor-at-large of *Saturday Review* and editor of *Change,* whose article on "The Forgotten American," as originally printed in *Harper's Magazine,* bore beneath the title the rousing injunction, "You better pay attention to the son of a bitch before he burns the country down."

The two readings that conclude this book turn to a pair of fundamental issues in the public life of contemporary Americans. In the first, nine observers discuss the factor of violence in American society. They are Hannah Arendt, professor of political science at the New School for Social Research; St. Clair Drake, professor of sociology at Roosevelt University; Clifford Geertz, professor of anthropology at the University of Chicago; Paul Goodman, educator, social critic, and America's most articulate anarchist; Michael Harrington, socialist leader and author of *The Other America;* Richard Hofstadter, professor of history at Columbia University; Thomas F. Pettigrew, professor of social psychology at Harvard University; David Riesman; and C. Vann Woodward. In the second selection, Gabriel A. Almond, professor of political science at Stanford University, shows how American character is expressed in American foreign policy and performance. Published in 1950, Almond's insights seem remarkably apt today, and it is fitting that this book of readings, having begun with the shaping of a new national character two centuries ago should end with a discussion of the significance of that character to the "new world" of the late twentieth century.

American Women and the American Character

DAVID M. POTTER

There is an old riddle which children used to ask one another concerning two Indians. One was a big Indian, the other was a little Indian, and they were sitting on a fence. The little Indian, the riddle tells us, was the big Indian's son, but the big Indian was not the little Indian's father. How, asks the riddle, can this be?

Boys and girls for a long time have found that this riddle succeeds very well in mystifying many people. And the fact that it does presents another puzzle as to why the riddle is hard to answer. If we were to state the question in more general terms: there are two human beings, one adult and one child; the child is the son of the adult, but the adult is not the father of the child, probably no one would have much difficulty in recognizing that the adult is the mother. Why then do the Indians on a fence perplex us? If we examine the structure of the riddle, I think we will find that it contains two devices which inhibit our recognition that the big Indian is a female. First, the two Indians are described as being in a very specific situation—they are sitting on a fence. But women, at least in our culture, do not usually sit on fences; if the two Indians had been roasting some ears of corn, or mending their teepee, how much easier the riddle would have been. Second, we are perhaps especially prone to think of Indians as masculine. If the riddle had said two South Sea Islanders, or perhaps, two Circassians, the possibility of their being female might occur to us much more easily.

But most of all, the riddle owes its baffling effect to the fact that our social generalization is mostly in masculine terms. If we said that the little Indian is the big Indian's daughter, but that the big Indian is not the little Indian's mother,

Reprinted with permission from David M. Potter, "American Women and the American Character," *Stetson University Bulletin*, LXII (January, 1962), pp. 1–22.

the possibility that the big Indian is the father would come to mind readily enough. For in our culture, men are still in a general category, while women are in a special category. When we speak of mankind, we mean men and women collectively, but when we speak of womenkind, we mean the ladies, God bless them. The word humanity is itself derived from *homo,* that is man, and the species is *Homo sapiens.* Neuter nouns or general nouns which are ambiguous as to sex—nouns like infant, baby, child, sibling, adolescent, adult, spouse, parent, citizen, person, individual, etc.—all take masculine pronouns. In our culture, a woman, at marriage, takes her husband's name. Though born a Cabot, if she marries Joe Doaks, Mrs. Joe Doaks she becomes and Mrs. Doaks she remains, usually for the rest of her life.

This masculine orientation is to be expected, of course, in a society which is traditionally and culturally male-dominated—in what we call a patriarchal rather than a matriarchal society. Even women themselves have connived at maintaining the notion of masculine ascendancy, and in the rather numerous concrete situations in which they actually dominate their men, they often dissimulate their control by pretending to be weak, dependent, or "flighty." In such a situation one must expect that men will be regarded as the normative figures in the society, and that, in popular thought at least, the qualities of the masculine component in the society will pass for the qualities of the society as a whole.

If this habit were confined to popular thought, it would hardly be worth examining. But it also sometimes creeps into academic and scholarly thought, which ought to have more rigor, and when it does so, it can sometimes distort our picture of society. Thus a writer may sometimes make observations on the traits or values of American men, and then may generalize these as the traits or values of the American people. If he did this deliberately, on the theory that since male values dominate the society, they must therefore be American values, we would have to concede that he is aware of what he is doing, even though we might question his results. But when he does so unconsciously, his method may easily lead him to assume first that since American men are dominant, the characteristics of American men are the characteristics of the American people, and that since women are people, the characteristics of the American people are the characteristics of American women, or in short, that the characteristics of American men are the characteristics of American women.

To avoid this trap, when one meets with a social generalization it is frequently worthwhile to ask concretely, does it apply to women, or only to the masculine component in the population? Does the statement that Prussians are domineering mean that Prussian women are domineering, or only Prussian men? Does the statement that Americans are individualistic mean American women as well as American men? The question seems worth asking, for it appears more than possible that many of our social generalizations which are stated sweepingly to cover the entire society are in fact based on the masculine population, and that if we took the feminine population into account, the generalization might have to be qualified, or might even run in an entirely different direction.

I

A notable example of this can perhaps be found in Frederick Jackson Turner's famous frontier hypothesis, stated so brilliantly at Chicago almost seventy years ago. The gist of Turner's argument was, of course, that the frontier had been a basic influence in shaping the character of the American people. Primarily, as he saw it, the frontier provided economic opportunity in the form of free land. When this free land was suddenly conferred upon a people who had previously been held in dependence by the land monopolies of the Old World, it made the American economically independent and this independence made him more individualistic and more egalitarian in his attitudes. Also, the necessity for subduing the wilderness by his own personal exertions, in a situation where he could not call upon doctors, dentists, policemen, lawyers, contractors, well-drillers, repairmen, soil analysts, and other specialists to aid him, made him more self-reliant.

Not even Turner's harshest critics deny that there was much truth in his observations, but many of them have pointed to his lack of precision, and it is fair to question to what extent Turner's generalizations applied to all frontier people, or to what extent they applied restrictively to frontier men. Sometimes it becomes clear that the life-process which he identifies with the frontier was primarily though not wholly an experience shared by men rather than by women. There is one famous passage, for instance, which begins, "The wilderness masters the colonist." Now *colonist* is a neuter noun, and could apply to a female colonist. But the passage continues to say that the wilderness, finding the colonist "European in dress, industry, modes of travel, and thought . . . takes him from the railroad car and puts him in a birch canoe [this sounds progressively less as if it could be a woman]. It strips off the garments of civilization and arrays him in the hunting shirt and the mocassin." Soon, this colonist hears the call of the wild almost as clearly as Jack London's dog, and when he does, "he shouts the war cry and takes the scalp in orthodox Indian fashion."[1] Here, at least, the pioneer in question is hardly a woman.

Certainly it is true that the frontier offered economic opportunity, and certainly, also, frontier women shared in some of the social consequences which flowed from the fact that this opportunity was available to their men. But is it not true, in cold fact, that the opportunities offered by the West were opportunities for men and not, in any direct sense, opportunities for women? The free acres of the West were valuable to those who could clear, and break, and plow and harvest them. But clearing and breaking, plowing and harvesting were men's work, in which women rarely participated. The nuggets of gold in the streambeds of California in 1849 represented opportunity to those who could prospect for them. But the life of the prospector and the sourdough was not a woman's life, and the opportunities were not women's opportunities. Similarly,

[1]Frederick Jackson Turner, *The Frontier in American History* (New York: Henry Holt and Co., 1920), p. 4.

the grass-covered plateau of the Great Plains represented economic opportunity for those who could use it as an open range for the holding and grazing of Longhorn cattle. But the individuals who could do this were men; the Cattle Kingdom was a man's world. Thus, when Turner says that "so long as free land exists, the opportunity for a competency exists," he means, in effect, an opportunity for males.

Again, it may bear repeating, there is no question here that the frontier influenced women as well as men. It had its Molly Pitcher and its Jemima Boone, as well as its Davy Crockett, and its Kit Carson. It left its stamp upon the pioneer women as well as the pioneer men. But when Turner states that it furnished "a new field of opportunity, a gate of escape from the bondage of the past," one must ask, exactly what was the nature of women's participation in this opportunity? Before this question can be analyzed, it is perhaps necessary to recognize that women's place in our society is invariably complicated by the fact that they have, as men do not, a dual status. Almost every woman shares the status of the men in her family—her father or her husband—and if this is a privileged position, she is a recipient of some of the privilege. This is an affiliated status, but if her men gain, she gains with them. Thus, if her family became landowners on the frontier, she participated in their advancement, and no one can deny that free land was, in this indirect sense, opportunity for her also. But woman also has a personal status, which is a sex status, as a female. As a female, on the frontier, women were especially dependent upon having a man in the family, for there was no division of labor there, as there was in settled communities, and most of the tasks of the frontier—the hunting, the wood-chopping, the plowing—could hardly be performed by women, though many of them, of course, rose to these tasks in time of emergency. In fact, the frontier was brutally harsh for females, and it furnished its own verdict on its differential impact upon the sexes. "This country," said the frontier aphorism, "is all right for men and dogs, but it's hell on women and horses."

If we accept Turner's own assumption that economic opportunity is what matters, and that the frontier was significant as the context within which economic opportunity occurred, then we must observe that for American women, as individuals, opportunity began pretty much where the frontier left off. For opportunity lay in access to independent employment, and the employments of the frontier were not primarily accessible to women. But in the growing cities, opportunities for female employment began to proliferate. Where the work of the frontier called for the strong back and the powerful muscles of a primeval man, the work of the city—clerical work, secretarial work, the tending of machines—has called for the supple fingers and the ready adaptability of a young woman, and it was in this environment, for the first time in America, that women found on any scale worth mentioning access to independent earning power. Once woman possessed access to such earning power, whether she used it or not, the historic basis for her traditional subordination had been swept away. The male monopoly upon jobs was broken, and the breaking of this monopoly was no less significant for American women than the breaking of the landlord's monopoly upon fertile soil had been for American pioneer men. As a symbol, the typewriter evokes fewer emotions than the plow, but like the plow, it played a vital part in the fulfillment of the American promise of opportunity and independence. The wilderness may have been the frontier for American men, and the cabin in the clearing the symbol of their independence, but the city was the frontier for American women and the business office was what gave them economic independence and the opportunity to follow a course of their own.

II

Another social generalization which is often stated as if it applied to all Americans, men and women alike, is that our society has experienced a vast transformation in the occupational activities of its people, and that we have passed from the independent, self-directed work, of the kind done by a land-owning farmer, to the regimented, externally-directed activity of the employee who labors for pay. In 1850, 63% of the gainfully employed workers in the United States were engaged in agriculture, and a high proportion of these were land-owning farmers—perhaps as nearly independent as people can be. In the past the farmer, more than most of his fellows, was in position to plan, decide, and act for himself—to maintain his own values without regard for the approval or disapproval of his fellow man, to work at his own pace, to set his own routine. But today, as the census figures show, the American who labors is no longer self-employed. In 1958, it was estimated that 50,000,000 people gainfully employed in the United States received salaries or wages, while only 8,000,000 were self-employed, which means that in general the American worker does not work for himself. He works under direction in an office or a factory. He does not decide what to do, when to do it, or for what purpose, but he waits for instructions which come to him through channels. Even the junior executive, despite his prestige, is no more a self-employed man than the factory worker, and if we may believe *The Organization Man* he is in fact considerably less independent after hours. With these ideas in mind, we speak in broad terms about the disappearance of the old forms of autonomous, self-directed activity.

Yet none of this applies in any sense to women, except for women who are employees, and although female employment has increased steadily to a point where nearly one-third of all women are employed it is still true that two out of three American women are not employees, but find their occupation chiefly in the maintaining of homes and the rearing of children. Millions of housewives continue to exercise personal choice and decision not only in arranging their own time-table and routine but also in deciding what food the family shall have and how it shall be prepared, what articles of purchase shall have the highest priority on the family budget, and, in short, how the home shall be operated. Despite strong tendencies toward conformity in American life, it is clear that American women exercise a very wide latitude of decision in these matters, and everyone knows that there are great variations between the regimes in various American homes. Indeed it seems fairly evident that the housewife of today, with the wide range of consumer goods available for purchase and the wide variety of mechanical devices to free her from drudgery, has a far broader set of alternatives for household procedure than the farm wife of two or three generations ago.[2] Moreover there are now great numbers of women working independently in their own homes, who a generation ago would have been working very much under direction as domestic servants in the homes of other women. If we based our social generalizations upon the experience of women rather than that of men, we might drop the familiar observation about the decreasing independence of Americans in their occupational pursuits. Instead we might emphasize that in the largest single occupational group in the country—the group which cooks and rears children and keeps house—there is a far greater measure of independent and self-directed work than there was in the past.

III

Closely connected to this question of the disappearance of the independent worker is another commonplace generalization, namely that the American people have become the victims of extreme specialization. Everyone is familiar with the burden of this lament: American industry has forced the craftsman to abandon his craft, and with it the satisfaction of creative labor, and has reduced him to operating a machine or to performing a single operation on the assembly-line as if he were a machine himself. Further, the complaint continues, modern conditions provide fewer and fewer opportunities for a worker to be an all-round person of varied skills and resources, as the American farmer used to be, and instead conditions make of him a diminished person, a narrow specialist hardly fit for anything save his narrow specialty.

Despite the exaggerated and somewhat hackneyed character of this outcry, it contains an important element of truth as regards the work of American male workers. But this generalization, too, is in fact applicable largely to the male component in the population rather than to the American people as a whole. For the American housewife is not a specialist, and in fact her modern role requires that she be far more versatile than her grandmother was, despite the greater skill of the grandmother in cooking, sewing, and other household crafts. A good housewife today must not only serve food to please the family palate, but must also know about calories, vitamins, and the principles of a balanced diet. She must also be an economist, both in her knowledge of the quality of the products offered to her and in her ability to do the impossible with a budget. She must not only maintain a comfortable home, but must also possess enough skill

[2]Robert Lynd, "The People as Consumers," writes that there is "probably today a greater variation from house to house in the actual inventory list of family possessions . . . than at any previous era in man's history." *Recent Social Trends in the United States* (New York: McGraw-Hill, 1933), pp. 857–911.

in interior decoration to assure that her own ménage will not seem dowdy or unappealing by comparison with the latest interiors shown in Hollywood films. She must not only rear children, but must also have mastered enough child psychology to be able to spare the rod and still not spoil the child. She must not only get the children ready for school, but must also, in many cases, act as a kind of transportation manager, participating in an elaborate car pool to convey them to and fro. In addition to all this, society now enjoins her not to rely upon the marriage vows to hold her husband, but to keep her personality and her appearance so attractive that he will have no incentive to stray. Whatever else she may be, she is certainly not a specialist, and even if she fails to meet all these varied demands upon her, her mere effort to do so would remove her from the category of specialists. If we based our social generalizations upon women rather than upon men, we might quite justifiably affirm that the modern age is an age of diversified activity rather than an age of specialization.

IV

The profound differences between the patterns of men's work and women's work are seldom understood by most men, and perhaps even by most women. In terms of the time-tables of life, however, the contrasts are almost startling. For instance, man usually begins work in the early twenties, labors at precisely timed intervals for eight hours a day and five days a week, until he is sixty-five, when his life as a worker may be cut off with brutal abruptness and he is left idle. Woman also usually begins work in the early twenties, perhaps in an office on the same time-table as a man, but after a very few years she becomes a wife, whose work is keeping house, and mother whose work is rearing children. As such she labors often for from fifty-one to fifty-six hours a week, and she does not have the alternation of work and leisure which help to lend variety and pace to the life of her husband. Her work-load will continue to be heavier than her husband's until the children are older, after which it will gradually diminish, and she may ultimately re-enter employment. But most women do not; they continue to keep house.[3] And as long as a woman does keep house, either as a wife or as a widow, she never experiences the traumatic, sudden transition from daily work as the focus of life to enforced idleness—the transition which we call retirement.

Another far-reaching consequence of the difference between man's work and woman's work is forcibly expressed in a recent public interest advertisement in *Harper's Magazine* by Frank R. Neu, entitled "We May Be Sitting Ourselves to Death." Neu presents some very impressive data about the poor physical fitness of a large percentage of American men, and about the deleterious effects of the sedentary life of Mr. Joe Citizen as an officeworker whose principal exercise is to

---

[3]In 1957, of the 21,000,000 women in the work force, 11,000,000 were wives. Female employment was highest (45%) in the age brackets 20 to 24, declined to 39% in bracket 25 to 44, rose to 40% in the bracket 45 to 64, and declined to 10% in the bracket 65 and over.

go around a golf course on an electric cart on the week-end. Then Mr. Neu says "Let's consider Jill, Joe's wife, for a moment. Chances are, on the basis of current statistics, Jill will outlive Joe by anywhere from five to 25 years. Medical science is not sure yet whether this is because Jill has different hormones from Joe or whether it is a result of the different roles which Joe and Jill fulfill in our society.

"The average suburban Jill is likely to be a homemaker responsible for rearing two or more children. It is safe to assume that any woman with this responsibility is going to get a lot of daily exercise no matter how many gadgets she has to help her do the housework. A homemaker does a lot of walking each day merely to push the buttons and start the machines that wash the clothes, cook the meals, and remove the dust. And she also does a good deal of bending each day to pick up after Joe and the junior members of the family. All in all, Jill is likely to get much more exercise than Joe. This may have a significant relationship to Jill's outliving Joe, who no longer hikes the dusty trail to bring home the buffalo meat and hides to feed and clothe his family."[4]

In the light of differences so great that they may radically alter the duration of life, it is again evident that a serious fallacy results when generalizations derived from the experience of American men are applied indiscriminately to the American people in such a way as to exclude the experience of American women.

V

As a further illustration of the readiness with which one can fall into a fallacy in this way, let me suggest one more generalization about Americans which has been widely popular in recent years. This is the proposition, formulated by David Riesman in *The Lonely Crowd,* that the American has been transformed, in the past century, from an inner-directed individual to an other-directed individual. A century or so ago, the argument runs, the American learned certain values from his elders, in his youth. He internalized these values, as matters of principle, so that, in Riesman's phrase, they served as a kind of gyroscope to hold him on his course, and he stood by them throughout his life whether they were popular or unpopular. When these values were involved, he did not hesitate to go against the crowd. Thus he was inner-directed. But today, says Riesman, in a universe of rapidly changing circumstances, where the good will of our associates is more important to our success than it ever was to the nineteenth century farmer, the American no longer internalizes his values in the old way. Instead, he responds very perceptively, very sensitively, to the values of others, and adjusts his course to meet their expectations. Indeed their expectations are a kind of radar-screen for his guidance. Thus he is other-directed, or to use an older and less precise term, he is much more a conformist.

[4] *Harper's Magazine,* Vol. 223 (Nov., 1961), p. 23.

Riesman does not discuss whether his thesis about "the changing American character" is applicable to American women, as well as to American men.[5] But we are entitled to ask, does he really believe that American women were so inner-directed as his analysis would suggest? Perhaps yes, if you believe that women have been more steadfast than men in defending the values on which the security of the home is based. But on the other hand, woman, historically, was a dependent person, and as a dependent person, she developed a most perceptive sensitivity to the expectations of others and a responsiveness in adapting herself to the moods and interests of others. She has always had a radar screen. If women are quicker to conform to the expectations of a group of other women than men are to a group of other men, and if we should say that this has been true in the past, what it would mean is that women have been other-directed all along, and that when Riesman says Americans are becoming other-directed, what he means is that American men are becoming other-directed. As women gain more economic and social independence, it might be supposed in terms of Riesman's own analysis, that more than half of the American people are becoming less other-directed rather than more so. With the gradual disappearance of the so-called "clinging vine" type, who dared not call her soul her own, this is, in fact, apparently just what is happening.

VI

If many of the generalizations which apply to American men, and which purport to apply to Americans generally, do not actually apply to American women, anyone who attempts to study the American character is forced to ask: to what extent has the impact of American historical experience been the same for both sexes, and to what extent has it been dissimilar? Viewed in these terms, the answer would probably have to be a balanced one. Certainly the main values that have prevailed in American society—the belief in individualism, the belief in equality, the belief in progress, have shaped the thought of American women as well as of American men, and American women are no doubt more committed to individualism, and to equality, and to progress, than women in many other societies. But on the other hand, some of the major forces that have been at work in American history have impinged upon men and upon women in differential ways. For instance, as I have already suggested, the frontier placed a premium upon qualities of brute strength and of habituation to physical danger which women did not possess in the same degree as men, either for biological or for cultural reasons. The result has been a differential historical experience for

[5]David Riesman, "The Lonely Crowd: A Reconsideration in 1960" in Seymour Martin Lipset and Leo Lowenthal, eds., Culture and Social Character: The Work of David Riesman Reviewed (Glencoe, Ill: The Free Press, 1961), p. 428, discusses an investigation by Michael S. Olmsted which showed that Smith College girls regarded themselves as more other-directed than men and regarded other girls as more other-directed than their group, but Riesman does not state what his own belief is in this matter.

American men and American women which must be analyzed if there is any basis to be found for asserting that there are differences in the character types of the two sexes.

What then, we might ask, have been the principal transformations that history has brought in the lives of American women? Surprisingly enough, this is largely an unexplored field, but there are certain answers which appear more or less self-evident.

One of these is that our society has, during the last century and a half, found ways to do most of its heavy work without the use of human brawn and muscle. Waterpower, steam power, electric power, jet power, and the power of internal combustion have largely eliminated the need for brute strength and great physical stamina in most forms of work. This transformation has emancipated men to a revolutionary degree, but it has even more strikingly emancipated women, for women are physiologically smaller than men, and they lack the muscular strength and physical endurance of men. As the factor of hard labor in human work is reduced and the factor of skill is enhanced, therefore, women have found that inequality in ability to meet the requirements of work is greatly diminished. This basic fact, by itself, has probably done more than anything else to promote the equality of women.

But if this is the most fundamental effect of the mechanization of work, mechanization has also had a number of other sweeping consequences. One of these is that it has destroyed the subsistence farm as a unit of American life, and the disappearance of the subsistence farm, in turn, has had the most far-reaching implications.

To appreciate this, we must remember what life was like on the subsistence farm. The only division of labor that existed in this unit was the primitive division between men and women. The men constructed the dwelling, planted and cultivated the crops, raised the cattle and hogs and poultry, sheared the sheep, and chopped wood for the stoves and the fireplaces. In short the man was the producer—the producer of food, of fuel, of the raw materials for clothing. The farm wife, in turn, not only cooked, kept house, and cared for the children, as modern wives still do, but she also performed certain other tasks. She used ashes to make her own soap, she put up vast quantities of preserved food, she spun fibers into cloth, and made cloth into garments. In economic terms, she and her daughters were processors. Together, they worked in a small, close-knit community, in which all lived very much together.

It hardly needs saying what happened to this typical unit of life in an earlier America. The use of machinery, the increased specialization of labor, and the development of an economy of exchange superseded it, and rendered it almost obsolete. Today a limited number of farmers with machines raise enough food for the entire population. Men go out to work instead of working on their own place, with their own sons, and their reward is not a harvest but a weekly wage or a monthly salary. Instead of "making a living" they make an income. All this is obvious, and oft-repeated. But what are the implications for the American woman?

Some embittered critics have retorted that modern woman, no longer a processor of goods, has lost her economic function, and that she retains only a biological function as mate and mother and a social function in the family. This loss of function, they would say, accounts for the frustration and sense of futility which seems to plague modern woman even more than it does modern man. But if we take a hard look at this argument, clearly it will not stand up. What has happened is that women have acquired a new role, in a new division of labor. With her husband away from the home, held by the compulsions of the clock, it falls to her, first of all, to use the family's income to take care of the family's needs. In short, while her husband has changed from a producer to an earner, she has changed from a processor to a consumer in a society where consumption is an increasingly important economic function.

The responsibilities of the consumer are no mean task. To handle them successfully, a person must be something of a dietitian, a judge of the quality of many goods, a successful planner, a skillful decorator, and a budget manager. The business of converting a monthly sum of money into a physical basis for a pleasant life involves a real art, and it might be counted as a major activity even if there were not children to rear and meals to prepare. But the increased specialization of the work of men at offices and factories away—frequently far away—from the home has also shifted certain cultural duties and certain community tasks in ever-greater measure to women.

In the Old World, upper-class men, claiming leisure as the principal advantage of their status, have made themselves the custodians of culture and the leaders in the cultural life of their communities. In America, upper-class men, primarily businessmen, working more compulsively and for longer hours than any other class, have resigned their cultural responsibilities to women and then have gone on to disparage literature and the arts because these pursuits, in the hands of females, began to seem feminine. Women have shouldered the responsibility, have borne the condescension with which their cultural activities were often treated, have provided the entire teaching force for the elementary schools, and most of the force for the secondary schools, and have done far more than their share to keep community life alive. This is another of the results, impinging in a differential way upon women, of the great social transformation of the last two centuries.

VII

So far as we have examined them, all of these changes would seem to operate somewhat to the advantage of woman, to have an emancipating effect, and to diminish her traditional subordination. No longer handicapped by a labor system in which biceps are at a premium, she has moved into the realms of employment, and has even preempted the typewriter and the teacher's desk as her own. If she has exercised a choice, which she never had before, and has decided to remain in her home, she has encountered a new economic role as a consumer rather than as a processor, with a broad range of activities, and with a new social role in keeping up the vigor of the community activities. In either case, the orbit of her activities is far wider than what used to be regarded as women's sphere, and it has been wide enough in fact to lead some optimistic observers to speak of the equality of women as if it were something which had reached some kind of absolute fulfillment and completeness about the time of the ratification of the woman's suffrage amendment in 1920.

Yet before we conclude our story with the ending that they all lived happily ever after, it is necessary to face up to the fact that women have not found all these changes quite as emancipating as they were expected to be. Indeed, much of the serious literature about American women is pessimistic in tone, and makes the dissatisfactions and the sexual frustration of modern American women its principal theme. Great stress is laid upon the fundamental dilemma that sexual fulfillment seems to depend upon one set of psychological attitudes—attitudes of submissiveness and passivity—while the fulfillment of equality seems to depend upon an opposite set—attitudes of competitiveness and self-assertion. At its grimmest level, this literature stresses the contention of Sigmund Freud that women instinctively envy the maleness of a man and reject their own sex. There is no doubt that these psychoanalytic views are important and that attention to questions of the sex life of an individual is basic, but a very respectable argument can be and has been made that what women envy about men is not their maleness in purely sexual terms but their dominance in the society and their immunity from the dilemmas which the needs of sexual and biological fulfillment on one hand and of personal fulfillment on the other pose for women.[6] The inescapable fact that males can have offspring without either bearing them or rearing them means that the values of family life and of personal achievement can be complementary for men, where they are conflicting values for women.

This one immutable and timeless fact, more than anything else, seems to stand forever in the way of the complete and absolute equality of men and women. Political and legal emancipation and even the complete equality of women in social relations and in occupational opportunities could not remove this handicap. So long as it remains, therefore, no one who finds a measure of

---

[6]Probably the best of the literature which emphasizes the sex frustration of the modern American woman is found in professional publications in the fields of psychology and psychoanalysis which do not reach a popular audience. In the literature for the layman, probably the best presentation of this point of view is Simone de Beauvoir's excellent *The Second Sex* (New York: A. A. Knopf, 1953), but other items have enjoyed a circulation which they hardly deserve. Two cases in point are Ferdinand Lundberg and Marynia F. Farnham, *Modern Woman: The Lost Sex* (New York: Harper, 1947) and Eric John Dingwall, *The American Woman: an Historical Study* (New York: Rinehart and Co., 1958). Denis W. Brogan's judicious and yet precise evaluation that Dingwall's book is "strictly for the birds" would be equally applicable to Lundberg. For an able argument that the condition of modern woman must be understood partly in social terms, and that the concept of "genital trauma" has been overdone, see Mirra Komarovsky, *Women in the Modern World: their Education and their Dilemmas* (Boston: Little, Brown and Company, 1953), pp. 31–52.

inequality still remaining will have to look for an explanation in social terms. But it is legitimate to ask whether this is the only remaining barrier to emancipation, or whether other factors also serve to maintain adverse differentials against woman, even in modern America, where she seems to be more nearly equal than she has been in any other time or place, except perhaps in certain matriarchal tribes.

There are, perhaps, two aspects of woman's role as housekeeper and as consumer which also contribute, in a new way historically, to work against the prevailing tendencies toward a fuller equality. These aspects have, in a subtle way, caused society to devalue the modern activities of women as compared with those of men, and thus may even have contributed to bring about a new sort of subordination.

One of these is the advent of the money economy, in which income is the index of achievement, and the housewife is the only worker who does not get paid. On the farm home, in the days of the subsistence economy, neither she nor her husband got paid, at least not very much, and they were economic partners in the enterprise of making a living. But today, the lowliest and most trivial job which pays a wage counts as employment, while the most demanding and vital tasks which lack the sanction of pecuniary remuneration do not so count. A recent and in fact very able book entitled *Women Who Work* deals, just as you would expect, not with women who work, but with women who get paid for their work. Sociologists regard it as an axiom that the amount of income is as important as any other criterion in measuring social status today, and in one sense, a woman's status may reflect the income of her husband, but in another sense it should be a corollary of the axiom that if income is esteemed, lack of income is followed by lack of esteem, and even by lack of self-esteem. If it needed proving, Komarovsky has shown that the American housewife tends to disparage herself as well as her work, as both being unworthy because they do not receive recognition in terms of cash income.[7]

If woman does not command respect as an earner, she is also likely to incur a certain subtle lack of respect for herself in her role as a consumer. For there is a strong tendency in some phases of American advertising to regard the consumer as someone who may be flattered or may be bullied, but who need not be treated as a mature person. Insofar as the consumer is an object of condescension, someone to be managed rather than someone to be consulted, someone on whom the will of the advertiser is to be imposed by psychological manipulation, and insofar as consumers are primarily women, it means that women become the objects of more than their share of the low esteem in which the consumer is held, and more than their share of the stultifying efforts to play upon human yearnings for prestige and popularity or upon human psychological insecurities. Anyone who recalls the recent publications about the rate at which the blinking of women's eyes increases when they view the display of goods in a supermarket,

---

[7] Komarovsky, *Woman in the Modern World,* pp. 127–153.

and the extent to which this display causes them to spend impulsively, rather than according to need, will recognize that the role of the consumer has not enhanced the dignity of women.[8] This aspect was very clearly and wittily recognized by Sylvia Wright in an article in *Harper's* in 1955, in which she dealt ironically with the assertion, which we sometimes hear, that America has become a woman's world.

"Whatever it is," she wrote, "I'll thank you to stop saying it's mine. If it were a woman's world, people wouldn't yammer at me so much. They're always telling me to do, be, or make something. . . .

"The one thing they don't want me to be is me. 'A few drops of Abano Bath Oil' they say, 'and you're not you . . . you're Somebody New lolling in perfumed luxury.' But I'm not allowed to loll long. The next minute I have to spring out in order to be Fire and Ice, swathed in satin, not a thing to do but look stark, and wait for a man to pounce. Turn the page, I've got to make sure it's Johnson's cotton buds with which I swab the baby. A few pages later, the baby gets into the act yelling for fullweight diapers. . . .

"I'm supposed to use a lot of make-up to keep my husband's love, but I must avoid make-up clog. I'm supposed to be gay, spontaneous and outgoing, but I musn't get 'expression lines.' [Expression lines are to wrinkles as morticians are to undertakers.]

"In the old days, I only had to have a natural aptitude for cooking, cleaning, bringing up children, entertaining, teaching Sunday School and tatting. . . .

"Now I also have to reconstitute knocked-down furniture and build on porches."[9]

If woman's status is somewhat confused today, therefore, it is partly because, at the very time when efforts to exploit her as a female began to abate, the efforts to exploit her as a consumer began to increase. And at the time when the intrinsic value of her work was gaining in dignity as compared with that of the male, the superficial value as measured in terms of money income was diminishing. The essential strength of her position has increased, but the combined effect of the manipulation by the media and the emphasis upon monetary earning as a standard for the valuation of work has threatened her with a new kind of subordination, imposed by the system of values which she herself accepts, rather than by masculine values imposed upon her against her will.

If a woman as a consumer in a world of producers and as an unpaid worker in a world of salaried employees has lost some of the ground she had gained by emancipation as a female in a world of males, even the emancipation itself has created some new problems for her. For instance, it has confronted her with a dilemma she never faced in the days when she was confined to her own feminine

[8]Experiments on the rate of eye-blink, as conducted by James M. Vicary, a leading exponent of motivation research, were reported in Vance Packard, *The Hidden Persuaders* (New York: David McKay Co., 1957), pp. 106–108.

[9]Sylvia Wright, "Whose World? and Welcome to It," in *Harper's Magazine*, vol. 210 (May, 1955), pp. 35–38.

sphere. This is the dilemma that she is now expected to attain a competence in the realm of men's affairs but that she must never succeed in this realm too much. It is well for her to be intelligent, but not intelligent enough to make a young man feel inferior; well for her to find employment and enjoy it, but not enjoy it enough to be unwilling to give it up for the cradle and the sink; well for her to be able to look after herself but never to be so visibly able that it will inhibit the impulse of the right man to want to look after her; well for her to be ambitious, but never ambitious enough actually to put her personal objectives first. When a man marries, no one expects him to cease being a commuter and to become a farmer because it would be good for the children—though in fact it might. But when a woman marries, her occupation becomes an auxiliary activity.

Here we come back to the presence of a fundamental dualism which has made the so-called "emancipation" of women different from the emancipation of any other group in society. Other emancipated groups have sought to substitute a new condition in place of an old one and to obliterate the old, but except for a few of the most militant women in a generation of crusading suffragettes, now almost extinct, women have never renounced the roles of wife and mother. The result has been that their objective was to reconcile a new condition with an old one, to hold in balance the principle of equality, which denies a difference, and the practice of wifehood and motherhood which recognizes a difference in the roles of men and women. The eternal presence of this dualism has not only caused a distressing amount of confusion and tension among women themselves; it has also caused confusion among their many volunteer critics. The result is that we encounter more wildly inconsistent generalizations about modern American women than about almost any other subject.

For example, modern woman, we are told, is gloriously free from the inferiority of the past, but she is miserable and insecure in her new freedom. She wields the purse strings of the nation and has become dominant over a world of increasingly less-masculine men who no longer trust themselves to buy a suit of clothes without their wife's approval. But also she does the routine work at typewriter and sink while the men still run the universe. Similarly, we are assured that the modern woman is an idle, parasitic, bridge-playing victim of technological unemployment in her own mechanized home, and also that she is the busy manager of a family and household and budget whose demands make the domestic chores of the past look easy by comparison. She escapes from reality into the wretched, petty little world of soap opera and neighborhood gossip, but she excels in her knowledge of public affairs and she became an effective guardian of literary and artistic values when her money-grubbing husband defaulted on the responsibility. She is rearing the best crop of children ever produced on this planet, by the most improved methods ever devised, while her overprotectiveness has bred "momism" and her unwillingness to stay at home has bred delinquency.

VIII

Clearly, we are still a long way from having arrived at any monotonous unanimity of opinion about the character of American women. Yet if we will focus carefully upon what we really know with some degree of assurance, we can perhaps begin the process of striking a balance. We certainly know, for instance, that many of the trends of American history have been operative for both men and women in somewhat the same way. The emphasis upon the right of the individual has operated to remove legal disabilities upon women, to open many avenues to gainful employment, to confer the suffrage, and so on. Even our divorce rate is an ironic tribute to the fact that the interests of the individual, and perhaps in a majority of cases the individual woman, are placed ahead of the protection of a social institution—namely the family. The rejection of authority in American life, which has made our childrearing permissive and has weakened the quality of leadership in our politics, has also meant that the relation of husband and wife is more of a partnership and less of an autocracy in this age and in this country than at any other time or place in Western civilization. The competitive strain in American life has impelled American women as well as American men to strive hard for their goals, and to assert themselves in the strife—indeed European critics complain that they assert themselves far more strenuously than European women and entirely too much for the tranquility of society.

On the other hand, we also know that the experience of women remains in many ways a distinctive experience. Biologically, there are still the age-old facts that women are not as big as men and not as strong; that the sex act involves consequences for them which it does not involve for the male; that the awareness of these consequences conditions the psychological attitudes of women very deeply; and that motherhood is a biological function while fatherhood is, in a sense, a cultural phenomenon. Historically, there is the formidable truth that the transformations of modern life have impinged upon men and women in different ways. The avenues of employment opened to men are not the same as the avenues of employment opened to women. The revolution in our economy has deepened the division between work in the home and work outside the home by according the sanction of monetary reward to the one and denying it to the other—thus devaluing in a new way work which is distinctively woman's. The economic revolution, while converting most men from producers to earners, has converted most women from processors to consumers, and the exploitation of the consumer has, again, added a new devaluation to woman's role. Society has given her the opportunity to fulfill her personal ambitions through the same career-activities as a man, but it cannot make her career aspirations and her family aspirations fit together as they do for a man. The result of all this is a certain tension between her old role and her new one. More of an individualist than women in traditional societies, she is by no means as whole-heartedly individualistic as the American male, and as a study at Berkeley recently showed, she still hesitates to claim individualism as a quality of her own.[10] If she enters the competitive race, she does so with an awareness that the top posts are still pretty much the monopoly of men, and with a certain limitation upon her competitive commitment. In short, she is constantly holding in balance her general opportunities as a person and her distinctive needs as a woman, and when we consider how badly these two go together in principle, can we not say that she is maintaining the operative equilibrium between them with a remarkable degree of skill and of success?

The answer to my childish riddle was that the big Indian is the little Indian's mother. To say that she is a squaw is not to deny that she is an Indian—but it is to say that she is an Indian for whom the expectations of the masculine world of Indians, or of Americans, do not apply. It is to say that her qualities and traits, whether she is an Indian, or an American, will reflect the influence of the same sweeping forces which influence the world of men, but that it will reflect them with a difference. In this sense, what we say about the character of the American people should be said not in terms of half of the American population—even if it is the male half—but in terms of the character of the totality of the people. In this sense, also, attention to the historic character of American women is important not only as a specialty for female scholars or for men who happen to take an interest in feminism, but as a coordinate major part of the over-all, comprehensive study of the American character as a whole. For the character of any nation is the composite of the character of its men and of its women and though these may be deeply similar in many ways, they are almost never entirely the same.

[10]John P. McKee and A. C. Sheriffs, "Men's and Women's Beliefs, Ideals, and Self-Concepts," in *American Journal of Sociology,* LXIV (1959), pp. 356–363.

The Search for Southern Identity

C. VANN WOODWARD

The time is coming, if indeed it has not already arrived, when the Southerner will begin to ask himself whether there is really any longer very much point in calling himself a Southerner. Or if he does, he might well wonder occasionally whether it is worth while insisting on the point. So long as he remains at home where everybody knows him the matter hardly becomes an issue. But when he ventures among strangers, particularly up North, how often does he yield to the impulse to suppress the identifying idiom, to avoid the awkward subject, and to blend inconspicuously into the national pattern—to act the role of the standard American? Has the Southern heritage become an old hunting jacket that one slips on comfortably while at home but discards when he ventures abroad in favor of some more conventional or modish garb? Or is it perhaps an attic full of ancestral wardrobes useful only in connection with costume balls and play acting—staged primarily in Washington, D.C.?

Asking himself some similar questions about the New England heritage, Professor George W. Pierson of Yale has come forth with some disturbing concessions about the integrity of his own region. Instead of an old hunting jacket, he suggests that we call New England "an old kitchen floor, now spatter-painted with many colors." He points out that roughly six out of every ten Connecticut "Yankees" are either foreign-born or born of foreign or mixed parentage, while only three have native forebears going as far back as two generations, and they are not necessarily New England forebears at that. "Like it or not," writes Pierson, "and no matter how you measure it—geographically, economically, racially or religiously, there is no New England Region today." It has become instead, he says, "an optical illusion and a land of violent contrast and change." And yet in spite of the wholesale and damaging concessions of his essay, which

Reprinted with permission from C. Vann Woodward, *The Burden of Southern History*, rev. ed. (Baton Rouge: Louisiana State University Press, 1968).

he calls "A Study in Denudation," he concludes that, "as a region of the heart and mind, New England is still very much alive."

One wonders if the Southerner, for his part, can make as many damaging admissions of social change and cultural erosion as our New England friend has made and come out with as firm a conclusion about the vitality of his own regional heritage. More doubt than assurance probably comes to mind at first. The South is still in the midst of an economic and social revolution that has by no means run its course, and it will not be possible to measure its results for a long time to come. This revolution has already leveled many of the old monuments of regional distinctiveness and may end eventually by erasing the very consciousness of a distinctive tradition along with the will to sustain it. The sustaining will and consciousness are also under the additional strain of a moral indictment against a discredited part of the tradition, an indictment more uncompromising than any since abolitionist times.

The Southerner may not have been very happy about many of those old monuments of regional distinctiveness that are now disappearing. He may, in fact, have deplored the existence of some—the one-horse farmer, one-crop agriculture, one-party politics, the sharecropper, the poll tax, the white primary, the Jim Crow car, the lynching bee. It would take a blind sentimentalist to mourn their passing. But until the day before yesterday there they stood, indisputable proof that the South was different. Now that they are vanished or on their way toward vanishing, we are suddenly aware of the vacant place they have left in the landscape and of our habit of depending upon them in final resort as landmarks of regional identification. To establish identity by reference to our faults was always simplest, for whatever their reservations about our virtues, our critics were never reluctant to concede us our vices and shortcomings.

It is not that the present South has any conspicuous lack of faults, but that its faults are growing less conspicuous and therefore less useful for purposes of regional identification. They are increasingly the faults of other parts of the country, standard American faults, shall we say. Many of them have only recently been acquired—could, in fact, only recently be afforded. For the great changes that are altering the cultural landscape of the South almost beyond recognition are not simply negative changes, the disappearance of the familiar. There are also positive changes, the appearance of the strikingly new.

The symbol of innovation is inescapable. The roar and groan and dust of it greet one on the outskirts of every Southern city. That symbol is the bulldozer, and for lack of a better name this might be called the Bulldozer Revolution. The great machine with the lowered blade symbolizes the revolution in several respects: in its favorite area of operation, the area where city meets country; in its relentless speed; in its supreme disregard for obstacles, its heedless methods; in what it demolishes and in what it builds. It is the advance agent of the metropolis. It encroaches upon rural life to expand urban life. It demolishes the old to make way for the new.

It is not the amount of change that is impressive about the Bulldozer Revolution so much as the speed and concentration with which it has come and with which it continues. In the decade of the forties, when urbanization was growing at a swift pace in the country as a whole, the cities of the South's fifty-three metropolitan areas grew more than three times as fast as comparable cities in the rest of the country, at a rate of 33.1 per cent as compared with 10.3 per cent elsewhere. For every three city dwellers in the South at the beginning of that decade there were four at the end, and for every five farm residents there were only four. An overwhelmingly rural South in 1930 had 5.5 millions employed in agriculture; by 1950, only 3.2 millions. A considerable proportion of these Southerners were moving directly from country to suburb, following the path of the bulldozer to "rurbanization" and skipping the phase of urbanization entirely. Rural Negroes, the most mobile of all Southerners, were more likely to move into the heart of the urban areas abandoned by the suburban dwellers. In the single decade of the forties the South lost a third of its rural-farm Negro population. If the same trend were continued through the present decade, it would reduce that part of the colored population to about one-fifth of the Negroes living in the region.

According to nearly all of the indices, so the economists find, economic growth of the South in recent years greatly exceeds the rate maintained in the North and East. The fact is the South is going through economic expansion and reorganization that the North and East completed a generation or more ago. But the process is taking place far more rapidly than it did in the North. Among all the many periods of change in the history of the South it is impossible to find one of such concentration and such substantive impact. The period of Reconstruction might appear a likely rival for this distinction, but that revolution was largely limited to changes in legal status and the ownership of property. The people remained pretty much where they were and continued to make their living in much the same way. All indications are that the bulldozer will leave a deeper mark upon the land than did the carpetbagger.

It is the conclusion of two Southern sociologists, John M. Maclachlan and Joe S. Floyd, Jr., that the present drive toward uniformity "with national demographic, economic, and cultural norms might well hasten the day when the South, once perhaps the most distinctively 'different' American region, will have become in most such matters virtually indistinguishable from the other urban-industrial areas of the nation."

The threat of becoming "indistinguishable," of being submerged under a national steamroller, has haunted the mind of the South for a long time. Some have seen it as a menace to regional identity and the survival of a Southern heritage. Premonitions of the present revolution appeared during the industrial boom that followed the First World War. Toward the end of the twenties two distinctive attempts were made by Southerners to dig in and define a perimeter of defense against further encroachment.

One of these entrenchments was that of the twelve Southerners who wrote *I'll Take My Stand*. They sought to define what they called "a Southern way of life against what may be called the American or prevailing way," and they agreed "that the best terms in which to represent the distinction are contained in the phrase, Agrarian *versus* Industrial." Agrarianism and its values were the essence of the Southern tradition and the test of Southern loyalty. Their credo held that "the whole way in which we live, act, think, and feel," the humanist culture, "was rooted in the agrarian way of life of the older South." They called for "anti-industrial measures" which "might promise to stop the advances of industrialism, or even undo some of them."

Even in 1930 the agrarians were prepared to admit "the melancholy fact that the South itself has wavered a little and shown signs of wanting to join up behind the common or American industrial ideal." They admonished waverers among the younger generation that the brave new South they contemplated would "be only an undistinguished replica of the usual industrial community."

Three decades later the slight "wavering" in the Southern ranks that disturbed the agrarians in 1930 would seem to have become a pell-mell rout. Defections came by the battalion. Whole regiments and armies deserted "to join up behind the common or American industrial ideal." In its pursuit of the American Way and the American Standard of Living the South was apparently doing all in its power to become what the agrarians had deplored as "only an undistinguished replica of the usual industrial community." The voice of the South in the 1950's had become the voice of the chamber of commerce, and Southerners appeared to be about as much absorbed in the acquirement of creature comforts and adult playthings as any other Americans. The twelve Southerners who took their stand in 1930 on the proposition that the Southern way stands or falls with the agrarian way would seem to have been championing a second lost cause. If they were right, then our questions would have already been answered, for the Southerner as a distinctive species of American would have been doomed, his tradition bereft of root and soil. The agrarian way contains no promise of continuity and endurance for the Southern tradition.

Two years before the agrarian pronouncement appeared, another attempt was made to define the essence of the Southern tradition and prescribe the test of Southern loyalty. The author of this effort was the distinguished historian, Professor Ulrich B. Phillips. His definition had no reference to economic institutions but was confined to a preoccupation with race consciousness. The essential theme of continuity and unity in the Southern heritage, wrote Professor Phillips, was "a common resolve indomitably maintained" that the South "shall be and remain a white man's country." This indomitable conviction could be "expressed with the frenzy of a demagogue or maintained with a patrician's quietude," but it was and had been from the beginning "the cardinal test of a Southerner and the central theme of southern history."

Professor Phillips' criterion of Southernism has proved somewhat more durable and widespread in appeal than that of the agrarians. It is not tied so firmly to an ephemeral economic order as was theirs. Nor does it demand—of the dominant whites, at least—any Spartan rejection of the flesh pots of the American living standard. Its adherents are able to enjoy the blessings of economic change and remain traditionalists at the same time. There are still other advantages in the Phillipsian doctrine. The traditionalist who has watched the Bulldozer Revolution plow under cherished old values of individualism, localism, family, clan, and rural folk culture has felt helpless and frustrated against the mighty and imponderable agents of change. Industrialism, urbanism, unionism, and big government conferred or promised too many coveted benefits. They divided the people and won support in the South, so that it was impossible to rally unified opposition to them.

The race issue was different. Advocates and agents of change could be denounced as outsiders, intruders, meddlers. Historic memories of resistance and cherished constitutional principles could be invoked. Racial prejudices, aggressions, and jealousies could be stirred to rally massive popular support. And with this dearly bought unity, which he could not rally on other issues, the frustrated traditionalist might at last take his stand for the defense of all the defiled, traduced, and neglected values of the traditional order. What then is the prospect of the Phillipsian "cardinal test" as a bulwark against change? Will it hold fast where other defenses have failed?

Recent history furnishes some of the answers. Since the last World War old racial attitudes that appeared more venerable and immovable than any other have exhibited a flexibility that no one would have predicted. One by one, in astonishingly rapid succession, many landmarks of racial discrimination and segregation have disappeared, and old barriers have been breached. Many remain, of course—perhaps more than have been breached—and distinctively Southern racial attitudes will linger for a long time. Increasingly the South is aware of its isolation in these attitudes, however, and is in defense of the institutions that embody them. They have fallen rapidly into discredit and under condemnation from the rest of the country and the rest of the world.

Once more the South finds itself with a morally discredited Peculiar Institution on its hands. The last time this happened, about a century ago, the South's defensive reaction was to identify its whole cause with the one institution that was most vulnerable and to make loyalty to an ephemeral aspect which it had once led in condemning the cardinal test of loyalty to the whole tradition. Southerners who rejected the test were therefore forced to reject the whole heritage. In many cases, if they were vocal in their rejection, they were compelled to leave the South entirely and return only at their peril. Unity was thus temporarily achieved, but with the collapse of the Peculiar Institution the whole tradition was jeopardized and discredited for having been so completely identified with the part abandoned.

Historical experience with the first Peculiar Institution ought strongly to discourage comparable experiments with the second. If Southernism is allowed to become identified with a last ditch defense of segregation, it will increasingly lose its appeal among the younger generation. Many will be tempted to reject their entire regional identification, even the name "Southern," in order to dissociate themselves from the one discredited aspect. If agrarianism has proved to be a second lost cause, segregation is a likely prospect for a third.

With the crumbling of so many defenses in the present, the South has tended to substitute myths about the past. Every self-conscious group of any size fabricates myths about its past: about its origins, its mission, its righteousness, its benevolence, its general superiority. But few groups in the New World have had their myths subjected to such destructive analysis as those of the South have undergone in recent years. While some Southern historians have contributed to the mythmaking, others have been among the leading iconoclasts, and their attacks have spared few of the South's cherished myths.

The Cavalier Legend as the myth of origin was one of the earlier victims. The Plantation Legend of ante bellum grace and elegance has not been left wholly intact. The pleasant image of a benevolent and paternalistic slavery system as a school for civilizing savages has suffered damage that is probably beyond repair. Even the consoling security of Reconstruction as the common historic grievance, the infallible mystique of unity, has been rendered somewhat less secure by detached investigation. And finally, rude hands have been laid upon the hallowed memory of the Redeemers who did in the Carpetbaggers, and doubt has been cast upon the antiquity of segregation folkways. These faded historical myths have become weak material for buttressing Southern defenses, for time has dealt as roughly with them as with agrarianism and racism.

Would a hard-won immunity from the myths and illusions of Southern sectionalism provide some immunity to the illusions and myths of American nationalism? Or would the hasty divestment merely make the myth-denuded Southerner hasten to wrap himself in the garments of nationalism? The danger in the wholesale rejection of the South by the modern Southerner bent on reaffirming his Americanism is the danger of affirming more than he bargains for.

While the myths of Southern distinctiveness have been waning, national myths have been waxing in power and appeal. National myths, American myths have proved far more sacrosanct and inviolate than Southern myths. Millions of European immigrants of diverse cultural backgrounds have sought and found identity in them. The powerful urge among minority groups to abandon or disguise their distinguishing cultural traits and conform as quickly as possible to some national norm is one of the most familiar features in the sociology of American nationalism. European ethnic and national groups with traditions far more ancient and distinctive than those of the South have eagerly divested themselves of their cultural heritage in order to conform.

The conformist is not required nor expected to abandon his distinctive religion. But whether he remains a Protestant, a Catholic, or a Jew, his religion typically becomes subordinate or secondary to a national faith. Foreign observers have remarked that the different religions in America resemble each other more than they do their European counterparts. "By every realistic criterion," writes Will Herberg in his study of American religious sociology, "the American

Way of Life is the operative faith of the American people." And where the mandates of the American Way of Life conflict with others, they take undisputed sway over the masses of all religions. Herberg describes it as "a faith that has its symbols and its rituals, its holidays and its liturgy, its saints and its sancta," and it is common to all Americans. "Sociologically, anthropologically, if one pleases," he writes, the American Way of Life "is the characteristic American religion, undergirding American life and overarching American society despite all indubitable differences of region, section, culture, and class." Differences such as those of region and section, "indubitable" though he admits them to be, he characterizes as "peripheral and obsolescent."

If the American Way of Life has become a religion, any deviation from it has become a sort of heresy. Regionalism in the typical American view is rather like the Turnerian frontier, a section on the move—or at least one that should keep moving, following a course that converges at not too remote a point with the American Way. It is a season's halt of the American caravan, a temporary encampment of an advancing society, eternally on the move toward some undefined goal of progress. If the encampment of regionalism threatens to entrench or dig in for a permanent stand, it comes to be regarded as "peripheral and obsolescent," an institutionalized social lag.

The same urge to conformity that operates upon ethnic or national minorities to persuade them to reject identification with their native heritage or that of their forebears operates to a degree upon the Southerner as well. Since the cultural landscape of his native region is being altered almost beyond recognition by a cyclone of social change, the Southerner may come to feel as uprooted as the immigrant. Bereft of his myths, his peculiar institutions, even his familiar regional vices, he may well reject or forget his regional identification as completely as the immigrant.

Is there nothing about the South that is immune from the disintegrating effect of nationalism and the pressure for conformity? Is there not something that has not changed? There is only one thing that I can think of, and that is its history. By that I do not mean a Southern brand of Shintoism, the worship of ancestors. Nor do I mean written history and its interpretation, popular and mythical, or professional and scholarly, which have changed often and will change again. I mean rather the collective experience of the Southern people. It is in just this respect that the South remains the most distinctive region of the country. In their unique historic experience as Americans the Southerners should not only be able to find the basis for continuity of their heritage but also make contributions that balance and complement the experience of the rest of the nation.

At this point the risks of our enterprise multiply. They are the risks of spawning new myths in place of the old. Awareness of them demands that we redouble precautions and look more cautiously than ever at generalizations.

To start with a safe one, it can be assumed that one of the most conspicuous traits of American life has been its economic abundance. From early colonial days the fabulous riches of America have been compared with the scarcity and want of less favored lands. Immense differentials in economic welfare and living standards between the United States and other countries still prevail. In an illuminating book called *People of Plenty*, David Potter persuasively advances the thesis that the most distinguishing traits of national character have been fundamentally shaped by the abundance of the American living standard. He marshals evidence of the effect that plenty has had upon such decisive phases of life as the nursing and training of babies, opportunities for education and jobs, ages of marriage and childbearing. He shows how abundance has determined characteristic national attitudes between parents and children, husband and wife, superior and subordinate, between one class and another, and how it has molded our mass culture and our consumer oriented society. American national character would indeed appear inconceivable without this unique experience of abundance.

The South at times has shared this national experience and, in very recent years, has enjoyed more than a taste of it. But the history of the South includes a long and quite un-American experience with poverty. So recently as 1938, in fact, the South was characterized by the President as "The Nation's Economic Problem No. 1." And the problem was poverty, not plenty. It was a poverty emphasized by wide regional discrepancies in living standard, per capita wealth, per capita income, and the good things that money buys, such as education, health, protection, and the many luxuries that go to make up the celebrated American Standard of Living. This striking differential was no temporary misfortune of the great depression but a continuous and conspicuous feature of Southern experience since the early years of the Civil War. During the last half of the nineteenth and the first half of the twentieth centuries, when technology was multiplying American abundance with unprecedented rapidity, the South lagged far behind. In 1880 the per capita wealth of the South, based on estimated true valuation of property, was $376 as compared with $1,186 per capita in the states outside the South. In the same year the per capita wealth of the South was 27 per cent of that of the Northeastern states. That was just about the same ratio contemporaneously existing between the per capita wealth of Russia and that of Germany.

Generations of scarcity and want constitute one of the distinctive historical experiences of the Southern people, an experience too deeply embedded in their memory to be wiped out by a business boom and too deep not to admit of some uneasiness at being characterized historically as a "People of Plenty." That they should have been for so long a time a "People of Poverty" in a land of plenty is one mark of enduring cultural distinctiveness. In a nation known around the world for the hedonistic ethic of the American Standard of Living, the Southern heritage of scarcity remains distinctive.

A closely related corollary of the uniquely American experience of abundance is the equally unique American experience of success. During the Second World War Professor Arthur M. Schlesinger made an interesting attempt to define the national character, which he brought to a close with the conclusion that the

American character "is bottomed upon the profound conviction that nothing in the world is beyond its power to accomplish." In this he gave expression to one of the great American legends, the legend of success and invincibility. It is a legend with a foundation in fact, for much can be adduced from the American record to support it and explain why it has flourished. If the history of the United States is lacking in some of the elements of variety and contrast demanded of any good story, it is in part because of the very monotonous repetition of successes. Almost every major collective effort, even those thwarted temporarily, succeeded in the end. American history *is* a success story. Why should such a nation not have a "profound conviction that nothing in the world is beyond its power to accomplish"? Even the hazards of war—including the prospect of war against an unknown enemy with untried weapons—proves no exception to the rule. The advanced science and weaponry of the Russian challenger are too recent to have registered their impact on the legend. The American people have never known the chastening experience of being on the losing side of a war. They have, until very recently, solved every major problem they have confronted—or had it solved for them by a smiling fortune. Success and victory are still national habits of mind.

This is but one among several American legends in which the South can participate only vicariously or in part. Again the Southern heritage is distinctive. For Southern history, unlike American, includes large components of frustration, failure, and defeat. It includes not only an overwhelming military defeat but long decades of defeat in the provinces of economic, social, and political life. Such a heritage affords the Southern people no basis for the delusion that there is nothing whatever that is beyond their power to accomplish. They have had it forcibly and repeatedly borne in upon them that this is not the case. Since their experience in this respect is more common among the general run of mankind than that of their fellow Americans, it would seem to be a part of their heritage worth cherishing.

American opulence and American success have combined to foster and encourage another legend of early origin, the legend of American innocence. According to this legend Americans achieved a sort of regeneration of sinful man by coming out of the wicked Old World and removing to an untarnished new one. By doing so they shook off the wretched evils of feudalism and broke free from tyranny, monarchism, aristocracy, and privilege—all those institutions which, in the hopeful philosophy of the Enlightenment, accounted for all, or nearly all, the evil in the world. The absence of these Old World ills in America, as well as the freedom from much of the injustice and oppression associated with them, encouraged a singular moral complacency in the American mind. The self-image implanted in Americans was one of innocence as compared with less fortunate people of the Old World. They were a chosen people and their land a Utopia on the make. Alexis de Tocqueville's patience was tried by this complacency of the American. "If I applaud the freedom which its inhabitants enjoy, he answers, 'Freedom is a fine thing, but few nations are worthy to enjoy it.' If I remark on the purity of morals which distinguishes the United States," complained Tocqueville, " 'I can imagine,' says he, 'that a stranger, who has been struck by corruption of all other nations, is astonished at the difference.' "

How much room was there in the tortured conscience of the South for this national self-image of innocence and moral complacency? Southerners have repeated the American rhetoric of self-admiration and sung the perfection of American institutions ever since the Declaration of Independence. But for half that time they lived intimately with a great social evil and the other half with its aftermath. It was an evil that was even condemned and abandoned by the Old World, to which America's moral superiority was supposedly an article of faith. Much of the South's intellectual energy went into a desperate effort to convince the world that its peculiar evil was actually a "positive good," but it failed even to convince itself. It writhed in the torments of its own conscience until it plunged into catastrophe to escape. The South's preoccupation was with guilt, not with innocence, with the reality of evil, not with the dream of perfection. Its experience in this respect, as in several others, was on the whole a thoroughly un-American one.

An age-long experience with human bondage and its evils and later with emancipation and its shortcomings did not dispose the South very favorably toward such popular American ideas as the doctrine of human perfectibility, the belief that every evil has a cure, and the notion that every human problem has a solution. For these reasons the utopian schemes and the gospel of progress that flourished above the Mason and Dixon Line never found very wide acceptance below the Potomac during the nineteenth century. In that most optimistic of centuries in the most optimistic part of the world, the South remained basically pessimistic in its social outlook and its moral philosophy. The experience of evil and the experience of tragedy are parts of the Southern heritage that are as difficult to reconcile with the American legend of innocence and social felicity as the experience of poverty and defeat are to reconcile with the legends of abundance and success.

One of the simplest but most consequential generalizations ever made about national character was Tocqueville's that America was "born free." In many ways that is the basic distinction between the history of the United States and the history of other great nations. We skipped the feudal stage, just as Russia skipped the liberal stage. Louis Hartz has pointed up the complex consequences for the history of American political thought. To be a conservative and a traditionalist in America was a contradiction in terms, for the American Burke was forever conserving John Locke's liberalism, his only real native tradition. Even the South, in its great period of reaction against Jefferson, was never able fully to shake off the grip of Locke and its earlier self-image of liberalism. That is why its most original period of theoretical inspiration, the "Reactionary Enlightenment," left almost no influence upon American thought.

There is still a contribution to be derived from the South's un-American adventure in feudal fantasy. While the South was not born Lockean, it went through a Lockean phase in its youth. But as Hartz admits, it was "an alien child in a liberal family, tortured and confused, driven to a fantasy life." There *are* Americans, after all, who were not "born free." They are also Southerners. They have yet to achieve articulate expression of their uniquely un-American experience. This is not surprising, since white Southerners have only recently found expression of the tragic potentials of their past in literature. The Negro has yet to do that. His first step will be an acknowledgment that he is also a Southerner as well as an American.

One final example of a definition of national character to which the South proves an exception is an interesting one by Thornton Wilder. "Americans," says Mr. Wilder, "are abstract. They are disconnected. They have a relation, but it is to everywhere, to everybody, and to always." This quality of abstraction he finds expressed in numerous ways—in the physical mobility of Americans, in their indifference or, as he might suggest, their superiority to place, to locality, to environment. "For us," he writes, "it is not *where* genius lived that is important. If Mount Vernon and Monticello were not so beautiful in themselves and relatively accessible, would so many of us visit them?" he asks. It is not the concrete but the abstract that captures the imagination of the American and gives him identity, not the here-and-now but the future. " 'I am I,' he says, 'because my plans characterize me.' Abstract! Abstract!" Mr. Wilder's stress upon abstraction as an American characteristic recalls what Robert Penn Warren in a different connection once described as "the fear of abstraction" in the South, "the instinctive fear, on the part of black or white, that the massiveness of experience, the concreteness of life, will be violated; the fear of abstraction."

According to Mr. Wilder, "Americans can find in environment no confirmation of their identity, try as they may." And again, "Americans are disconnected. They are exposed to all place and all time. No place nor group nor movement can say to them: we are waiting for you; it is right for you to be here." The insignificance of place, locality, and community for Thornton Wilder contrasts strikingly with the experience of Eudora Welty of Mississippi. "Like a good many other [regional] writers," she says, "I am myself touched off by place. The place where I am and the place I know, and other places that familiarity with and love for my own make strange and lovely and enlightening to look into, are what set me to writing my stories." To her, "place opens a door in the mind," and she speaks of "the blessing of being located—contained."

To do Mr. Wilder justice, he is aware that the Southern states constitute an exception to his national character of abstraction, "enclaves or residual areas of European feeling," he calls them. "They were cut off, or resolutely cut themselves off, from the advancing tide of the country's modes of consciousness. Place, environment, relations, repetitions are the breath of their being."

The most reassuring prospect for the survival of the South's distinctive heritage is the magnificent body of literature produced by its writers in the last three decades—the very years when the outward traits of regional distinctiveness were crumbling. The Southern literary renaissance has placed its writers in the vanguard of national letters and assured that their works will be read as long as American literature is remembered. The distinguishing feature of the Southern school, according to Allen Tate, is "the peculiar historical consciousness of the Southern writer." He defines the literary renaissance as "a literature conscious of the past in the present." The themes that have inspired the major writers have not been the flattering myths nor the romantic dreams of the South's past. Disdaining the polemics of defense and justification, they have turned instead to the somber realities of hardship and defeat and evil and "the problems of the human heart in conflict with itself." In so doing they have brought to realization for the first time the powerful literary potentials of the South's tragic experience and heritage. Such comfort as they offer lies, in the words of William Faulkner, in reminding us of "the courage and honor and hope and pride and compassion and pity and sacrifice" with which man has endured.

After Faulkner, Wolfe, Warren, and Welty no literate Southerner could remain unaware of his heritage or doubt its enduring value. After this outpouring it would seem more difficult than ever to deny a Southern identity, to be "merely American." To deny it would be to deny our history. And it would also be to deny to America participation in a heritage and a dimension of historical experience that America very much needs, a heritage that is far more closely in line with the common lot of mankind than the national legends of opulence and success and innocence. The South once thought of itself as a "peculiar people," set apart by its eccentricities, but in many ways modern America better deserves that description.

The South was American a long time before it was Southern in any self-conscious or distinctive way. It remains more American by far than anything else, and has all along. After all, it fell the lot of one Southerner from Virginia to define America. The definition he wrote in 1776 voiced aspirations that were rooted in his native region before the nation was born. The modern Southerner should be secure enough in his national identity to escape the compulsion of less secure minorities to embrace uncritically all the myths of nationalism. He should be secure enough also not to deny a regional heritage because it is at variance with national myth. It is a heritage that should prove of enduring worth to him as well as to his country.

Black Rage

WILLIAM H. GRIER and PRICE M. COBBS

THE SHADOW OF THE PAST

Americans characteristically are unwilling to think about the past. We are a future-oriented nation, and facing backward is an impediment to progress. Although these attitudes may propel us to the moon, they are deficient when human conflict needs resolution. They bring white Americans to an impasse when they claim to "understand" black people. After all, the thoughts begin, the Negro is also an American and if he is different it is only a matter of degree. Clichés are brought forth and there is a lengthy recitation of the names of famous Negroes. Long association has bred feelings of familiarity which masquerade as knowledge. But there remain puzzles about black people; all is not understood, something is missing.

For if the black American is to be truly understood, his history must be made intelligible. It is a history that is interwoven with that of this country, although it is rarely reported with candor. In recent years superficial studies of Negroes have been made. For those few who truly search, the past of the black man is seen reflected in his daily life.

It is evident in character structure and child-rearing. It can be heard on a Sunday morning in a Baptist church. It reveals itself in the temper of the ghetto and in the emerging rage now threatening to shatter this nation, a nation the black man helped to build. A few black people may hide their scars, but most harbor the wounds of yesterday.

The black man of today is at one end of a psychological continuum which reaches back in time to his enslaved ancestors. Observe closely a man on a Harlem street corner and it can be seen how little his life experience differs from that of his forebears. However much the eternals differ, their inner life is remarkably the same.

On a cold morning one of the authors sat watching a group of black men. They were standing outside an office for casual laborers in clusters of four or five. Some were talking and gesturing, but from a distance one could detect apathy in most.

These were the "hard-core" unemployed. Their difficulties could be blamed on lack of education, personal maladjustments, or just plain laziness and such a judgment would be partially correct. The greater truth was that they were black. Because of this fact, they had little chance of obtaining favorable or permanent work. They were doomed to spend endless gray mornings hoping to secure a day's work.

A truck drove up and they stiffened. There was a ripple of excitement as a white man leaned out of the cab and squinted. As he ran his eyes past the different men, one could almost hear his thoughts.

This one is too thin . . . that dark one looks smart-alecky and is probably slow . . . the boy way in the back there might do.

No imagination is required to see this scene as a direct remnant of slavery. Move back in time and this could be an auction block. The manual labor is the same and so is the ritual of selection. The white man involved in the selection feels he is only securing a crew. But, then, so did his forefathers. In addition, the psychic structure of the black men being selected has altered little since slavery. To know this is deeply troubling—and frightening.

A city erupts in fury. Its residents are appalled and outraged. Biracial committees are appointed and scapegoats appear from everywhere. Instead of wretched housing and stifling unemployment, outside agitators and wily Communists are said to be the most important causes. Always the basic reasons are at best minimized and at worst denied. After three centuries of oppression the black man is still thought to need a provocateur to inflame him!

History is forgotten. There is little record of the first Africans brought to this country. They were stripped of everything. A calculated cruelty was begun, designed to crush their spirit. After they were settled in the white man's land, the malice continued. When slavery ended and large-scale physical abuse was discontinued, it was supplanted by different but equally damaging abuse. The cruelty continued unabated in thoughts, feelings, intimidation and occasional lynching. Black people were consigned to a place outside the human family and the whip of the plantation was replaced by the boundaries of the ghetto.

The culture of slavery was never undone for either master or slave. The civilization that tolerated slavery dropped its slaveholding cloak but the inner feelings remained. The "peculiar institution" continues to exert its evil influence over the nation. The practice of slavery stopped over a hundred years ago, but the minds of our citizens have never been freed.

To be a bondsman was to experience a psychological development very different from the master's. Slavery required the creation of a particular kind of person, one *compatible* with a life of involuntary servitude. The ideal slave had to be absolutely dependent and have a deep consciousness of personal inferiority.

His color was made the badge of that degradation. And as a final precaution, he was instilled with a sense of the unlimited power of his master. Teachings so painstakingly applied do not disappear easily.

The white man tried to justify the lot of the slave in many ways. One explanation made the slave a simple child who needed the protective guardianship of a benevolent parent. For many whites this distortion has persisted to the present. A modern version holds that black people are little different from other citizens save for a paucity of education and money. The reason for these deficiencies is left vague. The observer is left with the comfortable feeling that blacks are stunted in growth, have profligate ways, and are uninterested in learning. This attitude obscures the multitude of wrongs and the ruthless oppression of blacks, from slavery to now.

The Negro man of eighty told a story. He was twelve and a playmate was tied in a cage waiting to be taken away and lynched. The shackled boy stood accused of raping a white woman.

The old man recalled the fright which caused him to run away the next day. From that time on he never knew a home. His years were spent roaming about the country. He became an itinerant preacher, forever invoking God, but always too terrified to return to his place of birth. When asked why, he would reply: "The white folks down there are too mean."

For most of his life he was tortured by memories. Every place he stopped, he soon became frightened and moved on. Sometimes in the middle of a sermon he would cry out: "How could they do that to a boy?"

This old man is even now living in one of our cities. He continues to preach in storefront churches. At times he may encounter whites who smile benevolently at his quaintness and apparent exaggerations. But his memories are real and his hatred, however masked, is a burning fire.

Because of an inattention to history, the present-day Negro is compared unfavorably with other racial and ethnic groups who have come to this country. Major differences in backgrounds are ignored. The black man was brought to this country forcibly and was completely cut off from his past. He was robbed of language and culture. He was forbidden to be an African and never allowed to be an American. After the first generation and with each new group of slaves, the black man had only his American experience to draw on. For most Negroes, the impact of the experience has been so great as to even now account for a lack of knowledge of their past.

. . . .

The black experience in this country . . . began with slavery and with a rupture of continuity and an annihilation of the past. *Even now each generation grows up alone.* Many individual blacks feel a desperate aloneness not readily explained. The authors have heard stories telling of each generation's isolation from every other. Non-black groups pass on proud traditions, conscious of the benefit they are conferring. For black people, values and rituals are shared and indeed transmitted, but with little acknowledgment of their worth. The Jew achieves a sense of ethnic cohesiveness through religion and a pride in background, while the black man stands in solitude.

. . . The white American has created a blindness for himself which has a peculiar effect on blacks. In psycho-therapeutic sessions Negroes are preoccupied with determining just how many of their difficulties are a consequence of the prejudice of whites. And while there is sometimes the tendency to attribute everything to white cruelty, there is often the opposite tendency—a determination not to see. They may insist that white oppression has never exerted any influence on their lives, even in the face of such realities as police brutality, job and housing discrimination, and a denial of educational opportunities. It is a powerful national trait, this willful blindness to the abuse of blacks in America. It is a blindness that includes the victim as well as the crime.

An eighty-seven-year-old woman was born in the deep South, the result of a union between one of the black "girls on the place" and the son of the white landowner. Years later she was told how, at her birth, the white mistress of the "big house" heard that her son had fathered a child. The young mother was summoned to bring the child for an audience with the grandmother.
The old lady admired the child, and noting her fairness suggested that she be taken and raised as white.
The mother objected: "She is my child and I'll keep her."
Even into old age, this Negro woman admired the courage of her mother. She spoke about the thin line separating the races. A flip of the coin could decide whether one was "colored" or "white."

The relationship between black and white is complex. This association has affected the white partner less than the black, but the effect on the white partner has had more significance since he has been the policy maker. An analysis of the relationship tells much about the American national character. Attitudes of the kind directed toward blacks, rooted deep in the fabric of this country, clearly have significant influence on many decisions. A nation which has made the despising of blacks a unique element of its identity is at a profound disadvantage when called upon to lock arms with people of other lands and form a brotherhood of nations.

A focus on the black partner yields information of a different sort. To be "colored" has meant far more than riding in the back of the bus. To be sure, there is great misery in being the last hired and first fired and relegated to decaying sections of town, but there is enduring grief in being made to feel inferior.

The old woman may have been fortunate in her awareness of that early choice. She is at least mindful of some of the factors in that selection. For most of her people, this is rarely the case. Their treatment is designed to impress them with their lowly position. The role of inferiority into which they have been cast has affected them deeply, but if the wounds are not physical, they are easily ignored.

The American black man is unique, but he has no special psychology or exceptional genetic determinants. His mental mechanisms are the same as other men. If he undergoes emotional conflict, he will respond as neurotically as his white brother. In understanding him we return to the same reference point, since all other explanations fail. We must conclude that much of the pathology we see in black people had its genesis in slavery. The culture that was born in that experience of bondage has been passed from generation to generation. Constricting adaptations developed during some long-ago time continue as contemporary character traits. That they are so little altered attests to the fixity of the black-white relationship, which has seen little change since the birth of this country.

Long ago in the United States basic decisions were made. The most important of these made color the crucial variable. This began as the cornerstone of the system of black slavery. After refinements, it has remained to become imbedded in the national character. Persisting to this day is an attitude, shared by black and white alike, that blacks are inferior. This belief permeates every facet of this country and it is the etiological agent from which has developed the national sickness.

. . . .

White citizens have grown up with the identity of an American and, with that, the unresolved conflicts of the slaveholder. White Americans are born into a culture which contains the hatred of blacks as an integral part.

Blacks are no longer the economic underpinnings of the nation. But they continue to be available as victims and therefore a ready object for the projection of hostile feelings. Throughout the country they are highly visible, by now useless for exploitation, and demanding participation in the affairs of the country.

Because there has been so little change in attitudes, the children of bondage continue to suffer the effects of slavery. There is a timeless quality to the unconscious which transforms yesterday into today. The obsessions of slave and master continue. Both continue a deadly struggle of which neither is fully aware. It would seem that for most black people emancipation has yet to come.

A harried young mother, having exhausted the resources of several social agencies, turned to the psychiatrist as a last resort.

She had a pretty face but she was obese and wore frazzled clothes. As a result, she looked like a shapeless, middle-aged woman. On the first visit she wore an ill-fitting red wig which fell forward over her eyes. She made motions to right it, only to have it lodge over her ears.

She told of her difficulties by describing various crises. The younger children were sick and two older boys had disappeared the previous evening. A riot had broken out on that same evening and she feared for the safety of her sons.

She lived with her five children in a rat-infested apartment. She had never been married and most of her twenty-six years had been spent in public housing projects, living on welfare grants. With five children, she ran out of money near the middle of the month.

Then her mother, who could scarcely afford it, would help her buy food. If the groceries were paid for, her roof would begin leaking, and once again she would call the housing office, only to be insulted.

The final blow involved problems with a "raunchy nigger." He had lived with her for several months and had disappeared when the last welfare check was late.

The most bitter outburst was reserved for the Welfare Department. It was headed by a "boss man" who, she believed, found delight in harassing black women. No one had any privacy. The woman next door awakened in the middle of the night, trembling with fright, to discover that the noise at the window was a social worker peering in to determine if a man was sleeping there.

The patient despised public charity, but having stopped school after the ninth grade, she found her meager skills of little use. Some of her neighbors worked as domestics, but only those with few or no children. If a woman had more than two young children, she could not earn enough to pay a sitter. On and on she went. Through most of her narrative she maintained her composure. But as she was relating an incident of little consequence, the tears came and, as she wept, her strength was revealed.

She continued to talk of her life and its burdens. In a short lifetime she had been subjected to great suffering, but she was not defeated. With genuine humor she could acknowledge and laugh at her shortcomings. In the midst of tears, she became warm and chuckled as she related an incident about her children. Hidden in despair was a distinctive vitality. It came out when she told of her church work or a meeting with a friend. As she spoke, her natural generosity was apparent.

At the end of the hour she dried her eyes, rearranged her wig, and strode out. As she moved, a particular style came through. She was depressed, upset, angry, and had her share of problems. She moved slowly, but her head was high. She disappeared down the hall. One knew that in the agony of her life was the beauty and torment of the black experience in this country.

If the resources and imperfections of this young woman were unique to her, her story would not assume such importance. Familiar concepts could adequately describe her intrapsychic conflict. We would search her past for early trauma, distorted relationships, and infantile conflicts. The social milieu from which she came would be considered but would not be given much weight. Our youthful subject, however, is black and this one fact transcends all others.

She perceives herself and her surroundings in a manner deeply influenced by this fact. The dismal quality of her life shows how little society thinks of her. Six generations have passed since slavery, and her view of life's possibilities is the same as that of a slave on a Georgia plantation. The reluctant conclusion is that her assets and liabilities are the same as that slave's. She is wily, resourceful, and practiced in the art of survival. But, like her "soul sister" in bondage, she is a victim from the time of her birth. This society has placed her at a disadvantage from which she cannot recover. However visible her deficiencies, the true burdens are subtle and strike at her soul. For the more we become immersed in her problems, the more her life spells out a tragedy.

She meets her problems with ordinary defenses. But *her* difficulties have existed for hundreds of years. The pathology she shows is common to most Negroes.

The curbing of her aggression began at an early age. It was in large measure determined by a society that is frightened of her. Beneath her passivity lies anger which might otherwise be directed at white people. As a consequence, we see the dependency about which so much has been written. This is another legacy of slavery. In the morning of her life, she saw her mother and other black adults vulnerable to the whim of white persons. From this it would seem logical that she could become as helpless in this society as her enslaved ancestors. To be prevented from growing and maturing is to be kept in a state of dependency.

The means by which she controls her anger have a direct link to the silent war between master and slave. She must be cautious. This may be why she speaks of the "boss man" with such bitterness. She sees him as free to hurt her, while she can never act on her hate for him. That they are both trapped in such an unequal contest is again a tribute to the unchanging nature of America.

In meeting the world, she seems defensive, as if protecting herself from a thousand slights. Her armor, however, guards against real danger. The suspiciousness may seem excessive, but to relax can be to invite disaster. If these types of character traits are seldom encountered in whites, it is because they do not face the same assaults or grow up in the same climate of hatred. As a result, this woman exhibits emotional weariness. The reality of being alternately attacked, ignored, then singled out for some cruel and undeserved punishment must extract its toll. That penalty may be a premature aging and an early death in some black people. To be regarded always as subhuman is a stultifying experience.

It is people like our patient whom the nation now fears. Some feel that she threatens the basic social structure. There is a dread that Negroes will impoverish the country by proliferating on welfare rolls. Recently there has been a fear that they will gain political control of the cities now that whites are fleeing to the suburbs. No one can doubt that white America is afraid.

If our black woman could wipe away the tears, she would laugh. Reflect if you will: the most powerful nation on earth, afraid of the poorest, least educated, most leaderless ten percent of its population. Truly the white American projects his own hostility onto the latter-day slave. How else to understand his terror?

Our young patient weeps for good reason. She has seen her hopes soar only to be frustrated. But where her parents retreated into their black world, she is now demanding more of the white man's world. After three centuries of oppression, along with other black people, she has made a vow.

I will take it no longer.

We weep for the true victim, the black American. His wounds are deep. But along with their scars, black people have a secret. Their genius is that they have survived. In their adaptations they have developed a vigorous style of life. It has touched religion, music, and the broad canvas of creativity. The psyche of black men has been distorted, but out of that deformity has risen a majesty. It began in the chants of the first work song. It continues in the timelessness of the blues.

For white America to understand the life of the black man, it must recognize that so much time has passed and so little has changed.

"BAD NIGGER" AND "POSTAL CLERK"

One of the constant themes in black folklore is the "bad nigger." It seems that every community has had one or was afraid of having one. They were feared as much by blacks as by whites. In the slave legends there are tales of docile field hands suddenly going berserk. It was a common enough phenomenon to appear in writings of the times and to stimulate the erection of defenses against this violent kind of man.

Today black boys are admonished not to be a "bad nigger." No description need be offered; every black child knows what is meant. They are angry and hostile. They strike fear into everyone with their uncompromising rejection of restraint or inhibition. They may seem at one moment meek and compromised—and in the next a terrifying killer. Because of his experience in this country, every black man harbors a potential bad nigger inside him. He must ignore this inner man. The bad nigger is bad because he has been required to renounce his manhood to save his life. The more one approaches the American ideal of respectability, the more this hostility must be repressed. The bad nigger is a defiant nigger, a reminder of what manhood could be.

Cultural stereotypes of the savage rapist-Negro express the fear that the black man will turn on his tormentors. Negro organizations dread the presence of the bad nigger. White merchants who have contact with black people have uneasy feelings when they see a tight mouth, a hard look, and an angry black face. The bad nigger in black men no doubt accounts for more worry in both races than any other single factor.

Granting the limitations of stereotypes, we should nevertheless like to sketch a paradigmatic black man. His characteristics seem so connected to employment that we call it "the postal-clerk syndrome." This man is always described as "nice" by white people. In whatever integrated setting he works, he is the standard against whom other blacks are measured. "If they were all only like him, everything would be so much better." He is passive, nonassertive, and nonaggressive. He has made a virtue of identification with the aggressor, and he has adopted an ingratiating and compliant manner. In public his thoughts and feelings are consciously shaped in the direction he thinks white people want them to be. The pattern begins in childhood when the mother may actually say: "You must be this way because this is the only way you will get along with Mr. Charlie."

This man renounces gratifications that are available to others. He assumes a deferential mask. He is always submissive. He must figure out "the man" but keep "the man" from deciphering him. He is prevalent in the middle and upper-middle classes, but is found throughout the social structure. The more closely allied to the white man, the more complete the picture becomes. He is a direct lineal descendant of the "house nigger" who was designed to identify totally with the white master. The danger he poses to himself and others is great, but only the surface of passivity and compliance is visible. The storm below is hidden.

A leading Negro citizen came to a therapy session with his wife, who was suffering from a severe and intractable melancholia. She had several times seriously attempted suicide. The last attempt was particularly serious. She was angry with her husband and berated him for never opening up and exposing his feelings.
For his part, the husband remained "nice." He never raised his voice above a murmur. His wife could goad him, but he was the epitome of understanding. He was amenable to all suggestions. His manner and gestures were deliberate, studied, and noninflammatory. Everything was understated. During the course of treatment he was involved in several civil rights crises. His public life was an extension of his private one, and he used such words as "moderation" and "responsibility." His entire life was a study in passivity, in how to play at being a man without really being one.

It would be easy to write off this man as an isolated passive individual, but his whole community looks upon his career as a success story. He made it in the system to a position of influence and means. And it took an aggressive, driving, determined man to make it against the odds he faced. We must ask how much energy is required for him to conceal his drive so thoroughly. And we wonder what would happen if his controls ever failed.

Starting with slavery, black people, and more particularly black men, have had to devise ways of expressing themselves uniquely and individually and in a manner that was not threatening to the white man. Some methods of giving voice to aggressive masculinity have become institutionalized. The most stylized is the posture of "playing it cool."

The playing-it-cool style repeats itself over and over again in all aspects of black life. It is an important means of expression and is widely copied in the larger white culture. A man may be overwhelmed with conflict, threatened with an eruption of feelings, and barely maintaining his composure, but he will present a serene exterior. He may fear the eruption of repressed feelings if they bring a loss of control, but an important aspect of his containment is the fear that his aggression will be directed against the white world and will bring swift punishment. The intrapsychic dynamics may be similar in a white man, but for the black man it is socially far more important that the façade be maintained.

. . . .

Black men have stood so long in such peculiar jeopardy in America that a *black norm* has developed—a suspiciousness of one's environment which is necessary for survival. Black people, to a degree that approaches paranoia, must be ever alert to danger from their white fellow citizens. It is a cultural phenomenon peculiar to black Americans. And it is a posture so close to paranoid thinking that the mental disorder into which black people most frequently fall is paranoid psychosis.

Can we say that white men have driven black men mad?

CHARACTER TRAITS

Traits of character and patterns of behavior that appear more often in black people than in other groups can all be traced to various aspects of life in America. Cultural anthropologists have searched intensively and interminably and have found no contemporary evidence for the persistence of African patterns of culture. The experience of slavery was unbelievably efficient in effacing the African and producing the American Negro. As a result, the cultural and characterological patterns developed by American Negroes provide a unique picture of a people whose history was destroyed and who were offered in its stead a narrow ledge of toil on which to live and grow and nurture children. All that is uniquely Negro found its origin on these shores and provides a living document of black history in America.

The interaction among members in black families is increasingly responding to many of the pressures which shape life in other ethnic groups in America. The superficial aspects are the most readily affected, in part because deeper themes and roles are more resistant to change and because the instruments of change are aimed precisely at the superficial aspects of life. But beneath the apparent similarities there run consistent threads—ways of life shared by most black people.

The black family is first of all an extended family. Relatives more readily share the responsibilities of child-rearing. Members of the family more often come to the aid of a troubled member.

In a child-guidance clinic which served a large number of black children, it was found easy to take a black child out of an explosive home situation and lodge him temporarily with a relative in the South. This generally produced good long-term results. Among whites, relatives *and the immediate family* were more resistant to such solutions.

When a brother is asked where *home* is, he is likely to answer promptly: "Montgomery, Alabama," even if he has lived in Cleveland, Ohio, for the past forty-seven years. Home is where the land was and where "one's people" are. The answer might be further refined with the explanation: "Montgomery is my home but all my *people* are in Birmingham." Where my people are is part of my essential self and where I first dug my fingers in soil is a vital part of me. Geography is thus part of the extended identity as is the extended family.

It has a further implication. Away from one's home and people, one is merely a sojourner. However long one lives away from home, the roots reach back to one's people. Cleveland may represent merely a forty-seven-year visit away from home. When death comes, the body is taken home. Thus our brother is never in a true sense a Clevelander. However much his community makes him feel an outsider, he himself provides an additional increment of alienation. As a protective device, he says it was never his city anyway.

The viciousness of life in America for black men makes them remove themselves even further. If I establish first that I am a stranger in your land, I will at least avoid the shock of being attacked in my own home by kinfolk. We are strangers and I dwell for a while in your world—therefore, whatever you do to me cannot truly come as a surprise.

In this world of strangers black men make a home wherever they can. Any black man in a white environment can establish a relationship with another black man by a glance or an easy salutation such as "Hey, bro"—and he has a colleague.

In years gone by a most delightful relationship existed between porters and waiters on passenger trains and the infrequent black traveler. A man could put his child on the train, press a dollar into the hand of the porter, and ask him to "look after her"—and he could rest easy. It was a source of pride for train employees to lavish care and affection on their brethren. The charm of a dining-car waiter in caring for a frightened black girl would have to be seen to be appreciated. It was as if these men were thumbing their noses at the railroad company as they provided million-dollar service to impoverished black travelers. This small body of true aristocrats has lately fallen on hard times, but some future complex of services will no doubt find dark men extending a special hand of welcome to dark brothers.

More than any other place, however, the barbershop is the black man's way station, point of contact, and universal home. Here he always finds a welcome— a friendly audience as he tells his story and a native to give him the word on local doings.

The bickering, the sniping, the backbiting so often said to characterize black people in their relationship with one another seems so very much to be the rivalry of siblings. Underlying it all is a feeling that "you're no better than I." It is an unfortunate corollary of such a feeling of "sibship," but it is probably a small price to pay for the comfort and the web of support provided by a brother-hood.

The family is broad; the self has roots in many places. The brother has several selves and many homes. A creature of prey must have more than one haven.

"It's a poor rat that don't have but one hole."

A black mechanic who had a good income as owner of his own repair shop dissipated his profits and when pressed by creditors ran crap games in his place of business to raise money. Reminded that he had a major investment in his business which was jeopardized by the gambling, he threw up his hands and said: "I'll never make nothing no way."

He was an excellent mechanic and had demonstrated above-average ability from his earliest years. He was raised in the South and at the age of ten was maintaining complicated machinery. With little formal schooling he nevertheless became skillful at various machine operations. He had developed a potentially thriving business single-handedly. But what he later described so eloquently was his lack of faith in that which he accomplished with his own hands. The ownership of property had been a source of misery for his father. White rivals, with the collusion of southern courts, had overnight taken the fruits of years of labor. He himself as a young man had been swindled by white men. The crucial factor here is that he had no recourse. The courts, the state, the citizenry—all were poised to accuse *him* if he objected to being robbed.

In his behavior he seemed to be saying that he could not hope to accumulate goods from his own labor. They could be taken away so swiftly that it was better not even to consider them his own. The more he owned, the more anxious he became. He turned then to luck; if fortune smiled he was saved. Otherwise he faced bankruptcy.

A man cannot develop an intense emotional investment in land if it can be taken away at any moment. The interlocking of business interests in any community, particularly in the South, can effectively prevent a black man from accumulating goods by denying him funds and supplies, and, in general, blocking his access to commerce. If by some chance he does acquire land or goods, they can be taken away by the same association of business interests in his community. The reader who is skeptical probably bases his doubts on his own experience, but black people have been robbed of their goods as well as their labor throughout their sojourn in this country.

In the 1950's a young white southern lawyer, newly returned from a New England law school, was assigned a case by his law firm involving a Negro woman and her property. He soon realized that his task was to have the woman committed to an institution as insane and to arrange for the acquisition of her property by a client of the law firm. He resigned from the firm and took on the woman's defense. He learned of similar cases and, by defending them, earned the enmity of his colleagues. Threats were made on his life and he fled the state for his own safety.

The brother with property in the South is highly visible and is usually the target for business rivals. What would otherwise be healthy competition becomes under these circumstances a deadly game of defense in which the most he can hope for is to avoid capture. Retaliation is out of the question.

Thus for black people the ability to divorce oneself emotionally from an object is necessary for survival.

The mechanic's response is neurotic but the surrounding reality fosters his symptom. Does anyone know of a community where a small businessman who happens to be black does not face greater problems of survival than his white confreres? And if such is the case, does not his fate really lie with chance rather than his own effort?

To label this response improvident, to call the man naive or inexperienced in the ways of business, is to close one's eyes to the nature of the society in which he lives. It is a refusal to recognize the social soil in which his attitudes grow.

The journals of slaveowners tell of their exasperation when their slaves refused to work or worked poorly or broke farm tools. They attributed such behavior to "poor moral fiber," shiftlessness, and stupidity. One wonders who is stupid, the slave who dawdles or the owner who expected him to do otherwise.

And one wonders how long a man can maintain enthusiasm for thrift, diligence, and hard work when the rewards so earned are denied and when the goods so earned are stolen.

We suggest that there is no more subtle student of American society than the black man, and when he suspects that he is called to a race where there is no prize, he simply declines to run.

One additional word on the matter of property. The land to which Africans were brought and which their labor made great was simply an outpost in the wilds of North America when they first were pressed into bondage. Their labor produced tobacco, the first significant agricultural product to supplement the precarious shipping industry. When in the early 1800's the European demand for cotton made it a prime cash crop, blacks were imported in huge numbers. When cotton became king, it rested solely on black backs. Cotton, or the slaves who produced it, moved this nation from a colonial outpost in 1800 to an industrial giant of the twentieth century. The labor of blacks and its product were the bridge and, importantly, the only bridge from world insignificance to world dominance in slightly more than a century. As certain as is history—America is the wealthiest nation in the world because of the labor of black men.

One further item: when a slaveowner found his land exhausted from too intense cultivation of cotton, he sold the slaves to purchase machinery and fertilizer which would allow him to diversify his crops. From this point of view, blacks occupied a central place in the nation's economy.

The Civil War came at a time when cotton no longer held its pre-eminent position and when industrialization was on the rise. The time had passed when the labor of black slaves made such an overriding difference to the economy of the country. Their labor in the fields would be important for another sixty years, but by 1865 the future of the country was secure and the cynic may be excused if he notes that the national repugnance for slavery developed only at a time when its loss did the nation little harm.

Since 1865 the most significant economic development for blacks has been the systematic theft of the lands acquired by this agricultural people. The labor required for an ex-slave to lay hold of an eighty-acre plot of land was prodigious, but the speed with which he could be robbed of it was dizzying.

Quite aside from the moral issue, the historical picture makes America's treatment of blacks somewhat more comprehensible. They were brought here to be exploited and that exploitation has continued to this very date. Robbed of lands, they were denied worthwhile employment in the growing industrial complex. They were drafted into the labor force in times of stress and need, such as war, as easily as they were drafted into military service. When the emergency was past, they were dismissed. They were swept into commercial enterprises as laborers when they could be used tactically—as, for example, by the growing auto industry to spike the guns of organized labor or indeed by organized labor to undo the automakers. In all these involvements they were pawns—kept poor, uneducated, and powerless.

Now the purpose of this shuttlecock game in which the brother is the cock was not lost on dark men. They and their labor have always been used for the enrichment of white men. And as the idea of private property is so important in American society and acquisitiveness has become a virtue, it is not surprising that black people have on occasion developed a uniquely flexible concept of ownership.

Men reduced to the status of non-persons and removed from the protection of the social code can hardly be expected to honor the responsibilities imposed by that code. And men (now emancipated) excluded from all benefit of the social order, indeed preyed upon by that social order, may wear lightly the injunction that (a white man's) property is sacred. No, we grant that it is likely that blacks steal more than whites, but we suggest that there is no more efficient way to produce a thief than to steal a man's substance and command that he hold his peace.

THE PSYCHIC COSTS OF RACE HATRED

It seems inaccurate to apply the term "racial prejudice" both to Negroes' feelings about white people and to their feelings about themselves. There seems to be confusion about the quality of one's feelings if one is a victim of racial prejudice. The fact of the matter is that black people are inclined to regard the white man as superior. There are examples without number in the patois and the everyday behavior of millions of blacks which speak for the fact that they do indeed feel that the white man is intrinsically better.

Caution must be exercised in distinguishing feelings of inferiority from emulation of the majority by a minority concerned with survival. But, even taking this into account, there remains an increment of feeling which says emphatically: "White is right."

For a black man to straighten his hair chemically, to have what is known as a "process," is a painful, dangerous procedure. The result is a slick pompadour which in no way save one resembles a white man's hair. Only in that it is straight and not kinky does it appear less black and more white.
Negroes have always referred to straight hair as good—and kinky hair as bad.

Black people feel that white people are smarter, and here there is a subtle refinement. It is not that they see themselves in a real sense personally as stupid. It is rather that they look upon themselves as average and the white man as "supersmart." Black racists are fond of recounting the evil genius of the American white man, and a careful hearing of their words tells clearly that, though they *say* that they no longer look up to Charlie, this is by no means the case. They have simply reversed the moral value placed on his acts. Now they are evil and perfidious, whereas before they were glorious and enviable. But they continue to be brilliant acts of genius, executed by omniscient men. It is a pity that too many of these voices calling Negroes to blackness still preach a thinly veiled version of white supremacy.

Consider too what would be proper conduct if one were an oppressed member of a helpless minority held in effective bondage by a majority which not only has numbers in its favor but is a majority of intellectual supermen as well. If a person had such a view, he would develop an extremely suspicious way of life. He would adopt a frightened, cornered, panicky, paranoid way of thinking.

We suspect that many of the black racists exhibit a paranoid style of life because they feel they are facing an enemy of supermen, not simply an enemy which outnumbers them.

Such an attitude need not be confined to racists.

A black professional was conversing with a younger man about a new project. He answered several questions about the proposal, some parts of which involved confrontation with white professionals. The older man was held in high esteem by black people in the community. He had a distinguished record of service on community-wide committees and boards. To an outsider, he was as comfortable at a mixed cocktail party as in his office. His professional activities were wide and multiracial. By almost any measure he would be regarded as successful.

As the exchange continued, to each question the older man raised an objection. He warned against angering "them." "They" might not like it; "they" would have thought of it first; "they" would have a different and therefore better proposal. He got angrier as the discussion continued. "They" became increasingly synonymous with all white people.

He finally became exasperated and ended the conversation with "Don't you know Charlie never sleeps?"

It must be apparent how profoundly damaging such an attitude can be to the achievement of black people. In the United States at this time the essential competition between men is an intellectual one. The essential judgment of one's usefulness rests on one's intellectual capability, and if one fails in *fair* competition, it is an intellectual failure. Second only to making certain that black people have a fair chance is the necessity that they be free of corrosive attitudes about their intellectual inferiority.

In the area of ambition and striving there is a further consequence of this attitude. The conviction that Charlie is shrewder saps a black man's drive. It is a discouraging task to compete against a superman even if he is "super" only in one's own mind. Humans being what they are, it provides an opportunity to opt out of the struggle altogether and develops an attitude of "What's the use? Why fight it? You can't possibly win struggling as ordinary men struggle; ordinary men sleep nights and Charlie never sleeps."

The only way out, if indeed it can be so considered, is a poor one at best and the price paid for success is terribly high. We speak of those Negroes who make it by emulating the white man. They accept as a fact that Negroes are not so smart as white people and decide to reject their blackness and, insofar as possible, embrace whiteness. They identify with white men in every way and add to that a contempt for black people. In the process they gain some of the "white man's magic." They acquire some of the superior qualities they attribute to him. They may as a result feel more competent, but it is a direct function of their feeling that "other Negroes" are incompetent. In this way they develop a contempt for themselves, because, however much they avoid it, they remain black, and there are things about themselves that will yet remind them of their blackness and those reminders will evoke feelings of self-hatred and self-depreciation.

To the extent that emulation of the white man is rewarded by society, the individual will find confirmation of his belief that this is the proper course. If he achieves status and wealth, these gains may well be saying to him that "white is right." His psychic division widens and his hatred of self grows. The more success he gains, the more he feels white people are in fact smarter, and the more convinced he is that black people are stupid.

For any person growing up in the often anti-intellectual climate of America, it is difficult, whether he be black or white, to develop an accurate assessment of and a healthy respect for his own intellectual endowment. Imagine how difficult this is when every element in the milieu says that your kind is stupid and their kind is smart. A society which can deal out such severe punishment and which can offer such magnificent rewards is most persuasive, however foolish its message may be.

Black men hear on all sides that success lies in being like white people, who establish the standard of wisdom. Is it any wonder, then, that this consequence of racial prejudice is deadly to the intellectual flowering of black people? And is it any wonder, then, that in a desperate attempt to avoid it, many latter-day chauvinists adopt an anti-intellectual posture? They fail to see that by this very stance they reveal themselves as victims of the same American creed of white superiority.

. . . .

For black and white alike, the air of this nation is perfused with the idea of white supremacy and everyone grows to manhood under this influence. Americans find that it is a basic part of their nationhood to despise blacks. No man who breathes this air can avoid it and black men are no exception. They are taught to hate themselves, and if at some point they discover that they are the object of this hatred, they are faced with an additional task, nothing less, for the imperative remains—Negroes are to be despised.

Thus the dynamics of black self-hatred are unique. They involve the child's awareness that all people who are black as he is are so treated by white people. Whatever hostility he mounts against white people finds little support in the weakness and the minority status of black people. As it is hopeless for him to consider righting this wrong by force, he identifies with his oppressor psychologically in an attempt to escape from his hopeless position. From his new psychologically "white" position, he turns on black people with aggression and hostility and hates blacks and, among the blacks, himself.

Racial prejudice, therefore, is a pitiful product of systematized cruelty, in which frightened people climb onto the stand with the oppressor and say: "Yes, we hate them too!" They are opportunists, wretched and terrified, but going with a winner.

BLACK HERO

History may well show that of all the men who lived during our fateful century none illustrated the breadth or the grand potential of man so magnificently as did Malcolm X. If, in future chronicles, America is regarded as the major nation of our day, and the rise of darker people from bondage as the major event, then no figure has appeared thus far who captures the spirit of our times as does Malcolm.

Malcolm is an authentic hero, indeed the only universal black hero. In his unrelenting opposition to the viciousness in America, he fired the imagination of black men all over the world.

If this black nobleman is a hero to black people in the United States and if his life reflects their aspirations, there can be no doubt of the universality of black rage.

Malcolm responded to his position in his world and to his blackness in the manner of so many black boys. He turned to crime. He was saved by a religious sect given to a strange, unhistorical explanation of the origin of black people and even stranger solutions to their problems. He rose to power in that group and outgrew it.

Feeding on his own strength, growing in response to his own commands, limited by no creed, he became a citizen of the world and an advocate of all oppressed people no matter their color or belief. Anticipating his death by an assassin, he distilled, in a book, the essence of his genius, his life. His autobiography thus is a legacy and, together with his speeches, illustrates the thrusting growth of the man—his evolution, rapid, propulsive, toward the man he might have been had he lived.

The essence of Malcolm X was growth, change, and a seeking after truth.

Alarmed white people saw him first as an eccentric and later as a dangerous radical—a revolutionary without troops who threatened to stir black people to riot and civil disobedience. Publicly, they treated him as a joke; privately, they were afraid of him.

After his death he was recognized by black people as the "black shining prince" and recordings of his speeches became treasured things. His autobiography was studied, his life marveled at. Out of this belated admiration came the philosophical basis for black activism and indeed the thrust of Black Power itself, away from integration and civil rights and into the "black bag."

Unlike Malcolm, however, the philosophical underpinnings of the new black militancy were static. They remained encased within the ideas of revolution and black nationhood, ideas Malcolm had outgrown by the time of his death. His stature has made even his earliest statements gospel and men now find themselves willing to die for words which in retrospect are only milestones in the growth of a fantastic man.

Many black men who today preach blackness seem headed blindly toward self-destruction, uncritical of anything "black" and damning the white man for diabolical wickedness. For a philosophical base they have turned to the words of Malcolm's youth.

This perversion of Malcolm's intellectual position will not, we submit, be held against him by history.

Malcolm's meaning for us lies in his fearless demand for truth and his evolution from a petty criminal to an international statesman—accomplished by a black man against odds of terrible magnitude—in America. His message was his life, not his words, and Malcolm knew it.

Black Power activism—thrust by default temporarily at the head of a powerful movement—is a conception that contributes in a significant way to the strength and unity of that movement but is unable to provide the mature vision for the mighty works ahead. It will pass and leave black people in this country prouder, stronger, more determined, but in need of grander princes with clearer vision.

We believe that the black masses will rise with a simple and eloquent demand to which new leaders must give tongue. They will say to America simply:

"GET OFF OUR BACKS!"

The Forgotten American

PETER SCHRAG

There is hardly a language to describe him, or even a set of social statistics. Just names: racist-bigot-redneck-ethnic-Irish-Italian-Pole-Hunkie-Yahoo. The lower middle class. A blank. The man under whose hat lies the great American desert. Who watches the tube, plays the horses, and keeps the niggers out of his union and his neighborhood. Who might vote for Wallace (but didn't). Who cheers when the cops beat up on demonstrators. Who is free, white, and twenty-one, has a job, a home, a family, and is up to his eyeballs in credit. In the guise of the working class—or the American yeoman or John Smith—he was once the hero of the civics book, the man that Andrew Jackson called "the bone and sinew of the country." Now he is "the forgotten man," perhaps the most alienated person in America.

Nothing quite fits, except perhaps omission and semi-invisibility. America is supposed to be divided between affluence and poverty, between slums and suburbs. John Kenneth Galbraith begins the foreword to *The Affluent Society* with the phrase. "Since I sailed for Switzerland in the early summer of 1955 to begin work on this book. . . . " But *between* slums and suburbs, between Scarsdale and Harlem, between Wellesley and Roxbury, between Shaker Heights and Hough, there are some eighty million people (depending on how you count them) who didn't sail for Switzerland in the summer of 1955, or at any other time, and who never expect to. Between slums and suburbs: South Boston and South San Francisco, Bell and Parma, Astoria and Bay Ridge, Newark, Cicero, Downey, Daly City, Charlestown, Flatbush. Union halls, American Legion posts, neighborhood bars and bowling leagues, the Ukrainian Club and the Holy Name. Main Street. To try to describe all this is like trying to describe America itself. If you look for it, you find it everywhere: the rows of frame houses overlooking the belching steel mills in Bethlehem, Pennsylvania, two-family brick houses in Canarsie (where the most common slogan, even in the middle of a political campaign, is "curb your dog"); the Fords and Chevies with a decal American flag on the rear window (usually a cut-out from the *Reader's Digest,* and displayed in counter-protest against peaceniks and "those bastards who carry Vietcong flags in demonstrations"); the bunting on the porch rail with the inscription. "Welcome Home, Pete." The gold star in the window.

When he was Under Secretary of Housing and Urban Development, Robert C. Wood tried a definition. It is not good, but it's the best we have:

He is a white employed male ... earning between $5,000 and $10,000. He works regularly, steadily, dependably, wearing a blue collar or white collar. Yet the frontiers of his career expectations have been fixed since he reached the age of thirty-five, when he found that he had too many obligations, too much family, and too few skills to match opportunities with aspirations.

This definition of the "working American" involves almost 23-million American families. The working American lives in the gray area fringes of a central city or in a close-in or very far-out cheaper suburban subdivision of a large metropolitan area. He is likely to own a home and a car especially as his income begins to rise. Of those earning between $6,000 and $7,500, 70 per cent own their own homes and 94 per cent drive their own cars.

94 per cent have no education beyond high school and 43 per cent have only completed the eighth grade.

He does all the right things, obeys the law, goes to church and insists—usually—that his kids get a better education than he had. But the right things don't seem to be paying off. While he is making more than he ever made—perhaps more than he'd ever dreamed—he's still struggling while a lot of others— "them" (on welfare, in demonstrations, in the ghettos) are getting most of the attention. "I'm working my ass off," a guy tells you on a stoop in South Boston. "My kids don't have a place to swim, my parks are full of glass, and I'm supposed to bleed for a bunch of people on relief." In New York a man who drives a Post Office trailer truck at night (4:00 P.M. to midnight) and a cab during the day (7:00 A.M. to 2:00 P.M.), and who hustles radios for his Post Office buddies on the side, is ready, as he says, to "knock somebody's ass." "The colored guys work when they feel like it. Sometimes they show up and sometimes they don't. One guy tore up all the time cards. I'd like to see a white guy do that and get away with it."

What Counts

Nobody knows how many people in America moonlight (half of the eighteen million families in the $5,000 to $10,000 bracket have two or more wage earners) or how many have to hustle on the side. "I don't think anybody has a single job anymore," said Nicholas Kisburg, the research director for a Teamsters Union

Council in New York. "All the cops are moonlighting, and the teachers; and there's a million guys who are hustling, guys with phony social-security numbers who are hiding part of what they make so they don't get kicked out of a housing project, or guys who work as guards at sports events and get free meals that they don't want to pay taxes on. Every one of them is cheating. They are underground people—*Untermenschen.* . . . We really have no systematic data on any of this. We have no ideas of the attitudes of the white worker. (We've been too busy studying the black worker.) And yet he's the source of most of the reaction in this country."

The reaction is directed at almost every visible target: at integration and welfare, taxes and sex education, at the rich and the poor, the foundations and students, at the "smart people in the suburbs." In New York State the legislature cuts the welfare budget; in Los Angeles, the voters reelect Yorty after a whispered racial campaign against the Negro favorite. In Minneapolis a police detective named Charles Stenvig, promising "to take the handcuffs off the police," wins by a margin stunning even to his supporters; in Massachusetts the voters mail tea bags to their representatives in protest against new taxes, and in state after state legislatures are passing bills to punish student demonstrators. ("We keep talking about permissiveness in training kids," said a Los Angeles labor official, "but we forget that these are our kids.")

And yet all these things are side manifestations of a malaise that lacks a language. Whatever law and order means, for example, to a man who feels his wife is unsafe on the street after dark or in the park at any time, or whose kids get shaken down in the school yard, it also means something like normality—the demand that everybody play it by the book, that cultural and social standards be somehow restored to their civics-book simplicity, that things shouldn't be as they are but as they were supposed to be. If there is a revolution in this country—a revolt in manners, standards of dress and obscenity, and more importantly, in our official sense of what America is—there is also a counter-revolt. Sometimes it is inarticulate, and sometimes (perhaps most of the time) people are either too confused or apathetic—or simply too polite and too decent—to declare themselves. In Astoria, Queens, a white working-class district of New York, people who make $7,000 or $8,000 a year (sometimes in two jobs) call themselves affluent, even though the Bureau of Labor Statistics regards an income of less than $9,500 in New York inadequate to a moderate standard of living. And in a similar neighborhood in Brooklyn a truck driver who earns $151 a week tells you he's doing well, living in a two-story frame house separated by a narrow driveway from similar houses, thousands of them in block after block. This year, for the first time, he will go on a cruise—he and his wife and two other couples—two weeks in the Caribbean. He went to work after World War II ($57 a week) and he has lived in the same house for twenty years, accumulating two television sets, wall-to-wall carpeting in a small living room, and a basement that he recently remodeled into a recreation room with the help of two moonlighting firemen. "We get fairly good salaries, and this is a good neighborhood, one of the few good ones left. We have no smoked Irishmen around."

Stability is what counts, stability in job and home and neighborhood, stability in the church and in friends. At night you watch television and sometimes on a weekend you go to a nice place—maybe a downtown hotel—for dinner with another couple. (Or maybe your sister, or maybe bowling, or maybe, if you're defeated, a night at the track.) The wife has the necessary appliances, often still being paid off, and the money you save goes for your daughter's orthodontist, and later for her wedding. The smoked Irishmen—the colored (no one says black; few even say Negro)—represent change and instability, kids who cause trouble in school who get treatment that your kids never got, that you never got. ("Those fucking kids," they tell you in South Boston, "raising hell, and not one of 'em paying his own way. Their fucking mothers are all on welfare.") The black kids mean a change in the rules, a double standard in grades and discipline, and—vaguely—a challenge to all you believed right. Law and order is the stability and predictability of established ways. Law and order is equal treatment—in school, in jobs, in the courts—even if you're cheating a little yourself. The Forgotten Man is Jackson's man. He is the vestigial American democrat of 1840: "They all know that their success depends upon their own industry and economy and that they must not expect to become suddenly rich by the fruits of their toil." He is also Franklin Roosevelt's man—the man whose vote (or whose father's vote) sustained the New Deal.

There are other considerations, other styles, other problems. A postman in a Charlestown (Boston) housing project: eight children and a ninth on the way. Last year by working overtime, his income went over $7,000. This year, because he reported it, the Housing Authority is raising his rent from $78 to $106 a month, a catastrophe for a family that pays $2.20 a day for milk, has never had a vacation, and for which an excursion is "going out for ice cream." "You try and save for something better; we hope to get out of here to someplace where the kids can play, where there's no broken glass, and then something always comes along that knocks you right back. It's like being at the bottom of the well waiting for a guy to throw you a rope." The description becomes almost Chaplinesque. Life is humble but not simple; the terrors of insolent bureaucracies and contemptuous officials produce a demonology that loses little of its horror for being partly misunderstood. You want to get a sink fixed but don't want to offend the manager; want to get an eye operation that may (or may not) have been necessitated by a military injury five years earlier, "but the Veterans Administration says I signed away my benefits"; want to complain to someone about the teen-agers who run around breaking windows and harassing women but get no response either from the management or the police. "You're afraid to complain because if they don't get you during the day they'll get you at night." Automobiles, windows, children, all become hostages to the vague terrors of everyday life; everything is vulnerable. Liabilities that began long ago cannot possibly be liquidated: "I never learned anything in that school except how to fight. I got tired of being caned by the teachers so at sixteen I quit and joined the Marines. I still don't know anything."

At the Bottom of the Well

American culture? Wealth is visible, and so, now, is poverty. Both have become intimidating clichés. But the rest? A vast, complex, and disregarded world that was once—in belief, and in fact—the American middle: Greyhound and Trailways bus terminals in little cities at midnight, each of them with its neon lights and its cardboard hamburgers; acres of tar-paper beach bungalows in places like Revere and Rockaway; the hair curlers in the supermarket on Saturday, and the little girls in the communion dresses the next morning; pinball machines and the *Daily News,* the *Reader's Digest* and Ed Sullivan; houses with tiny front lawns (or even large ones) adorned with statues of the Virgin or of Sambo welcomin' de folks home; Clint Eastwood or Julie Andrews at the Palace; the trotting tracks and the dog tracks—Aurora Downs, Connaught Park, Roosevelt, Yonkers, Rockingham, and forty others—where gray men come not for sport and beauty, but to read numbers, to study and dope. (If you win you have figured something, have in a small way controlled your world, have surmounted your impotence. If you lose, bad luck, shit. "I'll break his goddammed head.") Baseball is not the national pastime; racing is. For every man who goes to a major-league baseball game there are four who go to the track and probably four more who go to the candy store or the barbershop to make their bets. (Total track attendance in 1965: 62 million plus another 10 million who went to the dogs.)

There are places, and styles, and attitudes. If there are neighborhoods of aspiration, suburban enclaves for the mobile young executive and the aspiring worker, there are also places of limited expectation and dead-end districts where mobility is finished. But even there you can often find, however vestigial, a sense of place, the roots of old ethnic loyalties, and a passionate, if often futile, battle against intrusion and change. "Everybody around here," you are told, "pays his own way." In this world the problems are not the ABM or air pollution (have they heard of Biafra?) or the international population crisis; the problem is to get your street cleaned, your garbage collected, to get your husband home from Vietnam alive; to negotiate installment payments and to keep the schools orderly. Ask anyone in Scarsdale or Winnetka about the schools and they'll tell you about new programs, or about how many are getting into Harvard, or about the teachers; ask in Oakland or the North Side of Chicago, and they'll tell you that they have (or haven't) had trouble. Somewhere in his gut the man in those communities knows that mobility and choice in this society are limited. He cannot imagine any major change for the better; but he can imagine change for the worse. And yet for a decade he is the one who has been asked to carry the burden of social reform, to integrate his schools and his neighborhood, has been asked by comfortable people to pay the social debts due to the poor and the black. In Boston, in San Francisco, in Chicago (not to mention Newark or Oakland) he has been telling the reformers to go to hell. The Jewish schoolteachers of New York and the Irish parents of Dorchester have asked the same question: "What the hell did Lindsay (or the Beacon Hill Establishment) ever do for us?"

The ambiguities and changes in American life that occupy discussions in university seminars and policy debates in Washington, and that form the backbone of contemporary popular sociology, become increasingly the conditions of trauma and frustration in the middle. Although the New Frontier and Great Society contained some programs for those not already on the rolls of social pathology—federal aid for higher education, for example—the public priorities and the rhetoric contained little. The emphasis, properly, was on the poor, on the inner cities (*e.g.*, Negroes) and the unemployed. But in Chicago a widow with three children who earns $7,000 a year can't get them college loans because she makes too much; the money is reserved for people on relief. New schools are built in the ghetto but not in the white working-class neighborhoods where they are just as dilapidated. In Newark the head of a white vigilante group (now a city councilman) runs, among other things, on a platform opposing pro-Negro discrimination. "When pools are being built in the Central Ward—don't they think white kids have got frustration? The white can't get a job; we have to hire Negroes first." The middle class, said Congressman Roman Pucinski of Illinois, who represents a lot of it, "is in revolt. Everyone has been generous in supporting anti-poverty. Now the middle-class American is disqualified from most of the programs."

"Somebody Has to Say No ..."

The frustrated middle. The liberal wisdom about welfare, ghettos, student revolt, and Vietnam has only a marginal place, if any, for the values and life of the working man. It flies in the face of most of what he was taught to cherish and respect: hard work, order, authority, self-reliance. He fought, either alone or through labor organizations, to establish the precincts he now considers his own. Union seniority, the civil-service bureaucracy, and the petty professionalism established by the merit system in the public schools become sinecures of particular ethnic groups or of those who have learned to negotiate and master the system. A man who worked all his life to accumulate the points and grades and paraphernalia to become an assistant school principal (no matter how silly the requirements) is not likely to relinquish his position with equanimity. Nor is a dock worker whose only estate is his longshoreman's card. The job, the points, the credits become property:

Some men leave their sons money [wrote a union member to the *New York Times*], some large investments, some business connections, and some a profession. I have only one worthwhile thing to give: my trade. I hope to follow a centuries-old tradition and sponsor my sons for an apprenticeship. For this simple father's wish it is said that I discriminate against Negroes. Don't all of us discriminate? Which of us . . . will not choose a son over all others?

Suddenly the rules are changing—all the rules. If you protect your job for your own you may be called a bigot. At the same time it's perfectly acceptable to shout black power and to endorse it. What does it take to be a good American? *Give the black man a position because he is black, not because he necessarily works harder or does the job better.* What does it take to be a good American? Dress nicely, hold a job, be clean-cut, don't judge a man by the color of his skin or the country of his origin. What about the demands of Negroes, the long hair of the students, the dirty movies, the people who burn draft cards and American flags? Do you have to go out in the street with picket signs, do you have to burn the place down to get what you want? What does it take to be a good American? *This is a sick society, a racist society, we are fighting an immoral war.* ("I'm against the Vietnam war, too," says the truck driver in Brooklyn. "I see a good kid come home with half an arm and a leg in a brace up to here, and what's it all for? I was glad to see *my kid* flunk the Army physical. Still, somebody has to say no to these demonstrators and enforce the law.") What does it take to be a good American?

The conditions of trauma and frustration in the middle. What does it take to be a good American? Suddenly there are demands for Italian power and Polish power and Ukrainian power. In Cleveland the Poles demand a seat on the school board, and get it, and in Pittsburgh John Pankuch, the seventy-three-year-old president of the National Slovak Society demands "action, plenty of it to make up for lost time." Black power is supposed to be nothing but emulation of the ways in which other ethnic groups made it. But have they made it? In Reardon's Bar on East Eighth Street in South Boston, where the workmen come for their fish-chowder lunch and for their rye and ginger, they still identify themselves as Galway men and Kilkenny men; in the newsstand in Astoria you can buy *Il Progresso, El Tiempo;* the *Staats-Zeitung,* the *Irish World,* plus papers in Greek, Hungarian, and Polish. At the parish of Our Lady of Mount Carmel the priests hear confession in English, Italian, and Spanish and, nearby, the biggest attraction is not the stickball game, but the *bocce* court. Some of the poorest people in America are white, native, and have lived all of their lives in the same place as their fathers and grandfathers. The problems that were presumably solved in some distant past, in that prehistoric era before the textbooks were written— problems of assimilation of upward mobility—now turn out to be very much unsolved. The melting pot and all: millions made it, millions moved to the affluent suburbs; several million—no one knows how many—did not. The median income in Irish South Boston is $5,100 a year but the community-action workers have a hard time convincing the local citizens that any white man who is not stupid or irresponsible can be poor. Pride still keeps them from applying for income supplements or Medicaid, but it does not keep them from resenting those who do. In Pittsburgh, where the members of Polish-American organizations earn an estimated $5,000 to $6,000 (and some fall below the poverty line), the Poverty Programs are nonetheless directed primarily to Negroes, and almost everywhere the thing called urban backlash associates itself in some fashion with ethnic groups whose members have themselves only a precarious hold on the security of affluence. Almost everywhere in the old cities, tribal neighborhoods and their styles are under assault by masscult. The Italian grocery gives way to the supermarket, the ma-and-pa store and the walk-up are attacked by urban renewal. And almost everywhere, that assault tends to depersonalize and to alienate. It has always been this way, but with time the brave new world that replaces old patterns becomes increasingly bureaucratized, distant, and hard to control.

Yet beyond the problems of ethnic identity, beyond the problems of Poles and Irishmen left behind, there are others more pervasive and more dangerous. For every Greek or Hungarian there are a dozen American-Americans who are past ethnic consciousness and who are as alienated, as confused, and as angry as the rest. The obvious manifestations are the same everywhere—race, taxes, welfare, students—but the threat seems invariably more cultural and psychological than economic or social. What upset the police at the Chicago convention most was not so much the politics of the demonstrators as their manners and their hair. (The barbershops in their neighborhoods don't advertise Beatle Cuts but the Flat Top and the Chicago Box.) The affront comes from middle-class people— and their children—who had been cast in the role of social exemplars (and from those cast as unfortunates worthy of public charity) who offend all the things on which working class identity is built: "hippies [said a San Francisco longshoreman] who fart around the streets and don't work"; welfare recipients who strike and march for better treatment; "all those [said a California labor official] who challenge the precepts that these people live on." If ethnic groups are beginning to organize to get theirs, so are others: police and firemen ("The cop is the new nigger"); schoolteachers; lower-middle-class housewives fighting sex education and bussing; small property owners who have no ethnic communion but a passionate interest in lower taxes, more policemen, and stiffer penalties for criminals. In San Francisco the Teamsters, who had never been known for such interests before, recently demonstrated in support of the police and law enforcement and, on another occasion, joined a group called Mothers Support Neighborhood Schools at a school-board meeting to oppose—with their presence and later, apparently, with their fists—a proposal to integrate the schools through bussing. ("These people," someone said at the meeting, "do not look like mothers.")

Which is not to say that all is frustration and anger, that anybody is ready "to burn the country down." They are not even ready to elect standard model demagogues. "A lot of labor people who thought of voting for Wallace were ashamed of themselves when they realized what they were about to do," said Morris Iushewitz, an officer of New York's Central Labor Council. Because of a massive last-minute union campaign, and perhaps for other reasons, the blue-collar vote for Wallace fell far below the figures predicted by the early polls last fall. Any number of people, moreover, who are not doing well by any set of official statistics, who are earning well below the national mean ($8,000 a year), or who hold two jobs to stay above it, think of themselves as affluent, and often use that word. It is almost as if not to be affluent is to be un-American. People who can't use the word tend to be angry; people who come too close to those who can't become frightened. The definition of affluence is generally pinned to what comes in, not to the quality of life as it's lived. The $8,000 son of a man who never earned more than $4,500 may, for that reason alone, believe that he's "doing all right." If life is not all right, if he can't get his curbs fixed, or his streets patrolled, if the highways are crowded and the beaches polluted, if the schools are ineffectual he is still able to call himself affluent, feels, perhaps, a social compulsion to do so. His anger, if he is angry, is not that of the wage earner resenting management—and certainly not that of the socialist ideologue asking for redistribution of wealth—but that of the consumer, the taxpayer, and the family man. (Inflation and taxes are wiping out most of the wage gains made in labor contracts signed during the past three years.) Thus he will vote for a Louise Day Hicks in Boston who promises to hold the color line in the schools or for a Charles Stenvig calling for law enforcement in Minneapolis but reject a George Wallace who seems to threaten his pocketbook. The danger is that he will identify with the politics of the Birchers and other middle-class reactionaries (who often pretend to speak for him) even though his income and style of life are far removed from theirs; that taxes, for example, will be identified with welfare rather than war, and that he will blame his limited means on the small slice of the poor rather than the fat slice of the rich.

If you sit and talk to people like Marjorie Lemlow, who heads Mothers Support Neighborhood Schools in San Francisco, or Joe Owens, a house painter who is president of a community-action organization in Boston, you quickly discover that the roots of reaction and the roots of reform are often identical, and that the response to particular situations is more often contingent on the politics of the politicians and leaders who appear to care than on the conditions of life or the ideology of the victims. Mrs. Lemlow wants to return the schools to some virtuous past; she worries about disintegration of the family and she speaks vaguely about something that she can't bring herself to call a conspiracy against Americanism. She has been accused of leading a bunch of Birchers, and she sometimes talks Birch language. But whatever the form, her sense of things comes from a small-town vision of national virtues, and her unhappiness from the assaults of urban sophistication. It just so happens that a lot of reactionaries now sing that tune, and that the liberals are indifferent.

Joe Owens—probably because of his experience as a Head Start parent, and because of his association with an effective community-action program—talks a different language. He knows, somehow, that no simple past can be restored. In his world the villains are not conspirators but bureaucrats and politicians, and he is beginning to discover that in a struggle with officials the black man in the ghetto and the working man (black or white) have the same problems. "Every time you ask for something from the politicians they treat you like a beggar, like you ought to be grateful for what you have. They try to make you feel ashamed."

The imponderables are youth and tradition and change. *The civics book and the institution it celebrates—however passé—still hold the world together.* The revolt is in their name, not against them. And there is simple decency, the language and practice of the folksy cliché, the small town, the Boy Scout virtues, the neighborhood charity, the obligation to support the church, the rhetoric of open opportunity: "They can keep Wallace and they can keep Alabama. We didn't fight a dictator for four years so we could elect one over here." What happens when all that becomes Mickey Mouse? Is there an urban ethic to replace the values of the small town? Is there a coherent public philosophy, a consistent set of beliefs to replace family, home, and hard work? What happens when the hang-ups of upper-middle-class kids are in fashion and those of blue-collar kids are not? What happens when Doing Your Own Thing becomes not the slogan of the solitary deviant but the norm? Is it possible that as the institutions and beliefs of tradition are fashionably denigrated a blue-collar generation gap will open to the Right as well as to the Left? (There is statistical evidence, for example, that Wallace's greatest support within the unions came from people who are between twenty-one and twenty-nine, those, that is, who have the most tenuous association with the liberalism of labor.) Most are politically silent; although SDS has been trying to organize blue-collar high-school students, there are no Mario Savios or Mark Rudds—either of the Right or the Left—among them. At the same time the union leaders, some of them old hands from the Thirties, aren't sure that the kids are following them either. Who speaks for the son of the longshoreman or the Detroit auto worker? What happens if he doesn't get to college? What, indeed, happens when he does?

Vaguely but unmistakably the hopes that a youth-worshiping nation historically invested in its young are becoming threats. We have never been unequivocal about the symbolic patricide of Americanization and upward mobility, but if at one time mobility meant rejection of older (or European) styles it was, at least, done in the name of America. Now the labels are blurred and the objectives indistinct. Just at the moment when a tradition-bound Italian father is persuaded that he should send his sons to college—that education is the only future—the college blows up. At the moment when a parsimonious taxpayer begins to shell out for what he considers an extravagant state university system the students go on strike. Marijuana, sexual liberation, dress styles, draft resistance, even the rhetoric of change become monsters and demons in a world that appears to turn old virtues upside down. The paranoia that fastened on Communism twenty years ago (and sometimes still does) is increasingly directed to vague conspiracies undermining the schools, the family order and discipline. "They're feeding the kids this generation-gap business," says a Chicago housewife who grinds out a campaign against sex education on a duplicating machine in her living room. "The kids are told to make their own decisions. They're all mixed up by situation ethics and open-ended questions. They're alienating children from their own parents." They? The churches, the schools, even the YMCA and the Girl Scouts, are implicated. But a major share of the villainy is now also attributed to "the social science centers," to the apostles of sensitivity training, and to what one California lady, with some embarrassment, called "nude therapy." "People with sane minds are being altered by psychological methods." The current major campaign of the John Birch Society is not directed against Communists in government or the Supreme Court, but against sex education.

(There is, of course, also sympathy with the young, especially in poorer areas where kids have no place to play. "Everybody's got to have a hobby," a South Boston adolescent told a youth worker. "Ours is throwing rocks." If people will join reactionary organizations to protect their children, they will also support others: community-action agencies which help kids get jobs; Head Start parent groups, Boys Clubs. "Getting this place cleaned up" sometimes refers to a fear of young hoods; sometimes it points to the day when there is a park or a playground or when the existing park can be used. "I want to see them grow up to have a little fun.")

Can the Common Man Come Back?

Beneath it all there is a more fundamental ambivalence, not only about the young, but about institutions—the schools, the churches, the Establishment—and about the future itself. In the major cities of the East (though perhaps not in the West) there is a sense that time is against you, that one is living "in one of the few decent neighborhoods left," that "if I can get $125 a week upstate (or downstate) I'll move." The institutions that were supposed to mediate social change and which, more than ever, are becoming priesthoods of information and conglomerates of social engineers, are increasingly suspect. To attack the Ford Foundation (as Wright Patman has done) is not only to fan the embers of historic populism against concentrations of wealth and power, but also to arouse those who feel that they are trapped by an alliance of upper-class Wasps and lower-class Negroes. If the foundations have done anything for the blue-collar worker he doesn't seem to be aware of it. At the same time the distrust of professional educators that characterizes the black militants is becoming increasingly prevalent among a minority of lower-middle-class whites who are beginning to discover that the schools aren't working for them either. ("Are all those new programs just a cover-up for failure?") And if the Catholic Church is under attack from its liberal members (on birth control, for example) it is also alienating the traditionalists who liked their minor saints (even if they didn't actually exist) and were perfectly content with the Latin Mass. For the alienated Catholic liberal there are other places to go; for the lower-middle-class parishioner in Chicago or Boston there are none.

Perhaps, in some measure, it has always been this way. Perhaps none of this is new. And perhaps it is also true that the American lower middle has never had it so good. And yet surely there is a difference, and that is that the common man has lost his visibility and, somehow, his claim on public attention. There are old liberals and socialists—men like Michael Harrington—who believe that a new alliance can be forged for progressive social action:

From Marx to Mills, the Left has regarded the middle class as a stratum of hypocritical, vacillating rear-guarders. There was often sound reason for this contempt. But is it not possible that a new class is coming into being? It is not the old middle class of small property owners and entrepreneurs, nor the new middle class of managers. It is composed of scientists, technicians, teachers, and professionals in the public sector of the society. By education and work experience it is predisposed toward planning. It could be an ally of the poor and the organized workers—or their sophisticated enemy. In other words, an unprecedented social and political variable seems to be taking shape in America.

The American worker, even when he waits on a table or holds open a door, is not servile; he does not carry himself like an inferior. The openness, frankness, and democratic manner which Tocqueville described in the last century persists to this very day. They have been a source of rudeness, contemptuous ignorance, violence—and of a creative self-confidence among great masses of people. It was in this latter spirit that the CIO was organized and the black freedom movement marched.

There are recent indications that the white lower middle class is coming back on the roster of public priorities. Pucinski tells you that liberals in Congress are privately discussing the pressure from the middle class. There are proposals now to increase personal income-tax exemptions from $600 to $1,000 (or $1,200) for each dependent, to protect all Americans with a national insurance system covering catastrophic medical expenses, and to put a floor under all incomes. Yet these things by themselves are insufficient. Nothing is sufficient without a national sense of restoration. What Pucinski means by the middle class has, in some measure, always been represented. A physician earning $75,000 a year is also a working man but he is hardly a victim of the welfare system. Nor, by and large, are the stockholders of the Standard Oil Company or U.S. Steel. The fact that American ideals have often been corrupted in the cause of self-aggrandizement does not make them any less important for the cause of social reform and justice. "As a movement with the conviction that there is more to people than greed and fear," Harrington said, "the Left must . . . also speak in the name of the historic idealism of the United States."

The issue, finally, is not *the program* but the vision, the angle of view. A huge constituency may be coming up for grabs, and there is considerable evidence that its political mobility is more sensitive than anyone can imagine, that all the sociological determinants are not as significant as the simple facts of concern and leadership. When Robert Kennedy was killed last year, thousands of working-class people who had expected to vote for him—if not hundreds of thousands—shifted their loyalties to Wallace. A man who can change from a progressive democrat into a bigot overnight deserves attention.

What Generation Gap?

JOSEPH ADELSON

Can the truth prevail against a false idea whose time has come?

The idea that there is a generation gap is not totally false, perhaps. But it is false enough, false in the sense of being overblown, oversimplified, sentimentalized. This may be too strong a way of putting it. Let us say, then, that the idea of a generation gap is at the least unexamined, one of those notions that seems so self-evident that we yield to it without taking thought, and without qualms about not taking thought.

Once we examine the idea, we find it is almost too slippery to hold. What do we mean by a generation gap? Do we mean widespread alienation between adolescents and their parents? Do we mean that the young have a different and distinctive political outlook? Are we speaking of differences in styles of pleasure-seeking: greater sexual freedom, or the marijuana culture? Or do we simply mean that the young and the old share the belief that there is a significant difference between them, whether or not there is?

These questions—and many others one might reasonably ask—are by no means easy to answer. Few of them can in fact be answered decisively. Nevertheless, enough information has been accumulated during the last few years to offer us some new understanding of the young. As we will see, this evidence contains some surprises; and persuades us to cast a very cold eye on the more simpleminded views about this young generation and its place in our society.

Parents and Children

One definition of generational conflict locates it in rebellion against parental authority, or in the failure of parents and their adolescent youngsters to understand and communicate with each other. (In short, "The Graduate.") On this particular issue, there is, as it happens, abundant evidence, and all of it suggests strongly that there is no extensive degree of alienation between parents and their children. Vern Bengtson, one of the most careful scholars in this area, has collected data from more than 500 students enrolled in three Southern California colleges. About 80 percent of them report generally close and friendly relationships with their parents; specifically, 79 per cent feel somewhat close or very close, 81 per cent regard communication as good, and 78 per cent feel that their parents understand them all or most of the time.

Essentially similar findings have emerged from Samuel Lubell's perceptive studies of college youth. He reports that only about 10 per cent of the students he interviewed were in serious discord with their parents, and there was in most of these cases a long history of family tension. Any clinician working with college-age students would agree; among the rebellious or alienated, we find that their troubles with their families go back a long way and surfaced well before the college years.

In some respects the findings of Bengtson and Lubell are not really surprising. What they do is bring us up to date, and tell us that a long-established line of findings on adolescence continues to be true. A few years ago my colleague Elizabeth Douvan and I studied 3,000 youngsters of 12 to 18, from all regions of the country and all socio-economic levels. We concluded that there were few signs of serious conflict between American adolescents and their parents; on the contrary, we found that it was more usual for their relationships to be amiable.

The recently published study by psychiatrist Daniel Offer—of a smaller group, but using more intensive methods of scrutiny—arrives at much the same conclusion. Incidentally, there is no support for the common belief that the adolescent is hostage to the influence of his friends and turns away from parental guidance. A number of studies, here and abroad, tell us that while peer opinion may carry some weight on trivial issues—taste, clothing and the like—on more central matters, such as career and college choice, it is parental opinion that counts.

Whatever the supposed generation gap may involve, it does not seem to include deep strains between the young and their parents. The idea of the adolescent's family milieu as a kind of *Gotterdämmerung,* as the scene of a cataclysmic struggle between the forces of authority and rebellion, is exaggerated. As Lubell put it: "we found both much less authority and much less rebellion than popularly imagined."

Politics

Those who are convinced that there is a generation gap also tend to identify youth in general with radical or militantly liberal beliefs. Thus, the young are sometimes seen as a New Breed, impatient with the political pieties of the past, less subject to that fatigue and corruption of spirit characteristic of the older generation of voters.

There is indeed a generational element in politics; there always has been. But to identify the young with liberal or left militancy makes sense only from the perspective of the elite university campus. Once we look at the total population of the young a decidedly different picture emerges. We have, for example, a brilliant and revealing analysis of the 1968 election by the University of Michigan's Survey Research Center, based upon 1,600 interviews with a representative national sample of voters. Perhaps the most interesting finding was that the under-30 voter was distinctly over-represented in the Wallace constituency, and that the Wallace movement outside the South drew proportionately more of its strength from younger than from older voters.

Some of the center's commentary on generational influences is worth quoting at length. "One of the most important yet hidden lines of cleavage split the younger generation itself. Although privileged young college students angry at Vietnam and shabby treatment of the Negro saw themselves as sallying forth to do battle against a corrupted and cynical older generation, a more head-on confrontation at the polls, if a less apparent one, was with their own age mates who had gone from high school off to the factory instead of college, and who were appalled by the collapse of patriotism and respect for the law that they saw about them. Outside of the election period, when verbal articulateness and leisure for political activism count most heavily, it was the college share of the younger generation—or at least its politicized vanguard—that was most prominent as a political force. At the polls, however, the game shifts to 'one man, one vote,' and this vanguard is numerically swamped even within its own generation."

To overemphasize the role of generational conflict in politics is to ignore or dismiss what we have learned over the years about the transmission of political sentiments. In the great majority of cases—it seems to average about 75 per cent in most studies—children vote the same party their parents do; it has often been noted that party preference is transmitted to about the same degree as religious affiliation. Political attitudes are also acquired within the family, though generally less strongly than party affiliation; among studies on this matter there is hardly one which reports a negative relationship between parental attitudes and those of their children.

My own research during the last few years has dealt with the acquisition of political values during adolescence, and it is patently clear that the political outlook of the parents, particularly when it is strongly felt, tends to impress itself firmly on the politics of the child. Thus, the most conservative youngster we interviewed was the daughter of a leader of the John Birch Society; the most radical was the daughter of a man who had—in 1965—ceased paying income taxes to the Federal Government in protest against our involvement in Vietnam.

The strongest recent evidence on this subject seems to come from studies of the student radical. These studies make it evident that the "rebellious" student is, for the most part, not rebelling against the politics he learned at home. Radical activists are for the most part children of radical or liberal-left parents; in many instances, their parents are—overtly or tacitly—sympathetic to what their children are doing. (This is shown in the letters written to the press by parents of the students expelled by Columbia and Chicago; the rhetoric of these letters reveals how strong the bond of political sympathy is between the parents and their children. For instance, a letter from a group of Columbia parents states: "We are, of course, concerned about the individual fates of our sons and daughters, but more so with resisting such pressures against a student movement which has done so much to arouse the nation to the gross horrors and injustices prevalent in our country.")

Values

Are the young abandoning traditional convictions and moving toward new moral and ideological frameworks? We hear it said that the old emphasis on personal achievement is giving way to a greater concern with self-realization or with leisure and consumption; that a selfish materialism is being succeeded by a more humanistic outlook; that authority and hierarchy are no longer automatically accepted, and are replaced by more democratic forms of participation; that rationalism is under attack by proponents of sensual or mystical perspectives, and so on.

The most ambitious recent survey on this topic was sponsored by *Fortune* magazine. *Fortune* seems to believe that its findings demonstrate a generation gap and a departure from "traditional moral values" on the part of many of the educated young. A careful look at the survey suggests that it proves neither of these propositions, but only how badly statistics can deceive in a murky area.

The *Fortune* pollsters interviewed a representative sample of 18-to-24-year-olds, dividing them into a non-college group, a traditional college group (largely upward-mobile youngsters interested in education for its vocational advantages), and a so-called "forerunner" group (largely students interested in education as self-discovery and majoring in the humanities and social sciences). Some substantial, though not surprising, differences are found among these groups—the "forerunners" are more liberal politically, less traditional in values, less enchanted about business careers (naturally) than the two other groups. But the findings tell us nothing about a *generation* gap, since the opinions of older people were not surveyed. Nor do they tell us anything about changes in values, since we do not have equivalent findings on earlier generations of the young.

What the findings do tell us (and this is concealed in the way the data are presented, so much so that I have had to recompute the statistics) is, first, that an overwhelming majority of the young—as many as 80 per cent—tend to be traditionalist in values; and, second, that there is a sharp division within the younger generation between, on the one hand, that distinct minority that chooses a liberal education and, on the other, both those who do not go to college and the majority of college students who are vocationally oriented. In brief, the prevailing pattern (of intra-generational cleavage) is quite similar to that which we find in politics.

The *Fortune* poll brings out one interesting thing: many of those interviewed—well over 80 per cent—report that they do not believe that there are great differences in values between themselves and their parents. This is supported by other investigations. Bengtson's direct comparison of college students with their parents demonstrates that they "shared the same general value orientations and personal life goals." He concludes that "both students and parents in this sample are overwhelmingly oriented toward the traditional middle-class values of family and career." From his careful study of normal middle-class high-school boys, Daniel Offer states flatly, "Our evidence indicates that both generations *share the same basic values*" (his italics).

Despite the impressive unanimity of these appraisals, the question of value change should remain an open one. It is hard to imagine that some changes are not taking place, in view of the vast social, economic and technological changes occurring in industrialized countries: the growth of large organizations, shifts in the occupational structure, the rapid diffusion of information, etc., etc. Yet the nature of these changes in values, if any, is by no means evident, and our understanding remains extremely limited.

We simply do not know which areas of values are changing, how rapidly the changes are taking place, which segments of the population they involve, how deeply they run, how stable any of the new values will turn out to be. Many apparent changes in "values" seem to be no more than changes in manners, or in rhetoric.

All in all, the most prudent assessment we can make, on the basis of the evidence we now have, is that no "value revolution" or anything remotely like it is taking place or is in prospect; and that if changes are occurring, they will do so through the gradual erosion, building and shifting of values.

Pleasure

Let us limit ourselves to the two areas of pleasure where generational differences are often held to be present: sex and drugs. Is there a sexual revolution among the young? And has a drug culture established itself as a significant part of youth culture?

Announced about 10 or 15 years ago, the sexual revolution has yet to take place. Like the generation gap itself, it may be more apparent than real. Support for this statement is provided by the Institute for Sex Research at Indiana University, which has just completed a new study, begun in 1967, in the course of which 1,200 randomly selected college students were interviewed. Comparing the findings with those obtained in its study of 20 years ago, the institute reports increasing liberalism in sexual practices but stresses that these changes have been gradual. One of the study's authors states, "There remains a substantial commitment to what can only be called traditional values." Most close students of the sexual scene seem to agree that the trend toward greater permissiveness in the United States probably began back in the nineteen-twenties, and has been continuing since. Sexual attitudes and habits are becoming more liberal—slowly. We are becoming Scandinavians—gradually.

The sexual changes one notes on the advanced campuses are of two kinds. First, there is a greater readiness to establish quasi-marital pairings, many of which end in marriage; these are without question far more common than in the past, and are more often taken for granted. Second, there is a trend, among a very small but conspicuous number of students, toward extremely casual sexuality, sometimes undertaken in the name of sexual liberation. To the clinician, these casual relationships seem to be more miserable than not—compulsive, driven, shallow, often entered into in order to ward off depression or emotional isolation. The middle-class inhibitions persist, and the attempt at sexual freedom seems a desperate maneuver to overcome them. We have a long way to go before the sexually free are sexually free.

As to drugs, specifically marijuana: Here we have, without much question, a sharp difference between the generations. It is a rare citizen over 30 who has had any experience with marijuana, and it is not nearly so rare among the young, particularly those in college. Still, the great majority of youngsters—almost 90 per cent—have had no experience with marijuana, not even to the degree of having tried it once, and, of course, far fewer use it regularly. Furthermore, a strong majority of the young do not believe marijuana should be legalized. What we have here, then, is both a generation gap and (as we have had before) a gap in attitude and experience within the younger generation.

It would be nice if we could keep our wits about us when we contemplate the implications of marijuana for our society. That is hard to do in the presence of hysteria on one side, among those who hold it to be an instrument of the devil, and transcendent rapture on the other, among those who see it as the vehicle and expression of a revolution in values and consciousness. In any case, the drug scene is too new and too fluid a phenomenon for us to foretell its ultimate place in the lives of the young. Drug use has grown rapidly. Will it continue to grow? Has it reached a plateau? Will it subside?

A more interesting question concerns the sociological and ideological factors involved in marijuana use. As marijuana has become more familiar, it has become less of a symbol of defiance and alienation. Lubell points out that just a few years ago the use of marijuana among college students was associated with a liberal or left political outlook; now it has become acceptable and even popular among the politically conservative. From what I have been able to learn, on some campuses and in some suburban high schools drug use is now most conspicuous among the *jeunesse dorée*—fraternity members and the like—where it succeeds or complements booze, and co-exists quite easily with political indifference or reaction and Philistine values. To put it another way, marijuana has not

so much generated a new life style—as Timothy Leary and others had hoped—
as it has accommodated itself to existing life styles.

Is there a generation gap? Yes, no, maybe. Quite clearly, the answer depends
upon the specific issue we are talking about. But if we are talking about a
fundamental lack of articulation between the generations, then the answer is—
decisively—no. From one perspective, the notion of a generation gap is a form of
pop sociology, one of those appealing and facile ideas which sweep through a
self-conscious culture from time to time. The quickness with which the idea has
taken hold in the popular culture—in advertising, television game shows and
semi-serious potboilers—should be sufficient to warn us that its appeal lies in its
superficiality. From another perspective we might say that the generation gap is
an illusion, somewhat like flying saucers. Note: not a delusion, an illusion. There
is something there, but we err in our interpretation of what it is. There *is* something going on among the young, but we have misunderstood it. Let us turn now
to the errors of interpretation which bedevil us when we ponder youth.

Parts and Wholes

The most obvious conceptual error, and yet the most common, is to generalize from a narrow segment of the young to the entire younger generation. With
some remarkable consistency, those who hold that there is a generation gap
simply ignore the statements, beliefs and activities of the non-college young, and
indeed of the ordinary, straight, unturned-on, nonactivist collegian. And the
error goes even beyond this: on the university scene, the elite campus is taken to
stand for all campuses; within the elite university, the politically engaged are
taken to reflect student sentiment in general; and among the politically active,
the radical fraction is thought to speak for activists as a whole.

It is not surprising to come across these confusions in the mass media, given
their understandable passion for simplification of the complex, and their search
for vivid spokesmen of strong positions. Thus, the typical TV special on the
theme, "What Is Happening to Our Youth?", is likely to feature a panel consisting of (1) a ferocious black militant, (2) a feverish member of S.D.S., (3) a
supercilious leader of the Young Americans for Freedom (busily imitating William Buckley), and (4), presumably to represent the remaining 90 per cent, a
hopelessly muddled moderate. But we have much the same state of affairs in the
quality magazines, where the essays on youth are given to sober yet essentially
apocalyptic ruminations on the spirit of the young and the consequent imminent
decline (or rebirth) of Western civilization.

Not too surprisingly, perhaps, the most likely writer of these essays is an
academic intellectual, teaching humanities or the social sciences at an elite university. Hence he is exposed, in his office, in his classes, to far more than the
usual number of radical or hippyesque students. (And he will live in a neighborhood where many of the young adolescents are preparing themselves for such
roles.)

On top of this, he is, like the rest of us, subject to the common errors of social perception, one of which is to overestimate the size of crowds, another to be attracted by and linger upon the colorful and deviant. So he looks out of his office window and sees what seems to be a crowd of thousands engaging in a demonstration; or he walks along the campus, noting that every second male face is bearded. If he were to count—and he is not likely to count, since his mind is teeming with insights—he might find that the demonstration is in hundreds rather than thousands, or that the proportion of beards is nearer one in 10 than one in two. It is through these and similar processes that some of our most alert and penetrating minds have been led astray on the actualities of the young; that is why we have a leading intellectual writing, in a recent issue of a good magazine, that there are "millions" of activist students.

It is not surprising, then, that both the mass media and the intellectual essayists have been misled (and misleading) on the infinite variety of the young: the first are focused upon the glittering surface of social reality, the second upon the darker meanings behind that surface (an art brought to its highest state, and its highest pitch, by Norman Mailer). What *is* surprising, and most discouraging, is that a similar incompleteness of perception dominates the professional literature—that is, technical psychological and sociological accounts of adolescence and youth.

Having attended, to my sorrow, many convocations of experts on the young, I can attest that most of us are experts on atypical fractions of the young: on heavy drug users, or delinquents, or hippies, or the alienated, or dropouts, or the dissident—and, above all, on the more sprightly and articulate youngsters of the upper middle class. By and large, our discourse at these meetings, when it is not clinical, is a kind of gossip: the upper middle class talking to itself about itself. The examples run: my son, my colleague's daughter, my psychoanalytic patient, my neighbor's drug-using son, my Ivy League students. Most of us have never had a serious and extended conversation with a youngster from the working or lower-middle classes. In our knowledge of the young we are, to use Isaiah Berlin's phrase, hedgehogs, in that we know one thing, and know it well, know it deeply, when we also need to be foxes, who know many things less deeply.

What we know deeply are the visibly disturbed, and the more volatile, more conspicuous segments of the upper middle class. These are the youngsters with problems, or with *panache*—makers and shakers, shakers of the present, makers of the future. Their discontents and their creativity, we hear it said, produce the new forms and the new dynamics of our social system. Thus, they allow us to imagine the contours of a hopeful new order of things or, contrariwise, permit us visions of Armageddon.

Perhaps so, but before judging this matter, we would do well to recognize that our narrowness of vision has led us to a distorted view of adolescence and youth. We have become habituated to a conflict model of adolescence—the youngster at odds with the milieu and divided within himself. Now, adolescence is far from being a serene period of life. It is dominated by significant transitions, and like all transitional periods—from early childhood to middle age—it produces more than its share of inner and outer discord. Yet we have become so committed to a view of the young based upon conflict, pathology and volatility—a view appropriate for some adolescents most of the time and for most some of the time—that we have no language or framework for handling conceptually either the sluggish conformity or the effectiveness of adaptation or the generational continuity which characterizes most youngsters most of the time.

Young and Old, New and Old

Another common error is to exaggerate the differences between young and older generations. Differences there are, and always have been. But the current tendency is to assume that anything new, any change in beliefs or habits, belongs to or derives from the country of the young.

This tendency is particularly evident in the realm of politics, especially on the left, where "young" and "new" are often taken to be synonymous. Is this really so? To be sure, the young serve as the shock troops of New Left action. But consider how much of the leadership is of an older generation; as one example, most of the leaders of the New Mobilization—Lens, Dellinger, Dowd and others—are in their forties and fifties. It is even more significant that the key ideologues of radical politics—such men as Marcuse, Chomsky, Paul Goodman— are of secure middle age and beyond. The young have, in fact, contributed little to radical thought, except perhaps to vulgarize it to a degree painful for those of us who can remember a time when that body of thought was intellectually subtle, rich and demanding.

For that matter, is New Left thought really new—that is, a product of the nineteen-sixties? I was dumfounded several weeks ago when I stumbled across a book review I had written in the nineteen-fifties, a commentary on books by Erich Fromm, Lionel Trilling and the then unknown Herbert Marcuse. My review suggested that these otherwise disparate authors were united in that they sensed and were responding to a crisis of liberalism. The optimistic, melioristic assumptions of liberalism seemed to be failing, unable to cope with the alienation and the atavistic revivals produced by technological civilization.

Thus, even in the sunny, sleepy nineteen-fifties a now-familiar critique of American society was already well-established. The seminal ideas, political and cultural, of current radical thought had been set down, in the writings of C. Wright Mills, Marcuse, Goodman and others, and from another flank, in the work of Norman O. Brown, Mailer and Allen Ginsberg. That sense of life out of control, of bureaucratic and technological things in the saddle, of malaise and restlessness were, in the nineteen-fifties, felt only dimly, as a kind of low-grade infection. In the middle and late nineteen-sixties, with the racial explosion in the cities and our involvement in Vietnam, our political and cultural crisis became, or seemed to become, acute.

What I am getting at is that there is no party of the young, no politics indigenous to or specific to the young, even on the radical left. The febrile politics of the day do not align the young against the old, not in any significant way. Rather, they reflect the ideological differences in a polarized nation.

What we have done is to misplace the emphasis, translating ideological conflict into generational conflict. We have done so, I believe, because it suits our various psychological purposes. On the left, one's weakness in numbers and political potency is masked by imagining hordes of radicalized youth, a wave of the future that will transform society. On the right, one can minimize the intense strains in the American policy by viewing it, and thus dismissing it, as merely a youth phenomenon—kid stuff. And for the troubled middle, it may be easier to contemplate a rift between the generations than to confront the depth and degree of our current social discord.

Present and Future

A third error we make is to see the mood of the young—as we imagine that to be—as a forecast of long-term national tendencies. In our anxious scrutiny of youth, we attempt to divine the future, much as the ancients did in their perusal of the entrails of birds. Yet consider how radically the image of the American young has changed within as brief a period as a decade.

Ten years ago, we were distressed by the apparent apathy and conformism of the young, their seeming willingness, even eagerness, to be absorbed into suburban complacency. We were dismayed by the loss of that idealism, that amplitude of impulse, we felt to be the proper mood of the young. By the early nineteen-sixties we were ready to believe that that lost idealism had been regained; the prevailing image then was of the Peace Corps volunteer, whose spirit of generous activism seemed so much in the American grain. And for the last few years we have been held by a view of youth fixed in despair and anger.

It should be evident that these rapid shifts in our idea of the young run parallel to changes in the American mood. As we moved from the quietude of the Eisenhower years, to the brief period of quickened hope in the Kennedy years, to our current era of bitter internal conflict dominated by a hateful war and a fateful racial crisis, so have our images of youth moved and changed. Yet, we were in each of these earlier periods as willing as we are today to view the then current mood of youth, as we saw it, as a precursor of the social future.

The young have always haunted the American imagination, and never more so than in the past two decades. The young have emerged as the dominant projective figures of our culture. Holden Caulfield, Franny Glass, the delinquents of the Blackboard Jungle, the beats and now the hippies and the young radicals—these are figures, essentially of our interior landscape. They reflect and stand for some otherwise silent currents in American fantasy. They are the passive and gentle—Holden, Franny and now the flower children—who react to the hard circumstances of modern life by withdrawal and quiescence; or else they are the active and angry—the delinquents and now the radicals—who respond by an assault upon the system.

In these images, and in our tendency to identify ourselves with them, we can discover the alienation within all of us, old and young. We use the young to represent our despair, our violence, our often forlorn hopes for a better world. Thus, these images of adolescence tell us something, something true and something false, about the young; they may tell us even more about ourselves.

Is America by Nature a Violent Society?

"Lawlessness Is Inherent in the Uprooted"

HANNAH ARENDT

It is highly doubtful that we know anything about the natural character of societies, but it seems evident that a country inhabited by a multitude of ethnic groups cannot even be said to possess that nearest equivalent to natural traits which is called "national character." If "like attracts like" is as natural for human society as that birds of a feather flock together, one could even say that American society is artificial "by nature." Still, it seems true that America, for historical, social and political reasons, is more likely to erupt into violence than most other civilized countries. And yet there are very few countries where respect for law is so deeply rooted and where citizens are so law-abiding.

The reason for this seeming paradox must probably be looked for in the American past, in the experience of establishing law against lawlessness in a colonial country—an experience which culminated, but was not ended, with the foundation of a new body politic and the establishment of a new law of the land in the American Revolution. For it was a similar experience that came into play in the colonization of the continent as well as in the integration of the many waves of immigrants during the last century. Each time the law had to be confirmed anew against the lawlessness inherent in all uprooted people.

I think that another peculiarity of American society is more relevant to the present situation. Freedom of assembly is among the crucial, most cherished and, perhaps, most dangerous rights of American citizens. Everytime Washington is unreceptive to the claims of a sufficiently large number of citizens, the danger of violence arises. Violence—taking the law into one's own hands—is perhaps more likely to be the consequence of frustrated power in America than in other countries.

We have just lived through a period when opposition to our bloody imperialist adventures—voiced first on the campuses, on chiefly moral grounds, and supported by an almost unanimous verdict of highly qualified opinion in the country at large—remained not only without echo but was treated with open contempt by the Administration. The opposition, taught in the school of the powerful and nonviolent civil-rights movement of the early nineteen-sixties, took to the streets, more and more embittered against "the system" as such. The spell was broken, and the danger of violence, inherent in the disaffection of a whole generation, averted, when Senator McCarthy provided in his person the link between the opposition in the Senate and that in the streets. He said himself that he had wanted "to test the system," and the results, though still inconclusive, have been reassuring in some important respects. Not only has popular pressure enforced an at least temporary change in policy: it has also been demonstrated how quickly the younger generation can become dealienated, jumping on this first opportunity not to abolish the system, but to make it work again.

The factor of racism is the only one with respect to which one could speak of a strain of violence so deeply rooted in American society as to appear to be "natural." "Racial violence was present almost from the beginning of the American experience," the splendid Report on Civil Disorders has put it. . . .

In the North, where I think the problem is more acute than in the South, we deal with a group uprooted through recent migration and hence no less lawless than other immigrant groups in their initial stages. Their massive arrival in recent decades has hastened the disastrous disintegration of the big cities, to which they came at a time when the demand for unskilled labor rapidly declined. We all know the consequences, and it is no secret that racist feeling among the urban population is today at an unprecedented high. It is easy to blame the people; it is less easy to admit the fact that, as things are handled now, those who stand most to lose and are expected to pay by far the greatest part of the bill are precisely those groups who have just "made it" and can least afford it. Impotence breeds violence, and the more impotent these white groups feel the greater is the danger of violence.

Just as "power checks power" (Montesquieu) so violence breeds violence. Unlike nationalism, which is normally limited by a territory and therefore admits, in principle at least, the existence of a "family of nations" with equal status for each, racism always insists on absolute superiority over all others. Hence, racism is humiliating "by nature," and humiliation breeds even more violence than sheer impotence.

The Negro violence we are witnessing now is political to the small extent that it is hoped to dramatize justified grievances, to serve as an unhappy substitute for organized power. It is social to the much larger extent that it expresses the violent rage of the poor in an overaffluent society where deprivation is no longer the burden of a majority and hence no longer felt as a curse from which only the few are exempt. Not even the violence for its own sake, preached by extremists—as distinguished from the rioting and looting for the sake of whisky, color television and pianos—is revolutionary, because it is not a means to an end: No one dreams of being able to seize power. If it is to be a contest of violence, does anybody doubt who is going to win?

The real danger is not violence, black or white, but the possibility of a white backlash of such proportions as to be able to invade the domain of regular government. Only such a victory at the polls could stop the present policy of integration. Its consequences would be unmitigated disaster—the end, perhaps not of the country, but certainly of the American Republic.

"What Is 'Natural' Today Need Not Be Natural Tomorrow"

ST. CLAIR DRAKE

However repulsive and shocking H. Rap Brown's quip may seem—"Violence is as American as cherry pie"—his motive in saying it must not obscure the fact that he was telling it like it is.

The American white-collar set have so little direct experience with violence that it is difficult for them to conceive of it as an ever-present reality—or possibility—in a person's daily life, although they know that the Indians were herded onto the reservations by force, that violence was used both to keep Negroes in slavery and to free them, and that assault and battery, rape and murder occur every now and then. The older people in the labor movement know something of the historic confrontations between trade unionists and the forces of law and order, though younger workers know almost nothing of the great labor struggles of the past. Negroes understand the reality of violence better than most Americans, for most of them have witnessed it in varied forms, even if they have not experienced it. But all Americans need to face the fact that American society—as compared with some others in the world—is a *very* violent society. Self-delusion is self-defeating. We can never lower the level of violence unless we admit that it is omnipresent and understand the forces that generate it.

To admit that "American society is by nature a violent society" is not to succumb to any kind of defeatist determinism, for the intensity of violence has been reduced in some areas of the national life over the past century and its patterning has undergone constant change. The episodes so vividly described in Louis Adamic's "Dynamite, The Story of Class Violence in America," could not possibly occur today. And the barbaric ritual of lynching that used to claim the lives of more than a hundred black men a year disappeared before World War II. The crucial centers of violence shift their locus, and more covert and sophisticated forms replace the cruder types of torture and murder. But violence has always functioned in America as a direct or indirect force for changing the status quo as well as for preserving it—and its practitioners seem never to feel guilty or apologetic.

The only interest groups in America which do not have a tradition of using violence to protect themselves from aggressors or to achieve group goals are the Afro-Americans. Yet the segregated Negro communities in America have been characterized by a high rate of *interpersonal* violence for the past hundred years—fighting among family members, brawls incident to drinking and gambling, mayhem and occasional homicide.

These are traits associated with the culture of poverty everywhere, induced by insecurity, frustration, overcrowding and inadequate incomes. Since twice as many families are below the poverty line among Negroes as among whites, a higher level of such violence is to be expected. It was characteristic of Irish, Italian and Polish communities in the United States before World War I, but for Negroes in the South during the same period the incidence of such violence was higher, because of the additional pressures placed upon them by an oppressive white society and the tendency of courts to be less concerned about the violence of Negroes toward one another than about aggression against white people.

From the end of World War II till 1964, the Northern ghettos were relatively quiet except for this interior violence. Meanwhile, the black people of the South were dismantling the entire caste structure in an amazing exhibition of well-organized nonviolent social action, undeterred by police dogs, water hoses and cattle prods. The white die-hard segregationists eventually turned to terrorism and assassination, ultimately taking the life of Martin Luther King himself.

In 1964, the "Harlem pattern" of rioting that had emerged more than two decades before was repeated in several cities, as some of the ghetto dwellers began to focus their aggression outward, venting their fury upon "Whitey's" property, though not his person. The incidents were usually set off as unplanned, spontaneous protests against a specifically vicious form of American violence that has rubbed the sores raw among ghetto dwellers—police brutality. But it is the stores of white men who do business in the black community that suffer the consequences of black wrath.

This type of violence has escalated, culminating in the arson and looting in more than 100 cities when Dr. King was assassinated. There is an ominous movement within the black masses away from the nonviolent Afro-American tradition and into the mainstream of the *American* tradition—of Shays's Rebellion and barn-burners; of the Molly Maguires and the Ku Klux Klan; of the draft riots of 1863 and John Brown's raid at Harpers Ferry. The black militants who have repudiated nonviolence and are making a bid for mass leadership will inevitably draw upon this tradition—as well as upon Frantz Fanon's "Wretched of the Earth," which is now their Bible.

Counterescalation will not eliminate these newly emergent patterns of ghetto violence. However, the transformation of life in the ghetto can—or, alternatively, the dissolution of the ghetto. An answer to labor's needs, not the use of the Army, ended labor violence in America. What is "natural" today need not be natural tomorrow.

We Can Claim No Special Gift for Violence

CLIFFORD GEERTZ

In a period which has seen the German massacre of the Jews, the communal horrors of Indian partition, the convulsive destructiveness of the last days of *L'Algerie Française,* the mass executions accompanying the Indonesian change of regime, the terrible civil wars in Nigeria and the Congo, and the wild riots in Sharpesville, it is difficult for the hardiest celebrant of The American Way of Life to claim for his country any special gift for violence. We are, it turns out, a people like any other. There is nothing particularly distinctive about the way we destroy one another.

The notion that "violence is as American as cherry pie" is one more cliché which we invoke to prevent our seeing our situation for what it is. Vague references to the frontier tradition, to the unsettledness of American life, to our exploitive attitude toward nature, or to our "youthfulness" as a nation provide us with prefabricated "explanations" for events we, in fact, not only do not understand, but do not want to understand. Easy generalizations about the sadism of motion pictures, comic books or prizefighting have the same effect: they permit us to avoid talking of matters about which we don't know what to say by allowing us to talk of ones about which we know only too much. There are many ways to evade issues, and for the educated classes (the uneducated ones have other devices) pop sociology, pop anthropology, pop psychology and pop history are among the best.

"Why was John Kennedy assassinated? Detroit burned? Martin Luther King murdered?" "Because America is by nature a violent society." Moliere's Doctor-in-Spite-of-Himself, explaining that the reason opium puts you to sleep is that it has dormitive powers, could hardly do better.

The fact is that the present state of domestic disorder in the United States is not the product of some destructive quality mysteriously ingrained in the substance of American life. It is a product of a long sequence of particular events whose inter-connections our received categories of self-understanding are not only inadequate to reveal but are designed to conceal. We do not know very well what kind of society we live in, what kind of history we have had, what kind of people we are. We are just now beginning to find out, the hard way; and the grasping at comprehensive self-characterizations, even unflattering ones, is but an indication that we do not want to learn too much about ourselves too quickly. Better to be left with familiar generalities, self-denunciatory if need be, than to go into the details of the matter and risk the even more frightening discovery that we don't know what is happening to us at all.

The risk is real enough, but I do not see how we can avoid running it. As the disorder grows, glib references to America's bloody heritage are not going to help much, if only because everybody else's heritage is bloody too, and we are going to have to find some more novel and, let us hope, more useful things to say about ourselves than that we are the spiritual descendants of Billy the Kid, John Brown, and Bonnie and Clyde.

There are many things which must be done if this country is to find its way out of the morass into which we have allowed it to drift. But not the least important—nor the least painful—is to clear the air of half-truths.

The Cold Violence of the Self-Righteous Is the Worst Kind

PAUL GOODMAN

There are two strains of violence in the American tradition that are psychologically and institutionally distinct and must be differently evaluated. The first is the violence of a dissenting, anarchic, pioneer disposition, brashly enterprising, jealous of its freedoms, and raw in history and culture. Brooking no interference, it may impatiently kill opposition. This is the strain of American Populism, where sovereignty finally resides in the general will rather than the laws; some of our best moments of constitutional growth have occurred by popular mutiny with fringes of lawlessness and violence, like the labor movement, the agrarian movement, abolitionism, the recent movement against the Vietnam war. Institutionally, it is the strain of absolute freedoms in the Bill of Rights—rights to speech, to assembly, to bearing arms. Needless to say, willful people can misinterpret the general will. And, of course, anarchic impatience can be senseless, as in the murder of Lincoln or Martin Luther King.

The problem is how to tame this strain of violence without losing the libertarian and equalitarian energy that it expresses. Our American violence of this kind is especially tragic because, as an uncultured people, we often turn on what is excellent, unique, and therefore insulting. I do not see any solution here except our slow cultivation of respect for the sacredness of life, and toleration, if not respect, for the eccentrically excellent. But, like Jefferson, I believe that we will best cultivate thinking citizens, not by imposing "law and order," but by encouraging even more popular initiative, disobedience and self-determination, however risky and arduous this path may be.

The second strain of American violence, however, has been and is far more virulent, and in my opinion it has no redeeming features. This is the violence of a self-righteous, callous, conformist and domineering majority that regards those who stand in the way, or do not shape up, as not quite persons, and does not hesitate to exterminate them. So we slew the Indians, held the Africans in slavery, exploited later immigrants, and now impose our empire on the various gooks and niggers of the world. I do not think this is properly called "racism," which is a form of paranoia. It is worse; it is squeamishness and pettiness to the point of dehumanization.

The arrogance of the powerful is not, of course, peculiar to America—think of the Romans and the British when they bore the white man's burden and, domestically, the *anciens regimes* of France and Russia. But we have immensely greater technology for mischief, and our half-educated suburbanism is unusually dangerous. The contrast is poignant between the technological brutality that we gloat about and the natural generosity that we also have as free and outgoing folk.

Self-righteous conformity is always grounded in anxiety, the need to blot out any threat to the conceit of one's own perfection; and this produces a cold, obliterating violence. It is appalling to notice in opinion polls how it is just those with the most years of schooling and the insecure *petits bourgeois* who want to bomb Hanoi, use nuclear weapons, and arm the police with tanks and Chemical Mace. There is a stern repression of feelings of flesh and blood in the interests of self-image and abstractions, like Law and Order. Lacking in empathy, these people cannot understand that, to the dispossessed, Law and Order mean precisely the run-around they have been getting.

Cold violence is not Wild West or berserk. It was probably a raw and bigoted man who killed Dr. King, but it will be by mean-spirited calculation that there will be a massacre this summer. Our frontier violence causes occasional tragedies, but the cold violence of organization men, technicians and bureaucrats slowly destroys children in schools, destroys Bentre to save it—and may blow up the world. A hundred years ago, the Ku Klux Klan grew out of an atmosphere of war and puritanic squeamishness, and we may well repeat the phenomenon.

In this process, those who are disregarded as not quite persons, who are treated brutally and who fear, not unjustifiedly, that they may be simply exterminated, desperately lash out with fire and riot, destruction and self-destruction. This more realistically threatens the self-righteous and domineering, and there is a downward spiral.

It was to interrupt exactly this spiral that Gandhi, A. J. Muste and Martin Luther King devised the method of popular non-violent confrontation. It is a way of forcing the smug and powerful to recognize the existence of other people, and thereby to rediscover themselves as human beings rather than automata. It personalizes conflict and makes possible the re-establishment of community, since in the end we must all live together. If this method is not "natural" to Americans, we had better learn it anyway, as second nature, for in the overcentralized and wrongly technologized conditions of modern times there is no other way of coping with cold violence.

Yet I do not grant that the method is un-American. Our Populism has always had only fringes of violence. Our courts have a spotty but pretty good record of defending protest. We have a fairly strong revulsion against authoritarian and militarist measures. The slow but majestic rise of popular opposition to the Vietnam war has certainly been impressive.

As in all revolutionary situations, there is a dilemma in our forward motion toward the profound changes necessary to meet profoundly new conditions. Disadvantaged people have the requisite revolutionary drive, but since they have no stake or say, their movements are taken over by demagogic dictators. Entrenched affluent people become narrow and reactionary and stubbornly have recourse to authoritarian repression. Both groups are anomic, have lost their sense of the commonweal, and indeed their common sense. The question is whether or not the American tradition, a tradition of constitution-making by a unique combination of assembly, protest, sporadic violence and legislative change, is still viable. At its best, its genius has been to produce new citizens precisely by the revolutionary process.

"It Is Dangerous to Raise up People's Hopes and Then Dash Them down"

MICHAEL HARRINGTON

Let me begin with an accurate cliché: The American experience has been, and is, particularly violent.

In the beginning, there were the vigilante justice of the frontier, the genocidal campaigns against the Indians, the restless mobility of a society in which many men asserted their identity rather than inheriting it and a gun was called The Great Equalizer. Later, after the West was pacified, the killing took new forms. The labor history of the United States is probably the bloodiest to be found in an industrialized nation and the most recent massacre, at Republic Steel on Memorial Day, 1937, is only 31 years behind us. I sometimes think that this intensity of the American class struggle is a function of the relative weakness of the American class consciousness. Workers and bosses did not confront one another as members of cohesive classes with distinct traditions but as egalitarian individuals in a grudge fight.

Our legacy of violence persists to the present day. Until the very recent changes in our censorship laws, the contrast between French and American policy in this area was most revealing. In Paris, young people were forbidden to see our gory films but permitted to view nudity; in New York, we were appalled by naked bodies and completely tolerant of mayhem.

After World War II, a number of factors gave new impetus to this American trait. The society was becoming almost completely urbanized, and traditional institutions, like the family and the church, cracked under the strain. At the same time, the maturing of the postwar baby boom vastly increased the crime-prone age group of 18 to 24. But, as in almost all things American, the violence provoked by this rapid change and ethical incertitude hurt some people more than others. More precisely, the poor—above all, the black poor packed into deteriorating ghettos—were the chief victims.

Crimes against the person, the President's Commission on Law Enforcement demonstrated a little more than a year ago, occur most often in the impoverished central city and least often in the affluent suburbs. This is part of the routine violence which this society visits upon its worst-off. As long as it stays in the ghetto, it is ignored; when it threatens the white middle class, it becomes a national problem.

But this everyday brutality of slum life, which grows out of poverty and despair, is not to be confused with riots. For the riots are a communal expression of the ghetto's anguish rather than individual tragedies induced by social conditions. These risings, the Kerner Commission documented, are not made by the most destitute but by young people, often employed in dead-end jobs, who see the society moving away from them despite their hard work. The Government bears a responsibility for this angry disenchantment, for Washington has, in recent years, promised boldly and performed timidly. The "unconditional" war on poverty was proclaimed more than four years ago; yet last January the Council of Economic Advisors announced that there had been an increase in substandard housing in the central cities. It is dangerous to raise up people's hopes and then dash them down.

To complicate matters further, there is not even an easy way to "buy off" these riots. For as people begin to make gains, they do not become satisfied and complacent, but rather, quite often, more demanding. It should not be a surprise that riots erupted in Detroit and New Haven with their socially-conscious municipal administrations. It is precisely when people are making progress, but not as fast as they want, that they explode.

Finally, there is the assassin, the man who kills a John F. Kennedy or a Martin Luther King. In times of extraordinary change, like ours, there is always the possibility of a paranoid response: Unable to understand the kaleidoscopic facts, a man sees in them the occult pattern of a conspiracy that justifies killing a deceitful leader. This psychology is most often met on the political right but, as Oswald may show, it has its left-wing variants as well. This demented vision can possess an isolated individual or it can inspire a terrorist group or even movement (Europeans recognize only the politically conscious, organized forms of the disease; they do not understand that Americans are as individualistic about their psychoses as about anything else).

If my analysis is correct, much of the violence in this society is unnecessary. If the slums were abolished within 5 to 10 years there would likely be a marked decrease in the commonplace homicides, rapes and assaults which the poor are driven to inflict upon one another. If the turbulent change in American society could be democratically subjected to social control there would perhaps be less incitement to paranoia. And if the nation actually honored its promises the disillusionment which brings people to riot could be wiped out.

With so many complex variables involved, it would be foolish to suggest simple solutions. Yet one might well ponder an incident from the life and times of Dr. King. In Montgomery during the bus boycott there were no special sermons on personal conduct, yet there was a marked decrease in crime among Negroes. The people had discovered a dignity and purpose within themselves and by changing their society they changed themselves. What the Montgomery Improvement Association could do, the United States of America could try to do.

"Spontaneous, Sporadic and Disorganized"

RICHARD HOFSTADTER

There is a small semantic trap in asking whether America is "by nature" a violent society. "By nature" suggests the possibility of an unchangeable national character. In this I do not believe. But I do think that America, by history and by habit, has been a violent society.

Americans seem to me to show a surprising tolerance of violence and a remarkably passive acceptance of the probability that it will recur. The feebleness of our efforts at gun control, even in the face of the grave crisis that is upon us, is an illustration of this passivity. But the distinctive thing about American violence is that it has been spontaneous, sporadic and disorganized. Traditionally, Americans were always strongly anti-militarist. What this meant was not that they had a penchant for pacifism but simply that they did not like standing armies—that they were against *institutional* militarism.

Again, it has long seemed to me that the case of the American labor movement is quite pertinent to this theme. As the laboring classes of the industrial world go, ours has been relatively lacking in class-conscious militancy, but no national labor history is so heavily marked by violent struggles in which lives and property were destroyed.

Race has always provided a background for violent conflict, whether in Indian wars, slave insurrections, lynchings or race riots. The race riots of 1919 were as formidable, though not as numerous, as the ghetto riots we have experienced in the last few years. The week-long Chicago riot of 1919, one of a number in the post-war period, left 15 whites and 23 Negroes dead, and 537 injured. The hiatus in major riots that occurred between the Detroit, Harlem and Los Angeles riots of 1943 and the riots of 1964 may have caused us to forget the frequency of this kind of violence in our history. But we are unlikely to forget it so readily again.

The historical catalogue of American violence is a formidable one. Mob action was already a force of some importance in the political life of colonial America. It goes on from there: a number of fitful rebellions, the long, ruthless struggle with the Indians, our slave insurrections, our filibustering expeditions, our burned convents and mobbed abolitionists and lynched Wobblies, our Homesteads, Pullmans and Patersons, our race lynchings, race riots and ghetto riots, our organized gangsterism, our needless wars.

There seems to be more truth than we care to admit in the famous dictum of D. H. Lawrence that (I am quoting from memory) "the essential American soul is hard, isolate, stoic and a killer." It exists, oddly enough, along with a remarkable tenderness about life under certain circumstances. It also exists along with a great readiness to declare ourselves for law and order, to admonish against violence, so long as we are not expected to do anything about it. We have, now, a mountain of fresh sermons against violence, but any zealot, any maniac, can still buy a gun if he has the price. This is one of the sacred rights of American manhood, and it will be hard to give it up, even after we have suffered within the span of a few years the murders of two cherished public men, and even after the black nationalists, in *their* quest for manhood, have started to take their cue from the whites.

Our Society Is Violent Not by Nature but by Structure

THOMAS F. PETTIGREW

Three days after the assassination of Dr. King, the National Rifle Association opened its annual meetings. Worried that the murder had "dramatically changed the emotional atmosphere" concerning gun controls, the executive vice president unashamedly made his position clear: "We oppose restrictions on the right of every American to purchase and own firearms."

This is more than a Washington gun lobbyist talking. The "right of every American" to possess instruments of violence is thought by many to be guaranteed under the Second Amendment of the Bill of Rights, though the limitation of the provision to "a well-regulated militia" is conveniently ignored.

America is complex, comprising many contradictions. But evidence abounds that, among other characterizations, it is a violent society.

Consider a sampling of the evidence. We were one of the few societies to countenance lynchings by the thousands. We routinely arm our police, an uncommon world practice. We still inflict capital punishment, even for nonhomicidal crimes. We prominently display violence, especially firearm violence, in our mass media and literature, with killers from Jesse James to Clyde Barrow often the heroes. We have a long and bloody history of mass riots, beside which present-day Negro rioting pales in comparison. And our record of assassinations of national leaders speaks for itself.

Homicide data document the pervasiveness of America's violence. Our rate is more than five deaths annually per 100,000 people. While some Latin-American nations have higher rates, the U.S. rate is twice that of Chile. The highest reported rate in Europe, Finland's, is less than half our rate. And the U.S. figure is roughly eight times that of England and Wales, and four times that of Japan, Australia, New Zealand and nearby Canada. Though these data are imprecise, such differences in magnitude are meaningful and startling.

Prevalent homicide in America is even more remarkable in view of the trend throughout the world for suicide and homicide to be inversely related. When suicide is high, as in such prosperous countries as Switzerland and Sweden, homicide is low. And when homicide is high, as in such poor countries as Nicaragua and Guatemala, suicide is low. But there are exceptions. Norway is low in both. The United States is relatively high in both, suggesting increased aggression expressed both inwardly and outwardly. . . .

A striking difference from Switzerland and Sweden is that our national wealth is not as evenly distributed. Thus, one hypothesis is that our unique pattern of sharp rates of both homicide and suicide is a result of large segments of poverty surrounded by great affluence.

Facile explanations of American violence as a simple legacy of the frontier require qualification. It is true that Latin-American countries, with their own frontier traditions, yield far higher rates than that of Spain. Yet Canada and Australia, with modest homicide rates, also have frontier origins. Clearly, our pattern is a product of particular circumstances, some of which are suggested by factors underlying the elevated homicide and aggravated assault rates of both white and Negro Southerners.

John Hope Franklin, in his book *The Militant South*, holds that the South had a developed violent tradition in the early 19th century, a tradition continued from frontier days by slavery and a restricted economy. He cites the region's greater use of firearms, dueling, vigilante groups, local militia and military training and titles during this period. And W. J. Cash shows how the Civil War further impeded the erosion of frontier traits and maintained the romantic, individualistic and violent "hell of a fellow" as a valued personality type.

Why, then, have Northern, rather than Southern, cities been struck hardest by recent race riots? In addition to greater fear of white reprisal, there is greater social control, especially from churches and extended kinship, in Negro communities in the South. And there are contrasting moods and expectations between Negro Southerners and Northerners. At least until the wanton murder of Dr. King, Negroes in the South held more hope for positive change and witnessed more actual improvement. But time runs out. Significantly, Atlanta, the most Northernlike city of the region, witnessed the first Southern riot in the modern motif last year. More may soon follow.

"Is America by nature a violent society?" More precisely, it is a violent society by structure—through its traditions and laws. We can begin to overcome our violent past by passage of the minimal gun legislation at present before the Congress; ultimately, we need uniform gun registration and sharp restrictions on gun sales over the counter as well as through the mails. We can lower our high homicide rates and prevent the assassination of our national leaders in part by fashioning modern firearms laws consistent with modern urban society.

"We Are Slowly Growing Less Uncivilized"

DAVID RIESMAN

In terms of liking cruelty and barbaric spectacle, America was less violent in the last century than many other countries, but in comparison with developments in other industrial societies, the process of pacification has taken longer, and remains incomplete. In the 19th century, we fought (apart from Indian skirmishes) four nondefensive wars: the Wars of 1812 and the Mexican War, both expansionist in aim; the Civil War, perhaps the most murderous in history up to that time; and the Spanish-American War (which was in turn followed by the guerrilla war in the Philippines, a precursor in some respects of Vietnam). Yet we are not so violent and so expansionist that we do not attempt to interpret our wars as defensive; both North and South in the Civil War saw the other side as bent on the destruction of their institutions.

As individuals and as a nation we tend to react to attack, or what we define as attack, with unmeasured violence, as we did in the mass bombing of German and Japanese cities, and the demand for unconditional surrender. In domestic affairs, our violence is distinctly uneven in distribution. Our young men learn early to be cowards about giving any sign of cowardice, and this means—particularly in the South and in the lower classes, but not only there—an outlook toward personal affront less fierce than that which Latin Americans call *machismo,* the cult of masculine prowess, but a somewhat subdued version of it: a fear of being thought calculating, prudent and unaggressive.

But in the more affluent and industrial sections—for example, among college students—there is more suicide than homicide. In the poorer parts of the country, notably in the Deep South, the reverse is true, among blacks as well as whites.

In social-class terms, there is a patrician, ascetic nationalism which is not personally violent but which encourages a patriotic belief in national honor which can lead to vicarious magnanimity or bellicosity, as in Theodore Roosevelt, Gen. Douglas MacArthur or John F. Kennedy. Throughout the society, but more common in the less-educated, are a hatred and fear of complexity, a liking for "action," which can become explosive either in personal or group conduct—and of course there are always available enough leaders from the educated to legitimate the violence of the less articulate.

Yet, current events to the contrary, I think we are slowly growing less uncivilized. Our large organizations, including the Army, demand cooperative people, and the patrician *machismo* of a General MacArthur, or its plebeian equivalent in a Gen. Curtis LeMay, is infrequent. Our wars of this century have been fought with decreasing hysteria and chauvinism. We learn much more today than in the past, thanks to the mass media, about the violence that does exist, and our highbrow arts tend to regard it romantically, but on the whole we are more sensitive to it, and like it less. However, we are still sufficiently anarchic as a people (we term this "individualism" and prize it) severely to restrict the powers of the Government in restraining us. (An example is the contempt toward our steadily less vindictive police among radicals and many educated people, as well as among the oppressed.)

Violence in America has been no one's monopoly. Marcus Cunliffe notes in a recent issue of *Commentary* that the Presidents who have been shot, or shot at, have been on the whole the strong and highly visible ones, targets for resentful white failures.

While blacks once confined their violence almost exclusively to their own area and to fellow blacks, now the blacks have gained enough self-confidence to take part in the democratic process and to begin to spread the violence around, although still with more rhetoric than vengeful assault, and, as well, more prone to attacks on property, symbolic and often festive, rather than on whites as such. One might even say that the relative restraint of most Negroes following Dr. King's assassination (notably in the dignity of the funeral itself) may be seen, given the provocation (and the rhetorical escalation that may substitute for, as well as promote, violence), as a tentative, and of course not irreversible, sign of the general decline of violence.

With the socially uncontrolled mechanization of farming, many poor blacks and whites with minimal educations have been uprooted from the Southern *machismo*-prone culture and thrown with no support and limited acculturation into the cities of the North, where, particularly if black, they must fend for themselves. This again reflects the lack of a strong national authority (save in foreign affairs) to move toward standardization of educational, farming, housing and other opportunities throughout the country and toward control of those technologies by which violence can become long-range, massive and imitable.

Our social fabric, as the Civil War might have taught us, is precarious. No other large industrial society has substituted color and ethnicity for social class as a basis of stratification and hence of tension. Our egalitarianism, which licenses verbal and sometimes actual killing of the prominent as well as the nameless, has brought us many economic and cultural triumphs; but it also means that our transition to a society both more evenly pacific and less unequal is likely to be long and painful. Martin Luther King sought to train Americans in the taxing discipline of nonviolent and inventive coercion. If we fail to distinguish violence from forceful pressures for change, and if we fail to appreciate the depth of what we are up against in ourselves and our history, and hence become despairing, ambivalent efforts at repression are likely to fail, and we may come to speak of the War between the States as Civil War I.

"Race Prejudice Is Itself a Form of Violence"

C. VANN WOODWARD

The phrase "by nature" implies an assessment of national character, the imputation of qualities assumed to be innate, deep-rooted, historic, fatefully ineluctable. Anyone who attempts such an exercise might ponder the success of attempts to capture the distinctiveness of English character in such phrases as Elizabethan, Puritan, Restorationist, Georgian, Victorian, Edwardian—and on to Swinging London. Over the centuries, American character has probably presented to the world as great a variety of conflicting images as historic England— puritanic and hedonistic, idealistic and materialistic, peaceful and warlike, isolationist and interventionist, conformist and individualistic, consensus-minded and conflict-prone.

I would say that America is part of an international culture of violence to which we have made distinctive contributions. The nations belonging to this culture differ much in the style and character as well as in the quality of violence they contribute. In addition to her obvious contributions to the technology and weaponry of violence, America might claim an innovative role in the style and variety of violence. Henry James described the business scene of his time as the "boundless ferocity of battle." Labor struggles in America have set international records of violence. Racial conflict, so far, has not. The brutality of success-at-any-price, however, the national cult of "making it," the escalation in verbal and literary violence, and the progress of mass media in communicating violence owe much to American know-how. This is not to deny to other countries—Germany, Russia, China, Indonesia and India, for example—their legitimate claims to distinctive contributions in both style and quantity of violence.

While assessments of national violence make sense only in comparative terms, it is a mistake to overlook striking internal variations in the character and amount of violence. For example, the homicide rate for blacks is far higher than among whites in all regions of the country, while the Negro suicide rate is only about one-third that for whites. Yet in spite of the low suicide rate, black violence is in another sense largely self-inflicted—in the sense that black people are its main victims. As Malcolm X so graphically illustrated in his *Autobiography,* the principal victim of "crime in the streets" is the Negro. The same is true of the ghetto riots.

Granting the significance of internal variations in violence, one should never overlook some national differences of vital importance. Obviously there is much in American culture and environment that tolerates, encourages, and even rewards violent behavior. As appallingly common as acts of violence are, however, they are mainly the deeds of individuals. Where they are the work of groups, they are most often "spontaneous," done in "the heat of passion." Conspiracy, ideology, religion and calculation have had relatively small parts.

So far, America, apart from the War for Southern Independence, has escaped great holocausts of internal violence. There is nothing in her record to compare with the political bloodbath in Russia before the Second World War, the horrors of genocide in Germany during the war, and the tragic mass killings between the Islamic and Hindu people of India after the war. The corpses in each country ran into the millions. More recently the domestic bloodbaths in Indonesia, Sumatra and Borneo have reckoned their corpses in the hundreds of thousands.

Race prejudice is itself a form of violence, and its expression is now the greatest threat of a cataclysmic and hitherto foreign scale of violence in America. Race riots are not new to America. The worst occurred in New York City in 1863, a week after the Battle of Gettysburg. The number killed was never known, but the most reliable estimate is about 70. No one of the riots from Watts to the present has claimed so many lives. The 125 cities that suffered disturbances in the week after Martin Luther King's assassination counted 43 dead. These killings are a disgrace to our country—but they are not numbered in the hundreds, the thousands, or the millions.

No special providence spares America from such an escalation. It is a source of wonder that in the many opportunities for tipping the scale from race riot to race war the tipping point has not been reached. There will be more opportunities.

It is obvious that we are going to have to live with racism and violence for some time to come. It is also clear that violence will continue to figure in foreign as well as in domestic disputes. We do not have to abandon hope of diminishing violence in both areas in order to acknowledge the desperate importance of preventing escalation to the holocaust stage in either.

American Character and Foreign Policy

GABRIEL A. ALMOND

Attitudes and opinions toward foreign policy questions are not only to be understood as responses to objective problems and situations, but as conditioned by culturally imposed qualities of character. These largely unconscious patterns of reaction and behavior strongly influence the perception, selection, and evaluation of political reality. At the level of mass opinion these "psycho-cultural" characteristics condition patterns of thought and mood on foreign policy problems. At the elite level they affect patterns of policy-making.

In order to speculate intelligently about the influence of these basic traits on foreign policy, it is first necessary to examine and analyze the most important interpretations of the "American character." Before specific judgment about the effect of these qualities on American foreign policy attitudes becomes possible, it is first necessary to discover what qualities Americans are alleged to have. . . .

In the systematic inventory which follows we have made an effort to include only those observations which have continually recurred and those which seem to have an inherent plausibility, recognizing that the criterion of "plausibility" is a purely subjective one.

1. General Value Orientation

The characteristic American value orientation would appear to consist of the following interrelated traits.

a. The degree of atomization in the United States is perhaps greater than in any other culture. The American is primarily concerned with "private" values, as distinguished from social-group, political, or religious-moral values. His concern with private, worldly success is his most absorbing aim. In this regard it may be suggested by way of hypothesis that in other cultures there is a greater stress on corporate loyalties and values and a greater personal involvement with political issues or with other-worldly religious values.

b. The "attachment" of the American to his private values is characterized by an extreme degree of competitiveness. He views himself and his family as in a state of competition with other individuals and families for success and achievement. American culture tends to be atomistic rather than corporate, and the pressure of movement "upward," toward achievement, is intense. Here again a hypothesis might be proposed that in other cultures individual competition for success tends to be more localized within specific classes or regions, tends to be subordinated to, or assimilated in, political competition, and tends to be muted by religious conceptions of life.

c. The American views himself and his family as in a state of competition with other individuals and families for values which are largely "material" in character. What he appears to want are the material evidences of success—money, position, and the consumer-goods of the moment. While the stress is toward money, or what money can buy, the important thing is not the money itself, but the sense of accomplishment or fulfillment which it gives. This sense of accomplishment rests on matching and exceeding the material standard of community and social class; it requires external approval and conformity. Because of the stress in the American value system on having what others want, and because of the great emphasis on the elaboration of material culture, the American tends to be caught up in an endless race for constantly changing goals—the "newest" in housing, the "latest" in locomotion, the most "fashionable" in dress and appearance. This love of innovation, improvement, and change tends to be confined to the material culture. Attitudes toward human and social relations tend to be more conservative. By way of hypothetical comparison it may be said that in other cultures the criteria of accomplishment are more stable. Religious salvation and political resentment provide greater consolation for the poor and the failures. The material culture tends to be hemmed in by tradition. The criteria of achievement have a more stable subjective basis in the sense of craftsmanship, esthetic and intellectual subtlety, and the fulfillment of social and religious routines.

d. There are certain derivative elements of this general value orientation which call for comment. First, intense individualistic competitiveness, in which the primary aim is to get more of what other people want, produces diffuse hostile tension and general apprehension and anxiety, which pervades every aspect of the culture including the competing unit itself, the family. The fear of failure and the apprehension over the hostility which is involved in one's relations with other persons produce on the one hand an extraordinary need for affection and reassurance, and on the other, an extraordinary tendency to resort to physiological and spiritual narcosis. In other words, as a consequence of being impelled by cultural pressure toward relationships in which one is aggressively pitted against others, the resulting unease and apprehension are characteristically mitigated by demands for external response, attention, and warmth, or by resort to escapism. Thus an excessive concern with sexuality, an excessive resort to alcohol, and, what is uniquely American form of narcosis of the soul—the widespread addiction to highly stimulating mass entertainment, the radio, movies, comics, and the like—provide culturally legitimate modes of discharging hostility and allaying anxiety.

Thus, by way of summary, the value orientation of the American tends to be atomistic rather than corporate, worldly rather than unworldly, highly mobile rather than traditional, compulsive rather than relaxed, and externally directed rather than autonomous. Needless to say, these are presented as hypothetical tendencies, which are supported only by an inadequate and quite heterogeneous body of evidence.

2. Value Expectations

The American is an optimist as to ends and an improviser as to means. The riches of his heritage and the mobility of his social order have produced a generally euphoric tendency, that is, the expectation that one can by effort and good will achieve or approximate one's goals. This overt optimism is so compulsive an element in the American culture that factors which threaten it, such as failure, old age, and death, are pressed from the focus of attention and handled in perfunctory ways. This belief that "things can be done" is coupled with a faith in common sense and "know-how" with regard to means. The American has a double approach to complex reasoning and theory. He has great respect for systematic thinking and planning in relation to technological and organizational problems. But even this type of intellectualism is brought down to earth by referring to it as "know-how." Know-how implies both the possession of formal technical knowledge and the capacity to improvise and overcome obstacles on the basis of a "feel" for the problem or the situation. In complicated questions of social and public policy there is a genuine distrust of complex and subtle reasoning and a preference for an earthy "common sense." Thus, in these important areas his compulsive optimism, his anti-intellectualism, and his simple rationalism leave the American vulnerable to deflation and pessimism when his expectations are thwarted and when threats and dangers are not effectively warded off by improvisations. This vulnerability is, to be sure, balanced by a certain flexibility and experimentalism, a willingness to try new approaches. If Americans typically avoid the rigidity of dogma in dealing with new problems, they also typically fail to reap the advantages of thoughtful policy-planning. What is involved here is not so much a net loss, but rather the failure to realize the net gain that would result from a greater intellectual discipline.

3. Attitudes toward Authority and Morality

The American tends to "cut authority down to his own size." He has a respect for achievement and a toleration of order-enforcing agencies, but a distrust of arbitrary or traditional authority. This attitude toward authority also carries over into the field of tradition and custom. Certainly the urban American, and many of the rural ones as well, are not seriously limited by traditional methods of doing things. They are iconoclasts with respect to earlier aspects of culture, and conformists in relation to the most recent value changes. They reject what was done in the past, and they conform to the new things that are being done *now*. But again this iconoclasm is especially noticeable in the sphere of material culture. A greater conservatism obtains in relation to social and political matters. This social and political conservatism is not unique to Americans. What seems to be unique is this combination of mobility of material values and fundamentalism with regard to social and political values.

Similar trends are observable in American attitudes toward moral norms. The norms of Christianity still constitute an important theme in contemporary American culture. Since these moral standards are in obvious and continual rivalry with the competitive ethic, Americans tend to suffer from ambivalence and conflicts in determining what is "proper." Under normal circumstances this conflict does not appear to have a seriously laming effect. It tends to be disposed of by adding a moral coloration to actions which are really motivated by expediency, and an expediential coloration to actions which are motivated by moral and humanitarian values. These tendencies are related to a rather widespread naive belief in the compatibility of morality and expediency. While this ambivalence is a factor which generally affects American behavior, there is also a characteristic pendulum movement between the two ethics. Thus, if generous actions, motivated by moral and humanitarian considerations, are accepted without gratitude, are misinterpreted, or are unrequited, a "cynical" rejection of humanitarianism may follow, resulting from the humiliation at having been "played for a sucker." To yield to humanitarian impulses in the "market place" or to moderate one's own demands in the light of "Christian" considerations, to give without the expectation of receiving, to suffer injury without retaliation—these are impulses which have a partial validity; but it is dangerous to give way to them since they dull the edge of competitiveness, confuse and retard the forward course of action.

Mood versus Policy

Since Americans tend to exhaust their emotional and intellectual energies in private pursuits, the typical approach to problems of public policy is perfunctory. Where public policy impinges directly on their interest, as in questions of local improvements, taxation, or social security policy, they are more likely to develop views and opinions resting on some kind of intellectual structure. But on questions of a more remote nature, such as foreign policy, they tend to react in more undifferentiated ways, with formless and plastic moods which undergo frequent alteration in response to changes in events. The characteristic response to questions of foreign policy is one of indifference. A foreign policy crisis, short of the immediate threat of war, may transform indifference to vague apprehension, to fatalism, to anger; but the reaction is still a mood, a superficial and fluctuating response. To some extent American political apathy is a consequence of the compulsive absorption of energy in private competitiveness. To inform oneself on public issues, to form policies on the basis of careful thought-taking, is hardly a task that is beyond the intellectual competence of a large proportion of the population. The intellectual demands of business life are in some respects as complicated as those of foreign policy. But the American has a powerful cultural incentive to develop policies and strategies relating to his business and professional career, and little incentive, if any, to develop strategies for foreign policy.

The orientation of most Americans toward foreign policy is one of mood, and mood is essentially an unstable phenomenon. But this instability is not arbitrary and unpredictable. American moods are affected by two variables: (1) changes in the domestic and foreign political-economic situation involving the presence or absence of threat in varying degrees, (2) the characterological predispositions of the population. Our knowledge of American character tendencies, meager as it may be, makes it possible to suggest potential movements of opinion and mood which may have significant effects on foreign policy.

1. Withdrawal-Intervention

Given the intense involvement of most Americans with private interests and pursuits, the normal attitude toward a relatively stable world political situation is one of comparative indifference and withdrawal. This was the case throughout the greater part of the nineteenth century, in the period between World War I and II, and . . . in the period immediately following World War II. The existence of this cyclical withdrawal-intervention problem suggests at least two serious dangers for foreign policy decision-making: (1) possible overreactions to threat; (2) possible overreactions to temporary equilibria in world politics. Under ordinary circumstances American emotion and action are directed with considerable pressure in the normal orbits of private competition. However, when threats from abroad became grave and immediate, Americans tend to break out of their private orbits, and tremendous energies become available for foreign policy. Thus, we see the explosions of American energy in World Wars I and II when, after periods of indifference and withdrawal, exceptional feats of swift mobilization were achieved. There is some evidence to suggest that the Russian threat may, if carelessly handled, produce dangerous overreactions. Thus the press conference of Secretary of State Marshall in the spring of 1947, in which he urged the American people to "keep calm," produced what amounted to a war scare. The volatility and potential explosiveness of American opinion must be constantly kept in mind if panic reactions to threat are to be avoided.

The danger of overreaction to threat is only one aspect of this withdrawal-intervention tendency of American opinion. Equally serious is the prospect of overreaction to temporary stabilizations in the world crisis. Because of the superficial character of American attitudes toward world politics, American opinion tends to react to the external aspects of situations. A temporary Russian tactical withdrawal may produce strong tendencies toward demobilization and the reassertion of the primacy of private and domestic values. The pull of "privatism" in America creates a strong inclination to self-deception. And while this is less characteristic of the informed and policy-making levels, it undoubtedly plays an important role here as well. The great American demobilization of 1945, both in the military establishment and in the civilian bureaucracy, and the hasty dismantling of war agencies and controls reflected the overwhelming eagerness to withdraw to private values and normal conditions. This movement was not based on a sober evaluation of the foreign situation and what this might require in military and political terms, but was a response to the overwhelming urge to have done with alarms and external interruptions and get back to the essential and important values.

2. Mood Simplification

Closely connected with the withdrawal-intervention pattern is a tendency which has to do with characteristic changes in the internal structure of American foreign policy moods. It has already been pointed out that under conditions of political equilibrium American attitudes toward world politics tend to be formless and lacking in intellectual structure. We define policy, as distinguished from mood, as consisting of a relatively stable intellectual structure including (1) explicit assumptions as to the values involved in domestic or international political conflict, (2) explicit evaluations of the relative costs and efficiency of alternative means of maximizing the value position of one's own country or political group. From the point of view of this criterion, American attitudes tend to range from unstructured moods in periods of equilibrium to simplification in periods of crisis. So long as there is no immediate, sharply defined threat, the attitude is vague and indefinite—e.g., apathetic, mildly apprehensive, euphoric, skeptical. When the crisis becomes sharpened American responses become more specific. Here American distrust of intellectualism and subtlety, the faith in "common sense," and the belief in simple answers lead to oversimplifications of the threat and the methods of coping with it.

While these tendencies are more characteristic of the "uninformed" general run of the population, they affect policy-makers as well. Thus during World War II, the Roosevelt shift from "Dr. New Deal" to "Dr. Win-the-War" reflected this need at the very highest level of policy-making to reduce the issues to simplified proportions. The "unconditional surrender" policy was a similarly oversimplified resolution of the moral and political problems of the war. The journalists and writers who directed American propaganda efforts in World War II solved their complex policy problems by the slogan of "the strategy of truth," which left to the lower-level, competitive policy-making process practically all of the important decisions of propaganda policy during the war. The policy of "non-fraternization" with Germans which was imposed on the American army of occupation similarly was understandable as a gratification of a need for moral simplism, but it bore only a slight relation to the complex and uncomfortable realities on which it was imposed. The entire sequence of American policies toward Germany had this character of mixed moral-expediential improvisations. At first these improvisations were motivated primarily by anti-German reactions; more recently the tendency is toward more pro-German improvisations. At the present time this tendency to oversimplify seems to be taking the form of reducing all the problems of world politics to a simple "East-West" conflict. There is considerable pressure to take as an ally any country or movement which is anti-Communist and anti-Russian.

It would, of course, be an exaggeration to attribute the same degree of "simplism" to policy-makers as might be expected of the "man in the street." But there can be little doubt that the process of foreign policy making is strongly influenced by this common-sense, improvisational tendency. Faith in policy-planning (which means in simple terms, taking the "long view," acquiring sufficient reliable information on which sound policy can be based, weighing and balancing the potential value of military, political, diplomatic, and psychological means in relation to proposed courses of action) has hardly taken root in the American policy-making process.

3. Optimism-Pessimism

The problem of shifts in mood from euphoric to dysphoric expectations is clearly related to those aspects of American opinion already described. The involvement in private concerns, coupled with an optimistic faith in good will, common sense, and simple answers, renders the American public vulnerable to failure. This reaction tends to result from the frustration of successive improvisations, none of which have been adapted to the complex character of the problem. Under these circumstances there are two possible dangers: (1) withdrawal reactions; (2) hasty measures motivated by irritation and impatience. The development of American attitudes toward Russia since the end of the war is an excellent illustration of this problem. During the war and in the period immediately following its termination there was a widely shared belief among Americans and among American policy-makers that the Russian problem could be readily solved by good will and the "man-to-man" approach. The continued thwarting of American overtures and concessions to the Russians now seems to have produced an attitude of hopeless pessimism. Pessimism certainly seems to be justifiable on the basis of the facts, but the negativism which has resulted may possibly constitute a danger if negotiation and bargaining with the Russians in principle is interdicted. The objective problem would seem to be one of choosing the time, the occasion, and the conditions when negotiation might lead to advantage. There is a similar danger of excessive pessimism in relation to potential allies. Perhaps there is a tendency toward a premature "writing off" of peoples whose social and political structures are unstable, countries which don't react with "American speed" to American proposals or which are not ready to commit themselves to the American "side" in as whole-hearted a fashion as we might desire.

4. Tolerance-Intolerance

The point has already been made that the American attitude toward authority, toward moral and ideological norms, contains conflicting elements. On the one hand, the American is not hemmed in by the mores and morals of "the horse and buggy days," and at the same time he is a conformist, a value-imitator. He is ready to try new things and new methods, but not if they make him look "different" or "peculiar." The truth of the matter would seem to be that, while he has loosened himself from the bonds of earlier moral standards and beliefs, he has not replaced these guides for conduct with any other set of principles. The autonomous conscience of Puritanism has been replaced by the "radar-directed" conduct of the "marketer." He tends to take his judgments as to what is right and wrong, proper and improper, from the changing culture as it impinges on him through the various social institutions and media of communication. This makes for a certain flexibility in attitudes toward other cultures and ideologies. But the flexibility is negative rather than positive. That is, the American has moved away from older moral and traditional norms without acquiring new bases of judgment. His toleration of difference therefore is unstable, and there is a substratum of ideological fundamentalism which frequently breaks through the surface and has an important impact on foreign policy. Thus in our efforts to stabilize the weakened and chaotic areas of Western Europe we have been prepared to go a long way in aiding "Socialist Great Britain" and the left-inclined powers of Western Europe. But there is a continual sabotage of this tolerance, frequent efforts at ideological imperialism, even occasional interferences at the administrative level, which are motivated by ideological fundamentalism.

In general, this intolerance of difference is more clearly expressed in periods of normalcy. Thus, even though the possibility appears to be remote, the prospect of a recrudescence of isolationism cannot be excluded. A tactical cessation of Russian pressure might produce just this kind of demobilization and withdrawal reaction and the reassertion of older principles of conduct. This is not to say that such a reaction would be decisive so far as policy is concerned; but it is a prospect which sound policy-planning should anticipate.

5. Idealism-Cynicism

In still another respect American moral predispositions may have consequences for foreign policy. The annoyance and irritation of the peoples of foreign countries over American self-righteousness is, on the whole, a relatively minor source of difficulty. Americans would appear to be happiest when they can cloak an action motivated by self-interest with an aura of New Testament selflessness, when an action which is "good business," or "good security" can be made to "look good" too. Similarly there is resistance among Americans over the straightforward expression of conscience-motivated behavior. What is "good" has to be represented as satisfying the criteria of self-interest. They are happiest when they can allay the Christian conscience at the same time that they satisfy self-interested criteria. In this regard the peoples of foreign countries are well protected, perhaps overprotected, by their own cynicism.

But there are a number of respects in which this moral dualism may produce more serious problems for the policy-maker. There would appear to be a certain cyclical trend in American moral attitudes. The great wave of idealism in the first world war gave way to the cynicism about foreign countries of the 1920's. The friendliness for our British and French allies of World War I gave way to bitterness over their defaults on their indebtedness. A little more than a decade ago the little country of Finland had a place at the very center of the American heart because she had kept up her payments on her war debts, while the European powers which had defaulted, and on the fate of which our security rested, were prevented from borrowing money in the American capital market. The chiliastic faith in the reasonableness of the Russians has now been supplanted by deep resentment over their base ingratitude.

American generosity and humanitarianism is a tentative phenomenon. Along with impulses toward good will and generosity, there is a deep-seated suspicion that smart people don't act that way, that "only suckers are a soft touch." In this connection a recent study which appeared in a popular magazine is of considerable interest. This investigation, claiming to have been based on "reliable sampling procedures," reflected a degree of religious piety among Americans considerably greater than had previously been estimated. Of greatest interest was its description of American attitudes toward ethics. It would appear that almost half of the sample was sharply aware of the conflict between what was "right" and the demands of secular life. A somewhat smaller proportion considered that religion influenced their activities in business, political and social life. Considerably more than half felt that their conduct toward neighbors was governed by the golden rule; but more than 80 per cent felt that their neighbors fell considerably short of the golden rule in their conduct toward their fellow-men.

Quite aside from the question of the full reliability of a study asking such "loaded" and personal questions, there seems to be confirmation here for the proposition regarding the moral dualism in the American character. The aspiration to conform to Christian ethical ideals is clearly present among most members of the culture, but there would appear to be a strong apprehension that such standards of conduct are inapplicable because the outside world does not behave that way. Hence any impulse toward ethically motivated generosity is impaired not only by the feeling that it will go unrequited, but that one's neighbors will ridicule it or attribute it to some concealed, self-interested motive.

It would appear to be a reasonable speculation from the foregoing findings that any action involving the giving or loaning of American wealth to foreign peoples, even though it be motivated by calculations of self-interest, activates this fear that "only a sucker is a soft touch." Under conditions of threat, such as those of the present, these doubts and suspicions about "giving things away" have been kept within manageable proportions. But in a period of temporary stabilization when the superficial aspect of the foreign situation encourages withdrawal reactions, these feelings may play a role of some significance.

6. Superiority-Inferiority

In a sense America is a nation of parvenus. A historically unique rate of immigration, social, and geographic mobility has produced a people which has not had an opportunity to "set," to acquire the security and stability which come from familiar ties, associations, rights, and obligations. It is perhaps not accidental that in the vulgarization of psychoanalytic hypotheses in America in the last decades one of the first to acquire popular currency was the "superiority-inferiority" complex. In more stably stratified societies the individual tends to have a greater sense of "location," a broader and deeper identification with his social surroundings. He has not *made* his own identity, while in America a large proportion of each generation is *self-made.* Being self-made produces a certain buoyancy, a sense of mastery, but it leaves the individual somewhat doubtful as to his social legitimacy. This sense of insecurity and uncertainty may add a strident note to American claims for recognition. This may explain the stereotype of the American abroad, confronted with complex and ancient cultures, taking alcoholic refuge in assertions of American moral, political, and technical virtue. It may also account for a feeling in the United States that American diplomats are no match for the wiliness and cunning of Old World negotiators. In other words, Americans typically overreact in their self-evaluations. They over- and under-estimate their skills and virtues, just as they over- and under-estimate the skills and virtues of other cultures and nations.

It is perhaps this quality among Americans—and among the American elites—which strongly militates against a balanced and empathic appreciation of cultural and national differences so essential to the development of an effective diplomacy. One may entertain the hypothesis that Americans tend to judge other nations and cultures according to a strictly American scoreboard, on the basis of which America is bound to win. It is difficult for Americans to accept a humane conception of cultural and national differences. Somehow, other cultural values must be transmuted into an American currency so that it becomes possible in a competition of national cultures to rate the United States as the "best all-round culture of the year."

There is a noticeable sensitivity among Americans on the score of cultural and intellectual inferiority. Only recently the American press cited the throngs of visitors to art museums exhibiting the Habsburg collection of paintings as effectively refuting European claims of American cultural inferiority. Feelings of crudeness and inferiority are not only expressed in the form of direct refutation by citing such evidence as the above; they also are frequently expressed in the tendency to equate esthetic and intellectual subtlety with lack of manliness—artists and intellectuals are "queers."

This superiority-inferiority ambivalence may manifest itself in policy-making in a number of ways. It may take the direct and perhaps more typical form of cultural arrogance—assertions of the superiority of the American way in politics, in economics, in social relations, in morality, or in the physical amenities of life. In this case the psychological mechanism involved is a reaction-formation; unconscious feelings of inferiority lead to the assertion of superiority. Or it may take the form of an admission of inferiority and an attribution of superiority to other cultures or elite groups. In either case there is an alienation from the real character and potentialities of the self. One either becomes an ideal and non-existent American—a *persona* American—or one rejects one's Americanism entirely and attempts to "pass," for example, into English or French culture. These formulations, of course, state the problem in the extreme for purposes of clarity.

These reactions have a selective appeal among the various elite groups. Thus American artists, writers, and intellectuals have historically tended to manifest inferiority feelings in the form of imitativeness, or in expatriation. It has been asserted that members of the American foreign service have tended to assimilate themselves too readily to foreign cultures and aristocratic "sets," perhaps at the expense of their American perspective. The tendency for American families of wealth and prestige to ape the English and Continental aristocracies is too well known to call for detailed comment. All of these groups have in common the quality of having differentiated themselves from the American pattern through extraordinary wealth, through artistic or intellectual deviation, or through long residence abroad. The more "representative" American—the Congressman for example—tends to manifest the simpler form of cultural arrogance.

Either inferiority or superiority feelings in relation to other cultures may have a negative effect on the national interest. Cultural arrogance may alienate other peoples, impair confidence in the United States among actual and potential allies, or aid in some measure in the mobilization of hostile sentiment among neutrals and potential enemies. Cultural subservience, particularly if manifested by American diplomats and negotiators, may result in real and unnecessary sacrifices of the national interest.

READINGS ON AMERICAN NATIONAL CHARACTER

This selective listing is intended to serve those whom curiosity or necessity impels to explore the recent literature of American character. It is limited to studies published in English since 1940, and it omits patently impressionistic or exhibitionistic writings. An asterisk (*) indicates that the title so marked contains a useful bibliography. Paperbacks and paperback reprints are identified by a dagger (†); in the case of paperback reprints the publishing data refer to the original hardcover issue. More extensive bibliographies will be found in *American Quarterly,* XV (Summer, 1963, Supplement), 271–88, and XXI (Summer, 1969, Supplement), 330–49.

ALBERT, ETHEL M. "Conflict and Change in American Values: A Culture-Historical Approach," *Ethics,* LXXIV (Oct. 1963), 19–33.
> Reflections on the nature, sources and meanings of contemporary value uncertainty, looking toward a general theory of values and value-change.

†ALMOND, GABRIEL A. "American Character and Foreign Policy," in Almond, *The American People and Foreign Policy* (New York: Harcourt, Brace & Co., 1950), ch. 3.
> Ambivalences in the American character make for instability in foreign policy.

BERGHORN, FORREST J. & GEOFFREY H. STEERE. "Are American Values Changing? The Problem of Inner- or Other-Direction," *Am. Quar.,* XVIII (Spring 1966), 52–62.
> Efforts to apply Riesman's concepts in studying contemporary and historical American child-rearing values lead to conclusion that, though the values have changed, "these concepts do not . . . seem viable categories of research."

BILLINGTON, RAY ALLEN. *America's Frontier Heritage* (New York: Holt, Rinehart & Winston, 1966).
> Explanations of American character that center on the agrarian experience, abundance or mobility "stem immediately or remotely" from the frontier hypothesis, and many of the values, behavior patterns and characteristic traits, developed on the frontier, persist powerfully into the present.

———. "How the Frontier Shaped the American Character," *Am. Heritage,* IX (Apr. 1958), 4 ff.
> Turner "was not far wrong when he maintained that frontiersmen did develop unique traits and that these, perpetuated, form the principal distinguishing characteristics of the American people today."

416

*†BOORSTIN, DANIEL J. *The Americans: The Colonial Experience* (New York: Random House, 1958).

A scholarly and provocative re-examination of early American thought and society, developing the main theses of *The Genius of American Politics.*

*†————. *The Americans: The National Experience* (New York: Random House, 1965).

The second of a projected three-volume study; emphasizes America's openness to innovation and experiment, ingenuity in communal organization and saving "vagueness." On significance of book as expression of (as well as investigation into) American character see John Higham's review in *New York Rev. of Books,* Nov. 11, 1965.

†————. *The Genius of American Politics* (Chicago: University of Chicago Press, 1953).

These historical observations on the "non-exportable uniqueness" of American political ideas and institutions constitute an important contribution to the analysis of characterological consensus.

BRIDGES, WILLIAM E. "Family Patterns and Social Values in America, 1825–1875," *Am. Quar.,* XVII (Spring 1965), 3–11.

Relates child-rearing practices to demands and expectations of American culture, finding an ambiguous relationship between family and marketplace; the family trained children for independence and mobility yet upheld the maternal values of "domestic solidarity" as checks on the success ethic.

†BROGAN, D. W. *The American Character* (New York: Alfred A. Knopf, 1944).

A once-over-lightly commentary on American values, institutions and behavioral styles "to encourage sympathetic understanding of the Americanism of America."

†CAWELTI, JOHN G. *Apostles of the Self-Made Man* (Chicago: Univ. of Chicago Press, 1965).

Examines American success ethic with particular attention to writings of Franklin, Jefferson, Emerson, Alger and John Dewey. The self-made man "persisted as a popular hero and as a central symbol . . . because Americans were able to synthesize, under his aegis, many conflicting strands of belief and aspiration."

COLEMAN, LEE. "What Is American? A Study of Alleged American Traits," *Social Forces,* XIX (May 1941), 492–99.

Analysis of most common trait ascriptions emphasizes "the amazing diversity of American life and character" and shows "the hazard involved in asserting that any trait is unqualifiedly American, to the exclusion of all opposing or modifying traits."

COMMAGER, HENRY STEELE. "The Ambiguous American," *N.Y. Times Mag.* (May 3, 1964), 16 ff.

An unambiguous recital of character traits: Americans are careless, generous, self-indulgent, sentimental, quantitatively materialistic, self-confident, complacent, arrogant, competitive, lawless, equalitarian, resourceful and adaptable. Interesting as example of popular presentation of American character.

†————. *The American Mind: An Interpretation of American Thought and Character since the 1880's* (New Haven: Yale University Press, 1950).

The first and final chapters summarize the salient characteristics of, respectively, the nineteenth- and twentieth-century American.

————. "Portrait of the American," in John W. Chase, ed., *Years of the Modern: An American Appraisal* (New York & Toronto: Longmans, Green & Co., 1949), ch. 1.

An historian's delineation of "some of the more pronounced traits of the American in the mid-twentieth century."

CRUSE, HAROLD. *Rebellion or Revolution?* (New York: William Morrow, 1968).

Explores the problem of "what America really is as a nation and the true nature of the Negroes' intrinsic relationship to the American reality."

†CUNLIFFE, MARCUS. "The American Character," in Cunliffe, *The Nation Takes Shape: 1789–1837* (Chicago: University of Chicago Press, 1959), ch. 8.

This portrait of the Jacksonian American by a British historian identifies character traits and polarities of orientation which, in general, "support the assertion that American 'national character' has not altered fundamentally since its early definitions."

CURTI, MERLE. "American Philanthropy and the National Character," *Amer. Quar.*, X (Winter 1958), 420–37.

"American experience in philanthropy has both expressed American character and . . . helped to shape it."

DECHARMS, RICHARD & GERALD H. MOELLER. "Values Expressed in American Children's Readers: 1800–1950," *Jour. Abnormal & Soc. Psych.*, LXIV (1962), 136–42.

Content analysis shows rise in "achievement imagery" from 1800 to about 1900, then steady decline. Results of this extension of McClelland's work "illustrate an interesting technique for obtaining objective data to investigate cultural hypotheses."

DEGLER, CARL N. "The Sociologist as Historian: Riesman's *The Lonely Crowd,*" *Am. Quar.*, XV (Winter 1963), 483–97.

Argues that other-direction has been "the dominant element in our national character through most of our history," and that evidence of characterological continuity may render Riesman's major categories "totally inadequate for purposes of historical analysis. . . . "

DENNEY, REUEL. "How Americans See Themselves," *Annals of the Amer. Acad. of Pol. and Soc. Sc.,* CCXCV (Sept. 1954), 12–20. Reprinted in Joseph J. Kwiat & Mary C. Turpie, eds., *Studies in American Culture: Dominant Ideas and Images* (Minneapolis: University of Minnesota Press, 1960), 16–26.

Perceptive critical commentary on approaches to the study of American character and problems of definition.

DU BOIS, CORA. "The Dominant Value Profile of American Culture," *Amer. Anthropologist,* LVII (Dec. 1955), 1232–39.

Schematic discussion of three major "focal" values—material well-being, conformity, and "effort-optimism"—and of the "strain for consistency in the American value system."

*DUHL, LEONARD J. "The American Character: Crisis, Change, and Complexity," *Jour. Nervous & Mental Disease,* CXXXVII (Aug. 1963), 124–34.

"Central to our American character is the ability to deal with crisis and to adapt. . . . The American character is now dissolved in crisis, and it is upon the resolution of such crisis that its newly emerging shape will depend."

*ELSON, RUTH MILLER. *Guardians of Tradition: American School Books of the Nineteenth Century* (Lincoln: Univ. of Nebraska Press, 1964), esp. chaps. 5, 7.

Chap. 5: American character is revealed, and American superiority affirmed, in schoolbook presentations of and judgments on the character of other nations. Chap. 7: schoolbooks express the linkages in the value system among practical creativity, material advancement, the Protestant Ethic, anti-intellectualism and anti-aestheticism, republicanism and patriotism

†ERIKSON, ERIK H. "Reflections on the American Identity," in Erikson, *Childhood and Society* (New York: W. W. Norton & Co., 1950), ch. 8.

"The functioning American, as the heir of a history of extreme contrast and abrupt changes, bases his final ego identity on some tentative combination of dynamic polarities such as migratory and sedentary, individualistic and standardized, competitive and co-operative, pious and freethinking, responsible and cynical. . . . "

FUCHS, LAWRENCE H. *Those Peculiar Americans: The Peace Corps and American National Character,* (New York: Meredith Press, 1967).

Peace Corps volunteers are characteristically American in exemplifying "the dominant values of American culture"—personal independence and self-reliance, activism and the "passion for achievement in work to prove the worth of the individual." They are atypical in that "they have questioned those values and have seen beyond them." Foreword by Riesman.

GILLIN, JOHN. "National and Regional Cultural Values in the United States," *Social Forces,* XXXIV (Dec. 1955), 107–13.

Regional "twists" and special emphases with respect to the national value system, here partially defined.

GINZBERG, ELI, ed. *Values and Ideals of American Youth* (New York: Columbia Univ. Press, 1961).

Papers and addresses from the 1960 White House Conference on Children and Youth.

GOLDSEN, ROSE K., MORRIS ROSENBERG, ROBIN M. WILLIAMS JR. & EDWARD A. SUCHMAN. *What College Students Think* (Princeton: D. Van Nostrand, 1960).

Report of the Cornell Values Study on values, attitudes, expectations, demands and beliefs of persons who will have a crucial role in shaping American character.

†GORER, GEOFFREY. *The American People: A Study in National Character* (New York: W. W. Norton & Co., 1948).

Perceptions and interpretations, sometimes barbed and often erratic, of a Freudian anthropologist. Revised ed., 1964, with minor modifications and an additional chapter of random observations.

*GREENSTEIN, FRED I. "New Light on Changing American Values: A Forgotten Body of Survey Data," *Soc. Forces,* XLII (May 1964), 441–50.

Views of Riesman, Whyte, Lowenthal *et al.* must be modified in light of data on children's choices of exemplars since 1890's which do not support hypothesis that "Americans have come to value personal achievement less in the past half century."

*HARTSHORNE, THOMAS L. *The Distorted Image: Changing Conceptions of the American Character since Turner* (Cleveland: Press of Case Western Reserve Univ. 1968).

This notable contribution to the historiography of American character examines efforts of 20th-century American intellectuals, aroused by problems of immigration, industrialization and war, to contrive alternatives to the frontier thesis for defining and explaining American character.

HARTZ, LOUIS *et al. The Founding of New Societies: Studies in the History of the United States, Latin America, South Africa, Canada, and Australia.* (New York: Harcourt, Brace & World, 1964).

Comparative analysis lends support to proposition that the "cultural fragment," broken off from the European whole, undergoes a process of "extrication, atrophy, and unfolding" that defines its character. Thus the "ultimate experience of the American liberal tradition" appears as model for the new societies here treated, each of which is distinctive, however, in being "a special blend of European national tradition, historical timing, racial encounter, accidental incongruity."

*HENNESSY, BERNARD C. "Psycho-cultural Studies of National Character: Relevance for International Relations," *Background, Jour. Internat'l Studies Ass'n,* VI (Fall 1962), 27–49.

Studies in national character "are not significant in the making, but may be so in the application, of national policy"; gives brief illustrations of possible uses of knowledge of national character.

†HENRY, JULES. *Culture against Man* (New York: Random House, 1963).

Polemic against the "pecuniary culture" that promotes the national character traits of hedonistic mindlessness, indiscriminate impulse-release, competitiveness and the drive to achieve, fearfulness and obsession with independence.

HOLLANDER, PAUL. "Leisure as an American and Soviet Value," *Soc. Prob.,* XIV (Fall 1966), 179–88.

Comparative examination of leisure as value leads to conclusions that both support and challenge "the so-called convergence hypothesis postulating a growing similarity between the United States and the U.S.S.R."

HSU, FRANCIS L. K. *Americans and Chinese: Two Ways of Life* (New York: Henry Schuman, 1953).

An extensive and provocative analysis of cultural contrasts from a "broadly Freudian" angle of vision. No other comparative study, of which we have all too few, approaches it in depth and scope.

————. "American Core Value and National Character," in Hsu, ed., *Psychological Anthropology: Approaches to Culture and Personality* (Homewood, Ill.: Dorsey Press, 1961), ch. 7.

Difficulties in defining American character, while substantial, are not insurmountable. "What we need to see is that the contradictory American 'values' noted by the sociologists, psychologists, and historians are but manifestations of one core value," namely, "self-reliance."

————. *Clan, Caste, and Club* (Princeton: D. Van Nostrand, 1963).

Constrasts the Hindu "approach to the world" (supernatural-centeredness or unilateral dependence) with the approaches of Americans (individual-centeredness or self-reliance) and Chinese (situation-centeredness or mutual dependence), emphasizing family relations and their implications for social character.

*HUNT, MORTON. *Her Infinite Variety: The American Woman as Lover, Mate and Rival,* (New York: Harper & Row, 1962).

"The emancipated middle-class American woman ... is more nearly a complete human being than any Western woman, save a handful of queens, viragoes, and salonières, since the days of the Roman Empire," yet she has not solved the problems of role ("married mistress"? "man's best friend"? "career wife"?): "which part or parts to choose, and how to combine them without disaster or else give up some of them without bitterness."

"Is America by Nature a Violent Society?" *N.Y. Times Mag.,* Apr. 28, 1968, 24 ff.

Between the killing of King and the killing of Kennedy, these observations by Hannah Arendt, St. Clair Drake, Clifford Geertz, Paul Goodman, Michael Harrington, Richard Hofstadter, David Riesman and C. Vann Woodward.

JACOB, PHILIP E. *Changing Values in College* (New York: Harper & Bros., 1957).

Finds "a striking homogeneity" of basic values among American college students: self-confidence, self-interest, conventional religious faith, morality with some elbow-room, privatism and tolerance.

†KENISTON, KENNETH. *The Uncommitted: Alienated Youth in American Society* (New York: Harcourt, Brace & World, 1965).

On the "new alienation" in America, here described as the "alienating society."

†————. *Young Radicals: Notes on Committed Youth* (New York: Harcourt, Brace & World, 1968).

On the character and content of a form of radicalism, based on interviews with leaders of Vietnam Summer, 1967.

KIMBALL, SOLON T. "Cultural Influences Shaping the Role of the Child" (1960), in Conrad M. Arensberg & Solon T. Kimball, *Culture and Community* (New York: Harcourt, Brace & World, 1965), chap. 12.

Among the cultural imperatives which "have been idealized for all members of [American] society" are mobility, independence, adaptability, the capacity for continued growth, and perpetual optimism.

†KLAPP, ORRIN E. *Heroes, Villains, and Fools: The Changing American Character* (Englewood Cliffs, N.J.: Prentice-Hall, 1962).

An impressionistic sociological survey and analysis of "the major social types of American society which serve prominently as its models." Argues that a "deterioration" of the national character is reflected in the currently "dominant role models of Good Joe-smart operator-playboy."

*KLUCKHOHN, CLYDE. "Have There Been Discernible Shifts in American Values during the Past Generation?" in Elting E. Morison, ed., *The American Style: Essays in Value and Performance* (New York: Harper & Brothers, 1958), 145–217.

A wide-ranging compendium of findings since 1941. Notes, *inter alia,* decline of Protestant Ethic, increase in "other-directedness," explicit valuation of "psychological health," emphasis on "individuality" as against "rugged individualism."

KLUCKHOHN, FLORENCE R. "American Women and American Values," in Lyman Bryson, ed., *Facing the Future's Risks: Studies toward Predicting the Unforeseen* (New York: Harper & Brothers, 1953), ch. 8.

The role of the American woman is "badly defined, shot through with contradictions, and in need of major alterations." Such alterations will have to accord with certain dominant values: "Individualism, a future-time orientation, a belief in mastering nature, the conception of human nature as evil but perfectible, and a high evaluation of men in action."

LASKI, HAROLD J. *The American Democracy: A Commentary and an Interpretation* (New York: Viking Press, 1948).

Comprehensive interpretation of American culture and character stressing the advance of technology and the system of business power.

LEE, EVERETT S. "The Turner Thesis Re-examined," *Amer. Quar.,* XIII (Spring 1961), 77–83.

"The Turner thesis is too simple an explanation for such complexities as American democracy and American character." Argues that it should be regarded as "a special case of an as yet undeveloped migration theory" because "there are few characteristics which are shared by so many Americans as migrant status and spatial movement."

*†LERNER, MAX. *America as a Civilization: Life and Thought in the United States Today* (New York: Simon & Schuster, 1957).

Encyclopedic observations and reflections "on the grand theme of the nature and meaning of the American experience."

†LIPSET, SEYMOUR MARTIN. "A Changing American Character?" in Lipset, *The First New Nation* (New York: Basic Books, 1963), ch. 3.

"A monistic materialistic interpretation of the correlates of American values and behavior sharply underestimates the extent to which basic national values, once institutionalized, affect the consequences of technological and economic change."

MARCELL, DAVID W. "Privacy and the American Character," *So. Atlantic Quar.*, LXVI (Winter 1967), 1–12.

Riesman's idea of other-direction helps explain and is reinforced by contemporary institutional threats to and devaluation of privacy; decline of privacy portends failure of liberal democracy.

MARTINDALE, DON. *American Social Structure: Historical Antecedents and Contemporary Analysis* (New York: Appleton-Century-Crofts, 1960), chaps. 1, 18.

The typically American constellation of traits includes "a strong practicality, a considerable anti-intellectualism, a genius for organization, a strong materialism, a tendency to moralize on every issue, a high level of personal dynamism, an unusual capacity for personal initiative and a strong sense of civil responsibility."

————. *Community, Character and Civilization: Studies in Social Behaviorism* (New York: Free Press, 1963), Pt. 4, chaps. 8, 9.

With the forming of an American national community—shaped by frontier experience, massive immigration and rise of mass society—a national goal-value system develops, destroying the goal-value systems of sub-communities (regional, ethnic, etc.) and re-grouping their fragments in a new pattern. Original carrier of national values was the "Yankee," now giving way to a type of character more consonant with the technological delights of "the packaged suburb."

MARX, LEO. *The Machine in the Garden: Technology and the Pastoral Ideal in America* (New York: Oxford Univ. Press, 1964).

Traces and evaluates "the uses of the pastoral idea in the interpretation of the American experience"; relates literature, general ideas and "cultural symbols" to "show how the pastoral ideal has been incorporated in a powerful metaphor of contradiction—a way of ordering meaning and value that clarifies our situation today."

*†McCLELLAND, DAVID C. *The Achieving Society* (Princeton: D. Van Nostrand, 1961).

Maintaining that "a particular psychological factor—the need for Achievement—is responsible for economic growth and decline," this influential study (itself a demonstration of high n-Achievement) casts light on aspects of American behavior and values. Main findings are summarized in McClelland, *The Roots of Consciousness*, chap. 2.

†————. "The United States and Germany: A Comparative Study of National Character," in McClelland, *The Roots of Consciousness* (Princeton: D. Van Nostrand, 1964), chap. 4.

Intense American concern with achievement and self-actualization is kept in check by other-direction, here declared to be "the psychological precondition of a democratic political system."

McLOUGHLIN, WILLIAM G. "Pietism and the American Character," *Am. Quar.*, XVII (Summer 1965), 163–86.

Takes a theme from H. R. Niebuhr's *The Kingdom of God in America* to argue that a "dynamic, sectarian form of pietistic-perfectionism" has had and continues to have a decisive, if ambiguous, influence on American character.

*†MEAD, MARGARET. *And Keep Your Powder Dry: An Anthropologist Looks at America.* New expanded ed. (New York: William Morrow, 1965).

The pioneer anthropological study of American character (1943). Mead remarks that "what value this book has now lies in the way it places a period ... in American culture and ... in our developing understanding of our own culture." New edition includes a new preface and introduction, the preface to the 1943 English edition, an updated bibliography, a bibliographical note on the vindication of psychocultural studies of large complex societies and a new concluding chapter of moral injunction.

†MEYERS, MARVIN. *The Jacksonian Persuasion: Politics and Belief* (Stanford: Stanford Univ. Press, 1957).

Character of Jacksonian America as revealed through political rhetoric; valuable discussion of Tocqueville's image of the American as "venturous conservative."

MILLER, DANIEL R. & GUY E. SWANSON. *The Changing American Parent: A Study in the Detroit Area* (New York: John Wiley & Sons, 1958).

Based on interviews with nearly 600 mothers in 1953, this study tends to confirm Riesman's observations on changing patterns of child training, here attributed largely to the general change "from entrepreneurial to bureaucratic experiences in American society. . . . "

MILLS, GORDON, ed. *Innocence and Power: Individualism in Twentieth-Century America* (Austin: Univ. of Texas Press, 1965).

Perspectives on American values and institutions from anthropology (Leslie White), economics (Clarence Ayres, Paul Samuelson), government (Louis Hartz), history (David Potter), literature (Frederick Hoffman) and philosophy (Charles Hartshorne).

*NASH, RODERICK. *Wilderness and the American Mind* (New Haven: Yale Univ. Press, 1967).

Delineates and interprets the changing American conceptions of wilderness, comprehended as natural condition, symbolic construct and "the basic ingredient of American civilization."

NOBLE, DAVID W. *Historians against History: The Frontier Thesis and the National Covenant in American Historical Writing since 1830* (Minneapolis: Univ. of Minnesota Press, 1965).

The set of American character is revealed in writings of major historians since Bancroft: "as long as the metaphysical distinction between European history and American nature remains, the American historian will carry the responsibility of being the chief theologian and political theorist of his nation. He must always explain how his country has achieved its uniqueness and he must always warn against the intrusion of alien influences."

NYE, RUSSEL B. *This Almost Chosen People: Essays in the History of American Ideas* (East Lansing, Mich.: Michigan State Univ. Press, 1966).

Essays on the ideas of progress, nationalism, free enterprise, mission, individualism, nature, equality.

PAYNTER, JULIE. "An End to Innocence," *Journal,* VII (Jan. 1969), 3–7.

Calls for new concepts of American character to take serious account of class, power and, especially, race: "Generalizations about our national character have been formed in white America and have been possible only, in effect, by reading black people out of the past."

PERRY, RALPH BARTON. *Characteristically American* (New York: Alfred A. Knopf, 1949).

Philosophical reflections on American values, thought and character with focal emphasis on the spirit of "collective individualism" and on the "characteristic American blend of buoyancy, collective self-confidence, measuring of attainment by competitive success, hope of perpetual and limitless improvement, improvising of method and organization to meet exigencies as they arise."

PIERSON, GEORGE W. "The M-Factor in American History," *Amer. Quar.,* XIV (Summer 1962 Supplement), 275–89.

"What made and kept us different . . . was, first of all, the M-factor: the factor of movement, migration, mobility."

———. "The Moving American," *Yale Rev.,* XLIV (Autumn 1954), 99–112.

Historical observations on the theme of horizontal mobility.

———. "A Restless Temper . . . ," *Am. Hist. Rev.,* LXIX (July 1964), 969–89.

Develops proposition that American mobility means "(1) new institutions patterned in part on free movement; (2) new relations with the physical environment based on a view of nature differing from the European; (3) a new concept of human fellowship or a decalogue of social conduct in some ways deviant form the Greco-Christian tradition; (4) even possibly a new attitude toward the self."

———. "Under a Wandering Star," *Va. Quar. Rev.,* XXXIX (Autumn 1963), 621–38.

An anxious inquiry into the contemporary effects of horizontal mobility on private attitudes and public policies.

POTTER, DAVID M. "American Individualism in the Twentieth Century," in Mills, ed., *Innocence and Power,* 92–112.

Though 19th-century individualism stressed self-reliance while 20th-century individualism has stressed nonconformity, both have placed "great weight upon the belief that individualism should serve as a means to group welfare rather than as a way of exalting man in isolation," yet neither "has had enough genuine concern for real group values" or "been willing to recognize that the tension between the individual and the group can never be treated as a simple antithesis. . . . "

POTTER, DAVID M. "American Women and the American Character," *Stetson University Bull.,* LXII (Jan. 1962), 1–22.

"The historic character of American women is important . . . as a coordinate major part of the . . . study of the American character as a whole."

†———. *People of Plenty: Economic Abundance and the American Character* (Chicago: Univ. of Chicago Press, 1954).

The importance of the historical dimension in the study of national character is shown in a perceptive investigation of the influence of economic abundance on American character.

†———. "The Quest for the National Character," in John Higham, ed., *The Reconstruction of American History* (New York: Harper & Brothers, 1962), ch. 11.

The contrasting images of American character—the American as individualist and idealist (Jefferson, Turner); the American as conformist and materialist (Tocqueville)—raise questions concerning the validity of generalizations about national character but may perhaps be partially reconciled in terms of a common American equalitarianism.

POWELL, THOMAS F. "American Values—What Are They?" *Soc. Ed.,* XXX (Feb. 1966), 83–87.

Distinguishes between professed values (e.g., individual liberties, equality of opportunity, equality before the law) and values that are "implicit in the characteristic behavior of Americans" (money, prestige, self-assertion). Calls for "rational synthesis" to overcome "schizophrenic conflicts" in national values: "Our overall purpose ought to be to *use* material wealth and power for the continuation of history's greatest experiment, the society open to talent."

RAPSON, RICHARD L. "The American Child as Seen by British Travelers, 1845–1935," *Am. Quar.,* XVII (Fall 1965), 520–34.

Lively commentary on the cultural implications of the American "cult of youth."

†RIESMAN, DAVID. *Individualism Reconsidered* (Glencoe, Ill.: Free Press, 1954).

———. "From Morality to Morale," in Alfred H. Stanton & Stewart E. Perry, eds., *Personality and Political Crisis* (Glencoe, Ill.: Free Press, 1951), 81–120.

Summary statement of the main themes of *The Lonely Crowd.*

———. "The Saving Remnant: An Examination of Character Structure," in John W. Chase, ed., *Years of the Modern: An American Appraisal* (New York & Toronto: Longmans, Green & Co., 1949), ch. 5.

Concise statement of the ethical imperative in Riesman's characterology. The "self-consciously autonomous people" are the "saving remnant" in an other-directed society.

———. "Some Observations on the Study of American Character," *Psychiatry,* XV (Aug. 1952), 333–38.

Comments on "some of the perplexities of working with the concept of character in a modern, highly differentiated society," especially with respect to questions of conformity and autonomy.

———. "Some Questions about the Study of American Character in the Twentieth Century," *Annals Am. Pol. & Soc. Sci.,* CCCLXX (Mar. 1967), 36–47.

A somewhat discouraged commentary on some of the complexities and bafflements which must be overcome for the study of American character to become worthwhile. The field should not be abandoned, yet "work on American national character has always seemed to me at best fragmentary and footloose."

————. "The Study of National Character: Some Observations on the American Case," *Harvard Library Bull.,* XIII (Winter 1959), 5–24.

Observations on the relations of history and historians to the study of national character, with particular reference to *The Lonely Crowd.*

†————. with Reuel Denney & Nathan Glazer. *The Lonely Crowd: A Study of the Changing American Character* (New Haven: Yale University Press, 1950).

†RISCHIN, MOSES, ed. *The American Gospel of Success: Individualism and Beyond* (Chicago: Quadrangle Books, 1965).

The editor calls this anthology a "pioneer effort to transcend the formal categories of sociology, literature, philosophy, religion, business management, economic theory, political science, social psychology and history in treating a theme central to the understanding of the American national character. The purpose is to explore and define what may be called the 'American Gospel of Success' by juxtaposing our inherited ideology with twentieth-century realities and the dilemmas of an economy shaped by the business mind."

ROBSON, WILLIAM A. "America Revisited," *Pol. Quar.,* XXXIV (Oct.-Dec. 1963), 339–53.

Americans are growing more sophisticated, modest and self-critical, while their basic characteristics continue to be those of "generosity, friendliness, a willingness to help others, respect for life, and a readiness to learn, combined with dynamic energy. . . . "

RUITENBEEK, HENDRIK M. *The Individual and the Crowd: A Study of Identity in America* (New York: Thomas Nelson & Sons, 1964).

Flaws in the American character are gloomily traced to "the difficulties that people in America have in establishing their identity both on the side of identification and on the side of individuation."

SANFORD, CHARLES L. *The Quest for Paradise: Europe and the American Moral Imagination* (Urbana: Univ. of Illinois Press, 1961).

An historical anatomy of the theme of natural innocence in American thought and sensibility; argues that "the Edenic myth . . . has been the most powerful and comprehensive organizing force in American culture."

SCHLESINGER, ARTHUR M. " 'What Then Is the American, This New Man?' " *Amer. Hist. Rev.,* XLVIII (Jan. 1943), 225–44. Reprinted in Schlesinger, *Paths to the Present* (New York: Macmillan Co., 1949), ch. 1.

An historian's reflective definition of American character and its determinants, with particular emphasis on "the protracted tutelage to the soil."

SHINN, ROGER L., ed. *The Search for Identity: Essays on the American Character* (New York: Inst. for Rel. & Soc. Studies, 1964).

Sixteen essays, partly analytical, partly homiletical, originating for the most part as addresses at the Institute's lecture series, winter, 1962–63. See especially the pieces by Baker, Blau, Clark, Fukuyama, Haselden, Lynn, Reissig and Shinn.

†SMITH, HENRY NASH. *Virgin Land: The American West as Symbol and Myth* (Cambridge: Harvard University Press, 1950).

Examines the 19th-century myths and images of the West and the western hero as keys to American values and character.

STROUT, CUSHING. "A Note on Degler, Riesman and Tocqueville," *Amer. Quar.,* XVI (Spring, 1964), 100–102.

Degler's critique of Riesman (above) "fails to take seriously enough the difference in method between the historian and the sociologist, and it tends to blur the limiting conditions of the thesis presented in *The Lonely Crowd.*"

†TAYLOR, WILLIAM R. *Cavalier and Yankee: The Old South and American National Character* (New York: George Braziller, 1961).

An examination of the self-images of America in pre-Civil War literature, focusing on the idea of the "divided culture." "The problem for the South was not that it lived by an entirely different set of values and civic ideals but rather that it was forced either to live with the values of the nation at large or, as a desperate solution, to invent others. . . . "

TUVESON, ERNEST LEE. *Redeemer Nation: The Idea of America's Millenial Role* (Chicago: Univ. of Chicago Press, 1968).
On the religious sources of the idea of the U.S. as chosen nation and world savior.

†WARD, JOHN WILLIAM. *Andrew Jackson: Symbol for an Age* (New York: Oxford University Press, 1955).
"Through the age's leading figure were projected the age's leading ideas"—the ideas of nature, providence and will—so that "of Andrew Jackson the people made a mirror for themselves."

†WECTER, DIXON. *The Hero in America: A Chronicle of Hero-Worship* (New York: Charles Scribner's Sons, 1941).
National character is revealed in the choice of national heroes whose selection is "an index to the collective mind and heart."

†WHYTE, WILLIAM H., JR. *The Organization Man* (New York: Simon & Schuster, 1956).
Argues a current shift in America from the Protestant Ethic to the "Social Ethic" among "the dominant members of our society."

WILLIAMS, ROBIN M. JR. "Changing Value Orientations and Beliefs on the American Scene," *Illinois in Transition: Proc. of the Ill. State of Society Conf. for Church Leaders* (Cooperative Extension Service, Univ. of Illinois—mimeographed), 116–32.
Examines changes and continuities in American values, using the schema developed in *American Society.* Concludes in general that changes have been overemphasized: "during the last half-century the verdict has to be 'the same main values—only more so.' "

———. "Individual and Group Values," *Annals Am. Acad. Pol. & Soc. Sci.,* CCCLXXI (May 1967), 20–37.
Studies of American values in the 20th century suggest some devaluation of work, achievement and racism, and some increase in positive emphasis on material comfort, humanitarianism, science and secular rationality, equality, nationalism and conformity to social pressure.

———. "Value Orientations in American Society," in Williams, *American Society: A Sociological Interpretation,* 2nd ed., rev. (New York: Alfred A. Knopf, 1960), ch. 11.
Schematic survey and classification of the patterns of interests, values and general orientations of American culture in relation to its total social structure. Originally published in 1951.

WINTHROP, HENRY. "American National Character and the Existentialist Posture," *Jour. Existentialism,* VI (Summer 1966), 405–19.
Strategies for advancing existentialism must take account of the prevailingly anti-existentialist bent of American character as shown in the taxonomies of Max Lerner and Orrin E. Klapp.

*WISHY, BERNARD. *The Child and the Republic: The Dawn of Modern American Child Nurture* (Philadelphia: Univ. of Pennsylvania Press, 1968).
"The history of the changing notions of the child and of the debates about child-rearing is . . . an important chapter in our ceaseless national inquiry about what is wrong with America and what America needs in order to be put right." This study covers the period 1830–1900.

†WYLLIE, IRVIN G. *The Self-Made Man in America: The Myth of Rags to Riches* (New Brunswick, N.J.: Rutgers Univ. Press, 1954).
Traces the history of the image and ideology of America's foremost exemplar of the Protestant ethic and "our most cherished conceptions of success" from Franklin to Bruce Barton.